UNDERSTANDING RELIGION IN GLOBAL SOCIETY

Kent E. Richter
College of DuPage

Eva M. Räpple
College of DuPage

John C. Modschiedler
College of DuPage

R. Dean Peterson
College of DuPage

WADSWORTH
CENGAGE Learning

Australia • Brazil • Japan • Korea • Mexico • Singapore • Spain • United Kingdom • United States

WADSWORTH
CENGAGE Learning™

Understanding Religion in Global Society
Kent E. Richter, Eva M. Räpple, John C. Modschiedler, and R. Dean Peterson

Publisher: Holly J. Allen

Religion Editor: Steve Wainwright

Assistant Editors: Lee McCracken, Anna Lustig

Editorial Assistant: Barbara Hillaker

Marketing Manager: Worth Hawes

Marketing Assistant: Andrew Keay

Technology Project Manager: Julie Aguilar

Executive Art Director: Maria Epes

Print/Media Buyer: Barbara Britton

Permissions Editor: Chelsea Junget

Production Service: Buuji, Inc.

Photo Researcher: Myrna Engler

Copy Editor: Kristina McComas

Cover Designer: Yvo Riesebos

Cover Image: Contrail at Dusk. Galen Rowell/CORBIS

Compositor: Buuji, Inc.

For product information and technology assistance, contact us at
Cengage Learning Customer & Sales Support, 1-800-354-9706
For permission to use material from this text or product,
submit all requests online at **www.cengage.com/permissions**
Further permissions questions can be emailed to
permissionrequest@cengage.com

Library of Congress Control Number: 2004103857

ISBN-13: 978-0-534-55995-3

ISBN-10: 0-534-55995-6

Wadsworth
10 Davis Drive
Belmont, CA 94002
USA

Cengage Learning is a leading provider of customized learning solutions with office locations around the globe, including Singapore, the United Kingdom, Australia, Mexico, Brazil, and Japan. Locate your local office at **www.cengage.com/global**

Cengage Learning products are represented in Canada by Nelson Education, Ltd.

To learn more about Wadsworth, visit **www.cengage.com/wadsworth**

Purchase any of our products at your local college store or at our preferred online store **www.ichapters.com**

Printed in the United States of America
    5 6 7 8 9   14 13 12 11 10
ED221

CONTENTS

13 RELIGION, PERSONALITY, AND THE INDIVIDUAL   332

14 RELIGION AND SOCIETY IN A GLOBAL AGE   359

PREFACE

The world is changing. We are living in dramatic times. Drastic alterations in economic, political, and cultural systems are afoot. This may be described as a time of *kairos* when the old structures associated with modernism are dying and something new is struggling to be born. This process of sweeping social change is often called globalization. Whatever name is attached to this process, it is dramatically altering the context for "doing religion."

This realization led us to produce a different kind of textbook. Specifically, we look at **the globalization process** and the global society that it is producing and use this matrix for studying the traditional areas associated with an Introduction to Religion class. The book begins with a discussion of the globalization process along with some of its implications for understanding religion. Then in each chapter we look at one or more areas where globalization is raising new questions for the topic of the chapter such as defining religion, ethics, or art. Global Byte boxes in each chapter also present topics from the news where religion and globalization are interacting to produce new dilemmas. These help students see that the topics covered in the text and the class do have real-life relevance. The final chapter of the book returns to the theme of global society to examine in more detail key religious issues found in the contemporary environment.

Interactivity is another important feature of this textbook. Students learn better and find courses more fun when they are able to actively interact with the materials presented. We have included two distinctive types of exercises to foster active learning. Each chapter begins with pictures and textual quotes on the initial pages and on the Wadsworth Web site (**http://religion.wadsworth.com/richter**) that center on major themes developed in the chapter. **Opening Questions** then encourage students to reflect upon these items as a way to prepare for studying this chapter. Each chapter ends with an invitation to go to the Wadsworth Web site and do **electronic exercises** as a way for students to further explore ideas presented in the text.

The electronic exercises are a unique part of this text. They are integrated carefully with the book itself to create an innovative learning experience for students. The electronic text contains both printed textual quotes and images that actively engage students to deepen their understanding of religion, moving through four increasingly more complex levels of knowledge and analysis. Each exercise asks students to:

1. Describe what is happening in the picture or text using concepts found in the chapter.
2. Compare the concept in the above with that found in another religion or religions employing additional materials presented on the Web site.

3. Make the connection between the concept(s) presented in this chapter with materials presented in yet another chapter.

4. Pose their own questions regarding these concepts and go on the Net to find answers to these questions.

Field tests of these exercises in our own classes have indicated that students find them challenging, but interesting and informative. Students usually indicate that the exercises are definitely worth doing!

Overall, the book's **phenomenonological approach** allows the claims, experiences, and beliefs of the followers of specific religions to be taken seriously. However, we do not shy away from presenting anthropological, historical, psychological, and sociological materials where these are relevant. At the same time, we caution students about avoiding the reduction of religious phenomena to merely non-religious explanations. The text also stresses the **internal logic** of given religions. We show how concepts in one area of a religion have implications for other areas as well. For instance, we point out that how a religion conceives of the Holy may color its understanding of how humans relate to the Holy, its rituals, or its ideas about salvation.

Teaching aids contained in the book include key points printed in the margins that carry on a running outline of the book, occasional marginal notes that elaborate on items students might not understand, boldfaced important items with definition in the body of the text, and an end glossary that references ideas or persons who might appear in several places in the book. **Ancillary materials** include a Test Bank containing true-false, multiple choice, short answer, and essay questions. An Instructors Manual with suggested answers to both the Opening Questions and Electronic Exercises also is available.

Finally we would be remiss if we did not gratefully acknowledge our research assistants, Ambereen Saddiqui and Nancy Johnson, whose tireless effort, patience, and excellent skills made this project much easier. We would also like to thank those colleagues who reviewed several stages of this project: Alan Altany, Marshall University; Tony Battaglia, California State University Long Beach; Herbert Berg, University of North Carolina at Wilmington; Steven Godby, Broward College; David B. Gowler, Oxford College of Emory University; Kay K. Jordan, Radford University; Sheila McGinn, John Carroll University; Calvin Mercer, East Carolina University; Stephen Sapp, University of Miami; William Soderberg, Montgomery College; Brian Wilson, Western Michigan University; and Ray Wright, University of Houston. Their thoughtful criticisms, insightful questions, and creative suggestions enlivened the whole writing process.

We hope that you the reader will find this book challenging and enlightening and that you will enjoy reading it as much as we enjoyed writing it. Please let us know of your reaction to our work.

Kent E. Richter
Eva M. Räpple
John C. Modschiedler
R. Dean Peterson
College of DuPage
Glen Ellyn, Illinois

ABOUT THE AUTHORS

Kent Richter is professor of Philosophy and Religious Studies at College of DuPage. He has a PhD in Religious Studies from Stanford University and an MA in Philosophy from Colorado State University. He regularly teaches world religions, Asian religions, and philosophy of religion. Special interests include comparative religious philosophy and the problem of evil. He has completed sabbatical travel in India and Turkey.

Eva M. Räpple is associate professor of Philosophy and Religious Studies at College of DuPage. She holds a PhD in Philosophy from the University of St. Andrews, Scotland, an MA in Theology from the Catholic Theological Union in Chicago, Illinois, and MA equivalents in Latin and theology from the University of Frankfurt, Germany. Dr. Räpple is the author of *The Metaphor of the City in the Apocalypse of John*.

John C. Modschiedler is professor of Philosophy and Religious Studies at College of DuPage. He holds a BA from Elmhurst College, a BD from Eden Theological Seminary, and an MA and PhD from the University of Chicago. He studied at Berlin Theological Seminary and at the Free University of Berlin, Germany, 1962–1965, with a World Council of Churches Ecumenical Exchange Scholarship and a Fulbright Scholarship. He has taught philosophy, ethics, and religious studies at Loyola University, New Orleans; William Rainey Harper College; and Elmhurst College.

R. Dean Peterson is professor of Sociology and Religious Studies at College of DuPage. He holds a BA in sociology and religion, an MA in sociology, and an MA in religion from Baylor University. His PhD is in historical theology from St. Louis University. His publications include *A Concise History of Christianity* (Wadsworth) and *Social Problems: Globalization in the 21st Century* (Prentice-Hall).

1 INTRODUCTION: STUDYING RELIGION IN GLOBAL SOCIETY

Getty Images/PhotoDisc Collection

The context for doing religion is changing. First modernization, and now globalization, means that religions are functioning in much different worlds than those in which they emerged. In some ways, the changes in society alter the content of religion and the ways in which religion interacts with society and people in that society. We discuss those changes and interaction patterns in this chapter. Please look over the pictures for this chapter found above and online (**http://www.religion.wadsworth.com/richter**), and read the following scriptural passages, then consider the Introductory Questions to prepare for reading this chapter.

Chi K'ang Tzu asked Confucius about government saying: "Suppose I were to kill the unjust, in order to advance the just would I be right?"

Confucius replied: "In doing government, what is the need of killing? If you desire good, the people will be good. The nature of the Superior Man is like the wind, the nature of the inferior man is like grass. When the wind blows over the grass, it always bends."

—Confucianism: The Analects 12:19

Religion that is pure and undefiled before God, the Father, is this: to care for orphans and widows in their distress and to keep oneself unstained by the world.

—Christianity: Holy Bible, James 1:27[1]

No sacrifice, no vow, no fast must be performed by women apart from their husbands; if a wife obeys her husband, she will be exalted for that reason alone in heaven.

—Hinduism: Laws of Manu 5:155 (Fieser and Powers)

And if your Lord had pleased, surely all those who are in the earth would have believed, all of them; will you then force men till they become believers?

—Islam: Holy Koran 10:99[2]

If the Torah had been given in fixed and inimitable formulations, it would not have endured. Thus Moses pleaded with the Lord: "Master of the universe, reveal to me the final truth in each problem of doctrine and law." To which the Lord replied: "There are no pre-existent final truths in doctrine or law; the truth is the considered judgment of the majority of authoritative interpreters in every generation."

—Judaism: Talmud, Sanhedrin 4:2 (Bokser and Bokser 11)

---

1. Unless otherwise noted, biblical quotations are cited from the New Revised Standard Version (NRSV) of the Bible, © 1989 by the Division of Christian Education of the National Council of the Churches of Christ in the United States of America, New York, NY.

2. Unless otherwise noted, quotations from the Holy Koran are cited from *The Koran*. Trans. M. H. Shakir. Electronic Text Center, University of Virginia. http://etext.virginia.edu/koran.html (accessed July 3, 2003).

INTRODUCTORY QUESTIONS

The previous scriptures and the pictures on the Web site deal with different ways that religions expect people to relate to society and also how religion itself fits into the world. Think of these as you reflect on these questions.

1. From the Confucian passage, what is suggested about how religious life might or should influence politics and society? Note the picture of the monastery in the wilderness. What does this say about how religion should connect with politics and society?
2. The quote from the Holy Koran suggests God could make us all believe in one religion, but it is evident that there are different religions. Why is that? Is it a good thing?
3. The Talmud (quoted in the last passage) is a collection of teachings from Jewish rabbis about how to understand the words of God revealed (they believe) to Moses. Does it suggest that "God's Word" changes? Who gets to say what God means? Can a religion change too much? Not enough?
4. The Christian quote seems to say that real religion is focused on moral action. If someone is a good person, is that the same as being religious? Are religious people good members of society? Are good members of society religious?
5. Some passages above suggest that there are specific social roles for women, for leaders, and for believers in general that are required by God and tradition. To what extent are the teachings of religion bound to a particular time in history? To what extent do religious teachings apply to all times and places? How does one distinguish between those that are bound to a particular time and those that have application to all times and places?
6. Does religion seem to "fit" better into a crowded society, as in the urban scenes on the Web site, or does it seem more vivid in nature? Do religions feel different depending on the context?
7. What other kinds of questions should we ask to begin the study of religion?

WELCOME

Welcome to the academic study of religion. We hope you will find the approach to religion presented in this book as exciting, challenging, and thought-provoking as we did when we took our first courses in religious studies many years ago. You may well find the perspective on religion presented in this book significantly different from any approach to religion you may have encountered in your previous religious training. For this is the academic study of religion, not personal religious study or personal devotion. One need not be "religious" to study religion; one need only be interested.

In studying religion academically, one uses the tools of scholarship developed through the centuries to seek a deeper understanding of the content of various religious traditions. This content focuses, of course, on what religions declare as truths about God or Reality, and on what religions do in the form of ritual and moral action. But it also includes the role of religion in individuals' lives and in the lives of the communities in which these individuals live. We study how religious traditions deal with the problems common to all humans and their societies, such as the place of religion in morality and the way religions explain death and the meaning of life. We analyze the interaction of religion and social change, how history changes religion, and how religion changes history. And there are a host of other related issues.

In this text, we employ a phenomenological approach to the study of religion. By **phenomenological approach** we mean a descriptive method by which scholars "try to accurately describe and interpret religious phenomena without making judgments about the truth of religious conceptions" (Schmidt 23). When using this technique, religious experiences and reports of these experiences, the language of religion, and the art, ritual, mythology, and meanings of religion are all taken seriously. These elements of religion are not trivial but say very important things about human beings, their problems, their place within the universe, and, perhaps, the nature of the cosmos itself. Moreover, the phenomena of religion provide us with the basic data whereby we can analyze religious traditions and make comparisons among them.

Phenomenology involves describing and interpreting religious phenomena without making judgment about their ultimate truth.

In this approach, we will describe a variety of religious phenomena from diverse cultures and societies. Moreover, we will also investigate phenomena that until fairly recently have not been part of traditional religious studies, for example, texts or rituals among people indigenous to North America and African Americans. We are therefore using a cross-cultural as well as a multicultural approach in which different religious traditions are compared according to the various dimensions of religious experience. These dimensions are chosen because they allow us to focus on religious traditions from a kaleidoscope of different perspectives and themes, which together should guide us in our understanding of human religious beliefs. An important goal in this dimensional analysis is to discern differences and similarities by comparing religious phenomena. We describe religious phenomena and also inquire about their functions in religious contexts. In other words, we not only describe religious phenomena but also explore their meaning as experienced in human life. This broader approach should help us to gain insights regarding essential aspects of religious worldviews.

cross-cultural analysis—examination taking into account various cultures

multicultural analysis—examination across diverse ethnic and racial groups (e.g., feminist perspective)

Comparing religious phenomena is an important aspect of phenomenology.

However, the consideration of which dimensions of religious life should be studied is a key question that is often debated. For our purposes, the dimensions of religious experience we have chosen for study correspond to our chapter headings and are as follows:

1. Studying Religion in Global Society
2. What Is Religion?
3. The Absolute, the Ultimate, the Holy
4. Origins and Founders
5. World Scriptures
6. Myths, Stories, and History
7. Suffering and Evil
8. Religion and Art

9. Ritual
10. Religion, Morality, and Ethics
11. Religious Experience
12. Salvation and the Meaning of Life
13. Religion, Personality, and the Individual
14. Religion and Society in a Global Age

Although the dimensions are discussed in separate chapters, they are not different entities but are intrinsically interwoven. They are dynamic patterns, which interact and exhibit influence on each other. We will therefore also investigate how one dimension relates to another one. In particular, the exercises will give you many opportunities to explore these dynamic patterns among the dimensions. We have included the following quick reference guide (Table 1.1) in order to give you a way to compare some of the differences among important religious traditions. Each of the concepts presented in the quick reference is expanded in the printed version and in the electronic text on the Web site.

The main approach we employ is to study religions as *religious* phenomena. Yet this is one possible method among a variety of other disciplines that also provide valid insights regarding religions. Other disciplines, such as history, sociology, anthropology, and psychology, can enhance the phenomenological study of religion. These will be used as appropriate. Still, our main focus is on a comparative, nonjudgmental approach to religious traditions.

In this chapter, we set the stage for students' further studies by addressing the key question of why one should study religion. Then we look at a unique feature of this book: the interplay of religion and globalization. Finally, we point students toward the integration of the printed text and an electronic workbook (found on the Wadsworth Web site, **www.cengage.com/religion**).

WHY STUDY RELIGION?

Some students may have taken the course for which this text is used because they are interested in the class and its material, religion. Others may have taken it because the class is a part of a broader Religious Studies major. However, the majority of students likely have taken this religious studies course because it is part of the liberal arts or general education requirements for a degree. Unfortunately, many students do not believe the wide array of classes they are forced to take outside of their major have much value, and therefore many undergraduate students need to be convinced that this study has some relevance to their general education. In short, they ask, "Why do I have to take general education classes?" and perhaps, "Why should I study this topic in particular?"

For one thing, a broad range of courses in "general education" may assist students in developing skills needed in future careers. For instance, the ability to read, do math, gather information, organize information, analyze it, draw conclusions, and present this material in written and verbal form are skills in demand across the spectrum of career options. In fact these skills may be even more important than the specific knowledge students obtain in their majors. This is so simply because knowledge is developing so rapidly that what a student learns

Skills acquired in general education courses will be important throughout your working career.

Table 1.1 World Religions Compared

Concept	Tribal Religion	Hinduism	Jainism	Buddhism	Confucianism
The Absolute, the Holy	High God, various spirits, spiritual energy, ancestors	Brahman, various gods (e.g., Vishnu, Rama, Shiva, Kali)	Tirthankara, ultimate wisdom	Nirvana, Emptiness, "Perfection of Wisdom," Buddha Mind	Tao, Cosmic Order, perfect virtue and character of the "Gentleman"
Origins and Founders	Mythical ancestors	No specific persons, legendary Rishis "hear" gods	Mahavira	Siddhartha Gotama, the Buddha	K'ung Fu-tzu, Confucius; Mencius
Scriptures	None, often nonliterate cultures	Vedas, Upanishads, epic texts including Bhagavad Gita	Agamas, especially the Angas	Pali Canon, other additions, sermons of the Buddha	The Five Classics; the Four Books (esp. C's Analects)
Suffering and Evil	Disease, etc., often from offended spirits or ancestors	Samsara (cycle of rebirth), illusory world, bad karma	Birth/rebirth, karma	Samsara, ignorance, craving/desire	Disharmony of society, evil character (esp. of ruler)
Major Rituals	Offerings, relations to spirits/ancestors, healing, rites of passage	Puja (ritual worship, offerings), "sacred thread," bathing	Puja, fasting	Meditation, offerings to monks, honoring the Buddha	Ritual propriety, honoring ancestors, honoring Confucius
Ethical and Moral Ideals	Various codes of social cohesion	Caste duties, devotion to a god	Nonviolence (ahimsa), honesty	"Precepts," monastic rules, "compassion"	Virtues of character, benevolence, wisdom, filial piety, etc.
Community Structures	Tribal organization, shaman as religious specialist	Caste system, priest class, renouncers, guru	Monastic/laity distinction, temple priests	Monastic/laity, Arhat, Sangha, Bodhisattva, teachers	Popular temple system, structured social order
Salvation and Afterlife	Spirit world, ancestors, some reincarnation	Reincarnation, karma, bhakti/jnana, union with Brahman	Purification/asceticism	Enlightenment, moksha, meditation/wisdom	Proper family burial, ancestor spirit

Concept	*Taoism*	*Shinto*	*Judaism*	*Christianity*	*Islam*
The Absolute, the Holy	Tao, the order and "way" of life and nature	The "Kami," gods or spirits or forces	The One God, Jahweh	One God, the Holy Trinity, Jesus the Christ	One God, Allah
Origins and Founders	Lao Tzu; Chuang Tzu	None specific	Abraham, Moses	Jesus of Nazareth, the Christ; St. Paul and Apostles	Muhammad
Scriptures	Tao Te Ching, Chuang Tzu	Kojiki, Nihongi	Torah, Tanakh, Talmud	Bible: Old and New Testaments	Holy Koran; Hadith and Islamic law
Suffering and Evil	Disharmony of nature, striving and desire	Pollution, ritual uncleanness (esp. touching the dead), social shame	Sin, disobedience to God	Sin, separation from God	Denying God's supremacy
Major Rituals	Popular divination, popular worship of deities	Worship of kami, temple and home shrines	Shabbat worship, Passover, Yom Kippur	Worship, Christmas/Easter, Baptism/ Eucharist	Daily prayers, Ramadan fast, Hajj
Ethical and Moral Ideals	"Actionless action," effortless spontaneity, not striving	Social duty, honoring kami	Ten Commandments, 613 Commandments of Talmud	Ten Commandments, "laws of love"	Ritual obedience, Islamic law
Community Structures	Popular temple priesthood, social withdrawal	Social order, devotion to family/nation	Nation, descendents of Abraham, rabbis/teachers	Baptized members, some monks/priests, "ministers"	Imams, general equality of believers
Salvation and Afterlife	Union with Tao, accepting death	Harmony with gods, good life, ancestors	Nation/security, eternal life with God, obedience	Heaven, saved by Christ (by grace)	Heaven/hell, right obedience outweighing sin

today in classes may soon be obsolete. The skills noted above actually amount to "learning how to learn," and this ability is a key to future success in any field.

The purpose of education is living.

While specific academic skills and the general skill of knowing "how to learn" are very important, education has a much deeper aim. Some have said, "The purpose of an education is not a job. The purpose of education is living." The idea here is that education can help people have a deeper and more meaningful existence. In addition, educated people may live more responsible and ethical lives because their education has challenged them to be aware of alternative ways of living and to examine their own society and lives. Such an approach also helps people be more responsible and better-informed citizens in their societies. This is especially important in democratic societies where citizens are expected to make complex decisions that give them input into the direction of their nations. This development of a more complete person is so important that religious studies along with related disciplines, such as art, music, dance, languages, history, and philosophy, are called humanities. That is, these disciplines are intended to "humanize" people.

Courses like religious studies help to humanize you.

"Okay," one may say, "the humanities may 'humanize' me, but why do I need to study religion as such?" One answer, or rather a whole series of answers, to this question was offered by Martin Marty, one of the foremost historians of Christianity in the United States. Calling academic study "an exuberant adventure," Marty offers 10 reasons for teaching and studying religion.

Religion kills.

1. "Religion motivates most killing in the world today. Any number of violent confrontations today have an underlying religious dimension. These conflicts can be found from the Middle East to Afghanistan and from India to Malaysia to the United States. Politicians and citizens alike must pay attention to the involvement of religion in numerous violent political, economic, and social movements. Additionally, Marty notes that religion may kill in more subtle ways, such as oppression and repression.

Religion heals.

2. "Religion contributes to most healing in the world today." In the field of medicine in both the modern and the undeveloped world, religion often provides the motivation for those who help, and to the extent that peacemaking and reconciliation are a kind of healing, religion often plays a constructive role. Numerous hospitals, clinics, and health organizations globally have their origins in the world's religions.

3. "Religion is globally pervasive; there is a great deal of it." The vast majority of our planet's 6 billion people identify with one religion or another. Ironically, this situation exists in spite of the supposed secularization of modern societies. This irony is put in perspective by Marty's pithy comment: "In the academy you *get* to study why, in a world we choose to call secular, religion grows and intensifies."

Religion is the soul of culture.

4. "Religion has a long past, and its tentacles are culture-wide." A great deal of the world's art, architecture, music, literature, and dance has its source in religion. Even much so-called "secular art" employs religious questions, images, and themes. In this sense, religion has been called the "soul of culture."

5. "Religion is hard to define and thus a tantalizing subject." Most religious studies textbooks try to define religion all the way from "a con-

ventional and institutional definition" to "a label for every kind of 'ultimate concern.'" Thus, as Marty notes, "religion" can be defined so vaguely that critics declare, "if everything is religious, nothing is." The study of religion, therefore, inquires deeply into "the limits and scope of religion," carefully trying to decipher the mystery of this vast subject. And, as Marty adds, "that inquiry inspires many others."

There is an undeniable religious dimension in many aspects of human life

6. "Religion, however defined, helps explain many other activities." The dialogical fields of study, such as the psychology of religion, religion and psychological studies, religion and literature, the Bible as literature, sociology of religion, religion and society, religious social ethics, and philosophy of religion, are solid indications of the interrelatedness of religion with its cultural contexts. Another example in that same vein is evident in the work of Max Weber, a major pioneer in sociology. His influential book, *The Protestant Ethic and the Spirit of Capitalism* (1958), deals with the relationship between religion and economics. Some philosophers, like Karl Marx, might say that we explain religion by explaining economics, but Weber suggests it is the other way around. Rather than reducing religion to something else that "explains" it, the study of religion may lead to an understanding of religion as a unique arena of human experience, which in turn helps us to explain many other facets of human experience.

Religion often motivates some of the most positive and most negative aspects of human behavior.

7. "Religion is protean." Referring to the Greek mythological figure Proteus, who could change shapes at will, Marty is pointing out that we study a broad range of human activities when we look at people's religions. "In the name of religion people dance, act, make music, fight wars, abuse some, liberate others, seek to effect justice, reinforce prejudice, fight addiction, and do other. . . activities." So when one studies religion, one discovers a broad range of human activities, all of which are worth studying.

pluralism—a condition characterized by a multitude of different groups (i.e., ethnic, religious, social class, and so on)

8. "Religion is one of the most revealing dimensions of pluralism." That is, when we look at the many different ways that people live lives of meaning and purpose all over the world, religion is one of the major points of difference we discover. Even in our own multicultural society, the plurality of religions is one of the key elements of diversity. Thus "understanding the lover or the neighbor or the enemy often demands knowledge of religion."

9. The study of religion is practical. In the political realm, in the realm of advertising, in personal relations, not taking religious sensibilities into account can lead to ruin. It would be a joke, if not an insult, to advertise to a Jewish community your butcher shop's sale on pork chops. Similarly, it might not be a good idea for a U.S. diplomat to schedule a high-level meeting with Arabian politicians on a Friday at noon. Muslims have special prayers at this time, and Jews do not eat pork.

10. "Religion as a subject matter or a dimension of culture has attracted a scholarly cohort of experts." That is, when one studies religion, one sits beside many other great scholarly minds that have become embroiled in this fascinating quest. "People have been thinking about the modern study of religion for a century," Marty notes, and the sources, commen-

taries, reformations, and revivals of religious ideas stretch back to the beginnings of civilized history. You meet here literally the greatest and most influential minds of all time. (20, 48)

Marty's ultimate point in advancing these reasons for studying religion is that the appropriate attitude toward its study is not that you have "got to" study religion, but that you "get to." In the process one may gain insights into far more than the "strictly" religious. After all, these are, as Huston Smith calls them, "Our Great Wisdom Traditions." And here one might find benefits never imagined.

PREPARING FOR GLOBAL SOCIETY

Martin Marty's reasons for studying religion are many, and perhaps they are persuasive. But now, as our world changes and evolves, there is one more reason to study religion: For the first time in history, we are evolving into a global society. At a very minimum, this means that whether one is conducting business, doing politics, or traveling, people all over the globe are more and more likely to encounter someone unlike themselves, and in particular this may mean someone of a different religion. Therefore, in order to have comprehension of, to work with, and to foster communication with these different people, we will need to understand their religion. Moreover, this need is not abstract (*someday* I may encounter someone of a different religion) but is immediate. That is, even now most societies are becoming more ethnically and religiously diverse. The chances are that the new neighbor who moves next door may be a Christian, Jew, Hindu, Muslim, or Jain. Thus learning about religions new to us may, in our global society, be simply inevitable.

Understanding religion may help you understand your neighbor.

Talking about the global society, the global village, postindustrial society, or the Information Age is becoming commonplace. In the mass media and in any number of scholarly disciplines, from the social sciences to the arts to religious studies to philosophy, globalization is a process to be confronted. **Globalization** is a massive process of social change resulting from the growing interconnectedness of human social, cultural, economic, and religious life that is altering human activities on a planetarywide scale. Although perhaps no one yet has a definitive answer to explain the transition process now occurring, some type of dramatic change is clearly afoot. It is equally clear that religion is intimately involved with this change at two levels. First, religion is part of those forces that, on the one hand, promote the globalization process, and, on the other hand, resist the globalization process. Secondly, the globalization process is creating a much different context for "doing religion" or being religious than has ever appeared in human history. As a result, we have chosen to make globalization an important theme of this educational system.

Globalization is redefining the context for "doing religion."

In this section, we begin our examination of the interaction of religion and globalization by looking at the backdrop necessary for understanding the major changes now occurring. Initially, we present some background concepts necessary for coming to grips with globalization. Next, we look at pervasive social change from traditional to modern societies. Finally, we offer some thoughts on the interaction of modernism and religion. With this background, we will then turn our attention to the worldwide development of global society.

■ SOCIAL CHANGE AND TIME

We begin our review of important ideas for understanding the transition to global society by looking at two ancient Greek concepts of time that are important for our study. The first of these is *chronos,* which is the basis of the English word *chronological.* By **chronos,** the Greeks meant the step-by-step ordering of time. In other words, time units are arranged as seconds, minutes, hours, days, weeks, months, years, and so on. This concept includes a view of the past ("This happened two years ago"), a present ("This is happening now"), and a future ("This will happen two years from now"). So events including significant social changes can be placed within this sequence. Thus it is possible to say that the Modern Period began in the 1500s.

Placing events in some type of past sequence of events is what most people with a European heritage understand as history. Yet, some caution is in order at this point. The events of history are seldom as obviously clear-cut as most people assume. This is especially true when we are talking about major social changes. For example, many scholars would contend that the Modern Period began in the 1800s, not the 1500s. These scholars contend that modernization truly originated when urbanization and industrialization began dramatically altering the way people lived in Western Europe—a process that eventually would spread to the United States, Canada, and much of the rest of the world.

History is a "flowing stream," not an ordering of carefully separated chronological events.

We do not have time to enter into the fine points of that debate now. It is enough to say that the 19th century may have been a focal point of this change to modern society, although clearly the modernization process began several centuries before and is still continuing in many parts of the world today. This brings us to a major point: History is more of a "flowing stream" than a clearly separated ordering of chronological events. So when we speak of globalization or the development of a global society, we are discussing an ongoing process that began some time ago and is likely to continue for some time in the future.

At the same time, this does not mean that all moments are of equal importance in the process of historical change. Some eras obviously are more important than others. This brings us to a second Greek concept of time—*kairos.* For the ancient Greeks, a **kairos** is a moment in history which is "pregnant with expectancy." That is, a *kairos* is a particular moment when social, economic, political, technological, religious, and other forces come together in dynamic tension to create a situation when a dramatic, large-scale change is occurring or will occur at any moment. Literally, the image is of a pregnant woman who will give birth at any moment. Everything is ready. Yet, everything is waiting for exactly the right moment for the birth to occur. *Kairos* (pl. *kairoi*) is the word translated in the Christian New Testament where Paul says Jesus came in "the fullness of time" (Galatians 4:4). That is, Jesus came at a moment in history when, according to Paul, God had prepared just the right conditions for the arrival of His Son. *Kairoi* also are referred to by such terms as times of paradigm shifts or watersheds in history.

In times of *kairos,* an individual or small group of people can have a truly dramatic impact for better or worse on the course of events. In addition to Jesus, we can argue that a host of historical figures, such as **Siddhartha Gautama** (the Buddha, ca. 563–ca. 483 BCE, or BC on the Christian calendar), **Lao Tzu**

(604–531 BCE), **Confucius** (551–479 BCE), **Socrates** (ca. 469–ca. 399 BCE), **Plato** (427–347 BCE), **Aristotle** (384–322 BCE), **Augustine of Hippo** (354–430 CE, or AD on the Christian calendar), **Muhammad** (ca. 570–632), **Martin Luther** (1483–1546), **Adolf Hitler** (1883–1945) and **Mahatma Mohandas Gandhi** (1869–1948), all came in "the fullness of time." Certainly, for better or worse, each of these people had an effect on large portions of humanity and significantly altered the future of the world.

A kairos is not a total break with the past.

Although these people and their various *kairoi* in the world produced changes in the direction of history, it should also be noted that these moments do not represent a total break with the past. When these times of change appear, the ideas, values, and religious and social structures that developed during the previous age seem to cease to function properly and to command people's loyalty. Thus these ideas and structures may be replaced with something new. Nevertheless, the old assumptions and ways often provide the seed ground for the growth of new concepts and systems of the emerging age. For instance, democracy is a set of political beliefs and systems supported by religious ideology that emerged as a prime characteristic of the Modern Period, and democracy is even now remaking much of the developing world. Yet it may be noted that citizens of those countries that have been democratic longest may be losing faith in the democratic process and are therefore seeking alternatives to the ballot box, such as the court system or pressure groups, to find justice or make their viewpoint heard. Yet, whatever new structures emerge likely will carry many of the principles and assumptions of democracy.

We may be in a period of kairos where the Modern Period is ending and the Global Society is beginning.

Globalization represents a kairos on a planetary-wide scale.

To sum up, from one point of view history can be seen as a *chronos* in which one era "unfolds" into another. It is difficult to determine where one period ends and another begins. At the same time, social, historical, political, economic, technological, and, of course, religious forces do come together to produce moments of history "pregnant" with change. These are *kairoi*. At the beginning of the 21st century, we may be at one of these watershed moments. The Modern Period that began with the Protestant Reformation in the 1500s is coming to an end, and the Global Society is struggling to be born. What is truly unique about this *kairos* is that it is occurring on a planetwide level. For the first time in history, people are being called upon to transcend traditional boundaries of family, village, tribe, and nation to see themselves as "citizens of the world," with all the complex and frightening implications that transition may hold. From the Laplands of northern Russia to the deserts of Saudi Arabia to the rainforests of the Amazon, people of all kinds are being integrated into a global system whether they like it or not. For better or worse, massive change is afoot. To understand this change, we must look more closely at the Modern Period, since it is the "modern" ideas and social systems that may now be reaching their limits, and it is out of these systems that the new Global Society will emerge.

■ THE MODERN PERIOD

This is not the place to do a detailed history of the Modern Period, of course, but to understand globalization it is necessary first to see some of the ideas and social systems characteristic of the modern era. These ideas and systems are now so widespread in contemporary societies that it may be surprising to find that they are not natural, nor have they always existed. In fact, the items we discuss next demonstrate how traditional societies and modern societies are quite different.

Perhaps the best way to understand the characteristics of modernism, then, is to look briefly at the type of societies modern ones replaced, namely the pre-modern or "traditional" society. As we have noted in other contexts, the real-life shift from very traditional to ultramodern societies is a continuum, not an utterly abrupt event, and the line between the two may not be not as sharp as we indicate. Nevertheless, the break between pre-modern and modern societies is significant, indeed in some ways a break so stark that sociologists often refer to this change as the Great Dichotomy. So, although this discussion oversimplifies complex changes, it is useful for seeing the momentous changes that have occurred over the last 500 years and that they themselves are in the process of being altered.

First, let us consider traditional societies. These societies by and large were rural and small scale, meaning that before the modern period, the overwhelming majority of people lived in very small groups with a strong sense of community. Relationships were personal and obligations assumed moral significance. That is, people related to people as known individuals—people they knew personally. The obligations were moral, and often religious, in nature. People assumed obligations to one another because it was the right thing to do and it was demanded by their religion. Obligations also were widespread, meaning they included almost a total commitment to the members of the community. So if people were ill, their houses burned down, or their children were in need, the community felt obliged to render assistance.

In these traditional societies, people may have had some sense of their individuality, but the societies were communal in their orientation, so the individual was relatively unimportant. The group (the family, the tribe, the village, the religion) was more important than the individual, who was expected to make sacrifices for the group. For example, young people did not choose their mates. Instead, their parents or others selected a mate for them, with the choices made more for the good of the family or tribe than for the happiness of the married couple. After all, it was taken for granted that the wisdom of elders was the proper authority for the functioning of the group. Standing up and asserting one's individuality in such a context was unthinkable.

Similarly, there was little diversity in traditional societies. People tended to be of a single ethnic group, with a single way of life, and of a single religion. Thus one's identity was closely tied up with one's ethnic group and one's religion, since indeed religion and ethnic culture were for the most part one and the same. For instance, in traditional India to be an Indian was to be a Hindu and vice versa. Consequently, the boundaries between the members of one traditional society and the next were clear, since being a member of the group, of the tribe, of the religion, and of the ethnic group were pretty much the same thing. A person outside the group was easily recognized as both ethnically and religiously different.

The worldview of traditional societies was sacred or spiritual. That is, life in the material world of day-to-day activities was rooted in the sacred realm, not in the material. For instance, if a person was ill, roots, herbs, or medicinal concoc-

The Great Dichotomy refers to the vast differences between traditional and modern societies.

Traditional societies are rural societies where there is a strong sense of community and moral obligation (often based on religion).

In traditional societies, the group, not the individual, was important.

The worldview of traditional societies was spiritual.

tions would be given him or her, not merely as medicines, however, but as parts of a religious **ritual** carefully performed so that healing could take place. The medicine man or woman who prepared the concoctions often was also a shaman who cared for other religious elements necessary for the society's well-being, such as rituals involved in planting and harvest and protection from spirits. Thus all of human society was situated in a great sacred web that composed the spiritual cosmos, without the harsh division between the material and the spiritual that many of us experience. The material world itself was seen as alive with spirit.

shaman—traditional healing man or woman

All of this tradition, the sense of community and sacredness of pre-modern culture, began to be undermined by the changes that began with the Protestant Reformation of the 16th century. Of course, what came to be known as modernism evolved over the last 500 years, but by the 19th century, it was obvious that a different kind of social system was emerging. To begin with, this society was urban and industrial. Not only had the place of residence and means of making a living changed, but the basic patterns of life and the assumptions of the society also had altered radically.

Modern societies are industrial and urban.

First, people no longer lived in small groups but in larger cities. It was no longer simple to know the people around you or to know whom to trust. Consequently, the sense of community began to dissolve, and people no longer felt the obligations of kinship, one to another. Relationships therefore assumed a new basis, becoming founded only on legal, limited contracts, instead of personal relationships. For instance, if you buy a new calculator, it will come with a warranty (a type of contract) that has nothing to do with who you are or whom you know. If your warranty is for 90 days and the calculator ceases to work after 91 days, the company has no legal obligation to repair or replace your calculator, nor do they feel any moral obligation to make amends even if the product was clearly defective. Relationships are no longer based on moral or religious duty but become based on rational expediency and legal requirements.

Relationships become limited and contractual in modern societies.

With the advent of modernity, the sense of community was further undermined by the fact that modern societies tended to be more pluralistic. By pluralistic, we mean that modern nation–states bring together people of diverse ethnic, religious, class, and vocational backgrounds. Thus, the original sense that one's community is one's ethnicity, which is also one's religion and one's identity, was severely weakened. This change can be further illustrated by the modern development of a variety of volunteer and professional organizations (such as Boy Scouts, the Lions Club, Mothers Against Drunk Drivers, the American Medical Association, the American Academy of Religion, and so on) for which membership has nothing to do with one's traditions or natural, ethnic identity. Community, in this way, becomes something artificial, however helpful it may be as a source of entertainment, prestige, or personal identity.

The loss of community identity brings us to two other main characteristics of modern societies. First, modern societies tend to have an **individualistic worldview** that focuses on individual versus collective interest. That is, the individual has assumed an importance never before seen. The individual, not the group, is the important entity and has come to be the basis of society. Not only has individual happiness come to the forefront, but individual rights have become a primary concern. The individual is assumed to have absolute rights that must be protected against various collectivities, whether government, majority groups,

Modern societies are individualistic.

religion, business, or even the family. While the stress on the individual and his or her rights has many benefits, individualism also may be undermining the basis for society (Bellah et al.).

Secondly, modern societies stress the rational. It is assumed that rationality underlies, or at least should underlie, business actions, political judgments, and intimate relations. Of course, rationality was seen as the primary characteristic of human beings as far back as Aristotle, Greek philosopher of the 4th century BCE. But it was the French philosopher Rene Descartes (1596–1650), the so-called "father of modern philosophy," who was determined to build his whole philosophy on the fact of human reason—the one thing, he believed, that one could not question. Sensory information, ideas about the world, and even the reality of one's own body, he claimed, were potentially doubtful. But the one thing Descartes believed he could not question was, "I think, therefore I am."

The key point of this Cartesian emphasis is, perhaps, that Descartes was no longer satisfied with believing what tradition and culture had bequeathed. Indeed, it was his emphasis on personal rational inquiry that led shortly to another famous rationalistic dictum of the European Enlightenment, *sapere aude,* or "know for yourself." No longer could one take for granted that men and women were spiritual beings created in the image of God and that human virtues such as compassion, love, and morality flowed from human's spiritual nature. Thus the emotional, spiritual, moral, and religious elements of the human person, if they were to be accepted at all, had to be verified by rational inquiry, being viewed by some philosophers as mere holdovers from pre-modern, prescientific times.

Indeed, science as most of us today understand it emerged during the Modern Period as another powerful force for shaping modern societies. The scientific method became *the* way to know truth, while revelation (scripture), intuition, and tradition were thought to be purveyors of half-truth, at best. Science, the modernist proclaims, bases its conclusions on verifiable evidence; that is, evidence that can be in some way counted or measured by objective criteria. Of course, one immediate victim of the scientific focus on measurement and objectivity was the traditional sense of the spiritual nature of the cosmos. In fact, because the spiritual cannot be readily measured by objective means, spiritual phenomena were seen as irrelevant, or worse, as deceitful illusions.

Ultimately, the loss of the spiritualized natural world of traditional societies led to a **mechanistic, materialistic vision of the cosmos.** By this we mean that the universe came to be seen as a large machine composed of dead matter, rather than of life and spirit, and by the same token, all activity in this materialistic universe, both natural and human, was merely the result of laws of nature. Thus the universe became disenchanted, or what philosopher and advocate of transpersonal spirituality Ken Wilber calls a flatland universe (243). By flatland universe he means a universe limited to the material realm and therefore devoid of meaning or purpose. As a result, all physical objects, from rocks to plants or animals or even humans, simply perform their biological functions according to fixed laws. Thus there is no purpose to their individual existence nor is there any direction in evolution. Moreover, within the flatland universe there are no hierarchies. Not only is every person equal to every other person, but every living being is equal to every other living being. That is, a plant, gnat, fish, whale, and human have

Modern societies stress rationality.

European Enlightenment— 18th century philosophical movement characterized by skepticism toward uncritical universalistic claims and trust in human reasoning

Modern societies are scientific.

Modernism has a mechanistic, materialistic view of the universe.

In the flatland universe every being is equal to every other being.

equal value in the web of life. Ironically, this meant that the Modern Period, which began with the grand presumption of the value of human rationality, eventually concluded with the idea that humans really are no different from other animals. With all values lost to scientific methodologies, there no longer remained any more reason to punish a criminal for murder than to punish a child for swatting a fly. "That's ridiculous!" we might say. Nevertheless, it seems to have been the logical outcome of a material universe devoid of spirit, depth, and meaning.

■ RELIGION IN MODERN SOCIETIES

Animosity has existed between science and religion in the modern world.

It should not be surprising that a good bit of animosity has characterized the relationship between religion and modernism. Many people are aware of the ongoing battle between science and religion. In fact, if people see conflict between the modern world and religion, it is seen in battles at various levels between scientific tenets, inquiry, and discoveries, and religious resistance to scientific approaches and discoveries. For instance, in the early part of the 20th century conservative Christians strongly opposed the teaching of evolution in the classroom. They succeeded in having laws passed establishing biblical understandings of creation as the basis of teaching the beginnings of the universe and forbidding the teaching of evolution. These laws were challenged in the famous Scopes Monkey Trial held in 1925 in Dalton, Tennessee. The trial ended in the conviction of a young biology teacher, John Scopes, for violating the anti-evolution law. The conviction was overturned on appeal.

Creation Science—the belief that biblical stories of creation are supported by scientific data

To some degree, this battle continues today in the conflict between scientific evolutionists and Creation Science advocates in school districts across the United States. Creation Science advocates hold that biblical stories of the creation of the universe and life are as scientific as is materialistic evolution. They argue that biblical stories of creation should be taught alongside evolution as alternative explanations of origins. Many conservative Christians still resist sending their children to public schools where the theory of evolution is taught. It is worth noting that many Christians have been successful in reconciling their religious views to scientific perspectives. They live quite comfortably in a world that combines scientific views along with a deep and meaningful religious faith.

There is a fundamental conflict between materialistic modernism and religion.

Still, there is a fundamental conflict between materialistic versions of modernism and religion. Religion insists that at root the universe is grounded in the Sacred, the Holy, or the spiritual, and that recognizing this is essential to truly understanding the material world, along with human beings, their possibilities, and their failures. Yet, with the rise of rationality and science, the mechanistic, materialistic worldview of modernism came to dominate many people's thinking. Religion found itself on the defensive more and more. Western Christianity, especially, has seen the greatest pressure from modernism, but everywhere modernism spreads, the religious world feels under attack.

The attack on religion is more than imaginary. Modernism brought with it a doctrine of secularism that often is pursued with "religious zeal." (See Box 1.1.) **Secularism** is a philosophy that seeks to remove society from under the dominance of religion and to place it under the guidance of rational humanism. **Humanism** is a philosophy where humans, along with their well-being, needs,

Box 1.1	Impious Europe

The material from Martin Marty mentions several times the ongoing conflict between secularization and religion. We discuss this in greater detail later in this chapter. At this point, we offer a case study of the interaction of the secular and religious by reviewing excerpts from an article by philosopher Roger Scruton.

"I was brought up in the England of the 1950's . . . [where] . . . you could be confident that God was an Englishman, who had a quiet, dignified, low-key way of visiting the country each weekend while being careful never to outstay his welcome. In today's England, God is a foreigner, an illegal immigrant with aggressive manners and a way of intruding into every gathering . . . In the presence of this new God, the voice of the English churches becomes ever weaker, ever more shy of doctrine, ever more conciliatory and ill at ease.

". . .Those brought up in our postreligious society do not seek forgiveness because they are by and large free of the belief they need it. This does not mean they are happy; indeed, the high rates of juvenile crime, promiscuity, and drug dependence suggest the opposite. It does mean that they put pleasure before commitment and can neglect their duties without being crippled by guilt. And since religion is the balm for guilt, those brought up without religion seem, on the surface, to lose the need for it.

"But only on the surface. You don't have to be a believer to be conscious of a great religious deficit in our society. We saw its effect during the strange canonization of Princess Diana, when vast crowds of people congregated in places vaguely associated with the princess's name, to deposit wreaths, messages, and teddy bears . . . She became a sacrificial offering, and therefore a saintly intercessor before the mysteries that govern the world. . . .

"Even if we mourn the post-Enlightenment loss of faith, it is sometimes said that we should welcome the fact that rational argument father than blind superstition now governs public opinion. The social and political movements that are currently most influential in Europe—the ecological movement, the movement for 'animal rights,' the movement toward political union—are, in their activist component, almost completely closed to rational argument. . . .Behind the façade of reasonableness in each of those movements lurks a fortified orthodoxy, ready, if challenged, to punish dissent.

". . . We have abandoned those aspects of religion that provide genuine guidance in time of spiritual need. The instinctive awe and respect toward our own being that the Romans called pietas has . . . vanished from public life of Europe . . . Discussions of embryo research, cloning, abortion, and euthanasia—subjects that go to the heart of the religious concept of our destiny—proceed in once-Catholic Europe as though nothing was at stake beyond the expansion of human choices. Little now remains of the old Christian idea that life, its genesis, and its terminus are sacred things, to be meddled with at our peril."

Source: Scruton, Roger. "Impious Europe." *Wilson Quarterly.* Winter 2003: 56–60.

and happiness, determine the nature of good and evil. This, in essence, makes humans the measure of all things and changes the basis for society, morality, and relationships. For instance, historically most people probably assumed that human morality, relationships, and societies were rooted in the spiritual realm and, therefore, related to religion. So it is that for centuries the governance of Western European societies was based upon "the divine right of kings." But with the rise of modernism, that basis shifts to humans themselves, with contemporary democracies resting on "the consent of the governed."

Moreover, secular philosophy often sees religion as more than "misguided," as a dangerous force that must be actively rooted out from spheres of public influence. As a result, many secular democracies try to remove religion from public debates, government, and education. This even occurs in countries where the vast majority of citizens are religious. A whole series of conflicts are ongoing globally between secularization and religion, as we see in later chapters. (See especially Chapter 10: Religion, Morality, and Ethics and Chapter 14: Religion and Society in a Global Age.) Religions born in traditional societies (which amounts to most religions) have found it difficult to adjust to other aspects of modern societies as well. For instance, religions often assume a sense of community and moral obligation that, as we have seen, was undercut by the forces of modernization with its rabid individualism. Similarly, modernistic pluralism and flatland relativism have tended, on the one hand, to bring together people of diverse backgrounds, while on the other hand to deny that there is any way to establish the truth or even relative merit of religious concepts, practices, or morality. The net result of this combination of forces is that people tend to make religion an individual and private experience. This is apparent in such statements as, "Well, you have your religion and I have mine; so let's not fight."

Modern people tend to see religion as an individual and private experience.

Although this permits personal commitment and may lessen conflict, it undermines the role of religion in society and cuts off the present from the possible benefits of the religious wisdom of the past. It also assumes incorrectly that religion has no social function, but it is entirely personal. Additionally, it ignores the commonalities of religions, the ability for people of different faith traditions to cooperate on common concerns like environmental problems, and the power of faiths to produce positive social change. Such a trite statement discounts the fact that religions themselves recognize higher and lower forms of faith and have a fair degree of agreement on what a higher form (or level) of religion looks like.

Religions have significant areas of agreement and recognize what higher forms of religion look like.

In summary then, the relationship of modernism and religion is ambiguous at best. On the one hand, modernism has produced a number of contributions to social development—for example, modern technology, medicine, and increased production—that have received favorable, though not uncritical, treatment from many forms of contemporary religion. Other aspects, like improvements in civil rights, human rights, and social justice, enjoy widespread religious support. However, still other aspects, such as environmental destruction, exploitation of the less fortunate, growing discrepancy between the wealthy and the poor, and some scientific advances, have drawn the ire of religious groups around the world. The undermining of community, growing consumerism, and the lack of moral commitments have been targeted by various religious groups as well. Still, the real dispute between religion and modernism centers on the religious sense that there is something sacred in or behind the universe, in contrast to the mechanistic, materialistic model of modernism. Ultimately, because of the dominance of this mechanistic model of the universe, religion sits uncomfortably indeed in the modern world.

consumerism—making the goal of life to consume more and more products

GLOBALIZATION AND THE CREATION OF GLOBAL SOCIETY

Globalization represents an unfolding of trends originating in modernism.

Earlier in this chapter we wrote about this moment in history as a time of *kairos* in which something that transcends modernism is struggling to be born. To some degree, globalization is a coming to completion of trends that began during the modern period or even before. For example, the concept of human rights is a prime force for individual and social justice in the emerging global society. The idea of human rights *per se* is, of course, very old and traceable in part to the concepts of the human and civil obligations of ancient Greek culture. More recently, the ancestors of universal human rights were the political and civil rights of citizens spelled out in documents like the United States' *Bill of Rights.* But it was not until very recently, in 1948, that the notion of universal, global human rights came to the forefront with the *United Nations Universal Declaration of Human Rights.*

Globalization also represents a clear break from the Modern Period.

We see in this example that globalization is, on the one hand, a further development of modern trends, but we can see in the same example that globalizing forces are remaking the modern world, even as modernism remade the world of traditionalism. Human rights are indeed a coming to fruition of earlier trends, but they also are something entirely new. Earlier rights were limited in scope. The *Bill of Rights,* of course, is only a national, not a global document, and it applies only to U.S. citizens even today. Moreover, when it was initially created, the rights spelled out in the document did not even apply to all people living within the borders of the country, but only to white males who owned property. Poorer white males, as well as all women, Native Americans, African Americans, and so on, only gradually gained their full rights as American citizens.

Human rights are associated with people because they are human.

Thus the *Universal Declaration* is a radical idea precisely because it recognizes certain rights attached to all humans simply because they are human. It applies to all, regardless of sex, race, ethnicity, religion, creed, station of birth (rich or poor), and age, and as absolute rights that cannot (at least theoretically) be denied them under any circumstances. Additionally, enforcement of these rights is not limited to an individual nation (as in the case of citizens' rights) but is given over to the community of nations individually and collectively. Furthermore, the *Universal Declaration* has become a basis of extending globalization. That is, injustices all over the globe are being addressed in the name of human rights. For instance, the abuse of women in various countries around the world is being fought in the name of human rights. It is no longer possible for a nation to justify abuse by saying, "It is our custom or our religious belief to treat women in this (abusive) fashion." They now have to answer to the assertion of universal rights that are understood to transcend local customs and beliefs.

So with globalization, as the case of human rights exemplifies, something old is dying, and something new is struggling to be born. Globalization in general is a process that is occurring right now, carrying with it some major shifts in human groups and in worldviews. It is necessary then, finally, to define this worldwide trend and to consider its effects on all human endeavors, especially considering the interactions between the emerging global society and religion.

■ GLOBALIZATION

Globalization, as we noted earlier in this chapter, is the growing interconnectedness of the realm of human activity on a worldwide scale along with the transforming impact of that interconnectedness. Globalization, to some extent, is connected with the spread of Western Civilization. The spread of Western Civilization began in the 16th century, as western European countries began several centuries of worldwide exploration and conquest. Though various western European powers had worldwide empires, a single global society did not exist and not all peoples were an active part of any developing global society. Some remained relatively isolated. To a large measure, World War II brought an end to those relatively isolated groups of people who were not really integrated into the emerging global system. For example, numerous peoples on isolated islands of the South Pacific had previous contact with the modern world but were reasonably free to pursue their traditional lives. World War II brought that part of the world onto center stage. The overall result was that these peoples have been progressively integrated into the global system and that integration is overrunning their traditional way of life, for better or worse. In fact, now there are very few, if any, peoples who have not had significant and transforming contact with the outside world.

This growing transformation resulting from interconnectedness is much more than a simple spreading of Western Civilization or even modernism. Instead a transformation is occurring in such a fashion that a new worldwide culture is being formed. By **culture** we mean a shared way of life which binds people or peoples together into a society. In other words, globalization is creating a common way of life for all the peoples of the world that is binding them into what philosopher and theologian Pierre Teilhard de Chardin (1881–1955) called "planetary-wide society" (*The Phenomenon of Man*).

A word of caution is in order before proceeding with the discussion of globalization. It is true that modernization and now globalization are tremendously powerful social forces that transform earlier types of societies. However, recognizing this does not mean that everyone or all peoples welcome the globalization process. In fact, many individuals, groups, and peoples resist, sometimes violently, the incursion of the changes sparked by globalization. This opposition comes from a number of different sources with varied interests. For instance, native peoples may resist destruction of their traditional cultures by forces of globalization. Others resist the exploitation of the environment or the poor that is magnified by globalization. Still others oppose the perceived threat to their religion posed by globalization.

Globalization is not welcomed by all.

Secondly, the creation of a planetary-wide society or a global culture does not mean that there is no room for considerable local variations. For instance, even though human rights are said to be universal (applying to all people everywhere), some variations are possible on local levels. This is most obvious when we are talking about what is known as social and economic rights. The *Universal Declaration* says that all citizens should have access to quality health care. However, whether access is granted through a type of government-supported health system or through a system provided by private companies and hospitals could be open to local interpretation. Or the type of medical care could vary according to local practices. Some societies might choose to rely entirely on Western scientific medicine while others might choose to rely on local medicine, such as Chinese herbal medicine in combination with Western medicine.

The globalization process is occurring on two levels—objective globalization and subjective globalization (Robertson). By **objective globalization** we mean "the increasing planetary interconnectedness of human social activity and the worldwide effects or repercussions of that activity" (Peterson, Wunder, and Mueller 16). Most people probably are aware of globalization at this level. These are things which are external, are obvious, and can be measured in some fashion. For example, there is now, more than ever, worldwide commerce connecting all regions of the world. There is more travel between the countries of the world as well. And where goods or people may not physically travel between different parts of the world, still more telephones, faxes, and computers spread information throughout. There are globe-spanning institutions, such as the International Court of Justice, the World Bank, and the United Nations, which make possible pursuing justice, funding international projects, taking some form of global political action, and the like. Companies advertise to global audiences: McDonald's sells hamburgers (or a rough equivalent) literally all over the world. The 2000 Olympic Games in Sydney, Australia, witnessed the participation of 198 of the world's 208 nations. The games were aired to an estimated television audience of 3 billion, or half of the world's population.

What is less apparent is that this level of interaction is actually transforming the way societies, nations, and regions conceive of themselves and of their place in the cosmos. For instance, when speaking of such issues as environmental decay and the threat posed by weapons of mass destruction, we sometimes ask our students, "After considering the possibility that our actions can end life on this planet, what is the only race that really counts?" Sooner or later, some student will come up with the answer, "The human race." This is an answer that one would not hear until very recently. This indicates an awareness that the fate of all peoples is connected at least at the basic level of survival.

This answer also suggests more fundamental changes are occurring at the level of individual and group consciousness. This basic impact is what is referred to as subjective globalization. **Subjective globalization** is "the social redefinition of identities and worldviews that emerges from the human confrontation and dialogue caused by objective globalization" (Peterson, Wunder, and Mueller 16). Precisely because it is remaking who we are on the inside, the process of subjective globalization is often personally troubling and the source of intergroup conflict. While we cannot discuss this topic in depth at this point, we note a few key elements involved with subjective globalization.

Probably the most troubling element in the redefinition involves identity. **Identity** is the way individuals and peoples understand themselves along with the ways they see themselves relating to other peoples, the natural world, and the spiritual world. Anthropologist Kay Milton argues that the boundaries that used to separate people are breaking down. These are being replaced by any number of discourses occurring on a worldwide level, where ideas, values, worldviews, practices, and beliefs are exchanged across traditional cultural, religious, and national boundaries. This not only makes global communication possible, but

Globalization occurs at two levels—objective and subjective

Subjective globalization involves a remaking of the interior worlds of individuals and groups.

Globalization is remaking individual and group identities.

also erodes traditional identities based on factors like ethnic group (i.e., Kurds, Zulu, Mosquito Indians), nation, and religion. In turn, these discourses lay the groundwork for defining oneself, one's people, one's nation, and one's religion in more universal terms.

Sociologist Wendell Bell notes that throughout human history there has been a strong tendency for people to live in progressively larger groups—from very small roaming bands to clans, from ethnic groups to nation–states, to even larger political, economic and religious units, and finally, possibly to a global society. Each of these levels may be a component of personal and community identity; hence, the transitions from one identity to another may produce confusion, uncertainty, and conflict, as one's identity in a family must expand to include one's identity in a village, or one's identity in an ethnic group gives way to being, say, a citizen of the United States. Certainly, the movement toward global society is also troubling, as many individuals and peoples feel that their personal and group identity is threatened and that their cherished way of life is being undermined. Indeed, one of the characteristics of emerging global society is that the profusion of identities already apparent in modernism is becoming more complex, and the traditional boundaries between groups is becoming more and more blurred.

Personal and group identities are threatened by globalization.

Another key element in subjective globalization involves shifts in personal and collective value systems. A **value system** involves the desired patterns of life, states of being, or outcomes of social life by which individuals and collectives measure the quality of their existences and the direction of their activities. A value system helps an individual or society define what is desirable and undesirable as well as how rewards and punishments, rights and duties should be distributed. A value system has to do with the ethical, moral, and justice dimensions of individual and social life. The most foundational shift in values occurring with globalization is moving away from value systems based on local standards toward those involving wider frames of reference. This shift is often expressed as a movement from particularism to universalism.

Particularism means the tendency to assess what is desirable and undesirable in terms of local values. That is, a tribe may use its own values to determine the proper relations between husbands and wives. On the other hand, universalism means finding standards for determining what is desirable or undesirable that apply to all people everywhere. Following the above example, a tribe might be called upon to determine the proper relations between husbands and wives on standards thought to apply to all people, such the *Universal Declaration of Human Rights*. But this can be problematic, since the values developed for a particular way of life might conflict with a more universal view. Should the "universal" standard for how a man treats his wife (or wives) overrule the cultural standards that have been in place for centuries? Should local American (or Canadian or Nigerian or Thai) standards for assessing political corruption dominate or should more widely recognized standards be applied? Should a country orient its economy toward meeting the needs of its citizens or risk participation in the global economy, which might cause harm to the standard of living of some citizens? These are the kinds of questions that exemplify the ongoing conflict between particularism and universalism on an array of fronts.

There is widespread conflict between particularism and universalism.

Finally, a profound reorientation in people's understanding of the universe and their relation to it seems to be occurring along with globalization. We noted earlier in this chapter that modernism tended to see the universe in a mechanistic, materialistic fashion. This led to **rational instrumentality** as the dominant mode of engaging the universe. Rational instrumentality means that human reason can be used to manipulate the universe and its component parts to suit human needs and desires. This approach is based on the assumptions that the universe is a dead machine and that humans, as thinking beings, are superior to the material world. As we saw above, the superiority of humans to the natural world has been severely challenged even within the circle of materialist thinkers, with the result that humans have come to be viewed as creatures among other creatures of the world.

Rational instrumentality is giving way to a re-enchanted universe.

Thus the dominance of a materialistic view of the universe is being challenged as we move into the 21st century, and a new model of the universe may be emerging, along with new images of how people operate in this universe. We might call this process re-enchanting the universe. By **re-enchanting** we mean there is a strong tendency to see the material universe as alive with spirit. In fact, some suggest that the essential character of the universe is spiritual, not material (Snyder). To some degree, this is a return to assumptions about the universe that were dominant prior to modernism. That is, most traditional peoples and religions saw the world as alive with spirits and demons and assumed a fundamental spiritual character to all of existence.

A spiritualized universe is altering how people relate to the material world.

Yet, something more than a simple return to traditional **animism,** a belief in the spiritual character of material phenomena and the universe itself, is afoot. The "spiritual" character of the universe is to an even greater extent being recognized and promoted by science itself, as we discuss later in this book. If the universe is alive with spirit, then humans' place in it is significantly altered. Humans can no longer attempt to manipulate thoughtlessly the material world but somehow must commune with it. Humans are no longer separated from and superior to the universe but progressively see themselves as part of the greater web of life that integrates all beings into a larger whole. Thus the new global community may include not only all people, but all living things of the planet. On this point, science and some kind of a spiritual view of the world seem at last to agree.

On all of these points, whether we consider the shift and broadening of community identities, challenges to local value systems, or the re-enchantment of the natural world, there are profound implications for religion. Thus globalization is a force to be reckoned with not only in the human affairs of economics and politics, but also in the very human world of religion.

■ RELIGION, GLOBAL SOCIETY, AND TWO AXIAL PERIODS

So far in this chapter, we have set the context for discussing the operation of religion in the contemporary world. We now turn our attention to how religion and global society interact. It is beyond the scope of the present chapter to do a thorough discussion of religion in global society. Instead, we confine ourselves to a few opening comments at this point. We present more detailed discussion as appropriate throughout this book.

Religion is intimately involved with two great axial periods in human history.

The First Axial Period set the stage for subsequent history.

Upanishads— Hindu sacred texts composed between 8th and 6th centuries BCE

Several tantalizing lines of thought could be pursued at this juncture. One of these is the involvement of religion in stimulating the two great axial periods in history. Following the lead of the German philosopher, Karl Jaspers (1883–1969), religious writer and editor Ewert Cousins maintains that contemporary globalization has its origins in the First Axial Period of history. The basic meaning of axial period can be grasped by thinking about the axle on your car. The axle is that point around which the tire rotates. So an **axial period** is an era of time around which subsequent history rotates.

The **First Axial Period** was an era stretching from approximately 800–200 BCE in which huge changes in human thought occurred, changes that in turn set the foundation for much of history until the present day. This period peaked about 500 BCE and produced major changes in thinking in three widespread areas of the world. In China, Lao Tzu and Confucius laid the groundwork for Chinese philosophy. In India, the Upanishads laid the foundation for new directions in Hinduism, while the Buddha and **Mahavira** (ca. 599–ca. 527 BCE) produced the foundations for Buddhism and Jainism, respectively. In Persia, **Zoroaster** (ca. 628–551 BCE) delved into the struggle between good and evil, while the Jewish prophets Elijah (ninth century BCE), the first Isaiah (eighth century BCE), and Jeremiah (seventh century BCE) linked true religion with social justice. Not much later, Greek philosophy developed, culminating in the thought of Socrates, Plato, and Aristotle, who laid the basis for the logical exploration of the universe, explored civil virtues, and developed complex metaphysical systems. Cousins contends that though these leaders were philosophers and religious teachers, their insights transformed all elements of human culture. Their impact is still felt today.

Along with the transformation of culture, a change occurred in the consciousness of humankind. The tribal mentality that dominated up to the First Axial Period was concerned with the rhythms of nature and fertility, as well as with the rituals that were often seen as somehow sustaining the cycles of the cosmos. The psychological emphasis was on the collective (i.e., on being members of the tribe), which gave emotional identity and security but left little room for individual development, responsibility, or spirituality. The new consciousness that developed in the First Axial Period stressed the individual knowing oneself, reflection on nature and society, and personal development. This self-reflective consciousness made the way for individual spirituality seem as a subjective (and perhaps inward) journey. Often this journey was tied with the quest for true morality. In the long run, the new consciousness led to a split between heaven and earth, between the material and the spiritual that we have seen characterizing much modern thought. It also led to the extreme individualism that may be undermining the very institutions upon which humans depend.

Cousins contends that the **Second Axial Period**, which is now reshaping human consciousness, is marked by moving away from divergence to convergence. That is, the classical religions resulted in moving into diverse patterns of thought, ritual, and philosophy. This allowed them to develop a rich tapestry of concepts and expressions of religious truth. Still, within the last hundred years, there have been any number of efforts to bring diverse religions together in creative contacts for dialogue on theological and practical issues. A defining characteristic of these efforts is the growing global consciousness we discussed above. This growing consciousness does not mean that religions are interested in becoming the same; rather, they seek both to celebrate their diversity and to find common ground, especially in the global effort to deal with the humanmade problems that threaten life on Earth. Those religions participating in this process hope to bring the moral power and accumulated wisdom of the world's diverse faith communities to the task of solving the problems of human and nonhuman life.

■ RELIGION, UNIVERSALISM, AND PARTICULARISM

The section above alludes to religion's involvement in creating and/or finding universals. Certainly one of the results of the First Axial Period was a belief in universal experiences and principles that applied to all people. For instance, most tribal peoples were concerned with serving their gods in the hope of providing prosperity, power, fertility, or other desirables for themselves. However, in most tribal religions, there was little thought to the relation of their gods to other peoples' gods, nor was there much of an idea of a god or gods for all people. Thus the Hebrews' god in the initial parts of Jewish scriptures was the god of Abraham, Isaac, and Jacob (the three earliest founders of the Hebrews' religion), but there seems to have been little concern for claiming that this was the one true god or the god who should be followed by Canaanites or Moabites (other tribes in the region). While conflicts with surrounding tribes were seen as conflicts between the gods of those tribes and the Hebrews' god, there was little effort to convert neighboring clans to the Hebrews' religion.

The First Axial Period saw a movement toward universalism.

This began to change with the First Axial Period. For instance, Jewish prophets began to speculate on the mission of the Jews to the world. The pressing question for these prophets was, "What does it mean to be God's chosen people?" The most important answer to this question derived by the prophets was that the Jews were to be a witness for God to the world. God was the God of all people, not just the Jews. The Jews were God's chosen instrument to bring His salvation to the world. Likewise, the Tao was seen as operating throughout the universe with all people, not just Chinese tribes. The enlightenment experienced by the Buddha was possible for all people, not just Indians, by following the universal teaching of the Buddha.

So historically and in the contemporary period, religion has been deeply involved with the growing quest for universals. At the same time, religion frequently is embroiled with the assertion of particularism. That is, religions have been and continue to be deeply involved in the creation of boundaries between groups as well as the assertion of the supposed superiority of one group over others based on religious differences. On the positive side of particularism, religion

Religion frequently is involved in the quest for universals along with the assertion of particularism.

helps cultures maintain their identity and protect their cherished way of life against the onslaught of outside forces related to globalization. On the negative side, the assertion of religious particularism may lead to prejudice, discrimination, and even violence against persons of different religions. Ironically, the religious quest for common ground and toleration apparent in contemporary life exists alongside rising religious bigotry and persecution. Interestingly, both trends often are seen in all religions. For example, there are Muslims who are working with other religions toward common goals, while at the same time other Muslims are deeply committed to advancing violently their brand of Islam against followers of other religious traditions.

■ RELIGION IN A RE-ENCHANTED UNIVERSE

We indicated that religion had a difficult time within the mechanistic, materialistic universe supported by most modern science. To some degree, religion and science have been seen as presenting alternative, incompatible understandings of the cosmos. Religion, it seems, advocated a subjectively experienced, intuitive, spiritual universe, while science advanced an objectively observed, rational universe operating according to discoverable laws. Thus while religion gave people a sense of nature's beauty and purpose, science seemed to provide mechanistic explanations, which, through technology, helped to solve many of the practical problems faced by modern people. So while religion might promise miracles or supernatural aid, it was science, the modernists believed, that would solve our problems of producing food, treating illness, and advancing human knowledge, all without assistance or interference from unpredictable outside spiritual forces.

The emerging spiritual view of the universe found in science will lay the ground for a deeper explanation of reality.

Nevertheless, there has arisen in some quarters a growing lack of faith in science to deliver on all its promises, while many have found the rational world of science emotionally unrewarding. As a result, a resurgence of spirituality marked the last few decades of the 20th century. As we have noted, science itself may be moving toward a much more "spiritual" view of the cosmos, and it is possible that this more spiritual view of the cosmos now advocated by both some branches of science and religion may provide a fruitful plane for creative dialogue. In turn, this dialogue may allow an exploration of yet deeper elements of reality. Science and religion together, in a combined effort to describe a meaningful, rather than mechanistic universe, may now be in a position to contribute to a more comprehensive understanding of our world and of ourselves, helping to define a new global society.

CONCLUSION

All of these changes are upon us, and one rightly faces the increasingly global future with both hope and fear. But in all these changes, religion is and will continue to be a powerful force both for and against the events of a post-modern world. This textbook in general, and this chapter in particular, invite you to study religion, one of the most challenging areas of contemporary life. At once, religion is one of the oldest human pursuits as well as one of the most current. Religion informs, encourages, and inspires both the best and the worst in human beings. It has moved men and women to heroic sacrifice and motivated great compassion, while it has also been a factor stimulating the greatest achievements in thought, ethics, art, literature, music, dance, and architecture. At the same time, it has been a source of some of the greatest acts of hatred, bigotry, and genocide in human history. Religion has been and continues to be a two-edged sword, cutting for both good and evil in the broad and varied lives of individuals and societies all over the world. Religion is a powerful force with which we must reckon—for better or worse. We hope this text will provide you the tools for a more in-depth understanding of the broad range of human religion and how it will continue to fit into the changing world that you are bound to inherit.

■ INTERACTIVE EXERCISE

Please continue your exploration of Religion in Global Society by going to the interactive exercise for this chapter online (**http://www.religion.wadsworth.com/richter**).

WORKS CITED

Holy Bible. New Revised Standard Version. New York: Oxford UP, 1989.

Law of Manu, Sacred Books of the East. Vol. 25. Oxford: Oxford UP, 1886.

Bellah, Robert N., et al. *Habits of the Heart: Individualism and Commitment in American Life.* Berkeley: University of California Press, 1985.

Bokser, Ben Zion, and Baruch Bokser. *The Talmud: Selected Writings.* New York: Paulist Press, 1989.

Cousins, Erwert H. *Christ of the 21st Century.* New York: Continuum, 1998.

de Chardin, Pierre Teilhard. *The Phenomenon of Man.* New York: Harper Torch Books, 1965.

Fieser, James, and John Powers. *Scriptures of the World's Religions.* Boston: McGraw/Hill, 1998.

Leys, Simon (trans.). *The Analects of Confucius.* New York: Bantam Books, 1997.

Marty, Martin E. "An Exuberant Adventure: The Academic Study and Teaching of Religion." *Religious Studies News,* Vol. 12, No. 3 (September 1997): 20, 48.

Milton, Kay. *Environmentalism and Cultural Theory.* New York: Routledge, 1996.

Peterson, R. Dean, Delores F. Wunder, and Harlan L. Mueller. *Social Problems: Globalization in the Twenty-First Century.* Upper Saddle River, NJ: Prentice Hall, 1999.

Robertson, Roland. *Globalization: Social Theory and Global Culture.* Newberry Park, CA: Sage, 1992.

Schmidt, Roger. *Exploring Religion.* Belmont, CA: Wadsworth, 1980.

Scruton, Roger. "Impious Europe." *Wilson Quarterly.* (Winter 2003): 56–60.

Shakir, M. H. (trans.). *The Koran.* Electronic Text Center. http://etext.virginia.edu/koran.html (accessed July 3, 2003).

Snyder, Howard A. *Earth Currents: The Struggle for the World's Soul*. Nashville, TN: Abingdon, 1995.

Weber, Max. *The Protestant Ethic and the Spirit of Capitalism*. Trans. Talcott Parsons. New York: Scribner, 1958.

Wilber, Ken. *A Brief History of Everything*. Boston: Shambhala, 1996.

FOR FURTHER READING

Barbour, Ian. *Religion in an Age of Science: The Gilford Lectures*. Vol. 1. New York: HarperCollins, 1990.

Beyer, Peter. *Religion and Globalization*. Thousands Oaks, CA: Sage, 1994.

Bokser, Ben Zion, and Baruch Bokser. *The Talmud: Selected Writings*. New York: Paulist Press, 1989.

Cousins, Erwert H. *Christ of the 21st Century*. New York: Continuum, 1998.

Fieser, James, and John Powers. *Scriptures of the World's Religions*. Boston, McGraw/Hill, 1998.

Huntington, Samuel P. *The Clash of Civilizations and the Remaking of the World Order*. New York: Simon and Schuster, 1996.

Milton, Kay. *Environmentalism and Cultural Theory*. New York: Routledge, 1996.

Robertson, Roland. *Globalization: Social Theory and Global Culture*. Newberry Park, CA: Sage, 1992.

Smith, Huston. *Beyond the Post-Modern Mind*. Revised ed. New York: Crossroads, 1989.

Snyder, Howard A. *Earth Currents: The Struggle for the World's Soul*. Nashville, TN: Abingdon, 1995.

Teasdale, Wayne, and George F. Cairns, eds. *The Community of Religions*. New York: Continuum, 1996.

Wapner, Paul. *Environmental Activism and World Civil Politics*. Chatham, NJ: Chatham, 1996.

Wilber, Ken. *A Brief History of Everything*. Boston: Shambhala, 1996.

Yogananda, Paramahansa. *A World in Transition: Finding Security in Times of Change*. Los Angeles: Self-Realization Fellowship, 1999.

2 WHAT IS RELIGION?

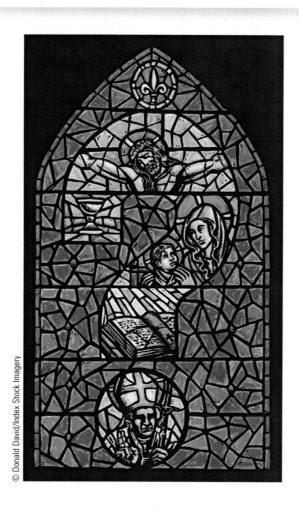

© Donald David/Index Stock Imagery

We can imagine some students having the following conversation: "Doesn't everybody know what we mean by *religion?*" "I know what my religion means to me." "Well, I guess there are those who aren't religious or don't have any religion." "Maybe it does need to be defined or explained for some people." In this chapter, we present some of the most important definitions and understandings of religion. Please look over the pictures for this chapter found above and online (**http://www.religion.wadsworth.com/**

richter), and read the following scriptural passages, then consider the Introductory Questions to prepare for reading this chapter.

> *Now faith is the assurance of things hoped for, the conviction of things not seen. . . . By faith we understand that the worlds were prepared by the word of God, so that what is seen was made from things that are not visible.*
> —Christianity: Holy Bible: Hebrews 11:1, 3

> *This day have those who disbelieve despaired of your religion, so fear them not, and fear Me. This day have I perfected for you your religion and completed My favor on you and chosen for you Islam as a religion.*
> —Islam: Holy Koran 5:3

> *Zilu asked how to serve the spirits and gods. The Master [Confucius] said: "You are not yet able to serve men, how could you serve the spirits?" Zilu said: "May I ask you about death?" The Master said: "You do not yet know life, how could you know death?"*
> —Confucianism: The Analects 11:12

> *Indifferent to all sensual delights, Mahavira cheerfully wandered from place to place, speaking very little. In the winter he would meditate in the shade, and in summer he would expose himself to the blazing heat of the sun. Thoroughly purifying himself, disciplining his mind, body and speech, Mahavira became completely calm and equanimical.*
> —Jainism: from the Acaranga-sutra and the Kalpa-sutra

> *Abdu'l-Baha said: ". . . All God's prophets have brought the message of love. None has ever thought that war and hate are good. Every one agrees in saying that love and kindness are best."*
> —Baha'i: "The Universal Love" by Abdu'l-Baha

INTRODUCTORY QUESTIONS

These pictures and scriptural quotations suggest different aspects of what it means to be religious. Perhaps it is primarily about belief, or about moral action, or about ritual. Look at these pictures and read the quotations as you consider the questions below.

1. The Christian religion often speaks of faith. Is faith the central attitude of religion? What does the word *faith* really mean?

2. The Baha'i religion claims to bring together all religions and claims that God meant all religions to teach love and peace. Do you think this is so, given what religions do and say in the world? If someone does preach war or hatred, can we conclude he or she is not really religious?

3. Mahavira is praised in Jainism as a "Tirthankara" who purified himself by self-denial and self-inflicted pain. The statue of Gotamesvara, another Tirthankara, shows a saint who stood still and did nothing until vines grew up around his body. Does this kind of withdrawal seem like "purity" of religion? Why or why not?

4. Imagine Pentecostal Christians praying with their hands raised up high and a Muslim man reading the Holy Koran. Could both of these be "worship"? If God himself has "perfected" religion for us, as in the quote from the Holy Koran, maybe the Pentecostals are sincere enough, but sincerely wrong in the manner in which they are worshipping God. How does that strike you? Does this contradict what you know or have been taught?

5. Compare both the worshippers in question 4 to the moral activity of Mother Teresa. All of them are "doing something" with their religion, but perhaps Mother Teresa seems more morally active, rather than just performing some ritual. Does her "activity" seem to you more properly religious? Might ritual and morality *both* be important?

6. Apparently, Confucius thinks that concerns about spirits or the afterlife are relatively unimportant. Does such an idea make you think Confucius could not have been really teaching religion? Does religion *have* to be about gods or spirits or the afterlife?

WHAT IS RELIGION?

If there were a consensus among scholars as to what religion is, we could simply cite the definition or description, and there would be no need for this chapter. However, as is often the case, neither life nor the religious dimension of human experience is that simple. The range of possibilities in attempting to define religion goes all the way from overgeneralization to oversimplification, from paradox to perspectival or reductive, from playful or humorous to despair or disparaging, to "no religion," as in "there is no such thing." For example, just as the great philosophical theologian of the early Christian church St. Augustine (354–430) "defined" time by saying, "If you do not ask me what time is, I know what it is; if you ask me, I do not know" (Saint Augustine 264), so also could religion be "defined" in the same way the Supreme Court of the United States defined pornography: "We can't *define* it, but we recognize it when we see it." In this chapter we examine a number of different definitions of religion to help you begin to appreciate the complexity involved in trying to define exactly what religion is or is not.

There are many definitions of religion.

A major scholar in the history of religions, Jonathan Z. Smith, writes:

It was once a tactic of students of religion to cite the appendix of James H. Leuba's Psychological Study of Religion *(1912), which lists more than fifty definitions of religion to demonstrate that "the effort clearly to define reli-*

gion in short compass is a hopeless task." Not at all! The moral of Leuba is not that religion cannot be defined, but that it can be defined, with greater or less success, more than fifty ways. . . "Religion" is not a native term; it is a term created by scholars for their intellectual purposes and therefore is theirs to define. It is a second-order, generic concept that plays the same role in establishing a disciplinary horizon that a concept such as "language" plays in linguistics or "culture" plays in anthropology. There can be no disciplined study of religion without such a horizon. (281–282)

Smith means by this that, for all the difficulties we may have in trying to focus in on a good definition of religion, we cannot shirk the intellectual duty of at least trying to define it. While there may not be a "right" definition, any of the many definitions we might find or construct can be more or less helpful in truly understanding this astonishing phenomenon we all experience, whether personally or as mere observers. So, although it is bound to be difficult and open to considerable challenge, we simply must try our hand at defining our topic, being willing to refine and develop our definitions as we go. Trying to define religion, therefore, is not an act of fruitless guessing, but an important process of trying to understand something vital and difficult.

■ ETYMOLOGICAL AND DICTIONARY RESOURCES

Given the challenge of defining religion, we might begin to get at the meaning of the word starting with its etymology, the meaning of its roots. According the *Oxford English Dictionary (OED)*, religion is connected earlier with the Latin *relegere*, to read over again, but later with the Latin *religare* (*re*, back; *ligare*, to bind). This latter connection is the idea usually favored by modern scholars in explaining the force of the word. Thus religion from *religare* suggests to bind back, to be bound to some important idea or value. According to other sources, this "binding" is reminiscent of being bound to a promise. Thus Schmidt et al. write:

In Latin, the root word for religion means "to bind."

> *In early Roman times,* religio *signified the oaths and obligations that families observed in relationship to powers external to human beings. Individuals who were diligent in performing their obligations were* religiosi *(devout or pious), and the places in which such duties were performed were considered religious, or sacred. The Roman philosopher* **Cicero** *(ca. 45 BCE) noted that* religio *was derived from the root* religere, *a term meaning "to gather together" and "to go over again" in the sense of one who is careful and constant in performing ceremonies in the service of the gods. Early Christians understood* religio *to signify the careful performance of rites and duties in respect to God. (4)*

When coming across any word whose meaning may be unfamiliar, it may be helpful to see whether any part of it is like a word one already knows, which, in turn, may help one to understand its meaning. For example, even though religion begins with *re*, you may recognize the *lig* part as looking like the word *ligament*. And what does a ligament do? It binds bone to bone, muscle to cartilage. Similarly, one's religion may bind one back to a strong commitment one has to the object of one's faith. The word ob*lig*ation makes the same point.

Religion may mean faith in or worship of some One or Thing, but some religions have neither.

After the etymology, the *OED* offers the following succinct definition pertinent to our inquiry: "A particular system of faith and worship." Perhaps this is the conception of religion that many people would take for granted, particularly in cultures dominated by Christianity. But those who have some familiarity with the religions of the world other than Christianity might realize that the worship part of the definition does not seem always to apply. Indeed, the concept of worship may be quite inappropriate for religions without an object of worship, such as Buddhism or Confucianism. Indeed, the Confucian quotation at the beginning of this chapter suggests strongly that the worship of spiritual beings is certainly *not* what Confucius taught.

We can see that dictionary definitions do not necessarily settle our problem. Indeed, that may be why dictionaries often offer multiple definitions of words, especially of difficult philosophical terms like religion. Thus the *OED* follows the above definition of religion with another, more elaborate definition. Religion, it says, is

> *Recognition on the part of humans of some higher unseen power as having control of one's destiny, and as being entitled to obedience, reverence, and worship; the general mental and moral attitude resulting from this belief, with reference to its effect upon the individual or the community; personal or general acceptance of this feeling as a standard of spiritual and practical life.*

Here again we recognize the definition's presumptions about worship. We might also note that this definition has problems because not all religions think in terms of a higher power—that being, power, or person one worships. The relatively small religion of India called Jainism, for example, explicitly denies the importance of gods and elaborates, rather philosophically, reasons for denying the idea of an ultimate Creator. As with some sects of Buddhism, Jainism prefers to stress salvation in terms of self-effort. Gods are irrelevant.

Another definition provided by the *OED* is "Devotion to some principle; strict fidelity or faithfulness; conscientiousness; pious affection or attachment." This definition appears to be more neutral, but of course it would not satisfy those whose religion is more (or less) than steadfast adherence to a principle. That is, we could easily note that for many people their personal religion is not, in this sense, very religious. Or stated less paradoxically, it is easy to see that many people are not very devoted to their religion. This is not meant as a criticism but only as an observation. In fact, it seems simply evident that for many people, other interests besides religion occupy their time and lay claim to their devotion. Roman Catholic marathon runners might well spend much more time and energy training for the marathon than they do practicing worship or ritual. Thus they would be showing much more devotion to their running and training than they do to their Catholicism. Nevertheless, if we would say they practice running "religiously," we mean it only as a metaphor. Roman Catholicism remains their religion, even if they show more devotion to their running.

In all these dictionary definitions of religion we could certainly find problems. Yet despite the ambiguity in the definitions regarding the term, we should not, as was noted above, simply despair or give up on finding some kind of helpful direction. Thus, aside from the dictionary, scholars have labored long to define our term, and a number of definitions of religion have become some of the more well-known within the field of religion. We shall go through some of these and then try to determine whether any observations regarding them can help us with any kind of taxonomy, or systematic categorization, of religion.

■ DEFINING RELIGION

There have been numerous scholarly attempts to define or describe religion, and the definitions themselves come in various forms. For example, some definitions of religion are said to be monothetic, while others are polythetic. Other definitions are considered functional. The term *monothetic* comes from the words *mono*, meaning one, and *thesis*, a proposition or affirmation. Thus monothetic definitions of religion try to "identify a single, decisive trait that all members of a class invariably have in common . . ." (J. Smith 4). For example, saying that all religions are defined by having "supernatural beings," or "the sacred," or "the ultimate" would be monothetic definitions. We will see more of this kind of definition shortly.

A polythetic (*poly,* many; *thesis,* as above) definition would tend to replace the "single, decisive feature" with "a *set* of *features or properties*" that defines religion. Thus, we will see definitions of religion that stress not just one criterion of religion but a whole series of qualities. Indeed, as our effort to define religion develops, we will find that a focus on the sacred will include implications about ritual, morality, and a number of other aspects of life, all of which may be religious.

Finally, functional definitions focus on religion's "capacity to serve human needs. For example, religion has been defined functionally as a form of social control, as morality tinged with emotion, as a way of investing life with meaning" (Schmidt et al. 9). This means that we might try to define religion not by specifying what it contains but by indicating what it does, especially what it does for people psychologically and socially. When we discuss how religions help to satisfy people's need for meaning or how religions help to organize society, we are considering functional aspects of religion.

From our perspective, the human elements of thought, action, passion, and will, along with the entire religious dimension of human experience itself, provide the most elemental categories for defining religion. Thus any and all definitions, descriptions, understandings, or interpretations of religion will have to be polythetic, even if some central aspect of religion can be identified at its core. Note as we continue how many aspects of religion seem to be parts of a definition, even as a fully applicable definition eludes us. The multifaceted nature of religion may become evident. Perhaps the exercises for this chapter will also provide some insight into the multifaceted nature of the phenomenon of religion.

■ RELIGION AS RITUAL

Because of its ties to the etymology of the word *religion,* perhaps a good place to begin is with a definition that focuses on the repetitive ritual activity involved. In his book *Religion: An Anthropological View,* Anthony F. C. Wallace states that

> *Religion is a set of rituals, rationalized by myth, which mobilizes supernatural powers for the purpose of achieving or preventing transformations of state in [humankind] or nature. (107; see also Hall, Pilgrim, and Cavanagh 6)*

monothetic—
containing one thesis or proposition

polythetic—
containing a variety of criteria

functional—
pertaining to functions

Here Wallace stresses the human element of action—doing or performing a ritual. This is not the only kind of religious action one might perform, and soon we will contrast ritual with another form of action, morality. Still, the relation of religion to ritual is easy to see. When the Hindu devotee enters a temple and places a red dot on his or her forehead, this is ritual. Similarly, when the Jewish believer performs the Seder, when the Roman Catholic Christian makes the sign of the cross, when the Native American performs a rain dance, when the Muslim faces **Mecca** to pray, or when one utters a simple prayer of thanks before a meal—all this is performing a ritual. And doing these things, many people believe, makes one religious.

Of course, ritual is really only one element of religious life and therefore, perhaps, ought not to be raised to the level of providing a definition of religion. Indeed, ritual is important enough to warrant a full chapter in this text, but it is also clear that there are rituals, from handshakes to celebrating the Fourth of July, that are not really religious. We shall discuss such matters in some depth later.

Seder—elaborate dinner, performed by Jews to commemorate the Exodus from slavery

Religion may mean performing a religious ritual.

Box 2.1   Global Byte
Yes, But Is It a Religion?

An aspect of globalization among various groups in the United States of America seems to be a development away from organized religion in favor of spiritual movements. While the major traditional institutionalized religions are often scrutinized and viewed with suspicion in regard to traditional practices, ritual action, and beliefs, many groups find a spiritual dimension in alternative trends.

In the beginning of 2004, with the recent announcement of the detection of the first cow suffering from mad cow disease, organizations like Sanctuary Farms suddenly gained new popularity. The purpose of Sanctuary Farms is to promote compassion for America's most abused animals, among these are turkeys, pigs, cows, and sheep. The founders of the community began their campaign by tracing practices in slaughterhouses on videotape and making those practices known to television audiences as well as using them as evidence in court. Today, they run a 175-acre farm, which serves as a living space and shelter for animals taken from "dead piles" at slaughterhouses or farms. In addition, the farm provides education for visitors and volunteers, supports a store, and circulates publications to further their goals in raising awareness in the campaign against the cruelty of American food production, in which animals are treated as objects rather than sentient beings. Volunteers are asked to follow a vegan lifestyle. This requires them to follow a diet without meat, dairy products, eggs, honey, or other animal byproducts; not to wear leather, silk or wool clothing; and to use care items that have not been tested by animals and do not include animal by-products.

The organization is certainly not a traditional religious group. Nevertheless, it uses the word *sanctuary* for the farm, indicating the spiritual dimension of the pursuit to preserve animal rights. Its overall goal, to foster compassion to all sentient beings, also globally connects the followers with more traditional religious groups, such as Buddhists and Hindus as well as many Native Americans. So we are left with the question, "Is the Sanctuary Farm movement a religion?"

Source: "Sanctuary Farm Applauds Ban on Butchering of Sick Animals," *New York Times.* 2 January, 2004: B1.

■ RELIGION AS MORAL CONDUCT

If ritual is seen as religious activity, then another form of religious action alluded to earlier is ethical or moral action on the part of a religious person. As written in the Hebrew Scriptures, religion may be defined with the words and emphasis of the prophet Amos:

> *I hate, I despise your festivals,*
> *and I take no delight in your solemn assemblies.*
> *Even though you offer me your burnt offerings and grain offerings,*
> *I will not accept them;*
> *and the offerings of well-being of your fatted animals*
> *I will not look upon.*
> *Take away from me the noise of your songs;*
> *I will not listen to the melody of your harps.*
> *But let justice roll down like waters,*
> *and righteousness like an everflowing stream.*
>
> *Amos 5: 21–24*

The point here seems, like ritual, to emphasize the proper behavior of religion, but unlike ritual, indeed in direct contrast to ritual, the Jewish scripture here clearly demands justice and righteousness. In a similar vein, Jesus also said: "Not everyone who says to me, 'Lord, Lord,' will enter the [realm] of heaven, but only the one who does the will of my Father in heaven" (Matthew 7: 21). In this context of "righteous action" it is easy to understand the indirect definition of religion on the part of Christian theologian Albrecht Ritschl (1822–1889). For Ritschl, true religion was doing the righteous, the moral, the ethical, or the good deed, not the performance of any ritual. According to a treatment of Ritschl by H. Richard Niebuhr (1894–1962), an important Christian theologian who did significant work in the sociology of religion,

Religion may be the performance of moral conduct, of "good deeds."

> *The Christian can exercise his calling to seek the kingdom of God if, motivated by love of neighbor, he carries on his work in the moral communities of family and economic, national and political life. Indeed "family, private property, personal independence and honor (in obedience to authority)" are goods that are essential to moral health and the formation of character. Only by engagement in civic work for the sake of the common good, by faithfulness in one's social calling, is it possible to be true to the example of Christ. . . . the founder of the Christian community is at the same time the moral hero who marks a great advance in the history of culture. (qtd. in Niebuhr 97–98; emphasis added).*

Thus, true religion is following Jesus, who, according to Ritschl, is the "moral hero": not so much the Son of God or the Divine/Human One but the most perfect human being who ever lived, the imitation of whom is the Christian's true religious obligation. Writing in the context of ethics, Christian theological ethicists Waldo Beach and H. Richard Niebuhr further characterize Ritschl as one who "centered his attention on the historic Jesus of Nazareth, rather than on the metaphysical God–man, as the Saviour of man through the *moral perfection of his personality*. . . . He made of the Kingdom of God an earthly goal, 'the moral unification of the human race, through action prompted by universal love to our neighbor'" (445; italics added).

Whether or not this is an accurate assessment of Christianity, the point clearly is to define genuine religion as a kind of behavior, specifically moral behavior. We might have to consider if being moral is necessarily being religious; certainly many moralistic **atheists** would like to be considered good, ethical human beings but steadfastly not religious ones. But on the other hand, we might expect that some kind of moral response would be part of a religious commitment. We shall in a later chapter consider the relation of religion and morality. For now, let us admit that the two are not necessarily identical but that they are often closely intertwined.

■ RELIGION AS FEELING

Another influential definition of religion was that of Christian theologian and philosopher **Friedrich Schleiermacher (1768–1834)**, who defined religion as "a feeling of absolute dependence" or "the absolute feeling of dependence." This feeling, Schleiermacher suggested, is something *experienced emotionally* or non-rationally. This does not mean that the religious feeling is *ir*rational but that it is felt or experienced, in contrast with doctrines and beliefs that may be thought out or intellectually believed based on reason (13; see also 19, 34, 40, 125). Feeling is also in contrast to actions ritually performed, such as those discussed above. Feeling is emotion, not ideas or actions.

Religion may be a feeling or an emotion.

Nevertheless, feeling here does not mean any kind of emotion. As Joseph Dabney Bettis points out,

> *This moment of self-awareness does not accompany our involvement with any object in the world or the world as a whole because these relationships are always reciprocal. Rather it is an awareness of the fact that we and the objects of our environment, which are reciprocally related, are both, in their relatedness, dependent and not self-sufficient. The "absolute feeling of dependence" is not merely the "feeling of dependence" carried to the absolute. It is a . . . type of awareness. We give the name "God" to the correlate of this feeling of absolute dependence. (142)*

Thus Schleiermacher's intent is to relate this "feeling of absolute dependence" to something beyond the world, something greater and more wonderful than any merely earthly dependence. It is not absolute dependence on one's car for transportation, or on one's parents for tuition money. Of course, the more desperate one's situation, the more these merely earthly dependencies might qualify as a kind of religious feeling. Perhaps you have had the experience of feeling absolutely dependent upon the person who can fix what desperately needs fixing, or who can help you get your computer to do what you just could not figure out how to do on your own, without whom you simply could not proceed. Perhaps more dramatically, imagine that you are in a cave large enough for guided tours and you have been told at one point that all the lights will be turned off. You may also have been cautioned to sit down or to hold onto something like a railing because you may lose your balance in the dark. Indeed, when the lights go out in such an environment, you may become completely disoriented because there is *no* light whatsoever. This is *absolute* darkness, an absolute blackness in which you cannot see your hand in front of your eyes, and you may realize with a hint of fear your utter lostness. Lost indeed: in such a world there would be literally nowhere to turn, no direction or sense even of where to begin. This is "a feeling of *absolute dependence!*". . . on the railing, . . . and someone turning the lights on again!

A similar understanding was reflected in a classic book, *The Idea of the Holy* by Rudolph Otto (1869–1937), a Christian theologian who also believed that religion was a feeling. For Otto, this feeling could be described as an experience of the *mysterium tremendum,* the tremendous mystery of the holy. He described this as a sense of the numinous, a presence at once wonderful and eerie. It is a sense of the power of the holy, the nonrational (again, not *irrational*) experience of the sacred above and beyond and in contrast to the commonplace phenomena of the worldly experience of the senses (12–30).

mysterium tremendum— Lat. fear-inspiring mystery

Those Latin words, *mysterium tremendum,* spoken in one's deepest, most tremulous and ominous voice, begin to express the feeling of what Otto meant. It may be like the kind of experience that gives one that "tingling feeling up and down your spine" or just the kind of goose bumps that have nothing to do with being cold. Although the word *awesome* has lost some of its weight due to its current overuse, the experience of truly being awestruck is something like what Otto was attempting to convey. We shall have occasion to develop Otto's concept of the holy later, and we shall look in Chapter 3: The Absolute, the Ultimate, the Holy at the objects of the holy that are, perhaps, the central fixture of religion. Here, in this section, we note the human element of feeling, emotion or passion— something other than that which can be put into words, defined, or "captured" by the intellectual mind. Religion, it seems, is something one must feel, something otherwise ineffable, inexpressible, and just as difficult as defining love or any of the other human emotions. It brings to mind the awe-inspiring prayer of Shankara (early eighth century CE), a great Hindu philosopher and mystic. His prayer began with the invocation, ". . . Thou, before whom all words recoil" (qtd. in Smith 60). Here indeed "words recoil," for the experience of this wonder is not something to define or describe. It is something to feel.

■ RELIGION AS ULTIMATE CONCERN

Related, perhaps, to the emphasis above on the emotional sense of dependence or of the awesomeness of the holy, a potentially more neutral version of this focus on religious feeling uses the terminology of the *ultimate* as something many religions have in common. When something is "ultimate," we could say it is the final, the most important, the first or last basis and foundation of everything else. Indeed, the word *ultimate* comes to us, oddly enough, from Greek grammar, in which the final syllable of a word was called the *ultima*. For our purposes, and perhaps for a definition of religion, a focus on the "ultimate" then becomes the sense of finding that which is the final ground of life.

Religion is whatever is of ultimate concern to the individual or the culture.

The "object" that one finds ultimate may, of course, be quite varied. It may be "a spiritual being, an impersonal absolute, or a way of being," as Schmidt et al.

have suggested (7). But whatever the ultimate may be, Paul Tillich (1886–1965), a major German–American philosophical theologian, has argued that this concept is really the best basis for defining religion. He wrote:

> *Religion is the aspect of depth in the totality of the human spirit. . . . What does the metaphor* depth *mean? It means that the religious aspect points to that which is ultimate, infinite, unconditional in [humankind's] spiritual life. Religion, in the largest and most basic sense of the word, is ultimate concern. And ultimate concern is manifest in all creative functions of the human spirit. (81)*

Thus, whatever is of ultimate concern to someone is that person's religion.

We already noted above, when considering the dictionary definition of religion as "devotion," that there seems to be a considerable possibility that what one finds most important may not exactly be religious. Tillich, of course, was well aware of this problem and called it the "demonization" or the "profanization" of the true focus of religion. That is, it seems evident that people can, and often do, take other ideals and causes as their ultimate concern. This, he said, results in "quasi-religions—ideologies, such as nationalism or socialism, which claim the loyalty or veneration of their followers with the intensity of the theistic religions." According to Tillich, "we are faced by two opposing dangers: on the one hand, . . .secularization. . . —a process of becoming more and more empty or materialistic without any ultimate concern; and on the other hand, demonization, which makes one particular religious symbol, group, usage, world view—or whatever—absolute" (Tillich and Brown 4–5). That "whatever" can include money, power, sex, clothes, automobiles, collectibles, and, one dares to say, even sports—the "shrine" in the home being the television room, the local place of worship being the sports bar, the cathedral being the city stadium, and the denomination or branch of religion being the major league involved.

Whatever the dangers of defining religion as ultimate concern, there seems to be some significance to Tillich's point that religion serves to ground people's lives and to provide a final anchor to the significance of human action. Thus, another version of Tillich's understanding may be that of "John B. Magee, the author of *Religion and Modern Man,* who offers the following definition: 'Religion is the realm of the ultimately real and ultimately valuable' [22, 29, 32]. Here religion is defined as the true and ultimate measure of people's existence, the final test of life's meaning" (Hall, Pilgrim, and Cavanagh 7–8).

Religion may be that which is "meaning-giving."

Similarly, Max Weber (1864–1920), a singularly eminent figure in the history of sociology, provides another important definition of religion. He defined religion as "a *meaning-giving* activity that serves emotional and social, as well as cognitive, functions." Religion, he argued, is "a way of investing life with meaning in response to those features of human existence (suffering, evil, and death) that are not resolvable in scientific terms [cf. Weber 1]. As anthropologist Clifford Geertz observed, "religious symbol systems provide a context for making suffering 'bearable, supportable, something, as we say, sufferable'" (qtd. in Schmidt et al. 9).

All this is to say that there is good sense in defining religion as a kind of basis for life, a source of grounding, meaning, and significance. And when one traces back the meaning of life to its final basis, one finds the ultimate, one's proper and necessary ultimate concern. Again, there is reason also to question a definition of religion that offers too easily the possibility of defining nationalism or sports as genuine religion. But there is also a profound point to seeing religion as a final source of the meaning of life.

■ RELIGION AS BELIEF

Religion may mean affirming a belief.

While we have just described definitions of religion that stress feeling without words of description, other definitions of religion concentrate on the words or ideas usually present and often central in religion. This is the religious aspect of belief, or the fact that religions often include a belief system. Belief, here, refers to a kind of cognitive assent, an agreement with the truth claims a religion might make about realities and powers beyond the ordinary. It probably also involves a certain commitment or self-investment in such ideas. Certainly, for many people, and especially in the Western or Abrahamic religions, this emphasis on believing may be centered on belief in God or gods, in deities or spiritual or supernatural beings. Of course, there are also important beliefs in nonreligious or atheistic ideologies, such as nationalism; free-market, free-enterprise capitalism; or antireligious **Marxist–Leninist–Stalinist communism.** However, such beliefs may not seem religious to most of us, and indeed some scholars in anthropology have maintained that "belief in Spiritual Beings" or "belief in superhuman beings and in their power to assist or harm. . . is the core variable which ought to be designated by any definition of religion" (Tylor 383). Specifically, ". . . 'religion [is] an institution consisting of culturally patterned interaction with culturally postulated superhuman beings'" (Spiro 94).

When these beliefs solidify and become institutionalized, then either assent or consent to a prescribed belief is the key issue for the authorities and believers involved. Perhaps the most salient examples are the various creeds within Christianity, which came to be the ultimate criterion for inclusion or membership within the group. The very word **creed** comes from the Latin word *credo,* meaning "I believe," and the effect of this early Christian emphasis on creeds was to define oneself and proper membership in the Christian church by what one believed. Thus the failure to believe the **orthodox** (straight teachings) creeds, or the refusal to deny beliefs deemed **heterodox** ("other teachings"), became the criterion for exclusion, excommunication, or even execution. Specific examples of creeds include the Apostles' and the Nicene Creed within Christianity, but there are other creeds from other religions. The Islamic Shahada, the declaration that "There is no God but Allah; Muhammad is the Prophet of Allah," is, like a creed, the kind of confession which, when uttered publicly and with full knowledge of its meaning, constitutes entry into and membership in Islam. In a way, these declarations of belief are like pledges of allegiance or loyalty oaths in the secular world. But our emphasis here is that, within religion, sometimes the most prominent defining quality is the element of human thought, for example, the mind and its intellect affirming a belief, a **doctrine** or a teaching. In this way, belief sometimes sees thoughts as the predominant element, rather than the human elements of ritual action or religious passion or emotion.

▪ NOT RELIGION BUT FAITH

Closely related to the definition of religion as belief might be the consideration of religion as faith. Indeed, this term is itself troublesome and may require significant consideration before we grasp exactly what it means. One definition of religion as faith is a kind of negative definition coming from an entirely Christian perspective. We think here of Karl Barth (1886–1968), one of the most influential Christian theologians of the 20th century. From an entry in *A Dictionary of Christian Theology,* Barth's position is summarized as follows:

> *Religion . . . is hardly a biblical word at all. It occurs not at all in the English versions of the Old Testament and only about five times in the New Testament, where it represents different Greek words. . . . The Old Testament strongly opposes the "religion" of the surrounding Canaanite peoples and of Assyria and Babylon because of the crudities and immoralities of the worship of the nature-gods* (baalim). *Similarly the New Testament sees little connection between the revelation in Christ and the pagan religions of the Roman Empire. Karl Barth (the most prolific, modern, Christian theologian) has good biblical support for his claim that the Christian faith is not a religion at all. Religion for Barth is human piety, human self-justification and human conjecture: faith is that which God creates in us. (288–289)*

In other words, religion, with its rituals and feelings and even its beliefs, is not really faith. Religions, in this sense, are largely a human construction that have little to do with the work of God in the human heart. Barth himself, in a vocabulary common to theological disputes, argues that religion is human or "natural theology," whereas Christian faith is "revealed theology." Real faith, the turning of the heart toward God, is not the human construction of actions and ideas about God but is the human response to God's original action of self-revelation to humankind, without which there could not even be anything known as natural theology (*The Epistle to the Romans* 246, 248; see also *A Kart Barth Reader* 28–29).

Religion may be a matter of faith, which is more than belief or ritual or other human activities.

▪ RELIGION AS FOCUS ON THE SACRED OR HOLY

With all these definitions of religion, there are clearly important insights, as well as troubling concerns. Certainly religion deals with ritual and morality as behaviors that flow from belief, and clearly beliefs and faith are crucial aspects that try to describe and hold on to the content of religion. At the same time, human feelings are clearly involved and hint at the significance and the inexplicable ultimacy of that which we take to be the object of our religious attention. All this makes sense of what we call religion.

But when the focus is on the *object* of religious belief rather than its expression in words or even its effect on our emotions or behavior, then some definitions of religion emphasize the sacred or the holy. Here we might stress the absolute or the infinite—a transcendent reality that characterizes the focus of reli-

Religion may mean focus on the sacred or holy.

gion and separates religious beliefs and actions from the profane, the secular, the relative, the finite.

We have already seen a hint of this idea in the section on religious feeling above, in which the ideas of Schleiermacher and Otto focused on feelings of dependence and awesomeness. Our point here, however, is not about the feelings, but about the object itself, that essence, energy or divine person that is the source and focus of meaning and emotion. This is what Otto called the Holy. We often call it the Sacred. The meaning, however, includes in both cases an emphasis on that which is the great reality beyond or over us, perhaps even within us, yet still something profound and wondrous enough to be the source and meaning of all that religion is about.

One way to understand this focus on the holy is to consider the more particular emphasis on a monotheistic understanding of the divine. Some would argue that religion is simply not properly religion unless it is explicitly monotheistic. That is, religion, one might argue, should always point us back to God, with a particular emphasis on the *relationship* between the one God and humankind. This is evident in Judaism's central creed, the Shema (the Hebrew word for *hear*): "Hear, O Israel: The Lord is our God, the Lord alone" or "The Lord our God is one Lord" (Deuteronomy 6:4). Likewise in Christianity, **St. Thomas Aquinas** (1225–1274), one of the principal saints of the Roman Catholic Church and declared by a pope to be the official philosopher/theologian of the Church, wrote that "the term religion 'denotes properly a relation to God'." It "excludes any other object except the one God as appropriate for religious relations." Similarly in Islam, the Holy Koran states: "Your God is one God. . . . There is no God but God!" (20:98). As Hall, Pilgrim, and Cavanagh have expressed it: "In [this] monotheistic view neither humanism, nor communism, nor any feeling, ritual activity, or belief that does not express a relationship to this monotheistic God is properly religious because religion is essentially a relationship to one God who is conceived of as the only divine being" (6–7).

Clearly the emphasis on relating all religious practice, belief, and feeling to the one God helps to define religion and to distinguish it from other important, but not religious, concerns. At the same time, we saw early on that there are clear cases in which religions other than the three listed in the previous paragraph do not focus their ultimate concern on God. Buddhism, Jainism, and Confucianism, as we noted above, each may include somewhere in their systems certain deities or supernatural beings, but in none of these religions do gods seem to be the ultimate object. So it seems as though defining religion by the focus on God is too narrow.

Nevertheless, we might well consider that in those religions in which gods are not ultimate, something else is. **Nirvana** or the **Buddha Mind**, the pure soul of the Tirthankara or the Tao of Heaven—all these suggest, even in the nontheistic religions, that something greater than we, greater than our world and our secular concerns, is the final and most important focus of all that religion is about. Perhaps this object of "ultimate concern," to use Tillich, is the proper focus of our sense of the *mysterium tremendum*, to echo Otto. Perhaps we may not yet say if "God" is the proper word for this holy source. Indeed, one famous giant in the field of the history of religions, Mircea Eliade, admitted that perhaps "no definitive definition is possible, because each tradition has a unique perception of the sacred." Yet nevertheless, he "regarded the sacred as 'the one unique and irreducible element' of religion" (qtd. in Schmidt et al. 7 [Chap. 1, Note 15, p. 672], from Eliade but not found in the original on p. 1, as cited). As with Eliade, in this text we shall try to develop this emphasis on the sacred and the holy as the central aspect of religion. That will be the focus of Chapter 3.

■ RELIGION: SUCCINCT AND INCLUSIVE DEFINITIONS

As a concluding perspective for the sake of the student who "wants an answer," the definition of religion from another major figure in the study of religion, and three other final definitions of religion, whose major differences are basically ones of length, can be considered. In his classic book, *The Varieties of Religious Experience,* William James (1842–1910) defines religion as ". . . the feelings, acts, and experiences of individual men in their solitude, so far as they apprehend themselves to stand in relation to whatever they may consider the divine" (42).

Moojan Momen provides one of the briefest definitions of religion: "Religion is humanity's response to what it experiences as holy" (27). We can see here an emphasis similar to ours above on the centrality of that which is sacred, including in the definition all the ways that humans respond to it. Thus we might imagine that the responses include the behaviors of morality and ritual, the various feelings of awe and dependence, and even the formation of beliefs and creeds. Momen himself elaborates on his definition by saying: "The best . . . definitions usually end up with words such as:

> *Religion is that human activity that acknowledges the existence of another reality transcendent to or immanent within this physical world and that seeks to describe and put human beings into a correct relationship with that reality, in ways that may involve correct knowledge, beliefs and values, correct personal and social activity, correct ethics, correct law, or participation in correct social institutions. (27)*

In this definition, we find elements of those concerns for behavior, feeling and belief that have been previously discussed.

In a manner similar to Momen's, Hall, Pilgrim, and Cavanagh offer a succinct definition intended to be inclusive: "Religion is the varied, symbolic expression of, and appropriate response to that which people deliberately affirm as being of unrestricted value for them" (11; italics removed). Here again we see reference to both expression (meaning as beliefs, feelings) and response (in ritual, in ethics), but the focus this time is not on the holy, but on something of "unrestricted value." Here we see, perhaps, Tillich's ultimate concern in new words. Or here, too, we see a reference to the holy after all.

Finally, the definition offered by *The New Columbia Encyclopedia* attempts to be more specific and inclusive:

> *religion, a system of thought, feeling, and action that is shared by a group and that gives the members of that group an object of devotion; a code of behavior by which an individual may judge the personal and social consequences of his actions; and a frame of reference by which an individual may*

relate himself to his group and his universe. Usually, religion concerns itself with that which transcends the known, the natural, or the expected; it is an acknowledgment of the extraordinary, the mysterious, and the supernatural. The religious consciousness generally recognizes a transcendent, sacred order and elaborates a technique to deal with the inexplicable or unpredictable elements of human experience in the world or beyond it. (2299)

Here again, more elaborately and fully stated, we see the many elements of religion we have tried to explore. Consider the references to "thought, feeling and action"; consider, too, the final "concern" with something beyond the normal arena of the world, for example, with something "extraordinary, the mysterious and the supernatural." Perhaps, the holy is the center, the hub of religion, from which many spokes radiate, holding together the full, ever-turning wheel of human religion.

RELIGION AS ILLUSION

Before we leave this ongoing effort to define religion, it is only fair to consider those definitions of religion that see it as illusion, as misinterpretations or misconceptions of reality. Many of these definitions are **reductionistic;** that is, they try to show how religion can be reduced to merely human inventions to fulfill psychological needs or other functions. Others, however, can be metareligious, suggesting perhaps that there is religious meaning beyond what most of us think of as religion. We shall briefly consider both types.

Certainly there is some temptation to think of religion as a kind of human weakness or human error, as human projections enabling human beings to explain and make sense of their otherwise inexplicable experiences of "undeserved" suffering and ultimately death. An early proponent of this view was the philosopher **Ludwig Feuerbach** (1804–1872), who held that religious feeling is simply a product of human yearnings projected beyond the naturalistic materialism of human experience (Feuerbach and Eliot 2; see also 10–14, 19). In Feuerbach's own words,

Man—this is the mystery of religion—projects his being into objectivity, and then again makes himself an object to this projected image of himself thus converted into a subject; he thinks of himself is [sic; as] an object to himself, but as the object of an object, of another being than himself. Thus here. Man is an object to God. (29–30)

By all this Feuerbach meant that human beings really only crave a greater, better, more secure human life. What we really worship, he claimed, is ourselves, "Man" written with capital letters and projected into the universe, imagined to be a being greater than the disappointing mankind that we know all too well. Disappointed with "man," we long for "Man," and thus we invent "God." And that, Feuerbach claimed, is religion.

Perhaps the most well-known representatives of this understanding of religion are **Karl Marx** (1818–1883) and **Sigmund Freud** (1856–1939). In perhaps his

metareligious definition—definition in which religious meaning "surpasses" the mere level of what is generally perceived as religion

most famous words, Marx, a social and political philosopher who is the father of Marxist–Leninist–Stalinist communism, defined religion as "the sigh of the oppressed creature, the heart of a heartless world, and the soul of soulless conditions. It is the opium of the people. . . . Religion is only the illusory sun which revolves around man as long as he does not revolve around himself" (Marx and Engels 41). These famous words, influenced by Feuerbach, suggest that religion is an invention of people who want more in life, and who, in place of a better world, are given a false world of gods and salvations. In the words of Hall, Pilgrim, and Cavanagh: "According to this definition all the beliefs, practices, and attitudes of religion reflect a distorted and essentially immature response to the universe as it actually is." (7)

Religion may be an illusion, a distortion of reality.

As for Sigmund Freud, the very title of his book, *The Future of an Illusion*, indicates his perspective on religion. For Freud, any language that does not give factual information is ultimately meaningless. The scientific mind is incompatible with religion: "There is no appeal to a court above that of reason." The religious illusion is wish-fulfillment, by which humankind attempts to make a harsh life tolerable, and is unverifiable. And the difference between illusion and delusion is only one of degree: In an illusion the distortion of reality is hidden; in a delusion it is obvious. According to Freud, religion is illusion, but some religious beliefs go beyond that to being delusional (Ricoeur 234–235). Thus, for Freud, religion is again a kind of invention of the dissatisfied. People who wish they had a loving father on earth construct the delusion of a Father in Heaven; those who wish to escape moral guilt invent a loving Savior.

Of course, most of these reductionistic definitions of religion are questionable. Our purpose here, however, is not really to defend religion or to try to assert what it really is. It is useful to note, indeed, that not all redefinitions of religion that seek to deny religion, as we know it, are entirely negative. In some cases, people we might recognize as religious themselves would argue that real religion goes beyond religion. Or, if that sounds too mysterious, consider here a non-Western, "no-religion" definition suggesting that from the perspective of the conventional language that ordinary people speak—"people language"—there are different, opposing religions and different, opposing definitions of religion. But from a higher spiritual perspective, there is no religion.

> *Such people speak of "Christianity," "Islam," "Buddhism," "Hinduism," "Sikhism," and so on. . . . Then, there is the language which is spoken by those who understand reality (Dhamma), especially those who know and understand reality in the ultimate sense. This is another kind of language. . . . We can call it "Dhamma language."*

> *Those who have penetrated to the essential nature of religion will regard all religions as being the same. . . . However, those who have penetrated to the highest understanding of Dhamma will feel that the thing called "religion" doesn't exist after all. . . . Thus the phrase "No religion!" is actually Dhamma language of the highest level. . . .*

> *One who has attained to the ultimate truth sees that there's no such thing as "religion." There is only a certain nature, which can be called whatever*

we like. We can call it "Dhamma," we can call it "Truth," we can call it "God," "Tao," or whatever, but we shouldn't particularize that Dhamma or that Truth as Buddhism, Christianity, Taoism, Judaism, Sikhism, Zoroastrianism, or Islam, for we can neither capture nor confine it with labels and concepts. Still, such divisions occur because people haven't yet realized this nameless truth for themselves. They have only reached the external levels . . . (Bhikku 1–4)

It may, of course, seem a little ironical to be using a Buddhist set of definitions to explain religion in terms that claim to transcend all religions, including Buddhism. Yet this is not altogether a rare idea. Many Hindu mystics, too, think that beyond the multitude of religions there is only a pure insight, a oneness that is "no religion." Certainly such a mystical view is worthy of further consideration, though it is beyond the scope of what we can consider here. Yet it is useful to note that there are philosophers and mystics who might say that our study of religion is, from the outset, a study of something misleading.

mystic—person claiming insights into mystery transcending common reality and human knowledge

RELIGION: INDIVIDUAL AND SOCIETY

As a transition to bring our efforts to define religion back to a discussion of globalization, we might note two different emphases one could make in discussing where the power and the importance of religion is seen the most. Just as a basic distinction within humankind is between the individual and the group, some important definitions of religion focus on one or the other.

■ THE SOLITARY INDIVIDUAL

Religion may mean "what the individual does with his/her own solitariness."

Emphasizing the individual, Alfred North Whitehead (1861–1947), a major British–American philosopher whose work has been called *process philosophy*, and whose thought has spawned *process theology*, has defined religion as "what the individual does with his own solitariness." He wrote:

Religion is solitariness; and if you are never solitary, you are never religious. Collective enthusiasms, revivals, institutions, churches, rituals, bibles, codes of behaviour, are trappings of religion, its passing forms. . . what should emerge from religion is individual worth of character. . . . The great religious conceptions which haunt the imaginations of civilized [humankind] are scenes of solitariness: Prometheus chained to his rock, Mahomet [Muhammed] brooding in the desert, the meditations of the Buddha, the solitary Man on the Cross. It belongs to the depth of the religious spirit to have felt forsaken, even by God. (6–9)

Elaborating on this definition, Hall, Pilgrim, and Cavanagh state that

For Whitehead, the essence of religion lay in humanity's confrontation with "the awful ultimate fact, which is the human being, consciously alone with itself, for its own sake." We need to keep in mind, however, that it is pos-

sible for a person to be solitary in this sense while she or he is actually with other people; the solitariness is an inward state, not a public one. (7)

integrity—Lat. *integer*, whole, complete, perfect, virtuous

The parallel to this from ancient Greek philosophy begins with Socrates' "Know thyself" and is further immortalized in Shakespeare's (1564–1616) *Hamlet:* "To thine own self be true" (1.3). Integrity—being true to oneself—is the essence of religion.

■ RELIGION: SOCIETY AS TRANSCENDENT

Society itself may be the center of religious valuation.

The counterpart or the antithesis to this definition of religion is that of sociologist **Emile Durkheim** (1858–1917), who sees "religion as a 'science of social control' grounded in a society's sense of the sacred." In Durkheim's words (Schmidt et al. 9),

A religion is a unified system of beliefs and practices relative to sacred things, that is to say things set apart and forbidden, beliefs and practices which unite into one single moral community . . . all those who adhere to them. (qtd. in Schmidt et al. 9)

Schmidt et al. continue:

For Durkheim, the sacred is not a supernatural being but an aggregate of human values perceived as transcendent and authoritative for group life. Religious beliefs and practices conceal the collective ideal, but humans are not mistaken in insisting on the importance of these beliefs and practices as they consecrate those values and conventions that sustain communal life. (9)

Here the point is to stress the fact that, although we might tend to declare religion a thoroughly private matter, it is really a way of forming community. People have traditionally found themselves living near others with similar values and similar beliefs. Religion has long been a kind of glue for society, something that declares and sanctions transcendentally the ideals that hold a society together. With this emphasis, "society and not the individual provides the center for religious valuation. Religious beliefs, practices, and attitudes are directed toward the expression of what a society of people holds to be of central importance" (Hall, Pilgrim, and Cavanagh 7).

It might seem evident that religion involves both society and the individual, but as is evident in the above discussion, sometimes one is emphasized over the other. This is also true in historical periods and in specific cultural contexts. We noted in Chapter 1 that, as the Modern Period gives way to globalization, there is a loss of continuity in the cohesive social unit. One's neighbors and even one's friends may be people of different religions, with different ideals. Yet as we are forced to enter into this global community, religion cannot merely lock itself away in personal subjectivity, nor can we stand to have religion become a vehicle for the kind of violence that seeks to force its own individual ideals upon the world. Thus as we seek in this chapter to define religion, globalization offers new challenges.

■ Defining Religion in a Global Community

In the preceding discussion, struggling to define religion according to its many facets, noting the mixture of individual and social emphases, and even acknowledging that some may define religion by denying it completely, all these explorations may seem like merely an academic exercise. Perhaps it just does not seem to have much to do with the real world. As it turns out, what is religion or what is not religion may have a great deal to do with the real world. Another related question that is important is what is a true or legitimate religion? In the first chapter, we indicated that this book might help us understand our neighbors. Consider the following imagined, but not unrealistic scenario.

Suppose a conservative Christian lives on a cul-de-sac. His or her neighbors consist of a Marxist, a Muslim family, and two families from Asia, one Confucian and the other Buddhist. A discussion with the Marxist neighbor might include a dialogue something like this:

Christian: "You're a Marxist. Isn't Marxism a religion?"

Marxist: "No, Marxists are atheists."

Christian: "I know that. But Marxism is a way of life with a system of ethics, which gives direction to your life. There are sacred texts, such as the writings of Marx and Lenin. You have an idea of an ultimate state, the 'classless society'—a kind of Nirvana. It has all the hallmarks of a religion."

Marxist: "You're right, but Marxism has no god and no other-worldly salvation. It is not a religion."

Confusion will only increase when the Christian talks with his Confucian neighbor. To the Christian, Confucianism may certainly seem like a religion, with elaborate rituals and a sense of ethics rooted, somehow, in heaven. But the neighbor may or may not agree. Some would say that Confucianism is a philosophy or a system of social ethics but not a religion.

The Buddhist neighbor would perhaps agree more readily with the Christian that Buddhism is a religion. It speaks of salvation, includes rituals, and even offers devotion to the Buddha. But the conservative Christian may believe that the Buddhist religion is not legitimate, since the salvation it offers fails to recognize God or the need for a savior. It may be religion, but it may also be a false religion that leads the unwary astray.

The Muslim neighbor would likely agree with the Christian on this. Both of these religions focus on a single, ultimate God, and both focus on a need for salvation and a threat of hell if one fails to be a proper believer. However, the Christian and the Muslim neighbor might disagree about one another's religions. The Christian may see the Muslim still as lost and in need of salvation through Jesus Christ. The Muslim neighbor may have the same problem with Christianity, seeing it as a confused effort to worship God, dangerously prone to the "idolatry" of worshiping Jesus. Or perhaps, since in Islam Christians may be seen as "people of the Book" (the religious tradition dating back to Abraham), the Christian might, just might, be a "believer," though still a confused one. As a result, both the Muslim and the Christian may try to convert the other neighbors on the cul-de-sac, but they may also be trying to convert each other.

■ GLOBALIZATION, WORLD BUILDING, AND WORLD MAINTENANCE

In the imaginary neighborhood described, people are confronted with the questions "What is religion?" and "What is legitimate religion?" In a very real way, given globalization, these questions have considerable import beyond the relationships in one's neighborhood. In Chapter 1, it was noted that globalization is a sweeping social change that is remaking the face of our planet. It not only affects social and political institutions, but it also is reshaping our group and individual identities. People often turn to religion to root themselves in changing times. To understand why this is so, we will look at the work of sociologist Peter Berger.

In a book called *The Sacred Canopy*, Berger holds that life in the physical and social environments is really quite chaotic. Whether dealing with nature or humans, we simply do not know what to expect. Humans cannot function in the midst of such uncertainty. To prevent the ravages of such uncertainty, *each society must build its own world.* This world consists of social structures, such as family, politics, an economy, and, of course, religion. It will have positions in that structure, like father, mother, child, priest, teacher, and students. Each of these will have behavioral expectations or norms, which direct peoples' behavior. Each world, each community, will have values that tell people what is important and what is unimportant. These worlds contain complex belief systems that tell people how things operate, who the people of this society are, and how they fit into the larger material and physical universe. It is this socially constructed world that makes the physical world and the people in it understandable and predictable. It is this socially constructed world that stands between the people of a society and the horrors of chaos (see Berger and Luckmann).

Yet Berger maintains that these socially constructed worlds are notoriously unstable. Once these worlds are created, *world maintenance* becomes a deep problem. That is, each society must defend its world against change and disintegration. In fact, defending its way of life is a preoccupation of most societies. Societies have a variety of mechanisms to defend their social worlds. The most important and effective of these is simply teaching new members what they are to believe, how they are to behave, how they are to worship, what their careers will be, and the like. Societies also have a wide variety of rewards they can dole out for conforming behaviors and punishments they can give out for deviant behavior. Thus socially constructed worlds have built-in systems for maintaining their uniqueness. Nevertheless, as the world changes, socially constructed normality is remarkably precarious.

So Berger argues that every society is an exercise in world building and world maintenance. How does religion operate in this process? It turns out that religion is very important in both parts of the process. Religion frequently contributes to world-building activities. The norms, values, beliefs, and ethics of religions are embodied in the socially created world. For instance, there is little doubt that Confucian ideas strongly influenced the creation of Chinese, Japanese, Korean, and other Asian and Southeast Asian societies. It is equally clear that Orthodox Christianity had and has a strong influence on Russian society to this very day, in spite of its years under the control of essentially atheistic communism.

On the other hand, there is a strong tendency for religion to support the existing social arrangements of a given society. So, the violation of the beliefs, customs, and values of a given social world (society) often not only brings punishment from secular authorities but from religious sources as well. Indeed, religion is all the more deeply involved in this process of maintaining the social system, insofar as there is a strong tendency in societies to take their ways and practices and elevate them into the supernatural realm. That is, the human-created systems, norms, values, and beliefs that make up a given social world are often seen as somehow reflecting the fundamental laws and structure of the universe. Or to put it another way, our ways, customs, and social structure are not merely our creation but reflect the very pattern of the cosmic Tao, or the commandments that God would have us to follow. In short, our ways are God's ways! The reason for this is obvious. If the expectations, beliefs, and structures of our social world are simply human creations, then humans can change them. Instability and uncertainty result. But if our social world is really created by God, or is a reflection of the "Tao of Heaven," then it is eternal and beyond change. This leaves the world we have created safe and secure and gives us a mighty fortress against the threat of chaos.

As the dramatic changes of globalization proceed, therefore, religion is all the more active in both world building and world maintenance. As citizens of the world, like the inhabitants of our fictional neighborhood above they find themselves surrounded by beliefs and practices that do not seem to be legitimate religion, or even religion at all, individuals may be faced with a need to rebuild their religious understanding of the world. Thus many movements, such as interfaith dialogues and the Council for a Parliament of the World's Religions can be found worldwide. These movements represent universalism, an effort to redefine religion in ways that seem more inclusive. Similarly, religions worldwide are meeting with other religions and philosophies to discuss areas of disagreement and agreement and to bring the collective moral power of religions to bear on the pressing problems of humanity. Religions engaging in these encounters hope that the collective moral ideals they embody will form the basis for a more just world order. Thus redefining religion to more clearly include Confucianism, while also stressing perhaps the moral function, could help people form a new social order in the global community.

In contrast, as globalization threatens the self-definition of local communities and individual cultures, religion rises up to defend itself against disintegration. Those religious movements such as fundamentalism, seeking to rediscover and to keep strong the "fundamentals" of religion and culture, are engaged in world maintenance. These movements stress particularism. That is, they see modernization and globalization as a threat to a valuable, cherished way of life that has been the very definition of a community for generations. Thus they attempt to use religion as a bulwark against threatening change.

■ CHANGE, NEW RELIGIONS, SECTS, AND CULTS

It should not be surprising that modernization and globalization produce widespread and diverse religious reactions, given Berger's contentions about the necessity of world building and maintenance. Some of these reactions take the forms

Council for a Parliament of the World's Religions—an assembly of religious and spiritual leaders, which fosters the advance of international interreligious dialogue

fundamentalism—movement characterized by strict adherence to principles

particularism—focus on particular interests

sect—group generally regarded as differing from generally accepted religious institutions of a culture

cult—group following a specific ideology or religious belief

of new religions, sects, and cults, especially in contrast to the more standard accepted religious institutions of a culture. Here again, we confront the important issue of how we define and legitimate religions, since a world-maintaining structure will tend to support the accepted religion, while viewing with suspicion developments of new sects and cults.

A foundational discussion of how new sects relate to the accepted religion of a culture was provided by two academic colleagues, sociologist Max Weber and theologian Ernst Troeltsch, in what has come to be called the "church–sect continuum." Weber later added a sociological description of cults into this typology, and other scholars through the years have introduced many further refinements and modifications. For instance, Christian theologian H. Richard Niebuhr introduced the concept of *denomination* as a type of religious organization that stood somewhere between the church and sect poles of the continuum (see Niebuhr, *The Social Sources of Denominationalism)*. There is some danger in these terms, inasmuch as church and denomination seem to focus on specifically Christian institutions. So keep in mind as we explain these terms that we are looking at some generalizations regarding the relation of established religious systems to developments of breakaway groups and new religious developments. We will consider this relation in terms of church, sect, and cult.

A "*church* organization in this typology is one that dominates the culture in which it is operating. It is so dominant that other religious organizations are excluded from the society. Because of this, church-type organization is largely at peace with its surrounding culture. Membership in the religion is taken for granted; membership is by birth. It is also mandatory. Thus the organization is inclusive, in that all citizens of a society are considered members. Salvation, too, is taken for granted, given probably through the socially accepted religious rituals like the sacraments. Leadership in the church is professional, meaning that there are requirements, such as education and participation in certain rituals, which must be met before one can become a leader. Worship is formal and dignified. Close approximations to the church-type organization might include the Roman Catholic Church in Western Europe during the High Middle Ages or the Russian Orthodox Church in Russia during the 19th century. It may also include the form Confucianism takes (or at least used to take) in China and the elaborate Buddhist institutions of Tibet.

A sect-type organization is the polar opposite. Sects are generally small. They often have evolved out of a more established religion. They not only are in conflict with their parent religion but also are at odds with the surrounding culture. In fact, one of the chief characteristics of a sect is its hostility to its mother religion and even to its mother culture. Therefore, it cannot be presumed that one is born into membership, but rather one must join by conversion. People may have to report some type of personal experience with the Holy before they are allowed to join. Membership, then, is exclusive, meaning it is limited only to the few who have experienced salvation or been especially called. Most people are considered outside of those who will share in salvation. Since the mother religion controls the institutions of education that provide the credentials of leadership, leaders in a sect may have little or no formal professional education. Certainly, professional education, like a seminary degree, is not required for sect leaders. The emphasis is on the leaders having some type of experience with the Holy, such as receiving a call from God to be a minister or prophet, which justifies their leadership. Worship is usually loosely structured, spontaneous, and, frequently, emotional. The many storefront churches that dot poor neighborhoods in American cities are good examples of sects. The Falun Gong sect in modern China is also an example (see Box 2.2).

Cults share the characteristics of sects, including the hostility to the dominant culture(s), but they are somewhat distinct. At least in their initial phases they tend to have a loose organizational pattern, which may center round the experiences of a charismatic leader. A charismatic leader is a person who is seen by others as particularly gifted, who may have a "magnetic personality," and who may have had some new experience with or revelation from the Holy which makes his or her teaching and leadership especially poignant. Perhaps the key difference between sects and cults is their understanding of their respective missions.

Sects and their leaders generally grow out of some more established religion and see themselves as somehow trying to return to the purity of that tradition, which has been corrupted by the more established forms of that religious tradition. For instance, many Baptists evolved out of the Calvinist branch of the Protestant Reformation in the 17th century. Part of their appeal was their call to return to the practices of early Christianity, such as conversion to Christianity, as opposed to being born into the faith. Similarly, the Baptists emphasized "believer's baptism," the ritual baptism of a person only after a personal experience of salvation. This amounts to adult baptism, as opposed to infants being baptized at birth. These changes emphasized for the Baptists a return to personal commitment and personal salvation, as opposed to the ritual normality and presumptuous membership of the established church.

Cults, like sects, may evolve out of an established religion but represent a radical break with that religion. The leader's experience has produced insights that move the cult beyond those found in their religious heritage, so while a sect is reforming or repurifying the church, a cult may be the beginning of a new religion altogether. The origins of The Church of Jesus Christ of Latter-Day Saints (Mormons) provide a good example of this phenomenon. Its founder Joseph Smith (1805–1844) had a series of revelations in the early 19th century, which eventually lead him and his followers to break with established Christian organizations and traditional theology. Though Smith's followers may have claimed to be Christian, many of their theories on a variety of topics depart significantly from accepted Christian doctrines. They even added a new scripture, The Book of Mormon, translated from inscribed golden tablets Smith unearthed, as a supplement to the Christian Bible with equal or even greater authority. Latter Day Saints' doctrine seems to be a combination of Christian theology with several philosophies and ideas present in American culture at that time. Indeed, cults tend to bring together in new, creative combinations ideas drawn from a variety of religious, philosophical, and/or secular sources. Thus, as the experience of the Mormons points out, cults ultimately tend to create new religions.

We have shown that when scholars speak of sects and cults, as well as using the term *church* in this context, they are defining specific types of religious organizations. They do not mean anything specifically Christian, nor do these labels necessarily carry positive or negative connotations. However, this usually is not the case in the general population. When most people speak of sects and cults,

How to define religion is a tremendous problem for scholars, for students, and, perhaps at times, "average citizens" also. How do we decide what is a legitimate religion deserving of human rights protections, and what is a harmful or dangerous organization that a government may seek to suppress for the sake of public order and the good of society?

The answer to these questions is not always clear. However, it is obvious that authorities and others will manipulate definitions of religions to fit their purposes. For instance, the term *cult* has ominous meanings in the West and other places as well. If a group can be successfully labeled a cult, measures can be taken against the targeted group that cannot be taken against a religion. A good example of this is the contemporary treatment of the Falun Gong in China.

The Falun Gong (also known as Falun Dafa) is a religious movement founded in 1992 by **Li Hongzhi**. The movement grew rapidly, if quietly. Falun Gong is a variation of an ancient Chinese practice of *qigong*, which seeks to perfect the body and mind by slow physical exercises (similar to *tai chi*) and meditation. These are combined with efforts to cultivate moral character in day-to-day life based on the "supreme principles" of the universe—Truthfulness, Benevolence, and Forbearance. Practitioners claim improved physical and mental health, tension release, and more energy from the discipline. The Falun Gong claim "tens of millions of people in over forty countries" (Falun Dafa 1). Interestingly, Falun Dafa members themselves deny that they are a religion. They insist they are a "network for transmitting information and practices" (ReligiousTolerance).

The bulk of Falun Gong's troubles with the Chinese Communist government began after an April 1999 silent protest in Beijing against government policies. The government labeled Falun Gong a "dangerous cult." Borrowing terms from the Western anti-cult movement (discussion follows), the government claimed the "cult" engaged in mind control, its aims were political not spiritual, it inculcated members in dangerous superstitions, it endangered members' lives, it undermined authority, and it threatened social stability. Authorities responded to this supposed threat with a protracted, harsh campaign, which included destroying more than two million publications, videos, and cassettes. Thousands were imprisoned for brief or longer periods. Many were tortured and some were killed. Often, those imprisoned, sent to mental institutions, or placed in labor farms for "reeducation" were sentenced without trial or with trials that did not meet the minimum requirements for protecting people's legal, constitutional, and human rights. Thousands still remain in detention. The persecution continues (Amnesty International). It is worth noting that the campaign against dangerous, superstitious cults extends to numerous religious groups, including evangelical and Roman Catholic Christians.

Sources: "Falun Dafa: A Brief Introduction." 2001. http://www.falundafa.org/eng/overview.htm (accessed July 1, 2002); ReligiousTolerance. "Falun Gong & Falun Dafa: What it is, what it does, and why the Chinese government is so terrified of it." 2001. http://www.religioustolerance.org/falungong.html (accessed July 1, 2002); and Amnesty International. "China." *Amnesty International Report 2001.* 2001. http://web.amnesty.org/web/ar2001nsf/webasacountries/CHINA?Open Document (accessed July 1, 2002).

the terms are given derogatory meanings. To most, a sect, but more especially a cult, is a deviant organization to be feared and fought. Judging from the Chinese government's labeling of the Falun Gong not as a religion but a "dangerous cult," the detrimental meaning of cult is not limited to Western cultures. If the Chinese government acknowledged the Falun Gong as a religion, then the Chinese government could be accused of denying the "freedom of religion," which apparently it does not wish to do.

Because of the negativism associated with the terms *sect* and *cult,* many scholars have started to use concepts like "new religions," "alternative religions," and "new religious movements." Throughout history, and especially at times of dramatic social change, the established church may well find itself confronted with breakaway movements and even entirely new movements that grow in the fertile soil of an unstable society. Thus, the movements that emerge as new religions may be unhappily labeled cults. We can expect such change and such mistrust when new religious organizations and activities appear as a reaction to modernization and globalization.

■ THE SOCIAL CONSTRUCTION OF DANGEROUS CULTS

At this point it may seem frustrating that more and more distinctions arise to categorize religions. One may well wonder if any of this concern over church, sect, and cult has anything to do with real life or genuinely important changes in the world.

It turns out that how you label (define) existing or emerging religions is very important. The labels (definitions) we place on various religions determine their legitimacy as well as society's reaction to these religions. These labels can have tremendous implications for how people in a culture, along with their political, legal, and economic systems, treat existing and emerging religions, as well as the adherents to these religions. To illustrate this point, sociologist Rodney Stark tells the following fable:

> Consider a particular new religion. Like most of these groups, it can be identified as a cult because it displays three typical cultic features. First, it claims to have extensive new religious truths—a set of new doctrines that are very different from those taught by conventional churches. Second, the source of these new teachings is a young man who claims to have received them directly from God. Third, the leader requires obedience and encourages his followers to abandon their current lives and become full-time followers.
>
> Understandably, the parents of many of these followers are upset and angry about the exploitation of their children by this self-proclaimed messiah. Their worst fears are confirmed by well known clergy who issue public warnings about the dangers of this cult and the dangers of all authoritarian religions led by deluded fanatics. The growing outcry soon forces the government to act: The leader is crucified between two thieves. (ix)

Those familiar with the Christian Gospels will recognized this as an adapted version of the story of Jesus, and the "particular new religion" refers to emerging Christianity. Clearly, most Jews in the first century of the Christian era did not accept Jesus as the Messiah (Christ). To many of them, such an idea was crazy and perhaps Jesus was demented as well. To many Jewish leaders, Jesus not only was a threat to their authority, but he also was undermining the whole social, religious, and political order.

Those Romans familiar with events in Judea at the time of the crucifixion likely were confused about or indifferent to the Jewish outcry against this would-be messiah. The situation would change, however, in the following centuries as Christianity gained more adherents in the Roman Empire. Roman officials became convinced of the threat presented by this dangerous cult and initiated campaigns against it. Average Roman parents may well have had much the same reaction as first century Jewish parents when their children started joining the strange, new, subversive movement.

The point should be obvious by now: all established religions at one time were emerging religions. How they were viewed by people at the time of their emergence was much different from how they were viewed once they had established themselves as older, "traditional," legitimate religions. The church of today was the sect, or even the cult, of yesterday. And how much we trust (or mistrust) the church, simply because it is the established way of doing things, and how much we fear (or are fascinated with) a cult, simply because it is new, does make a difference in how we live.

■ A Contemporary Example

This dynamic is as evident today as it has been in the past. Whether we see emerging religions, on the one hand, as new religions or alternative religions or, on the other hand, as sects or cults has serious ramifications. Sociologist David Bromley amply illustrates this point when he discusses "The Social Construction of Subversion."

Bromley points out that a number of new religious movements appeared in the United States during the 1960s. The 1960s were a period of social upheaval, which many Americans found threatening. During the 1960s, new social movements touted new lifestyles and questioned the foundations of American culture. Initially, many labeled these alternatives as "hippie." In the 1970s, the "Hippie movement" as such began to lose steam. As this happened, the quest for alternative lifestyles started to take on overtly religious forms. Many of the emerging religions, such as the "Moonies," the Children of God, or the Transcendental Meditation movement, attracted the same type of relatively affluent, fairly well-educated young people who were drawn to the social protests and hippie activities of the 1960s.

At this point, emerging religions became the focus of parental and social anxiety. An anticult movement started to take shape. Eventually, this movement was able to place a wide range of nonconventional religious groups, philosophies, and lifestyle alternatives (such as vegetarianism or practitioners of traditional medicine, i.e., non-Western, "nonscientific" medicine) under the cloud of dangerous cults in the minds of many Americans.

The anti-cult movement proceeded to credit these cults with a host of vices, such as mind control, authoritarian and intolerant leadership, stealing the free will of followers, child abuse, and a multitude of other evils. These cults and their leaders were seen as so powerful that the average person could not resist falling under their diabolical control. As a result of these efforts, many Americans came to believe a vast evil conspiracy was afoot that represented a threat to the family, democracy, Christianity, and morality.

In turn, these supposed attributes came to be the basis of all sorts of questionable practices against cults, their leaders, and their followers. For example, hearings were held before various political bodies, where the cult menace was discussed. Laws were passed in some states, which allowed parents to obtain legal custody of their adult children when they joined one of these objectionable religions. Note here that these were *adult* children who were legally free and mentally capable to make decisions in any other areas of their lives. Parents were then allowed to commit their children to mental institutions or to place them under the control of mental health/cult experts who might engage in all sorts of questionable practices to "deprogram" the converts. Remember, the greatest crime or bit of "insanity" most of these converts had committed was to exercise their recognized American right to choose their religion. Bromley proceeds to demonstrate that as the cult scare began to recede in the late 1980s, the same accusations and tactics of the anti-cult movement were transposed into the anti-Satanist frenzy of the 1990s.

Beyond this, sociology professor James T. Richardson and graduate student Barend van Driel show how much of the ideology and tactics of the American anti-cult movement was exported into the anti-cult movements in Europe. In spite of their common roots, the results of the anti-cult movements in these countries varied greatly depending on the culture of the nation in which they were operating. Thus the results of anti-cult movements efforts were much different in Holland, England, France, and Germany.

The anti-cult movement, therefore, was successful in whipping up a frenzy against emerging religions. But in what sense is this frenzy a social construction? By social construction we mean that more of the reaction to cults was the result of social definition than it was of some type of objective data documenting the actual operations to the religious groups themselves. That is, spurred on by some churches and denominations, the media, "cult experts," and the like, large segments of American society came to see the emerging religions as dangerous and greatly overestimated the threat that most of these groups posed to individuals, families, and society. Moreover, much of the supposed subversion of emerging religions is not supported when scientific social research is conducted. For instance, Richardson and van Driel discuss the results of an especially sound study of cults conducted for the Permanent Commission for Public Health of the Dutch government. The data from this study agree with "what most social scientists have repeatedly stated" (157), namely, that they cannot support accusations of coercion, mind control, lack of free will choice, or "ideological totalitarianism."

None of this is to say that all emerging religions are benign and wonderful additions to any nation's cultural tapestry. But it is to say that what we expect as social normality determines what gets labeled a cult, and the word *cult* is itself loaded with negative meanings. Once again, how we define our terms, and the emotional and conceptual attachments that go with our words, are very important to how we understand our culture, our neighbors, and ourselves.

CONCLUSION

In this section, we have seen how religion plays a key role in a society's world-building and world-maintenance activities. New religions or variations of old ones often appear as part of the process of social changes, and many of these movements support, rather than threaten, the societies in which they appear. The definitions of religion or, at least, of legitimate or illegitimate religions have tremendous importance when these labels are applied to these new groups by the larger society in which the emerging religions dwell.

In the same way, how we define religion in general is important to how we carry on any discussion of the topic. A discussion that too narrowly defines religion mono-thetically, or that fails to allow us to include in our discussion the wide diversity of world beliefs, actions, and emotions that make up the essential elements of world religions, would bias the discussion from the outset. At the same time, a definition made so broadly that it required us to consider Marxism, sports, or the Madonna fan club as "religions" would leave us with no clear ideas on which to focus our thoughtful analyses. For these reasons, we have offered here a lengthy consideration of the many elements that go into what humanity calls religion. In the chapters that follow, we look with more detail at many of these issues.

■ INTERACTIVE EXERCISE

Please continue your exploration of defining religion by going to the interactive exercise for this chapter online (**http://www.religion.wadsworth.com/richter**).

WORKS CITED

Saint Augustine. *Confessions.* Translated with an Introduction by R.S. Pine-Coffin. New York: Viking Penguin, 1961.

Amnesty International. "China." *Amnesty International Report 2001.* 2001. http://web.amnesty.org/web/ar2001nsf/webasacountries/CHINA?Open Document.

Banton, Michael, ed. Corp. Author: Association of Social Anthropologists of the Commonwealth, and Jesus College. Conf. Author: Conference on New Approaches to Social Anthropology. *Anthropological Approaches to the Study of Religion.* A.S.A. Monographs; 3. New York: F.A. Praeger, 1966.

Barth, Karl. *The Epistle to the Romans.* A Galaxy Book. New York: Oxford University Press, 1980.

Barth, Karl, et al. *A Karl Barth Reader.* Grand Rapids, MI: Eerdmans, 1986.

Beach, Waldo, and H. Richard Niebuhr. *Christian Ethics.* New York: Ronald Press, 1955.

Bellah, Robert Neelly. *Beyond Belief: Essays on Religion in a Post-Traditional World.* Berkeley: University of California Press, 1991.

Berger, Peter L. and Thomas Luckmann. *The Social Construction of Reality*. Garden City, NY: Doubleday, 1966.

Bettis, Joseph Dabney. *Phenomenology of Religion: Eight Modern Descriptions of the Essence of Religion*. Harper Forum Books. New York: Harper & Row, 1969.

Bhikku, Buddhadasa. "No Religion," 1–4.

Bromley, David. "The Social Construction of Subversion." In *Anti-Cult Movements in Cross-Cultural Perspective*. eds. Shupe, Anson, and David G. Bromley. Religious Information Systems, Vol. 16. Garland Reference Library of Social Science, Vol. 913. New York: Garland, 1994, pp. 49–75.

Durkheim, Emile, Carol Cosman, and Mark Sydney Cladis. *The Elementary Forms of Religious Life*. New York: Oxford University Press, 2001.

Eliade, Mircea. *Patterns in Comparative Religion*. Meridian Books. Cleveland, OH: World, 1963.

Falun Dafa. "Falun Dafa: A Brief Introduction." 2001. http://www.falundafa.org/eng/overview.htm (accessed July 1, 2002).

Feuerbach, Ludwig, and George Eliot. *The Essence of Christianity*. Harper Torchbooks. New York: Harper & Row, 1957.

Freud, Sigmund. *The Future of an Illusion*. Garden City, NY: Anchor Books, 1964.

Hall, T. William, Richard B. Pilgrim, and Ronald R. Cavanagh. *Religion: An Introduction*. San Francisco: Harper & Row, 1985.

Harris, William H., et al. *The New Columbia Encyclopedia*. 4th ed. New York: Columbia University Press, 1975.

James, William. *The Varieties of Religious Experience: A Study in Human Nature*. New York: Mentor; New American Library, 1958.

Magee, John Benjamin. *Religion and Modern Man*. New York: Harper & Row, 1967.

Marx, Karl, and Friedrich Engels. *On Religion*. New York: Schocken Books, 1967.

Momen, Moojan. *The Phenomenon of Religion*. Boston: Oneworld, 1999.

Niebuhr, H. Richard. *Christ and Culture*. 50th anniversary expanded ed. New York: HarperCollins, 2001.

———. *The Social Sources of Denominationalism*. Cleveland, OH: Meridian Books/World, 1929, 1957.

Otto, Rudolf. *The Idea of the Holy*. A Galaxy Book. New York: Oxford University Press, 1958.

ReligiousTolerance. "Falun Gong & Falun Dafa: What it is, what it does, and why the Chinese government is so terrified of it." 2001. http://www.religioustolerance.org/falungong.html (accessed July 1, 2002).

Richardson, Alan. *A Dictionary of Christian Theology*. Philadelphia: Westminster Press, 1969.

Richardson, James T., and Barend van Driel. "New Religions in Europe: A Comparison of Developments and Reactions in England, France, Germany, and the Netherlands." In *Anti-Cult Movements in Cross-Cultural Perspective.* eds. Shupe, Anson, and David G. Bromley. Religious Information Systems, Vol. 16. Garland Reference Library of Social Science, Vol. 913. New York: Garland, 1994, pp. 129–170.

Ricoeur, Paul. *Freud and Philosophy: An Essay on Interpretation.* New Haven, CT: Yale University Press, 1970.

Ritschl, Albrecht, et al. *The Christian Doctrine of Justification and Reconciliation.* Clifton: New Jersey Reference Book Publishers, 1966.

"Sanctuary Farm Applauds Ban on Butchering of Sick Animals." *New York Times.* (January 2, 2004): B1.

Schleiermacher, Friedrich. *The Christian Faith.* Harper Torchbooks. New York: Harper & Row, 1963.

Schmidt, Roger, et al. *Patterns of Religion.* Belmont, CA: Wadsworth, 1999.

Shakespeare, William. *Hamlet.* New York: Methuen, 1982.

Smith, Huston. *The World"s Religions.* San Francisco: HarperSanFrancisco, 1991.

Smith, Jonathan Z. *Imagining Religion: From Babylon to Jonestown.* Chicago: University of Chicago Press, 1988.

Spiro, Melford E. "Religion: Problems of Definition and Explanation." In *Anthropological Approaches to the Study of Religion.* ed. Michael Banton. London: Tavistock, 1966, p. 94.

Stark, Rodney. In *New Religions as Global Cultures: Making the Human Sacred.* eds. Hexham, Irving, and Karla Poewe. Boulder, CO: Westview Press, HarperCollins, 1997, p. ix.

Taylor, Mark C. *Critical Terms for Religious Studies.* Chicago: University of Chicago Press, 1998.

Tillich, Paul. "Religion." In *Man's Right to Knowledge,* 2nd Series, 81. New York: Columbia University Press, 1954.

———. *What Is Religion?* New York: Harper & Row, 1969.

Tillich, Paul, and D. Mackenzie Brown. *Ultimate Concern.* New York: Harper & Row, 1965.

Tylor, Edward Burnett. *Primitive Culture.* Vol. 1. New York: Harper, 1958.

Wallace, Anthony F. C. *Religion: An Anthropological View.* New York: Random House, 1966.

Weber, Max. *The Sociology of Religion.* Boston: Beacon Press, 1963.

Whitehead, Alfred North. *Religion in the Making.* Living Age Books. New York: Meridian Books, 1960.

FOR FURTHER READING

Bellah, Robert Neelly. *Beyond Belief: Essays on Religion in a Post-Traditional World.* Berkeley: University of California Press, 1991.

Berger, Peter L., and Thomas Luckmann. *The Social Construction of Reality.* Garden City, NY: Doubleday, 1966.

Carmody, Denise Lardner, and John Tulley Carmody. *Native American Religions: An Introduction.* New York: Paulist, 1993.

Kung, Hans, and Julia Ching. *Christianity and Chinese Religions.* New York: Doubleday, 1989.

Momen, Moojan. *The Phenomenon of Religion.* Boston: Oneworld, 1999.

Niebuhr, H. Richard. *Christ and Culture.* 50th anniversary expanded ed. New York: HarperCollins, 2001.

Schechter, Danny, ed. *Falun Gong's Challenge to China: Spiritual Practice or "Evil Cult"?* New York: Akaschi Books, 2000.

Smith, Jonathan Z. *Imagining Religion: From Babylon to Jonestown.* Chicago: University of Chicago Press, 1988.

Subhuti, Dharmachari (Alex Kennedy). *Buddhism for Today: A Portrait of a New Buddhist Movement.* Wiltshire, UK: Element, 1983.

Taylor, Mark C. *Critical Terms for Religious Studies.* Chicago: University of Chicago Press, 1998.

Tillich, Paul. *What Is Religion?* New York: Harper & Row, 1969.

3 THE ABSOLUTE, THE ULTIMATE, THE HOLY

Getty Images/PhotoDisc Collection

Within all religions, it seems, there is some hint of an Absolute or Ultimate Reality that gives people a glimpse of glory and provides the meaning behind everything the religion teaches. Is there more to reality than meets the eye? Is there some great mystery to capture our consciousness and to give value to life? In the pictures for this chapter, above and online (**http://www.religion.wadsworth.com/richter**), and in the following quotations, we find various religions' discoveries, or efforts, to express "The Holy." Review these pictures and scriptural passages, and then think about the Introductory Questions that follow to prepare for reading this chapter.

In the year that King Uzziah died, I saw the Lord sitting on a throne, high and lofty; and the hem of his robe filled the temple. Seraphs were in attendance above him; each had six wings: with two they covered their faces, and with two they covered their feet, and with two they flew. And one called to another and said: "Holy, holy, holy is the LORD of hosts; the whole earth is full of his glory." The pivots on the thresholds shook at the voices of those who called, and the house filled with smoke. And I said: "Woe is me! I am lost. . . ."

—Judaism: Isaiah 6:1–4

In the beginning was the Word, and the Word was with God, and the Word was God. He was in the beginning with God. All things came into being through him, and without him not one thing came into being. What has come into being in him was life, and the life was the light of all people. The light shines in the darkness, and the darkness did not overcome it. And the Word became flesh and lived among us, and we have seen his glory, the glory as of a father's only son, full of grace and truth.

—Christianity: The Gospel of John 1:1–5, 14

"Those who know Brahman," replied Angiras, "say that there are two kinds of knowledge, the higher and the lower. The lower is knowledge of the Vedas [scriptures]. The higher is knowledge of that by which one knows the changeless reality. By this is fully revealed to the wise that which transcends the senses, which is uncaused, which is indefinable, which has neither eyes nor ears, neither hands nor feet, which is all-pervading, subtler than the subtlest—the everlasting, the source of all. As the web comes out of the spider and is withdrawn, as plants grow from the soil and hair from the body of man, so springs the universe from the eternal Brahman."

—Hinduism: Mundaka Upanishad (Prabhavananda and Manchester 43)

Great King, just as, although the great ocean exists, it is impossible to measure the water or to count the living beings that make their abode there, precisely so, great king, although Nibbana [Nirvana] really exists, it is impossible to make clear the form or figure or age or dimensions of Nibbana, either by an illustration or by a reason or by a cause or by a method. Great king, a person possessed of magical power, possessed of mastery over mind, could estimate the quantity of water in the great ocean and the number of living beings dwelling there; but that person would never be able to make clear the form or figure or age or dimensions of Nibbana.

—Buddhism: Questions of King Malinda (Stryk 112–113)

The Way [Tao] can be spoken of, but it will not be the constant way;
The name can be named, but it will not be the constant name.
The nameless was the beginning of the myriad creatures;
The named was the mother of the myriad creatures.
Hence constantly rid yourself of desires in order to observe its subtlety;
But constantly allow yourself to have desires in order to observe what it is after.
These two have the same origin, but differ in name.
They are both called dark, darkness upon darkness, the gateway to all that is subtle.

—Taoism: Tao Te Ching 1 (Chan 445)

INTRODUCTORY QUESTIONS

These passages and the pictures on the website portray several different images of the Absolute. Please think about the following as a way to prepare for considering the materials covered in this chapter.

1. Can you see something similar in Isaiah's description of God and the vision of Christ in the "Transfiguration"? Can you see the same thing in the description of Nibbana or the Tao?
2. Is Brahman God? Say why or why not.
3. What might Ayer's Rock have to do with religion? Consider a storm at sea or dark and high mountains. Imagine the impression on native peoples.
4. Why is Isaiah afraid? Is there any relation between his fear and God's glory? Is there any "fear" associated with any of the other objects described or depicted above?
5. What does the inside of a mosque have to do with God? What is so great about an Empty Circle?
6. How is greatness expressed in these quotations and the pictures? Can you link that greatness to the inexpressibility of the Tao or of Brahman? Are God and the revealed Word, also ultimately inexpressible?

7. Try making a list of adjectives that might describe any of the Sacred Beings depicted or mentioned. Try making a list of nouns to name them all.

INTRODUCTION

As hinted in the previous chapter, there is *something* about religions that makes them religious, that gives them the feel of being sacred or holy. The "feel" is difficult to describe; indeed, it may not be enough merely to describe a feeling without going on to attempt a description of the "Something" that is believed to provoke it. In the quotations on this chapter's title page, God and Christ, Nibbana (Nirvana) and the Tao are mentioned, as well as representations of the Zen Buddhist's Empty Circle and the Aborigine sacred site of Ayer's Rock in Australia. What is it about these things—one is rightly hesitant even to use the bland word "things"—that sets them apart and makes them the focus of what we call religion? In what way is a first century Jewish man like Jesus or an abstract concept like the Tao, let alone a curiously drawn circle or a large, orange rock, the proper object of devotion and the source of meaning for thousands or millions of people? To answer such questions and to proceed at all in the exploration of any religious phenomena, we must look for the essential core of religion in the mysterious, holy "Something" that makes religion into religion.

The Holy Absolute is the mysterious "Something" at the core of religion.

THE HOLY AND THE NUMINOUS EXPERIENCE

Anyone who has ever stood in Yosemite Valley and stared upward at the thousand-foot monolithic face of El Capitan, or ever stood on a beach during a raging storm at sea, or any one of those particularly awe-inspired people who, during a particularly active lightning storm, pulls up a chair to watch—such people have probably felt a tinge of what might be called religious feeling. Before the word awesome came to describe movies and pizza, it was used to describe something so wondrous that it inspired awe, that dumbstruck, entranced awareness of the power and glory, or the simplicity and uniqueness, of some object. The "awe" in "awesome" is more than a reaction of pleasure or enjoyment, certainly not just casual entertainment. It might be a kind of astonishment, yet not necessarily surprise, as when one sees majestic mountains close up; it is by no means unexpected, yet it is still something more than we could have fully imagined beforehand. Size and power, beauty and delicacy, all can evoke this sense of astonishment, not for being exactly new, but for being wonderful, a vision before which we simply stand silent to watch. It is here, perhaps, that an insight into religion begins.

Powers of nature may easily inspire this experience when they both entrance and terrify. It is a remarkable emotion that at once attracts us with glory and makes us afraid for our lives. There is something here, we might be thinking, that is great, greater than I, something by which I may be threatened. It is not the threat of antisocial violence or incurable illness, but a threat that is intrinsically connected with the greatness we watch with entranced wonder. **Immanuel Kant** (1724–1804), an 18th-century German philosopher, describes the aesthetic experience of seeing in art or nature certain grand and powerful figures that at once provide pleasure and "outrage the imagination." By their sheer size, or by their wild activity, they overwhelm our senses, so that we experience a "momentary check," at once attracted and repelled by the almost-threatening greatness. Such wonders of nature create in us an **experience of the sublime** as the object of our senses or contemplation is greater than we can encompass, beyond control, yet lovely with wonder (Kant 91).

The wonders of nature may inspire awe, pleasure, and threat.

Influenced by Kant but much more sensitive to and focused upon the specifically religious aspects of such experience, the early 20th-century philosopher Rudolf Otto tried to describe in such terms the fundamental religious experience. He called it an **experience of the numinous.** In the famous phrase quoted in the previous chapter, he described this numinous experience as a sense of the *mysterium tremendum et fascinans,* the tremendous and fascinating mystery. He wrote:

Rudolf Otto described the encounter with the Holy as mysterium tremendum et fascinans.

> The feeling of it may at times come sweeping like a gentle tide, pervading the mind with a tranquil mood and deepest worship. It may pass over into a more set and lasting attitude of the soul, continuing, as it were, thrillingly vibrant and resonant, until at last it dies away and the soul resumes its "profane," non-religious mood of everyday experience. It may burst in sudden eruption up from the depths of the soul with spasms and convulsions, or lead to the strangest excitements, to intoxicated frenzy, to transport, and to ecstasy. It has its wild and demonic forms and can sink to an almost grisly horror and shuddering. It has its crude, barbaric antecedents and early manifestations, and again it may be developed into something beautiful and pure and glorious. It may become the hushed, trembling, and speechless humility of the creature in the presence of—whom or what? In the presence of that which is a mystery, inexpressible and above all creatures. (12–13)

Like Kant's "sublime," the numinous is something that both attracts and staggers, something that puts a check on the imagination and holds us spellbound. But even more than the sublime, the numinous seems inescapably to hint at something beyond the things that are evident to the natural senses. Something, we might admit, is great and wonderful to our senses, but there is also something beyond our senses, perhaps beyond the natural *per se.* This feeling, then, hints at something which is above nature, literally that which is "supernatural." And thus, for Otto, the greatness of the numinous is necessarily beyond our conceiving (*mysterium*), its power daunting (*tremendum*), and its glory attractive (*fascinans*).

Of course, it is not enough to describe experience as such. We noted in Chapter 2 that a monothetic definition of religion, focused only on personal experience, might leave us talking not about religion but about how we feel. Similarly, it is not enough only to deal with Otto's *mysterium* as merely the theoretical abstractions of a speculative philosopher. Later in this text, we will have the opportunity to discuss the role of inner experience in religious life, as well as a chance to mention how philosophers past and present have tried to argue and discuss the nature and existence of Ultimate or Absolute Reality. But arguably more important than experiences and philosophies are the descriptions of the "who or what" the religious person finds awesome. That is, religious awe seems to be about Something, a great and wonderful Something (let us capitalize it for now) that appears to the religious soul as the source and object of the grandeur he or she experiences. And this is, as suggested in the previous chapter, the hub of the vast, turning wheel that is religion.

So far, of course, we continue to deal with an abstraction, or a metaphorical "hub" that refers to the Unnamed. But our point for this chapter is that the religions themselves do try to specify what, or who, this "Something" is. We can return to the examples supplied at the front of this chapter, or turn to other examples that accompany this book, to see where the religious "Something" is named and described. In the chapter introduction, it is God, Brahman, or the Tao; it is perhaps more obscurely Nirvana, an empty circle or a great, orange stone. Of course, much of this may be imagery, but whether name or imagery, in many cases we find here an attempt to convey that sense of having found a greatness that both awes us and transcends us. Sometimes the fearsome aspect is prominent, as in the case of the Hindu goddess Kali. One need only consider her bloody rampage in defeating an army of evil giants, a rampage so full of bloodlust that only the recognition of her husband, Shiva, among the corpses could slow her fury. From the *tindolo* "ghosts of power" that are thought to cause disease among the Melanesian islanders to the converted demons of the Tibetan Buddhists, there are clear cases where the very threatening nature of the sacred is evident. At other times, this great power is more mildly suggested simply in the conceptual ineffability, the rational inaccessibility of this "Something." Here, it —this "Something"—is felt to be more than we can quite contain, certainly more than we can quite describe, like the Tao in the preceding excerpt. Ironically, then, "beyond description" becomes one of the ways that we describe the great reality that transcends us, and thus becomes one of the criteria by which we consider its greatness. One way or another, with stories or pictures or concepts we can barely understand, we find that religions all over the world try to give some name to the "hub" of their way of life.

So we talk of a "Something" unique and wonderful, beyond us and yet with us, somehow the source and the goal of all we are and know. It is powerful and, perhaps, terrifying; it is perhaps benign and mysterious. But somehow it is a source of being or power or wisdom, a source greater than all that is merely earthly. It is the object of the numinous experience, the awesome, the wonderful and terrifying mystery. Perhaps we do not quite know how to name it. But for the purposes of our general study, let us call it the Absolute, or the Ultimate, or the Holy.

THE ABSOLUTE, ULTIMATE, AND HOLY

The words chosen in this context present an attempt to convey certain aspects of the "Something" that possibly we can, after all, understand, at least in some provisional ways, even if the Absolute itself can never quite be comprehended. For example, we can say that the object of religion, generally described, is the "Absolute." By this term, we mean that this great reality is not merely the prod-

Religious awe is about the great Something that is encountered.

ineffability— incapability of being described or explained; beyond words

The Something may be described as the "Absolute."

uct of some prior creation or deeper reality. Literally, the word suggests something that cannot be dissolved or be broken down into components and explained away. It is irreducible. We can think of this as similar to the end product of arithmetic factoring, the breaking down of a number into its factors of multiplication. For in the end, all of the factors must be prime numbers, and once one finds a prime number as a factor, there is no more reduction. Thus the prime numbers are, so to speak, final and irresolvable. Western philosophers, like the 13th-century Roman Catholic theologian Thomas Aquinas, used previous Greek philosophical ideas to speak of God as "simple." Obviously this did not mean God was "simple minded" but rather meant that God is a basic and final unity, not composed of parts but a single, integrated whole (see Pegis 28ff). The Absolute cannot be taken apart or put together, cannot be composed of pieces somehow more fundamental. God to these Christians, like the Tao to the Taoists, is simply the final answer and explanation for what we see and know, and beyond it there is no prior or deeper reality to find.

The Something may be described as the "Ultimate."

As final source and goal, we might call it the Ultimate. In the famous quotation from the Christian theologian Paul Tillich, given in the last chapter, religion *per se* was described as a kind of ultimacy. The ambiguity in Tillich's claim has been noted, as in one way he describes some "ultimate concern" of the religious person but in another way speaks of the Absolute, which is itself, *in* itself, the Ultimate. For our purposes here, let us stress that "ultimate" does not refer only to a person's "concern," but to an Ultimate Being. This is well-illustrated in Islam, where, in the process of daily prayers, Muslims bow and submit themselves to God with the declaration "Allahu akbar"—God is most great. The comparative language here really seems to say "God is greater," emphasizing that God's greatness is more than any other greatness we know. This may seem obvious to followers of those religions in which there is only one God, for it would seem unavoidable that the one God is the ultimate being. But even in the **Vedas**, the ancient scriptures of Hinduism where a multiplicity of gods is taken for granted, extreme greatness, even ultimate greatness, is attributed to the gods, first one, then another. Thus, the god "who by birth was chief of the Gods, the most wise," is **Indra**, who "became the Gods' protector with his strength and power." But at the same time, the god who is "wise and self-effulgent, shall be supreme above all forever" is **Aditi**. And of **Rudra** it is said, "The power divine of this sovereign Lord, the ruler over the world, never diminishes . . . for there is none more mighty than you" (Kishore 44ff.). In all such praise, one may wish for more consistency, but one cannot miss the imputation of final and ultimate greatness.

In Hinduism, many gods are described as "Most Great."

The ultimacy of the Absolute might also be seen in the suggestion that all reality rests not in itself but on some deeper and greater reality, which in turn rests on nothing else. Here we mean that somehow all reality, all that we see, hear, taste, and touch, has its existence not in itself but in something else, something more final. Thus the "Ultimate" is often seen as, in some sense, responsible for the existence of everything else. Or, to say it another way, all natural reality is seen as in some way dependent on a supernatural Ultimate Reality.

The Ultimate may be seen as the foundation upon which everything that exists rests.

On this point, many religions speak of the Ultimate as a **creator**, a Being responsible for the existence of all other things by an act of will. All things, to borrow again from Thomas Aquinas, are contingent, existing not on their own strength but by virtue of a greater power. "Contingent" means that all natural objects, every tree or person, mountain or raindrop, exist only because of how they were formed by something else. They depend, or are contingent upon, something else. The creator God, however, is noncontingent, existing by virtue of His own being alone. This, Aquinas explained, means that everything we see around us, ourselves included, apparently could exist or might not have existed. Obviously if my parents or the carpenter who built a table had not existed, then I or that table would not have existed. Surely, Aquinas would emphasize, we do not create ourselves and cannot be, by the very nature or our derived being, capable of existence without some outside help. But ultimately, it seems, we must search out that one Being, that one Creator, who is responsible for all things but who Himself is not created by anything. Thus God, to the Roman Catholic theologian, is the Ultimate: There is none beyond Him (see Pegis 26).

Thomas Aquinas argued that God was the Creator, the noncontingent Being upon which all contingent beings depend.

emanation— literally, an act of proceeding out from the Ultimate Reality

In some cases, however, the Ultimate Reality is not technically a creator, willfully making or calling into being the things that exist, and yet it still is seen as the source or fountainhead of all that exists. For example, **Brahman** in Hindu mystical thought, or the **mana** of Polynesian native religion, seems not to have made the worlds of being but to have become them, emanating out from themselves and becoming or energizing reality from within. Like "The Force" of the *Star Wars* saga, these are not powers that stand outside the cosmos but are ultimate powers somehow within the physical universe. Thus, instead of creation, philosophers speak of emanation, a self-unfolding from unity into plurality. Brahman, *mana* or, for that matter, the Force, does not stand outside the universe like an artist creating a picture but is more like the picture itself moving and organizing itself into objects, life, and order. Like a boiling stew in a giant cauldron, the material of all reality overflows itself, spreads, hardens, and becomes the world of time, space, and physical reality. Consequently, one may not quite properly speak of a Creator God in this image, and yet it is clear that this eternal and all-pervasive "stew" is the final, the Ultimate Reality, from which all else derives its being. Thus both creation and emanation clearly suggest concepts that qualify as "Ultimate Reality," beside which there is no deeper source to find and no later goal to pursue.

Finally, this Absolute, this Ultimate Reality may also be described as "the Holy." Although this term has taken on a largely moralistic tone—"holier-than-thou"—its original meaning seems to have suggested rather the quality of something being unique and distinct. That is, the Holy seems to refer to something somehow different from all we imagine and describe, set apart in a kind of purity all its own. This word's Latin equivalent, *sanctus*, has given us the roots in English of a broad range of religious terms: sanctify, saint, sacred; and in some of these terms again the moral tinge seems prominent. But technically, the words "holy" and "sacred" describe something "set apart," somehow distinct from all other things, either as their source or simply as the mysterious "wholly other." Here again the Holy is inscrutable and mysterious, as the numinous experience suggests; it is beyond description, inaccessible to human minds and human touch; it is final and ultimate, irresolvable and irreducible into parts and pieces. And thus when Moses, the great prophet of Judaism, stands before the burning bush on Mt. Sinai and asks God His name, God tells him only, "I AM that I am" (Exodus 3). Similarly, the description of the eternal mystical Brahman of Hinduism can only be described as *neti–neti*, "not this and not that" (see Bresnan 42).

The terms "Holy" and "Sacred" indicate that which stands apart.

Of course, we also use the term "holy" as a more general adjective to describe any number of objects associated with temples, churches, and mosques the world over. But clearly this use is by extension, using it as a general adjective when it is most properly applied only to a single object. To borrow an example from Aristotle, a Greek philosopher of the 4th century BCE, we might say that a person has healthy blood or even a healthy appetite; but it is clear that the word "healthy" really applies to the person herself, and that the blood and the appetite are healthy because they belong to a healthy person. Similarly, the word "holy" is applied to other things, like sacred books and holy persons, because each is "set apart" and "made distinct" for special use based on its special association with the Holy itself. All such holy objects are emphatically *made* special, *made* different from the ordinary, different from all that is secular, or literally "of the world." And then the Holy-in-Itself, or the word "Holy" *per se*, applies only to that which is above everything else, beyond or behind all that is "made special." The Holy-in-Itself is intrinsically holy, set apart, unique unto itself, and thus somehow behind, or above or beyond, all we can see, hear, measure, and think.

Objects, books, or people we recognize as holy are made *holy by their dependence on a "Holy" that is totally distinct from this finite world.*

So it is that as globalization brings the world's religions into our own backyards, we find that each religion has its own center, its own hub. Each seems to find there, variously named and described, a great holy Something that is the foundation and meaning upon which any description of religion must finally rest. It is the Ultimate and the Absolute, the source of all that we think and experience, and at the same time mysterious, beyond what we can quite hold or know. It is the Holy and the source of holiness for all sacred objects; it is the final existence and the source of existence for all that is. Thus, it is the object of our deepest religious sense and the focus of the experience of the numinous.

THE LOGIC OF THE ABSOLUTE

As you read the scriptures at the beginning of the chapter the "feel" for the numinous might be more or less pronounced. One can hardly expect a textbook to create the religious experience of the numinous for students, of course. However much we may quote and stress the scriptures and images of world religions with all the poetry we can muster, some people will be touched but others merely confused. Some may stand before the storm over the ocean and see only waves and sand. But at least one might consider how and why the Absolute plays the central role it does in religious participation. Whether one agrees or not, one can at least understand why the Tao, Nirvana, and God stand at the core of their respective religions and how they make sense of all that the religions teach as they stretch across the globe.

There is a kind of simple logic one can follow to see this. By working backwards through some of the ideas suggested describing the wide range of sacred objects made holy by their relation to the Holy-in-Itself, one can see how the holiness of even the most minor religious object takes its power, so to speak, from some greater and ultimate being. To begin, try to imagine any holy or sacred element in any religion and ask what makes it so holy or sacred. For example, consider the "holy water" of Christian baptism, or the Holy Koran of Islam; or think about a sacred stupa in India that houses some relic of the Buddha; or think

stupa—burial mound or tower-like form with Buddhist relic

about the great sage Confucius himself. Why are these things or people sacred? As suggested in Figure 3.1, each of them has a holiness derived from some other ideal, from something, we might say, "more holy." But eventually, as one asks in turn what makes the next object or person in the chain holy, one must come to the great "Something," a presumed reality that is simply holy in itself. This is the Absolute, the Ultimate, the Holy *per se*.

Conceptually, then, the Absolute/Ultimate/Holy is that from which the many objects and people of a given religion derive their own greatness, their own "holiness." Indeed, the religions themselves seem to have their substance and their essence here; it is this that seems to make the entire religion *religious*. Thus the Absolute may also be the final source of meaning and value in individual lives. That is, just as one can trace the holiness of the "holy water" to the holiness of God, one might trace the value of one's job, one's family, one's life choices to the value of serving God or being in God's presence. Here again, the ultimacy of the Absolute is evident, and we shall see in ensuing chapters how religion often works to guide behavior and hope, in ritual, ethics, and the meaning of life.

Of course, other objects may thrill us, and other causes may move us to action. Indeed, often we want to serve other ideals and work toward other goals quite independently of any religious motive. In fact, we may desperately want a new car, or be inspired to fight poverty or world hunger, much more than we pursue any goal or value of our own religion. For some people, in fact, such concerns take the place of religion, providing life with all its guidance and ritual while nevertheless failing to develop a central core one would conceivably call "holy." Such systems of thought and action—if they are "systems"—have been called functional equivalents of religion.

> *Nonreligious systems that organize and give meaning to people's lives have been called "functional equivalents" of religion.*

Imagine a man who owns a '63 Thunderbird, washes it every Saturday, buys magazines about it, joins a club of similar owners, drives a thousand miles every summer to join these owners at a rally, and generally works throughout his life for the joy and excitement of his car, along with all it means. He and his group might therefore have their pilgrimages and rituals, their ideals and icons, even stories of past owners, treated almost as saints and **prophets**. For this man, "Thunderbird-ism" is a functional equivalent of religion, a way of organizing life and its meaning around some central reality that yields direction, community, and hope. Perhaps other examples, more realistic ones, would be better: Consider the devoted and confirmed Marxist or the avid and dedicated Olympic athlete. For all these people, one object, one goal, one ideal is the focus of their energy and desire. And yet, arguably, none of this is religion.

In these cases, their "systems" function like a religion, but unless there is some sense that behind all these objects there lies hidden a kind of mysterious and inherent finality, then we do not quite have religion. Of course, one can imagine—perhaps strangely—the belief that one's Thunderbird or sports team is really "more than a car" or "more than an athletic event." Or, perhaps more reasonably, one might imagine in the "devout" Marxist something like a picture of heaven in the ideal Marxist future, the "classless society" in which all people are free, hardworking, equal and united. We might feel with this Marxist a sense of the wonder and utopian glory of this humanist heaven, a beauty and meaning almost mysterious and not quite within human comprehension. In such specula-

Holy Water ◄——— Blessed by ◄——— Priest sanctified ◄——— Church instituted ◄——— Jesus part of ◄——— Triune God
          Priest   by Church   by Jesus   Trinity

Figure 3.1 "Logic" of the Holy and Holiness in Christianity

tive ways, we might actually turn Thunderbird-ism or Marxism into religions but only, we might note, if one thinks the car or the "classless society" is absolute, ultimate, and holy. People may wash their cars "religiously," and devotion to their car may function like a religion in some people's lives, but it is not the religion of car-ism until the car takes on the sense of the Absolute and Holy.

Thus, it might be a good exercise in understanding the logic of the Holy to imagine ideals and activities that human beings have elevated in their lives to ultimate and ideal principles and yet that are not "religions." Whether or not one's gang affiliation or one's desire for a vacation to Disneyland is the strongest motivation in one's current activities, one can repeatedly ask "What makes this so valuable?" until it seems one has reached some end. And only if that end somehow sits outside and beyond us, somehow mysterious, enthralling and dynamic, can we say we are dealing with "religion." And this is not to challenge or to demean anyone's commitments or ideals. Indeed, ironically, it suggests that often one's religion might not be one's highest interest. That is, we have noted already that one's devotion to God, for example, might not be "ultimate" in one's life, even though God is, by religious definition, the "Ultimate" Being. In this way, if one stops to think logically through the bases of value and meaning, one can see the difference between even a part-time believer's "God" and a full-time athlete's race. In fact, there is something curiously common about the possibility of our Olympic runner admitting that his "religion" is about "God," even if he is, at least for now, much more interested in getting to the Olympics than in getting to worship services.

Thus, it is true that religions serve a variety of important functions in a person's life, but not everything that serves such functions is therefore religion. The function of a religion in a person's life might include its power to motivate and direct human life, its ability to create and sustain community, and its wealth of inspiration and encouragement to action and discipline. But it is not true that any ideal or object that motivates us, creates communities, or inspires action is therefore a religion. Nevertheless, if that source of direction, meaning, and community stretches us beyond ourselves and our world, beyond our concepts of everyday things to the greatness and terrifying wonder of the *mysterium tremendum,* then we may speak of religion proper. Here again, the Holy is the hub, and all these personal and social functions are the spokes that make up the "wheel" of religion. Given this point, we may study all the chapters that follow in this text as efforts to explain morality, experience, ritual, community, and so on, as they relate to their "hub," the Absolute.

For a system to be the functional equivalent of religion, it must bring a sense of ultimacy to followers.

Box 3.1 Picturing Religion and Globalization

Ecumenism and the Parliament of the World's Religions

In Chapter 1 we discussed Ewert Cousin's *(21st Century)* ideas regarding the contemporary age being a Second Axial Period in which the religions of the world are "coming together." One example of this is a widespread, multi-faceted movement referred to as the "ecumenical movement." The Ecumenical Movement proper refers to a movement within Christianity that started as a cooperative effort on the part of various Protestant denominations to further missionary activity. The Ecumenical Movement became one of the defining religious directions of the 20th century. The Movement rests on an agreement to suspend disagreement over differences in theology, ritual, and church organization while finding areas where denominations could cooperate.

It resulted in dialogues among the three major branches of Christianity (Roman Catholic, Orthodox, Protestant), collaboration on numerous religious and moral issues, and such things as ecumenical worship services, especially at universal holidays like Christmas and Easter. The most dramatic effect has been the union (or virtual union) of numbers of Christian groups. For instance, early in 2001 several major Lutheran groups united in full fellowship with the Episcopal Church in the United States. The Lutherans and Episcopalians agreed to recognize each others' sacraments, exchange of pastors, some unity of denominational offices, and the like. How far the actual merger of the denominations will go is still unclear.

Although the Ecumenical Movement *per se* is within Christianity, the currents which fostered it are felt across the religious spectrum. The Parliament of the World's Religions is a good example. The First Parliament of the World's Religions was held in Chicago in 1893 as part of the Columbian Exposition. While the meeting was called a "world parliament," the vast majority of participants were from liberal Protestant denominations. Few groups outside of the Protestant mainstream were present. In spite of this, Buddhists and Hindus were represented, and the First Parliament gave the United States its initial serious exposure to these faiths.

In the late 20th century, a committee formed to resurrect the parliament idea. The Second Parliament of the World's Religions was held in 1993 in Chicago. This time the emphasis had changed from a "show and tell" by different religions to an effort to bring the moral power of religion to bear on pressing world problems. To this end, the Parliament issued *Toward a Global Ethic*, authored largely by the Roman Catholic theologian Hans Küng. The Parliament brought together more than 8,000 leaders and adherents from a wide spectrum of faiths from across the globe to discuss the role of religion in dealing with the problems of the 21st century.

The Third Parliament of the World's religions was held in Cape Town, South Africa, in 1999. Here more than 7,000 representatives of diverse religious groups gathered to worship, to celebrate projects that assisted in global healing, and to study a host of religious, social, environmental, and economic issues. As part of this meeting, the Parliament issued *An Appeal to Guiding Institutions* to follow the principles of the *Global Ethic* in deciding matters of environment, justice, education, health, and gender around the world. A Fourth Parliament of the World's Religions is planned for the near future.

CONCEPTIONS OF THE ABSOLUTE

None of the previous descriptors of Ultimate Reality goes so far as to say that there is an evident uniformity among the world's religions on just how one ought to characterize the Absolute or Holy. As a brief look at world scriptures indicates, there are many different words that the religious cultures of the world have used to name and describe this final and Ultimate Reality. And it is overly optimistic, perhaps, to assume that somehow, behind them all, there is some single, overarching, one "Absolute" that is merely described in all these different ways. Hoping for a global perspective, perhaps, it is tempting to assert, for example, that "all the gods of all the religions are but different names for the one Absolute." Indeed, some great religious teachers, such as the Hindu mystic **Ramakrishna** (1836–1886) or the prophet of the Baha'is, **Baha'ullah** (1817–1892), have declared such an ultimate unity of religious ideas. We cannot study these claims at this point, but it should be noted that the declarations of a higher religious unity are themselves based upon claims of greater visions (for Ramakrishna) or new revelations (for Baha'ullah). But for those of us with no such special claims, declaring all religions' "gods" to be differing versions of the same God or ultimate principle is presumptuous. Moreover, if we are to take the religions for what they say of themselves, we cannot deny or ignore the evident differences in their descriptions of the Absolute. For the Tao of Taoism is not (at least for our phenomenological study) the Allah of the Muslims, nor is the **Christian Trinity** the same as the Hindu Brahman. Indeed, without claiming a "higher" insight, we must meet the diversity and disagreements of the world's religions honestly and face the descriptions of the Absolute they offer as genuine variety, not easily reducible to a single vision.

In spite of similarities, there are significant differences in descriptions of the Absolute.

■ THEISM

Within the variety of religious views of the Holy, there are clearly those conceptions of the Absolute that are personalized. These we might call "gods," and its philosophical conception we call theism. Theism (from the Greek word *theos*, god) is thus a belief in the Absolute conceived of as a God or gods, suggesting that the Ultimate Reality is a personal being, a consciousness that thinks and plans and feels in some sense like we do. God or the gods might choose and act, or work wonders in the world to display their power or displeasure. These beings get angry but may also forgive and love and aid human beings with their supernatural power. Thus they act, though in a higher and grander way, something like humans themselves act in their relations with one another, person to person. This is the meaning of theism as a belief in a "personal divine being."

Theism sees the Absolute as a personal being.

Of course, a theologian might quickly insist that the personalization of God/gods need not limit such beings to our understanding of what personality and mind and emotion imply. Saying that God/gods are like minds, even like human minds in their relational qualities, personalities, and potential for emotion, does not imply that they are "merely" human. If God is a mind, a personal being, He/She is (or They are) more fully understanding and loving and powerful than we can really comprehend. Thus, the personal nature of the Ultimate should not necessarily contradict its absolute character. Though "person-like," the ultimate reality is still a great and terrifying mystery somehow beyond the stretch of human comprehension.

■ POLYTHEISM

There can in some views, of course, be many gods. This is **polytheism**, and in some polytheistic religions the list of gods might be very long. Some parts of the early Hindu Vedas read like a veritable roll call of divinities, declaring the power and majesty of each, and beseeching each for his or her aid and blessing. "I invoke Indra and Agni, the great Soma-drinkers for the sake of Mitra, the friend and benefactor of all," declares one of the opening sections, while a page away the text calls, "Mitra and Varuna I invoke; may Varuna be our chief guardian, may Mitra defend us" (Kishore 14-15). Similarly, the ancient religions of Egypt, Greece, and Rome describe many gods, indeed offering a mythical family tree describing the birth of gods from other gods, their relations of kinship, and their various wars and disputes. Isis and Osiris procreate and bring forth the god Horus for the Egyptians; Zeus is made the brother of Hades and Poseidon among the Greeks. Shinto has a similar mythology, with the creator gods Izanagi and Izanami creating the Japanese islands, as well as their divine children, by sexual procreation. In all such polytheisms, whichever of the gods we may describe, whether some Jovian "king of the gods," or one's personal focus of unrivaled devotion, it seems that no single god is alone and unique. This may itself raise a problem in our logic of the Absolute, inasmuch as we might expect there to be only one "ultimate." Yet inescapably, it seems that the gods of polytheism *share* holiness, exhibit it "more or less," and perhaps even pass it on to their children,

In polytheism, there is no supreme and holy god.

like an inherited characteristic. Indeed divinity in some religions' pantheons may be a quality the gods have acquired, either through the fortunes of life, like Ma Ssu in China, or by virtue of their own extreme meditative disciplines, like some of the Vedic gods.

The Iliad—Greek epic tale of the battle of Troy

It is perhaps tempting to see the gods of polytheism as somewhat too anthropomorphic, all too human. The list of Zeus's sexual exploits, recited on Mount Ida in *The Iliad* (see Book XIV) certainly makes him seem like a rather lascivious patriarch, and indeed early Christian writers like **Justin Martyr** (100–163) and **Tertullian** (160–230) explicitly defended their religion by pointing out how bad an example such gods were of anything like divinity. Similarly, someone from outside the Hindu culture of India might wonder why the Hindu goddesses associated with Shiva, the Devis, seem so often to be revealed as bloody and violent. Manifested as Durga, she is the demon-slaying, animal-sacrificing goddess, and we have already seen her as Kali, the Black Goddess, whose very clothes and jewelry are the severed arms and heads of her victims. Here, these pictures present us with beings whose apparent bloodlust might not even seem human, let alone divine. Of course, the usual response to such a critique is that many of these images of sexuality or violence are open to interpretation and may be considered symbolic. Thus, Kali's bloodlust is a sign, not of her mere violence but of her power to defeat evil.

Ultimately, of course, the point of all these deities may not be that we like them all but that we see their glory, or at least the glory of one of them. Indeed, the very wantonness of Zeus or the violence of Kali might not seem justified to some of us mortals, but then it does not need to be. That is, this very antinomian activity might itself be evidence of the gods being beyond our usual categories of understanding. And so Kali's battlefield frenzy only shows her to be all the more tremendous and beyond our control, thus all the more divine. And in the end, the divine power of Zeus or Kali lies not only in sex or violence but in the fact that they are gods, beings of another kind, beings beyond the mortal world. Their power for war or lust need not be justified to us mortals at all, for they remain gods even if the motives and actions of gods sometimes seem less than divine.

■ ANIMAL SPIRITS AND ANCESTORS

*Sometimes poly-
theism assumes
the form of ani-
mism.*

Closely related to polytheism are certain forms of animism, a view common among the world's native religions and becoming popular in current pagan and neo-pagan revivals. On this view, the objects of nature are themselves imbued with souls (Latin: *anima;* pl., *animae*), and so the tree or the deer is somehow more than an object of nature. It is a person, a being, and thus one interacts and interrelates with these soul-filled objects as one would with one's neighbor. Like the gods of more theologically elaborate polytheisms, these nature spirits may indeed be relatives of the living and must certainly be considered, honored, or prayed to when the difficulties of life and the cycles of time demand their cooperation.

The actual line between animism and polytheism is vague. It certainly seems strange indeed that natural objects, once imbued with spirit or soul, may be considered distinct personal beings. This is especially evident perhaps in the personification of the sun, the moon, the earth, and the sky. Mother Earth–Father Sky personifications, as represented in typical Navajo sand paintings, reveal both the inner living spirit of "inanimate" nature and the personifying tendency of polytheism. Gender is also revealing, not so much perhaps for the sexual implications in myth, as in the creation story of Shinto mentioned above, but to represent the seminal rain and the receptive, fertile soil. It should be no surprise that native people, whose lives are so closely bound up with the natural rhythms of seasons and the lives and cycles of animals and crops, should find these beings to be more than "inanimate." Indeed they are fully "animate" beings of soul, with whom we communicate and interact.

*Ancestor spirits
are also wor-
shipped in the
world's religions.*

Ancestor spirits, too, may be worshipped, venerated, and feared in various religions of the world. Here also, a vaguely polytheistic sense of the plurality of spiritual beings is assumed, and proper interaction with these spirits is required. In the dreams and visions of tribal shamans, the dead can direct and heal the living with supernatural power. But the dead can also haunt the living and afflict them with diseases and catastrophes. Many African tribal cultures, for example, consider the "living dead" to be those spirits of deceased relatives who yet participate in human affairs. Consequently, the tribal shaman or "witch doctor" may appeal to these spirits, seeking them in dreams for their help with guidance and healing. At the same time, they are also the source of sickness and poverty when they are displeased.

Less ominously, but perhaps more famously, the Confucian religion also focuses heavily on ancestor spirits. In the Confucian traditions, disembodied ancestors are treated with a markedly spiritual reverence, and the living respond to them with a strict concern for ritual and obedience. For most traditional Chinese, a household shrine contains a scroll that lists ancestors' names five generations or more into the past, and daily incense is offered to these ancestor spirits, alongside other household gods. Similarly, the living relatives in Chinese society take good care of the ancestral gravesite with an annual spring ritual or cleaning and more incense offerings. Generally, the living are urged "to serve the dead as they were served while alive" (Chan 104). So here again the many spirits of the many dead are venerated and served, as they may be contacted, feared, and appeased in numerous tribal groups throughout the world.

Thus, in all such cases, whether dealing with gods, spirits of the dead, or the animate beings of nature, concern for such greater beings is pervasive, and their character and qualities cover a broad range from the gentle and generous to the threatening and capricious. While the Hindu goddess **Parvati** may be a source of beauty and the blessings of wealth, Kali is a horror and rampage of blood; as the Native American "Grandfathers" of Black Elk's vision are gentle and directive, the spirits of the dead among the Yoruba of Africa are a constant threat to life, health, and welfare. Yet in all such cases, this very power of destruction may be part of the awesome greatness and the inspiration of worship and ritual for many of the gods, just as glory and beauty and generosity inspire the worship and praising of other gods in these polytheistic and spirit-focused religions.

Destructive power may be part of the awesome greatness of the divine.

■ MONOTHEISM

In other religions, especially those descended from Judaism, there is generally a strong and uncompromising contrast brought out against any polytheistic or animistic suggestion. These religions—Judaism, Christianity and Islam—insist instead that there can be only one God, and thus we find an emphatic monotheism. Here the one God, the "God Almighty," is given an absolutely unique authority, shared with no other being. Islamic scripture, perhaps especially, stresses again and again the aloneness of God, explicitly at times in contrast not only to the polytheists of Arabia but even to the Christians. Thus the Holy Koran, the sacred text of Islam, declares condemnation against all polytheists, those who have other gods "associated" with Allah, saying, "Surely Allah does not forgive that anything should be associated with Him, . . . and whoever associates anything with Allah, he devises indeed a great sin" (4:48). And to the Christians the Holy Koran commands: "Believe therefore in Allah and His apostles, and say not, Three [i.e., the Trinity]. Desist, it is better for you; Allah is only one God; far be it from His glory that He should have a son" (4:171). Indeed, for Muslims, any such hint of "other gods" is a drastic philosophical and moral error called **shirk,** the "associating" of anything with God as if it could be on God's level. In Islam, unequivocally, God is one and alone and "most great."

Judaism, Christianity, and Islam hold to an emphatic monotheism.

In the early scriptures of Judaism, on the other hand, some scholars have suggested that various Bible passages acknowledge and even declare the existence of other gods. Thus in Psalm 97, for example, the "other gods" are called upon to worship YHWH (Yahweh). Even at Sinai, the command to "have no other gods before Me" seems to acknowledge the existence of such beings, even as it commands the worship of the one God alone. Yet even here, it is clear that Yahweh,

Box 3.2   Global Byte:
          A 21st-Century Theology?

Unitarianism, or Unitarian Universalism, is not a new movement. Its doctrines trace back to the beginning of the Christian Protestant Reformation in Europe in the 16th century, and some say its theological roots go all the way back to the disputes about the divinity of Jesus in the third and fourth centuries. As the name suggests, the original issue involved the assertion of the "unity" of God, in contrast to the traditional claim that God is a Trinity, or three "persons" in one God. The "Universalism" title was adopted because Unitarians chose to believe that no one could go to hell, that God would save everyone universally. The Unitarian Universalists, therefore, denied that Jesus was the "Son of God" in any theological sense and stressed instead that God calls all people to be His children, loving and saving them all without distinction, with corresponding implications that we, God's children, ought to turn to love and serve others.

The Ultimate Reality concept assumed by Unitarian Universalism is an interesting paradox that, in some ways, marks a general religious problem in a global age. As Unitarianism evolved, its desire to be all-inclusive led to an interest in distancing itself from its Christian roots. Thus in the 18th century, some Unitarians preferred to call themselves "Free Christians," because the Unitarian title seemed only to be an argument against traditional Christianity. Today, many Unitarians would prefer not to speak of God in any Christian terms, indeed perhaps not to speak of "God" at all, as they emphasize instead the desire to make religion accessible to any belief and any doctrine.

Something of this development and its theological difficulty can be seen in a recent article in the *Unitarian Universalist World* magazine by Forrest Church, minister of the Unitarian Church of All Souls in New York City. In "A Theology of the 21st Century," he wrote that Universalists "need not believe in the old Universalist God—or even employ the word God." This religion is, after all, intended to be "nondoctrinal." At the same time, Dr. Church notes the need within the Unitarian Universalist Church for "unabashedly evangelical Universalists," people willing to declare and to spread its message of tolerance and unity. In a way, it seems, Unitarian Universalists must avoid making any statements about the nature of the Absolute, and yet they must indeed make some statements based upon some idea of "a power that is greater than all and yet present in each." It is theology without theology.

If theology in general amounts to an effort to speak rationally about God and to analyze its religious implications, it is possible that any theology for the 21st century would find itself in the process of trying to find a religious basis for strong moral commitments even while it tries to avoid doctrines of God. Whether or not Dr. Church and the Unitarian Universalists have found this theology is perhaps best left for the reader to decide. But as we have seen, this may be a task for many religions in a global age, as identifiable theological claims and efforts to be inclusive in a pluralistic world seem to be conflicting ideals.

Source: Church, Forrest. "A Theology for the 21st Century" in *UU World* (Nov/Dec 2001), http://www.uua.org/world/2001/05/feature1.html (accessed April 25, 2004).

the great "I AM" revealed to Moses on that mountain, is the "God of gods" and is not to be confused with any putative "other gods" as if they were genuine rivals. Some scholars even suggest that this monotheistic emphasis, after all, was the real point of the creation story in Genesis 1: It is not an effort to describe how God created but rather to insist that only the Creator God is truly God and that

He whom the Hebrews worship in fact created the sun and moon, the animals, and the lands that are worshipped as gods by the surrounding pagans.

Monotheism, then, is different, often emphatically different, from the kind of polytheism, animism, or ancestor worship that populates the spiritual world with a multitude of sacred beings. And yet there is also a very significant similarity between God, the gods, and the variety of spirits; namely, that they are all persons. This does not mean, of course, that they are all human beings but rather that there is something here like a human mind, a personality, a consciousness of will and temperament. This implies that we human beings may interrelate with the Absolute as one being to another; we may "talk" to them and they to us. There is, moreover, a suggestion of the possibility of love, as well as anger and punishment. We may talk of revelation and conversation, fear and friendship, interaction and interrelation in the face of the divine. These gods, or God, may be self-aware, conscious Creators and may plan and act in human history, doing miracles to save, awe, or punish the religious few or the entire world. They become for their followers the objects of wonder and worship or prayer and ritual supplication. They can become dreaded enemies, close friends, or intimate lovers.

Ancestor worship, animism, polytheism, and monotheism all insist that the spiritual power(s) have a personality.

■ THE NONTHEISTIC ABSOLUTE

The description of the Absolute as a deity, God or gods or spirits of many kinds, may seem a common and obvious notion of the Ultimate Reality, that which is at the center of religion. Indeed, as globalization has spread the ideas of dominant cultures around the world, especially those of the great monotheistic faiths that have molded most of Western culture, theism as a description of the Absolute may be something we take for granted. But in many religions, the Absolute is best understood impersonally. This means that the Absolute is not considered a person, a relational being with a mind somewhat akin to our own. Rather, an impersonal Absolute is more likely conceived of as a great substance, an impersonal essence, or some general abstraction of spirit or being itself. One might say that instead of imagining some great Person in the sky, think of the Sky itself.

Perhaps we need some examples. At the beginning of the chapter, Brahman and Tao are mentioned in their respective religions, but it is evident that these are not persons, not "gods" as such. They are forces of existence, but they are not beings to whom one prays or whom one fears or loves. Instead Brahman is perhaps more like the matter and form of the universe, the great oneness from which all is derived and to which all returns. The Tao, we might suggest, is also no deity but more like an order or harmony, that from which everything takes its pattern and within which all things move in their multifarious rhythms. This idea, we might generalize, is like the concept of a great Oneness, the "One without a second" mentioned in the Hindu scriptures. For such a concept, we may use the term monism, describing a metaphysical view that all reality is part of this single unity. The "mono" prefix asserts here the singularity and unity of the Absolute as surely as it does in monotheism; yet in this concept there is no *theos*, no god, no personhood.

Monism describes the view that there is a single unity of all beings to the degree that only the One exists.

This great oneness of all being is thus emphasized to suggest an Absolute Reality somehow "beyond" individuality and distinction. Look again at the

Brahman concept noted earlier and in the opening excerpt from the **Upanishads.** Throughout the texts of mystical Hinduism, Brahman is equated with the impersonal inner soul, or Self (**Atman**), of all living beings. But precisely because the ultimate reality is in all beings, it cannot be any one particular being. It is, as the scriptures say, *neti–neti,* "not this, not that." Thus, while Brahman is the essence of all things, it is beyond all appearance, not really evident in the many different things we see. Similarly, Brahman is said to be *satchidananda,* pure Being, Consciousness, and Bliss, but at the same time it is certainly not *a* being or *a* consciousness, not an individual in any sense we recognize as relational. Thus when compared to the world of plurality in which we live, the mystics find the Absolute Being everywhere, the One as the great reality within all things. Everything, though it seems to be individual and distinct, is really one thing, the only thing that truly exists, and therefore all things are, in some sense, one reality. This is monism.

A related but subtly distinct notion is the concept of pantheism, a term that literally means "all is God." Here the root *theos* does suggest a "god," and yet it would be misleading to think it implies a relational "person," as in traditional theism. Thus pantheism suggests that "God," whatever energy or power that is conceived to be, is in all things in a way that does not necessarily deny their plurality; nevertheless, the sense in which "all things are God" does deny that anything relates to God as to a personal being. As the *Stanford Encyclopedia of Philosophy* puts it, "Pantheism is non-theistic, but not atheistic. It is a form of non-theistic monotheism or even non-personal theism . . . [but most pantheists] do not believe God is a person or anything like a person." Thus the point remains that there is no relation or personal interaction with the Absolute here, for the simple reason that there is no "other" with which it may relate. That is, since all *is* "God," there is no real relationship between the Absolute and anything else. Thus the "divinity" here is not "He" or "She" or "They" but rather "It." And the connection between the Absolute One and the broad plurality of objects and animals, persons and plants is not technically relational, not a matter of communication, love, or anger, but rather, ultimately, the connection of identity. I do not pray to or worship this Ultimate Being. Rather I *am* the Ultimate Being, as are the lumberjack, the tree, and the ax he uses to chop it down. This is unlike monism insofar as there is indeed a relation between lumberjack, tree, and ax. For the pantheist, plurality is maintained between things, but all things are equally "divine." For the monist, the distinctions between these apparently discreet entities are the mere illusion of the unenlightened. Thus the pantheistic animist may say that *mana* is the spiritual substance that empowers all living things, while the monistic spiritual teacher of the Upanishads declares to his student, "You ARE Brahman" in such a way that the student's sense of individual identity is an illusion.

We cannot supply here a complete distinction between pantheistic and monistic concepts of the Absolute, but we can stress that in both notions there is a denial of the personal nature of "God" and a tendency instead to see the Absolute as within, not beyond, the multitude of things we see, or seem to see. By this logic, the causal relation of the monistic or pantheistic Absolute to the world around us is more likely to be described as emanation than as creation, as these concepts were defined above. For our purposes here, the point is to note that with emanation, the Absolute does not stand outside of creation like a painter before a picture, but rather it unfolds itself and *becomes* creation, is itself within and throughout the reality of nature like the soul of the world. So, as we saw, Brahman is at once the single Ultimate Reality and also the inner soul (Atman) of all things: Brahman–Atman. Similarly, the Tao of Taoism is not "beyond" the world but is itself the source of "the ten-thousand things." Thus we might say a monistic Absolute is immanent, the ultimate Holy somehow spread throughout the world and within the person; in contrast, the creator God of monotheism might be described as **transcendent,** beyond and outside of the world He creates from nothing.

Ultimate Reality unfolds itself, becomes creation in nontheistic traditions; the Creator of theistic traditions creates the world and cosmos from nothing.

■ SUMMARY

The various concepts of the Absolute that we have attempted to study in this section—polytheism, monotheism and monism (or pantheism)—offer us three (or four or many more) distinct ways of seeing how people have characterized the Absolute: a multitude of deities and spirits, each perhaps less than infinite, or each a sign of the Infinite itself; a single, final deity, encompassing all relational ideals in Himself/Herself; and a single, final, but impersonal force and substance, somehow all things, scattered throughout or hidden behind the things we see. In all these cases, there is something mysterious and tremendous and fascinating about the One, the gods, the spirits, or God, a quality perhaps at once fearsome and wonderful. We have tried to convey this majesty, mystery, and admitted ambiguity in words like "Holy," "Absolute," and "Ultimate." Even if such words are inadequate, they attempt to communicate something about the central core of religious life, the absolute "Something" around which the practices, experiences, and attitudes of religion revolve. Our efforts to define this Absolute may indeed fail, but such concepts applied to the God, gods, spirits, and ancestors of the world's religions, to their *mana,* Brahman, Tao, Allah, or Holy Trinity, help us to begin the kind of study that takes seriously what the religions say is the focus of their own devotion.

RELIGIOUS DISAGREEMENT IN A GLOBAL COMMUNITY

In the many religions of the world, distinctions of the sort just noted are often strict and uncompromising: The monotheistic God of Islam finds no place for the many gods of the idolaters; the Oneness of D. T. Suzuki's Zen finds error upon error in a Christian monotheism that looks outward for God instead of inward for the Buddha Nature. But it is also true that the various interpretations of the Absolute mix and mingle or stretch and expand to absorb or include one another. Thus for some polytheists, Allah and Christ may be but other gods in the glorious **pantheon,** and to the Hindu mystic, all gods, Hindu or Judaic, are but playful masks on a faceless and nameless Absolute. In many tribal cultures, the roughly pantheistic reality, expressed above in the concept of *mana,* exists within or behind the various gods and spirits and ancestor ghosts that populate the

idolator—someone worshipping idols, images, or objects that are representative of a god/gods/God unseen realm. All of these might be considered strategies for explaining and exploring the differences among the world's conceptions of the Absolute and thus ways in which the disagreements between religions might seem less stark. In a world grown smaller through the technological developments of modernity, we cannot help but meet, it seems, people with whom religious disagreement seems unavoidable, and so some strategy for explaining how religions interrelate seems necessary. At the same time, ironically, these strategies are themselves varied and, perhaps, irreconcilable.

■ EXCLUSIVISM

Three main strategies exist, and within each there are myriad interpretations and reactions. Some religions are exclusive, claiming that the final and absolute description of their God or Truth is simply a fact and, therefore, that all contradictory claims are false. This approach, known as exclusivism, need not be cruel or imperialistic, but it is often uncompromising, at least on central conceptions of the Absolute. Because the self-revelation of the one God is Truth, the monotheist might say, we cannot merely ignore the mistake of polytheism or, indeed, atheism. Similarly, because the way to salvation of the Buddha's teaching is precise and necessary, numerous pitfalls of misunderstanding and seduction make it impossible to find salvation any other way. The point is that the Truth, whether as monotheistic belief or Buddhist salvation, cannot grant easy compromise nor accept heresies as equally valid alternative descriptions. Without denying that the reality of God is greater than anyone can fully grasp, exclusivist conceptions of the Absolute simply insist that there are still some claims about "God" that are false, perhaps catastrophically false. Monotheists do not generally claim to know God completely, but they do claim to know something of God truly. And if anything at all can be declared of God truly, then it seems unavoidable that some opposing claims about God are just mistaken or, for example, excluded.

This exclusivism seems to have its harshest form, as we might expect, when religions speak of salvation and damnation. How terrible it might seem to an outsider if a religion declares that those who choose not to follow God or who fail to find enlightenment are simply lost. And whether "lost" implies a further series of lifetimes of suffering or an eternity in the sorrows of some darkly depicted Hell, the implications of this exclusion are harsh indeed. Yet from the exclusivist's position, such potential loss is only the logical result of a claim of truth and the genuine responsibility of human choice. Thus when Yahweh, the God of the Jews, is said to be a "jealous" God (Exodus 20:4), we should not understand that jealousy as a weakness of envy or bitterness. It is, rather, a call by the one absolute God to the simple justice of acknowledging His unique ultimacy. And when the Buddha declares that there is no salvation in any "way" that continues to hold a belief in "the self" (as in the *Abhidharmakosha* of Vasubandhu), he is not damning anyone but only stating that some mistaken beliefs make it impossible for one to find liberation. Nevertheless, for those living in a varied, global community, where the Buddhist monk's visitor could be a Christian or a monotheist's neighbor may be Hindu, such exclusion may seem harsh, even if it is logically defensible.

Exclusivism mentions that there is only one correct understanding of the Holy Absolute.

The harshest implication of exclusivism is excluding from salvation those who do not follow the correct tradition.

■ INCLUSIVISM

In contrast, a religious inclusivism might suggest that others' "truths" are already, to one extent or another, included within the truths of one's own religion's descriptions of the Absolute. Thus others' gods or others' methods might be secondary versions of our own, alternative names for the God or higher monistic essence that is the Holy truly. Thus personalistic gods might be seen as playful, temporary personae of the impersonal Absolute. The Absolute, one could say, is really the impersonal Oneness of being, but it can be considered in any of a thousand forms, any "god" or "spirit" you want to worship, like an "educational tool" for spiritual beginners. In this way, worshippers of the Hindu god Vishnu might maintain that all divine persons, from Krishna to Christ, are avatars or manifestations of Vishnu himself. The ultimate deity is therefore Vishnu, but this god is willing to take any name or form people will follow for their salvation and for the preservation of the world. Similarly, a universalistic Christian might declare that when Christ came to save "all people," that is exactly what he did, whether they agree or not.

Yet even here, the irony from a global perspective lies in the fact that inclusive religious views often include others only by changing them or by finding a truth higher and broader than the "partial truths" of others. Thus, the Hindu might "include" Islam by declaring that Allah is merely one of the possible forms and names of the Ultimate Impersonal, but this is done at the expense of denying the utter finality and uniqueness of Allah that is a central insistence of the Holy Koran. That is, the Hindu may smile benignly and say, "Yes, your worship of Allah is also good because Allah is one of the forms of Vishnu," but this would hardly be flattering to the Muslim. Similarly, Islam claims a kind of inclusion of Christianity by finding Jesus to be a great prophet of God. But here, too, the cost is the denial of the crucial Christian understanding of Christ as unique savior.

Perhaps most intriguing as an example of religious inclusivism is the Baha'i faith, which explicitly seeks to assert a universal unity of religions. Throughout the ages of human history, they claim, the one God has revealed Himself to all cultures, to prophets of every age, and it is from these that we have the world's religions. Thus, all religions are valid because they are all religions of the one God. This sounds inclusive and accepting, and it may be seen as an ideal religion for a global community. Indeed, the prophet of the Baha'is, Baha'ullah, declared that all religions were "ordained by God and are reflections of his Will and Purpose." The irony of this claim, however, is that that this "unity of religions" seems to make such an inclusive statement only by declaring that all religions, even those without a focus on God, were really originally focused on God. Thus 'Abdu'l-Baha wrote: "The founder of Buddhism was a wonderful soul. He established the oneness of God, but later the original principles of his doctrines gradually disappeared" ('Abdu'l-Baha 158). Here the Buddha is included as a "wonderful soul" but only by declaring that the Buddha really taught a form of monotheism. Surely this would seem odd to the Buddhist.

The point here is not to critique the Baha'i religion but to see that religiously inclusive claims seem to succeed by changing another's religious view to fit one's own. Indeed, inasmuch as the uniqueness of the Christians' Savior or of the Buddha's **Dharma** is itself exclusive, an inclusive religion that tries to fit them in perhaps cannot help but change their meaning. Arguably, concepts of the Absolute capable of including alternative conceptions of the Holy would, in the very process of inclusion, exclude the exclusivists. It would be ironic indeed if, in my inclusivism, I were to insist that you are included in my religion because I understand your religion better than you do, whether you accept my interpretation of your religion or not.

■ PLURALISM

A genuine pluralism holds there are many truths not reducible to one.

The third strategy for relating one religion's conception of the Absolute to another's involves the notion of pluralism. A genuine religious pluralism would suggest that there are simply many truths, ultimately not reducible to any one nor explicable in any single term. While logically problematic, this effort is attractive for avoiding, though not resolving, the apparent disagreement among the religious conceptions of the Absolute. Here, if one can be careful enough not to let one's philosophical effort decay into another inclusivism, all religious views of the Absolute can be declared "true," whatever their form and whatever contradictions may exist between them. Of course, there may be severe ethical difficulties for the consistent pluralist, and it might be the concept of "truth" itself that suffers the most. For it is difficult to see how the genuine pluralist can justify taking a moral stand on any issue, no matter how atrocious, and we might wonder how a pluralist can deny the importance of apparent contradictions while trying to say anything at all about the Absolute.

But however severe such problems may be for logical philosophers or however we may have to wrestle out the ethical difficulties in a later chapter, perhaps for our purposes here it is useful just to grant some kind of pluralism in the wide descriptions of the Holy and say that, somehow, they are all "right." This is an attractive view, especially once again given the fact of global intercommunication and humanity's apparent need to learn cooperation. Yet even for our study, it should be acknowledged that philosophical pluralism is not likely to be congruent with what the religions actually say of themselves. For although we are *de facto* pluralists in a pluralistic society—that is, we cannot help but admit that there are many religious views, and we are not allowed, by law, to force anyone to change—what many of the religious scriptures of the world themselves declare of their admittedly limited understandings of the Absolute may not be so open. Perhaps all we can do is confess the descriptive fact of religious disagreement and look at each religion's own efforts to describe how it includes or excludes the others.

Thus, it is finally possible that none of the concepts used to name and describe the Absolute is ultimately broad enough to encompass all the religions of the world in their self-spoken diversity. Even if some translators of the Upanishads call Brahman "God," and various mystics of different traditions call God "the Real," we may not be able to find a name for the Holy that accurately conveys all that the world's religions want to say. Nor is that our purpose here; we are not proposing a religious solution to religious disagreement. For us, the point is to find terms broad enough to be used across traditions, even if none of the traditions would accept such terms as very helpful names for the Absolute. At the same time, we need to describe the Absolute in terms sufficiently narrow to rule out those things that are the center of the functional equivalents, like the Marxist state or one's '63 Thunderbird. It is clear, for example, that using the term "God" for all the great realities that are the central Absolute of the world's religions would probably be too narrow, inasmuch as the ancestor spirits or the Tao seem not to qualify. By the same token, calling them all a "life focus" or a "source of ritual and meaning" would clearly be too broad. Thus we hold onto our key words—the Absolute, the Ultimate, the Holy—to try to designate that which may, by its very nature, be beyond designation.

Yet to be precise, these terms are attempts to escape that paradox, attempts to give a label to that phenomenon within the world's religions that cannot adequately be labeled, just as the word "indescribable" is itself a descriptive term for that which is beyond description. As time goes on, we can each judge how successful such terms might be.

■ GLOBALIZATION AND DIVERSITY

In Chapter 2 we discussed various ways in which religion is defined. In this chapter, we have talked about a number of diverse ways in which the Absolute may be viewed. One of the appealing points of the array of religions is the marvelous patchwork of their diversity. How will globalization affect this diversity? The answer to this question may well be found in the contradictory trends generated by the globalization process.

In Chapter 1, we discussed how globalization was creating two contradictory forces in a variety of areas, including religion. These are the trends toward particularism and universalism. As a result, we see any number of movements in all religions that assert their particularity against what they see as the threatening movement toward watering down or destroying their unique identity. For instance, at the *Parliament of the World's Religions,* there were a number of protesters against what they understood as religious compromise or, worse, toward some effort to establish a single world religion. Thus, Muslim protesters proclaimed, "The Koran is the answer, not the World Parliament," while Christian dissidents asserted, "Jesus is the Savior, not the World Parliament." Still other carried placards labeling the Parliament as a plot of "Free Masons," "Zionists," "Secular Humanists," and a host of other nefarious plotters. Most of the protesters were peaceful, but others threatened violence. The threat of violence caused the South African police to project a strong presence at and around the meetings of the Parliament.

Globalization has specified a number of particularist movements asserting their own uniqueness.

On the other hand, the Ecumenical Movement and a spate of meetings worldwide, such as the Parliament, do presume the quest for universals. That is, there is a strong push in a wide range of interreligious contacts to find common ground in theology, as well as in facing the pressing practical problems of humanity. However, finding common ground does not mean the creation of a universal religion. Clearly, that is not likely to happen anytime soon, if it ever happens or even if it is desirable in the first place. For one thing, such a universal agreement would require that the religions involved, as we noted above, would have to sacrifice core doctrines and practices that are at the heart of their identities.

The Ecumenical Movement rests on the quest for universals, but does not deny various religions' uniqueness.

So the quest for universals does mean finding common ground, but it also means recognizing the elements that make the religions involved different from the start, especially in their understanding of the Absolute. At the very least, this means toleration of differences. However, true common ground and cooperation mean more than just toleration. They mean respecting, and perhaps learning from, the differences. Can an Islamic emphasis on the oneness of God help a Christian to understand the Trinity? Can a tribal culture's view of the Absolute in the spirits of nature help a monotheist to learn the value of the creation? Such an effort to learn and respect may provide the basis for creative growth in understanding other people's religious beliefs, as well as an increasing appreciation for the depth of one's own religious tradition.

In short, globalization does not mean the development of a single world religion or ignoring differences amongst humanity's religions. As argued above, the avoidance or overcoming of disagreement may be impossible. But globalization may force us all to recognize and to appreciate the diversity in unity along with the unity in diversity.

CONCLUSION

The evaluation of our terminology and the varying descriptions of how one might understand the Holy can only take place with further study. And, as the focus of this text has suggested all along, that further study can best be pursued by going to the primary sources. Therefore, as you do the exercises on the Web site **www.cengage.com/religion**, try to apply terminology about the Absolute and the Holy, the transcendent and the immanent. See if you can distinguish ideas of Ultimate Reality that are monotheistic from those that are polytheistic, monistic, or pantheistic. As always, these exercises are meant to give you a chance to work with these ideas and see how, or if, they help you understand the religions of the world, including perhaps your own.

■ INTERACTIVE EXERCISE

Please continue your exploration of the Absolute by going to the interactive exercise for this chapter online (**http://www.religion.wadsworth.com/richter**).

WORKS CITED

Holy Bible. New International Version. Grand Rapids, MI: Zondervan, 1984.

'Abdu'l-Baha. Some *Answered Questions.* Wilmett, IL: Baha'i Publishing Trust, 1997.

Bresnan, Patrick. *Awakening: An Introduction to the History of Eastern Thought.* Upper Saddle River, NJ: Prentice Hall, 1999.

Chan, Wing-tsit. *A Sourcebook in Asian Philosophy.* Princeton, NJ: Princeton University Press, 1963.

Church, Forrest. *A Theology for the 21st Century.* UU World. Nov/Dec 2001, http://www.uua.org/world/2001/05/feature1.html (accessed April 25, 2004).

Corrington, R. H. *The Melanesians: Studies in Their Anthropology and Folklore.* New York: Dover, 1972.

Homer. *The Iliad.* New York: Walter J. Black, 1942.

Kant, Immanual. *Critique of Judgment.* Oxford, UK: Oxford University Press, 1982.

Kishore, B. R. *Rig Veda.* New Delhi, India: Diamond, 1998.

Koller, John, and Patricia Koller. *A Sourcebook in Asian Philosophy.* New York: Macmillan, 1991.

Levine, Michael. "Pantheism." *The Stanford Encyclopedia of Philosophy.* 1997. Edited by Edward N. Zalta, http://plato.stanford.edu/archives/fall1997/entries/pantheism/#Ath (accessed April 29, 2004).

Martyr, Justin. *First and Second Apologies (Ancient Christian Writers #56).* Boston: Paulist, 1997.

Mayeda, Sengaku. *A Thousand Teachings: The Upadesasahasri of Sankara.* Albany, NY: State University of New York Press, 1992.

Mutahhari, Murtaza. *Fundamentals of Islamic Thought.* Berkeley, CA: Mizan, 1985.

Otto, Rudolf. *The Idea of the Holy.* Oxford, UK: Oxford University Press, 1982.

Paper, Jordan, and Lawrence G. Thompson. *The Chinese Way in Religion.* 2nd ed. Belmont, CA: Wadsworth, 1998.

Payne, Robert. *The Fathers of the Western Church.* New York: Dorset, 1989.

Pegis, Anton. *Introduction to St. Thomas Aquinas.* New York: Modern Library, 1948.

Prabhavananda, Swami, and Frederick Manchester. *The Upanishads: Breath of the Eternal.* London: Mentor, 1948.

Stryk, Lucien. *The World of the Buddha.* New York: Grove Weidenfeld, 1968.

Suzuki, D. T. *The Field of Zen.* New York: Perennial Library, 1970.

Tertullian. *Apology and De Spectaculis.* Boston: Harvard University Press, 1977.

Zabilka, Ivan. *Scientific Malpractice: The Creation/Evolution Debate.* Lexington, KY: Bristol, 1992.

4 ORIGINS AND FOUNDERS

Getty Images/PhotoDisc Collection

Almost all religions have stories that trace their legendary beginnings. Some of these simply recount myths about supposed origins while others trace their roots to more or less historical founders. In this chapter, we discuss many issues concerning the stories religions tell about how they started. As a way of preparing for the materials in the chapter, please look over the pictures above and online (**http://www.religion.wadsworth.com/richter**) and the following quotations, then answer the Introductory Questions that follow.

When I was thus in the act of calling upon God, I discovered a light appearing in my room, which continued to increase until the room was lighter than at noonday, when immediately a personage appeared at my bedside, standing in the air, for his feet did not touch the floor. . . . He called me by name, and said unto me that he was a messenger sent from the presence of God to me, and that his name was Moroni; that God had work for me to do; and that my name would be had for good and evil among all nations.

—Mormonism: from "The Origin of the Book of Mormon" (Smith ii)

I am the Creator, the true and real God. I have the preordination for this Residence. At this time I have appeared in this world in person to save all mankind. I ask you to let Me have your Miki as My living Temple.

—Shinto (Spoken to Zenbei Nakayama concerning his wife Miki, as she was possessed by a god [*kami*] to become the foundress of the Tenrikyo sect of Shinto): *A Short History of Tenrikyo* (70).

Wanblee [the Eagle Spirit] kept the beautiful girl with him and made her his wife. The eagle's wife became pregnant and bore him twins, a boy and a girl. When the waters [of the flood] finally subsided, Wanblee helped the children and their mother down from his rock and put them on the earth, telling them: "Be a great nation, become a great Nation, the Lakota Oyate."

—Religion of the Brule Sioux Indians: "How the Sioux Came to Be" (Erdoes and Ortiz 95).

The speech is measured out in four quarters, the sages with insight know it. The three kept in close secret cause no movement, the fourth is the division that is talked about. God is one, but the sages call Him by various names.

—Hinduism: Rig Veda I.164 (Kishore 39–40)

96.1: Read in the name of your Lord Who created.
96.2: He created man from a clot.
96.3: Read and your Lord is Most Honorable,
96.4: Who taught (to write) with the pen
96.5: Taught man what he knew not.

—Islam: Holy Koran 96:1–5

INTRODUCTORY QUESTIONS

1. The picture of Jesus and the picture of the Buddha counting on his fingers represent both as teachers. How are they the same? How are they different? Consider as you think about this what you learned about Jesus and the Buddha in the last chapter.
2. Miki Nakayama becomes a vehicle for the revelation of "the true and real God." Does this seem to be much different from the call of Muhammad or the revelation to Joseph Smith? In what way?
3. Note there are two pictures of the Buddha. Traditionally, his hand positions tell us that in the first he is teaching but in the second he is not. How do both pictures tell something about the Buddhist religion?
4. The wife of the Eagle, along with her twin children, becomes the source of the nation and the religion of the Lakota Oyate. Would you consider them "prophets," like Muhammad? Why, or why not?
5. Lao Tzu appears very jolly on his ox. Would you be surprised to see a picture of Jesus so jolly? Why?
6. What different roles do the many human figures play in these pictures and quotations? See if you can generally describe how people become the sources for their religious truths. Are there nonhuman sources of religious truths?

APPROACHES TO ORIGINS

There is an immediate difficulty when one attempts to discuss the origins of any religion. It is a temptation, for example, to consider primarily the history and the sociological structures of a specific time and place and consider them to be the real forces that create a people's religious views. For example, the "origin" of Christianity, we might say, lies in the politics and sociological dissatisfactions of first century Jews, their desire for liberation, and their inability to rebel effectively against the Roman authorities. Or the "origin" of Hinduism perhaps lies only in the "conquest" of the Indus Valley civilization by the nomadic Aryans in the 16th century BCE. As Hindus mixed their cultures, so they mixed their gods. Certainly, such a view is not entirely false, but it does fail to get at the issue of founders and origins that is the central point we intend to discuss here. Indeed, these social and historical origins are probably not what most religious people would recognize as the origins of their own religions. It is important therefore to distinguish between what one might call "external" explanations of a religion's origins and the religion's own "internal" explanations. The methodology of this chapter shall emphasize the latter.

"External" explanations are those imposed from outside of a religion; "internal" explanations are those that come from within a religion.

■ "EXTERNAL" APPROACHES TO ORIGINS

It is certainly tempting, and undoubtedly useful, to describe the origins and founders of religion by using "external," or we might say "scientific," approaches. In discussing the history of religions, for example, there are many attempts to explain the development of religious ideas along evolutionary lines.

Studies in the early 20th century, such as those by Edward Burnett Tylor (1832–1917) and James Frazer (1854–1941), concluded that religion emerged out of the uncertainty of life and the need of primitive peoples to understand, hopefully even to control, the world around them. Enticed perhaps by the success of Darwinian thinking, these anthropologists concluded that religion emerged and changed throughout human history as beliefs in magic, nature spirits, gods, and God evolved, in that order. As in biological evolution, such ideas lived and survived or died out depending on how well, and to what extent, they helped various cultures survive in their environments. In this way, these anthropologists looked at the origins and developments of religion like a biologist might look at the origins and developments of a species of fish.

Religious skeptics may see religion in terms of psychological and sociological manipulation.

Similarly, other theories that explain the origins from an "external" perspective might appeal to us, especially if we are religious skeptics ourselves, by explaining the source of religion not as the product of evolution but of human invention. That is, a religious skeptic might be inclined to interpret the origins of religion in terms of psychological needs or sociological manipulation. For example, just as parents might invent the ideas of Santa Claus or the Boogie Man to constrain a child's behavior, so religion, the extreme skeptic might argue, was invented in ancient times just to keep the masses in line. The philosopher and writer **Ayn Rand** (1905–1982), as an example of such a skeptic, laments the long history of Western culture, in which nations were run—and human creativity and freedom were suppressed—by the deadly union of powerful despots and religious justifications. As the "Attilas" ruled by ruthless power, she says, so the "Witch Doctors" helped to keep the people suppressed by pointing them to mystical worlds and by teaching them other-worldly values that go against our natural inclinations to work hard, get ahead, and become independent. Thus, religion was used to oppose the real, material values of life and to justify the abominations of the conquerors. Rand declares:

For Ayn Rand, "Attilas" and "Witch Doctors" form an exploitative alliance.

> *Thus Attila and the Witch Doctor form an alliance. Attila loots and plunders; the Witch Doctor exhorts the victims to surpass their selfish concern with material property. Attila slaughters; the Witch Doctor proclaims to the survivors that scourges are a retribution for their sins. (20)*

For Karl Marx, religion is the "opium of the people."

As previously noted, Karl Marx would have probably agreed with Rand, ironically enough, since Rand disagreed so vehemently with Marxism. Thus, to use Marx's famous line, religion is "the sigh of the oppressed creature, . . . the opium of the people" (McLellan 64).

Other popular declarations about the true origins of religion are equally destructive. Sigmund Freud, most famously, presumed that religion is not the result of divine interaction with human beings, but it was rather the result of subconscious drives. Chapter 2: What is Religion refers to his book *The Future of an Illusion,* in which he argues that moral self-constraints and the inevitable fear of death inescapably produce in the human subconscious an anxiety and unhappiness that simply must be overcome. Thus, the needy human psyche constructs a "heavenly Father" to be a "benevolent providence" that is more powerful than the forces and uncertainties of nature and that promises us, somehow, complete fulfillment of our desires. He concludes about religious origins that "religion would thus be the universal obsessional neurosis of humanity; like the obsessional neuroses of children, it arose out of the Oedipus Complex, out of the relation to the father" (Pals 73).

All of these "external" attempts to explain the origins of religion can be quite useful. But of course they all remain "external"; that is, they attempt in different ways to analyze religion with an explanation that, to a large extent, describes religion using the lens of an external model as, for example, provided in sociological or psychological modes of analysis. If, however, we are to attempt to explore religion phenomenologically, our study emphasizes what the religions themselves say about their origins.

■ THE "INTERNAL" OR PHENOMENOLOGICAL APPROACH

Scientific approaches to religious origins often are guilty of reductionism.

Attempts to explain religious origins as social evolution, psychological construction, or socioeconomic manipulation are in danger, we might say, of "reductionism," the tendency to explain something away by reducing it to simple explanations. Of course, in one sense these theories do discuss the origins of religion, and they can all be helpful and revealing, insofar as psychological, sociological, and even economic forces do play significant roles in how religions develop and how they are lived. Indeed, there will be significant elements of psychology and sociology of religion in this text. But there is the danger of misunderstanding the phenomenon of religion as believers experience it if such theories are allowed to "reduce" religion to nonreligious causes. Such "reductionistic" approaches to religion are not our intention here. In the first place, they are, of course, speculative and would require a full study of psychological or sociological theories to begin a valid defense or challenge to such theories. But more importantly, they are certainly not what the religious believer himself would describe as the phenomenon of religion. That is, though an evolutionary model of religious origins might be like explaining the biological origins of a fish, such views would be quite foreign to those people who actually live and breathe the religion, as foreign perhaps as the idea of evolution would be to the fish.

phenomenological method—the process of study whereby one tries to describe the phenomena of religion as they are found, not as they are explained by outside disciplines

As noted before, the method used in this book is the so-called phenomenological method. This term has been used to refer to the notion of explaining phenomena simply as they are observed, without any evaluation of whether they are true or false. In this case, our concern is less with where the theorist might say religion *really* comes from than with what believers themselves say of the origins of their beliefs and practices.

A phenomenological approach to religion takes seriously what believers say about the origins of their religion.

This is not to say that there are no psychological or sociological conditions that influence, and indeed may determine, how religion in fact evolves or develops. It may well be that religion emerges into human consciousness out of fear of death or because primitive peoples dreamed of their departed parents. It may well be that religion on a personal level is somehow psychologically founded on an inner need for security, or perhaps on a social level it is a vast political conspiracy to assert and cement the power of monarchs and semi-divine rulers. All this is, of course, possible, but it is also by no means the exclusive dimension of religion. Above all, it seems problematic to say that religion is nothing more than psychological or social forces. For if one says religion is merely the result of psychological needs or sociological manipulations, then such theories seem to reduce

Table 3.1	Models of Interpretation for Origins of Religions
External approach (using a model or lens to analyze religion)	▪ Religion as evolutionary process
	▪ Religion as human invention, fulfilling psychological or sociological needs
	▪ Religion as socio-, economic, or political ideology
Internal approach	▪ Study and analysis of phenomena of religion as described by believers

religion to something that is, in itself, not religious. Theories, analyzing religion through external lenses, may become somewhat like distractions: temptations to move away from our phenomenological approach and to take a view of religious origins that the believers and devotees of the world's religions would not themselves recognize, let alone acknowledge.

Thus in this phenomenological study, we will look for insights into what religions view as their own origins. The religions themselves tell us where they come from—of course, more or less explicitly, perhaps with a number of different viewpoints even within the same religion. They tell us, more or less, who spoke the first words or gained the founding insight of this religion, or from whom or what we learned the practices of worship or devotion that continue to guide us. Believers and devotees recognize their own stories of origins and their own founders as the sources from which religious belief and practice "truly" come, regardless of what Frazer may say of evolution or what Freud may say of psychological needs.

Devotees use stories of origin and founders to explain how their religion came about.

What do religious people say about the origins of their own traditions? As may well be expected, there is no single story, or even a single formula, that religions follow to explain how religion begins. It might be expected that there should be some kind of logical coherence between the variation in the stories of founders and origins and the variations observed in the last chapter on the religions' concepts of the holy and the sacred. For as God is different from Brahman, or ancestor spirits differ from the Tao, so the prophets differ from seers, and shamans from sages.

▪ FOUNDERS

Founders are humans through whom new religious insight came.

Religious origins, of course, can be found in the examination of religious "founders." These **religious founders** are the men and women (though indeed mostly men) who in some way or another became recognized as the bringers of new insight. Thus, unlike the more general "origins," the founders are explicitly human individuals, often historically recognizable. Yet they are not just average people. These famous few are religious founders because they found or heard some message or teaching from God, from the gods, or from a human wisdom deeper and more profound than most people have ever experienced. These people saw or heard or experienced a great truth about the Absolute, whether God or the Tao, and they passed that truth along, motivated by compassion for the lost or driven by the overwhelming spirit of the divine. And thus they became the prophets and sages of new religions.

Many of the examples of these famous founders are easy enough to find, especially since in several cases the religions themselves are named after these founders. Confucianism, Buddhism, and Christianity, in particular, refer in their titles to specific persons, and no one seriously contests that these men really lived, breathed, walked, and taught in the world of time, space, and history that we ourselves experience. Thus, Confucius (China, 551–479 BCE), **Siddhartha Gotama the Buddha** (India, 563–483 BCE), and Jesus (Galilee, 4 BCE– 29 CE) became the source of the religions that bear their names and titles. It might be argued whether or not they would have wanted to be named as founders of a religion. For example, some suggest that Confucius never intended to form some religious organization, let alone one that would worship him and bear his name. Similarly, though historically many writers have named "Mohammedanism" after the founder **Muhammad** (Arabia, 570–632 CE), Muslims rightly insist that their religion should be called Islam. Nevertheless, what we recognize immediately in religions named—even erroneously—for their founders is that these religions are to a considerable degree what they are because of what is attributed to these individuals, these founders.

Many religions trace their origins to figures that are more or less historically identifiable.

Other human founders are, of course, more difficult to find. **Lao Tzu** (China, 600–500? BCE), the supposed writer of the fundamental text of Taoism, the *Tao Te Ching,* may not have been a historical personage at all. However, certainly tradition credits him with founding the religion that, in this case, does not bear his name. The guru **Nanak** (India, 1464–1539), for the Sikhs; **Mahavira** (India, 599–527 BCE), the "great hero" of Jainism; and **Moses** (ca. 1250? BCE), or even **Abraham** (ca. 1800? BCE) of Judaism might all be mentioned as well. There are also a small number of women who might be named here. As noted already in the opening quotations, **Miki Nakayama** (Japan, 1798–1867) was thought to have become possessed by a benevolent *kami,* the god-spirits of Shinto. More recently, **Mary Baker Eddy** (United States, 1821–1910) discovered her insights into the "science" of Jesus' healing miracles and so became the founder of the sect of Christian Science.

Many founders are legendary rather than historical.

Of course, some religions might have no human founders at all, and of this we will speak later. Other religions might have had human founders, but they were lost in the obscurity of a distant past. Certainly it is difficult to name the legendary "Rishis," or seers, of ancient Hinduism who supposedly heard the message of the Vedas from the gods themselves. And for many tribal cultures, the origins of their practices and beliefs lie in an antiquity of primal ancestors, legends of whom go far in explaining religious practices as well as the source of the world of nature, of specific animals, and indeed, of all time and space.

Yet for our purposes, it is important to distinguish all these founders not merely on the basis of which religion they represent, or even whether they are male or female, historical or legendary. For again, these are not perhaps the most important distinctions in the minds of the believers themselves. But there are other distinctions, central to an understanding of those religions, and confusion about such distinctions can create confusions about the entire religion.

■ PROPHETS

It is common in English to use the term *prophetic* or *prophecy* to refer primarily to foretelling the future. This understanding comes from the popular sense that, according to the Christian Bible, the prophets of the Old Testament foretold the coming of Jesus, and that the New Testament culminates with foretellings of the end of the world. But the primary sense of the term *prophecy* might be much more straightforward than that. From the word roots, apparently the word *prophecy* means essentially to "speak forth," or simply to "declare." This is, of course, a special kind of declaration, a declaring of truths that a mere human alone could not know. Thus, "declaring" the answer to an arithmetic problem is not prophecy; declaring to the world the message of God is.

And this, perhaps, is the essential defining characteristic. For the prophets, especially of the Abrahamic religions—Judaism, Christianity, and Islam—have always been men and women who received a message from God and passed it on for the benefit of humanity. Indeed, in Islam the Arabic term *rasul* is often simply translated "messenger." Muhammad, indeed, perhaps stands as the clearest example of a prophet; certainly to the Muslim he is the very archetype, the virtual embodiment of how a prophet responds to God's call, conveys God's message, and lives out a life worthy of his calling.

Both during his lifetime and throughout the following centuries, Muhammad has served as the ideal model for Muslim life, providing the pattern that all believers are to emulate. He is, as some Muslims say, the "living Koran"—the witness whose behavior and words reveal God's will. (Esposito 11)

But of course, Muhammad's revelation of God's will is not first of all in his behavior but in his reception and transmission of a message. As one of our chapter's opening quotations recounts, Muhammad, it is said, was spoken to by God through an angel's voice, telling him to "recite." That is, he was told to declare the words that God would give him. Hadith stories give even more detail of how the angel "pressed" upon Muhammad to force him to recite these revelations, even though he himself was unable to read (see Peters 50–53). The implication, as John Esposito emphasizes, is that the holy scripture that Muhammad received and recited is the Holy Koran, a word that itself means "recitation." Thus, these are very literally the words of God, and Muhammad himself "is merely an instrument or a conduit; he is neither author nor editor of the Koran, but God's intermediary" (Esposito 21).

A prophet, then, so perfectly exemplified by Muhammad, is one who receives a word of God and speaks it forth. But, of course, Muhammad is not the only example of a prophet, and indeed even within Islam a number of prophets are named and acclaimed as true messengers of God. In fact, some Muslims might protest calling Muhammad the "founder" of the religion of Islam precisely because they would believe him to be only the final messenger. He was not, they say, the only prophet but rather the "Seal of Prophets," the last and perfect prophet in a long line of men and women chosen by God to deliver His words.

Certainly the prophets of Judaism, besides being mentioned with some praise in the Holy Koran, are in fact the prior model of what a prophet should be, inasmuch as the prophets of Judaism predate Muhammad by hundreds, even thousands, of years. Thus, Moses might have been our better, since prior, example.

Moses was the first of the biblical prophets.

For he, too, received the word of God and spoke it forth. In the famed story of the Exodus, the escape of the people of Israel from their slavery in Egypt, Moses was told to speak to the elders of Israel, and even to the Pharaoh of Egypt, in the name of "the God of Abraham, Isaac and Jacob." Even though Moses protested that he was not a good speaker, God insisted:

> Then the LORD said to him, "Who gives speech to mortals? Who makes them mute or deaf, seeing or blind? Is it not I, the LORD? Now go, and I will be with your mouth and teach you what you are to speak." (Exodus 4:11–12)

The prophets of Judaism are numerous. Micah, Amos, Isaiah, Jeremiah, and Ezekiel are prominent in the Hebrew Bible, having entire "books" named after them and focused on the revelations they received from God. Other books of the Holy Bible, books called "The Prophets," or the *Nevi'im* by Jewish believers, clearly focus on the prophetic work of Daniel, Amos, Hosea, Joel, and others. Prophets named in the historical "chronicles" of Judaism, like Nathan and Elisha, do not have a specific "book" of their prophecies, but their prophetic role was the same, as all these men were chosen by God to deliver His message. Some, like Moses, actually protested being chosen, but God's will and God's words were overwhelming. Jeremiah felt that he was too young to be a prophet, but God insisted otherwise (Jeremiah 1:6). Ezekiel, more ominously, was warned that if he did not speak out God's words, then he himself would become guilty (Ezekiel 33:8). Some were symbolically touched on the lips; Ezekiel ate a scroll that contained the words of God, a scroll that tasted as sweet as honey in his mouth (Ezekiel 3).

In the Christian view, the issue is more complicated. There are certainly prophets, inasmuch as men and women within the Church were apparently chosen to deliver God's messages. But these would not be founders, by any means, but servants of the growing body of believers. The founder for Christianity is, of course, Jesus, and it would be incorrect to call him a prophet, at least according to Christian belief. He is acclaimed to be the fulfillment of Old Testament messianic prophecies, predictions that the "anointed one" would indeed come and "deliver Israel from bondage." In that sense, Jesus is indeed taken to be a prophet like Moses. As written in the Gospel of John:

messianic prophecy— prophecy proclaiming the coming of the Messiah

> The woman said to him, "I know that Messiah is coming" (who is called Christ). "When he comes, he will proclaim all things to us."
> Jesus said to her, "I am he, the one who is speaking to you."
> Just then his disciples came. They were astonished that he was speaking to a woman, but no one said, "What do you want?" or, "Why are you speaking with her?"
> Then the woman left her water jar and went back to the city. She said to the people,
> "Come and see a man who told me everything I have ever done! He cannot be the Messiah, can he?"
> They left the city and were on their way to him. (4:25–30)

For Christians, Jesus is the fulfillment of prophecy and the Messiah (Christ) who will deliver his people.

But he is also taken to be a king, like David. And ultimately, Christians consider Jesus more than a prophet or a king, designations that will be discussed shortly. For now, let it be emphasized that this interpretation of Jesus, whether as merely a prophet or as the Son of God, is hardly a minor issue. It is, perhaps, the single, most significant issue that separates Christians and Muslims the world over.

Yet these "founders" are special not for having discovered some truth on their own but for having been chosen by God as a messenger, one who hears the word of God and delivers it to others. Just as a king might choose some individuals to carry his decrees to cities and villages across the realm, so God chose individuals to bring His law, His directions, His truths, to all who would believe.

And this, of course, shows the significant connection between this specific concept of founders and a concept of the Sacred. It makes little sense to speak of prophets in this sense apart from a concept of God as personal, active agency. The God of Islam or Judaism is not merely a force or impersonal absolute but a Spirit, perhaps a Mind, as we have noted in Chapter 3. And thus it is consistent here to speak of prophets who have, in some mysterious way, communicated with God and received a message to be handed on. Moreover, it is clearly part of the greatness and sovereignty of God that generally the prophet does not choose to come to God, but rather God clearly chooses the prophets, sometimes whether they like it or not.

■ SAGES

Some religions are founded by sages or particularly wise people.

With the idea of prophets in mind as men and women chosen by God to hear God's words and to speak them forth in God's name, there may be a useful contrast between founders who are prophets and those who are *sages*. This word is chosen to name a category of religious figures whose wisdom and insight that helped form their religion was, in some way, purely their own. That is, sages like Confucius or the Buddha were certainly not prophets in the sense we have discussed, for they did not hear a message from God or speak it forth under His direction. Indeed, as we have seen, the very concept of the prophet goes along with the monotheistic concept of the Holy, rather than with a concept of the Tao or the Buddha Mind. Thus, none of the "sages" could have heard a message or even been "chosen" by God. Instead these great founders of religion saw for themselves some deeper truth or hidden reality. Like the prophets, they pass a message on to their followers and to the entire world, but unlike the prophets, they are not messengers of God or "conduits" of a divine word. They are, rather, wise men, devout and dedicated to finding the Way (Tao) or the Truth (Dharma) that the world so drastically needs to understand. They are discoverers, not discoverers of foreign lands or arcane sciences but of ultimate human happiness, and of the Absolute Reality itself.

Dharma—in Buddhism, the message of the Buddha in general, translated as the Truth or the Law of the Buddha

Sages, then, are extraordinary people who have seen a sacred truth. The Buddha, for example, though recognized from his birth as a future savior of the world, was not traditionally considered a divine incarnation or a messenger of gods. Indeed, it is suggested in the legends of his life that the gods themselves waited upon his words, listened to his sermons, and rejoiced to hear the liberating message. Brahma, the great creator god of Hinduism, is said to have come to him shortly after his enlightenment and to have begged him to preach his message to the suffering world (Debary 70). Thus, the Buddha was by no means commanded by God to speak in God's own name. Rather, he spoke his own Dharma, his own Truth, which he had discovered himself in the depth of his own meditative effort and which he went on to teach in response to the need of gods and people. Consequently, he declared after his own enlightenment, "Here on this spot I have fulfilled my cherished goal; I now rest at ease in the truth" (69). And so the prince Siddhartha Gotama become the Enlightened One, the Buddha.

Confucius and Lao Tzu, the respective founders of Confucianism and Taoism, also represent sages, though of a somewhat different stripe than the Buddha. As philosophers of China, these men would not have thought so much in terms of enlightenment and liberation as they would have been looking for the Way, the Tao. For there is nothing in their stories to suggest some sudden illumination or liberation from attachment to the desires of life, and indeed, such a concept of liberation would be foreign to the Chinese mind. But rather, both of them seem only to have been teachers, yet wise and insightful beyond the norm.

Confucius was born around 550 BCE and spent his mature life as a wandering teacher. We have seen in Chapter 3 that his religious ideals were not focused on gods or spirits but emphasized rather the cultivation of virtuous character. Thus, he pointed ultimately to the Way, the Tao, and the need to become Chun-tzu, the Superior Man. In all this moral and religious direction, Confucius found his sources in careful observation of human nature and in his own understanding of the ultimate order of things, the Tao. Perhaps even more accurately, he found his sources in sages more ancient than himself, great leaders and teachers of the past who had discovered, as he was rediscovering, the proper order and balance of society and the glorious Way (Tao) of social harmony. Long after his death in 479 BCE, Confucius himself was deified, raised to the status of a divine ancestor in the popular worship of Confucianism. But for his own teaching, he remained a man, though a very wise, cultivated man. Thus, there is no event in Confucius' life in which he was called to be a prophet. Rather, in the brief but famous autobiography in the *Analects* (2:4), he describes his own cultivation as a sage:

At fifteen my mind was set on learning. At thirty my character had been formed. At forty I had no more perplexities. At fifty I knew the Mandate of Heaven. At sixty I was at ease with whatever I heard. At seventy I could follow my heart's desire without transgressing moral principles. (Chan 22)

Lao Tzu is more of a mystery. Traditionally declared to have been an older contemporary of Confucius, Lao Tzu is now thought to have been perhaps an invention, or if he was real, it is unlikely that he wrote the great Taoist classic, the *Tao Te Ching*, which is attributed to him. Nevertheless, he remains embedded in tradition as the founder of Taoism. Yet here too, the man is by no means a prophet, receiving any divine message. He is rather a sage, a great sage, whose insight into the harmony of life and the flow of nature gave us, according to the tradition, the remarkable poetry and profundity of philosophical Taoism. Thus, he (or at least the author of the *Tao Te Ching*, section 20) comments:

I seem drifting in the sea;
Like the wind blowing about, seemingly without destination.

The multitude all have a purpose;
I alone seem to be stubborn and rustic.
I alone differ from others,
And value drawing sustenance from Mother (Tao). (Chan 150)

Our point in all this is to emphasize that the fundamental preface of every great prophet, "Thus says the Lord," is something one would never hear from Confucius or Lao Tzu or the Buddha. These latter are indeed "founders" of their respective religions (admitting various historical uncertainties), but it is significant to point out that their work is nevertheless importantly different from that of the prophets. Inasmuch as all of these founders point beyond themselves to that which is final and ultimate in itself, for example, to the Holy or the Absolute, they are indeed founders of religions. But precisely because they point to different concepts of the Absolute, the basic differences in their roles and emphases, indeed in their very words of declaration, become evident. For a prophet like Muhammad is different from a sage like Lao Tzu, precisely as Allah differs from the Tao.

■ OTHER FOUNDERS

There are numerous other founders and major developers of religions who do not fit into the tidy designations of prophet and sage. Some of these do not fit so well simply because they are not exactly founders but might be reformers or developers of religion. One might think, for example, of Paul, who for Christianity is a formative figure but who would not, at least according to the biblical traditions, be considered the founder of Christianity. Of course, insofar as Paul is responsible for writing Christian letters and insofar as he is a central figure in the spreading of Christian beliefs, he is undeniably one whose words are akin to prophecy. But his title, along with other early disciples of Jesus, is *apostle,* which literally means "one who is sent." Like a prophet, he was "sent" by Jesus to proclaim a message; he mostly wrote personal letters, and these, perhaps to his own surprise, became the scriptures of Christianity.

In the two major Chinese religions noted in this discussion, both Confucius and Lao Tzu had their respective second-generation disciples whose own books became significant seminal texts. **Chuang Tzu** (369–286 BCE) developed Taoist thought in a text that might actually predate the *Tao Te Ching.* **Mencius** (372–289 BCE), for his part, took up Confucius' teachings in his own book, which became so completely accepted as orthodox Confucianism that it became one of the *Four Books* used in civil service examinations throughout Confucian China.

With Buddhism, especially, we see a line of important teachers who established significantly distinct schools of Buddhism that followed the Buddha by many years, even many centuries. The perhaps legendary **Bodhidharma** (d. 532) and the so-called 6th Patriarch **Hui-neng** of China (638–713) might be called the founders of that specific branch of Buddhism called Zen. And notably, some founders of Buddhist sects, like Nichiren (Japan, 1222–1282), were considered living Buddhas. Shall we consider these men "founders" or not?

With other religions there is less confusion on this point. Indeed, at its clearest there is Islam, which unequivocally asserts that there are not, and cannot be,

Some "founders" of religions are more reformers or developers of their religions.

Christianity, Confucianism, Taoism, and Buddhism all have "second generation" authors who further developed their traditions.

sect—a subdivision of a major religion; a denomination, for example, Baptists and Lutherans for Christianity, Shi'a and Sunni in Islam, Pure Land and Zen in Buddhism. There are, of course, sub sects within the sects as well.

Reformers seek to "purify" existing religions, not found new ones.

Gnostics—early Christian group, emphasizing mystic-spiritual knowledge

For Christians, Jesus was the Word of God incarnate, not just a prophet.

For four centuries after Jesus' death, Christians struggled with the meaning of the Trinity and the Incarnation.

any prophets after Muhammad. Certainly, in Christianity there were tremendous changes and development brought about by the reformers of the 16th century, men like Martin Luther and John Calvin. But here, too, the tradition would never call them founders or even developers of the religion. They might be "founders" of specifiable sects of Christianity, one could argue, but it seems not founders of Christianity, *per se*. At best, these "reformers" would be just that: men who had clarified and reformed the original faith, cleansing it, they hoped, from the corruptions of the ages since the original founder, Jesus.

The Case of Jesus

Jesus is a notably unique example of a founder. As pointed out earlier, it may be tempting, and indeed in Islam it is necessary, to call Jesus a prophet. But for orthodox Christian doctrine, he is much more. Indeed, in Chapter 3, we noted that Christianity has as its Ultimate Reality the one God, the same Yahweh (the Christians would say) who was revealed to Moses. And yet God to the Christians is not the basic, unqualified unity emphasized by Jews or by Muslims. Rather for them, God is *triune*, one God in three persons, the eternally interrelational trinity of Father, Son, and Holy Spirit.

The term *incarnation* literally means "enfleshed," "put into a fleshly body," "embodied." But what was thus put into a body? For Christians, the unique answer refers to a "person" of God Himself, the eternal Word (*Logos*). This term, *logos,* Greek for "word" or "reason," was used in John's gospel to name the person of the Christian triune God who became incarnate as Jesus. It had been used previously by various Gnostics, by the Jewish philosopher **Philo** (20 BCE–50 CE), and even by the ancient Greek philosophers to describe the reason or order of nature, the rationality of God, or the creative principle of the cosmos. For John the evangelist, the "Word" was neither an impersonal power of the cosmos nor a merely spiritual aspect of God. Thus, John's spiritual claim is bold and radical when he declares, "In the beginning was the Word, and the Word was with God and the Word was God. . . . And the Word became flesh and dwelt among us" (John 1:1, 14). Thus, Jesus of Nazareth, the son (as was supposed) of Joseph the carpenter, is acclaimed to be the son of God. For Christians, Jesus, the "founder" of their faith, is not merely a prophet nor simply a sage.

Over the next four centuries after Jesus' death, Christians debated their understanding of the Trinity and the Incarnation. Jesus was, it seemed clear to them, divine, and yet they could not deny the Jewish root of their belief that declared the oneness and uniqueness of God. Consequently, because it strives to maintain monotheism and yet to declare its founder divine, Christianity struggles for a unique concept of its founder, who is neither prophet nor sage but somehow both and more. Thus, the Christian view of its founder, Jesus Christ, is a key element in the distinction and disagreement between Christianity and other faiths, including the other monotheistic Abrahamic religions, Judaism and Islam. And again, this should not entirely be a surprise. For the Christian view of Jesus differs, say, from the Islamic view of Muhammad (or even the Islamic view of Jesus) precisely because the Christian view of the eternal triune God differs from the Islamic emphasis on the unity of God.

The Case of Hindu Avatars

The concept of a founder as an incarnation of God fits much more easily into Hinduism than it does into Judaism or Islam. As we have seen, the Ultimate Reality in Hinduism can be understood as an unmanifest, impersonal One, Brahman, and yet also understood to manifest itself in millions of divine forms. In Hinduism, therefore, gods abound, many of them believed to have been physically manifested on earth, incarnated in human and nonhuman forms. And there is no reason to suggest there could not be more.

Undoubtedly, the most famous of the manifestations of god in Hinduism are the avatars of Vishnu, especially Krishna and Rama. The term *avatar* literally means "descent," the "coming down" of Vishnu to inhabit the world. As Krishna says to the warrior Arjuna in the *Bhagavad Gita* (4:6), "Though myself unborn, undying, the lord of creatures, I fashion nature, which is mine, and I come into being through my own magic. Whenever sacred duty decays and chaos prevails, then I create myself, Arjuna" (Miller 50).

Thus, like the Jesus of Christianity, Krishna and Rama and many other beings are, in a sense, incarnations of deity. But of course the differences are profound. Precisely because the gods are many, the incarnations are many and the forms are endless. Vishnu, himself but one of the many gods, has manifested, according to the tradition, as the fish that saved the first man from a great flood, as the tortoise that assisted the gods in churning the ocean into a nectar of immortality, and as the half-man, half-lion Narasimha, who defeated the great demon, Hiranyakashipu. It is precisely because polytheism, or at least the polytheistic manifestation of the unmanifest Brahman, is a thoroughly accepted concept of the Holy, that a multitude of manifestations of Vishnu is unproblematic.

Indeed, Vishnu himself is only one of the gods who has had many manifestations. We might note especially the wives of the god Shiva, who are the multiple forms of the goddess Devi. For Hindu shaktas, the millions who worship the wife of Shiva in any of her many forms, she is both the "power" (*shakti*) of Shiva and a goddess of many forms in her own right. As Durga, she killed the dreaded buffalo demon; as Parvati, she is the gentle wife of Shiva and mother of Ganesh; as Kali, she is the black goddess of bloody carnage whose wild rampage of gore defeated an army of giants and nearly destroyed the world.

Yet all these gods and goddesses are a problem in the discussion of founders precisely because they are almost too divine. As "founders," they are not teachers, sages, saviors, or prophets so much as they are, simply, gods. Like Jesus, they might be called "incarnations," but of course they are incarnations already of a plurality of gods, who are themselves, arguably, manifestations of the one, ultimate Brahman. It is also difficult to know if we can—or if we should even try to—place figures like Krishna and Kali, let alone the great man-lion Narasimha, in recorded history. Whether or not Jesus was the Son of God, his place in history seems unquestioned, and the actions of more recent founders, like Muhammad, are easily given specifiable dates. Even the more obscure Lao Tzu was—and, for many, still is—taken to have lived in the sixth century BCE and to have been visited by Confucius in 518 BCE. But for the "descents" of Vishnu and the incarnations of Devi, historical contexts are more problematic. Certainly, Krishna is said to have been born in the city of Mathura as the son of King Vasudeva and Queen

---

The concept of God incarnate fits better into Hinduism than Judaism or Islam.

avatar—incarnation of a god

Krishna—avatar of Vishnu

Rama—avatar of Vishnu

Devi—mother goddess incarnate in multiple forms.

It is difficult to see the many gods of Hinduism as founders because it is impossible to place them in a particular time in history.

Box 4.1	Global Byte
	The Founder of Baha'i

In this chapter, we have made a distinction between origins that may be mythological and founders who are historical figures whose stories are told with some degree of factual accuracy. Of course, the accuracy of the stories of these founders is obscured when they supposedly are gods or, simply, by the passage of time that allows history to become mixed with legend and myth. A good example of a historical founder where the basic details of his life are fairly clear and factual is Bahá'u'lláh, the main originator of the Bahá'í faith, one of the world's newest major religions.

BAHÁ'U'LLÁH (1817-1892)

Founder of the Bahá'í Faith

Born in 1817, Bahá'u'lláh was a member of one of the great patrician families of Persia. The family could trace its lineage to the ruling dynasties of Persia's imperial past, and was endowed with wealth and vast estates. Turning His back on the position at court which these advantages offered Him, Bahá'u'lláh became known for His generosity and kindliness which made Him deeply loved among His countrymen.

This privileged position did not long survive Bahá'u'lláh's announcement of support for the message of the Báb [a messenger who predicted the coming of a new prophet of peace]. Engulfed in the waves of violence unleashed upon the Bábís after the Báb's execution Bahá'u'lláh suffered not only the loss of all His worldly endowments but was subjected to imprisonment, torture, and a series of banishments. The first was to Baghdad where, in 1863, He announced Himself as the One promised by the Báb. From Baghdad, Bahá'u'lláh was sent to Constantinople, to Adrianople, and finally to Acre, in the Holy Land, where He arrived as a prisoner in 1868.

From Adrianople and later from Acre, Bahá'u'lláh addressed a series of letters to the rulers of His day that are among the most remarkable documents in religious history. They proclaimed the coming unification of humanity and the emergence of a world civilization. The kings, emperors, and presidents of the [19th] century were called upon to reconcile their differences, curtail their armaments, and devote their energies to the establishment of universal peace.

Bahá'u'lláh passed away at Bahjí, just north of Acre, and is buried there. His teachings had already begun to spread beyond the confines of the Middle East, and His Shrine is today the focal point of the world community which these teachings have brought into being.

Source: http://www.bahai.org/article-1-2-0-6.html (accessed February 12, 2004).

Devaki, and he is the noble teacher of Arjuna during the great war described in the Mahabharata. Yet historical placement of such events is unlikely. It is quite possible that such legends have their distinctly historical roots, but as Ainslie Embree has suggested, "neither the events they narrate nor the time scale in which they are set are 'historical.' While scholars, both Western and Indian, tried to find a historical base in this material, they found it difficult" (633).

At the same time, questions of historicity with respect to some "founders," and perhaps for most of them, might be irrelevant. For the point of many of their legends, and perhaps especially about the avatars and manifestations of the Hindu gods, is certainly not about history. In most cases, the point is that we learn, as in the case of Rama, to follow their divine example, or, as with Krishna's instructions to Arjuna, that we heed the divine message. And above all, it seems that the point in most cases is that we recognize the glory of the gods and goddesses themselves whom we are to worship.

In the end, finding founders in Hinduism is difficult overall. Ironically, the easiest to find in this ancient religion might be the most recent. For just as Vishnu is thought to have become manifested in many forms, so even his avatars are believed to have become manifested. Thus, Hinduism contains a strong tradition of living gods, gurus, or teachers who, for their spiritual impressiveness and wise teaching, are recognized, sometimes by their own words, as latter-day incarnations of Hindu gods. For example, Swami Narayan (1781–1830) was considered to be an incarnation of God, of Krishna, who manifested himself into the world in order to bring stability and to rebuild the moral values of India. More recently, Anandamayi Ma (1896–1982) was considered by her devotees to be the incarnation of the mother goddess, of Devi herself. Both sects that they founded continue to this day.

Looking for the ancient founders of Hinduism, we find ourselves lost in antiquity. Tradition says that the Vedas, the ancient scriptures of Hinduism, were "heard" by ancient seers or rishis. Thus, like prophets, they received from the gods a kind of message that they passed on to humanity. Yet the Vedas themselves are not apparently declarations of the biblical "Thus saith the Lord." They are themselves rather hymns and prayers, praises and appeals to the gods. More like the work of hymn writers or sages, the Vedas are nevertheless said to be *sruti* scripture, "heard" from the gods, as opposed to the later *smriti* scripture, "recalled" from old times. Yet exactly when the Vedas were "heard," and by whom, or in what sense they are words of gods and not merely of sages—all this remains obscure.

So, as all of these foundations of Hinduism are clouded in legend and quite unspecific, the "founding" of Hinduism is a mystery. Consequently, when scholars talk of Hindu origins, they often refer less to the religious than to the historical contexts that brought about the development of Vedic literature. So we could discuss the evolution of Shiva from the ancient Indus Valley Civilization's god of animals or bring Vishnu from his obscurity in the pantheon of Aryan Civilization. But this would merely push the same problem of finding "founders" farther back into the mysterious past. It might also run the risk of missing our emphasis on trying to see the religion through the eyes of believers. For certainly, the current worshipper of Vishnu does not see him merely as an obscure Vedic god who rose to prominence by being confused with popular gods of later legends. Rather, he is the great God of Preservation, manifested throughout time for his own purposes. And how we today originally received this information about him is, perhaps, of minimal importance.

So perhaps we must sometimes just leave the origins of religion in obscurity. Indeed, we might note that the boast of the believers might not be in the religion's founder but rather in the religion's ancient roots. And it might thus be precisely in the *lack* of a founder that a religion in general, and Hinduism in particular, might claim to transcend human history.

ORIGINS

There are, of course, more obscure cases of religious origins, especially in those religions that seem to have no founding, no specific dates or persons that were the sources of religious information. Looking at the ancient roots of more animistic religions, like the tribal religions or even Shinto, we find that origins are again lost in myth and legend.

In Shinto, for example, the founding of new sects, like Tenrikyo, has already been noted, and the foundress, Miki Nakayama, might in an extended sense be called a prophetess. But Shinto itself pre-existed written Japanese, and the earliest texts and stories that relate the beginning of the religion are really the myths that relate the beginnings of Japan. It is apparent to historians that the Shinto religion might have evolved from the shamanic tribal religions that still occupy the most remote parts of Japan, but here again we find speculation that goes beyond the scope of our study. Thus the question, "Whence our religion?" would have to be answered by the follower of Shinto with the same stories that answer the question, "Whence our world?" and there would follow stories of ancient gods who made the Japanese islands and set the first emperor on the throne.

Though Shinto may refer to a founder, the religion predates historical figures and lie in myths associated with the founding of Japan.

It is, in fact, primarily with the tribal religions, which Shinto arguably resembles, that we find the origins of the religion set into myths of emergence. These stories are often placed in very ancient times, telling not only how the various aspects of the world came into being but also how the people were involved in these developments. For the Australian Aborigines, their tribal ways are believed to be some 50,000 years old, set not only into their cultural and ritual practices but even into the land itself. Ancient ancestors, they would say, at one time walked the face of the earth, participating in the creative work of the world that put in place the mountains and trees and animals themselves. In this same creative work, usually called the "Dreaming," the land was formed and with it the rituals and social structures of aboriginal religion. In many cases, these directions on how to live were handed down from a high god to the original ancestors of the aboriginal people. Thus, in either case, the mythical ancestors who were at once the product and the source of creation were also the source or at least the vehicle of religious revelation (Noss and Noss 24).

One interesting extension of this kind of religious revelation is the fact that, in a metaphorical sense, the very land itself can, in some cases, be part of the "founding," or at least part of the origins, of a religion. Certainly among the Australian tribal peoples the land is indeed more than mere object. It may actually be the ancestors themselves, somehow magically ossified in the creative work of the Dreaming, and thus the message, the direction of the ancient ancestors, is not merely lost in some distant past. For the land is here and now, and these cliffs, these rocks, this bush, all in some way or another continue to embody the direction and creative origination expressed in the ancient myths. They *are* the presence and direction of the ancestors and the creator gods.

In a sense, the land itself may be a factor in the founding of religion for tribal people.

kami—spirits and deities of traditional Japanese religion

As with tribal religions, where nature itself is alive, Japanese Shinto might urge followers to see that the gods, the kami, are not in a distant heaven but perhaps in this mountain or in that grove. Thus, perhaps, the mountain and the grove themselves have something to tell. Consequently, a grove or other sacred site may be marked with the *shimenawa,* a braided rope draped between poles or trees as if marking the entryway into holy ground. The trees and mountains themselves, thus, reveal the holy and become "founders," in a way, of sacred practice.

In China the scale broadens. There the entire natural order of things is assumed to be evidence of the Tao, the Way. Thus for the Taoist, the variety of animals and the myriad distinctions of action and response in nature show that harmony and change represent the movement and fluid harmony of the Tao itself. In this light, Kuo Hsiang comments, "Birds and animals and the myriad things are contented with their endowment. Emperor Yao and Hsu Yu were tranquil in their circumstances. This is the perfect reality of the universe" (Chan 327).

In Chinese religion, birds, animals, and aspects of nature may teach us about the Tao.

On this larger scale, the earth itself, especially personified as female, is for many people a clear source of the revelation of the Absolute. In many ancient civilizations, images of a "Mother Goddess" are taken to be early depictions of the fertility of earth and animal. These goddesses, furthermore, are thought to have evolved into various other goddesses, such as in India, where, in spite of the lower class status women often are accorded, goddess worship remains a powerful religious expression. Thus, the fertile earth is itself the representation of Devi, the eternal goddess. In Vedic times, the earth goddess Prithivi was a minor figure, but goddess worship revived in later Hinduism, and the many forms of the wives of the gods took on a power of their own. Thus, these goddesses, especially the wives of Shiva, became the Shaktis, female beings of power, especially Durga and Kali. We have already discussed "gods as founders"; here the point is that the power of the goddesses can be revealed through the fertility and the creative power of the earth itself.

In these and many more ways, the "inanimate" objects of nature—though many tribal people would hardly consider natural objects inanimate, i.e., soulless —become for many peoples the revelation of the divine. From the breadth of nature herself to her harmonious movement, to the trees and mountains and to the stones, any of these natural objects can seem to be the "prophets" and "sages" of religion. Indeed, as Noss comments, the veneration of stones, "from pebble to boulder," is a practically universal phenomenon going back to prehistoric times (15). A fascinating example of this phenomenon can be found in the collection of "spirit stones" in China. An exhibit at the Art Institute of Chicago displayed numerous stones of strange and exotic shapes that had been taken in ancient China to be signs "of remote and sacred mountain peaks or of Taoist paradises." Thus, these stones seem to play a prophetic role, revealing to the viewer something of the mysteries beyond our sight. As the museum guide quotes from Lin Youlin's *Stone Compendium of the Plain Garden:*

The objects of nature reveal the divine for many people.

> *Large stones, characterized by jagged ridges, are all found among the Five Sacred Peaks. The habitations of those who can effect transformations [Taoist practitioners] are among what the Taoist books call cavern-heavens, blessed realms, and numinous traces. In all these places can be found strange blue and green stones. (Little 17)*

Overall, the suggestion that nature itself can "prophesy," or can be the source of revelation about the gods or the "paradises" beyond us, is an abstract but not uncommon theme. Indeed, as might be expected, even in the Abrahamic, monotheistic religions, nature and natural objects can be seen as revelations of

God. Especially when these religions speak emphatically of the creative power of God, nature is a source of the knowledge of God, as a picture or a poem can tell us a great deal about the artist who created it. Thus, Christian theologians since the Middle Ages have spoken of knowing God as shown in the "general revelation" of nature, alongside the knowledge of God gained from the "special revelation" of scripture that was given through the prophets. In this sense, the poetry of King David in the Judaic Psalms speak thusly:

In the Judaic tradition, nature "prophesies" to the hand of the Creator. In the Middle Ages, Christian Theologians called this general "revelation."

> 1: *The heavens are telling the glory of God; and the firmament proclaims his handiwork.*
> 2: *Day to day pours forth speech, and night to night declares knowledge.*
> 3: *There is no speech, nor are there words; their voice is not heard;*
> 4: *yet their voice goes out through all the earth, and their words to the end of the world.*
> *In the heavens he has set a tent for the sun . . . (Psalm 19:1–4)*

In a variety of ways, nature and her objects act as religious founders. Human artifacts, too, of course, can be described as "revealers" of the Absolute, although at this point we may be slipping into a discussion of symbolism. Religions all over the world have developed their own symbologies in order to offer believers, perhaps especially those who cannot read the scriptures, some kind of adequate invitation and instruction on the nature of the gods or of God. From totem poles to stained glass windows, human artifacts have been constructed and symbols produced to remind us of who or what is greater than humans, beyond us and invisible.

GLOBALIZATION, THE MOTHER GODDESS, AND HISTORY

In Chapter 1 we indicated that globalization represents a coming together of forces growing out of modernism and those that represent a break with the Modern Period. Two of these trends are particularly relevant for shedding light on the interaction of religion and globalization, along with the question of origins and founders addressed in this chapter. The first of these is the re-enchanting of nature as a reaction against materialistic visions of the universe. That is, modernism tended to stress the mechanical model of the natural world, using physics and chemistry to explain the life and balance of nature. Western religions that seemed to place God outside nature as a distant "clockmaker" seemed to participate in this view. And both this traditional religious view and the mechanical picture of nature have, perhaps, appeared to lead historically into problems like pollution and environmental degradation. Dissatisfaction with these views of nature, then, has led to a new "spirituality" that often takes the form of some effort to "commune" with nature or, at least, to establish some innovative, spiritual relationship with the natural world.

The Modern Period's mechanistic view of the universe is consistent with the "clockmaker" god of Deism.

Globalization also is associated with an emphasis on objectivity, which may undermine religious views and stories.

At the same time, the second trend of globalization is the spread of the modern ideal of doing scientific, objective history. It may be surprising to find that the idea of trying to study history in an objective fashion is only about two centuries old. The stress on science so characteristic of modernism led to the development of techniques to discover the objective validity of historical truth. The emphasis on objective truth led to the discounting of myths, legends, and unsupported stories as mechanisms for conveying truth. This is why, if we find some element of a story is not objectively factual, we may say, "Oh, that's just a myth," meaning it is untrue and not worthy of serious consideration.

This is a very limited and unfortunate understanding of myth and other types of religious stories, as will be discussed further in Chapter 6: Myths, Stories, and History. But for the moment, this line of inquiry is beyond the scope of our consideration. What is important is how teachings of the new spirituality may conflict with objective history, and, in turn, how this may call into question the origins of religions.

One form that the new spirituality of global society takes is a "return" to "nature religions" wherein worship, ritual, and practice focus on the forces of nature. In the United States, the rise of Wicca is a good case study. Wicca now has as many as 200,000 adherents in this country (Allen 1). Wicca claims to be a rediscovery of the ancient pagan religions replaced by Christianity in Western Europe. It focuses on the worship of the life-giving, female "Mother Goddess" along with her male counterpart.

About two-thirds of the followers are women who call themselves Witches, with a capital "W," to distinguish themselves from those witches considered as being in league with the devil in Christian thought. According to Wicca's teaching, ancient pagans knew the Mother Goddess as maiden, mother, and crone—the three stages in the life of a woman—and that this emphasis tended to honor the value of women's lives more than religions with a male God. In conjunction, Wiccans insist that the societies in which the Mother Goddess religion was practiced were matriarchical (female dominated), egalitarian, and harmonious. These practices and ideals of Wicca are said to predate Christianity and to have been preserved by centuries-old covens operating underground to avoid persecution by Christian authorities.

For some time, historians and archeologists seem to have provided support for Wicca's claims. We noted the presence of female goddesses in Hinduism and as part of many tribal societies, and this may have included early hunting and gathering societies. This presence of numerous goddesses led some scholars to posit a Mother Goddess who preceded later dominant male deities. For instance, Merlin Stone claims that in hunting and gathering societies, females were essentially equal to males and were revered as the source of life. These societies were closely bound to nature and were directly dependent on what nature provided. In these early, nature-dependent societies, the chief deity was a female Mother Goddess. It was only when societies settled into permanent villages with farming as the means of production that things started to change. The new societies used more advanced technology (usually controlled by men), accumulated surpluses of foodstuffs and other forms of wealth, and developed stratification. Men came to dominate women, and male gods came to dominate female goddesses.

Charlotte Allen notes that a radical change in scholarly opinion has occurred in recent decades. To make a long story short: Wicca probably was founded in 1950, not centuries ago; the rituals, practices, and beliefs of Wicca are of relative recent origin, not attributable to pre-Christian pagans; peaceful, female-

---

(margin notes)

Wicca—movement claiming to rediscover ancient pre-Christian nature-oriented rituals, beliefs, and practices

Wicca is a good example of the flourishing new nature religions.

Wicca traces its origins to the pagan nature religions that predated Christianity in Europe.

dominated societies did not exist; and there probably never was a single, female Mother Goddess. In other words, the facts of objective history conflict with the very stories that define and give meaning to Wicca. Where does this leave followers of Wicca, who seem to derive meaning and well-being from their religion but who also hold to the importance of scientific history as a means of finding truth?

This is not an isolated case. In fact, most Western religions have had to face the dilemma of what to do when their cherished beliefs are challenged by historical research. For instance, traditionally Moses was said to be one of the founders of the Jewish, Christian, and Muslim faiths. Modern research has shown that the stories regarding Moses are likely to be a mixture of fact and legend. As an example, Moses is said to have written the first five books of the Bible—collectively, the Books of Moses or the Torah. Yet, modern research has led scholars to suggest that this cannot have been the case because, for example, some passages refer to events after Moses' death.

For some Jewish, Christian, and Muslim believers, this and other historical facts make very little difference to their basic faith. But to others, such historical findings are seen as a threat to their faith. We can only speculate what will happen as globalization causes scientific norms of objectivity to spread into non-Western societies. As this occurs, the global trend in favor of such historical research may well conflict with the equally global trend of seeking "ancient" wisdom and "earth-based" spirituality, as well as with the spirituality of many societies' traditional religions.

CONCLUSION

The point of this chapter has been to describe the various ways in which religions understand their own origins. In many cases, there stands a single person at the beginning, one who has heard the message or discovered the arcane truth, which then becomes the foundation of belief for millions. Whether their biographies are historical or wildly encrusted with legend, these prophets and sages and incarnations are believed somehow to have tapped directly into the mystery of the Holy and then to have delivered their insights to the rest of us. Believers in turn thankfully acknowledge their greatness and sometimes even worship these founders.

Yet it cannot be said that all religions have such founders. In many cases, as we have seen, the roots of a religion lie in obscurity and very possibly in the twists and jumbles of collected stories and undecipherable myths. From unnamed ancestors, from acts of mysterious gods, and from the stones and mountains around us, religious visions and practices are born. And here, too, the followers point with reverence to these beginnings and find there a hint of the mystery that their religions try to describe and celebrate with love and fear.

In all this variety of founding and origination, religions are born, and for the believer, the myths and legends and histories that surround their sages, prophets, and ancestors help to evoke that sense of awe and wonder at the Absolute that seems to lie at the root of religious consciousness. Yet for the critical thinker, there are many questions. As noted with the case of Wicca, we may eventually challenge the historical claims of these religions' stories as, for example, one might in all honesty want to know if Jesus really walked on water or if Lao Tzu ever lived at all. Yet ironically, there may be many believers for whom the historicity issue is peripheral or even irrelevant. And whether, say, legends of the Buddha's life or stories of ancient ancestors even should be read as if they *intend* to be historical is something we must consider as we interpret these tales. How to read such literature is an issue to consider in Chapter 5: World Scriptures, and Chapter 6: Myths, Stories, and History.

For now, critical questions might be raised about how a religion's idea of its own origins and founders cohere, or fail to cohere, with its own beliefs about the Holy and the Sacred. It has already been suggested, for example, that the concept of the prophet fits well with the monotheistic religions but is not very clearly a useful concept in Chinese religion. In Sikhism, notably, as it developed in distinct contrast to both Hinduism and Islam, the exact status of the founder Nanak raises an interesting set of questions. In one sense, he is very much like a prophet, as defined in this chapter. Yet he could not be called a prophet in 15th century India, given its Islamic context, since it is clear and emphatic in Islam that there are no "prophets" after Muhammad. Thus he, along with his successors, was called a *guru*, which means "teacher." At the same time, he was neither a common "teacher" of Hinduism nor, as is sometimes claimed of Hindu gurus, an incarnation of a god. Understanding exactly what title we might attribute to Nanak may therefore depend a great deal on his story and on how we understand the Sikh idea of Sat Nam, the True Name of God.

Just as valuable in such studies is the consideration of how religions are alike and how they differ. There are similar concepts of prophets among the Abrahamic religions precisely because they share a common foundation in their shared concept of monotheism. Sages share similarities in Taoism and Confucianism because they are both Chinese religions in which the Tao, the Way of the cosmos, is studied as the proper pattern of life. But perhaps the Buddha, too, should be called a sage and therefore is more like Confucius than he is like Moses. And if this seems too obvious to be helpful, consider that the Pure Mind, or Nirvana, for the Buddhist is significantly different from the idea of God for monotheists. By extension, it is interesting to consider what it would mean to argue that Jesus to the Christian is more like Krishna than like Muhammad, since, in a way, Jesus is considered divine. Such points of comparison might well mark the key distinctions between religions and underscore the most dramatic issues of differences between religions, differences over which people have fought and died.

▪ INTERACTIVE EXERCISE

Please continue the exploration of origins and founders by going to the interactive exercise for this chapter online (**http://www.religion.wadsworth.com/ richter**).

WORKS CITED

Holy Bible. New International Version. Grand Rapids, MI: Zondervan, 1984.

Allen, Charlotte. "The Scholars and the Goddess." *Atlantic Monthly Magazine*. January 2001. http://www.theatlantic.com/cgi-bin/01issues/2001/01/allen.htm (accessed January 16, 2001).

Bahá'u'lláh (1817–1892) Founder of the Bahá'í Faith. http://www.bahai.org/article-1-2-0-6.html (accessed February 12, 2004).

Brown, Harold O. J. *Heresies: The Image of Christ in the Mirror of Heresy and Orthodoxy from the Apostles to the Present*. Grand Rapids, MI: Baker, 1984.

Chan, Wing-tsit. *A Sourcebook in Chinese Philosophy*. Princeton, NJ: Princeton University Press, 1963.

Coburn, Tomas B. *Encountering the Goddess*. Albany: State University of New York Press, 1991.

deBary, W. T. *The Buddhist Tradition*. New York: Vintage, 1972.

Erdoes, Richard, and Alfanso Ortiz. *American Indian Myths and Legends*. New York: Pantheon, 1984.

Embree, Ainslie, and Carol Gluck. *Asia in Western and World History*. Armonk, NY: Sharpe East Gate, 1997.

Esposito, John L. *Islam: The Straight Path*. Oxford, UK: Oxford University Press, 1998.

Hallstrom, Lisa Lassell. *Mother of Bliss: Anandamayi Ma*. Oxford, UK: Oxford University Press, 1999.

Kishore, B. R. *Rig Veda*. New Delhi, India: Diamond, 1998.

Little, Stephen. *Spirit Stones of China*. University of California Press (for The Art Institute of Chicago), 2000.

Mackenzie, Donald A. *India: Myths and Legends*. London: Senate, 1994.

McLellan, David. *Karl Marx: Selected Writings*. Oxford, UK: Oxford University Press, 1977.

Miller, Barbara S. *The Bhagavad Gita*. New York: Bantam Classics, 1986.

Noss, David, and John Noss. *A History of the World's Religions*. New York: Macmillan, 1994.

Pals, Daniel L. *Seven Theories of Religion*. Oxford, UK: Oxford University Press, 1996.

Peters, F. E. *A Reader on Classical Islam*. Princeton, NJ: Princeton University Press, 1994.

Rand, Ayn. *For the New Intellectual*. New York: Signet, 1961.

Reed, A. W. *Aboriginal Stories of Australia*. Terrey Hills, Australia: Reed, 1980.

Smith, Joseph. *The Book of Mormon*. Salt Lake City, UT: Church of Jesus Christ of Latter Day Saints, 1973.

Stone, Merlin. *When God Was a Woman*. Fort Washington, PA: Harvest, 1976.

Stryk, Lucien. *The World of the Buddha*. New York: Grove Weidenfeld, 1968.

Tenrikyo. *A Short History of Tenrikyo*. Rev. ed. Tenri, Japan: Headquarters of Tenrikyo Church, 1958.

FOR FURTHER READING

Allen, Charlotte. "The Scholars and the Goddess." *Atlantic Monthly Magazine*. January 2001. http://www.theatlantic.com/cgi-bin/01issues/2001/01/allen.htm (accessed January 16, 2001).

Amstrong, Karen. *Islam: A Short History*. New York: Random House, 2002.

Carrithers, Michael. *The Buddha*. New York: Oxford University Press, 1983.

Ehrman, Bart. D. *Jesus: Apocalyptic Prophet of the New Millennium*. New York: Oxford University Press, 1999.

Fung Yu-lan. *A Short History of Chinese Philosophy*. New York: Macmillan Paperbacks, 1960.

Khalidi, Tarif. *The Muslim Jesus*. Cambridge, MA: Harvard University Press, 2003.

Schüssler, Fiorenza. *In Memory of Her: A Feminist Theological Reconstruction of Christian Origins*. New York: Crossroad, 1992.

5 WORLD SCRIPTURES

Getty Images/PhotoDisc Collection

For most religious people today, scriptures are seen as one of the major sources of religious authority—even if a minority regularly read scripture. Scriptures are the means by which most religions have been passed on throughout recorded history to this day. Differences over the interpretation of scripture—for example, disagreements over the "true" meaning of scriptures—have divided religious folk ever since the original scriptures came into being. These issues are presented and discussed in this chapter. For now, please look over the pictures found above and on the Web site (**http://www.religion.wadsworth .com/richter**), and read the following passages, then consider the Introductory Questions that follow to prepare for reading this chapter.

And this Koran is not such as could be forged by those besides Allah, but it is a verification of that which is before it and a clear explanation of the book, there is no doubt in it, from the Lord of the worlds. Or do they say: He [Muhammad] has forged it? Say: Then bring a chapter like this and invite whom you can besides Allah, if you are truthful.

—Islam: Holy Koran, 10:37–38

With honest wrath [Martin Luther] untwisted and pulled together where the ancient spider [Roman Catholicism] had spun longest and most carefully. He handed the holy books over to everyman—so that at last they got into the hands of the philologists, that is to say, the destroyers of every belief which rests on books.

—Friedrich Nietzsche on Protestant Christianity: *Gay Science*, section 358

First of all you must understand this, that no prophecy of scripture is a matter of one's own interpretation, because no prophecy ever came by human will, but men and women moved by the Holy Spirit spoke from God.

—Christianity: Holy Bible, 2 Peter 1:20–21

A special transmission [of Truth] outside the scriptures, not founded upon words or letters. By pointing directly to [one's] mind, it lets one see into [one's own true] nature and thus attain Buddhahood.

—Buddhism: "Bodhidharma's Poem" (Dumoulin 85)

Confucius said, "I transmit but I do not create. I believe in and love the ancients. . . . I was not one who was born with knowledge; I love ancient [teaching] and earnestly seek it."

—Confucianism: The Analects 7:1, 19

Moses received the Torah from Sinai and committed it to Joshua, and Joshua to the elders and the elders to the prophets; and the prophets committed it to the men of the Great Congregation. These said three things: "Be deliberate in judgment"; "Raise up many disciples"; and "Make a hedge for the Torah."

—Judaism: Mishnah, Aboth Aboth 1.1

INTRODUCTORY QUESTIONS

1. In the first quotation, it is evident that Muslims believe the Holy Koran to be an absolutely unique book. Think of other books you know. Are scriptures in general, or maybe the Holy Koran in particular, really so unique? What makes a book "scripture" in the first place?

2. Confucius is well-known for writing many of the central books that are the "classics" of Confucianism in particular, and of Chinese culture in general. But he claims no special knowledge; rather he is only saying again what ancient "sages" have discovered. Can such books be "scripture"? How might they be like, but different from, a book like the Holy Koran (or the Holy Bible), which is said to be revealed to human beings by God?

3. In the pictures on the Web site, William Farel holds the Holy Bible aloft as a sign of its final authority and importance. The famous Buddhist monk, Hui-neng, is seen tearing up the scriptures to indicate that real spiritual insight does not come in written words. How seriously do you think one should take written scripture in thinking through one's own religion?

4. Jewish rabbis quote the Mishnah text to point out that the written text of the Torah, the books of Moses, is only part of the message of God and that any good teacher needs to deliberate and evaluate the scriptural text to construct a "hedge" of interpretation. Do you think truly divine scriptures need a "hedge" of interpretation, or do they "interpret themselves"?

5. In the picture of St. Matthew writing his Gospel, it is suggested that he is "inspired" by God. The quote from the New Testament, too, declares that writers were "moved" by God to write their scriptures. Ironically, in the picture of Ganesh, he is a god who does the writing as recited by a human. The Holy Koran is said to be God's own words in Arabic, and Muhammad was only memorizing what he was told. How is "inspiration" like "dictation"? Does that distinction make you trust or mistrust the words of some scripture more or less?

6. With great disdain for religion, Friedrich Nietzsche notes that religions based on scripture have a big problem. Once, the Pope could tell us what to believe, but then others read the scriptures and told us what they think it means, until finally scholars and skeptics took up the book. Whom should we trust to say what the scriptures mean? Popes, priests, scholars, average people? Is reading scripture as "democratic" as reading any other book?

7. Having been betrayed by treaties many times, Osceola, in the picture on the Web site, is showing disdain for the written word. In the Bodhidharma poem, too, writing is not taken as being necessary or even useful for religious enlightenment. Is a written promise better than a spoken one? Is a written religious revelation better than storytelling or direct one-to-one teaching? Why?

WORLD SCRIPTURES

A Christian children's song that is very common in the United States goes, "Jesus loves me, this I know, for the Bible tells me so." Significant in this simple song is not only the central theology of Jesus Christ but also the evident appeal to authority. The average Christian child singing this little song does not likely think through the profound importance of its appeal to the Bible, but in a very real sense the reference to scripture in these lines is nearly as important as the reference to Jesus. For it is important to believe in Jesus' love, the Christian might say, but it is also important to know where the Christian teachings come from. It is not only a question of what is believed but also a question of who says so.

Scripture is a central aspect of much religious practice, as it supplies a basic source of religious teaching an authority.

In many religions, the "Who says so?" question is answered with some kind of appeal to scripture. By scripture, one most commonly understands something like a book, some kind of writing, for example, a script. Yet clearly the term denotes something more: a writing that also has unusual authority, an importance and assumed truth that make it clearly not just another average book. Thus, of course, in that song, the Christian appeals not just to some book but to the Bible. And this book is taken to be "the word of God."

Such a powerful appeal to the authority of a text is, of course, not unique to Christianity. Parallel to the Christian song, one might imagine a Muslim singing that Allah is the only God, "for the Holy Koran tells me so." Even in traditional Hinduism, there is a strong sense of the most basic authority of teachings coming from their most fundamental scripture, the Vedas. Some have suggested that, in the admittedly difficult process of defining "Hinduism," one possible point to note is the acceptance of the authority of the Vedas. Ninian Smart, in fact, suggests Hindu "orthodoxy" can be "defined by the acceptance of the authoritative value of the revelation (*sruti*) which includes the Vedas" (54). This may be especially true since the fifth century BCE, when rejection of the Vedas was one of the marks of rival Indian religions, like Buddhism and Jainism. In such examples, we come to see that the authority of written scripture is not only a key element in religious belief but is even a defining dividing line between religions.

As with Hinduism, what is orthodox or generally accepted in a religion often depends on the acceptance or rejection of particular scriptures.

The importance of scripture in the world's religions, therefore, may seem obvious. Indeed, this text has taken for granted that the authority of religious teaching is often found in some kind of scripture. That is why we start our chapters with brief, mostly scriptural quotations, as if to say, "Look, here are some basic points the religions of the world say about themselves." Similarly, we encourage and facilitate the students' discovery of extra portions of scripture (online Holy Bible, Holy Koran; extra texts at our Web site) in order to give readers more context and explanation for the points we try to make about the many religions we observe. This is only reasonable, since part of teaching and learning about religion must involve the attempt to say not just what some teacher or modern writer thinks about the religions but what the religions say about themselves. As much as possible, therefore, it seems reasonable to try to go back to the religious sources, the scriptures, as a way of finding out what religions really teach.

Scriptures are key to understanding the teachings of most religions.

And of course this is true not only for scholars and writers and students. The need to "get back to the scriptures" may be especially important for seekers of religious meaning. Indeed, it may be clear from the previous chapter that few of us can claim to be prophets of God or sages of cosmic wisdom ourselves.

Consequently, we are left with the hope of finding God's message or cosmic wisdom by reading the prophets' and sages' words. This seems a reasonable approach to any personal, spiritual study of religion.

Yet we would be mistaken if we did not also admit right away that what the many religions of the world mean by scripture, and the amount of authority they grant to a written text, is not quite unanimous. For some, the appeal to scripture—as in the children's song—may be ultimate and final. If the Holy Bible—or the Holy Koran, etc.—says something, that settles it. In other religions, however, while there is clearly some kind of writing that believers appeal to for guidance, the real authority of that scripture may not be very prominent. Indeed, the picture of Hui-neng tearing the scriptures represents perhaps the farthest extreme in how religions understand the centrality of the written word. In the famous Zen story portrayed in that picture, the Sixth Patriarch of Chinese Zen Buddhism, as Hui-neng was called, was himself illiterate and had no great book-learning of Zen. Indeed, he insisted that book-learning was not the point of Zen at all. Instead, the Zen student should seek an intuitive insight of his or her own. Thus, even the Zen master of today might declare that if you think to find enlightenment in a text, you are fundamentally misguided. In fact, recalling the Zen poem quoted at the beginning of this chapter, if you are too dependent on "words and letters," the master might just tear up the scriptures before your eyes.

The irony in the Zen story, of course, is that there came out of the famous story of Hui-neng a very important text called *The Platform Sutra of the Sixth Patriarch,* and that scripture became—again, quite ironically—a central and informative document of Zen Buddhism as it developed in China. Heinrich Dumoulin, in fact, says that "The main elements in the Zen movement of the age are constellated in this work. Its privileged position is clear already from the title: in Buddhism the word *sutra* is commonly reserved for writings representing direct transmissions of the words of the Buddha. *The Sutra of the Sixth Patriarch* came to occupy a key place among the sacred texts of the Zen school" (123). Nor is this merely a later historian's assessment of the importance of this text. According to the stories of Hui-neng, this same teacher who tore the texts of his students later declared that this new text was a decisive sign of true teachings. He said, "You ten disciples, when later you transmit the Dharma, hand down the teaching of the one roll of the Platform Sutra; then you will not lose the basic teaching. Those who do not receive the Platform Sutra do not have the essentials of my teaching" (Yampolsky 173). This is irony indeed.

The point of this story told here is that, even when we might expect there to be an explicit rejection of the authority of scripture, the authoritative use of scripture is still often prominent. Even in Zen, various scriptures have different amounts of authority, different power to claim to be read as the central teachings of that religion. Thus, even in Zen, the scriptures themselves become central fixtures of a religion. Exactly where these scriptures are thought to originate, exactly how authoritative and final they might be, can vary a great deal from one religion to another, and even within the same religion. But to one extent or another, the student of religion will find some kind of scripture playing a role in religions throughout the world.

One primary exception to this generalization, however, might be the ambiguous role that written scripture comes to play in Tribal Religion. Insofar as being

While some religions make scripture their central authority, in others, scriptures is not very prominent.

sutra—traditionally a "sermon" of the Buddha, thus in text the written transcription of the Buddha's teaching; from earliest Buddhism, sutras are taken as collections of the Buddha's sermons and therefore as fundamental authoritative texts

Dharma—in Buddhism, a general term for the "truth" or "law" of the Buddha, thus all that the Buddha taught and exemplified

Even when and where written scripture is apparently rejected as a main authority, there are still central uses of scripture.

The various scriptures of a religion may have varying degrees of authority to the claim of being central to that religion.

nonliterate—having no written language—can be a defining characteristic of tribal cultures, it is not surprising that such cultures would have their religious teachings and religious authority not set in any writing but conveyed in storytelling. Such oral cultures, as they are sometimes called, may have a genuine mistrust of the written word as something static and dead, certainly not interactive like a good storyteller would be. Walter Ong, in his book on *Orality and Literacy,* has noted that oral communication tends to serve a community in a way that writing does not. Because memorization and direct communication are needed in an oral culture, he notes, stories tend to be "conservative" and "empathetic." This means that oral cultures use their spoken dynamics to hold the tribal group together. Storytelling keeps the people united as a whole community by maintaining a memorized story that they can all relate to and that they all find familiar. Such stories do not invite analysis but rather promote an acceptance of standard forms and standard ways. Writing, in contrast, invites the individual to consider ideas in the abstract and to stand at a distance. Writing tends to divide the tribe, while oral storytelling keeps it united. (See Ong, Chapter 3.)

We shall discuss later some of the issues in religion proper that have tended to work against the acceptance of written scripture. But in spite of such perspectives, the overwhelming use of scripture in world religions is evident. Of course, that does not mean that what the Muslim and the Hindu, or the Buddhist and the Christian, mean by "revelation" or "authority of scripture" is the same. Nor does it mean that when these believers read their various scriptures they use the same tools of interpretation. These are further matters to explore.

SOURCES OF SCRIPTURE: WRITERS AND REVELATION

One of our opening quotations says that scripture comes from God. Even without being a skeptic—one who might just assert that scriptures are all human inventions—it is not necessarily true that all religions see scripture as coming directly from a divine source. As noted previously, the picture of the god Ganesh writing the Mahabharata, a great epic tale of Hinduism, is particularly fascinating. In it, the god is merely the scribe, and the source of the scripture is a human poet. We also noted that the Buddhist sutras are primarily the sermons of a man, Siddhartha Gotama, who became enlightened and so was called the Buddha. It seems that scriptures, therefore, are indeed special, but exactly why they are special is not as easy as saying they are "from God."

Of course, even with scriptures that claim to be from God, "God" is not usually listed as the author of a text. Indeed, you will note in this book's bibliographical material that, as we quote the Holy Bible or the Holy Koran, we do not list "God" as the author of either. And that does not necessarily mean we are unbelievers. It means, rather, that a book claiming to be a "revelation," for example, something revealed to humanity from God, is not so simple as saying God wrote a book. These scriptures did not, after all, simply appear miraculously in the world, nor were they spoken aloud to the world at large. Rather the traditions of religions like Judaism and Islam say that God chose specific individuals to hear His message and to spread it into the world. These are the prophets, men

In oral cultures, storytelling is more important than scriptures.

Ganesh—the elephant-headed god of Hinduism, a son of the god Siva; he is known for being a "remover of obstacles," as well as being the scribe of the Mahabharata

Not all religions teach that scripture comes "from God."

and women who were chosen as spokespersons for God, or for one of the gods. We have already discussed some examples of such persons in Chapter 4: Origins and Founders. Our point here is to note that there is an obvious logical link between the status of the writer of a text and the text itself being labeled scripture. To claim to be a prophet is, in a way, to claim to be writing revealed scripture, and vice versa. If we authors of this textbook were to claim that this text is itself a holy scripture, we would also be claiming for ourselves a kind of prophetic status. Happily, we do not.

As we noted in the previous chapter, however, not all religious founders should be called prophets, and by the same token, not all scripture should be considered prophetic. We noted in Chapter 4 that besides prophets there are sages and even divine incarnations that have given messages to the people of the earth, messages deemed sacred. And just as these terms for founders differ, so do their methods of revelation. For we might note that while the scriptures of Islam, the Holy Koran, must be considered a direct dictation of God's words, no such concept could apply to Buddhism. Certainly, the sagely Buddha is as much the sacred founder of Buddhism as Muhammad is the prophetic founder of Islam. But just as sages differ from prophets, so the "revelation" of the scriptures of Buddhism differs from those of Islam.

It is perhaps worth stressing that in the case of Islam, the holy scriptures must be considered the direct words of God and are emphatically not the words of Muhammad. Indeed, we might note that Islamic doctrine tends to emphasize that Muhammad himself was illiterate and therefore did not even write the words down himself. Instead, say the Muslims, others wrote and memorized the Arabic recitation of the Holy Koran as Muhammad spoke. But Muhammad himself was not the author, for his central job, so to speak, was to openly receive, memorize, and then recite to others the perfect words he received through the angel Gabriel. And Gabriel, too, the doctrine declares, is only a conduit. For the Arabic words of the Holy Koran are said to be the perfect and untranslatable words of God Himself, as if copied from an eternal book in heaven. Thus, in the end, although we regularly refer to Muhammad as the source of the Holy Koran, it is vitally important in Islam to see that these holy words were literally recited to Muhammad aloud, or into his consciousness, and were in turn recited by Muhammad to others. Indeed, the word *Koran* itself means "recitation." Thus, there is in the Holy Koran nothing of the wisdom or personality of Muhammad himself. If one wants something of Muhammad's personal views and practices, one must turn to the secondary scriptures of Islam, the Hadith. But for the pure and perfect word of God, there is only the Holy Koran, the unspoiled dictation of God's own words.

One will not find, but should also not expect, such a claim from Buddhism. The Buddha, we noted, is not a prophet but a sage. We meant by this that the Buddha did not even intend to receive a dictation from a divine being. Indeed, such a notion would have made no sense to Siddhartha Gotama. Instead, we find in the Buddhist scriptures the wisdom of the Buddha. These are his *sutras*, his sermons, containing his own unparalleled insights. Now, a Muslim might reasonably disregard so meager a claim—a scripture that is merely the wisdom of a man. But for the Buddhist, this is a universal wisdom that comes from the perfect, enlightened mind, revealing (if that is the right word) insights meant for the salvation of

Labeling a writing "scripture" implies a status for the writer or revealer that is beyond the ordinary.

Scripture may be revealed as the "dictation" of God's own words as in the claim of the Holy Koran in Islam.

Hadith—collection of sayings and deeds by Mohammad and his followers

Scripture may be the insightful, enlightened wisdom of a sage as in the claim of Buddhism.

all humanity. The Buddhist scriptures, therefore, are not a dictation from God, but they are the final authority of the Truth, the Dharma, nevertheless.

This difference between Islam and Buddhism should not surprise us, for we have seen from the beginning that different notions of the Sacred imply different ideas about other parts of religion. If Nirvana, or the pure Buddha-Mind itself, is "the Holy" of Buddhism, it is clearly different from Islam right at its core, where—for Muslims—Allah, God alone, is the Absolute. Thus, there is no Buddhist prophet, and there does not need to be one. The Buddhist scriptures, therefore, are also not dictations from a divine being, and there does not need to be one. The words of the Buddha are rather a universal wisdom meant for the liberation of all beings.

Scripture may be the writing of people whose words are "inspired" by God, though perhaps not dictated as in the case of the Bible.

Besides dictation and wisdom, the notion of inspiration offers a fascinating, if less clear, middle position. In the Tanakh (the Bible of the Jews, known to others as the Hebrew Bible or the Old Testament) and the Christian Bible, for example, we see much writing that is taken as scripture and revealed, in some sense, to prophets. Some Jews and Christians believe in verbal inspiration, but many others do not see scriptural text as the dictated words of God, though this scripture is seen as the Word of God. The fascinating distinction here is that the writers of these texts revealing the word of God were also writing from their own hearts. One might note, for example, that among the four accepted Gospels of the Christian New Testament, there are differences in emphasis and phrasing, differences in expected audience, and differences in the stories the writers chose to relate. Historical problems aside, Christians might explain such differences simply by noting that these scriptures are not merely dictated, but neither are these words merely the wisdom of these particular writers. Rather, the Christians say, these writings are inspired by the Holy Spirit. However God chose to do so, He seems to have used these writers' personalities and interests, even as He revealed His own will and words. Thus, you find much of the personality of writers like David and Jeremiah, Matthew and Paul in the writings of the Bible. Yet the orthodox believers of Judaism and Christianity nonetheless believe these words to be the revelation of God.

The writings of the authors of Jewish and Christian scripture reflect these authors' personalities, though believers feel the Word of God "shines through" these works.

Our point so far is to stress that there are a number of books that claim to be religious scripture, revealing in some sense or another the great mysteries of the Sacred. But it is also true that those who dismiss appeals to scripture by saying, "Oh, there are thousands of books that people say come from God," are quite mistaken. There are actually very few such books, especially if one considers how many other books there are in the world. But what they have in common is some kind of special claim to being revelation about the Sacred. Even with this commonality, however, they do not all claim the same kind of origination. For dictation is one thing; human wisdom is something else, and inspiration is different from both. Yet in these examples, the different methods of revelation fit with their different concepts of what (or who) the Sacred Reality is. We should expect such consistency.

AUTHORITY AND CANON

Although scriptures come into the world's religions in different ways and with different amounts of importance, we have shown through the connection between scripture and founders that there is at least a certain level of authority in all religious scripture. People all over the world read and pay attention to their written scriptures because they believe they lead us to the truth about the Sacred. This Holy Bible or Holy Koran, these Vedas or Sutras, unlike all others, the believer might say, are the source of special, sacred insight. Like quoting a famous astronomer or physicist when you want to say something authoritative about galaxies, the religious believer quotes his or her scriptures because he or she believes this book is the ultimate authority on the subject of religious truth. And as we have seen, this authority of scripture is united with some kind of special claim about the author.

Consequently, the authorship of religious texts is often a central concern in establishing and maintaining the authority of scriptures. For Muslims, this is a point of pride and assurance with respect to the Holy Koran. For it is a clear doctrinal assertion that just as the words of God were dictated perfectly to Muhammad and recited perfectly to others, so those words have been perfectly preserved even to the present. There is no question of origin here: one prophet chosen to recite one divine message, which is contained in one version of one book. Thus, Muslims claim, the authority of scripture is secure.

When the authorship of a particular text is in doubt, however, it can be quite reasonable to further question whether or not the text qualifies as scripture. During the early centuries of the Christian era, long before there was any centralized authority in the Church to declare what is scriptural and what is not, the different churches scattered through the Roman empire were met with choosing which writings were authoritative. Generally, it seems they focused on writings by first-generation apostles and those who had known Jesus directly. However, they also seemed to have had a general concept of what teachings a scripture *should* contain. Thus, the Gospel of Matthew was accepted easily enough, since it was both orthodox and written by a direct disciple of Jesus. But the Book of Hebrews was a problem. It seemed orthodox enough (unlike the Gospel of Thomas, a noncanonical gospel), but in dispute was that a "witness to the Gospel" did not write it; therefore, its authority remained questionable.

The formation of the Christian Bible presents a fascinating case of the process of canonization. This term refers to the making of a canon, an official body of literature generally accepted as authoritative. In the case of Muhammad and the Holy Koran, there was little question, since all official scripture had to come through Muhammad, and because there was, from the time of Muhammad through the formation of the final scripture 24 years later, a central authority capable of enforcing a decision. For Christianity, however, rather like for Buddhism, there was a large collection of writings to choose from, and the scattered groups decided among themselves what seemed like scripture and what did not. This was a very imprecise process (barring theological doctrines about the guidance of the Holy Spirit), and consequently, though the earliest listing of New Testament writings appears almost complete by about 180 CE, the canon may not have been really complete until about 250 and was not formally declared by a council document until 367 (see Bainton 36–37). Even this declaration was not by a council of the whole church. It is well-known that even during the Reformation in the 16th century, prominent theologians like **Martin Luther** (1483–1546) considered dropping problematic New Testament texts like the Book of James. Luther did remove several books from the end of the Old

Muslims believe that one prophet was chosen by God to recite one version of the Divine book: the Holy Koran.

Canonization can be a long process of determining which writings are scripture and which are not, as was the case of the Christian Bible.

canon—an officially accepted body of literature, especially a collection of writings taken together as scripture

Testament, designating these apocrypha (writings) that did not carry the authority of the scripture. The Council of Trent (1545–1563) was a council of the Roman Catholic Church called to deal with issues raised by the Protestants. It chose to affirm these books removed by Luther as part of the Old Testament. The Protestant challenge to scripture never affected the orthodox Christianity. Thus, Roman Catholics and Orthodox Christians have several books in their Old Testament not accepted as scripture by Protestants. However, all three accept the same scriptural books in the New Testament.

Canonization in Buddhist scripture is another interesting story. Tradition states that, soon after the death of the Buddha, his closest disciples met to declare what they had heard the master teach. Thus, the core of the Buddhist scriptures is taken to be the Buddha's sermons, his direct teachings, as remembered and recited by his followers, collected then in what is called the "Three Baskets," or the Tripitaka. These scriptures remain the only authoritative texts for the more conservative branches of Buddhism, for example, the Theravadin sect, and because they were eventually written in the **Pali** language, they are often referred to as the Pali Canon. Exactly *when* this recitation process took place is difficult to determine, of course. Moreover, the problem for Buddhism was that other sects, especially the Mahayana sects, began to develop not long after the Buddha's death, and these sects, too, developed scriptures. So who has the proper canon?

Mahayanists, of course, claimed that their scriptures, too, were the words of the Buddha. Conservative Hinayanists, however, complained that these new scriptures had only recently appeared and they seemed, moreover, to teach ideas outside the orthodoxy of the Pali Canon. Mahayanists, in reply, simply claimed that the scriptures were hidden or lost for a time. And the traditional Mahayana explanation for the changes and variations of the message is that the Buddha had many different messages, different compassionate teachings for the different types of people who needed to hear his message. Like the loving father of foolish children caught unawares in a burning house, one famous Mahayana parable teaches, the Buddha offers many different enticements to lure the people from the dangers of samsara, to save them from rebirth (Robinson and Johnson 82; also Strong 133ff). Thus the new Mahayana scriptures are just different sermons of the Buddha, ones the Hinayanists did not hear. Of course this looks a bit suspicious: new, "lost" scriptures with new, unusual teachings. But who shall decide what the Buddha really said? Evidently, it was up to the different schools to choose. Thus, Buddhism became and remains a widely divergent set of teachings, with different canons of scripture all claiming to be the message of the Buddha.

These examples from the world's religions are only intended to show how complex and variable the process of canonization might be. Obviously, there is great need to decide who spoke or wrote these words and upon what authority. Where there is no political power or centralized authority in an early religious development, the canon of scripture is open to interpretation and development, resting ultimately on community consensus. Where there is such power and authority, as with Islam or, in a different way, Confucianism, the canon can simply be declared, and woe to those who differ. Yet even in these religions, history is not without evidence of dissident voices claiming that the central scriptures have been changed or lost. It is well-known, for instance, that Shi'ite Muslims contend there have indeed been corruptions of the text of the Holy Koran, as the dominant Sunni

In the case of the Buddhist scriptures, the Tripitaka (Three Baskets of Discourses) are believed to represent the teachings of the Buddha and are recognized by all branches of Buddhism as scripture.

samsara—in a general sense, the process of reincarnation into different mortal beings

Mahayanist and Hinayanist Buddhists disagree on the scriptural authority of other "new" writings.

Muslims eliminated references to the authority of Ali, whom Shi'ites insist should be the proper successor to Muhammad (see Peters 183–184). Valuable and even necessary as scripture might be for many of the world's religions, therefore, it seems evident that appeals to scripture are never without points of dispute, and this is even before we get to problems of reading and interpretation.

We have seen, then, that scripture is a curiously central and curiously difficult notion in itself. When we appeal to scripture, do we mean these words were dictated from God, inspired in human hearts, or that they are simply the universal wisdom of a sage, like Confucius or the Buddha? In any collection of such writings, can we be sure that these writings are the ones properly chosen to be included in a canon, and if so, why? Such questions suggest that all religious scriptures require us to consider what "scripture" means and to consider problems of revelation, authority, and canon. So if you think it is easy to pick up a scriptural text and announce that this is the word of God, think again. We do not say that such appeals to scriptural authority are unwarranted or unnecessary. Arguably, most religious believers in the world quite rightly appeal to scripture as a foundation of belief and practice. Indeed, as we have seen, it is ironic that even when some religions (like Zen Buddhism) would downplay the value of scripture, still scripture appears and takes on a central and authoritative role. Thus, scripture is perhaps vital to religious life but by no means an easy notion to explore in its history and authority. We shall see this complexity again as we turn to consider the science of scriptural interpretation.

Disputes occur about scripture even before thorny questions of interpretation are considered.

INTERPRETATION OF SCRIPTURES

We have seen that the scriptures of the world's religions have varying amounts of authority, varying ways of being appeals to a higher wisdom. Yet for all this difficulty of understanding exactly what scripture is, we have seen that scriptures play a prominent role in many religions—sometimes the absolutely central role—in defining what the followers are to believe and to do. Thus, scripture, for all its uncertainty, needs to be read and understood.

This process of understanding, however, is made all the more difficult by the fact that we need to interpret what we read. Some may hope that we could all just pick up a text claiming scriptural authority, read it, and know directly what God or the Buddha meant to tell us. If only we could open the text and read the words, surely (one might hope) we have also understood what it means. This might be the assumption of those who presume a kind of scriptural literalism, an approach to scripture that would take the letter-for-letter meaning of words and derive a clear meaning of the text in general. Unfortunately, it is not always so easy. Indeed, it might be more accurately suggested that no one can really read a text literally. Thus a science of interpretation is necessary for those who are truly trying to understand the meaning of a religious text.

Understanding the meaning of scripture is not as simple as taking the literal meaning of that scripture.

■ INTERPRETATION AND LITERAL READING

All understanding of scripture is ultimately interpretation. In any religion, even those people whose current language is also the original language of their scriptures do not escape the fact that their understanding of their sacred writings is

All understanding of scripture is ultimately interpretation.

also interpretation. For example, a Muslim in Egypt or Saudi Arabia may speak Arabic fluently and the Holy Koran is itself originally in Arabic, but nevertheless, when the modern Egyptian or Saudi reads the Holy Koran, interpretation takes place as the old words are brought into the modern context.

Interpretation is, of course, all the more evident in cases of translation. It is something of an obvious refrain that "all translation from one language to another is also interpretation," since a translator must choose meanings of words in the translation language that are closest to what he or she thinks was meant in the original language. That involves interpretation. Thus, those whose language is not that of the original scriptures are all the more subject to the necessity and inevitability of interpretation. For modern Hindus, for example, reading the Vedas is like Christian Roman Catholics using Latin. The Vedic **Sanskrit** is no longer a living language, and therefore, understanding what the original scriptures mean requires one to translate the ideas into one's own modern thought. Interpretation is therefore inescapable.

Consequently, a "literal" meaning of scripture is, arguably, impossible. Therefore, the contrast is not really between a "literal" understanding of scripture and an "interpretative" understanding of scripture, since all reading is interpretive. What people really mean by a literal reading of scripture, therefore, is really one kind of interpretation, ultimately one among many choices of how scripture may be understood. Literal reading, too, is *an* interpretation. To be sure, the extant original text—to the extent that any variants among the most ancient manuscripts or documents are not seriously troublesome—has its rightful claim to importance *as that which has been transmitted to us,* but no matter by what method it is understood, it will still be received in the hearer's or reader's mind as *an interpretation.* Moreover, to quote David Tracy, a significant Christian theologian of our time, in this regard: "There is no nonsituational basis for any interpretation" (Grant and Tracy 170). The more technical way of expressing this would be to say that "except for a strict fundamentalist. . . it is inconceivable that any contemporary [interpreter of scripture]" would not take the historical critical method of interpretation into account (153).

We shall elaborate later on what is meant by the *historical critical method* and historico-critical exegesis of scripture, but for the moment, a brief example to help make this point. Just as some English words of Shakespeare's time meant something different in his day than they do today, so also various words in the original languages of scripture had different meanings when they were written than they do today. Perhaps, indeed, the old words have little meaning at all because they are now so obscure. In Shakespeare's day, a "nice" person was a person who conned others—a negative connotation—not someone who would be thought of as "nice" today—a positive connotation. In Shakespeare, "to die" can mean to have sexual intercourse. A similar, simple, classic example from the first book of the Bible is the verse that says Adam "knew" his wife Eve, and she bore him a son (Genesis 4:1). Not every English-speaking person would necessarily realize that "to know" in that context means to have sexual intercourse. The point, then, is that in order to understand what scriptures mean, the reader simply must take history and context into account. The words alone are not enough; one must interpret.

The conflict over scripture is not between a literal meaning and an interpretation but disputes among different ways of interpretation.

Very few approaches to scriptural interpretation would not consider the historical critical method.

historico-critical exegesis—various methods of interpreting text by studying the historical context

On our way to an understanding of the problem or challenge of interpreting scripture, we shall begin by noting that the interpretation of scripture and the recognition of its necessity can be seen within scripture itself. There are several Christian examples. In the Book of Acts in the New Testament (Acts 8:30–31), Philip the Apostle heard an Ethiopian reading the prophet Isaiah and asked, "Do you understand what you are reading?" He replied, "How can I, unless someone guides me?" And he invited Philip to help him. Evidently, reading was one thing; understanding was another. Later, the Apostle Paul, writing his letters to his earliest converts, explicitly interprets scripture when he says: "Now this is an allegory. . ." (Galatians 4:24). In terms of Paul's whole Jewish and Christian experience, "His interpretation of scripture cannot possibly be what it was in his pre-Christian life. The Old Testament remains scripture; but it is no longer [the] letter [of the law], but [the spirit of the law, that is, the] Spirit; no longer Law, but a ministry of grace. . . . A specifically Christian interpretation of the Old Testament has come into existence" (Grant and Tracy 27). Finally, Jesus as portrayed in the **Gospels** clearly respects the Holy Scriptures of his time: "Do not think that I have come to abolish the law or the prophets; I have come not to abolish but to fulfill" (Matthew 5:17); yet he frequently says, "You have heard that is was said to those of ancient times. . . . But I say to you . . ." (Matthew 5: 21, 27, 31, 33, 38, 43). Thus, Jesus himself thereby interprets or reinterprets scripture.

Even Jesus himself interpreted or reinterpreted Hebrew scriptures.

Midrash—collection of commentaries on the Hebrew Bible

Talmud—collection of Jewish law and teaching

Judaism and Islam have their examples of traditions of interpretation.

Within Judaism there are similar examples. In the Tanakh (written in Hebrew and Aramaic) the fact that 1 and 2 Chronicles repeats much of what is in 1 and 2 Samuel and 1 and 2 Kings is an indication that there needed to be several interpretations of the events involved. More recently, the very existence of the Midrash (Hebrew: to examine, to investigate), which is a verse-by-verse interpretation of the Jewish Scriptures, and the Talmud (Aramaic from Hebrew: learning), which is the oral law of the Jews with elucidations, elaborations, and commentaries by rabbis as distinct from the written laws, are both significant historical evidence of the need for interpretation. In both cases, it is clear that the rabbis are saying, "Yes, the Torah is what God has said; now we need to understand what it means."

In Islam, the existence of the **Hadith** is further proof of the need for clarification and the inevitability of interpretation of the Holy Koran. The Holy Koran, as we have seen, is considered the direct revelation of God's own words in perfect Arabic. Indeed, the very title, Koran, means recitation. But to fully understand how to apply the teachings of God, Muslims appeal to the *Hadith* (Arabic: story, news), the collection of stories about the words and actions of Muhammad. As a secondary revelation, this collection allows Muslims to interpret the words of God. Indeed, historically speaking, any interpretation of a Koranic passage that could not be supported by Hadith was originally rejected.

inerrancy—exemption from error

The stress on interpreting scripture may lead to relativism—people making the scriptures mean anything they want.

As we speak of the need for interpretation, of course, there is a danger of relativism. Some people might conclude from this discussion that literally any interpretation of scripture is possible, and therefore that the "truth" of revelation is dependent on the individual, just as "beauty is in the eye of the beholder." This relativism, however, would seem to be the opposite of the kind of absolutism asserted by those who would hold to the inerrancy of scriptures. Is the word of God allowed to mean anything the merely human mind wishes to find? Is a presumed essence, the real meaning God intended, lost to the need and desires of one's personal situation? Scholars, it seems, would admit that ". . . today that objectivity in the interpretation of the work of the human spirit is an elusive aim; the interpreter always reads something of his own thought into what he interprets. . ." (Grant and Tracy 61). But does that prevent Holy Scriptures in the Judeo-Christian-Islamic traditions from being either "spoken by God" or the Word of God, such that there remains ". . . no question of its inspiration or authenticity" (8)? How is this apparent gap between inerrancy and the need for interpretation to be bridged?

Of course, one possibility has been to find an authority, which could inalterably determine the meaning of scripture (Grant and Tracy 73). In Judaism, those **rabbis** who today see themselves as Orthodox, as distinct from Conservative or Reform Jews, claim that authority for themselves. Within Christianity, given that the scriptures were created within the Church and preserved by **apostolic succession,** that authority is claimed by the Roman Catholic Church (73–75), culminating in 1870 in the doctrine of **papal infallibility.** Thus, Roman Catholicism is the "true Church," the true interpretation, as opposed to Eastern Orthodox or Protestant churches. In Protestantism, as Nietzsche noted in our opening quotation, scripture was to be given up to the interpretation of the individual. This helps to account for why there are so many different Protestant denominations.

In Islam, after any variant versions of the Holy Koran were ordered destroyed (Warraq 85), its canon was established as The Holy Koran, and it came to be considered by its most fundamentalist and conservative adherents as ". . . the eternal, uncreated, literal word of God sent down from heaven, revealed one final time to the Prophet Mohammed as a guide for humankind (2:185)" (Esposito 19).

Thus, the Holy Koran, Muslims insist, cannot have been influenced by the circumstances under which it was revealed, can contain no mistake, and cannot be superseded by any new discovery (compare Muir qtd. in Warraq 86). From this, it follows that it is even unfitting to translate the Holy Koran, for, as noted, any translation is an interpretation and therefore cannot carry the weight of the original (Smith 231–235). But even given only the Arabic original, differences of interpretation exist within Islam. For example, the Islamic mystics, the Sufis (Arabic: *suf,* wool; because of coarse woolen garments worn to protest the finery of wealth), argue that in their interpretation of the Holy Koran ". . . Allah presents himself as both 'the Outward [*al-zahir*] and the Inward [*al-batin*]'" (57:3). Consequently, although orthodox, Sunni Islam may construct their doctrines and laws based on the outward meaning of the Holy Koran, the Sufis chose to focus their understanding of Allah on the inward, direct encounter with God in their own lifetime (Smith 258–259). Thus, some Sufis' interpretation of the nearness of God to the human soul resulted in statements that the orthodox Muslims found heretical. We shall see examples of this later in Chapter 11: Religious Experience.

So interpretation occurs even in those religions stressing most vigorously the unity and clarity of their scriptures. Indeed, we have argued that in a very real way interpretation is inescapable. The point, therefore, for a reader of religious scripture is perhaps not simplistically to claim a "literal" use of scripture but to understand how some interpretations differ from others. Rather than claiming an ability to get a "pure" understanding of scripture, it is perhaps wiser to be con-

One answer to relativism is to have some authority who claims the sole or final right to interpret the scripture.

Even with an Arabic original of the Holy Koran, varying interpretations of the holy scripture exist.

Sufis—mystic Muslim sect

Sunni—member of one of the Islamic divisions

Since interpretation always occurs, we need to understand how methods of interpretation differ from one another.

scious and forthright about the tools we use in the process of interpretation. The science of interpretation is called hermeneutics.

■ CLASSICAL HERMENEUTICS

Over against the literalistic claims of a simple reading of scripture stands the historical fact that scriptures have indeed been, and continue to be, interpreted in various ways. This has culminated in the development of a science of interpretation referred to as hermeneutics (Greek: *hermeneuein,* to interpret). Without going into a detailed history of the various ways and methods of interpreting scriptures, we can list and explain some of them briefly, much of which is derived from the classical hermeneutics of the Christian tradition.

hermeneutics—
science of interpreting text

Literal Meaning

The *literal* sense is the "dictionary meaning" of the words. But we have already noted that even the literal reading of scripture is a kind of interpretation. For one chooses to read for literal meaning as one option among many, and within a lit-

Even those inter-
pretations of scrip-
ture stressing lit-
eral meanings still
distinguish
between such
things as the con-
notative and deno-
tative meanings of
words.
eral reading there is often both the connotative (extended, implied) as well as the denotative (direct) meaning of the words. For example, the word *son* means directly the biological male child of a man or woman; it may also connote a special moral relation of obedience or dependence. Indeed, the very fact that we distinguish between denotative and connotative meanings of words is already an indication of the ambiguity of language. Furthermore, the fact that some scripture is written as parable or poetry implies the intention to tap the richness of language for meaning beyond the words themselves. We shall deal with this notion more in the next chapter.

Mystical Meaning

Besides the literal meaning of scripture, earlier scholars referred to other possible interpretations under the genus of the ". . . *mystical* or *spiritual* [or intellectual] sense [as] an additional meaning, based on the view that the literal sense does not exhaust the meaning of the words" (Wood vi; *NIB*, I, 89). This approach may be further subdivided. For example, in the *allegorical* sense of a passage of scripture, allegories are presumed to lie behind the literal sense and to speak figuratively or symbolically of the hidden spiritual truth that transcends the literal sense of a sacred text. For example, the manna eaten by the Israelites (Exodus 16:31; John 6:31–34) may be interpreted allegorically as the bread of the Eucharist (the Christian sacrament of holy communion) (Wood vi).

Biblical scholars
early on insisted
that mystical or
spiritual meanings
of scriptures could
be found.
The *typological* interpretation of a passage of scripture ". . . presupposes a *historical* connection between the events, persons, or things in the Old Testament and corresponding ones in the New Testament." For example, just as the ark (the *type*) saves Noah's family and the animals, so also the Church (in this case, the *anti-type*) saves believers (Wood vi). In the New Testament book of Hebrews, the Old Testament figure Melchizedek (Psalms 110:4) prefigures Jesus Christ in the New Testament (Hebrew 5:5 *passim*). However, "while the epistle to the Hebrews represents the most thorough analysis of the Old Testament in typological terms which we possess in the New Testament, there are many other examples of typology" (Grant and Tracy 33).

Finally, there are both anagogical and tropological meanings. In an *anagogical* interpretation ". . . the meaning [of a text] is raised from earthly subjects to heavenly." The text may literally say something about earthly life, but its spiritual meaning reveals to us something of heaven. Similarly, a *tropological* interpretation is one ". . . whereby the reader finds a moral lesson in the words" (Wood vi). Again, whatever the literal meaning of a passage, there is a deeper meaning, in this case, a moral lesson. Interestingly one can find four different meanings—the literal, the allegorical, the anagogical and the tropological—in the classical example of Jerusalem in the New Testament in Galatians 4:22–26: "Historically [Jerusalem] means the city of the Jews; allegorically it signifies the church of Christ; anagogically it points to that heavenly city which is the mother of us all; and tropologically (or morally) it indicates the human soul" (Grant and Tracy 85).

Theological Meaning

As a final development of classical hermeneutics in the Christian tradition, we can add the theological meaning. A *theological* interpretation concerns itself with what scriptures say about God that lends itself to the formation of doctrines or

The theological approach stresses what doctrines may be developed from scripture.

teachings regarding the theological meaning of scriptures beyond their historical or literary value (Wood vi). For example, as part of the history of interpretation we must simply acknowledge at this point that the first major schism within the established Christian Church was the split that resulted in the Roman Catholic Church and Eastern Orthodox Christianity in 1054. The next major break was that of the Reformation led by Martin Luther and others in the 16th century, which resulted in Protestant Christianity. In the broadest possible sense, it can be observed that in each branch of Christianity a slight emphasis on a different aspect of the Holy Trinity—God the Father (Roman Catholicism), God the Son (Protestantism), and God the Holy Spirit (Eastern Orthodoxy)—is the result of perhaps even an unintended focus that comes from a theological understanding of scriptures. Notably, within the Christian scriptures themselves the word *Trinity* cannot be found and must, therefore, be an interpretation. Thus, reading scripture particularly to gain or to apply a theological doctrine is yet one more way in which scripture, however authoritative its divine words, yields to human interpretation.

■ MODERN HERMENEUTICS

Besides the classical methods of interpreting scripture listed above, there are more recent developments in hermeneutics that have been central to the interpretation of scriptures for more than a century. This is the *historical critical method,* which refers to a number of ways of interpreting ancient texts by studying as well the historical context in which they were written or in which the narrative supposedly occurred. What an ancient writer might have meant by certain words, or indeed whether or not the supposed ancient author could even have used such words, are all matters of historical study. And again, this historical critical method has been applied most forcefully to the reading of the Christian Bible, although it is beginning to receive wider use in the interpretation of scriptures of other religions as well.

The historical critical method stresses the necessity of understanding the context in which scripture developed.

Critical Methods

We begin with the first steps of applying the historical critical method by distinguishing between lower and higher criticism. The former meant trying to establish from various ancient manuscripts what the most accurate original text was and what it said. This was also known as *text* or *textual criticism.* The latter meant any other issues of interpretation that presented themselves as historical problems, such as authorship, historical context, and so on (compare Holladay, *NIB,* I, 131). An integral part of higher criticism is *source criticism,* which seeks to determine the possible oral and written sources of scriptures, including their chronological or historical formation. Where, for example, did the writer of Matthew's gospel or the prophet Muhammad get the ideas that became part of scripture? *Traditio-historical criticism* investigates the history of the traditions formed by the communities of faith that produced the scriptural texts. In all these cases, the job of the student or scholar is to try to establish the nature of the original text, its authorship, and its sources by studying its historical context (Holladay 132).

The lower criticism tries to establish which text is closest to the original, while the higher criticism deals with historical problems.

Form criticism focuses on the various forms of literature found in the scripture.

Form criticism is a part of the previous method but seeks to analyze and categorize specifically the literary forms or genres of a scriptural text. Such forms include ". . . narrative, legal material, wisdom sayings, prophetic oracles, [and] liturgical texts . . ." (Holladay 133), as well as prayers, confessions, poetry, hymns, miracle stories, parables, letters, sermons, and even apocalyptic material. Here, the point seems to be to consider how the text functions, and did function historically, as a form of literature, since how we understand a text is at least largely determined by what kind of story or poem, and so on, we think the text is meant to be. We shall see more of this problem in Chapter 6: Myths, Stories, and History.

Other forms of the historical critical method include *redaction criticism,* which is interested in how a tradition's texts have been edited or redacted to reflect various theological perspectives; *composition criticism,* which goes beyond individual instances of redaction criticism to see their effect on the whole text; and *canonical criticism,* which focuses on the final form of the text and its role in the final canon (Holladay 133–135). In these cases, the point of critical analysis is to determine as well as we can what construction and reconstruction a text might have gone through in order to give it an internal coherence or to make it fit into a larger scriptural context. These are all methods for trying to understand historically how a scriptural text was constructed so that we can understand perhaps what it means.

Redaction criticism focuses on how scripture texts have been edited for various purposes.

There is, of course, some controversy to such methods. Some may see the historical critical method as a pernicious effort to undermine the authority of scripture. For example, if we were to find in the Torah, the five books of Jewish scripture supposedly written by Moses, certain words or ideas that could not have been common at the time of Moses, then we might conclude that Moses himself did not really write these texts. Similarly, if the story of Krishna as chariot driver for the warrior Arjuna in the Hindu **Bhagavad-Gita** is supposed to describe an historical event 3,000 years before the Common Era, then there is some mistake, since there were apparently no chariots in India at that time. Or finally, simply to ask about the historical "sources" of Muhammad's ideas seems to deny the fundamental Islamic view that these words, verbatim, were given to Muhammad by God. Thus, such historical study may seem to threaten scriptural authority, even though the study of history surely seems to be a necessary fundamental effort to understand the meaning of any written text.

Emphasis on the Reader

Some forms of critical method focus not on the text *per se,* but on how it is received. That is, it is one thing to discuss historically how a text was composed, what its words historically meant, and so on, but it is another to discuss how it appealed to its audience, what kind of people were intended to be its expected audience, and how different people bring different understandings to their own personal reading of scripture. These different critical emphases bring out for us one of the more important facts of hermeneutics: that a text does not, so to speak, exist in a vacuum but that it is necessarily delivered through the mind and ideas of readers. Thus, who reads scripture, *when* they read it, and what *ideas* they bring to that reading are part of what a scripture means.

There are still historical-critical aspects of this approach. For example, *audience criticism*, as its name implies, seeks to ascertain the original audience for the text. It is often noted, for example, that Matthew seems to have written his gospel intending his audience to be Jewish readers, whereas Luke wrote with non-Jews in mind. What are the implications of such a fact for interpreting these two writings? Such a question may well require the study of a social history that would include a sociological analysis of the communities in which the scriptures arose. All of this should help to provide an enriched understanding of texts by reconstructing their socio-political environments (compare Holladay, *NIB*, I, 134–136).

Reader-response criticism focuses on the reader of the scripture and how the reader responded in his/her historical context.

Such an approach—and there are many others that similarly focus on the context of the reader—exemplifies an important emphasis on the general notion of **reader-response criticism.** Here, "more attention is paid to how a text is received than to how it originated or how it is arranged." That is, some hermeneutical emphases stress that how a text is received may be more important, more truly a matter of the "meaning" of the text, than what that text actually says. Indeed, at its most extreme, we might argue that it is the reader and not the text that is the real creator of meaning (Holladay 143–144).

Some approaches to interpretation emphasize a kind of "conversation" between the text and the reader.

This emphasis on the interpretive role of the reader is well-represented in David Tracy's masterful summary of interpretation theory in his contribution to *A Short History of the Interpretation of the Bible,* by Robert M. Grant with David Tracy. Emphasizing the hermeneutical theories of Hans-Georg Gadamer, Tracy points out that ". . . no interpreter enters the process of interpretation without some prejudgments," with such prejudgments interwoven into "the very language we speak and write" (156–157). Therefore, he argues, we need to enter into the process of interpretation as if it were a kind of "conversation," a two-way communication in which a text speaks to us and we, in turn, respond. This requires what Tracy calls "correlations," a sense that some point of the text must appeal to the preunderstandings of the reader, which in turn help to interpret the text. In other words, in the real interpretive "conversation" between a religious text and its readers, "neither text nor interpreter, but only the conversation between both can rule. Interpreters cannot abandon their preunderstanding, nor can the claims of texts to the attention of that preunderstanding be abandoned. Text and interpreter must be allowed to be mutually critical" (171–173).

Who a person is and where he or she comes from has a key role in interpreting scripture.

All this, Tracy concludes, is just a way of saying that a religious text must answer to the way people in a religious community think, even as the religious text changes the way people in that community think. That is why who the people are and what their history has taught them are important parts of what a scripture means to them. This realization has led in modern times to the idea that in our day and age there are certain groups whose various social locations give them a distinct understanding of their respective scriptures. For example, reflecting the many books and articles that have been written in that vein, *The New Interpreter's Bible,* Vol. I, has separate articles devoted to "Reading the Bible as . . . African Americans, . . . Asian Americans, . . . Hispanic Americans, . . . Native Americans, and . . . as Women." All this is to recognize that who you are and where you come from has a profound effect on what you will think the scriptures mean.

Of course this, too, can be a controversial point, and it is likely that two opposite errors can follow from its consideration. For some scriptural literalists (we might say "fundamentalists"), this idea of the human aspect of interpretation might simply be rejected. Such believers would perhaps be insulted by the idea that the Holy Bible or the Holy Koran or the Vedas can be given meaning only by being understood within the context of real, living societies. In contrast, people on the other end of the spectrum might leap to the conclusion that any scripture thousands of years old cannot really have anything to say to modern people. The first will want to say that scripture has its own pure, clear message; the latter might insist that scripture itself "can just mean anything you want." Both claims are false. Instead, scripture and the people who follow it are an interpretive team, a conversation in which the words of God (let us say) become the understandings of mortals.

All we have said in this section has been to suggest that the process of the interpretation of scripture is by no means a simple matter. Or to put it in another, more potentially confusing way, even for those who think the interpretation of scripture is easy, it is still not an easy matter. That is, within those religions that put their scripture forward as a central and necessary revelation, there is no simple consensus on how to read it. For Muslims, personal interpretation (*ijtihad*) is frowned upon, insofar as, given the decisions of jurists and scholars in the construction of Islamic Law, there is no need for such a dangerous practice. Jews, on the other hand, recognize that the word of God is open to the interpretation of the community, something that must be deciphered from the actual text of the Tanakh. Christians traditionally stand somewhere in between, indeed everywhere in between.

CREEDS AND PHILOSOPHIES

We have seen that scripture in the world's religions takes on a variety of roles and emphases, yet throughout it plays a central role in religious epistemology (the study of knowledge). People refer to scripture as a way of appealing to prophets or sages and, by extension, as a way of appealing to God himself or of finding a universal wisdom about the Sacred. But we have also seen that there is a great deal of complexity hidden in the appeals to scripture, and that it takes a shrewd, often scholarly mind, to follow the historical and linguistic twists and turns that scriptural authority and interpretation presume. Perhaps that is why we often find creeds.

Statements of doctrine and confessions of belief, like creeds, develop out of the authority of scripture.

The word **creed** comes from the Latin word for belief. Especially the early Christian creeds would start with the word *credo*, "I believe," and go on to recite the basic beliefs of the Christian religion. These creeds were probably developed at first out of confessions of faith, in which people would openly recite their beliefs and thereby "confess" to the world their deep spiritual commitments. J. N. D. Kelly points out that in the early history of Christianity, before there was a central authority or even an agreed-upon body of scripture, various churches formed an "outline message" of the Christian faith to be used in church ceremonies. Thus, when a pagan Roman converted to Christianity, he or she would recite this formula in order to say, yes, I am a Christian, and here are the things

I believe. These formulae, in a sense, made it easier to state the basic and central parts of the religion and to summarize what that meant to a new believer. This, at least, was especially true of Christianity.

Christianity, in fact, provides us with probably the primary example of a religion for which doctrine is central. Because Christianity emphasized *belief,* essentially trusting that Jesus is the Christ who is one's savior, and also because Christianity formed its central ideas over a period of time without the benefit of a centralized authority, having the right belief, the "straight teaching," was of primary concern. This indeed is what **orthodox** means, the straight teaching, which from the first decades of Christianity settled into short creedal statements that could summarize the truths of the faith.

Harold Brown, in fact, argues that Christianity defined itself during its formative years primarily by being challenged in its central beliefs. That is, Christian thinkers of the first three centuries were often responding to "heresies" when they were trying to decide what orthodoxy really was. For in a religion in which salvation depends on belief, to change the beliefs is to jeopardize everyone's salvation. Thus, Brown notes, the earliest declarations that "Jesus is Lord!" required later elaborations on how Jesus was related to God, whether Jesus was the "natural" or "adopted" Son of God, and whether Jesus was also truly human or only appeared to be human. In this way, says Brown, Christian doctrine emerged as the necessary attempt "to spell out the significant concepts of the Gospel and place them in relationship to the individual and the world" (7).

All of this is easiest to see in the Christian religion, in which the early history required brief statements of belief, a ritual practice for new converts to confess their commitment to Jesus, and eventually a detailed theology to make sense of what Christianity really means. It is less easy to see in other religions wherein statements of belief are not ritually central. In Islam, the famous "first pillar" of the faith is a basic statement of belief, specifically belief in God and Muhammad. This statement, called the **shahadah,** simply declares, "There is no God but Allah, and Muhammad is His messenger." The simplicity of this statement, coined for Islam in the seventh century, was and remains a contrast with some of the very complex creeds of Christianity that had appeared by that time (compare, for example, the Chalcedonian Creed of 451).

In other religions in which orthodoxy is even less an issue, we seldom find creedal statements. There are other kinds of ritual declarations of one's devotion, of course, such as the "Three Refuges" in Buddhism, by which one declares one's intent to "take refuge in the Buddha, the Dharma and the Sangha." This statement is more about one's intention to seek salvation in Buddhism than it is a statement of what is believed. Yet hidden here is reference to *the Dharma,* a notion in Buddhism that refers to the Truth that the Buddha saw and taught. This Dharma is most commonly summarized in the list of teachings called the Four Noble Truths.

Described sometimes as a simple recipe for understanding what is wrong with the world and how to escape it, the Four Noble Truths can be summarized as follows:

1. Life is suffering.
2. The cause of suffering is desire.

The ideas of beliefs and creeds have played a central role in the history of Christianity.

In Islam, the statement of the sha-hadah *is a simple creed.*

Creeds are seldom found in religions in which orthodoxy is not a key concern.

Buddhism lists teachings, not as creeds, but as useful summaries of the Buddha's wisdom.

3. We can stop the suffering by stopping the desire.
4. The way to learn to stop desire is the Noble Eightfold Path.

This summary, though not used as a creed, is nevertheless a simplified doctrinal formula that can help to summarize the mass of teachings left by the Buddha. Consequently, for those seeking "refuge" in the Truth of the Buddha, we find a basic formula we can use to begin to follow his teachings. Notably, this summary ends with the hint of another summary, another numbered list. In fact, one finds that early Buddhism is particularly fond of numbered lists as ways to understand the world and the teachings of Buddhism. There are Four Noble Truths, an Eightfold Path, Three Marks of Existence, Five "Piles" that define a person's life, and a Twelvefold Chain of Causation. While these lists do not function in Buddhism as confessional creeds—since "believing" is not a central issue in Buddhism—these lists do help one to summarize the insights of the Buddha, keeping them in mind while one seeks salvation and takes refuge in the Buddha's wisdom.

The lack of a creed does not mean that a religion has no system of beliefs.

As we look into religions like Taoism or Shinto, it becomes very difficult to find anything like a creed or a statement of orthodoxy. We will comment shortly on why that is so, but for now let us make this last point. The lack of creeds or orthodoxy does not mean that a religion has no doctrine. Statements of what a religion asserts as true can be found in any faith, including those that claim to have no such statements. We saw at the beginning of this chapter that there is a curious irony in the fact that sometimes a religious teacher writes a book to explain why his teaching needs no books. Similarly, there are statements in religions even about why the religion needs no statements, or why its statements cannot be understood as statements. Everywhere we go in the world, people continue to think about their religions and to formulate those religions into ideas expressed in language. And even statements of how little we can know of God, of the Tao, or of Brahman become statements about the Holy.

More complex statements of belief, systems of belief, form as philosophies. We can note existence of complex philosophies throughout the world's religions.

And this, perhaps, is how religions become philosophies. Within all cultures, it seems, there are people with a curiosity and a talent for analyzing the ideas of religion and trying to explain and explore those ideas. Writers like Thomas Aquinas in Christianity, **Shankara** (700?–750?) for Hinduism, **Wang Yang-ming** (1452–1529) the Confucian, the Muslim **Averroes** (1126?–1198), and many, many others are recognized in one sense as religious devotees. But even more, the work of such writers is deeply analytical and carefully philosophical. Detailed statements about what God himself must be like, or how the world cannot be what it seems, or why there is suffering, or how diversity comes into existence—these very arcane and intellectual discussions have been analyzed with great rigor and brilliance by such thinkers. And while they do not tend to produce popular creeds, their ideas influence millions of followers, whether the followers have even heard of them or not.

Philosophers like these writers have developed detailed theologies, cosmologies, ethics, anthropologies, psychologies, and other studies of what is true, based upon their understanding of scriptures, of the words of founders, and ultimately of the Sacred itself. These philosophies, of course, can be as complex and difficult as the scriptures themselves, and so perhaps those who actually use such philosophies are the few with a need and a desire to make intellectual systems of religious beliefs. For most believers, simpler statements of belief, and indeed very simple creeds, are often all we need and all we want. Of course, for some religious people, beliefs and belief systems are not very important at all, and indeed in some religions, any belief is automatically suspect, just because it *is* a belief. We shall look at *anti-doctrine* next.

ANTI-DOCTRINE AND INEFFABILITY

All scripture and all doctrine, obviously enough, rely upon words. Words are pretty useful things, when one thinks about it, and indeed one probably cannot even think about how useful words are without using words to do the thinking. When words are used to form statements of truth, they help direct our actions and save our lives. Imagine how useful it was for some primitive humans to be able to say to others where to find food or to watch out for danger. When words are written, these truths can be conveyed beyond the reaches of normal time and space. That is, a written sentence like this one might well outlive its authors, might outlive you readers, and can stretch far beyond what we writers could have spoken to the people we know in our limited geographic area. And finally, when we can state truths and agree on them, we form communities and make friends, precisely because of what we say. This is, in a sense, what doctrine does for everyone: it helps them define themselves for others and thereby learn to recognize friends.

There are limits to what words, especially written words, can do.

As useful as words and scripture and doctrinal statements might be, however, we cannot end this chapter without considering the limits of language and religious contexts in which there is a self-conscious rejection of words, scripture and doctrine. Remember from our pictures for this chapter the famous etching of the Buddhist Patriarch, Hui-neng, tearing scripture to pieces, as well as the picture of the Native American leader, **Osceola** (1804–1838), stabbing his knife through the useless pages of a written treaty. Though their motives are different, it seems clear that in these two cases there is little respect for the written word, indeed a self-conscious rejection of what words mean and what they convey.

For Osceola, there is probably little appreciation for a written treaty because it was evident to him that these written words had little binding power. For a Native American, the more meaningful words of religious tradition would doubtless be spoken, not written. We noted early in this chapter that the spoken word, especially for native peoples, often carries with it the idea of a transmission of sacred stories, and therefore it creates a kind of social unity in the experience of a shared heritage. And with Osceola in particular, especially when it comes to treaties and agreements, he would certainly appreciate proper action over powerless script.

In the Zen tradition, all words are problematic insofar as they may hinder attaining ultimate truth because words make reality seem dualistic.

For Hui-neng the matter is different. In the Buddhist religion, or at least in the developing Zen tradition, all language is problematic, insofar as language by nature makes us think in **dualistic** terms. That is, language and words, spoken or written, necessarily express truth about reality in terms of subject and object: I (subject) see the sky (object), God (subject) loves me (object). But this, at least according to the Zen teacher D. T. Suzuki, immediately divides reality, and therefore cannot *explain* reality. For Zen enlightenment, Suzuki insists, true wisdom,

Prajna, sees reality as a whole, without any divisions created by language. Therefore he writes, "The worst enemy of Zen experience . . . is the intellect, which consists and insists in discriminating subject from object. The discriminating intellect, therefore, must be cut short if Zen consciousness is to unfold itself" (136–137). Thus, all language keeps us from enlightenment.

For such examples, it seems that practice and experience take precedence over language. We must see this hierarchy of values as a genuine religious possibility, wherein what a scripture or a doctrine or a creed might say about a religious view is much less important than what one feels about or how one obeys one's religion. Indeed, for some philosophers and theologians who stress the problems caused by different religions having opposing religious claims, the resolution to religious disagreements might be to see them as having unity regarding religious morality or religious experience. "Doctrine divides, but service unites"; "doctrine divides, but love unites." Such sayings that one can quickly find with a simple Internet search are stressing this general problem of language and suggesting something better: Words divide us from one another, but our hearts and our actions make us one.

Of course, the irony of all this is that, even to state such a moralistic or experiential transcendence of language, one seems to need to speak. That is not to say that morality and experience are unimportant. Indeed, we must take such aspects of religion as seriously as we take religious text and religious doctrine, which is why we also have chapters in this text about religious morality and religious experience. But the irony remains that in all these chapters, we write words, you read words. Perhaps inescapably, we all speak in words trying to communicate what we think about what we do and about what we feel, including what we do and what we feel about religion. If words divide us by creating doctrine, they also bind us together by allowing us to communicate, to share what we believe about morality, experience, and yes, about doctrine. And in all religions, even in which the use of texts or the use of language is disparaged, it is only through written and spoken words that we study these phenomena and learn, as the reader studies and learns from this text.

SCRIPTURE, CHANGING WORLDS, AND GLOBALIZATION

Even given the importance of scripture to religions, it is sometimes difficult to understand the emotions that arise in conflicts over the nature or interpretation of scripture. Religious movements, job loss, forced migrations, and, even violence have resulted from controversies regarding scripture. Some insight into why this is so may be found in the work of sociologist Peter Berger.

In a book called *The Sacred Canopy* (1967), Berger holds that life in the physical and social environments is really quite chaotic. Whether dealing with nature or human behavior, we simply do not know what to expect. Humans cannot function in the midst of such uncertainty. To prevent the ravages of such uncertainty, *each society must build its own world.* This world consists of social structures, such as family, politics, an economy, and, of course, religion. It will have positions in that structure like father, mother, child, priest, teacher, and students.

Each society must build its own world to make life predictable for its citizens.

Each of these will have behavioral expectations or norms, which direct peoples' behavior. Each world, each community, will have values that tell people what is important and what is unimportant. These worlds contain complex belief systems that tell people how things operate, who the people of this society are, and how they fit into the larger physical and spiritual universe. It is this socially constructed world that makes the physical world and the people in it understandable and predictable. It is this socially constructed world that stands between the people of a society and the horrors of chaos.

Yet, Berger maintains that these socially constructed worlds are notoriously unstable. Once these worlds are created, *world maintenance becomes a deep problem*. That is, each society must defend its world against change and disintegration. In fact, defending their way of life is a preoccupation of most societies. Societies have a variety of mechanisms to defend their social worlds. The most important and effective of these is simply teaching new members what they are to believe, how they are to behave, how they are to worship, what their careers will be, and the like. Societies also have a wide variety of rewards they can dole out for conforming behaviors and punishments they can give out for deviant behavior. Thus socially constructed worlds have built-in systems for maintaining their uniqueness. Nevertheless, as the world changes, socially constructed normality is remarkably precarious.

So Berger argues that every society is an exercise in world building and world maintenance. How does religion operate in this process? It turns out that religion is very important in both parts of the process. Religion frequently contributes to world-building activities. The norms, values, beliefs, and ethics of religions are embodied in the socially created world. For instance, there is little doubt that Confucian ideas strongly influenced the creation of Chinese, Japanese, Korean, and other Asian and Southeast Asian societies. It is equally clear that Orthodox Christianity had and still has a strong influence on Russian society to this very day, in spite of its years under the control of essentially atheistic communism.

On the other hand, there is a very strong tendency for religion to support the existing social arrangements of a given society. So the violation of the beliefs, customs, and values of a given social world (society) often not only brings punishment from secular authorities but from religious sources as well. Indeed, religion is all the more deeply involved in this process of maintaining the social system, insofar as there is a very strong tendency in societies to take their ways and practices and elevate them into the supernatural realm. That is, the human-created systems, norms, values, and beliefs that make up a given social world are often seen as somehow reflecting the fundamental laws and structure of the universe. Or to put it another way, our ways, customs, and social structure are not merely our creation but reflect the very pattern of the cosmic Tao or the commandments that God would have us follow. In short, our ways are God's ways! The reason for this is obvious. If the expectations, beliefs, and structures of our social world are simply human creations, then humans can change them. Instability and uncertainty result. But if our social world is really created by God or is a reflection of the "Tao of Heaven," then it is eternal and beyond change. This leaves the world we have created safe and secure and gives us a mighty fortress against the threat of chaos.

Each society must maintain its socially constructed world.

Religion is involved in both world building and world maintenance.

As the dramatic changes of globalization proceed, therefore, religion is all the more active in both world building and world maintenance. As citizens of the world find themselves surrounded by beliefs and practices that do not seem to be legitimate religion, or even religion at all, individuals may be faced with a need to rebuild their religious understanding of the world. Thus many movements, such as interfaith dialogues and the Parliament of the World's Religions, can be found worldwide. These movements represent universalism, an effort to redefine religion in ways that seem more inclusive. Similarly, religions worldwide are meeting with other religions and philosophies to discuss areas of disagreement and agreement and to bring the collective moral power of religions to bear on the pressing problems of humanity. Religions engaging in these encounters hope that the collective moral ideals they embody will form the basis for a more just world order.

Religion is involved in the search for universals necessary for creation of a global society and in the particularistic defense of groups threatened by globalization.

In contrast, as globalization threatens the self-definition of local communities and individual cultures, religion rises up to defend itself against disintegration. Those religious movements such as fundamentalism, seeking to rediscover and to keep strong the "fundamentals" of religion and culture, are engaged in world maintenance. These movements stress *particularism*. That is, they see modernization and globalization as a threat to a valuable, cherished way of life that has been the very definition of a community for generations. Thus, they attempt to use religion as a bulwark against threatening change.

While all of this may speak to the role of religion in changing times, it does not address directly the question of why so much attention is given to conflicts regarding scripture. The answer to this is found in the idea that scripture shows the holy and perhaps unchanging nature of the spiritual and material universe. To say this differently, scriptures are those documents that anchor the socially constructed world in the eternal. When scriptures are questioned or reinterpreted, the constructed world staving off chaos and resting on those scriptures quakes. This allows the threat of chaos to creep into believers' psyches.

Battles over scripture also reflect battles over those worlds associated with that scripture.

Not only do modernization and spreading globalization threaten the socially constructed worlds, but also the methods of scriptural interpretation associated with these trends may call for a serious examination of religious "truth," as well as those worlds resting on that scripture. Therefore, controversy regarding scripture and scriptural interpretation involves not only a "battle for the Bible" (or whatever scripture is being examined) but also a battle for the socially constructed world associated with that scripture. As modern methods of interpretation, like the historical critical method described previously, spread to religions other than Christianity, passionate controversies regarding scripture also are spreading.

CONCLUSION

Reading and understanding scripture is not easy. But for religious life, neither is it dispensable. We have suggested in this chapter that there us a tremendous depth of analysis and criticism involved in thoughtful reading of scriptural text, but we have also noted that scripture and revelation are deeply entwined in the historical and doctrinal roots of religions all over the world. Even religions that in many ways deny the value of scripture often use authoritative writings, and for other religions, the authoritative writings are the very bedrock of all the religious truths that follow. Thus, the Holy Bible, Holy Koran, the Vedas, and even the Platform Scripture of the Sixth Patriarch are texts people have read and continue to read in order to know what they need to understand and what they need to do in order to be a true follower of a sacred path. In admitting the complexity of reading and understanding scripture, the difficulties on both a global and personal level, we have in no way intended to suggest that scriptures can be abandoned, or that they have no inherent value or meaning. Quite the contrary: We have only tried to insist that whatever scripture one reads, one must read thoughtfully. But this is no more than we should already have expected from a sacred text.

■ INTERACTIVE EXERCISE

Please continue your exploration of world scriptures by going to the interactive exercise for this chapter online (**http://www.religion.wadsworth.com/richter**).

WORKS CITED

Bainton, Roland H. *Early Christianity*. New York: Van Nostrand, 1960.

Brown, Harold O. J. *Heresies: The Image of Christ in the Mirror of Heresy and Orthodoxy from the Apostles to the Present*. Grand Rapids, MI: Baker, 1984.

Dumoulin, Heinrich. *Zen Buddism: A History*. Vol. 1. New York: Macmillan, 1988.

Esposito, John L. *Islam: The Straight Path*. 3rd ed. Oxford, UK: Oxford University Press, 1998.

Grant, Robert McQueen, and David Tracy. *A Short History of the Interpretation of the Bible*. 2nd ed. Rev. and Enlarged. Philadelphia: Fortress, 1984.

Holladay, Carl R. "Contemporary Methods of Reading the Bible." In *The New Interpreter's Bible*. Vol. 1, 131. Nashville, TN: Abingdon, 1994.

Kelly, J. N. D. *Early Christian Doctrines*. New York: Harper and Row, 1960.

Lester, Toby. "What Is the Koran?" *The Atlantic Monthly*. January 1999. http://www.theatlantic.com/issues/99jan/koran.htm (accessed January 12, 2004).

Ong, Walter J., ed. *Orality and Literacy: The Technologizing of the Word*. New York: Methuen, 1988.

Peters, F. E. *A Reader on Classical Islam*. Princeton, NJ: Princeton University Press, 1994.

Robinson, Richard H., and Willard L. Johnson. *The Buddhist Religion: A Historical Introduction*. 4th ed. Belmont, CA: Wadsworth, 1997.

Smart, Ninian. *The World's Religions*. Cambridge, UK: Cambridge University Press, 1998.

Smith, Huston. *The World's Religions*. San Francisco: HarperSanFrancisco, 1991.

Strong, John S. *The Experience of Buddhism: Source and Interpretations*. Belmont, CA: Wadsworth, 1997.

Suzuki, D. T. *Zen Buddhism*. Garden City, NY: Doubleday Anchor Books, 1956.

Warraq, Ibn. *The Origins of the Koran: Classic Essays on Islam's Holy Book*. Amherst, NY: Prometheus, 1998.

Wood, James D. *The Interpretation of the Bible*. London, Duckworth, 1958.

Yampolsky, Philip B. *The Platform Sutra of the Sixth Patriarch*. New York: Columbia University Press, 1967.

FOR FURTHER READING

Berger, Peter. *The Sacred Canopy: Elements of a Sociological Theory of Religion*. Garden City, NY: Doubleday, 1967.

Grant, Robert McQueen, and David Tracy. *A Short History of the Interpretation of the Bible*. 2nd ed. Rev. and Enlarged. Philadelphia: Fortress Press, 1984.

Ong, Walter J., ed. *Orality and Literacy: The Technologizing of the Word*. New York: Methuen, 1988.

Strong, John S. *The Experience of Buddhism: Source and Interpretations*. Belmont, CA: Wadsworth, 1997.

Suzuki, D. T. *Zen Buddhism*. Garden City, NY: Doubleday Anchor Books, 1956.

6 MYTHS, STORIES, AND HISTORY

In traditional societies, religious and other cultural beliefs and practices are transmitted through stories. Is it any wonder that in societies that have writing, stories convey useful information, including treasured ideas about religion? Many types of religious stories are used in religions. Some should be understood as literal and factual, but many others were never intended to simply convey historical or factual information. In this chapter, we discuss the many types of religious stories and how these should be understood. For now, please look over the pictures for this chapter on the Web site (http://www.religion .wadsworth.com/richter), and read the following passages, then consider the Introductory Questions that follow as a way to prepare for reading this chapter.

The righteous flourish like the palm tree, and grow like a cedar in Lebanon. They are planted in the house of the LORD; they flourish in the courts of our God. In old age they still produce fruit; they are always green and full of sap, showing that the LORD is upright; he is my rock, and there is no unrighteousness in him.

—Judaism: Psalm 92:12–15

O you who believe! When you rise up to prayer, wash your faces and your hands as far as the elbows, and wipe your heads and your feet to the ankles; and if you are under an obligation to perform a total ablution, then wash (yourselves) and if you are sick or on a journey, or one of you come from the privy, or you have touched the women, and you cannot find water, betake yourselves to pure earth and wipe your faces and your hands therewith, Allah does not desire to put on you any difficulty, but He wishes to purify you and that He may complete His favor on you, so that you may be grateful.

—Islam: Holy Koran 5:6

A blind horse trotting up an icy ledge—
Such is the poet. Once disburdened
Of those frog-in-the-well illusions,
The scripture-trove's a lamp against the sun.

—Zen Buddhism: Satori poem by Kosen, 1808–1893 (adapted from Stryk 357)

Shu [Brief] and Hu [Sudden] discussed how they could repay the kindness of Hun-tun [Chaos]. "All men," they said, "have seven openings so they can see, hear, eat and breathe. But Hun-tun alone doesn't have any. Let's try boring him some!" Every day they bored another hole, and on the seventh day Hun-tun died.

—Taoism: Taoist Parable from Chuang Tzu (Watson 95)

Duryodhana's pride and wickedness had gone beyond all bounds. He had neither pity nor mercy nor good sense. In his madness, he even ordered that Draupadi's clothes should be stripped from her as she stood in the assembly; he thought this would be the best way to disgrace the proud queen and bring her to shame. Lord Krishna then came to her rescue and worked a miracle. As Dushahsana stripped her of one garment, another one appeared upon her. As that was torn away, another came in its place, and another and another and another!

—Hinduism: The Mahabharata (Rao, Rameshwar, and Narayan 76–77)

For I handed on to you as of first importance what I in turn had received: that Christ died for our sins in accordance with the scriptures, and that he was buried, and that he was raised on the third day in accordance with the scriptures, and that he appeared to Cephas, then to the twelve. Then he appeared to more than five hundred brothers and sisters at one time, most of whom are still alive. . . .

—Christianity: I Corinthians 15: 3–6

INTRODUCTORY QUESTIONS

1. The miniature picture found on the Web site represents the text of Revelation 21, which describes how God brings to earth a "New Jerusalem" at the end of time. Should we understand such a story like we understand a history book? How is it the same? How is it different?
2. Psalms are poems. How does knowing that the psalm is poetry change the way you read it, as opposed to, say, reading the instructions taken from the Holy Koran? Describe how the illumination of the Ingeborg Psalter enhances an understanding of the text.
3. The Zen poem is about enlightenment (*satori*). Look at this poem alongside the psalm. How does poetry help express some things? How does poetry fail to express other things?
4. St. Paul refers to the story of Jesus' life and resurrection. Such stories are, of course, unusual (since they contain miracles), and yet he refers to witnesses. Does that make it more dependable than, say, a story about creation, as depicted in the Shinto art?
5. How can we understand a story by Chuang Tzu? Why would such a story be in a text of "scripture"? If a teacher has a serious point to make, why doesn't he or she just teach it clearly?
6. The script in the painting by Hakuin reads: "[Zen is] a direct pointing to the human mind. See into your nature and become Buddha!" Is this poetry? Are there languages "outside of language"? Describe the role of brush and ink in Zenga.

TEXT AND LANGUAGE

We noted in the previous chapter on scripture that sacred texts play a very important role in religious traditions. Though they raise for the believer a number of problems regarding interpretation and history, they are often the primary source of authority, thought to be revealed to humanity through sages and prophets. Yet it is not the text itself, a mere book of so many pages or so many verses that commands our attention. It is, rather, the content of the book, its stories and myths, its lessons and instructions that lead the believer and capture his or her attention. Indeed, sometimes it is the very sound and form of the words, their holy language that is somehow a source of power or a focus of religious concern.

An indication of the importance of religious language can be found in the elaborate measures and care that are given to the precise form of the written word. Consider, for example, the text of the Holy Koran. As previously noted, Muslims believe the Holy Koran to have been revealed verbatim to Muhammad, not mediated through inspiration or through Muhammad's personality or cultural context. Thus this text, in Arabic, is the revealed word of Allah, and as such it should not be translated from the original Arabic into any other language, lest it lose the authenticity of the word of God. Throughout the world, Muslims are therefore required to recite the Holy Koran in Arabic, even if they themselves do not quite understand the language. Indeed, all over the world, many Muslims do not speak Arabic as their own native tongue and could not carry on a conversation in Arabic; yet precisely because the Arabic version of the Holy Koran is alone the pure word of God, they learn to recite the text of the holy book verbatim in Arabic. Thus, the Holy Koran is a striking example of the language of a holy text being sacrosanct.

Islam is certainly not the only religion that safeguards the sacredness of the holy word with an insistence on the preservation of original language. In traditional Hinduism, Sanskrit, the language used in the major rituals of brahmanical Hinduism, plays a significant role. Yet here the focus is not on the written but spoken word, which again has been preserved as accurately as possible over thousands of years through exact memorization. Indeed in much brahmanical ritual, precise recitation of the Sanskrit words of the Vedas is required if the Brahmin priests are to achieve the desired ends, as somehow the words themselves are the source of power. And as with Arabic for many Muslims, most Hindus do not understand Sanskrit; indeed, most Hindus have never read the Vedas. Nevertheless, it is well-known by all pious Hindus that the priests must know the Vedas and must know them exactly as written in Sanskrit, for it is in this precise language that the great rishis first heard these revelations.

rishis—mythic seven sages in Hinduism

In some cases, the text of scripture may be considered so sacred it cannot be translated from its original language.

Other religions are less concerned with the original language of their scripture and allow for the primary content of revelation to be available in various translations. Christianity, for example, never attributed the same significance to the original Hebrew of its Old Testament or the original Greek of its New Testament as other religions. This is somewhat ironic, since the Old Testament is roughly equivalent to the Jewish Tanakh, and Judaism, in contrast, has always stressed the importance of reading Hebrew. For example, there are elaborate techniques and strict rules involved in the copying of the Jewish **Torah**—Jewish Law consisting of the five books of Moses, the first five books of the Hebrew scriptures and considered the most sacred part of the Jewish scripture—so that every stroke and jot of the Hebrew text in the sacred writings must be perfect. When a young Jewish boy comes of age and is initiated into the adult religious community through the Bar Mitzvah ritual, learning to read Hebrew is a necessary part of the process. But for Christians, there has never been a single authoritative and original language of scripture, and in this context, translations have had to assume the role of the authoritative "original" text.

Latin, of course, became the holy language of the Roman Catholic Church and her Bible, even though neither the Hebrew nor the Christian Bible was originally in Latin. This is all the more ironic given the fact that Jerome's famous fifth-century **Vulgate** translation into Latin remained the standard for the trained Roman Catholic clergy long after Latin ceased to be a living language, even though Jerome's intention was precisely to translate the Bible into the "vulgar," or common language, of his day. Even earlier, the **Septuagint** (ca. 285 BCE) had been adopted from the Jews as the standard Greek translation of the Tanakh, and it, along with texts and fragments of the original Greek New Testament, became the basis for many other versions, including Martin Luther's translation into German. His work, along with the development of the printing press, allowed for a wide distribution of the Bible among the common people. Such a development in the treatment of the holy word significantly influenced theological concepts of Protestantism as well as the history of Christianity overall.

Yet while scholars and translators struggle over ancient texts and produce new ones, and while many of the pious learn or at least memorize sacred languages, the content of these scriptures is also important. As powerful as the very words of Sanskrit may be when breathed by the Brahmins during a Hindu ritual, most Hindus know much better the stories of the gods and the great epics of their battles and encounters on earth. Though we noted that the focus on "original language" among Christians might be less dramatic than that of Muslims and Brahmins, Christians as well frequently recite the stories of the biblical text to support their belief in God, Christ, and the Holy Spirit. Thus, even if language *per se* is not central, the stories and the content of the sacred biblical text are well-known, embedded deep in the hearts of believers.

Thus, we look not only at the actual human language of the world's scriptures but also at their stories and lessons, wisdom and poetry. For we have seen the immense authoritative role sacred scriptures occupy in religious traditions. So if we are going to understand the power these texts exhibit, we must understand the kinds of language they use, a factor that plays a major role in the special treatment they frequently receive in contrast to "ordinary" language.

LANGUAGE GAMES

Since certain traditions attempt to safeguard the original version, it seems at least questionable whether language simply is a set of words inscribed with meaning. As a matter of fact, the immense variety of literary traditions in religious contexts demonstrates that language hardly can be contained in specifically designed boundaries. As modern theories of interpretation emphasize (see the previous chapter), words are not entities that have a certain and simple meaning, but

---

Bar Mitzvah— literally, son of commandment, initiation rite, ritual which marks the assumption of observing the commandments

Unlike Judaism and Islam, Christianity has never had a single official language for its scripture, though for a long time Latin assumed that status in Roman Catholicism.

rather texts, including sacred texts, become meaningful while human beings read or hear those texts. In other words, the words alone do not carry a fixed meaning in themselves, but at least to a certain extent, meaning depends on the context in which these words are heard, including the lives and minds of those who hear the words. Thus, we must think of the language of the text of the Bible, the Holy Koran, the Vedas, and other scriptures as more complex than we might at first realize. Understanding the complexity of language not only helps one interpret scripture but also assists one in understanding many of the contemporary global controversies surrounding religions.

The contexts in which words are given and "heard" may be as important as the words themselves in understanding their meaning.

To introduce this complexity of meaning, we can refer to Ludwig Wittgenstein (1898–1951), a German philosopher of language who had an immense impact on modern thought. In his analyses of meaning, Wittgenstein compared language to a game, suggesting that the rules of the game are analogous to the rules of language. In a game of chess, for example, among those playing the game the rules provide a certain pattern or ordered form of life. Players do not always follow the same pattern in applying the rules, which is to say that millions of different moves are possible. Yet rules remain if the players are to have a game at all. With language, then, we have a similar "game." There is a certain regularity in language, a structure of rules and types of speech that nevertheless allows for an immense flexibility in language. Consequently, just as chess figures can be moved around in a million different ways, different combinations of words can be used in different contexts or styles to produce a multitude of different meanings. Moreover—and this is somewhat unlike chess but perhaps a lot like playing cards—there is not just one set of existing rules for language, for language is dynamic, with new words and even new language games being invented as others become outmoded and disappear altogether. Thus Wittgenstein wrote:

Language contains rules but permits flexibility as well.

> *But how many kinds of sentence are there? Say assertion, question, and command?—There are* countless *kinds: countless different kinds of use of what we call "symbols," "words," "sentences." And this multiplicity is not something fixed, given once for all; but new types of language, new language-games, as we may say, come into existence, and others become obsolete and get forgotten. . . . Here the term "language-game" is meant to bring into prominence the fact that the* speaking of language *is part of an activity, or of a form of life. (12)*

Accordingly, language is not an exact communication system, with easy one-to-one correspondence between word, objects, and actions. On the contrary, it allows for great variety and flexibility since it is embedded in real life. For example, the word "dog" sometimes refers to a four-legged animal that many Americans keep as pets, but sometimes it describes a villainous human, a homely girl, or even a kind of food. It might be used to depict the hopeless position in a disastrous situation as in the phrase "not standing even a dog's chance." Yet in all these uses we know what is meant by the word "dog" because we know the context of what is spoken. And we learn these interpretations because we live in the midst of real communication, not because we own a dictionary.

There is not a direct one-to-one correspondence between a word and its meaning.

Understanding, of course, becomes more complicated if we do not encounter live communication but deal with texts. However, mostly we just know—intuitively, experientially—that a poem is somehow different from a newspaper article or a college textbook about biology. Consider, for example, a famous poem by Joyce Kilmer:

> *I think that I shall never see*
> *A poem lovely as a tree.*
> *A tree whose hungry mouth is prest*
> *Against the earth's sweet flowing breast. (300)*

It would be pointless, and indeed rather silly, for a bright biology student to complain that this poem is evidently erroneous for confusing trees with suckling mammals. "A tree has no mouth," one might complain, "and the earth has no milk." Fine, but this clearly misses the point. Similarly, imagine a student who read her biology textbook and, when asked in class to comment on the chapter about trees and photosynthesis, commented, "It didn't move me, had no rhythm or imagery to awaken the real wonder of what a tree is." We suspect the biology teacher would be unimpressed. But our point is that actually both criticisms may be quite true. The error of the reader is not in his or her beliefs about the biology or the wonder of trees but in how he or she reads the literature. They both confused their language games, and the oddity of their interpretations is, as Wittgenstein might say, like trying to play chess with checkers' rules. To be aware that a text is written in a certain format, for example, as a poem and not an article in a scientific journal, gives us important clues about how to read it. To be familiar with the time period in which a specific text was written and being able to imagine the context also offers guidance in how to make sense of what we read. However, this knowledge does not strictly provide us with a definite "meaning" of the text. The rules of language games are not precise; they are not fixed but are flexible because human beings apply these rules in various real-life situations. Sometimes they change over time, sometimes people use them differently. Hence we cannot arrive at a single specific "meaning" of a text, but we will, most likely, find different readings.

Different persons may find different meanings to a text because they apply different language rules.

When looking at sacred stories and myths, we should take Wittgenstein's insights into consideration, reminding ourselves that these texts do not necessarily signify a "literal meaning" that can be extracted from the text simply by reading. Rather, we must see the myths, stories, lessons, and poems as games, dynamic entities that follow a variety of different rules. To try to identify those rules, or the forms of the language game, will therefore be a very important task in this chapter.

Understanding the particular "language game" used in a text is vital to grasping its meaning.

We should also keep in mind that most of these texts were written long ago by people who lived in a very different historical and cultural context. As one can easily imagine, this most often has significant implications on the ways these texts once were used. This might also mean that we probably are tempted to read them quite differently today.

MYTH

Let us, for example, take the word "myth." For most people perhaps, calling a story a "myth" amounts to denouncing it as something false. But for religious studies, the category of mythic language is something deeper than the simple denial of the story's literal truth. Indeed, as we shall see, speaking of myth is a way of trying to understand certain stories of world culture that has little to do with their literal meaning.

The Greek word *mythos* means "word" or "story." Traditionally, it has been used to refer to pagan stories, particularly Ancient Greek myths, in which gods and heroes and monsters conspired and battled. But this content is not the primary focus of mythic language. Myths originally were a means to communicate mysteries of the world or fundamental philosophical and religious beliefs, in which great events of even cosmic significance were explored in terms of their relation to the Sacred. So in short, **myths** are stories that try to communicate deep mysteries of the world and its relation to the Sacred. Thus, myths focus on the beginnings and the end of the cosmos, or on the origins of society or of some specific and important part of a people's culture. To characterize myths this way therefore, implies that this particular language game incorporates a complex range of sacred stories.

Some traditional examples of religious myths are easily recognized. The opening chapters of the Jewish and Christian scriptures contain the famous account of creation in which God creates the earth, sun, stars, and all life in "six days." On the other end of time, stories of final judgment are common in the Abrahamic religions. For example, Islamic scripture contains numerous warnings of Judgment Day, when God shall place in every individual's hand a book of his or her own deeds. Those whose book is placed into their right hands are the blessed; woe to those to whom God gives the book into the left hand! (Holy Koran 69:13–34).

Less dramatically, perhaps, myths like the stories of the Sage Kings of ancient China give no account of creation or judgment, but they do provide Confucianism a source of meaning and explanation. These ancient but questionably historical "kings," like Yao and Shun, are believed by Confucius to be the great, wise leaders of the past, who through their wisdom and virtue made China a great, peaceful, and prosperous nation. They then become symbols of how virtue and wisdom, especially in a ruler, harmonize the world in accordance with the Tao of Heaven. And in both Buddhism and, especially, Jainism, religions that explicitly avoid stories of creation, there are important assumptions about past Buddhas and past Tirthankaras, perfect and enlightened beings from very distantly past ages, whose wisdom and teaching are repeated in the words and examples of the historical founders of Buddhism and Jainism.

These cursory examples are meant only to show the breadth of mythic language and to suggest how one might begin to study myth. For more detail, let us examine the following emergence myth from the Hopi Indians closely to explore some of its complex aspects:

In the beginning there were only two: Tawa, the Sun God, and Spider Woman, the Earth Goddess. All the mysteries and power in the Above belonged to Tawa, while Spider Woman controlled the magic of the Below. In the Underworld, abode of the Gods, they dwelt and they were All. There was neither man nor woman, bird nor beast, no living thing until these Two willed it to be.

In time it came to them that there should be other Gods to share their labors. So Tawa divided himself and there came Muiyinwuh, God of All

Life Germs; Spider Woman also divided herself so that there was Huzruiwuhti, Woman of the Hard Substances, the Goddess of all hard ornaments of wealth such as coral, turquoise, silver and shell. Huzruiwuhti became the always-bride of Tawa. They were the First Lovers and of their union there came into being those marvelous ones the Magic Twins— Puukonhoya, the Youth, and Palunhoya, the Echo. As time unrolled there followed Hicanavaiya, Ancient of Six (the Four World Quarters, the Above and Below), Man-Eagle, the Great Plumed Serpent and many others. But Masauwhu, the Death God, did not come of these Two but was bad magic, who appeared only after the making of creatures.

And then it came about that these Two had one Thought and it was a mighty Thought—that they would make the Earth to be between the Above and the Below where now lay shimmering only the Endless Waters. So they sat them side by side, swaying their beautiful bronze bodies to the pulsing music of their own great voices, making the First Magic Song, a song of rushing winds and flowing waters, a song of light and sound and life.

"I am Tawa," sang the Sun God, "I am Light. I am Life. I am Father of all that should ever come."

"I am Kokyanwuhti," the Spider Woman crooned in softer note. "I receive Light and nourish Life. I am Mother of all that shall ever come." "Many strange thoughts are forming in my mind—beautiful forms of birds to float in the Above, of beasts to move upon the Earth and fish to swim in the Waters," intoned Tawa.

"Now let these things that move in the Thought of my lord appear. . . ."
(Leeming 36–37)

A first reaction from a modern reader probably will be surprise or even complete disagreement with the Hopi emergence story. Surely enough, scientific experiments have proven that the earth did not come about by Tawa, the Sun God, and Spider Woman, the Earth Goddess, "swaying their beautiful bronze bodies to the pulsing music of their own great voices, making the First Magic Song, a song of rushing winds and flowing waters, a song of light and sound and life" (37). At least according to scientific insights, the Hopi story is "a false story." Yet drawing this conclusion, again, misses the point of mythic language. Following Wittgenstein's analogy between games and language, we may consider that mythological stories follow completely different rules than scientific language. Perhaps our myth was never meant to answer the question of the origin of the universe in a systematic, physical manner. Maybe the story employs imagery, intuitive storytelling rather than precise language of the physical scientist. If so, then not recognizing the rules of the language game would mean that we as modern readers completely misunderstand the Hopi emergence story! But if this is the case, how may we understand the myth?

Mythic language follows different rules than scientific language.

We should start by exploring some of the admittedly complex aspects, which are characteristic for mythological stories. The major characters of the myth are evident: Spider Woman, Tawa, and the Magic Twins. Perhaps as we read we even create our own mental picture of these characters and their actions. Like poetry, the text invites the reader to imagine the first lovers, Tawa and Spider Woman, singing the Song of Life. This is the important point. Mythological sto-

Myths are invitations to imagine rather than concrete descriptions.

ries are incentives to imagine, to think and picture a reality that often evades concrete depiction. The Hopi story deals with the beginning of existence, the question: "Where do we, the Hopi people, come from?" The Hopi myth is therefore an attempt to explain a reality that otherwise is inexplicable—the very beginning of life—and to anchor that reality in the belief in a greater Reality, the absolute transcendent reality. Yet in contrast to fairy tales, the myth is not merely a fantastic invention; it is rather an attempt to depict the correlation between a known reality, the life we see around us, and what is conceived as absolute reality or truth.

We can see this explanatory but poetic pattern in other myths. How can we explain the origin of existence? How shall we understand our ultimate purpose? Let us connect creation and final judgment to the Absolute. Thus, creation and end-of-the-world stories are classical myths. Similarly, stories of Sage Kings help to explain to the Confucian mind who we are and, in a different sense, where we came from. And in a similar way, stories of past Buddhas and Tirthankaras tie the teaching and wisdom of our present faith to deeper, even infinite realities. Thus, myths provide a worldview based on a specific perception of reality as a whole, a unification of the importance of life and wisdom as we see it around us, with a greater, broader, deeper reality beyond the senses. In that sense, myths are not just an ancient phenomenon of nonscientific fantasy but are a versatile and essential language game in any culture that tries to communicate the depth and meaning of their central beliefs and values.

■ RECITATION AND PERFORMANCE

Myths use poetic language to express a relation between the profane and the Sacred Absolute Reality.

To understand myths, it is important to realize that their language is essentially poetic. We shall look specifically at poetry in a moment, but for now, saying mythic language is poetic means that, in contrast to literal depiction, the text is metaphorical, evoking imaginative thought that reaches toward the relation between the profane and what is considered sacred. As in poetic texts, there is deliberately more freedom in the use of spatial and temporal categories. While myths are not completely removed from historical reality, there is no necessity to represent space or time accurately according to our modern concepts. The focus is on whatever is considered significant. "See the movement of the sand. That is the life that will cause all things therein to grow," proclaims Spider Grandmother before disappearing from the sight of her newly created people (Leeming 39). For the Hopi Indians, growing their crops in the barren sands of the dry Southwestern desert even today means existence, and so the life-giving power of the sand amounts to a belief in the significance of being in this world. Time and space become essential time and essential space or, speaking in the terms of the Hopi, the myth provides guidance toward whatever is considered meaningful in the context of the Hopi tribe.

Myths are often performed or spoken.

The poetic nature of mythic language is also evident in the fact that much myth is more essentially a matter of performance than of description. While we encounter the Hopi myth here as written text, it is told as story orally or regularly reenacted in songs during Hopi ritual performances. Like communication in a theatre play, the dramatic presentation of the myth in ritual dances and songs provides a most impressive reiteration of significant aspects of the Hopi worldview and ensures the continuation of traditional Hopi values and beliefs. Generations of Hopi children are introduced to their cultural tradition through these dramatic performances in which they themselves become participants.

■ SOCIAL DIMENSION

While myths like the Hopi emergence story inspire imaginative thought about the ultimate significance of an Absolute Reality, they are also distinctively rooted in the experience of this world. We have seen that the very heart of the myth is the connection between lived experience and its greater, ultimate source. The following passage from the Hopi myth clearly indicates this concern:

> Then Spider Woman spoke to them thus: "The woman of the clan shall build the house, and the family name shall descend through her. She shall be house builder and homemaker. She shall mold the jars for the storing of food and water. She shall grind the grain for food and tenderly rear the young. The man of the clan shall build kivas of stone under the ground where he shall pay homage to his gods. (Leeming 38)

Myths often express the belief that the social structure of the group is rooted in Ultimate Reality.

A mythic vision also may serve as an impetus for transforming the present.

The implication here is that myth plays a powerful role in helping a society to organize itself or to make sense again of its social structure as somehow related to what is believed Ultimate Reality. Here, the Hopi myth designates certain tasks to the members of the community, thus organizing the social structure of a clan. Men and women are given specific roles, which are sanctified in the context of this story of origin. In a similar way, a classical Hindu creation myth in the Vedas (Rig Veda 10:90) describes how the world came about through the dismembering of an ancient man, **Purusha**. There, it is said that "His mouth became the Brahmin; his arms were made into the Warrior (*kshatriya*), his thighs the People (*vaishya*), and from his feet the Servants (*shudra*) were born" (Fieser and Powers 8). Here again, it is evident that the myth helps to substantiate a social order, the **Hindu caste system**. Thus, the order of society that the people live with daily has a meaning and value deeper and more significant than the social order itself.

Other myths may articulate historical events, support national identity and pride, and describe heroic triumphs over evil. They may relate a story of an ancient ancestor who formed the mountains or who raised the first wheat. Previously, we have primarily analyzed creation stories, emphasizing origins, yet myths encompass the complexity of human existence and, correspondingly, include an extensive range of topics. Rather than promoting a sanctified social structure, certain myths focus on possible change of certain worldviews. Mythic visions of a new world and future thus can provide incentive for transformation of past and present experiences. An example of such dynamic language can be found in Chapter 21 of the Book of Revelation in the Christian Bible. Here, the vision of a new heaven and new earth provides the stimulus to imagine a world transformed from its current situation. Yet while myths offer systems of interpretation for social structures, the important concern of myths is not the knowledge of this world but the correlation between what is known to what is believed to be true about the Absolute.

■ FALSE STORIES

In our discussion of the Hopi myth, the word "truth" plays an important but problematic role. We used Wittgenstein's analogy between language and games to clarify our understanding of different ways of using language. However, while it might be possible for us to appreciate the Hopi myth, in which the harmony and wisdom of Spider Grandmother is celebrated and enacted in the Hopi culture, we can hardly live according to the Hopi worldview. In that sense, the Hopi myth may indeed seem to be only a "false story." But it is more likely that our own myths are significantly different. In other words, we most likely follow different values and beliefs evident in different mythological stories.

Modern societies have myths as do ancient societies.

We might not recognize it, yet modern myths in our own culture are as abundant as ancient myths. One of the most persuasive modern mythmakers is Hollywood. Thinking about *Star Wars* or *The Lion King,* we might see that these stories provide a specific worldview for many Americans. *Star Wars* introduces a hero, Luke Skywalker, who surpasses his own limits and transcends his humanity, overcomes the inherited weakness of family, and yet maintains the family's sanctity. Similarly, the Lion King helps us imagine the overcoming of betrayal and the hope that virtue is rewarded, evil defeated. Even commercial advertisements like the Budweiser Frogs give us dramatized visualizations that persuasively reinforce beliefs and values in the American culture, values about leisure and entertainment, and the connection between such values as Budweiser beer. As commercial agents know, mythic language can be highly persuasive.

The power of myths does not depend on their literal truth but in their power to connect with people's lives.

More significantly, perhaps, less commercial myths influence us in the way we value democracy or capitalism. Take the image—true or not—of the poor immigrant family that comes to the United States and, through hard work and self-sacrifice, becomes economically successful and well-educated. Here we have a fine image of the success of a presumed economic system, whether we have ever known such a family or not. Myths like this therefore support and validate extant systems. Their power is not in their truth alone but in their power to connect people's lives to greater ideals.

Especially in the realm of religion, therefore, it is of utmost importance that language games are analyzed and explored for the implied goals. Myths are not "false" or "true" because of how they describe some past history or some future event. They are ways of describing, explaining, and reinforcing the values and order of our world. Mythic language is not used to make scientific or historical claims *per se.* Rather, myths are ways of communicating the deep relationship between our world and what is believed to be true about a deeper and greater reality. According to Charles Long, a historian of religions, in his major work, *Alpha: the Myths of Creation* (1963), for anyone who has studied the cultures of people who live in terms of an explicit myth, "the myth is a true story—the myth is a story about reality." (11) In an even more profound sense, Mircea Eliade, considered the foremost scholar in the field, writes in his *Myth and Reality:*

Myth narrates a sacred history; it relates an event that took place in primordial Time, the babbled time of the "beginnings." In other words, myth tells how, through the deeds of Supernatural Beings, a reality came into

Box 6.1   Global Byte

Myth, History, and the Difference It Makes

Judaism is apparently a very self-consciously historical religion. Its basic scriptural narratives are often historical in form and content, specifying dates of kings and leaders, noting world events and the role that God played in preserving His people throughout the ages. God made a covenant with Abraham, the scriptures say, promising him a land and a great nation. Some 450 years later, this was accomplished, say the scriptures, as Moses led that great nation out of slavery in Egypt, through the Wilderness of Sinai, and into the Promised Land. And to stress this historicity, the "Books of Moses" contain the common injunction from God Himself, telling His people not to forget what God has done for them. "Remember that you were slaves in Egypt and that the Lord your God brought you out of there with a mighty hand and an outstretched arm" (Deuteronomy 5:15).

The problem with historical language, however, is that people can try to find out independently if the events described really happened, and apparently within Judaism there is something of a brewing crisis. In a recent article, the title declares that within Judaism itself, "As Rabbis face fact, Bible tales are wilting." The gist of the story is that modern archeology seems to find no evidence of the great migration of the Hebrew people under Moses, no sign of their "conquest" of the Promised Land, and not even any real mention of the Hebrew people in the history of the Egyptians. One rabbi, David Wolpe, boldly summarizes, "The way the Bible describes the Exodus is not the way that it happened, if it happened at all."

So what happens to "historical" Judaism? Some might say, "Nothing." Rabbi Susan Grossman said, "The real issue for me is the eternal truths that are in the text," adding the question, "How do we apply this hallowed text to the 21st century?" For other Jews, however, it might seem that if the historical stories cannot be trusted, then there is no Promised Land, no "covenant with Abraham," no sense in being Jewish at all. Indeed, Orthodox Jewish rabbis generally continue to insist that every bit of the Torah is directly from God, and God does not err. And even some rabbis who begin to mistrust the "history" of the text admit that the "evidence" against the historicity of the stories may really be not proof that it did not happen but only the lack of historical evidence that it did happen. Perhaps. But the debate is clearly set, and it may revolve around whether we are to read the "history" as history, or the "history" as myth.

Source: "As Rabbis Face Facts, Bible Tales Are Wilting." *New York Times* [New York] March 9, 2002.

existence, be it the whole of reality, the Cosmos, or only a fragment of reality . . . Myth tells only of that which really happened (5–6).

Myths connect what we live with daily to the Absolute.

POETRY

Before going on to talk about historical and instructional religious language, let us look briefly at poetry *per se*. We have already said that mythic language is poetic, suggesting that it uses metaphor and imagery, and that it is not greatly concerned with accurate temporal or spatial descriptions. This seems clearly the case with poems in general. We noted earlier in the chapter that the poem by Joyce Kilmer describes trees as having mouths pressed against the "breast" of the earth. But no one pretends to take such a description as anything other than metaphor. To read a poem correctly, we must read it as a poem.

This holds true for religious poetry as well. Certainly the biblical Psalms offer numerous examples:

Hear my cry, O God; listen to my prayer.
From the end of the earth I call to you, when my heart is faint.
Lead me to the rock that is higher than I;
For you are my refuge, a strong tower against the enemy.
Let me abide in your tent forever, find refuge under the shelter
*   of your wings.*

                                                      (Psalm 61:1–4)

Poetic language in scripture must be understood as poetry, not literal descriptions.

Here, of course, it is not declared that there are "ends" to the earth. More theologically, it does not say that God is literally a "strong tower" or that God has wings. This is, of course, poetry, and these are images and metaphors meant to describe God's protection and care for His followers. The Jewish and Christian Bible is particularly abundant with such literature and offers the reader a challenge in proper understanding.

More extreme examples of the religious use of poetry can be found in Zen Buddhism, especially in the tradition of the "enlightenment poem." Here, poetry is, in a sense, required precisely because enlightenment itself is thought to be something that cannot be directly described. Having found perfect wisdom that transcends all language, there is, in some sense, no point of trying to describe enlightenment to those who have not experienced it. Yet the awakened Zen Buddhist does speak, and to express the inexpressible, he uses poetry. One example was in the opening quotations of this chapter; another, attributed to a Zen monk named Saisho (16th century), says:

Earth, mountains, rivers—hidden in this nothingness..
In this nothingness—earth, mountains, rivers revealed.
Spring flowers, winter snows.
There's no being nor non-being, nor denial itself.

                                                      (Stryk 353)

Our point here is not to interpret such a poem to explain its subtle references to enlightenment and religious experience. Rather, it is only to note that such a poem seems to say very little that is of direct explanation. Yet something great has happened in the awakening of this monk, something that transcends and yet is part of the everyday world of natural objects. There is even a hint at the end that no logic or language can explain what has been seen. From a Zen perspective, the ordinariness of "earth, mountains, rivers" somehow united with "nothingness" is brilliant; for most of us, perhaps, it is only a very odd and not very descriptive poem. But it is evidently an effort to express something of the inexpressible Absolute.

The oddity of some religious poetry does not mean, of course, that there is nothing of substance to learn from poetic language or that any poem can mean anything we like. Sometimes the poetic form is part of the mystery of the text, as it is for the Tao Te Ching, and it is no wonder that there are literally dozens and dozens of different translations of this book into English, each with its own interpretive direction. The Holy Koran, by contrast, is also poetic but should not be taken as "mere" poetry. Muslims insist, as we have noted before, that there is no text in the world that rivals the poetic force and the theological depth of the Holy Koran. It is, so say the faithful, both great poetry and the complete revelation of God's will.

The oddity of religious poetry does not mean that it contains nothing of importance.

For our purposes, the discussion of poetry is only to remind the reader of an obvious point: that poetry uses poetic language. Therefore, again as Wittgenstein suggests, we are well advised to read poetry according to the "rules" of the poetic "game." Thus, when Psalm 93 says, "The LORD . . . has established the world; it shall never be moved," it is a simple mistake to think this means the earth is the unmoving center of the universe. Such a conclusion is not just bad science; it is bad reading.

HISTORICAL LANGUAGE IN SCRIPTURE

We have spent some time trying to indicate that mythic and poetic language are unique ways of communication and experiencing the world and that, like all language games, they must be "played" according to their own rules. In particular, it might be one of the troubling temptations of modern readers, especially those mostly familiar with the Judeo/Christian readings of scripture, to confuse mythic language with historical language and, therefore, to expect that the meaning of a mythic story is primarily a description of past events. Thus, the famous "Usher Chronology" of 1650 boldly asserted that the creation described in Genesis took place on six consecutive days, starting on October 3rd (presumably a Sunday) in the year 4004 BCE. But as we have seen, this may be a mistake, not so much of an erroneous text but of interpreting a language.

It is common for modern reasons to mistake mythic language with historical language.

We say "may be" because it must also be acknowledged that some scriptures of the world's religions do seem to employ historical language and seem to intend that their readers understand their stories as descriptions of past events. And it is not our intention to assert that any particular myth (or poem) can only be read in one way. But how one reads a story—whether as myth or as history or as poetry—will have a dramatic effect on what one understands the story to mean, as well as on whether one interprets the story to be valid or accurate or personally valuable. Indeed, as we have seen, if we are to interpret creation myths, whether Judaic or Hopi, as scientific cosmology, we may simply have to say they are false. But if they are descriptions of how we understand the world around us, its origin and value, relating it to Absolute Reality, then we may have stories that offer insight into fascinating worldviews and religious concepts.

Since the late 19th century, an emphasis has been placed on discovering factual data when explaining causes for events.

We might have to pause here to clarify what we consider historical language. Since the late 19th century, an important focus in historical investigations has been on the critical research of facts and data to support a causal explanation of human events. Scholars therefore try to establish the validity of certain texts by analyzing historical facts. Under such assumptions, the fact, for example, that the

Roman historian Tacitus (55–122 CE) mentions Christians in a nonbiblical text becomes very important. Tacitus refers to Christians as people named after Christus, who suffered the death penalty under the reign of Tiberius (15.44). Historians interpret this reference as a significant support for historical events surrounding the death of Jesus. However, the focus on factuality and causal explanation is a perspective that ancient writers most certainly did not share with modern historical researchers. Although a historian like Tacitus does not write history completely removed from historical data, which include his reference to Christians, his foremost interest nevertheless seems to have been to understand human actions. To communicate such an understanding, he provides his readers with exciting historical narratives in which the people and actions come alive. Yet his purpose is not only to describe an historical event but to explore human nature. Thus, his narratives do not necessarily comply with the modern perception of historically accurate information.

■ "History" and Religion

"Historical" narratives in religion often are intended to convey something other than factual information.

As with Tacitus, historical narratives in religious contexts often serve a purpose much greater than the mere description of historical events. Instead, their purpose is to provide a worldview, an understanding of the past and its relation to the Sacred. Consequently, while it at least seems that the stories of some religious texts are indeed meant to be biographies and histories, accurate renditions of what real people in real times said and did are often missing. The most forceful example of this game of language, perhaps, is the Judaic religion. Once beyond the "myths" of the first eleven chapters of Genesis, the books seem to take on a historical specificity that attempts to make objective references to cities and people and places that might be evident to the readers. Thus, Abram leaves the cities of Ur and Haran, cities known as real places, and travels to lands where towns, peoples, mountains, and wells are named and known. Indeed, whoever wrote these portions of the text occasionally insisted that even the reader of his own time could find these landmarks, for example, the tomb of Rachel (Genesis 35:20; see also Joshua 4:9, 7:26, 10:27). The ongoing histories of the kings of Israel and Judah are also, apparently, meant to be historical claims about real people and their real actions. Dates are given relative to the rise and fall of known kings, historical events, and places, which we can trace to this day and function as historical reference points. And it is clear that part of the message of this "historical language" is precisely that it is to be remembered, as the people of Israel are told again and again not to forget what their "fathers" had done and not to forget the works that the Lord accomplished in the history of their nation.

Christians, as we might expect, picked up this historical consciousness from their Judaic roots. The Gospel of Luke and the Acts of the Apostles seem to be written explicitly as efforts to collect the biographical information about Jesus and about the early years of the Christian church. The writer indeed claims for his work: "to set down an orderly account of the events that have been fulfilled among us, just as they were handed on to us by those who from the beginning were eyewitnesses and servants of the word" (Luke 1:2). He further declares that he himself "carefully investigated everything from the beginning" in order to write "an orderly account" (Luke 1:3). However, Luke was not an eyewitness but wrote his gospel probably about 60 years after the death of Jesus. Most likely he was not even the first evangelist, an honor that is given to Mark (about 64–70 CE). Most importantly, however, Luke's focus was not primarily to provide accurate historical facts according to our perception of historical study today but to establish the authority of Jesus as the Christ in the biblical tradition as the one who fulfills the scriptures (Luke 24:27; also Matthew 26:56; Mark 14:49; Romans 1:2). Again, for our purposes in this text, it is not a question of whether or not Luke got accurate historical data or got it from reliable witnesses; it is rather a matter of what he seemed to believe he was trying to do and writing it in what we call the format of a historical narrative today.

Other religions also have elements of historical religious language in their scriptures, although they may not have the same kind of interest in historical narrative that one finds in Judaism and Christianity. Certainly in Buddhism, the biographical narrative of the Buddha's life is important and for many is intended and is read as history. Indeed, such biographical language is somewhat parallel to the story of the life of Jesus, with clear details about how the previous incarnation of the Buddha, depicted as a celestial white elephant, entered Queen Maya's womb and very precise descriptions of how the Prince Siddhartha traveled from his palace and saw for the first time the reality of sickness, old age, and death. The first written story of the Buddha's life seems to appear some 500 years after the Buddha's appearance, written by Ashvaghosha in the first century. Still, early Buddhist art and pilgrimage traditions tracing the path of the Buddha's life, and clearly predating any written biography, were important ways for early Buddhists to see how the Buddha lived. And believing that he really did live this way seems to have been an important part of one's own Buddhist experience.

It may appear strange, however, that most of the early scriptures of Buddhism do not emphasize the biographical narrative, but rather most of the literature is primarily instructive, most famously the sermons of the Buddha on the Dharma (the Truth of Buddhism) and the **Vinaya** (the discipline and rules of the *sangha* or Buddhist monastic order). Yet in another sense, there are important elements of historical language even in these **sutras,** insofar as they begin with reference to the place and setting of the Buddha's speech. "Thus have I heard," many of the sutras declare, and at the very least they seem to be trying to assert that the Buddha said these words in this place at this time. Thus, historical settings in scriptural literature can serve the purpose of establishing authority, showing when and how this information was obtained.

Another interesting example of this historical establishment of authority occurs in the Hadith literature of Islam, the second most important source of Islamic teaching after the Holy Koran. In the Hadith, stories of Muhammad's words and actions are preceded by careful lines of reference to the people who heard or saw these things, as well as reference to how these facts were transmitted from one hearer to the next. In this way, the "Thus have I heard" of the Buddhist sutras becomes, in the Hadith literature, a description of who heard the words of Muhammad, who heard the story next, and so on to the present author. For example, a Hadith may begin: "Narrated Anas ibn Malik from Malik ibn Sa'sa'a that Allah's Apostle [Muhammad] said. . . ." In this way, the authoritative word of Muhammad is established with historical language.

■ PROBLEMS OF "HISTORY"

In "historical language," the actual history often is difficult to discern.

Of course, in all this "historical language," the objective history may not be easy to discern. It is tempting to presume that any story of miracles and gods, however it may be placed within the context of real places, real people, and real times, must be false, and maybe we should relegate it to the category of myth. But as noted previously, it is a misunderstanding of both mythic and historical language to think that "history" means "true" and "myth" means "false." The issue of such language games, rather, is to read our texts carefully and thoughtfully, trying to sense the kind of rules established so that we do not expect to read mythological stories in the same manner we look at a historical narrative. That may indeed mean that historical language has a greater chance to be falsified for having made historically inaccurate statements, but this does not necessarily mean that historical language cannot offer insights into whatever is considered truth. And again, even "historical language" may not necessarily have as its main focus the relation of historical events.

Legends and epic tales may contain historical information but also have much nonfactual information.

The issue then might be to consider how we should expect religious followers to read their own texts. As we have seen, many do seem to insist that historical context and accuracy of placing events in time and space is valuable. Let us immediately admit, however, that there is a great deal of middle ground, such that many religious stories might be intended as historical language or might not. All that counts as legends and epic tales may contain pieces of historical information, and they may even be read historically by many. But it is difficult to know where history ends and enchanting tales begin. For example, an entire range of literature of Hinduism occupies a middle ground that might be called "epic literature," very much akin to the epics of Homer. The **Ramayana**, for example, is the tale of the wanderings of King Rama, as he, aided by his brother Lakshmana and the monkey deity Hanuman, battles the demon Ravana, who had stolen away Rama's wife. Another example is the poetic epic of the **Mahabharata**. Here, the five Pandava brothers, betrayed and robbed of their rightful inheritance of the kingdom, are exiled to the wilderness where they meet demons and gods in various adventures. They also develop a following of armies and amass powers in war, until finally the battle is fought to take back their rightful place in the kingdom. In this war, gods like Krishna and Shiva appear to counsel and guide, while great heroic exploits take place on and off the battlefield. But when did all this occur? Was there ever really a great war in the Bharat kingdom? Does it even matter?

Interestingly, there have been attempts to place the reign of Rama or the actions of Krishna during the Bharat war within some kind of recognizably historical time frame. Yet, as historian Romila Thapar has noted, this is a relatively recent phenomenon. It was not until the Muslim invasion, she suggests, that Hindus had much interest in specifying where Rama was born or where Krishna lived. Indeed, such questions may only have occurred to the Hindu mind as a later, "subconscious parallel with the prophet and the messiah" (69). That is, it may only have been a tendency to try to find a history within the epics after Hindus were more drastically introduced to those faiths for whom historical figures were central.

Although historical interest in the Hindu narratives is relatively late, recent efforts to place these events in history have flourished. Driven by the need to con-

Hindutva move-
ment—"Hindu-
ness" political
movement in
India attempting
to reclaim the
dominance of
Hindu culture

struct a political unity for Indian culture, the recent Hindutva movement has inspired speculation that the Bharat war, for example, must have occurred as early as 3100 BCE (Rajaram). Of course, such early placement would be fraught with anachronism, and thus historians like John Keay place any historical roots for such events in the Epic Period, 900 to 500 BCE. But even here, he notes, there are clear problems with stories of great kingdoms when in fact it seems that kingdoms were barely emerging as political realities. Ultimately, he says, there is just not enough concern for historical accuracy in the Hindu texts to find out if any real events or real persons were the basis for the accumulation of stories that became the great Hindu epics. "The historicity of a hero," he claims, "demands that his place and dates be established; no such figure graces Indian history until the Buddha illumines the scene after 500 BCE(39).

In finding historical roots, the Hindutva writers seek to establish a unity and identity for Hinduism beyond the religious amalgam labeled "Hinduism" by foreigners. Yet by the same token, they therefore open themselves to historical analyses that can easily show the error of placing marble palaces and horse-drawn chariots in events reportedly taking place in 3100 BCE. Similarly, the miracles of Moses and the exodus from slavery in Egypt may make for powerful "memories" that create a Jewish identity, defining the Jewish community and establishing the fulfillment of the Covenant, but they also raise questions about the archaeological and historical data of Palestine and Egypt in the second millennium BCE. If we had been there in the ninth century BCE and had seen a battle between forming kingdoms in the northern plains of India, or if we had been there and had seen the band of Hebrews leaving Egypt in 1250 BCE, would we really have seen the great acts of gods and heroes that are described there? Is there evidence left of the magnitude of these events? This is a difficult question to answer.

Historical lan-
guage may be less
than historical and
more than history.

But it is possible that historical language is both less than historical and more than history. German Biblical scholars, for example, have coined the term **heils-geschichte**, literally "salvation history," to describe the historical language of religious texts. This "salvation history" does not merely describe events in time and space but also interprets them as acts and intentions of God. Perhaps then, if we had stood on the walls of Jerusalem in 722 BCE and had seen the encampments of the armies of Sennacherib as they besieged the city, we would really have seen their fall into a mysterious sickness, leading to their withdrawal. And that might have been "history." But was it the work of the angel of death? Was this God's hand of deliverance? If we had seen those works of God in this history, that would be "salvation history."

In the end, then, historical religious language, like everything "religious" (as defined in this text), not only refers to events surrounding real people in real places, but it also necessarily seeks to connect those events and people to the Absolute. By opening the discussion to the "historical," this language game has different rules than, say, myth, and consequently historical language is arguable more dangerously open to falsification by historical study. At the same time, we cannot escape the nonhistorical, for example, explicitly religious, quality of this language game in its effort to find in "history" evidence of an Absolute Reality that transcends the world. That is perhaps both the power and the problem of religious historical language.

INSTRUCTION

All religions employ different types of language, though one type of language may dominate a given religion.

It should be obvious by now that there are many different language games that one might explore, and that within the general field of religion all of the language games can operate at different times and in different ways. We might note, too, that some religions could be expected to employ one language game more than another, inasmuch as the Tao of Taoism is unlike Yahweh of Judaism. The latter, we might expect, as God involved in the Covenant with the Jews, would inspire historical language and creation myth more than the former. Of course, we have by no means contended anything as simple as saying that Judaism is historical and Taoism is poetic. It is never so easy, and indeed, even discerning what language game is being used at any given time, or if what started out as "history" has changed to "poetry," or vice versa, it is often very difficult. Language in general is more variable than it might at times appear to the reader.

Happily, we might insert, there are aspects of religious language that are more straightforward than myth or poetry. We noted earlier in this chapter the contrast between the poem by Kilmer and a biology textbook that describes the chemical and physical properties of a tree, and after trying to interpret religious poetry, one may wish there were simply a religious textbook. Well, in fact there are some parts of religious literature that are at least more like a textbook than they are like poetry. We might call such literature "instructional." And like the biology book, it might be written with the intention of simply laying out information for the reader. Of course, we are dealing here with religion, not with trees, and "simple information" about God or Nirvana might be unavoidably problematic. Nevertheless, it is possible to find significant portions of religious literature that at least seem to be intended simply as instruction.

Most religions contain instructive language.

What kind of instruction are we dealing with here? Most likely, it seems, instructional language within religion focuses on two areas: belief and practice. In fact, much of what religious followers believe and much of what they do can be found in their scriptures and in other forms of religious literature as simple description. "Here is what we all believe," the scripture might declare, whether or not, in fact, "everyone" really believes it. Such a statement is rightly taken to be a declaration about doctrine, a statement of a truth claim about God or the nature of final judgment or about a thousand other things. "Here is what you should do and what you should not do," others might declare, and here again the point apparently is just to guide the followers.

Instructional materials in scripture take two forms: what we are forbidden to do and what we are to do.

Perhaps some basic examples of such instructive writing can be found in St. Paul's letters in the Christian New Testament and in a long list of the Buddha's sermons. In Paul's many letters, he is often evidently trying just to write Christian "information," clearly taking on the basic role of an instructor with information to divulge. Thus, for example, he starts his remarks on the Christian belief in the afterlife by informing the Christians in Thessalonica: "But we do not want you to be uninformed, brothers and sisters, about those who have died, so that you may not grieve as others do who have no hope" (1 Thessalonians 4:13). He then goes on to instruct the Thessalonians on what "we believe" about death and the resurrection. In other letters, Paul tells believers about the doctrines of salvation or how Judaism is related to Christianity, and many other aspects that Christians still read as instructions on proper doctrine. Similarly, he often writes instruction on proper behavior, telling husbands and wives in Colossae how to honor one another, or telling his disciple Timothy how the church should treat the older people and how they should choose their leaders. Of course, there are still disputes within Christianity about what Paul's words mean and how they are to be applied, but it at least seems that he intended these words to be read like instruction, not like a myth or a poem.

Similarly, in much of the literature of early Buddhism we meet the Buddha himself with disciples gathered around waiting for him simply to give instruction. A good example of this is found in the **Samyutta Nikaya**—that part of the Buddhist scriptures containing sutras or discourses either of the Buddha or his close disciples. After the declaration of where and when the Buddha spoke (see "history" earlier), the Buddha addressed the priests around him: "'Priests,' said he . . ., 'I will teach you, o priests, the burden, the bearer of the burden, the taking up of the burden, and the laying down of the burden,'" and then he proceeds to explain each of these four points successively (Warren 159–160). In other parts of the vast array of Buddhist scriptures, the Buddha instructs monks and nuns on how to run their monasteries, how to hold festivals, how to meditate, and even how to throw out of the community any monks and nuns who break specific rules (see "Pratimoksha Rules" in Conze 73–77). Again, whatever differences of opinion there may be between Buddhists about how to apply such rules, it seems clear that the intention of such literature, Buddhist or Christian, is basic instruction. Here's how to understand reality, say these teachers, and here's how to live.

An interesting but somewhat different subcategory of instructional text is called wisdom literature, especially evident in the Proverbs of the Hebrew Bible. Look at the following biblical verses:

Wine is a mocker and strong drink a brawler; and whoever is led astray by it is not wise. (Proverbs 20:1)

Riches do not profit in the day of wrath, but righteousness delivers from death. (11:4)

The crucible is for silver, and the furnace is for gold, but the LORD tests the heart. (17:3)

It is better to live in a corner of the housetop than in a house shared with a contentious wife. (25:24)

These verses first of all capture daily experiences and direct attention to common-sense notions among the members of the tribe, family, society, or nation. The very short structure of these aphorisms is easily inscribed into the memory. The purpose of these brief sayings therefore was not completely different in the ancient Middle East from what we have today in the quotations-of-the-day from the *New York Times*: namely, to notably characterize human experience and offer advice for different situations in life. However, in religious traditions such advice is not simply given because of common sense but receives its legitimacy from the religious belief of the people. In other words, these aphorisms are interesting examples of the correlation between daily life experience and what is believed to be Ultimate Reality. This is not merely aphoristic wisdom; it is wisdom from God.

Wisdom literature offers advice on day-to-day matters and relates these to the Ultimate.

Beyond such basic writings, of course, religions of all kinds can develop, and have developed, into complex and detailed philosophies and theologies. Often as a kind of second-generation phenomenon, men and women with philosophical minds arise within many religious traditions and set about systematizing the ideas, developing arguments and descriptions for their major religious ideas. We have already discussed philosophy and theology as an addition to "Scripture" in the previous chapter. For now, it can just be added that these writings, too, are sometimes an important part of religious instructional language. Thus, St. Augustine in the fourth century used philosophical categories from Plato to explore and explain Christianity, just as the Islamic philosopher and physician Avicenna (980–1037 CE) in the 11th century used Aristotle to explain Islam. Influenced by Mahayana Buddhism, Sankara in ninth-century India developed in detail the Hindu **Advaitin theories,** which claim the oneness of Ultimate Reality and hold Brahman is Atman (the soul). Likewise, the Neo-Confucians, like Wang Yang-ming in the 16th century, explained and restructured the ancient religions of China. All these philosophical and theological writers formulated and systematized doctrine, argued detailed points of theology or justified less-than-obvious points of behavior and belief, using careful argument and subtle explanations. And by quoting scripture and founders as authority, all of them tried to emphasize that this was no more than careful instruction in religious truth.

Philosophers and theologians expand upon, explain, and fine-tune teachings found in scriptures.

It should be clear by now, however, that there is nothing simple about reading a text that appears to be "careful instruction." For much instruction is also poetic, and much of the poetic instruction might refer to myths. Some instruction is even tongue-in-cheek, half-serious attempts to make a religious point by appealing to the readers' or hearers' sense of humor. We have already talked here about poetry and myth, and their mixtures with instruction might offer us numerous other examples. But the point for now is only to remind the student that no reading of scripture, not even "history" or "instruction," is simple.

HUMOR

Having mentioned humor, let us consider briefly this fascinating language game. An especially intriguing fact about humor is that jokes and anecdotes often begin as if they were true stories. Humor thus occasionally finds its fuel precisely in being able to confuse the listeners, hoping they will believe the narrative is history or instruction up until the punch line. At other times, humor works by twisting or grossly exaggerating what is well-known, thus surprising the audience with clever observations of daily life. Thus, the humorous is often simply the normal seen or expressed in new ways.

The trickster in Native American and other religions illustrates the use of humor to make religious points.

A notable case of humor invading traditional mythic language is the presence of the trickster in Native American myths. Here we see tribal cultures sometimes using odd tales of animals to explain how the momentous facts of life came to be. And often, these tales are intentionally humorous even if grave and serious in their apparent explanations. For example, Coyote is a classic trickster in some Native American tales, including stories that describe the relation between the native peoples and the white men. Two humorous stories tell of how Coyote trades with white men. In one case, Coyote brags to a white man of being a great trader, but, he explains, he needs his magical "cheating medicine" to really perform it well. The white man, wanting to see this "cheating medicine," loans Coyote his horse and his clothes so that the trickster can ride home quickly and get the medicine. But, of course, Coyote just rides away with the man's horse and clothes and never returns. In a similar tale, Coyote puts money up a burro's rear end and tells the white trader that if one kicks this burro in the stomach, this burro poops out money. Coyote demonstrates the phenomenon and sells the burro to the white man for a considerable profit (Erdoes and Ortiz 342, 371).

Gentle mockery is another form of humor used in scripture.

The tradition of gentle mockery, as a form of religious instruction, might be evident also in many standard jokes of Jewish humor. Notably, there are also jokes here that are somewhat self-mocking yet are revealing of the Jewish way of life and the Judaic attitude toward their own religion. It is a Jewish comment, for example, to say that "for every two Jews there are three opinions." The insight of such humor is precisely that Jews are trained and encouraged to argue and debate any topic, beginning with their own religious precepts. That is why the great corpus of Jewish literature, the **Talmud,** is essentially a book of prolonged argument by great rabbis about the meaning of the Torah. In one humorous tale, a young rabbi who gets drunk and is dumped by his friends into a graveyard awakens perplexed and wonders if he is dead. He decides to apply "Talmudic logic" and therefore reasons like this:

First, my powers of observation tell me I am in a cemetery. Therefore, I must be dead. But, secondly, I cannot be dead if my powers of observation are still working. The only logical conclusion, then, is that I am alive. Still, if I am alive, what am I doing in a cemetery? And on the other hand, if I am dead, why do I have to go to the bathroom? (Spalding 392)

In the Zen Buddhist tradition, we have already seen that straightforward teaching of Nirvana or Enlightenment is, in a sense, impossible, and we saw in conjunction with that fact the reliance upon poetry to express the experience of awakening. Some of the famous tales of enlightenment used as koans are clever tales of interplay between master and student that illuminate some important aspect of Zen teaching. In one story, the student is deep in meditation when the master interrupts and asks the student what he is doing. "I am becoming a Buddha," the student declares. The master then picks up a stone tile and begins to polish it with his hand. Distracted, the student asks the master what he is doing, and the master says he is making a mirror. "How can you make a mirror by polishing a tile?" the student asks. The teacher replies rhetorically, "How can you make a Buddha by practicing meditation?" (See Dumoulin 163.)

koan—instructive stories in Zen Buddhism meant to perplex the rational mind so that enlightenment can appear.

Perhaps the finest example that contains both the pleasant mockery of one's opponent and a sense of the inadequacy of normal instruction comes from the Taoist literature of Chuang Tzu. In many of the tales from Chuang Tzu, Confucius is used as a foil, sometimes made to be the confused or inadequate teacher of worldly, social virtues, and sometimes made to speak Taoist wisdom quite in contradiction to the principles of Confucianism. Thus, in one story, Confucius helps a student "forget everything," including "right and wrong" and the "rituals and music" that define Confucian ideals. And then, when the student succeeds in having no understanding and simply being "identical with the Great

Thoroughfare," Confucius humbly says, "with your permission, I'd like to become your follower" (Watson 87).

Having had all this labeled "humor," one might be disappointed that none of it is very funny. That's okay. Our point here is not merely to entertain, but of course it is nice if some entertainment is possible without losing either the message or the seriousness of the message. The point of noting humor here is then really just to acknowledge yet one more language game among the numerous possible language games, one more confusion perhaps in the great collection of words and stories and instructions that make up religious literature. Of course, the writers and speakers of religious literature have lives as broad as you and I, lives that contain lamentation, assertion, metaphor, exaggeration, humor, poetry, and maybe downright lies. And our job, as we read and as we listen, is the same with religious language as it is in all forms of communication: to listen and read carefully and thoughtfully and to try to understand what the writers and speakers mean. And whether we agree with some religious worldview or not, we might well understand what claims of metaphysical truth are being conveyed in religious instruction or what claims of history are being made in a legend of the distant past. Similarly, we can see what is humorous in some pieces of religious literature whether or not we think it is funny.

An awareness of various types of language games will help understand scriptures' meaning.

SILENCE

Saying nothing is also a way to communicate in religion.

It might well be noted that all of this discussion on the various uses of religious language—its stories, myths, poems, and jokes—overlooks the very important fact that sometimes saying nothing at all is also a way to communicate. This is especially true in religion in which we often deal with religious concepts that explicitly go beyond what can be fully known or fully described. There is an almost necessary element of the ineffable in religion, as we have noted since Chapter 2: What is Religion? In that discussion of the "Holy," it was observed that the Ultimate Reality is often said to be beyond description, beyond affirmation. Like the Brahman of Hinduism, it is *"neti-neti,"* and therefore, as the Tao Te Ching asserts, it is often true that

> *Those who are skilled (in the Tao) do not dispute (about it); the disputatious are not skilled in it. Those who know (the Tao) are not extensively learned; the extensively learned do not know it. (McIntyre Chapter 81)*

Zen Buddhism offers particularly notable examples of the preference for silence in a number of stories associated with the transmission of Zen enlightenment from teacher to student. One tale describes how the master Bodhidharma passes his authority as teacher to his student, Hui-k'o:

> *Nine years had passed and he [Bodhidharma] now wished to return westward to India. He called his disciples and said: "The time has now come. Why doesn't each of you say what you have attained?"*
> *Then the disciple Tao-fu replied: "As I see it, [the truth] neither adheres to words or letters, nor is it apart from them. It functions as the Way." The master said: "You have attained my skin."*

A nun Tsung-ch'ih said: "As I understand it, [the truth] is like the auspicious glimpse of the Buddha land of Aksobhya; it is seen once, but not a second time." The master said: "You have attained my flesh."

Tao-yu said: "The four great elements are originally empty; the five skandhas have no existence. As I believe, no Dharma can be grasped." The master said: "You have attained my bones."

Finally there was Hui-k'o. He bowed respectfully and stood silent. The master said: "You have attained my marrow." (Dumoulin 93)

Silence may as well be a form of communication with the Ultimate that is beyond description.

Silence, too, may be a form of communication, indeed a vital one when the point or concept to be communicated is beyond description. Does silence always mean that we have reached the end of description and moved into profound insight into the Ultimate Reality? Or does it sometimes mean we really have nothing to say? Even in everyday life, silence might be the quiet, consoling presence of a friend when we are sad, or it might be someone holding his or her tongue to keep from saying something mean, or it may be a very eloquent expression of anger. How do we know which? We watch and look; we search for context and probable intention. We choose our response depending on the meaning we think the "writer" of the silence intends, and of course we could be mistaken.

But that is the way with all language games. We have seen that trying to decipher text or speech is often a matter of trying to read between the lines what the author was trying to do, what language game the author was intending to play, and what game the reader is involved in interpreting the text. We have seen that it is not always obvious which language is intended, or indeed if there is more than one "game" being played. We decipher the rules from context and signs and from an occasional explicit reference to the form and content of the author's work. But we could be mistaken. Nevertheless, knowing we could err in how we read and comprehend text is no reason to avoid delving deeply into the religious language of the great spiritual texts of the world. It is a reason only for reading with care and thoughtfulness and with some humility.

GLOBALIZATION, HISTORY, AND FAITH

Earlier in this chapter we discussed historical materials as they related to scripture and other documents of faith. We indicated that the stress on scientific, objective history developed first in the 19th century in Western Europe and then spread to other parts of the modern world. By **scientific (objective) history,** we mean the approach to history based on the assumption that history is composed of factual events that can be investigated by objective data. In other words, people have come to believe that history is made up of facts and historians merely report these facts. This mindset is pervasive in the developed world. Thanks to modernization and globalization, it is spreading to most other regions of the world as well.

The assumptions associated with scientific history are relatively new.

It is important to re-emphasize at this juncture that this is a *new* approach. Most "historians" who wrote "histories" prior to the 19th century were not concerned with merely writing accounts of objective events but were writing with a particular purpose in mind. As a result, they often combined myth, legend, objective material, and their own interpretations of this material in their accounts. Thus, the Christian gospels along with other New Testament materials, such as the book of the Acts of the Apostles, were written to prove theological points or as tracts intended to bring various audiences like Jews or Greeks to believe that Jesus was the Messiah, the Son of God, and/or the eternal *Logos* made flesh. The goal of this writing was not to record the facts but to bring the audience to salvation.

The Christian writer of the Gospel of John makes exactly this point, "Now Jesus did many other signs in the presence of his disciples, which are not written in this book. But these are written so that you may come to believe Jesus is the Messiah, the Son of God, and through believing may have life in his name" (John 20:30–31). Earlier in this chapter we recommended that students realize that much historical writing is not objective history, but "salvation history." So it is that this type of literature needs to be read using the "language rules" appropriate for it.

Our point here is not merely to rehash earlier parts of the chapter. Rather, we want to look briefly at the impact of the spread of scientific history on communities of faith. The most immediate impact was on Western Christianity. We first review how Western Christians reacted to modern history. Then we propose that something similar to this is happening as objective history encounters faith traditions around the world.

Some of the impact already has been mentioned in this chapter. One outcome was an increasing effort to find verifiable evidence for the "historical" claims and events of religious traditions. A great deal of archeological and related historically oriented research has been undertaken in this vein. This has resulted in a vast expansion of knowledge regarding the socio-historical context of the development of various religions, including Christianity. This in itself has provided rich new sources for understanding and interpreting many of the world's religions.

Another more subtle, but perhaps more important, reaction is to change the standard of truth for religious materials. Scientific objectivity became the ultimate criterion for determining truth (see Chapter 1: Religion in Global Society). The insistence, therefore, became that religious stories and teachings not just be morally or religiously true but objectively true as well. For instance, it was no longer enough for the myths of a religion to define how the faithful understand their place in the universe, their relation to the spiritual world, and the meaning for their lives. Now they must be *factually* true as well.

In fact, for many Western Christians, "factual" (objective) truth of these stories became the prime issue. The defense of their faith became a defense of the historical reliability of their religious stories. Many came to believe that if even their mythical accounts were not factual, their entire faith was undermined.

So it is that there literally must be six (24-hour) days of creation, a single first man called Adam and a single first woman called Eve, a Garden of Eden, and a temptation by a talking snake in the Garden as indicated in the biblical book of Genesis, or all of the Christian faith was seen as invalid. To indicate that any of these were not objectively true was to deny the Christian faith. To question these even on the basis of reliable objective data creates great distress, produces a "battle for the Bible," and demands a vigorous, aggressive defense. If the scientific data seemed to support religious stories, then science and scientific data were acceptable. But if the data disagreed with the religious stories, then, at best, science was obviously mistaken; at worst, it was the tool of the Devil to lead the unwary astray.

Thus discussions of scriptures, socially constructed worlds, and historicity of religious stories became major issues for Christians feeling threatened by the emerging scientific, modern world. This lead to a number of backlashes against the challenges posed by modernism (see also Chapters 1: Religion in Global Society, 5: World Scriptures, and 14: Religion and Society in a Global Age). None of these is more important than the publication of *The Fundamentals* early in the 20th century in the United States. This series of pamphlets sought to define the fundamentals of the Christian faith that could not change in the face of modernism. "There are five fundamentals:

1. The inerrancy of the Scriptures (often coupled with a theory of verbal inspiration).
2. The virgin birth of Christ.
3. The satisfaction theory of the Atonement (as the only one taught in the Bible).
4. The physical, bodily Resurrection of Christ.
5. The impending return of the Lord. (Others held his earthly miracles were essential)." (Peterson 319)

We cannot go into each of these individually at this time. We need only to say at this point that all of these represent what was defined (rightly or wrongly) as *the* historical position of the church on these issues. These things could not be questioned from within or without the faith. It was this emphasis on the fundamentals that led to labeling those who opposed aspects of modernism as "Fundamentalists." The passionate defense of the fundamentals led to aggressive efforts to ferret out from pulpits, denominational offices, and educational institutions those who questioned these views.

As is implied previously, not all Christians had the same reaction to changes brought on by science, including those associated with scientific history. Many, if not most, Western Christians came to accept the data discovered by science and learned to live more or less comfortably with the implications of these data. This was the case even when these data contradicted traditionally held views, such as a literal six days of creation, Moses' authorship of the Torah, the authorship of the Christian Gospels by first-century disciples of Jesus, and, even, the historicity of Jesus' life and teachings as presented in the Gospels. This category of Christians are variously labeled "Modernists," "Moderates," and "Liberals." This category has had a long and continuing battle with Fundamentalists (or Conservatives or Evangelical Christians, as they prefer to be called in the United States).

A third category of reaction to the findings of modern historical and scientific findings also is apparent. This group believes that modern science and objective history do not support the stories and claims of religion. Since science provides the predominant worldview in today's world, they believe that, at best, religion is unnecessary and, at worse, it is dangerous and misleading. This category may

The publication of The Fundamentals was an important development in the reaction against modern science.

Those Christians who oppose selected parts of modernism came to be known as "Fundamentalists."

Those Christians who accommodate modern science and objective history are called Modernist (Moderate Liberals).

A third category of Westerners reacted by abandoning religion altogether (Secularists, Atheists, Agnostics).

be called Agnostics, Atheists, or Secularists. In any case, they have replaced a religious, spiritual understanding of humans and the universe with a materialistic, secular one.

We have seen all of the reactions above as modernism and globalization have spread scientific history worldwide. Hinduism, Buddhism, Judaism, Islam, and other religions have their fundamental, moderate, and secular factions. These do not necessarily share the same beliefs as their counterpoints in other religions. The key is that each category shares a common reaction to modernism and globalizing trends as well. Probably, moderates are the dominant category in all religions. However, the Fundamentalists are the most vocal. They also are most successful at putting together socio-religious movements to push their social and political agenda. They tend to be the most aggressive in promoting their perspective. On the whole, Moderates and Secularists tend to be more accepting of opposing viewpoints and more tolerant of pluralism.

CONCLUSION

Written or spoken language must be interpreted to be understood. This is especially true when we look at sacred texts. To simply lump all texts into a single category and assume the same language games apply to all types of religious literature leads to misunderstanding. To have understanding, we must know the type of language being employed, the language game being used, and the rules of interpreting that particular type of language.

Failure to employ the proper rules of the game may lead to misunderstanding, and even conflict. As we look at various religious-based bloodshed on a global scale, we are made aware that the "language games" are not just academic exercises. They have practical applications as well. Differences in understanding the "rules of the game" or applying different rules to the same scripture passage may lead to divisions within a given religious community and separate one religion from another. Since religion deals with the deepest emotions of humans, disagreement over language games can result in hatred and violent behaviors.

■ INTERACTIVE EXERCISE

Please continue your exploration of religious stories and myths by going to the interactive exercise for this chapter online (**http://www.religion.wadsworth.com/richter**).

WORKS CITED

"As Rabbis Face Facts, Bible Tales Are Wilting." *New York Times* [New York] March 9, 2002.

Conze, E. *Buddhist Scriptures*. Baltimore, MD: Penguin, 1959.

Dumoulin, Heinrich. *Zen Buddhism: A History*. Vol. 1. New York: Macmillan, 1988.

Eliade, Mircea. *Myth and Reality.* Trans. Willard R. Trask. New York: Hayser Colophon Books, 1963.

Erdoes, Richard, and Alfonso Ortiz. *American Indian Myths and Legends.* New York: Pantheon, 1984.

Fieser, James, and John Powers. *Scriptures of the World's Religions.* Boston: McGraw-Hill, 1998.

Frei, John. *The Eclipse of Biblical Narrative.* New Haven, CT: Yale University Press, 1974.

Keay, John. *India: A History.* New York: Atlantic Monthly Press, 2000.

Kilmer, Joyce. *Anthology of Catholic Poets.* New York: Liveright, 1955.

Leeming, David A. *The World of Myth.* New York: Oxford University Press, 1990.

Leggett, Trevor. *A First Zen Reader.* Ritland, VT: Charles E. Tuttle, 1960.

Long, Charles. *Alpha: The Myths of Creation.* New York: G. Braziller, 1963.

McIntyre, Stephen R. *Tao Te Ching.* 2003. Trans. James Legge. June 6, 2004. http://nothingistic.org.

Peters, F. E. *A Reader on Classical Islam.* Princeton, NJ: Princeton University Press, 1994.

Peterson, R. Dean. *A Concise History of Christianity.* 2nd ed. Belmont, CA: Wadsworth, 2000.

Rajaram, N. S. *Search for the Historical Krishna.* http://www.swordoftruth.com/swordortruth/archive (accessed November 26, 2003).

Rao, Shanta R., Shanta Rameshwar, and Badri Narayan. *The Mahabharata.* Chennai, India: Orient Longman, 1985.

Spalding, Henry D. *A Treasure Trove of American Jewish Humor.* New York: Jonathon Davis, 1976.

Stryk, Lucien. *The World of the Buddha.* New York: Grove Weidenfeld, 1968.

Tacitus, Cornelus. *The Annals and the Histories.* Chicago: Encyclopedia Brittanica, 1955.

Thapar, Romila. *Interpreting Early India.* Oxford, UK: Oxford University Press, 1992.

Warren, Henry Clarke. *Buddhism in Translations.* New York: Athaneum, 1982.

Watson, Burton, trans. *Chuang Tzu: Basic Writings.* New York: Columbia University Press, 1964.

Wittgenstein, Ludwig. *Philosophical Investigations.* Sec. 23. 2nd ed. Malden, MA: Blackwell, 2001.

FOR FURTHER READING

Armstrong, Karen. *The Battle for God.* New York: Ballentine, 2001.

Campbell, Joseph. *The Power of Myth: Joseph Campbell with Bill Moyers.* Ed. Betty Sue Flowers. New York: Doubleday, 1988.

Eliade, Mircea. *Myth and Reality*. Trans. Willard R. Trask. New York: Hayser Colophon Books, 1963.

Erdoes, Richard, and Alfonso Ortiz. *American Indian Myths and Legends*. New York: Pantheon, 1984.

Leggett, Trevor. *A First Zen Reader*. Ritland, VT: Charles E. Tuttle, 1960.

Leeming, David A. *The World of Myth*. New York: Oxford University Press, 1990.

Spalding, Henry D. *A Treasure Trove of American Jewish Humor*. New York: Jonathon Davis, 1976.

Suzaki, D. T. "Illogical Zen." *An Introduction to Zen Buddhism*. New York: Grove, 1964.

Wittgenstein, Ludwig. *Philosophical Investigations*. Sec. 23. 2nd ed. Massachusetts: Blackwell, 2001.

7 SUFFERING AND EVIL

Getty Images/PhotoDisc Collection

Sorrow and suffering, death and devastation seem to be all around us. For most religions, this fact is very important. Indeed, it is possible that the human response to suffering and the reality of evil around us are key elements to defining how religions function in human life. In the pictures found above and on the Web site (**http://www.religion.wadsworth.com/richter**), and in the scriptural quotations that follow, there are examples and religious responses to suffering and evil. Consider these cases and then think over the Introductory Questions that follow as a way to prepare for reading this chapter.

See, the Lord's hand is not too short to save, nor his ear too dull to hear. Rather, your iniquities have been barriers between you and your God, and your sins have hidden his face from you so that he does not hear.

—Judaism: Isaiah 59: 1–2

As he walked along, [Jesus] saw a man blind from birth. His disciples asked him, "Rabbi, who sinned, this man or his parents, that he was born blind?" Jesus answered, "Neither this man nor his parents sinned; he was born blind so that God's works might be revealed in him."

—Christianity: The Gospel of John 9:1–3

Suddenly Master Lai grew ill. Gasping and wheezing, he lay at the point of death. His wife and children gathered round in a circle and began to cry. Master Li, who had come to ask how he was, said, "Shoo! Get back! Don't disturb the process of change!" Master Lai said, "A child obeying his father and mother goes wherever he is told, east or west, south or north. And the yin and yang—how much more are they to a man than father or mother! Now that they have brought me to the verge of death, if I should refuse to obey them, how perverse I would be!"

—Taoism: Chuang Tzu (Watson 81)

Ngewo sent two messengers to a certain town to carry news of death and life. On the way, the dog met a woman cooking food for her child. He lay down and waited. But the toad had not stopped along the way. He reached the town first and entered, crying "Death has come!" Then the dog came running, crying, "Life has come!" But he was too late. The toad had brought death first. That is why people die.

—Mende Tribal Myth (Scheub 174–175)

INTRODUCTORY QUESTIONS

These passages and pictures suggest several different expressions of, and perhaps explanations for, the suffering we know in the world. Please consider the following questions as a way to prepare for reading this chapter.

1. As the Isaiah passage suggests, perhaps our suffering, including our separation from God, is our own fault. In the story of Noah's ark, depicted on the Web site, human suffering is again due to human "sin," and God

rows? If there is a God, would God be rightly angry at human behavior?

2. In the Mende myth, the coming of death is attributed to an almost whimsical error on the part of the dog. Does it seem that death is much more serious than this?

3. Master Lai seems to accept his suffering easily. Job, in the picture on the Web site, ponders his agony and wonders why God would inflict him with this terror. Why do you think these two pictures are so different?

4. If you were to take some religious view, how might you explain the similarities and differences between the depicted tornado and the death of the students at Columbine High School?

5. It seems in the end that Job's suffering was *not* divine punishment, and Jesus says explicitly that the blind man in the story is not suffering because of sin. What other reasons might there be for God to give or allow suffering?

6. The Buddha is shown in the process of starving himself as a means of gaining spiritual development. How might suffering be something a religious person would seek? Does this make sense to you?

7. If you try to take *no* religious position, how would you talk to a suffering Job? What would you say to the starving Buddha? To Master Lai?

INTRODUCTION

As we have seen, religions all over the world look beyond the world in a variety of ways to seek out the Holy, the Absolute. And we have also seen that the stories and myths that develop out of these religions often tie the Absolute to the world in fascinating and curious ways, hoping to make sense of life by imaging how that life came about and how life continues to depend upon the Reality beyond life. From the beginning, we have noted that the power and significance of religion lies not merely in some fanciful imagination but in the real effects and importance that religion has in the way we live and, indeed, in who we think we are. There is arguably no force in the world, even counting science and politics, that attempts to go so far making sense of our lives and defining our existence as does religion.

We will examine the breadth and significance of the effects of religion on human life as we continue through this book. We will note how morality and sense of purpose, hopes for meaning and the possibilities of immortality are all bound up with religious consciousness that sees their rationale in connection with the Absolute. These are all practical matters for very many people, and whatever science or political ideologies might assert about such beliefs and justifications, it remains true that the power of religion to guide life is pervasive. Indeed, one might argue that religion has at times, and perhaps still does, guide both science and politics.

Religions often are concerned with suffering.

As we look to these practical implications of religion, one of the most pressing issues has always been the connection between religions and suffering. Sorrow and disappointment, disease and death are facts of our existence, and as facts they cry out for explanation as surely as we wonder why the sun rises or the tides flow. For philosophical purposes and for convenience of reference, writers on this topic have often divided the sufferings and evils of life into two categories: moral evils and natural evils. The first term describes those acts of human beings that seem clearly villainous and evil. From world wars to petty jealousies, we find it more than obvious that human beings manage to perpetrate great evils upon one another. Without leaping into the discussion of ethics (see Chapter 10: Religion, Morality, and Ethics), we can argue that the Nazi genocide of the Jews was simply wrong, and that a conniving and vicious employee spreading intentionally cruel rumors about a co-worker is, though obviously less horrifying, also despicable. And so we may be driven to ask why such things occur, why there is such cruelty and heartlessness in this human heart—a heart, we might note, that equally prides itself on its religious zeal and morally idealistic aspirations.

Similarly, we wonder about "natural evils." Here we speak not of what humankind has done but about what nature has done to human beings. Earthquakes and tornadoes destroy villages and individual lives, while diseases eat up human bodies and decimate entire civilizations. These works of "evil" are not done by human hands, but they are certainly part of the pains of life. And whatever beauty we may have found in nature as evidence of the glory of God or the oneness of the **Wakan** beings of Sioux religion, nature is not evidently our constant friend. And so we wonder why there is disaster, as we wonder why human beings destroy other human beings.

Therefore, just as truly as the existence of the physical world around us calls us to understand our world through science and myth, so religions often develop their own theologies and myths to explain the world's suffering and to give it meaning. Indeed, as noted in the previous chapter, mythic stories often try to explore precisely these kinds of issues, rooting cosmic meaning in the reality of the Absolute. Thus mythic stories, from Pandora's Box to the Fall of Adam, are often a significant part of a religious worldview seeking to explain and make sense of our world. And as truly as God Almighty made the heavens and the earth, the Judaic believer might claim, so truly also does the story of sin and fall explain the sorrow and ugliness of our world.

This effort to explain suffering is a significant part of religion and is one of the key functional elements that makes religion work in believers' lives. In fact, it is arguably the most crucial functional element in religion, and as such it can sometimes become the key factor in explaining why people do or do not follow a religion. Is religion merely the superstitious response to the fear of death? Do we invent gods in the clouds only because we cannot control and because we continue to fear the rage of lightning and thunder? Perhaps. But as usual, reductionistic explanations are not our real purpose here. Nevertheless, it is valuable to consider this central functional role of religion, as it explains our lives of sorrow and loss, and to see how different religions seek to make sense of evil. We shall see, then, an overall theoretical explanation of how and why religions seek to explain suffering and evil, and we shall see, as suggested in the opening quotations of this chapter, that the way different religions explain the sorrows of life can vary greatly. But we will also see that these explanations are neither random nor irrational. Rather, they are intimately tied to the religiously rational connection between the world around us and the Absolute beyond us. That is, the sorrows and sufferings of life will find their specific religious meanings by relating to the specific religious Absolute that defines the core of each religion.

THE SACRED CANOPY

We have noted previously that it is possible, perhaps even tempting, to explain religion in general in terms of one of its functions, and that the explanation of human suffering is perhaps one of the most important functions of religion in human psychology. If we can understand our suffering, see it as the result of divine guidance or karmic retribution, at least the sorrows of our lives can make sense to us and seem less like the wild nonsense of a meaningless chaos. Of course, it is unnecessary to argue whether religion is *only* a means of psychological comfort in the face of sorrow. But we do need to consider how important religion is in providing a sense of meaning within chaos.

Socially constructed religious worlds help people stave off the chaos of life.

This point has been made by sociologist Peter Berger in a book entitled *The Sacred Canopy* (1967). Here, Berger suggests that it is precisely the chaos of life, especially disaster and suffering, that inspires the social construction of religious worlds. He means that life by itself, unfiltered and unexplained by concepts of spirit and divinity, can easily appear to us as chaotic and meaningless, and therefore all people hunger for explanation. We want to make this chaos into a cosmos, Berger suggests, for example, to change the wild unpredictability of the world into an ordered whole, make it into a "world." And religion is one of our tools for world building.

The problem, Berger argues, is described as **anomie**, a term meaning most literally the absence of order and law. When the world runs "normally," that is, when we live our lives with steady work and a dependable influx of food and basic comforts, we hardly notice life itself. But now and then we are met with "marginal situations," situations in life that threaten the core of our behavior and the comfort of our habits of survival. Crops fail when the rains refuse to fall, children get ill, people in society disagree and fight among themselves, and in all these cases we are pushed outside of the normality of life. That is why we ask about the purpose of life and wonder what these sorrowful events can mean. Death, says Berger, is "the marginal situation par excellence" (23). For here, whether we see the death of another or expect our own, life must be disrupted. And we cannot help but wonder why.

■ THEODICY

For Berger, this is above all a social problem, and society therefore comes together to construct an explanation. Thus religion is born. Regardless of whether this is an accurate explanation for the genesis of religion *per se*, we see in this theory that explaining suffering is a fundamental part of all religion, and thus all religion, Berger concludes, contains theodicy. Technically the word means "divine justice," having as part of its root the Greek word for "god," *theos*. We shall look later at specific theodicies— efforts to explain philosophically why God or the gods create or allow the suffering of their (presumably) beloved humans. For now, we might note that the word is, to an extent, inaccurate as Berger uses it, since many theodicies have nothing to do with God or gods. Nevertheless, for Berger, the term is taken to refer to any religious effort to make sense of suffering in the face of the Sacred. For if the Sacred is the very basis of meaning and order, then the social reality of suffering and death is a challenge not to be

For sociologist Peter Berger, theodicy means religious effort to make sense of suffering in the face of the Sacred.

ignored. "Every human order," he says, "is a community in the face of death. Theodicy represents the attempt to make a pact with death" (80). Invariably, he points out, we suffer and we die, and our religion owes us an explanation.

Perhaps it seems odd that religion in particular has this duty of explanation. One might consider that science, after all, tells us more accurately why we suffer. Indeed, modern medicine tells us much more clearly than some tribal shaman why we have pains in the liver or spots before our eyes. And it seems unlikely that a modern city dweller, even if sympathetic toward "the tribal way of life," would take an ailing child to the witch doctor. No, we expect that a medically trained professional will truly explain our suffering, and consequently a theodicy is not necessary. Headaches are caused by high blood pressure and death is from old age; divine wrath is irrelevant.

But such explanations miss the point. If two friends are caught in a lightning storm and one of them is struck and killed, we can well imagine that the survivor might later ask, "Why did this happen?" But it would be strange, and perhaps simply unkind, if we approached him in his grief and answered that the rain droplets in the sky build up an electric charge that needs to be discharged into the earth and that the electrical conduit of discharge just happened to be his friend. With such a causal explanation of how lightning strikes, the surviving friend is unlikely to respond, "Oh, that explains it! Thanks!" Indeed, all such physical explanations of why disasters occur, or of what makes us sick or why we die, are not enough. We seek not causal explanations but explanations offering meaning.

When people ask why suffering occurs, they are not looking for scientific (causal) explanations but religious explanations offering meaning.

Similarly, nature itself may seem to offer a scientific explanation of death and suffering, inasmuch as the evolutionary process known as "natural selection" is inherently built upon the idea of death. That is, from an evolutionary standpoint, there is no mystery to death, and indeed all the life we see around us, including the tremendous harmony of natural ecosystems, is unquestionably dependent upon a bloody kaleidoscope of death, especially death of the young and frail. It is well-known, for example, that sea turtles lay thousands of eggs on Mexican shores and leave those nests in months of sun for their eggs' incubation. Then, on one night, the thousands upon thousands of tiny sea turtles climb forth and frantically scramble to the sea. On the way, however, they are a massive feast for sea birds and other predators that literally eat as much as they can of these cute, little babies. For a thousand born, a hundred make it to the sea, where more predators, fish of many kinds, begin yet another feast. And thus the few that survive and perhaps live to adulthood do so only because so many died that the predators could not quite eat them all. It is a well-known evolutionary principle that a thousand times more young are born than can survive. Spiders lay eggs on paralyzed worms so their young can eat the worm alive; wolves drag down a young elk and eat its entrails while it yet breathes. Nature overproduces offspring by the thousands and thousands so that they can die, so that only the strong will live. Thus, nature improves and maintains her luxuriant species only with a million deaths, many a great deal more gory than what the worst of human criminals might have devised.

No, nature is not a model for us here. As Francis Schaeffer has pointed out, it was the observation that men are generally stronger than women that justified to the Marquis de Sade that men may rightly abuse women for their own pleasure (177). Nature is cruel as much as benign, he stressed, and if we are to look for meaning and moral hope, we need to look elsewhere. And thus people often look beyond nature, to "supernature," that is, to the supernatural. Even those who would find an overall harmony in some natural beauty may be presuming a unity and beauty in Nature (notice the capital) that makes it (or "Her") qualify as a sacred Absolute. Thus, the point might be made that religion, with its ultimate appeal to a higher Reality, is a natural place for humans to go when they seek some unity and meaning, some harmony and hope beyond the death and chaos of life. And just as we once traced the various "holy" objects of a specific religion to that great Something, the Absolute that is holy in itself, so here we trace the search for the meaning and purpose of suffering back to Something outside the world of death and sorrow. And this, for religious people, is the Holy.

Religions' answers to the "whys" of existence vary as much as the religions themselves.

This is the logic of religion's answer to the problems of suffering and death. Chaos and evils, the moral perpetrations of villainous humans and the wild, capricious disasters of an uncaring nature—moral evils and natural evils—cry out for explanation that goes beyond causal descriptions of physical forces. Yes, lightning strikes the earth, but why here, why now—why me? Religions answer such questions, or at least they try to, and the answers will, of course, vary as much as the religions vary. Overall, we might hope to find explanations of why such things happen at all, what lessons might be learned from this or that event, and what might be done in the future to avert such disasters—or to redeem them. Through it all, the religions of the world thus provide a sacred meaning, a "sacred canopy," to make sense of the senselessness of the world's suffering. How well the religions succeed in this endeavor to explain and comfort is a matter of philosophical contemplation and soul-searching reflection.

ORIGINS OF EVIL

It has long been a problem in the philosophy of the Western religions that the world of moral and natural evils is supposedly the creative work of a God of love and compassion. If, however, this God is good, why, we wonder, did God create a world so full of suffering? It is perhaps less recognized that the same problem exists in other religions. For it is clear that, for many Buddhist sects, we are supposed to be of pure minds, naturally endowed with an innately perfect consciousness, and yet we are deluded and misguided. In mystical Hinduism, similarly, we are all essentially "one with the One," part of the great purity that is Brahman. Yet somehow, the One became many, or at least seemed to, and the self-division of the great unity of being now constitutes the problem of human ignorance and worldly delusion. How shall we understand these things? If we begin to speculate on the sufferings and sorrows of life, we find that we must ultimately consider how suffering, whether physical pain or conceptual error, even *can* exist, given the reality of the Holy.

Religions must somehow reconcile a pure and, perhaps, loving Holy with the fact of suffering in the world.

■ THE "FALL"

For the primary theistic religions, an understanding of how evil begins is given mythic description. As we noted previously, these Abrahamic religions contain a standard myth intended to explore the nature of creation and the reason for its

The Abrahamic
religions link their
understanding of
the Fall (or sin) of
Adam and Eve in
the Garden of
Eden to the origin
of suffering.

brokenness. This is the myth of the Fall, or the story of Adam and Eve in the Garden of Eden. As noted in that discussion of myths, our point in this text is not to debate the historical claims that might be hidden or explicit in this myth but to note how the tale indicates the source and responsibility for suffering and sorrow. For in this tale, the garden, created pure and clean, watered by dew, full of fruit as the means for the sustenance of all living things, was apparently meant to be a kind of earthly paradise and was indeed created to be perfect by a loving God. But there was a single prohibition built into the system: "And the Lord God commanded the man, 'You may freely eat of every tree of the garden; but of the tree of the knowledge of good and evil you shall not eat, for in the day that you eat of it you shall die.'" (Genesis 2:16–17). And as the story progresses, it becomes clear that it is the breaking of this command not to eat from this particular tree that is the source of human trouble.

There are, of course, any number of interpretations of this story. Nineteenth-century Danish theologian Søren Kierkegaard (1813–1855) has noted, for example, that the prohibition given in the Garden of Eden could only have been a mystery to this first man, Adam. What could God have meant, warning that if he ate of this tree he would die? What is meant by "the knowledge of good and evil"? Perhaps Adam did not understand such ideas, but Kierkegaard suggests that Adam, nevertheless—and like Adam, all of us—had a consciousness of the significance of his own choices and a dreadful sense of his own responsibility (Kierkegaard 40–41). Other existential interpretations go even farther. Perhaps our very consciousness is awareness of responsibility, an awareness of the difference between what we are and what we might be. Thus "fallenness" is just a fact of the conscious mind, suggests Paul Tillich, whether there was a historical Adam or not (44).

Apart from such existential interpretations, the traditional story might be read as a possibly historical, as well as mythic, account of one man's responsibility for the evils of the world. For it is within this event, especially as the New Testament Christians interpreted it, that "sin came into the world." Thus with Saint Paul's interpretation, it is the sin of Adam that separates the human race, indeed the whole of it, from the perfection of bliss with God. And that in turn is the reason for the coming of Jesus as Savior.

Christians hold
that the Fall
brought sin and
suffering into the
world.

For our purposes, it might be especially emphasized that the story of the Fall does not end with the sin of Adam. It goes on, rather dramatically, to include God's curses on humanity. For once the children of God, however beloved, have broken trust with their Creator, they are no longer worthy of life in the blissful and peaceful garden. Their loss of innocence they have created themselves—as the story suggests in the imagery of their recognition of their own nakedness—but their loss of relationship to the world, that is God's doing. For in the story, God declares that, with this disobedience, "Cursed is the ground because of you; . . . by the sweat of your face you shall eat bread until you return to the ground, for out of it you were taken." (See Genesis 3:17–19.) Thus, our loss of harmony in the world follows from our disobedience to God, alongside our brokenness of soul. And so both natural evils and moral evils are born.

There is, of course, much more to the story, and books have been written to interpret its implications and presuppositions. But for our purposes, the point might be made that suffering and sorrow, evils of all kinds, are evidently the fault of humankind, especially of Adam and the primordial choice to disobey God in the Garden of Eden. Thus in the Jewish and Christian myth—a story echoed by Islam in Suras 20 and 7 of the Holy Koran—suffering and evil are explained, though by no means justified. And the lesson is that we have brought sorrow upon ourselves.

■ TRICKSTER MYTHS

Often a trickster is involved in stories of how evil and suffering came to be.

It is only to be expected, however, that where the Ultimate Reality is not a Creator God, especially not a God who makes prohibitions or can be disappointed in the human creation, the actual source of suffering and evil must lie somewhere outside of human disobedience or divine curses. Without a moral God, whether angry or merely disappointed, the cause of human woe may often be seen as almost whimsical, a mere error, almost a joke. Thus in many traditional cultures, native religions rely on trickster stories to explain how the world has gone awry. Particularly to explain death, these stories often relate that some being, probably an animal, was supposed to have made some decision or carried some message to humanity for their health and life but somewhere along the way he was distracted. In the excerpt that opened this chapter, the story of the dog that paused to eat along the way explains why death has come to humanity instead of life. It is obvious that, by all natural forces, the dog should have outrun the toad and easily carried to humanity the word of life. But, because of his distraction with food, he failed to deliver his message on time. And so death has come among us.

Other trickster stories echo this theme. Coyote, in the Native American Caddo legend, did not simply fail to deliver a message of life but in this case actually worked intentionally to make death eternal. According to the tale, the humans voted that their dead relatives should come back to life after a few days, and the chiefs, in fact, built a hut to hold the dead bodies, so that the spirit, embodied in a whirlwind, could be called back to reanimate the body. But, the story says, "Coyote saw it, and as the whirlwind was about to enter the house, he closed the door. The spirit of the whirlwind, finding the door closed, whirled on by. In this way Coyote made death eternal, and from that time on, people grieved over their dead and were unhappy" (Erdoes 471).

It is evident, then, that the trickster might sometimes be worse than merely distracted or mistaken. Sometimes he intentionally causes harm. Of course, in this Native American tale the Coyote's motivation is, apparently, just to avoid overpopulation. In other traditions, the cause of evil and suffering may be much more malevolent. The Holy Koran teaches, for example, that once having rebelled against God's commands, the evil angel Iblis—the Islamic equivalent of Satan—proceeds with malevolent intent to deceive and mislead the humans Allah had made. Thus in Islam, the gravest of all sufferings, the sin of idolatry and the fall into eternal hell, is an intended deception, a work of hatred. In fact, Satan himself declares before God, "I will certainly lie in wait for them (humankind) in Thy straight path. Then I will certainly come to them from before them and from behind them, and from their right-hand side and from their left-hand side; and Thou shalt not find most of them thankful." (Holy Koran 7:16–17).

7.14: In Islam, Iblis (Satan) had rebelled against Allah and chose to mislead the humans Allah had made.

Ultimately it seems misleading to consider the Devil of Islam or Christianity as a "trickster" of native traditions. Certainly, it seems the former's genuine malevolence is more emphatic. Still, our point here is that evil in some cases is attributed after all to creatures lower than a Creator God, creatures that, either through meanness or flippant whimsy, are responsible for the sorrows of humanity. Pointing to that meanness or error is then at least one way of explaining human suffering.

■ "IGNORANCE" AND ASIAN RELIGION

The actual cause of suffering is more difficult to find in Asian religions.

In many of the Asian traditions, any actual origin of suffering and evil is more difficult to find. In an almost humorous parable from Taoism, Chuang Tzu tells of two kings who used to visit one another by crossing through the land of Hun-tun. Hun-tun, whose name means "chaos" or "unformed," has no face and is, presumably, a symbol for the primordial, unformed, and unnamed Tao. But the two kings, thinking that somehow Hun-tun needs a face, decide to drill him seven holes. So each day they drilled another hole, says the story, "and on the seventh day Hun-tun died." One might find this story merely entertaining, but it might also be in Chuang Tzu to remind us that the imposition of human order onto the natural flow of the Tao can only cause troubles. Thus, once again, we are the cause of our own sorrows, though here there is no hint of sin or disobedience. It is rather simply the human error of trying to impose a human order on the Unnamed Tao.

It is not clear in such a story that any kind of historical or even semi-historical meaning is attached. Indeed, it seems clear that, like the story of Pandora's Box, we are not expected to place many of these tales in time but only to see them as lessons. Thus, the question of how evils and suffering originated may not be a very good question at all, insofar as the past tense verb seems to be looking for an answer that cannot be found. Perhaps for this reason, some philosophies of India have just avoided the question altogether. It seems evident, for example, that, according to the Vedanta system of Hinduism, we are said to all be one, indeed all reality is one with the Eternal One, Brahman. Yet it is just as evident that we fail to see that oneness, indeed that we thrive on our delusion of multiplicity and inherit from this error all the sufferings of life. So where does this error come from, if indeed all reality is the Pure Consciousness of Brahman? To this question there seems to be no answer, and perhaps intentionally so. For Sankara, the eighth century Hindu philosopher, simply calls this ignorance "beginningless." Its cause is simply our own existence, and the cause of our own existence, as if separate from the oneness of Brahman, is our ignorance (*avidya*). For this circle of life and death, the hopeful religious teacher suggests, there is a way out, but there is evidently no way in. That is, we may hope for liberation, salvation from the cycle of ignorance and rebirth (see Chapter 12: Salvation and the Meaning of Life), but there is no explaining how or why we are in the cycle to begin with. The problem is "beginningless." (See Mayeda's discussion of *avidya*, 76–79.)

Some Indian philosophies have given up the quest for why suffering came into the world.

Vendanta—
Hindu philosophical school based on the Upanishads

For some Hindu philosophers, ignorance of our oneness with the One (Brahman) is the cause of suffering.

A similar point with perhaps an even greater agnostic emphasis is given by Buddhism. In a famous parable, the Buddha responds to the question of our ignorance and suffering by describing a man shot with a poisoned arrow. For such a

Box 7.1 Global Byte
Religion, Politics, and Helping the Suffering

On December 26, 2003, a devastating earthquake struck the Iranian city of Bam, leveling the mostly brick and mud dwellings and killing an estimated 30,000 people. When disasters of this kind strike, relief agencies from all over the world respond with humanitarian aid: food, medicine, shelter, and even teams of dogs to search for survivors. Many of these agencies have a religious basis, as many religions in the world include specific moral commands to care for the suffering of others. Remarkably, the united efforts of religious organizations to respond to the suffering of others often helps to overcome people's barriers—both political and religious.

Iran is clearly an Islamic nation, one that has no great love for the United States and its Christian religion. Yet within the list of relief organizations that sent aid and workers directly to Iran after the quake, dozens of explicitly Christian groups appear, from Baptist World Aid, to Catholic Relief Services, to the International Orthodox Christian Charities. While there, the Christian agencies worked alongside Iran's own Red Crescent relief agencies, as well as the Islamic Aid and Islamic Relief foundations. Even the Taiwan Buddhist Tzu Chi Foundation was present. In response to human disaster, all these groups were welcomed, all worked side by side, and all helped to aid the suffering. It is not clear if all religions have an equal basis for works of charity and aid, for certainly each has its own distinct philosophies and ethics related to its own concept of Ultimate Reality. But in the case of Iran, religious relief agencies seemed to overcome many of these barriers, as they each responded to the dramatic human need.

While the United States has long been to Iran the "Great Satan," and while U.S. President Bush once called Iran a member of an "Axis of Evil," remarkable photos from Iran after the December 2003 quake showed Iranian troops guarding U.S. relief organizations. Even a U.S. Jewish relief agency was represented in Iran. Notably, it must be confessed that while the many religious groups from many nations responded to the need for charity, Iranian officials themselves stipulated that they would accept no aid from Israel. Evidently, in the face of great need many differences were put aside. Many, but not all.

Source: Reuters Foundation. "NGO's Responding to Iran Earthquake." *AlertNet*. December 31, 2003. http://www.alertnet.org/thefacts/reliefresources/107270583332.htm (accessed April 26, 2004).

man, the Buddha suggests, it is simply foolish to be concerned about where the arrow came from or what kind of arrow it is. The only issue of real concern is how to remove the arrow and to stop its poison (see Warren 120–22). The parable's point, it seems, is to insist that metaphysical questions about temporal origins are not very useful in resolving the problem of suffering. Instead, the Buddha explicitly insists that he does explain the causes of suffering in our lives—ultimately it is our own desire rooted, as with Hinduism, in ignorance—and this explanation is enough to guide one to salvation. We shall explore this point in detail below. But for now, we must see that in Buddhism, the problems of where ignorance comes from and of how enlightenment and ignorance can both be possible in the hearts and minds of finite beings are questions left unanswered.

Buddhism does not explain how suffering originated but focuses on removing the ignorance that perpetuates it.

This point goes on to suggest that the question of the origins of suffering may or may not be central to a particular religion's explanation of life. The story of the Fall in the Abrahamic religions might indeed be very important to understanding all that follows, perhaps especially in Christianity, in which the very center of the religion, the appearance of Christ, can be interpreted as God's way of undoing the original evil. But in other religions, such an origination myth is not very important. That is not to say, however, that explaining suffering and evil is, overall, unimportant. Indeed, it has been argued already, under the notion of the "sacred canopy," that religions are, in general, in the business of trying to explain our sorrows and sufferings, as well as our moral evils, in light of the ultimate, sacred Absolute. Thus, even if a religion does not stress in any way an origin-of-evil story, nonetheless there will almost certainly be strong references to human woe. At the very least, religions seem to want to offer a response to death, disease, and suffering, and how they do that will necessarily be related to how the original central notion of the Absolute has been set up. In other words, as we have argued all along, we should expect some reasonable continuity between how a religion explains (justifies, redeems, assuages) human suffering and the great reality that counts in that religion as the Absolute. To these examinations we now turn.

SUFFERING AND MONOTHEISM

Many explanations of suffering in monotheistic religions focus on human responsibility.

Tanakh—Jewish sacred texts composed of the Torah, five books of Moses, the Neviim, the prophets, and the Ketuvim, sacred writings. In Christian context, the Tanakh is generally referred to as the Old Testament or Hebrew Bible.

One important explanation in Judaism maintains that human suffering is punishment for violating the covenant with God.

We have seen that the Abrahamic religions share the myth of the Fall and its apparent implications about the responsibility of humankind for the physical evils of the world and for the moral evils of their own souls. There are other ways of interpreting suffering in monotheistic religions, of course, but many of them continue this theme of human responsibility. There is a great deal of Jewish emphasis, for example, on the concept of divine punishment. More agreeably stated perhaps, the Jewish historical doctrines emphasize God's insistence on human obedience to "the Covenant" and the severe consequences should the covenant be broken. For it is taught in the Tanakh that God chose the Jewish people as His own, a nation to represent Him on earth. To formalize this arrangement, the stories say, God made the Covenant with Abraham. As a consequence, the Jewish people needed to keep themselves pure, in accordance with the commandments, and for their obedience God would prosper them and extend their power and importance through all the world. "I shall be your God," so the covenant declares, "and you shall be my people."

Thus for the Jews, it was clear that health and prosperity were the direct result of remaining in good relation to Yahweh. But by the same token, defeat and disease, suffering and woe as a nation were evidently the result of having failed to keep covenant with God. The biblical texts of the histories of the kings of Israel and Judah are full of references to leaders whose evil or good deeds brought upon the nation God's judgment or blessing. Therefore, whether the entire nation fell or throve depended on the ability of the people to keep God's covenant. Far from being merely a description of an angry God, however, these stories also inspire the Jewish people to repent and to consider again the law of God as a gift. For although God warns them that He may punish four generations of children for the evils of the parents, in the same breath He promises mercy and compassion "to the thousandth generation of those that love God and keep His commandments" (Deuteronomy 5:10).

In Christianity and Islam, the emphasis seems to be a bit different. Given the change in the concept of the "covenant," this should not be surprising. Thus, for Muslims, whatever sufferings we may have to endure are universal, not for any "chosen people." As such, these struggles are tests, whereby we show whether we shall continue to submit to Allah. Similarly, but more specifically explored, Christians might describe their sufferings as opportunities to grow and, indeed, to glorify God with their patience (note the synonym, "long-suffering") and their willingness to love even their enemies. Thus, when the early believers experienced persecution, after having understood themselves to be saved by the work of Jesus' grace, these sufferings were not punishments or signs of divine anger but tests of endurance and the fires of purification. Indeed, Paul writes that the Christians may "boast in our sufferings, knowing that suffering produces endurance, endurance produces character, and character produces hope." And hope, he notes in the end, "does not disappoint us" (Romans 5:3–5).

Muslims may interpret suffering as a test of whether or not one will continue to submit to Allah.

There are other classic theistic answers to suffering, intended to encourage and strengthen the believer with the "sacred canopy" of divine purpose. Certainly the myth of the Fall alluded to earlier offers the important suggestion that evils are, in some sense, part of the moral choices made by human beings. Indeed, Christian philosophers, John Hick and C. S. Lewis have argued that there would be no genuine human choices, and therefore no genuine human free will, if we were not capable of committing acts of real evil. Thus, "moral evils" are necessarily the possible result of human freedom. Similarly, Hick goes on to say "natural evils" are necessary in a world where humans must freely respond to difficulty and danger. We can well imagine that God might have created a world that contained only ease and comfort but "such a world, however well it might promote pleasure, would be very ill adapted for the development of the moral qualities of human personality" (Hick 45). Thus suffering and evil are simply part of what God intended for our own moral development and moral freedom.

Christians may interpret suffering as an opportunity to grow in virtue and faith.

In the end, of course, the most prominent monotheistic response to the suffering and troubles of life might be the simple promise of salvation. Is there finally a "promised land," an expectation of final justice and purity? Believers might indeed hope that the trials and tribulations of earth are nothing compared to the glory and wonder that is promised in heaven. Again, Paul says, "I consider that the sufferings of this present time are not worth comparing with the glory about to be revealed to us" (Romans 8:18). Therefore, what seems like injustice now, and what appears to be the meaninglessness of innocent suffering in this world, all may be redeemed in heaven, where there is no darkness and where every tear is dried. We shall discuss salvation and afterlife in a later chapter, but for now it is easy to see why such hope of glory and peace might be a consolation and source of hope for the suffering.

Suffering may be seen as a promise for a great eternal reward.

One final point on theistic explanations of suffering might be needed. The classic story of Job in the Hebrew Bible is itself a mixture of explanations of the problem of evil, some about trials and tests, others about punishment for sin. In that story, Job is "a righteous man," as noted by God himself, and yet Satan, the "adversary," asserts that goodness is all too easy for a wealthy, respected, and healthy man like Job. God therefore gives Satan permission to "test" Job, and in the course of one day, the man loses family, wealth, and friends. Ultimately, Satan even takes away Job's health and inflicts upon him dire sores. And in one of the greatest pieces of religious literature, there ensues a discussion between Job and his friends about why all this occurred. In the course of this discussion, the friends insist that Job must be suffering as a punishment for his sins, since God is never unfair or unjust. Therefore, as we have seen above, the reasonable course of action is for Job to repent. Yet Job is sure that his sins, whatever they may have been, were not deserving of so grave a punishment; and in any case, he insists, God surely owes him an explanation of what he did and why it was so terrible. "Oh, that I had someone to hear me!" he cries out. "Here is my signature! let the Almighty answer me! Oh, that I had the indictment written by my adversary! Surely I would carry it on my shoulder" (Job 31:35–36).

The point of the book of Job, however, is apparently not about sin and punishment, as God eventually declares that the friends were in error. And it is evident in the tale that Job was in fact not being punished. Yet when God appears to Job "from out of the whirlwind," it is notable that God does not answer Job as the man wanted. Nor does God even explain that Satan, not He, was the one who inflicted the suffering. Rather, God answers Job with rhetorical questions:

> *Who is this that darkens counsel by words without knowledge? . . . Where were you when I laid the foundation of the earth? Tell me, if you have understanding . . . Shall a faultfinder contend with the Almighty? . . . Will you even put me in the wrong? Will you condemn me that you may be justified? Have you an arm like God, and can you thunder with a voice like his? (Job 38 and 40, various verses)*

Significant here is that God does *not* answer Job, and indeed, when so confronted, Job admits that he should not have made demands of God, and he "repents in dust and ashes." Yet, as we have said, it is clear that he did not suffer for his sins, nor is his repentance here about some secret evil that deserved punishment. Rather, we see that, in the end, perhaps the theistic point is that the absolute and eternal God does not owe us any explanation. Perhaps those who understand God to be absolute and sovereign must simply assert that "The Lord gives, and the Lord takes away. Blessed be the name of the Lord" (Job 1:21). This, too, is a response to the evils of life, a response perhaps quite appropriate to this monotheistic conception of the Holy.

The story of Job in the Hebrew scriptures does not give a final answer to why people suffer but asserts we must trust God even in suffering.

HAUNTING SPIRITS/HELPING SPIRITS

Traditional native religions do not always present a harmonious relation with nature spirits. Sometimes, these are quite capricious.

We have seen since Chapter 3 that many native traditions, while they may include in their religion some reference to a Creator God, usually focus more attention on the more immediate spirits. These spirits include the spirits of ancestors and the recently dead, as well as spirits of nature. In many cases, and perhaps especially in the more romanticized versions of nature religion where harmony with nature is taken for granted, the relationship to these beings is assumed to be benign. But it would be an error to presume that such native traditions find only peace and beauty in their relation to these beings. For in many cases, the spirits are capricious and frightening, responsible in fact for death, disease, and disaster within the tribe.

Relationships to ancestor spirits, for example, can sometimes go awry. As a case in point, we find that among the tribal cultures of Northeast Thailand the spirits of one's parents, and the spirits of one's ancestors more generally, ought to receive ritual offerings and "merit" from the living descendents. When this fails to occur—or so the explanations go—the ancestor spirits may become angry and "are capable of attacking living humans" (Tambiah 314). In some ways, this cause of affliction is like the theory of punishment by God, noted above, inasmuch as the sicknesses and disasters caused by the spirits are often in response to failures and errors made by the living. Thus sickness and trouble in childbearing may be the direct result of forgetting the ancestors or quarrelling within the living family. Apparently, then, the ancestor spirits are "moralistic" beings, concerned about the unity of the family, and they bring illness and trouble when the living fail to perform properly.

Tambiah's study also notes the afflictions caused by various nature spirits.(316–317) Spirits of one's own rice fields, for example, need to be placated with regular offerings so that the rice may grow and that the farmer may be kept safe from snakes. Other spirits reside in mountains or rivers and may afflict the casual passerby with fever or another minor illness. The general suggestion here is not that these spirits are concerned for the moral behaviors of the farmers and travelers but that they are rather capricious, simply mischievous, and may afflict people just because they want to.

Other kinds of spirits, especially among tribal cultures, can be the bringers of disaster and sorrow. Spirits of other human beings who have died young, especially by violent accident for men or in childbirth for women, are by nature unhappy spirits, never having found their proper fulfillment in life. Therefore they may haunt a village, bringing disease and disorder. The nats of Burmese tribal people are an undefined list of 37 spirits who haunt humans apparently just to be mean. Villagers explain that some have failed to honor the Buddha in a past life or have died unhappy. But some simply want to do harm. Malevolence apparently for its own sake is not beyond the possibilities of some of the fundamental spirits of tribal religion.

Of course, the attribution of malevolence to spiritual beings is not merely a tribal phenomenon, as evidenced by the existence of Satan or Iblis within the monotheistic religions described above. We have already seen how God allowed Satan to torment Job and how Iblis, chastised by God for failing to honor the human beings, promised to lead the humans into faithlessness and destruction. Notably, this being, technically speaking, is not to be understood as the counterpart to God, since Satan, too, is merely a creature made by God. Indeed in the later traditions, Satan is but one among the angels who has rebelled against God and been thrown from heaven. Thus, the Christian tradition describes Satan as Lucifer, the angel, who in his rebellion fell from God's presence and drew a third of the angels with him. These other "angels," then, make up perhaps the "demons" that torment human beings both on earth and in hell. It is notable that the attribution of illness to demons is common in the Christian New Testament, and indeed that exorcisms (casting out of demons) continue within Christian groups to this day, from Pentecostal to Roman Catholic.

KARMA AND REINCARNATION

Reincarnation, the belief that the spirit of a deceased person can be reborn into another living being, is a relatively common belief. Literally, it means that the spirit enters again into flesh, is re-embodied, so to speak. Among tribal peoples, this belief is most commonly invoked to explain the similarities between persons born generations apart, such that a great-grandchild might bear a marked physical or character trait similar to the great-grandfather, and so it seems the patriarch is reborn. The possibility of being reborn into nonhuman form is less common, though, again among some tribal peoples, this belief is also found. But it is especially among the traditions of India that we find perhaps the most fully developed exploration of this idea and especially its connection with the notion of karma. In this way karma becomes a classic way of explaining the sufferings of life.

Karma is easily understood—perhaps too easily—as a form of payback for one's deeds. The mechanics of the system are not altogether clear, but it is commonly assumed that the kind of deeds one performs in any given lifetime "come back" to one, either later in that lifetime or in another. We shall discuss this idea again in Chapter 10; for now, our interest lies in how this system of belief explains the suffering we know in this world. And of course, the notion is clear: As a kind of "payback," it can be inferred that whatever one suffers in life is due to what one has done in the past. That is, whether one suffers from disease or violence or accidental injury, one has, in some sense, brought it upon oneself. In short, you deserve whatever happens to you.

This notion of "deserving" ought not to be confused with punishments or rewards. All we can mean here is that if one does violence or causes injury, then violence or injury comes back rather automatically. There need not be, in this system, any wrathful deity or judging spirit; rather, the system works more like an echo, or a simple notion of moral cause and effect. Thus there is, technically speaking, no punishment here, but then neither is there any mercy. One cannot placate karma nor avoid its "wrath." What you sow is what you reap (to apply the biblical quotation), and there is no one to blame but yourself.

In one sense, of course, this idea helps to explain suffering quite well, and it helps also to give people a sense of ultimate fairness and justice. If we could see the violent criminal ultimately suffering from cancer or see the child molester struck by a meteorite, we could well imagine that the world does, after all, have this natural justice behind it. But, of course, it is not so simple: We see the innocent in tatters, children born diseased, and unnatural death come to the most gentle and humane. But this is where the doctrine of reincarnation fits in, for it can be suggested that the child born with leukemia or the gentle and wise old neighbor fallen victim to violence may indeed have "deserved" those sufferings as the result of actions in a previous lifetime. Indeed, in classical Hinduism there are believed to be natural levels of society, called castes, that give one a basic status in society and determine specific kinds of rights and duties. Thus, one may be born in a high caste, with all its religious and social privilege, or born in a low stratum of society, meant therefore to serve others and to do only the lowest and vilest kinds of labor for a meager subsistence. We saw in the chapter on myth that one way to justify this inequality of caste was through a creation myth; here we emphasize that the moral justification of the lower value of some persons can be understood as the result of how well they have served their social world in a previous life. And thus if the social stratification of caste seems to be fraught with injustice, it is woven through and through with a higher justice, one that stretches through generations and lifetimes.

Religions teaching reincarnation (rebirth in a different body) include the idea of karma as a way to explain suffering.

Karma is a kind of a "payback" for one's life deeds, but it is not exactly a simple system of reward or punishment.

Reincarnation may be used as an explanation of why the apparently undeserving suffer.

A famous Buddhist story makes this clear: Moggallana the Great was one of the Buddha's most brilliant followers, a pure and humble practitioner of the Dhamma (the Buddha's teachings), such that he was able to fly through the air and visit deities in the heavens. Yet, the story goes, having incurred the jealousy of some forest-dwelling ascetics, he was eventually surrounded and murdered by 500 assassins, who "broke his bones into bits." Later, as other followers of the Buddha were discussing this event, they pondered how this death seemed so unfair, so unjust a suffering for so good a man. Then the Buddha explained that this very Moggallana in a previous life had been a good, filial son who, nevertheless, at the instigation of his new wife, took his own parents out to the woods and killed them. Thus the Buddha explained:

> *Priests, the fruit of this one deed of Moggallana's was torment in hell for many hundreds of thousands of years, and death by pounding in a hundred existences, as suited the nature of his crime. Moggallana's death is therefore suited to his karma. (Warren 225)*

In Hindu and Buddhist systems of "higher justice," karma may stretch through many lifetimes and generations.

The explanations of the suffering of individuals through the explanations of karma are, therefore, relatively straightforward. One should recognize again that, in these explanations, there is not any appeal to a divine judge, nor is karma "angry" or wrathful. By the same token, of course, there is also no possibility here of divine mercy. We might also wonder about the "justice" of karma, inasmuch as we would perhaps expect there to be a connection between rewards or punishments and the identity of the individual agent. That is, we may be driven to ask why the individual Moggallana, not to mention the 99 other individuals who died by pounding, should suffer as individuals for the deeds of a different individual, namely, the young man who killed his parents. If I had been guilty of a heinous crime, no one would consider it justice to arrest my grandson, just because he had inherited my wealth; similarly, it may seem odd that the good man, Moggallana, should suffer for the deeds of the patricide just because he inherited the murderer's karma. But perhaps, in the end, it is wrong to consider karma as a "justice" system; it is, as we have suggested, more like a causal system than a judgment. If I shoot a bullet vertically upward and then stand in my place, that same bullet will come down to hit me; and if I should pass on before the bullet comes back and another should take that spot, the bullet will hit him just as surely. Justice or not, karma, like the bullet, must descend on whomever is next in line, and—justice or not—that explains why people suffer.

Karma is a causal system, not a system of justice.

▪ BUDDHISM AND DUKKHA

We have just seen that Buddhism, like Hinduism, asserts the law of karma as a basic explanation for the suffering of the world. Indeed, we noted that the story of Moggallana is a Buddhist tale, indeed a case from the later biographical constructions of the Buddha in which he clearly uses his omniscience to see into past lives and to discover people's karmic trails. But Buddhism is widely known for another point about the suffering of humanity, indeed a point for which traditional Buddhists often seem to require a special defense. For, at the risk of seeming unusually pessimistic, it is one of the most basic and fundamental statements of Buddhist doctrine to stress, not only that some people suffer from past karma, but indeed that all people suffer, and indeed all of life itself is suffering.

This doctrine, the doctrine of dukkha, is stated in the very first doctrine of the famous "Four Noble Truths" of Buddhism. In the first sermon of the Buddha, he declared that this "noble truth of suffering" means that, for all people, "birth is suffering, death is suffering, sorrow, grieving, dejection and despair are suffering. Contact with unpleasant things is suffering, not getting what you want is also suffering. In short, the five aggregates [composing human life] of grasping are suffering" (Fieser and Powers 84). The point, however, is not to be taken as simple pessimism. As defenders like Walpola Rahula argue, the claim here is simple realism, built not on a bare assertion contrary to human experience but on the facts of observation, especially the observation of impermanence (17).

Impermanence, indeed, seems to be the key to understanding the Buddhist doctrine of suffering. For the point is not that joy or happiness are fundamentally false but that they are fundamentally impermanent. As Rahula notes, "Enjoyment is a fact of experience; but this enjoyment is not permanent." Because nothing is lasting, because nothing has the kind of eternal substance that alone can fulfill our desires to hold onto what we like and to keep away what we do not like, all of our enjoyments simply must be ultimately frustrated. Thus Rahula adds that "when the situation changes, . . . when you are deprived of this enjoyment, you become sad, you may become unreasonable and unbalanced, you may even behave foolishly. This is the evil, unsatisfactory and dangerous side of the picture. This, too, is a fact of experience" (18).

Part of the point of this Buddhist "realism" is simply that suffering is a "fact of experience;" it is just the way things are, and there is no other reality, no God or heaven, to which one may flee for refuge. In some forms of Buddhism, especially in Tibetan art, this fact is often represented as the "wheel of life." In this famous depiction, life is shown to be a transient phenomenon with nothing substantial. Thus on the rim of the wheel, twelve sections mark the "chain of dependent origination," which shows how suffering is based upon birth, birth upon becoming, becoming upon grasping, grasping upon craving, and so forth, until in the twelfth step, all is rooted in the ignorance that thinks to find permanence in the world. Farther within the circle of life are shown the realms of rebirth, the arenas of heavens, earth and hells, in which sentient beings might be reborn. And in the center of the circle are three interwoven beasts—the snake, the pig, and the rooster—that symbolize the fundamental flaws of existence: greed, hatred, and delusion. And, perhaps, most notable in the picture is that the entire wheel is held in the clawed grasp and the fanged mouth of the demon "Time." Perhaps the essential point is, after all, that the entire realm of birth and rebirth, even if one is born as a king or a god, is part of the tiresome and troubled cycle of *samsara*, the cycle of karma and reincarnation. Thus, there is no escape from suffering other than to end the cycle itself.

Let us be clear: Buddhism has never called for suicide. For, as Rahula and other Buddhist writers have pointed out, though this idea of *dukkha* seems pessimistic, it is ultimately optimistic, for it teaches not only that suffering is all-pervasive but also that it can be stopped. Just as the wheel of life shows that suffering is the result of birth and rebirth, of craving and ultimately of ignorance, it

For Buddhists, suffering can be stopped by stopping craving and ignorance.

also shows, as the Buddha declared further into the Four Noble Truths, that suffering can be stopped with the removal of craving and ignorance. Thus with enlightenment, with the pure mind that sees the world in all its emptiness and selflessness, all the lust and craving for possession and existence is removed, and with this removal, there is no suffering. Remove the fuel from the fire, the Buddha taught, and the fire will simply go out, leaving quietude and simplicity. Remove the foolish belief in permanence and the attendant desires of life, and suffering ceases. This, then, is the Buddhist answer to the problem of evil.

BALANCE AND ACCEPTANCE

For Buddhists, life is not a struggle against a sea of suffering but an acceptance of the reality.

It may in fact be attractive to think of the answer to the sufferings of life, not as a fight and struggle against this "sea of troubles" but as a kind of acceptance. Already in Buddhism, we find stories that illustrate acceptance, such as the tale of Kisa Gotami. Upon the death of her infant son, she was, of course, distraught, and she sought the Buddha to have him save her child. Those more familiar with the famous stories of Jesus might expect a miraculous healing, but instead the Buddha sent Kisa Gotami, carrying her dead child in her arms, into a village to ask for a handful of mustard seeds. She was told, however, to accept the seeds only from a house where no one had died. What she found, of course, was that there was no such place, indeed that in every home someone had died. Thus death, she learned, is all-pervasive and unavoidable, and leaving her dead child in the forest, she sought to join the Buddha's order of nuns. As he told her in the end, "the law of death is that among all living creatures there is no permanence" (Stryk 174)

Such acceptance of suffering in Buddhism found resonance in the teachings of Taoism in China. Of course the theoretical foundations of Taoism, as we have seen in previous chapters, are different, but the harmony between Buddhist and Taoist teachings is nevertheless one of the factors that made the overwhelming success of Buddhism in China possible. For the Taoists, like the Buddhists, taught that suffering and illness are, after all, simply part of life. They were, we might argue, more positive, however, for the Taoist ideal, as we have seen, is that all things flow in a wholesome and harmonious order called the Tao. The Tao, noted in Chapter 3, is the Ultimate Reality, the unnameable and mysterious balance of *yin* and *yang*, famously symbolized by the black and white fluid circle of Taoist art. In this chapter, the point is that this symbol of balance and harmony indicates not that "life is suffering" but that death and sickness are, after all, half of the reality of life. As the Tao Te Ching says: "Heaven and Earth are not human; they regard all things as straw dogs" (Chan 141).

Taoism also teaches that suffering and death must be accepted as part of life.

To illustrate this concept of acceptance, we have already seen one of the famous stories of Taoist philosophy, given by Chuang Tzu. In that story, excerpted in this chapter's opening quotations, a Taoist sage, Master Lai, grows ill, though he is evidently in the prime of life. Yet he by no means resents his suffering. Indeed, he insists that it is *yin* and *yang* that have brought him to this point of death, and that it would be perverse of him to disobey them, even more perverse than to disobey mother and father. In the extended story, other masters join in the discussion as another man, Master Ssu, also grows ill, becoming, as the tale says, "all crookedy." Yet he, too, insists that there is no place for resentment:

> *I received life because the time had come; I will lose it because the order of things passes on. Be content with this time and dwell in this order and then neither sorrow nor joy can touch you. In ancient times this was called the "freeing of the bound." (Watson 81)*

We can see, perhaps, that this view of accepting the changes of life, including illness and death, are directly tied to a concept of the Absolute that describes the duality of highs and lows, health and sickness, and even life and death, as just mirrors of the Tao. They are thus no more to be resisted than the duality of male and female. And so, as Kisa Gotami leaves her dead child in the forest and seeks withdrawal and release, so the masters of the Tao learn to distance themselves from worry and concern over life. Chuang Tzu himself (another Taoist tale relates) therefore cries just a little at his own wife's death, but he is soon found singing and banging a drum. "It's like the change of the four seasons," he says: One change and she was born, another change and she is dead (Watson 113).

RESPONSES TO SUFFERING

We have already seen that there is an internal logic to religion, and indeed it should not surprise us that the kinds of explanations we find for the sufferings of life are directly tied to what each religion understands to be the Ultimate Reality. The direct connection between suffering and moral judgment, or suffering and moral trial, is clearly associated with the idea of God as a divine being who is Himself a moral judge and lawgiver. The general acceptance of suffering, on the other hand, apparently completely void of moral associations, is evident in Taoism, where the Ultimate Reality is not a morally concerned and relational being but an impersonal balance and indescribable order. Thus, each religion offers a distinct but comprehensible explanation for the woes of life and death, offering in turn a distinct and comprehensible implication for what we ought to do about it.

Each religion offers a distinct explanation of suffering that implies a "solution" to suffering.

We might well, in all these "answers," wonder how we *can* respond to the suffering of life. Let us not forget that these sufferings are not merely stories in religious texts; rather, the characters—Job, Kisa Gotami, Master Lai—represent us and our own parents, children, and friends. Shall we, when faced with leukemia in children or the death of a beloved parent, urge ourselves and our friends to "slip into the water and make no ripple?" Or shall we "rage against the dying of the light," as the poet Dylan Thomas urged his own dying father? It may not merely be a matter of taste, but it is likely far beyond to scope of this text to try to analyze all the possible answers.

The most reasonable acceptance of suffering is found in those religions where these are "just a part of the changes of life."

Nevertheless, the options may be noted. For we find most reasonable the acceptance of suffering and nonresistance when we see the world as a reflection of the Tao or see *dukkha* in the inescapable turning of the wheel of life. We recognize the "justice," perhaps, in the notion of karma and reincarnation, and find therein a strong motivation for improving our own actions and escaping the sorrows of karma. In dealing with spirits and gods, we find motivation for ritual action and social purity, concern that the ancestor ghosts and natural spirits do not become angry. Offerings and exorcisms are reasonable practices when the sorrows of life are the result of divine anger and spiritual oppression. And if the Holy is a moral and relational God, then perhaps we are mostly called to moral action, to prayers for mercy, and perhaps to the alleviation of the suffering of others in the name of God.

Suffering may be understood as a means of purifying the body from sin.

At its most extreme, suffering may be seen to have a positive, purgative value. That is, in some religions physical suffering is intentionally taken on because it purifies, makes one holy by forcibly denying the sins of pleasure and self-indulgence. Especially in those religious views where the sensual world is seen as in conflict with the Absolute, we may find that the highest saints torture themselves to prove that they have overcome the temptations of worldly life. Saddhus, holy men of India, can be found to this day performing severe punishments of the body (see Hartsuiker). In Jainism, there is an explicit tradition of *itvara*, or ritualized fasting to death. "Such a death," the scriptures say, "is a peaceful haven for all monks who are completely free from craving for life." (Fieser and Powers 67)

itvara—ritualized fasting in Jainism

Less extreme is the call to endurance and faith. We have already discovered the acceptance of suffering as part of the Tao and the realization in Buddhism that it is not our suffering but our desires (and ultimately ignorance) that are the real root of the problem. This acceptance does not take the suffering as good but rather finds a way to understand the suffering, seeing its causes and meaning in the larger religious picture. Somehow, this is similar to the theistic call to faith. We saw above in the emphasis on "sovereignty" that the proper reaction to the suffering of others and of ourselves—especially the latter—may be a call to patience and trust in God. The Christians of the New Testament are urged by the apostles, for example, simply to endure their persecution, realizing that they learn patience and become witnesses of Jesus' work on earth. Here, too, the suffering is not good or purgative in itself, but it can be endured when seen in the larger picture of God's plan.

To some extent, "Eastern" and "Western" religions may counsel patience and acceptance in the face of suffering, but they vary greatly on the fullest reaction to suffering.

Yet, as we might expect, the Taoist and Buddhist answers do not really resemble theistic faith in important ways. The Buddhist ideal, for example, is clearly one of dispassion and detachment. Christian willingness to endure suffering may, after all, be an imitation of Jesus himself, thus a willingness to know the pain and sorrow of life because of a greater good. There is no detachment or dispassion here. Indeed, it is interesting to compare the death scenes of the two great religious figures. The Buddha is usually shown lying on his side, a gentle smile on his face as he accepts death with detachment and dispassion. The Christ, in utter contrast, is often shown in agony and sorrow. Indeed, in contrast to the Buddha's dispassion, this suffering image is often called "the passion" of Jesus. The distinction may seem subtle, but it is important. For the religious view not only shows us our proper response to suffering but also declares its meaning and its reality. Thus, the Buddha's religious view shows him and the rest of us how to escape and transcend suffering; the Christ shows us how and why we must genuinely endure it.

In contrast to both perspectives, one might well complain that these religious views of suffering accept sorrow too much. Indeed, a stark atheistic complaint against all religion might argue that religious consolations just numb us to the reality of suffering and injustice, keeping us passive and complacent in the face of disease and injustice. This is perhaps one implication of Karl Marx declaring religion to be a drug, "the opiate of the people."

In fact, however, it seems that many religious views of suffering actually give us good reason to fight and to rage against sorrow and pain, as they suggest that the proper response is to struggle against the evils of life. Evident even in the story of Jesus and the encouragement to Christian martyrs, it is suggested that suffering is bad in itself. Certainly, the God of the Jewish scriptures, declared often to be a judgmental and punishing deity, is at least as often declared to be the one who comforts the sick and cares especially for those in need. In the famous passage from Isaiah, God chides His people for practicing their trite religious rituals and then insists that real physical care for others is the kind of ritual He prefers:

In spite of an element of acceptance, Abrahamic religions also demand struggling against suffering caused by injustice.

> *Is not this the fast that I choose: to loose the bonds of injustice, to undo the thongs of the yoke, to let the oppressed go free, and to break every yoke? Is it not to share your bread with the hungry, and bring the homeless poor into your house; when you see the naked, to cover them, and not to hide yourself from your own kin? (Isaiah 58:6–7)*

Here, the Jews as are told to defend the poor, to uproot injustice, and to be signs to the world that God Himself is good to people. For God Himself is to be known as "Defender of the fatherless," and those who follow His law should do likewise.

In many religions, then, the response to suffering is relatively passive, while in others it is active. Perhaps we find some sense in both, even if the balance and application of both is difficult to practice. For it does seem that the struggles of life and the very real and painful sorrows of sickness and death, especially the loss of those we love, ought to trouble us and move us. It is difficult to know if our rage and rebellion against the evils of the world, or our acceptance and "transcendence" of our own and others' suffering, is the greater spiritual response—or the greater error. We bear it, we fight it, we endure, and we turn to heal others. Or perhaps we deem it an illusion and let it pass with a nod of recognition. Which in all of these explanations for the sorrows of the world shall we embrace to inspire us in response? The answer one most immediately entertains may depend on which notion of the Absolute one accepts. And similarly, how one responds to suffering will help direct how one comes to understand the Sacred.

GLOBALIZATION AND AN UNSPEAKABLE EVIL

In this chapter we have discussed many theories about the causes and consequences of evil. We have seen that religions almost inevitably are concerned with suffering and evil, but they offer different explanations for suffering and diverse prescriptions for dealing with it. We take a bit different tact at this point. We look at how the great suffering and evil of the 20th century interacted with the globalization process.

With two world wars along with a number of smaller but deadly conflicts, numerous atrocities causing suffering and loss of life, and countless instances of plague, famine, and other natural disasters, the 20th century likely was the

The 20th century
likely has been the
bloodiest in his-
tory.

bloodiest century in history. In part, this was the case because there were simply more people around to suffer and die. Around 1850 for the first time in human history, the human population of the Earth reached one billion. Even with the destructive events outlined above, the human population increased dramatically so that by the year 2000 there were approximately 6.2 billion people on the planet.

In this section, we
focus on the un-
speakable evil of
the Holocaust and
the reaction to it.

Our purpose here is not to discuss all these natural and moral evils or the reactions to them. Instead, we look at the event that encapsulates evil more than perhaps any other—the Holocaust. Then we talk about some of the results of this unspeakable evil.

The Holocaust refers to the German Nazis' concerted effort to exterminate Jews and other "undesirables" from Europe and occupied territories during World War II. At least six million Jews, including one million children, were eradicated in German death camps. However, the Nazi program did not stop with the Jews but extended to Slavs, Roan (Gypsies), homosexuals, the mentally ill, and other categories of people deemed unfit. Some sources argue that as many as 26 million persons many have died in the Nazi death frenzy. Most of those killed were innocent civilians.

In the Holocaust,
Nazis produced an
industry of death
as they attempted
to eliminate
"undesirables,"
especially Jews.

Certainly, the Holocaust is not the first or last example of genocide, or the deliberate effort to wipe out a category of people. Numerous historical instances of genocide can be cited, and many other instances of genocide occurred in the 20th century, both before and after World War II. Yet, the Holocaust stands out in that it represents the most systematic, ferocious, and sustained program of extermination in human memory. The Nazis produced an industry of death. Their efforts were highly organized, employed all the tools of modern industry, required tremendous amounts of resources (physical and human), and were made more efficient by the use of modern science (for instance, many experiments were conducted on how to most efficiently kill their victims). When the full extent of the brutality of the Holocaust became obvious, much of the rest of the world recoiled in horror. The Holocaust may represent the worst example of absolute, unbridled evil that has ever existed.

Most, if not all, of the major religions of the world have subsequently condemned it. Be this as it may, the relation of religion, especially Christianity, is not that simple. There is a powerful line of argument that spells out how nearly 2000 years of a Christian culture that labeled Jews as "Christ killers" played a significant part in creating the social and philosophical context in which the Holocaust played out. Moreover, no major Christian group made an effort to condemn the Holocaust or acted to curb it when it was occurring. The complex relationship of Jews, Christians, and the Holocaust is carefully examined by historian James Carroll in his recent book *Constantine's Sword: The Church and the Jews, a History* (2001).

The relationship
between
Christians, Jews,
and the Holocaust
is incredibly com-
plex.

If the interaction of Judaism and Christianity in producing the Holocaust is complicated, the reaction of these groups to the Holocaust is equally complex. One of the greatest challenges faced by believers is how to make this meaningful. Christian and Jews believe that God speaks in the people and events of history. But what is God saying in the Holocaust? In fact, what kind of God would allow such a thing to happen? Would the God that led the Jews out of slavery in the biblical Exodus lead them into the hands of the Nazis for slaughter? Would the

Christian God who in Jesus Christ suffers and dies for the people he loves allow so many of his children to be sacrificed?

Many Christians and Jews question what, if anything, God meant by the Holocaust.

Should Christians somehow atone for the evil done to the Jews by other Christians? Should they pray for the dead for an intervention by the same Jesus they rejected when they were alive? Does this somehow denigrate the Jews and represent just another form of Christian arrogance? One thing is certain: Many Jews reject the intervention of Christians regarding the Holocaust especially when it seems the event is somehow "Christianized." Some argue that even the name "Holocaust" represents a Christian interpretation of this horror that should be rejected. Holocaust refers to the burnt offerings given to God in the temple. Thus, it indicates the Jews were a burnt offering to God, but to what end? Some Jews prefer to call the Nazi horror "*Shoah*." *Shoah* means "the desolation" or "the time when God was utterly and completely absent." They argue the Holocaust should be known by this uniquely Jewish concept.

Some see the *Shoah* is a turning point when evil was so great that mankind will never again allow such a thing happen. It has led some to abandon their faith altogether, while others have seen it as a reason to turn to religious faith. But perhaps even the effort to create meaning out of the Holocaust is self-defeating. Nobel Prize winning author and Holocaust survivor Elie Wiesel says this, "Auschwitz [one of the more infamous Nazi death camps] negates all systems, opposes all doctrines . . . They cannot but diminish the experience which lies beyond our reach" (qtd. in Carroll 6). Similarly, Jewish theologian Jacob Neusner argues, "What consequences, then, are to be drawn from the Holocaust? . . . I argue that none are to be drawn, none for Jewish theology and none for the life of Jews with one another, which are not there before 1933. Jewish theologians do no good service to believers when they claim 'Auschwitz' denotes a turning point" (qtd. in Carroll 6). Perhaps even reflecting upon the *Shoah* makes the unthinkable, thinkable.

Some theologians see the Shoah as a turning point in history; others say to endow the Holocaust with meaning is a mistake.

Whatever the ultimate meaning or lack thereof that may be drawn from the Holocaust, it has had one practical result with wide-ranging consequences for globalization. The Holocaust is the immediate cause of the United Nations' creation of the Universal Declaration of Human Rights (http://www.un.org/ Overview/rights.html). One of the first acts of the newly formed United Nations was to draw up this document that seeks to ensure member states will protect the political and civil rights, along with the social and economic rights, of people everywhere. One of its aims is to prevent occurrences like the *Shoah* from happening again. At this point, we look at its role in furthering globalization.

One direct result of the Holocaust is the United Nations' Universal Declaration of Human Rights.

The Universal Declaration is a significant advance in thinking about rights on several fronts. The most important of these is that it extends right protections to *all* people regardless of age, sex, religion, citizenship, religion, national origin, or station of birth (high-born or low-born). This is particularly significant because prior to this declaration, whatever rights were recognized were limited only to certain categories of people, such as males, adults, "freemen" as opposed to slaves, and citizens of the country granting the rights.

The idea of universal human rights advanced the cause of globalization on several fronts. Perhaps the most important of these is that it put to the forefront the idea that all people share a common human-ness and should be afforded equally respect, fairness, and justice. This is a boost to developing a consciousness of the sameness of all people that is necessary for the formation of a global society. The Universal Declaration also means that there are standards that are basic to human society that transcend and take precedence over the standards prevalent in a given country. That is, a society may wish to discriminate against minorities or conduct genocidal campaigns, but such activities represent a violation of human rights that must be stopped. It is significant that a number of interventions have been conducted by the United Nations or other agencies in countries where there were particularly blatant violations of citizens' rights. Genocides especially have been sorted out for action. Often these have involved the use of military power to stop bloodshed.

Finally, the Universal Declaration has been the basis for minority groups asserting themselves on a worldwide scale. For instance, women's groups have asserted their right to fair and equitable treatment in male-dominated societies. Likewise, indigenous groups have claimed the right to maintain the uniqueness of their cultures when these were threatened by larger economic or cultural forces. These and other similar appeals to universal standards are some of the most powerful forces driving globalization.

CONCLUSION

We see in the Holocaust the literally *global* influence of suffering on human thought and ideals. Perhaps in another way all suffering is "global," inasmuch as people everywhere know all too well what suffering is. Thus, we have seen that religions, likewise on a global scale, seek to respond to suffering with some explanation of its meaning or purpose. It is, of course, beyond the scope of this text to evaluate the philosophical and emotional adequacy of all of the religious explanations of evil and suffering that we have mentioned. But as a concluding point, let us at least note two more connections that will be addressed in this text. First, there is a clear connection between one's religious interpretation of the suffering of the world and one's religiously inspired ethical response. How we act in this world to relieve the suffering, or if indeed we act in this world to teach people to transcend the suffering, may both be considered acts of compassion. Indeed, one finds fascinatingly different forms of compassion in the story of Kisa Gotami, noted above, and parallel stories in which Jesus is said to have raised dead children to life (for example, in Mark 5). And both are labeled acts of great compassion. Their differences lie, however, in the logical connection between how these two religions view suffering, along with its meaning and its causes. We shall discussion religious ethics in Chapter 10.

Similarly, there is a direct connection between what a religion teaches about suffering and evil and how that religion teaches of ultimate liberation. Salvation, indeed, is a common theme in religion, though perhaps exactly what qualifies as "salvation" may differ widely from religion to religion, as we would expect. But again, we can also expect that there is some internal consistency in these ideas, a logical connection between how one views the sorrows and evils of life and how one expects them to be healed or redeemed. Much religious faith is inspired by the sorrows of life, and it is perhaps precisely because we suffer that we long for a new world, a world of redemption and justice, where "every tear is dried." We might regard this hope as "pie in the sky," or, worse, as a pitiful distraction from concerns of the real world for those too weak to struggle with reality. But it is true that a final redemption, a final hope, has a reasonable connection to our genuine concern with how we understand the meaning of suffering and evil. For some, sorrow and death, moral and natural evils are great and profound enough that there is a final answer only in the promise that "it will not always be this way." For that consideration, see Chapter 12.

In the end, whether we respond to the evils of the world with faith or acceptance, with struggle and tears, with mercy for others and hope for ourselves, or even with angry rebellion, we do so for reasons that often find their meaning in religious beliefs. That which is holy above all things may be the source or the explanation or the ultimate healing of our sorrows, and it is part of our humanness to want to understand this connection. Suffering and evil are powerful emotional and philosophical facts of life, crying out for explanation and response. And how we understand and respond to these facts says a great deal about who we are and about what we believe about the Holy and Absolute Reality.

■ INTERACTIVE EXERCISE

Please continue your exploration of suffering and evil by going to the interactive exercise for this chapter online (**http://www.religion.wadsworth.com/richter**).

WORKS CITED

Berger, Peter. *The Sacred Canopy: Elements of a Sociological Theory of Religion.* Garden City, NY: Doubleday, 1967.

Carroll, James. *Constantine's Sword: The Church and the Jews, a History.* New York: Houghton Mifflin, 2001.

Chan, Wing-tsit. *A Sourcebook in Chinese Philosophy.* Princeton, NJ: Princeton University Press, 1963.

Chuang Tzu. *Chuang Tzu: Basic Writings.* Trans. Burton Watson. New York: Columbia University Press, 1964.

Erdoes, Richard, and Alfonso Ortiz. *American Indian Myths and Legends.* New York: Pantheon, 1984.

Fieser, James, and John Powers. Scriptures of the World's Religions. Boston: McGraw/Hill, 1998.

Hartsuiker, Dolf. Sadhus, Mystic Holy Men of India. Rochester, VT: American International Distribution, 1993.

Hick, John. Philosophy of Religion. Englewood Cliffs, NJ: Prentice Hall, 1963.

Kierkegaard, Søren. The Concept of Dread. Princeton, NJ: Princeton University Press, 1957.

Lewis, C. S. *Problem of Pain.* New York: Collier Books, 1986.

Mayeda, Sengaku. *A Thousand Teachings: The Upadesasahasri of Sankara.* Albany: State University of New York Press, 1992.

Rahula, Walpola. *What the Buddha Taught.* New York: Grove Press, 1974.

Reuters Foundation, "NGO's Responding to Iran Earthquake," *AlertNet,* December 31, 2003. http://www.alertnet.org/thefacts/reliefresources/107270583332 .htm (accessed January 12, 2004).

Robinson, Richard H., and Willard L. Johnson. *The Buddhist Religion: A Historical Introduction.* 4th ed. Belmont, CA: Wadsworth, 1997.

Schaeffer, Francis. "How Should We Then Live?" *The Complete Works of Francis A. Schaeffer.* Vol. 5. Wheaton, IL: Crossway Books, 1994.

Scheub, Harold. *A Dictionary of African Mythology: The Mythmaker as Storyteller.* Oxford, UK: Oxford University Press, 2000.

Spiro, Melford E. *Burmese Supernaturalism.* Englewood Cliffs, NJ: Prentice Hall, 1967.

Stryk, Lucien. *The World of the Buddha.* New York: Grove Weidenfeld, 1968.

Tambiah, S. J. *Buddhism and Spirit Cults in Northeast Thailand.* Cambridge, UK: Cambridge University Press, 1970.

Tillich, Paul. *Systematic Theology.* Vol. I. Chicago: University of Chicago Press, 1957.

Warren, Henry Clarke. *Buddhism in Translations.* New York: Athaneum, 1982.

Watson, Burton, trans. *Chuang Tzu: Basic Writings.* New York: Columbia University Press, 1964.

FOR FURTHER READING

Berger, Peter. *The Sacred Canopy: Elements of a Sociological Theory of Religion.* Garden City, NY: Doubleday, 1967.

Carroll, James. *Constantine's Sword: The Church and the Jews, a History.* New York: Houghton Mifflin, 2001.

Chuang, Tzu. *Chuang Tzu: Basic Writings.* Trans. Burton Watson. New York: Columbia University Press, 1964.

Kierkegaard, Søren. *The Concept of Dread.* Princeton, NJ: Princeton University Press, 1957.

Laws of Manu. http://www.intratext.com/Y/ENG0162.HTM (accessed April 26, 2004).

Lewis, C. S. *Problem of Pain.* New York: Collier Books, 1986.

Rahula, Walpola. *What the Buddha Taught.* New York: Grove Press, 1974.

Warren, Henry Clarke, trans. *The Death of Moggall,nd.* 1896. http://www.sacred -texts.com/bud/bits/bits041.htm (accessed April 26, 2004).

SUGGESTED VIEWING

Schindler's List. Dir. Steven Spielberg. MCA Universal Home Video, 1994.

8 RELIGION AND ART

Throughout the centuries, art, in its multifaceted sheer endless variety, has played a very significant role in the context of religion. This chapter studies various forms of art in their religious contexts. Why are certain artistic expressions considered religious art? What are possible means of interpretation? What is the function of religious art? What kind of criticism has surrounded religious art? Questions like these will occupy our attention in the following chapter. Please use the quotations below and images above and on the Web site (**http://www.religion.wadsworth.com/richter**), to answer the Introductory Questions.

Moses said, "Show me your glory, I pray."

And he said, "I will make all my goodness pass before you, and will proclaim before you the name, 'The LORD'; and I will be gracious to whom I will be gracious, and will show mercy on whom I will show mercy. But," he said, "You cannot see my face; for no one shall see me and live."

And the LORD continued, "See, there is a place by me where you shall stand on the rock; and while my glory passes by I will put you in a cleft of the rock, and I will cover you with my hand until I have passed by; then I will take away my hand, and you shall see my back; but my face shall not be seen."

—Judaism: Exodus 33:18–23

And let [a person] fix his mind in this manner, and awaken deep faith and joy, and make an image of the Buddha with all its signs. Then he gains merit which is vast, and great, and measureless, and limitless, and which can be neither weighed nor counted.

—Buddhism: "The Merit of Making Images" (Van Voorst 110)

Let the same mind be in you that was in Christ Jesus, who, though he was in the form of God, did not regard equality with God as something to be exploited, but emptied himself, taking the form of a slave, being born in human likeness. And being found in human form, he humbled himself and became obedient to the point of death—even death on a cross. Therefore God also highly exalted him and gave him the name that is above every name, so that at the name of Jesus every knee should bend, in heaven and on earth and under the earth, and every tongue should confess that Jesus Christ is Lord, to the glory of God the Father.

—Christianity: Philippians 2:5–11

From the beginning all beings are Buddha.
Like water and ice, without water no ice,
Outside us no Buddhas.
How near the truth, yet how far we seek,
Like one in water crying "I thirst."

How vast is the heaven of boundless samadhi!
How bright and transparent the moonlight of wisdom!
What is there outside us, what is there we lack?
Nirvana is openly shown to our eyes.
This earth where we stand is the pure lotus land,
And this very body, the body of Buddha.

—Zen Buddhism: Hakuin Ekaku's *Chant in Praise of Zazen*)

INTRODUCTORY QUESTIONS

1. Should there be images of God/gods/goddesses? One of the "Ten Commandments" of Judaism/Christianity tells people not to make images. Why does that seem so different from the passage on making images in the Buddhist excerpt? Consider how the biblical passage Exodus 33:18–23 deals with the problem.
2. Philippians 2:5–11 has always been a key text in the debate about imaging God. Use an example of a representation of Jesus Christ to elucidate this.
3. The Dome of the Rock, one of the oldest Islamic works of architecture, carries a mosaic band above the arcades with an Arabic inscription (Kufic). Why does calligraphy receive such a heightened status in Islam? Use the inscription above the Arcades on the Dome of the Rock in Jerusalem as an example.
4. What is your impression looking at the statue of the Buddha seated on a Lotus flower? Please describe it. What can one learn from it?
5. Illustrate how language is used in the *Chant in Praise of Zazen* by Hakuin Ekaku. Try to explain the significance of the wording and structure of the poem in the context of Zen Buddhism.
6. Why, do you think, the picture of Chinese calligraphy is considered religious art?
7. As Nataraja the Lord of Dance, Shiva exhibits a manifestation of primal energy, designating the aspects of creation, preservation and destruction, illusion, and release. How does this representation differ most significantly from images or symbols referring to God in the monotheistic traditions?

RELIGION AND ART

If we were to go on a journey visiting famous places throughout the world, we most likely would encounter an amazing variety of religious art. Chances are that we would be exposed to a seemingly endless, often bewildering variety of religious artistic expressions. On this tour around the world, we would encounter stories of gods and goddesses hewn into stone on the outside of temple walls in India, listen to Gregorian chant that the believer experiences as communication with God, or discover the pleasing quietness of a Japanese Zen garden inviting the visitor to step into a new world of silence and meditation. The architectural magnificence of the Mosque in Damascus and the beauty of its mosaic would probably cause astonishment, while the quiet experience of a tea ceremony in Japan would leave the visitor with no doubt that he or she is participating in an artistic performance.

But what exactly is art, in particular religious art? Why are certain pictures, texts, sculptures, sounds, and dramatizations considered to be religious art? In one sense, it seems clear that religious art is simply art that carries with it some religious theme or religious purpose. As we have distinguished the religious from the non-religious in previous chapters, here, too, we will find interesting connections between art and the Absolute. But what, more specifically, are these connections? What kind of "themes and purposes" does art serve when it is bound up with the religious Ultimate? This chapter will inquire further into such questions. We shall find, as already suggested, that the forms of religious art are as varied as the religions themselves, and that their different functions within their religions can be equally variable. This should not come as a surprise. For just as the world's religions offer many conceptions of the Holy, so they find a multitude of forms and purposes for artistic expression.

There is a striking array of religious art worldwide.

ART AND EXPERIENCE

Throughout most centuries, art was prominently created in the context of religion and very often served as an integral part of religious beliefs and practices. Art, in particular pictorial and performance arts, have served to educate the people about religious ideas. This has especially been the case when the stories and myths of a tradition could not be conveyed in writing. And, of course, the myths and stories themselves—as we saw in Chapter 6: Myths, Stories, History—may overlap with artistic expressions in poetry, in epic and mythic narrative. Chanting and hymns abound throughout the world as music fills churches and temples with praise or magical power. And for much of the world's history, this was the primary use of such arts. This intrinsic correlation between religion and art is probably less prominent today, as modern and postmodern art, especially in secularized societies, have changed things considerably. Yet this does not necessarily imply that art even today is removed from religious contexts altogether, for they are often bound together as mutually reinforcing powers that try to express the deeper experiences of human life

For most of history, art was religious art.

We might, for example, consider the very powerful image of war, *Guernica,* by the Spanish painter and sculptor, Pablo Picasso (1881–1973). Although Picasso's piece is not a religious work, it addresses a question that most human beings are confronted with during their life, namely the question of evil and suffering, which, as discussed in the previous chapter, is also a central theme in religious contexts. The drama of war, inspired by the atrocities committed against civilians in a little Basque village in Spain, becomes, in Picasso's work, an emotionally comprehensible exploration of the human ability to inflict suffering, as well as a critical challenge to any heroic notion of warfare. Exhibited for the first time at the World's Fair in 1937, Picasso's *Guernica* engages the observer to reconsider humanity, especially regarding the meaning and sources of human suffering.

Even today, much art carries religious themes although the religious dimension may not be expressed directly.

Figure 8.1   *Guernica* by Pablo Picasso

Such a work of art has certain parallels in religious art. The Italian painter and sculptor Michelangelo Buonarroti (1475–1674) famously painted the *Fall of Humanity* in the Sistine Chapel, which depicts the myth of the fall, as described in the previous chapter. Here the artist offers a "visual explanation" of suffering caused by sinfulness compellingly located in the woman-faced serpent that deceives humanity and leads into death, as Christians would claim. In the Tibetan Buddhist depiction, the *Lord of Death,* also described in the previous chapter, offers another visualized interpretation of the source of suffering. In this picture, all existence is a circle, a cycle, and all is held in the grip of edacious time. In Hinduism, the goddess *Kali* is often depicted in her bloody rampage among the giants. Even if this is a battle against demons, its bloodthirstiness—severed heads for a necklace, arms for a skirt—seems to convey something of the gravity of life and the battle between good and evil. In a similar fashion, for those who listen to the dramatic presentation of the Christian passion narrative according to St. Matthew by the composer Johann Sebastian Bach (1685–1750), the music may initiate a deep experience of the reality of suffering that touches the senses. In all such religious art, as in Picasso's *Guernica,* some of the starkness of human reality can become part of experience, as all these artworks seem to express the horror of life or of death.

Of course religious art, like secular art, also takes on gentler themes, indeed glorious themes of redemption or, indeed, the wonder of the Absolute itself. But our point in these examples is to show that religious art takes the same themes as secular art but connects its meaning to the Sacred, while revealing something about humanity. It could be said that art works to "humanize the world for us—it presents things to us in a humanly approachable way" (Carroll 104).

Religious art may express many of the themes of secular art but connects these themes to the Sacred Reality.

Can we therefore say art conveys life experience? Is art thus a form of language? Narrative, poetic art, or Islamic calligraphy, of course, utilizes a system of words to communicate. Yet, not all art communicates with words, and, indeed,

calligraphy— artistic script

even in poetry and calligraphy, the meaning of the words alone is not the only, or, perhaps, even the primary purpose of the art. Indeed, art most often employs colors, shapes, sounds, materials, form, smell, or action to engage the observer or audience into a sense experience. The highly symbolic character of artistic expressions offers ambiguity in contrast to at least some distinct forms of language that are deliberately concerned with conceptualizations of experience. For example, to document a car accident in a police report, art would very likely be a highly troublesome tool, since an accurate record of the actual incident is needed. Ambiguity, therefore, would be a most undesirable quality. Art, on the contrary, with its appeal to the senses and emotions as well as its symbolic character, rather incites the imagination to explore reality beyond a mere factual and cognitive level.

Art causes people to use their imagination to carry them beyond the strictly factual realm.

Does this mean that all art makes the world accessible on an emotional level or engages the senses? Emotions and senses can certainly play a significant role in the confrontation with art. Yet, we might again argue that this is just one aspect of a very complex phenomenon, namely the interplay between art as object, the picture, music, sculpture, or any other artistic form and the subject who encounters it. We might think, for example, of the cosmic sound "OM" or the *enso*, the empty circle in Zen Buddhism. The focus here is on the process of creation, not on the product. Chanting or drawing essentially becomes an exercise in meditation. It seems these forms of art initiate a process of change in the ones who perform the sound or make the brushstroke, an act assisting in the process of the development of the self rather than an expression of human qualities. The focus is not expressive but the construction of the self. Art in this context initiates a process of overcoming the differences between cognitive and emotive qualities, the self and the other, or the mind and the body. The focus is on the creative experience that is evolving over a period of time. It may require weeks, years, or even ages.

The focus of art often is a process of creative experience.

It seems, then, that sometimes the purpose of art lies in the doing. Art in this sense is not focusing on the product of the artwork but on the meditative or ethical practice of producing art. Thus, art becomes ritual (see Chapter 9: Ritual). It is, however, true that artistic expressions may have the power to describe something about being human. Or rather, it more than "describes," for it excites the senses even while it conveys ideas. The believer confronted with religious art may both learn and feel something about the presence and the meaning of the Sacred.

Religious art may convey the presence or meaning of the Holy.

■ ART AS AN OPEN CONCEPT

Taking an "art-tasting" journey around the world, we would encounter another aspect of art in general, and of religious art in particular. It would become obvious that religious art exists in a sheer endless variety. Of course, to understand we might be aided by finding some common characteristics and some continuity in the content and forms of religious art within specific cultural contexts. But the task of exploring the same themes and the same forms of religious art becomes almost overwhelmingly difficult once we uncover the boundless diversity of religious art throughout the world. Yet this dazzling array is called "religious art," and within that genre we find similar themes and methods. How shall we begin to understand the variety within the unity?

One approach for dealing with the great variety of diverse examples of religious art might be to look at it under the aspect of family resemblances. In Chapter 6, we discussed Wittgenstein's proposition that language can be compared to a game. According to this theory, words are not merely a more or less successful effort to represent in words some external reality. They are, rather, part of a life-form, a way to live and communicate, such that the rules of language are analogous to the rules of a game. Just as there are many possible moves within the rules of a game of chess, there is likewise a great deal of creative variability in any language. In a similar way, art is dynamic and can be compared to a game. As there are rules in a game, there are certain rules for art, but what art "ought" to do depends on what "game" is being played. It is therefore important to appreciate art in the context in which it emerged. Understanding the purposes of art, finding the "family resemblances," can help one to see and understand differences between various works of art. If an artist were to paint in a completely new fashion, in a manner never seen before, such that there were absolutely no connection between his work and the art that was already known, the artist would be taking the risk that no one would understand his work. It is, therefore, important to identify patterns and criteria to appreciate art, even though these "rules" are not static configurations. As a matter of fact, art enjoys a greater variability than language or, to use the metaphor of the game again, its rules are more flexible. A possible way of considering art might therefore be to perceive it as "open concepts." As Morris Weitz points out:

> *The concept of art or of a work of art functions under a disjunctive set of conditions or criteria in which none is necessary and none is sufficient but each is not rejectable and each is a good reason for saying of something that it is a work of art. (237)*

As an example of the wide variety of art that can occur even within similar contexts, we may consider the diverse representations of the Virgin Mary as she has been captured in painting and sculpture through the centuries. Most paintings of the Virgin Mary portray her in a traditional style, borrowing its theme and manner from earlier well-accepted forms. This technique ensured that the artist's work could at once be recognized broadly and the viewers could readily connect its appearance with the religious biblical context. In contrast, Edvard Munch's (1863–1944) *Madonna* strips the Virgin Mary (quite literally) of her traditional form and color, giving her a kind of inaccessible ecstatic sexuality that was, for Munch, a deliberate protest against a tradition of pious art that idealizes sacred virginity and devotion. The work of Munch, therefore, appeared in opposition to long-established forms of devotional art, presenting a dramatic change of rules from traditional artwork. Nevertheless, the traditional images as the modern painting represent the Madonna and her sanctity as well as her womanhood (more evident in Munch). Thus, one may begin to understand important aspects of art by finding certain similarities as well as understanding their differences, by considering the historical contexts out of which each painting appeared. As this example shows, exploring artistic traditions according to family resemblances in the context of historical, religious, and cultural traditions can be a useful tool for the analysis of art.

To understand art, we must understand the "family resemblances" in the variety of art and discover the "rules" under which each family operates.

Art may be understood, in part, by looking at the cultural traditions and historical settings out of which the art comes.

Figure 8.2 *Madonna* (detail) by Edvard Munch

RELIGIOUS ART

So far, we have discussed art in fairly general terms. Yet what is religious art? It does not seem to be difficult to define religious art during the Medieval Period on the European continent since by and large art was directly or indirectly influenced by the major traditions of Judaism and Christianity, and, to a lesser degree, by Islamic traditions. Art during this period reflected the general conviction that the whole creation is seen and celebrated in art as the symbol of the Divine. The medieval artist contemplates God in the beauty of art.

However, as mentioned previously, the analysis becomes more difficult if we leave the specific geographical boundaries of civilizations characterized by Judeo-Christian tradition or reach into modern and postmodern times. Should *The Starry Night* by the Dutch painter Vincent Van Gogh (1853—1890) be called religious? What about Munch's *Madonna?* Or how can we assess a Zen garden in this context? To answer this question we might want to remind ourselves of the discussion about the numinous in Chapter 3: The Absolute, The Ultimate, The Holy. There, we referred to Immanuel Kant's philosophical justification of the numinous and the sublime. Kant, of course, did not raise the question of religious art. However, his proposition that the aesthetic experience is a way of imaginative mediation between the beautiful and the numinous has greatly influenced theories of art. According to Kant, an image or sculpture is not acclaimed as beautiful because it exhibits harmony or it accurately conforms to an idea or religious belief. Aesthetic experience, which Kant particularly exemplifies in the awe-inspiring encounter of natural phenomena, a startling, fascinating experience of limitlessness, is rooted in the mind's capability to transcend a mere reflection of the object and to move experientially towards the inaccessible noumenal. Kant claims, "Thus, instead of the object, it is rather the mind in appreciating it that we have to estimate as *sublime*" (Kant 500).

In religious contexts, the human being, faced with an infinitely overwhelming experience brought about by objects, imaginatively reflects upon this experience

aesthetic experience—experience inciting a sense of beauty

To some extent, religious art is profound because it conveys the sense of awe of the numinous experience.

Figure 8.3 *The Starry Night* by Vincent Van Gogh

and is transferred beyond the immediate experience, reaching towards what, in Chapter 3, was called (with Rudolf Otto) the *mysterium tremendum et fascinans.* Such transformation of the subject includes all human faculties. As Alain Besançon remarks:

> *The religious sublime is all of a piece, uniting all human faculties and realms of experience. It rids itself of the image and of the work of art, which are marked by their inadequacy. The religious sublime is a total sublime . . . anyone who arrives at this sublime is simultaneously or indiscriminately an artist, a moralist, a saint, a leader of the people. (233)*

Kant, similarly, believed that the power of art to convey an experience of the sublime transports humans "beyond themselves" and makes the experience more than just sensual. For him, this great transformative power was moral. He states:

For Kant, art had the power to transform a person morally.

> *That, too, which we call sublime in external nature, or even internal nature (e.g. certain affections) is only represented as a might of the mind enabling it to overcome this or that hindrance of sensibility by means of moral principles, and it is from this that it derives its interest. (Kant 508)*

In such philosophical considerations of the beauty of art, it seems high praise goes to the power of that beauty to initiate a process among humans to become more moral, more cultivated, certainly more than mere spectators. Moreover, Kant asserts that, in the reflection of art, the mind experiences and conceptualizes the work, initiates a fundamental change in perspective. In contrast to a medieval observer, who would perceive religious imagery as a reflection of divine glory, in a post-Kantian context, the mind of the spectator her/himself understands and forms a concept of the work.

This change in perspective has significantly influenced philosophers in their exploration of new theories of art, among these **Arthur Schopenhauer's** (1788–1860) theory of an "aesthetic ugliness," which leaves behind common prettiness. The German philosopher contends that if the artistic object is experienced as confrontational, non-pleasing, as offensive to the eye, the human being will actually be fortified. The will to overcome the experience of the ugly, he argues, or "the will to detachment," is necessary in order to free the subject of its ugliness and to permit the person to contemplate the sublime (Schopenhauer 260–262). One may think of Munch's *Madonna*. While it might not appear as unsightly to our modern taste, it certainly does not represent the traditional religious image of the Virgin Mary. On the contrary, its sexual attractiveness combined with religious symbolism, signified by the halo, distorts notions of religious piety. Yet does this mean that Munch's *Madonna* is not art? Schopenhauer would argue that the battle for willfully overcoming the expectancy of prettiness of the ordinary and the common frees the human being to gain insights into the deeper ideas manifest in art.

Schopenhauer believed that ugliness in art gives people "the will to detachment" that was necessary to contemplate the sublime.

In all this, it seems that the experience of the sublime in art, as well as in nature, raises us above ourselves. The religious sublime in particular corresponds to a spiritual experience, which may be captured in an artistic concept for representation of the ineffable or nondepictable. In short, by exciting the experience of the sublime, religious art enables human beings to imagine what cannot be seen or sensed fully. That is why even abstract art, like the chapel by the Latvian artist **Mark Rothko** (1903–1970) in Houston, Texas, or even, admittedly in a much broader understanding of the concept of the sublime, the simplicity of a Japanese tea ceremony or a Chinese drawing of nature can be seen as examples of religious art that excite the aesthetic experience of the sublime. It becomes a way to image the divine.

By exciting the experience of the sublime, religious art enables people to "see" what cannot be seen.

sublime—
absoluteness

■ IMAGING THE DIVINE: HINDUISM

O Goddess, by you everything is supported; by you is the world created;
By you is it all protected, and you always consume it at the end of time.
At the world's emanation you have the form of creation, in its protection
　you have the form of steadiness;
Likewise at the end of the world you have the form of destruction, O you
　who consist of the world!
You are the great knowledge, the great illusion (mahamaya), the great
　inside, the great memory,
The great delusion, The Great Goddess and also the great Demoness!
　You are primordial material (pakriti) of everything, manifesting the
triad of constituent strands (gunas) . . .
You are auspiciousness, the queen, modesty, intelligence, the knower.
Bashfulness, well-being, contentment, too, tranquility and forbearance are
　you.
Terrible with your sword and spear, likewise with cudgel and discus,

Figure 8.4   Chapel by Mark Rothko

With conch and bow, with arrows, sling and iron mace as your
   weapons . . .

(Coburn 290–291)

This hymn, which is part of the popular Sanskrit text *Devi Mahatyama* (fifth or sixth century CE), praises the all-inclusive characteristics of the Great Goddess in Hinduism. It is an extraordinary example of poetry that evokes the image of an all-encompassing divine reality. The text, throughout the centuries, has been an inspiration for artists. According to the hymn, Devi has the powers of creation, protection, and destruction, a supremacy that in the Hindu tradition is generally attributed to the gods Brahma, Vishnu, and Shiva. She encompasses paradoxical qualities, exhibiting great knowledge and great illusion, great insight, great memory, and great delusion. Simultaneously, she is Goddess and Demoness, primordial as well as manifest, and exhibits majesty and modesty. Shyness and forbearance, as well as her bellicose character, are all forms of Devi. The outward appearance of the great mother, as suggested in the text, is paradox, beyond the known reality. The contradiction in terms thus provokes the visualization of a divine reality of manifold characteristics, which has led to an endless variety of artistic representations of Devi in sculpture and imagery. To name just a few depictions, Hindus, therefore, praise the triumphant Durga, the forceful

The paradoxical nature of the Holy in Hindu religion has resulted in a multitude of contradictory artistic expressions.

warrior Kali, the goddess of learning Sarasvati, or Lakshmi the goddess of fortune and prosperity, all as Devi, the great goddess.

The poetic text is a mantra. The devout Hindu recites the hymn or performs the ritual of puja in front of the divine effigy, an act of devotion in which the word as well as its imaging connect the physical with the spiritual dimension and incite the mind to meditate upon the impossible (Coburn 56). The word, as well as the divine image or sculpture, is powerful for the believer.

So far we have only considered Devi, who offers a fascinating diversity of numerous representations in which all possible physical and spiritual qualities are united. Yet, of course, artistic sensibility is not limited to the example of the Great Mother but includes all gods in the Hindu tradition. Form in all its possibility is utilized to allow the mind to meditate. In this sense, artists have decorated Hindu temples with manifold sculptures that tell stories of the gods. Shiva and his wife Parvati come alive in an elaborate dance, a delicate tale in which the contact between the believer and the gods is enhanced on a most intrinsic sensual level. Ganesha, the elephant-headed son of Shiva and Parvati, carrying a bowl filled with sweets in his trunk, is venerated for his wisdom and knowledge. Hinduism, at least in its neverending variety of divine characteristics of its numerous gods and goddesses, emphasizes symbolic unity in incredible variety. Through the endless multiplicity of artistic representations, the believer is reminded that any easy categorization cannot encompass Ultimate Reality. Yet artistic form, in all its variety, offers a spur for the mind to meditate upon the Divine.

■ IMAGING THE DIVINE: THE MONOTHEISTIC TRADITIONS

While Hinduism, in some traditions, uses multiplicity to express symbolic unity, among the monotheistic traditions the dispute over the question of how to communicate what is essentially ineffable and nondepictable has been carried on throughout the centuries. The disagreement about the sacred image or icon has not only been the cause of numerous debates among theologians but also the source for fierce iconoclasm. It is interesting to follow some aspects of the discussion in the context of the monotheistic traditions.

In Judaism, the Torah offers a twofold path regarding the image of God. According to Genesis 1:27, "So God created humankind in his image, in the image of God he created them." This text provides an important suggestion that imaging God is possible, since a relation exists between humans and God. This notion is further assisted by the idea of God's involvement in the world. In the biblical text, God is not an abstract concept or a distant or formless Absolute but appears deeply engaged with His people through the covenant. He jealously, and at times angrily, guards the faith of His people (for example, Deuteronomy 6:13–15), while He also comforts them in suffering as a mother comforts her children.

> *Shall I open the womb and not deliver? says the LORD; shall I, the one who delivers, shut the womb? says your God. Rejoice with Jerusalem, and be glad for her, all you who love her; rejoice with her in joy, all you who mourn over her—that you may nurse and be satisfied from her consoling breast; that you may drink deeply with delight from her glorious bosom. As*

puja—Hindu ritual performance

The word, as well as the divine image or sculpture, is powerful for the believer.

Artistic form inspires the mind to meditate on the Divine.

iconoclasm—action of breaking or demolishing in particular religious images

a mother comforts her child, so I will comfort you; you shall be comforted in Jerusalem. You shall see, and your heart shall rejoice; your bodies shall flourish like the grass; and it shall be known that the hand of the LORD is with his servants, and his indignation is against his enemies. (Isaiah 66:9–14)

Here are images of God, not depicted *per se,* but possibly imagined nonetheless, inviting, as it were, a sense of how God could be pictured in representational art. Precisely because God is so much like the beings He created, so much like a mother, so much like an artisan of the world of nature, we might expect that representation of the Hebrew God Yahweh in art would be a common phenomenon.

Yet throughout history, to imagine God with human or anthropomorphic characteristics has often been perceived as the practice of **idolatry** in the monotheistic religions. The belief in God as the one and only all-powerful God was a struggle through most of Israel's early history. In Judaism, warnings and prohibitions against the making of idolatrous imagery continuously indicate that the religious commitment to the exclusive covenant was threatened by the attraction of gods and goddesses that could be awesomely represented and worshipped in images. Thus, the second commandment in the covenant epitomizes the prohibition against the worship of idols:

idolatry—worship of false gods

You shall not make for yourself an idol, whether in the form of anything that is in heaven above, or that is on the earth beneath, or that is in the water under the earth. You shall not bow down to them or worship them; for I the LORD your God am a jealous God, punishing children for the iniquity of parents, to the third and the fourth generation of those who reject me but showing steadfast love to the thousandth generation of those who love me and keep my commandments. (Exodus 20: 4–6)

Idolatry does not include *any* image, but certainly all images that are worshipped for their divine nature and magical powers become "idols." Of course, abstractions like money and fame might also be idols in a sense, but in biblical times the threat of idolatry was perceived in the fact that the nations probably worshipped many kinds of images, representing men, animals, and other beings that could be associated with natural powers. Thus, the natural phenomena became idols, along with representations of divine beings in pictures, statues, and amulets. The biblical texts thus reflect a struggle for what was believed the true conception of the God of Israel, a struggle that seems to have lasted until the radical purification of Israel in response to the Babylonian exile. Under Ezra, Haggai, Nehemiah, and Malachi, imagery was strictly banned; even the divine name, Yahweh, was not to be pronounced.

Christianity inherits the ambivalence towards images from the Hebrew tradition. The belief that, through Jesus, God has become human contributes yet another significant aspect to the discussion about divine imagery. The hymn cited by Paul in the letter to the Philippians (see the third opening quotation) contains an early Christian proclamation that proclaims the mystery of God becoming human. Jesus the Christ, this passage declares, was originally "in the form of

To Christians, the belief that God took on flesh in Jesus Christ leaves open the possibility that God could be depicted in art.

God," but took "the form of a slave," and was born into the world "in human likeness," thus "found in human form." Thus, a visible and therefore depictable human being, Jesus Christ, was believed to carry the image of the invisible God (2 Corinthians 4:4). Consequently, to picture God in analogy to His Son becomes a feasible possibility.

However, not everybody agreed on this matter. The hymn of Philippians 2:5–8 thus stands at the beginning of heated disputes within the Christian Church that have appeared and reappeared throughout the centuries. Since God Himself took on a physical likeness, may God therefore be depicted in physical form without the risk of idolatry? May at least the divine image be represented as something merely earthly, meant perhaps for those simple and ignorant people who could not otherwise fathom the concept of a transcendent reality? Do such images then actually enhance the knowledge of God? The **Church Fathers** exchanged their arguments in heated discussions about the symbolic nature of artistic representations, providing the theological arguments that served as guidance for future artists. Before these discussions, Christian art developed very slowly, mostly employing symbolic signs like the cross or the fish. But artistic depiction was given a more prominent role after the conversion of the Roman emperor **Constantine** (324 CE), taking on important political and social implications. One can see, for example, the grandiose representations of the *Christ Pantocrator* in Byzantine art or "Christ as philosopher". In these images, religious art changed dramatically from its humble beginnings, becoming a powerful, public proclamation of Christ as a religious figure and worldly leader.

Christian art began to flourish after the conversion of Constantine.

Islam offers a very different attitude towards images. While the biblical texts provide ample evidence of prohibitions against idolatry and the Koran frequently warns of idols (for example, Koran 21:57), there are no explicit guidelines. When asked about divine images, Muslims often cite Sura 59:24:

He is Allah the Creator, the Maker, the Fashioner; His are the most excellent names; whatever is in the heavens and the earth declares His glory; and He is the Mighty, the Wise.

As Bessançon rightly claims, it "requires a theological exegesis to deduce the prohibition on figuration from this verse" (78). Nevertheless, devout Muslims would not dare to imagine a figure of Allah nor would an artist create His image. Islam, therefore, is said to be strictly aniconic, which means the rejection of any kind of imagery depicting the Divine Reality. The only way divine nature can be known is through the revealed word, the verbal revelation of the uncreated Holy Koran. The reason for this absolute rejection of imagery, according to Bessançon, is the notion in Islam that God is infinitely distant. In contrast to Judaism and Christianity, in which figurative expression seems to suggest itself, Islam has no need to prohibit the image. That is, precisely because God is presented in the Bible with figurative images, physical imagery is invited and idolatry of the image is a danger. For Islam, God is too distant to be figuratively described; images are therefore inconceivable, and so there would seem to be no immediate danger of people being led astray by image-making. Instead, ritual practice and the word of the Koran offer guidance towards the invisible. It should not come as a surprise

exegesis — interpretation of a text

Muslims follow a strong prohibition against divine images of any kind.

that, in place of representational religious art, Islam brings forth superb calligraphy that celebrates the revealed word, as well as the architectural marvel of mosques with open courtyards that lead the gaze towards the endless vastness of heaven, and the beauty of mosaic pictures that symbolize paradise. Where God cannot be depicted, these artistic impressions instead become hints and illustrations of that which cannot be represented.

In all these cases, we see the difficulty of having representational art in those religions that find the Absolute in the holy uniqueness of a single Creator God. Of the three Abrahamic religions, Christianity is the most pictorial, indeed with direct representations not only of Jesus but even of God the Father. Probably precisely because God, to the Christian mind, has honored the physical form in the act of becoming Jesus Christ, that representational art can be justified. Yet, time and again, the danger of idolatry initiated contentious debates and struggles even among Christians. To picture God visualized as "Father" as Michelangelo did in the Sistine Chapel, would be a grave sin for Muslims. Again, this should not come as a surprise since for both Judaism and Islam the incarnation of God in Christ is not any part of the notion of the Holy.

■ THE ART OF BUDDHISM

So far, iconic art in the major theistic traditions has been discussed, including the polytheism of Hinduism and the monotheism of the Abrahamic faiths. Yet what about traditions like Buddhism, which have often been called both atheistic and aniconic? It might be expected that there would be no iconic representations if there were no gods to represent. But, of course, there are many depictions, both paintings and, especially, statues of the Buddha or of Bodhisattvas, sometimes in richly ornamented garments. What is the possible significance of these works of art?

> *Most Buddhists hold that the attention given to religious sculptures is not worship but paying respect.*

The majority of Buddhists maintain that the reverence given to images or Buddhist sculptures is not religious adoration or worship but respect. For example, the life story of the Buddha might be represented on a stele portraying important events are of significance for the Buddha's path to enlightenment. Among these are the birth of the Buddha, his enlightenment and teaching, and his death. But the point, evidently, is not merely to worship the Buddha at these stages of his life. Instead, the Buddhist emphasizes the spiritual qualities of the great teacher: his supreme wisdom, his boundless compassion, and his spiritual strength. The Buddha's life, therefore, provides guidance to the believer on his own path towards enlightenment. In a similar way, the sculpture of the Buddha Sakyamuni in a seated lotus posture is a lesson on meditation, a visualization of profound contemplation. Thus, Buddhists would say that the point of such art is not worship *per se* but respect for the great accomplishments of the great teacher, accomplishments that become models for the believer.

> *Tantric tradition—Buddhist teaching that emphasizes the bodily experience as the path to enlightenment*

Yet, there are other dimensions to Buddhist art. Especially in the Tantric tradition, art functions as a vehicle to self-transformation. Here, the focus of detachment, so prevalent in the strict Theravada tradition, is rejected, and imagery is used to lead the spiritual aspirant to an experience of unity with enlightened beings or with enlightenment itself. For this purpose, Tantric Buddhists employ the geometrical form of a *mandala,* which represents at its center a kind of cosmic connection, a sense of unity with divine wisdom. In practice, the *mandala* serves as the guide to self-realization via visualization, as one moves oneself through this stylized, visually represented room into the center. There, the meditator takes his own place as an enlightened being, since in Tantric Buddhism the devotee is the deity. Thus, the *mandala* is an important tool for meditation utilizing sensual and emotional appeal, as the senses and the emotions play an essential role in the ritual performances, intrinsically connected with Tantric images.

While Tantric Buddhism utilizes the sensual experience of colors, shapes, and forms to enhance visualization, Zen Buddhism, in contrast, appears as a constant protest against manifestation. The famous empty circle, the *enso* mentioned before, almost seems like a denial of visual guidance and direction, inasmuch as it is intentionally without content. Yet, it is still a guiding symbol, precisely because it is empty. As a matter of fact, Zen art might be best characterized by its paradoxical characteristics:

> *Zen demands being rather than representing, yet has inspired many different kinds of art. Zen teaches us not to merely hear, but to listen; not just to look, but to see; not only to think, but to experience and above all not to cling to what we know, but to accept and rejoice in as much of the world as we may encounter. (Addiss 6)*

Art, in the context of Zen, is a spur to search for awakening, refusing to settle for the merely visual appeal of representation.

The tea ceremony, for example, is a ritual of great aesthetic appeal yet deliberate in its simplicity and integrated into daily life. A few people come together, along a garden path lined with stones and a small pond, into a very modest hut. Inside, hot water is prepared, green tea is whisked, and the guests are served. Sweets are offered, balancing the taste of the tea. Nothing elaborate, and yet the highly sensory experience of taste, smell, and the sound of boiling water, connected with the serenity of the ceremony, provide an environment in which harmony and beauty offer a path to self-realization.

Ease seems to be a key aspect of Zen brushwork as well. Nothing is forced, but the flow of nature appears in the drawing, flowing from the deep attention and awareness of the artists. The sensory experience of nature is central to many works, not as mere visualization but as conscious realization and awakening of its true reality. In this sense, the focus is on the process of creation, not primarily on the artwork's lasting aesthetic value. In a fascinating analysis, Trevor Leggett suggests that even the simple figure of the Chinese symbol for "one," merely a single horizontal line, can be drawn in many misshapen ways, each error representing some form of inattention or unclarity of mind. Only the pure mind can draw this simple line perfectly (Leggett 222–223). Thus, art is more than depiction; it is a state of the enlightened mind.

In all its sincerity, Zen art can be deeply humorous. **Hakuin Ekaku** (1685–1769), an influential **Zen teacher** and artist, created superb works often mocking the overzealous devotee who pretends to have reached enlightenment. Famous is his drawing *Blind Men Crossing a Bridge* (Addiss 111), which portrays several men anxiously crawling across a bridge. The image is a metaphor for enlightenment. The ones whose minds are awakened see and do not need to struggle across

In Zen Buddhism, the empty circle is a guiding symbol precisely because it is empty.

Art may be more than a depiction of the Holy. It is an enlightened state of mind.

the dangerous currents of the river, as do the blind men in the drawing. The bridge, however, only seemingly provides the safe path, as it does not actually reach the other shore. Hakuin's bridge frankly exposes the shortsightedness of the mind carried away by illusion, yet it also gently encourages aspiration towards awakening.

Our discussion of Zen art would not be complete if we did not include an example of poetry, especially the so-called *haiku* form. The classic *haiku* poem consists of three lines, with each line exhibiting a certain number of syllables. A classic example is the frog *haiku* of Bassho (1644–1694):

Furur ike ya	*An old pond—*
kawazu tobikomu	*a frog jumps in:*
mizu no oto	*the sound of water*
	(Addiss 134)[1]

One should take some time to read the poem, and indeed read it aloud in the Japanese if possible. Can you imagine the jumping frog, hear the sounds of the splashing water, and see the ripples of the waves? The poem is characterized by an amazing harmony created through a balance of contrasting sounds and images. Each syllable, the Buddhist might say, captures an essence beyond words, although the words are incentives to explore the conscious realization of this essence. Thus, poetry may guide one toward timelessness, breaking through worldly reality, deepening insight towards awakening. Thus, the *haiku* poem is a startling example of artistic expression that gently encourages the development and construction of the self.

Poetry may guide one toward time-lessness, deepening insight toward awakening.

Zen art is surprising, paradoxical, a seemingly unending attempt to protest conceptualization while guiding the devotee towards emptiness and quietness. Other Buddhist art, as we have seen, is more representational yet not—at least for the more sophisticated follower—as an object of worship but a focus for veneration and respect. All this makes sense within the Buddhist religion precisely because, as we have seen, the Ultimate Reality is not conceived of in theistic forms. We would expect to find theistic imagery more evident in Hinduism, where a multitude of gods seems to invite a multitude of worshipped images. And indeed, this is precisely what we find. In comparison, there is less tendency to find direct representation of the one God in monotheistic religions, except in Christianity where that one God is believed to have taken on human form in Jesus. All this suggests a profound, but not really surprising, consistency between how a religion might use art and the way it conceives of the Absolute Ultimate Reality.

THE POWER OF ART

You might recall a moment in which an artistic image, the performance of a musician, or the grandeur of an architectural structure has overwhelmed you and left a feeling of far-reaching significance. Admittedly, this does not happen with all art, yet the fact that it does occur at all speaks for the impact that at least some art might exert on human beings. Sometimes art can be attached to certain ideas, like music attached to lyrics, so that the beauty of the art can influence the way

---

1. © 1989 Stephen Addiss. Reprinted with permission.

we receive the ideas. Art can inspire dedication to a cause, or it can distract from more important tasks. Religious devotion may be one of those causes or tasks. So the question here is whether art really aids religious devotion or is a deception and a distraction from what is truly the Absolute. In either case, it is evident that art has great power for influencing people's ideas and behaviors, but the problem is that the final religious value of art, like all power, can be ambiguous.

The age-old struggle between those who hold the qualities of persuasiveness of religious art in high esteem and iconoclasts, who would destroy the image or art in order to ensure the purity of the numinous, still continues. Plato, the ancient Greek philosopher, for example, maintained that artistic images could only provide a deficient similarity to the original form. That is, he believed that human souls at their best long to know "pure forms," spiritual realities that transcend the mere imitative objects of physical existence. And art, a mere imitation of imitation, is only a further distraction from "the Real." (Plato 598 b-c.) More recently, Kant's aesthetic theory mentioned previously prepared the path for modern iconoclasm by suggesting that art is a vehicle for experiencing the sublime and thereby pointing toward the highest ideals of moral freedom. Thus, the value of art is not in its intrinsic beauty but in the way one might be awakened by art to moral value (Kant 508). In his time, this meant that artistic beauty was no longer limited to images of the medieval hierarchical world, in which every aspect of art was to reflect the glory of God. Instead, art was set free to abandon traditional authority and subject it to critical assessment.

There is an age-old struggle between those who have high regard for religious art and iconoclasts.

Apart from such philosophical criticisms of the power of art, one might note that, even within religion, the potential of art to incite spiritual experiences, to arouse the senses, and to provoke emotional reactions remains ambiguous. Certainly, religions themselves use the appeal of art's attractiveness to propound their own messages. For example, on the inner face of the octagonal arcade of the Dome of the Rock in Jerusalem, attractive beauty and magnificent design greatly enhance the eloquence of the inscribed message:

In the name of God, the Merciful the Compassionate. There is no god but God. He is One. He has no associates. [the beginning of the shahada] Unto Him belongeth sovereignty and unto Him belongeth praise. He quickeneth and He giveth death; and He is Able to do all things . . . Muhammad is the servant of God and His messenger . . . , L//o! God and His angels shower blessings on the Prophet. O ye who believe! Ask blessing on him and salute him with a worthy salutation . . . The blessing of God be upon him and peace be on him, and may God have mercy. . . . O people of the Book! Do not exaggerate in your // religion [dini//kum] nor utter aught concerning God save the truth. The Messiah, Jesus son of Mary, was only a messenger of God, and His Word which He conveyed unto Mary, and a spirit from Him. So believe in God and His messengers, and say not "Three"—Ce//ase! [it is] better for you!—God is only One God. Far be it removed from His transcendent majesty that He should have a son. His is all that is in the heavens and all that is in the earth. And God is sufficient as Defender. The Messiah well never scorn b//e a servant unto God, nor will the favored angels. (Whelan 4)

Figure 8.5 "Judgment" hewn into stone at Autun, France

Muslims use architecture and beautiful calligraphy to express and enhance their message.

Prominently located above the heads of those who enter this holy Islamic place, the magnificence of the architecture and the splendor of the calligraphy certainly capture the eye. The inscription is clearly a religious message, claiming the uniqueness and the holiness of Allah. But it is also a political statement drawing unmistakable boundaries between the righteous and those who fall into the traps of false belief, namely Christians, who proclaim Christ as the Son of God. Art here, in all its beauty, serves to influence the believer to follow the Islamic religious faith and to disdain the error of the Christians.

Religious art is used as an educational tool.

Religious art has also been an effective educational source. For the Medieval or Renaissance person who was illiterate, scenes of final judgment centrally located above the main entrances of churches and cathedrals served as a storybook, representing the biblical text. Hewn into stone at Autun, France, is a pre-taste of the hellish punishment or the glorious salvation awaiting all souls in the future. Notably, during medieval times, this place in the church would also have marked the actual place in some Northern European cities where legal court decisions would have been executed (Barnes 8). Perhaps it is not merely coincidence that the scene brings to mind the image of a court, in which the judge reaches the final verdict. The institution of the law court provides the image, which compels the observer to make a connection between the legal judgments that happen around us and the heavenly judgment before which all souls must eventually stand. Thus, the concept of judgment on earth provides the concrete link to a world at the end of time, and the authority and power of eternal judgment conveys a sense of gravity to the earthly judgments of merely human courts. Social reality and religious belief here correspond closely in this artistic image, offering a frightening outlook for the believer.

Art may be a medium to bridge the gap between the social structure and the religious structure.

Figure 8.6 *Last Judgment* by Michelangelo

Michelangelo's Last Judgment presents a powerful drama of the horrible consequences of sin but also emphasizes the power of those claiming to forgive sins.

Michelangelo's *Last Judgment* in the Sistine chapel in Rome is another interesting example of religious art that enhances social structures. Situated prominently above the main altar, Jesus carries out the ultimate judgment over the souls. A dramatic scene develops in the picture. Captured for the ages is the horrified sinner, pulled into hell by dark forces, anxiously expecting the moment of terrifying punishment. Others are helped by angels to reach towards the heavenly realm. Artistic expressions do not only appeal to the cognitive ability of human beings but most often also provoke an emotional response, including pleasure, pain, fear, or interest, and therefore compel the observer to readily comply with the objectified symbolic system (Freedberg 317–344). Here we have not merely a discursive sermon about heaven and hell but rather frightening images that can provide an extraordinary example of persuasiveness. That is, Michelangelo's painting of the Last Judgment is simply intimidating in the commanding posture of Christ appearing in the human body, and in the frightening images of the chaotic hellish realm. A drama of the ultimate judgment in its irrevocability unfolds before the eyes of the observer and proclaims a fierce warning of the consequences of one's actions. But notably, these are consequences from which, according to the Roman Catholic tradition, the pope, bishops, and priests could absolve. Art, in this context, educates the believer, but it also provides a powerful tool in the hands of the ones who absolve from sinfulness. Here in the Sistine Chapel, political reality and religious belief coincide.

Art may also be used as a powerful tool for undermining religious and political structures.

This is not to say that Michelangelo's painting merely played into the hands of the ruling religious authority. The careful observer will notice several points of reference that can be reminders of the dangerous relationship between power and divine authority. A famous example is the sinner falling into hell, who carries a money bag around his neck, a constant reminder of the vice of avarice, which was especially tempting for those holding power. Thus, one might, from the same picture, be moved to seek refuge in the Roman Catholic rituals of absolution or to repent of the abuse of power and wealth. Art in general has the power to move the human being, but it is a power that can be used in many different directions.

■ RELIGIOUS ART IN A GLOBAL CONTEXT

Religious art has been freed from the "tyranny of place" that allows for exchange among artists worldwide.

Globalization, of course, also significantly influences art in general, and religious art in particular. The freedom from what Tyler Cowan calls the "tyranny of place" to a never-before-seen extent allows artists to access diverse expressions of art, exchange ideas, and immerse themselves in a multicultural environment (Cowan 5). Opportunities for international travel and accessibility even of remote places that still house some of the few indigenous people left in the world have dramatically augmented international exchange of art. In addition, the advances of information technology, as well as international trade, foster knowledge about, as well as trade of, artistic ideas and works on a scale never seen before. While this is of great significance for those who produce art, it also affects those who are interested in art, who consume, support, utilize, and/or purchase the work. Religious art is certainly not exempt from this dynamic exchange taking place in a global world.

The fact that religious art, as argued in this chapter, frequently correlates human experience with what is believed to be Ultimate Reality also inherently binds it to modern dynamics of globalization. This means religious art cannot escape the influences of the Western modern or postmodern culture, with its emphasis on otherness and difference, a focus that defies totality. David Tracy, referring to the medium of global communication, therefore claims:

> The new, participatory technologies of the global communications network are changing many social scientific readings of our situation. Our situation is no longer adequately described simply as "postindustrial," . . . but is

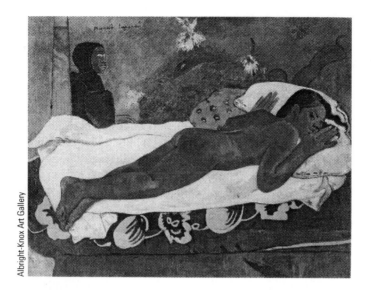

Figure 8.7 *Spirit of the Dead Watching* **by Gaugin**

more radically "postmodern." Here the cultural postmodern emphasis on diversity, difference, and otherness surprisingly meets a new technologically informed sense of participation. (Tracy, 241–242)

Accordingly, globalization affects art in a way that hardly can be categorized via a universal model. A frequent characteristic of art in general and religious art in particular actually becomes its multiplicity of diverse approaches emerging from an extraordinary increase in the exchange of ideas, forms, and the enhanced possibilities of exposure to artistic expressions. Direct and even simultaneous accessibility of Internet sources, for example, allows people throughout the world to view Tibetan sacred art, listen to the chanting of the Holy Koran, access beautifully illuminated Haggada manuscripts, or be exposed to pioneering of Tahitian culture in Gaugin's (1848–1903) painting, *Spirit of the Dead Watching*. In contrast to most cultural environments throughout history, technological advances greatly foster the focus on diversity, if only through enhanced accessibility of religious art.

One impact of globalization on religious art is to foster a greater appreciation of its diversity.

We may, of course, raise the question of whether such rapid exchange is desirable, whether it does not destroy the unique identity of various traditional forms of religious art mixing diverse aspects and thus stripping these from their original sacred context. So, we might argue that Gaugin's artistic exploration of the Tahitian people actually demystifies the original spiritual context. Similarly, the acquisition of Native American ceremonial objects, like the Kachina dolls, deprives those objects of their sacred quality. They simply have become souvenirs in the hands of tourists and therefore lose a religious value that was attributed to them before.

The globalization process may destroy the unique character of art by mixing it with other forms from different contexts.

In addition, many of the Native American artists, in particular those who sell their works in galleries, nowadays consider themselves primarily as reputable artists rather than creators of spiritual objects for a tribal ceremonial act. In other words, the religious significance of the work has changed dramatically. The work is viewed as a piece of art, while its role as spiritual tool becomes secondary or is forgotten, possibly lost completely. How much such loss is mourned depends on the way religious art is viewed and the importance that one might attribute to exchange as stimulant for creative new perspectives of artistic expressions. Ironically, the contact between Native Americans and Spanish and Mexican settlers provoked the Hopi production of Kachina dolls as well as trade of these objects. It is even debated whether Kachina dolls were carved before the tribe had any contact with Mexican/Spanish settlers (Cowan 57).

Such losses are also criticized in the context of "media imperialism," which explores the frequently used symbol of the powerful superimposition of American cultural imperialism via Hollywood and mass media (Crane 3). It is certainly true that American media occupies a prominent as well as highly influential place throughout the world, to a considerable degree fostered by the dominance of English as the most widely known language. Via such avenues, blockbuster movies like *The Matrix* are accessible throughout the world. Accordingly, American secular and religious values can be transmitted on an almost worldwide scale. Movies like *Star Wars* or *The Matrix* certainly do not explicitly use traditional religious imagery. Nevertheless, they have been of great interest to Christian allegorists and theologians since they take up religious issues. These movies, with their unusual approach towards essential questions and experiences in human life, exhibit profound influences on the viewers, partly because the surprising plots and constellation of imagery create new perspectives on traditional religious values and beliefs. In a global environment, such influences, enforced by Hollywood's power, transcend the boundaries of the American society and thus export postmodern values and spiritual messages to more traditional religious societies, at times inciting a clash of value and belief systems. Some countries, like for example Iran, restrict viewers from watching any foreign movies as long as those movies do not comply with the religious Islamic dress codes or political goals. This, nevertheless, has created a subculture of satellites and Internet access routes to exactly those sources that otherwise are restricted by the government. The market of artistic exchange thus cannot be completely stopped via such measures. On the contrary, it might be argued that interest in foreign artistic expressions is even heightened through the overpowering effects of Hollywood, as well as the ban on movies in certain countries.

But, even in a context of strong American dominance, the media market is much more diversified and complex and, interestingly, a number of foreign movies are becoming quite prominent. Some of the highly acclaimed movies, like the Iranian *White Balloon,* the co-winner of the Critic's Prize at the 1995 Cannes Movie Festival; or the Chinese movie, *The Road Home* (2001), which won prizes at the Sundance Festival and the Berlin Movie Festival, are just two examples of the complex artistic exchanges taking place in the world of moviemaking. *The Road Home* offers a subtle story that provides an intricate artistic picture of the virtue of filial piety in the Chinese tradition. The movie communicates to its audience a spiritual worldview fairly different or even absent from mainstream American moviemaking or from those viewers exposed to it in the Western World.

It therefore would be a mistake to see globalization only as the highly publicized export of American culture and worldview. While the more powerful soci-

Untraditional treatment of religious themes in American-made movies likely has strong implications for spirituality worldwide.

Globalization also allows movies from countries and religious traditions with different values to have exposure in the US and other western societies.

eties at times have an advantage in exporting artistic goods, there is also a growing interest in the unfamiliar, the different and otherness that at times can be found only in very small, remote communities. The plate seen here is made in the traditional characteristic manner of Iranian copper making; the ornaments clearly identify its Iranian origin and can be found there commonly in the marketplaces. Yet the motif, the crucifixion of Jesus, is a central Christian motif. Most likely, the artist was a Christian in or around Esfanhan, Iran. What is of interest to us is that the authors found the plate in the hands of Muslims for whom the motif of Christ crucified is highly objectionable. The Holy Koran states:

> *And their [Christians] saying: Surely we have killed the Messiah, Isa son of Marium, the apostle of Allah; and they did not kill him nor did they crucify him, but it appeared to them so (like Isa) and most surely those who differ therein are only in a doubt about it; they have no knowledge respecting it, but only follow a conjecture, and they killed him not for sure. (Sura 4:157)*

The mixing of themes from different religions may promote an interest in unfamiliar traditions.

Muslims consider Jesus as a prophet but do not believe that he died on the cross. To find Jesus pictured crucified on an Iranian plate provides an interesting example of the influence of art that, for some reason, merges religious values, if only on the level of transfer of the artistic object. In a way, boundaries that long have been maintained to differentiate the three monotheistic traditions are blurred in this exchange of the Christian image. Accordingly, one might argue that certain religious artistic expressions, since they are less strictly bound to doctrinal aspects of their respective religious context, can become tools in promoting interest in difference and otherness on the market of spiritual worldviews.

Another interesting phenomenon is the attraction of many Americans to Zen Buddhist art. The acclaim that the Zen master Hakuin has gained here in the Western world for his paintings to a large degree rests on a fascination with Zen methods and spiritual goals. These goals are attractive, at least to a degree, because their protest against conceptualization focuses on an aspect of artistic expression that is less prevalent in the Judeo-Christian and Islamic tradition. Again, the difference, the otherness allows for interest, fascination. Such development is enhanced, since the materials to make a Zen garden or perform the tea ceremony can now be purchased in many Western stores, and the philosophy is readily available in books and on the Internet. This may eventually transform these specifically Japanese traditions in the context of Western culture.

The spread of nonnative art to a society may produce a powerful backlash.

Yet the dynamic of powerful change, which enforces otherness, can be perceived as threatening the identity of certain religious groups while inciting fascination among others. This may produce a powerful backlash against the invading art. For example, after the second Gulf war in 2003, many Iraqi people who had been enjoying American pop music began to alter their taste. As a result, interest in traditional religious music flourishes again in Iraq while Islamic music suddenly is also appearing more frequently in Western markets and, for the first time in history, Serab Erener, a Turkish pop star, won the Eurovision, a major European pop contest.

Another fascinating area that is fundamentally reshaped by global dynamics is the role of women in religious societies. In this context, female artists often offer

Figure 8.8   *Untitled* by Shirin Neshat

The increasing role of women in religions is significantly altering how religious themes are treated in art.

a unique voice in a very complicated search for identity. The work of the Iranian born artist Shirin Neshat (1957–), for example, utilizes the medium of photography to epitomize the conflict between diverse cultural universes. Neshat, who lives and works in the United States, explores cultural differences in particular with regard to the role of women through her juxtapositions of traditional and nontraditional elements. Her images of veiled women, inscribed with poetry on their visible body parts, thus become emblems for women struggling to find their voice and identity in a rapidly changing world, a world that in significant ways is defined by religious parameters.

Globalization provokes the possibility of expanding insight into different religious contexts.

Through the process of globalization, artistic expressions become much more readily available to many people than ever before. They are not the privilege of the elite and can be accessed via Internet, in museums, as movies, all in all via any medium that art offers. This market of artistic ideas allows for change, for the recognition of differences and similarities, and most often fosters new creative developments while at the same time is also perceived as exceedingly threatening to religious identity and spiritual worldviews. A clash of worldviews is often the foundation for rejection of provocative artistic expressions. Yet, the few exam-

Figure 8.9   Crucifixion. Plate. Iran/Isfahan. Embossed metalwork. Diam. 39 cm. Artist unknown

ples given here also point to a chance that is inherent to the dynamics of global exchange, namely to enhance the prospects of expanding insights into different religious contexts.

CONCLUSION

Like language, religious art thus can be very influential and can serve as a political tool. By the same power, however, it can be a tool for political and moral reform, as well as a source of public education and personal encouragement. Moreover, precisely because art engages the senses and often excites an emotional response, it has been criticized, used as a powerful tool, or at times has been destroyed. Art can be exploited for its effective persuasive qualities, or it can be an exceptional inspirational source. Art in all its forms—painting, sculpture, music, poetry, drama—can do all these things and has done all these things. It is a remarkably powerful and versatile part of human culture.

Following Wittgenstein, one might say that art is analogous to a game, pertaining to certain rules. It does not carry an essence in itself, but rather like a game it provides the players with the material. Whether we think of the Zen artist who minimizes artistic expression to engage in spiritual transformation or the Hindu temple with its storybook of gods and goddesses, the dramatic Christian paintings of final judgment or the sweeping beauty of Islamic calligraphy, religious art seems to offer different tools for humans in their spiritual search. The nearly boundless multiplicity of forms with which art functions is matched only by the astonishing power it seems to have in moving the human heart.

■ INTERACTIVE EXERCISE

Please continue the exploration of art and religion by going to the interactive exercise for this chapter online (**http://www.religion.wadsworth.com/richter**).

WORKS CITED

Addiss, Stephen. *The Art of Zen.* New York: Harry Abrams, Inc.1989.

Barnes, Bernadine Ann. *Michelangelo's Last Judgment: the Renaissance response.* Berkeley: University of California Press, 1989.

Besançon, Alain. *The Forbidden Image: An Intellectual History of Iconoclasm.* Trans. Jane Marie Todd. Chicago: University of Chicago Press, 2000.

Carroll, Noël. *Philosophy of Art: A Contemporary Introduction.* New York: Routledge, 1999.

Coburn, Thomas. Translation of Devi Matayama. *Encountering the Goddess.* Delhi, India: Motilal Banarsidass, 1984.

Cowan, Tyler. *Creative Destruction.* Princeton, NJ: Princeton University Press, 2002.

Crane, Diane, Nobuko Kawashima, and Ken'ichi Kawasaki, eds. *Global Culture: Media, Arts,Policy, and Globalization.* New York: Routledge, 2002.

Freedberg, David. *The Power of Images: Studies in the History and Theory of Response.* Chicago, IL: Chicago University Press 1991.

Hakuin Ekaku. *Chant in Praise of Zazen.* Trans. The Montreal Zen Center. http://www.zenmontreal.ca/English/x04sheduleDaily.html (accessed August 1, 2002).

Kant, Immanuel. *The Critique of Judgment.* Trans. James Creed Meredith. Chicago: Encyclopedia Britannica, 1955.

Leggett, Trevor. *A First Zen Reader* Rutland, Vt: Charles E. Tuttle Company, 1960.

Plato. *The Republic VI-X.* Trans. Paul Shorey. Cambridge, MA: Harvard University Press, 1994.

Schopenhauer, Arthur. *The World as Will and Idea.* Vol 1. New York: AMS, 1977.

Tracy, David. "Public Theology, Hope, and the Mass Media." In *God and Globalization: Religion and the Powers of the Common Life.* Max L. Stackhouse and Peter J. Paris, eds. Harrisburg: Trinity International, 2000.

Van Voorst, Robert E. *Anthology of World Scriptures.* Belmont, CA: Wadsworth, 1999.

Weitz, Morris *The Opening Mind: A Philosophical Study of Humanistic Concepts.* Chicago: The University of Chicago Press, 1977.

Whelan, Estelle. "Forgotten Witness: Evidence for the Early Codification of the Koran." *Journal of the American Oriental Society.* Vol. 118 (1998): 4.

FOR FURTHER READING

Besançon, Alain. *The Forbidden Image: An Intellectual History of Iconoclasm.* Trans. Jane Marie Todd. Chicago: University of Chicago Press, 2000.

Coburn, Thomas. *Encountering the Goddess.* Albany, NY: State University of New York Press, 1991.

Davies, Stephen. *Definitions of Art.* New York: Cornell University Press, 1991.

Freedberg, David. *The Power of Images: Studies in the History and Theory of Response.* Chicago, IL: Chicago University Press 1991.

Ghose, Rajeshwari, with the collaboration of Puay-peng Ho and Yeung Chun-tong, eds. *In the footsteps of the Buddha: an iconic journey from India to China.* Hong Kong: University of Hong Kong, 1998.

Hattstein, Markus, and Peter Delius, eds. *Islam: Art and Architecture.* Trans. George Ansell et al. Cologne, Germany: Kˆnemann, 2000.

Schneider Adams, Laurie. *World Views: Topics in Non-Western Art.* New York: McGraw Hill. 2003.

IMAGES

Buonarotti, Michelangelo. *Last Judgment.* 1537-41. Fresco, Cappella Sistina, Vatican.

Gaugin. *Spirit of the Dead Watching.* 1892 (130 Kb). Oil on burlap mounted on canvas, 72.4 x 92.4 cm (28 1/2 x 36 3/8 in). Albright-Knox Art Gallery, Buffalo, NY. http://www.oir.ucf.edu/wm/paint/auth/gauguin/gauguin.spirit dead-watching.jpg (accessed May 31, 2003).

Gislebertus. *Judgment.* Cathedrale St-Lazare, Autun, Saone-et-Loire/France.

Jesus Crucified. Plate, Digital Image. Eva Maria Raepple, Esfahan/Iran.

Madonna. Artist Unknown. Spain. (Digital Image/Eva Maria Raepple).

Munch, Edvard. *Madonna* 1893-94; Oil on canvas, 90 x 68.5 cm; Munch Museum, Oslo/Norway.

Picasso, Pablo. *Guernica.* 1937. Museum Reina Sofia, Spain

Shirin Neshat. *Rebellious Silence.* 1994. Museum of Contemporary Iranian Artists. http://www.iranian.com/Arts/Dec97/Neshat/p6b.html (accessed May 31, 2003).

Van Gogh, Vincent. *The Starry Night.* 1889. Oil on Canvas, 73.7 x 92.1 cm. Museum of Modern Art, New York.

The Virgin in a Paradise Garden. 1415–1430. Tempera on oak, 20.2 x 16.2 cm. Wallraf- Richartz Museum, Cologne/Germany.

9 RITUAL

Getty Images/PhotoDisc Collection

R itual is part and parcel of religion. Religious ritual may be very simple or elaborate and complex. Moreover, rituals vary in how they are understood between religions and within a given religion. In this chapter we look at the complexities of religious ritual. As you prepare to read it, look at the picture found above and on the Web site (**http://www.religion.wadsworth .com/richter**), and the following quotations, then answer the Introductory Questions that follow to prepare for reading this chapter.

> *The Master Confucius said, "Without ritual, courtesy is*
> *tiresome; without ritual, prudence is timid; without ritual,*
> *bravery is quarrelsome; without ritual, frankness is hurtful."*
>
> —Confucianism: The Analects 8:2

Recite that which has been revealed to you of the Book [the Holy Koran] and keep up prayer; surely prayer keeps (one) away from indecency and evil, and certainly, the remembrance of Allah is the greatest.

—Islam: Holy Koran 29:44

He said to them, "I have eagerly desired to eat this Passover with you before I suffer; for I tell you, I will not eat it until it is fulfilled in the kingdom of God." Then he took a cup, and after giving thanks he said, "Take this and divide it among yourselves; for I tell you that from now on I will not drink of the fruit of the vine until the kingdom of God comes." Then he took a loaf of bread, and when he had given thanks, he broke it and gave it to them, saying, "This is my body, which is given for you. Do this in remembrance of me."

—Christianity: Luke 22:15–19

If the practice is properly carried out, one session of meditation is one session of Buddha; a day of meditation is a day of Buddha. Or, as the ancients have said, "One inch of meditation, one inch of Buddha; so inch by inch to the six-foot Buddha."

—Zen Buddhism: Amakuki Sessan's commentary on Hakuin's *Song of Meditation* (Legget 126)

Then, by means of the knowledge of the art of worshiping the lotus-eyed deity [Vishnu], he [the worshipper] should place water for bathing, cloth, sacred thread, ornaments, scents, flowers, incense, lamps, and edibles.

—Hinduism: *Puja* described in the Agni Purana (Smart and Hecht 212)

When Tzu-kung arrived [at the funeral], he found one of the dead man's friends weaving frames for silkworms, while the other strummed a lute. Tzu-kung hastened forward and said, "May I be so bold as to ask what sort of ceremony this is, singing in the very presence of the corpse?" The two men looked at each other and laughed.

—Taoism: Chuang Tzu, section 6 (Watson 82)

INTRODUCTORY QUESTIONS

In the pictures and scriptural quotations for this chapter, there are many different references to rituals like worship and funerals, prayers and holidays. Think of these examples as you consider these questions.

1. The first and second quotations declare something of the profound importance of ritual in Confucianism and in Islam. What are the benefits of following religious ritual, according to these claims? Do you think they are right?
2. The man worshiping with raised hands might be a Christian Pentecostal praising Jesus. Just from the form, it is unlikely that he is a Hindu worshiper doing *puja,* as described in the fifth quotation. Yet, they both look like "worship." What is worship?
3. Jesus' words above are the traditional basis for the Christian sacrament of the Lord's Supper (or Eucharist). What do you know about this ritual and how it is based upon these actions of Jesus? Do you think Jesus meant for this action to become a major, central religious ritual?
4. The wedding ceremony and the *Bar Mitzvah* depicted here are Hindu and Jewish rituals, respectively. There are, of course, also Jewish weddings and Hindu coming-of-age rituals. Can you think of other rituals that mark stages in life for these or other religions? What kind of stage of life seems to be sanctified here?
5. The man in white depicted here is a Sufi mystic of the Mevlevi order, or what is often called a Whirling Dervish. His dance is a kind of communication with God for some Muslim mystics, yet it may seem very different from the Muslim prayer suggested in the second quotation. Might the dance ritual be more like the Zen meditation mentioned in the fourth quotation?
6. The "Indian with a peace pipe" might seem like a cliché, but certainly, Christmas with Santa is an even worse cliché. What might be the real meaning of such ritual? Is it possible to forget or terribly misunderstand the rituals of others or even of ourselves?
7. What might be the point of the men laughing in the last story? Note that there is an almost humorous traditional rivalry between the Confucian emphasis on ritual and the philosophical Taoist suspicion that ritual is a distraction. Might there be reasons to reject ritual?

INTRODUCTION

Religion tells us a great deal about ourselves and about the world around us. Indeed religions apparently seek to tell about Ultimate Reality itself and to base all that exists and all beings in this Reality. Therefore, people read the sacred stories and embrace the sacred myths; they study their scriptures and look at the lives of their founders. All of this is done so that one might come to know better and better that which is of maximal importance in reality, the Holy. These points, at least, we have suggested in the foregoing chapters. However, we have not sought to explore what may truly be considered Ultimate Reality, or whether any particular religious scripture, or truth claim might be right. The fact remains that many people do seem to believe that the varying beliefs—historical, psychological, or metaphysical—are true (whatever that may mean), that they demand allegiance, not only knowledge. Indeed, they demand from us a response. Thus, when people follow a religion, they not only believe or assert certain "truths" of their religion, they also perform actions that are believed to be proper responses to the teachings of religions and their founders.

People perform certain acts as a response to the Holy.

These summary statements about doctrines and founders are, of course, less than subtle and may unfairly generalize. Previous chapters should already have offered more nuanced information. In this chapter, we turn to discuss religious responses, those activities that are done as part of one's relation to the Absolute. Such active religious responses might simply be broken into two kinds: ritual and morality, with ritual as the subjects of this chapter, ethics and morality of the next. Of course, as with most distinctions and categorizations in this book, it can easily be noted that the precise line between what is a ritual and what is morality is difficult to draw, especially, perhaps, within religion. For in a very real sense, there may be some ritual actions that, if not performed or if performed improperly, could be considered immoral; and indeed there are moral actions that, within both religious and nonreligious societies, take on a kind of ritual form.

But all this is getting ahead of ourselves, for we need to define these terms before making careful points about the nature of religious ritual and ethics. Here, the goal is to describe how most active responses to religious ideas qualify as ritual. We will also note a wide variety of ritual types and the fact that not all ritual is the same. This analysis will also attempt to investigate the relation between religions' primary rituals and what those religions teach about their own history, salvation, and theology. Thus, the nature of the Passover or Easter for Judaism and Christianity, respectively, is something quite different from how chanting or meditation works for Buddhism.

WHAT IS RITUAL?

ritual—repeated action believed to carry performative character in religious context

Although some people might find religious rituals tiresome or misguided, ritual *per se* is not easy to escape. In the broadest sense, ritual is nothing more than any kind of repeated action that carries with it some kind of extra, perhaps symbolic, significance beyond the action itself. That is, when we perform any kind of action again and again, carefully (or, perhaps, merely habitually) making the same motions with the same words, we are often trying to convey something significant. For example, one does not reach out, take another person's hand, and shake it just because shaking hands is an exercise or a quirk of muscle reaction. It has a kind of meaning, conveying a message of friendship or at least nonaggression. Indeed, some "secret" clubs and any number of undergraduates in the hallway may have very elaborate handshakes that signify a kind of bond, a way of recognizing one's friends. In older times, men would tip their hats, people would bow or curtsy; still today, soldiers salute, and even infants are taught to "wave bye-bye." All this is ritual. It is a stylized, repeated action with a meaning or significance beyond the action itself.

At the most basic level, rituals are repeated actions that convey meaning.

Religious ritual in particular, then, could be defined in this general sense, with one very obvious addition: reference or connection to the Sacred Ultimate Reality. Repeated, stylized actions and words that have their significance explicitly or implicitly tied to the Holy are, by definition, religious rituals. Just as we have specific rituals for saying hello to our friends, we might also have specific rituals for saying hello (so to speak) to God. When a Roman Catholic Christian enters a church, for example, there is a traditional ritual called genuflecting. One may see the believer pause before he or she sits, bow slightly, perhaps bending to one knee. He or she will also make a gesture with the hand, the "sign of the cross," across his or her own body. Of course, the significance and gravity of this kind of hello may be (we could hope) far greater than saying hello to a friend in the hallway, but it is, as ritual, very similar. Indeed, what could (or perhaps should) make it more significant is precisely that its object, the "friend" being greeted, is God.

Of course, not all rituals are ways of saying hello, either in hallways at school or in religious contexts. Some rituals, especially religious rituals, are reenactments or remembrances of some event in the mythic or historical past of a religious community. Other rituals more dramatically would be performed in order to make something happen in the world, or perhaps in ourselves. That is, some rituals are believed to be transformative, in that they intentionally change who humans are in relation to the Sacred. Or, perhaps, they purport to do miracles or magic, in a sense transforming the surrounding world. A different kind of ritual, perhaps one of the most common and universal, involves practices that are meant to sanctify important stages of human life, such as birth, puberty, marriage, and death. Yet other rituals are meant simply to be the proper recognition and worship of the Holy. These may be grand declarations of, or awe-filled responses to, the tremendous and attractive mystery of the Absolute. Or they might indeed be like saying hello to God.

Generally, then, religious rituals are repetitions of words and actions that relate us to the Absolute. But more specifically, they are meant to do a wide variety of things, depending on what they represent or reenact or attempt to effect. And across the religions of the world, their meanings and implications, though generally similar, will, of course, be vitally different, as different as God is from Nirvana or as Brahman is different from the Tao. Let us look at some specific examples.

RITES OF PASSAGE

Though we might think everyone's life is different and, especially across cultures, different people have different ideas about how life should go, the fact remains that there seem to be some rather basic stages that the average human life goes through. These stages, moreover, can sometimes involve rather dramatic changes in how one behaves or in what happens to one's body and mind. They also involve major changes in what society expects of a person and, indeed, what a person expects of him- or herself. We are not talking about the kind of changes that might rationally be adopted, like what to study in school or even (for some) what religion to follow. Rather, there are some changes of life that just happen to us and, indeed, they happen to everybody. The most obvious of these would be birth and death, but others might include puberty, and, for some people, marriage and/or having children, and even menopause for women.

These changes, or "passages" of life, can be scary. Very often, they involve changes to one's social status, changes in routines and fellowship, new and sometimes sudden shifts in one's own personal identity. Consequently, these passages can give anyone a drastic sense of the uncertainty of life and the need to learn to live a new way. Perhaps for this reason, religions all over the world have developed rituals that acknowledge, bless, and sanctify these passages. These are called **rites of passage**. There might, of course, be nonreligious rites of passage, such as a high school graduation, with all its "Pomp and Circumstance," or a 40th birthday party, complete with black balloons and jokes about being "over the hill." But religion in general, as mentioned many times, connects humans with the Sacred, and religious rites of passage express this connection through language, sound, smell, and/or action. In these rituals, the dramatic changes of life are given a connection to the Absolute, and in turn, a person is given blessing or purity, security, or an assurance of identity. That is, through repeated, formalized gestures, words, and actions, religious people are able to say, "This is my new identity," or "This is my place in the world." And that security is established and blessed by the person's connection to Sacred Reality, a connection recognized or even created by sacred ritual.

Religions all over the world have developed rituals that acknowledge the activity of the Holy at these transitions.

Following are examples of rites of passage. As noted, clearly birth and death are rather significant events in a person's life, and it is no surprise therefore that religions all over the world have developed rituals that acknowledge the role of the Sacred in the person's life at these stages. For example, it is clear that various rituals exist in the world's religions to dedicate, bless, or purify a newborn child. The **circumcision** ritual in Judaism explicitly marks the male child as a member of the Jewish ethnic group and therefore as a participant in the covenant with God. According to the Jewish tradition, this ritual marking of the male child's body was established as far back as the Patriarch Abraham, who was told by God that this mark on the body would be "a sign of the covenant between me and you," as part of what distinguished God's "Chosen People" from the rest of the world (Genesis 17). Thus, according to the tradition, the ritual self-identification of the child with his people is nearly 4000 years old, and it remains to this day a vital social ritual even for Jews who are not very religious.

Formula of Concord—statement of rules and norms agreed upon by the Lutheran groups of the late 16th century

Some Christian doctrine explicitly takes the Jewish circumcision ritual as the basis for its own practice of infant baptism. In the Lutheran Formula of Concord, for example, the writers of the "Epitome" directly refer to the circumcision verses of Genesis 17 to establish their claim that the baptism of children is both right and necessary (Tappert 498). As with Luther himself, the argument here is against the **Anabaptists**, who claimed that baptism should be performed only on those old enough to understand their faith. But the Lutheran doctrine here, along with **Calvinism, Roman Catholicism,** and many other branches of Christianity, argues that this children's ritual is precisely what makes them "children of God" (425). As with Jewish circumcision, the child is sanctified, made holy, and welcomed as a member of the blessed community.

Of all rites of passage, perhaps the most interesting are the rituals dealing with the transition from childhood into adulthood. These "puberty rituals" may seem odd to those of us whose cultures have overlooked the significance of puberty as a life-changing transition. But most cultures have recognized that here the boy becomes a man, the girl becomes a woman, and as such, the child becomes a responsible member of the community. In many cases, then, this includes the explicit responsibility of the new adult for his or her religious life. A classic case appears in Judaism, where traditionally a boy of 13 is said to become a counted member of the Jewish male community after taking instruction in the language and teachings of Judaism. This education culminates in a ritual, the **Bar Mitzvah,** in which the newly recognized man of 13 reads the Jewish scriptures, the holy Torah, and enters the adult community responsible before God for his own actions. The very title of the ritual translates as "Son of the Commandments," an indication that the boy is now responsible for his own obedience before God. In recent times, all but the most conservative Jewish groups have instituted a Bat Mitzvah as well, recognizing a "Daughter of the Commandments" alongside her male counterparts (Robinson 158–159).

Puberty rituals mark the transition from childhood to adulthood and the transition to a responsible member of the community.

In many tribal cultures, this adolescent rite of passage is particularly important. As such it often, especially for males, requires severe separation of the youth from the society, undergoing a "ritual death" before the boy can be reunited with the tribe and renamed a man (Beane and Doty165). In the "vision quest" of Native American religion, the boy may be isolated from his elders, left without food and going without sleep for some days, until a "vision," given by an ancestor or nature spirit, awakens him to the importance of his role in the tribe, and, in many cases, assigns him a new name, as in the case of Lakota Sioux tribal leader John Fire Lame Deer (Comstock 51–54). Among various Australian Aborigine tribes, the manhood ritual carries a component of bloodletting, often through circumcision. Here, the young man is taken away from the tribal camp and circumcised in order to prepare him for sexual activity, marriage, and family. However, at the same time, in these cultures the young man is finally taught the basic myths and histories of the tribe. As such, the newly recognized adults become responsible for the tribal relationship to the ancestors, a fully participating member of the religious community (Beane and Doty 183-184). In China, where the Confucian "Tao of Heaven" is the sacred model of human society, and especially the human family, the proper order of mourning and burial rituals is crucial. Ritual honoring of the dead parent is a vital part of how that person makes the transition from living relative to dead ancestor. Thus, specific attire and specific levels of ritual grieving, defined carefully depending on the relationship one had to the deceased, have been established in China since long before the Common Era. For example, a truly filial son would wear coarse sackcloth for as long as three years to honor the death of his parents; for a more distant relative, one could wear more comfortable clothing and would have to show grief for only some months (Thompson 36). It is because of these very formal ritual ways of commemorating the death of a relative that the Taoist rejection of formality, noted in our chapter's opening quotes, was such an outrage to the Confucian observers.

Death rituals are even more universal than birth rituals.

In Hinduism, the famed ritual of being cremated along the banks of the Ganges River, especially in the sacred city Varanasi, is rooted in the hope of purification and the improvement of one's next incarnation. According to the tradition, it is again the elder son who takes the lead role, shaving his head and becoming responsible for the purification of the parent's body. Burning of the body is, of course, symbolic of purification, as fire is broadly understood as a cleansing, purifying power. But it is especially the water of the Ganges River itself that aids the dead soul in becoming pure, as the river itself is a goddess, **Ganga Ma,** descended from heaven through the hair of the god Shiva. Thus, the faithful come from all over India to bring the bodies of their relatives to Ganga's banks. There, if all is performed rightly, the soul of the dead is purified and a good rebirth is assured. As the Mahabharata says, "For as long [for example, for as many years] as a person's bones remain in the waters of the Ganga, for so many thousands of years shall he prosper/be exalted in heaven" (13.27.31).

Hindus believe cremation on the bank of the Ganges ensures purification and a good rebirth.

Puberty, birth, and death rituals are only some of the rites of passage that recognize and sanctify the many stages along life's way. Perhaps the psychological importance of such rituals is hard for us to see, insofar as American culture, perhaps in the name of individual freedom, skips marriage for "living together" and allows the driver's license to take the place of the puberty ritual. However, it could be argued that precisely this lack of ritual has left many people insecure and uncertain of their identity and place in the community. The stages of life—most obviously death, but also marriage and puberty—are more terrifying than they seem perhaps. By establishing a link with the Sacred, the gravity of these events is acknowledged and the changes are sanctified.

■ OTHER TRANSFORMATIVE RITUALS

Rites of passage may be seen as an important part of a set of rituals more generally called **transformative rituals.** As the name suggests, transformative rituals deal with the transformation of the human being or of the world, by or for the power of the Sacred. The rites of passage are done because they are believed to initiate change, to transform. Similarly, other religious rituals are meant to transform the environment and to sanctify the world.

Some religious rituals are intended to sanctify the world.

Meditation rituals are a basic example. In many Asian traditions, meditation serves to transform the individual consciousness to create new attitudes or habits of attention that make one more apt to find enlightenment. In Buddhism especially, meditation techniques are detailed and varied, with some practices designed to induce trancelike states and others ordered simply to make one more aware of death and the futility of life. When a Theravada Buddhist monk or nun, **bhikku** or **bhikkuni,** for example, meditates on corpses, he or she is learning to form mental images and intending explicitly to become increasingly aware of the foulness of the body. According to the Buddhist text called the Visuddhimagga (fifth century CE), the monk or nun is to focus on the "ten impurities," presented as a rather disgusting list of how corpses may be torn apart, eaten by animals, or fall into various stages of decomposition (Warren 292). By visibly contemplating these corpses, the monk or nun is supposed to gain a kind of mental image of death, the "first trance" of Buddhist enlightenment. At the same time, seeing the foulness of the body and the inevitability of death and decay, the monk or nun should be led to break the attachment to sensuality and to conquer the physical lusts for life. Meditation thus transforms, helping the mental faculties to gain greater control and concentration, while the moral strength is increased against

Meditation rituals in Buddhism are intended to transform the monk and to bring his will and mind closer to enlightenment.

the temptations of the flesh. Thus overall the mind and will are brought closer to ultimate enlightenment (King 69–71).

Zen meditation may seem less moralistic, but its point is still dramatically transformative. As D.T. Suzuki describes *koan* meditation, one is to concentrate on an "irrational" teaching, such as "the sound of one hand clapping," not to find an "answer" but to transform one's consciousness. Concentration on the *koan*, he says, has the power to block the rationalizing mind and to allow the pure, transrational "Buddha Mind" to show through. He writes that the *koan* is intended "to make the calculating mind die," and although this sounds harsh, the ultimate intent is to drive the meditator deeper into the mind in order to find the pure Buddha within (138). Meditation, therefore, transforms the person, helping the aspirant to realize enlightenment.

Concentration on the koan in Zen Buddhism is intended to drive the follower to a trans-rational experience of the Buddha within.

Throughout the world's religions, there exist a wealth of rituals that, like meditation, use special actions and powers to change humans, to purify them, or to make them ready to meet the Divine. Ritual washings and baptisms are a common example. We already noted the role of Christian baptism in the birth ritual, as it transforms the child and takes him or her into the fellowship of faith. Even those Christians who do not practice infant baptism use baptism as, at least, a symbolic cleansing or, as believed, a symbolic death of the old sinner. Thus, the baptized Christian is "saved," "not as a removal of dirt from the body, but as an appeal to God for a good conscience, through the resurrection of Jesus Christ" (I Peter 3:21). Similarly, in Islamic prayer rituals, there is first required a washing of the face, neck, hands, and feet. These are largely symbolic actions, not really about being free of dirt but about the Muslim entering a state of purity, ready to begin his ritual conversation with God. Though it is not like Christian baptism if the latter is meant to cleanse one of sin, it is still "a habitual transaction about sins," a sort of "hygiene of the self" (Cragg 58–59). It may not affect forgiveness, but it symbolically confesses sin and prepares one to enter into the act of prayer.

Ritual washings or cleansings are used to indicate a symbolic cleansing of the self in many religions.

More dramatically, perhaps, some forms of self-transformative ritual are performed as self-inflicted punishments. Hindu **sadhus,** or holy men, perform any number of physical yogas that are meant to perfect a kind of self-control and self-mortification. One punishes the body to purify the soul. On the American continent, the Sun Dance of the native Sioux has the dancers pierce their own flesh with bones or sticks, after which the dancers are pulled or even raised off the ground by ropes tied to these piercings. The flesh tears and the blood flows, but in the end the dancer is purified and rededicated to the spirit of the people and the holiness of the land. One dancer reports,

> *It's not pain, it's ecstasy. We get the energy from the sun and from the contact with Mother Earth. You also feel the energy of the eagles, all the animals, all the plants that surround you, all the vegetation. That energy comes to sustain you. (Fisher 55)*

Some religions use ritual self-torture as a means of cleansing and purifying the self.

Thus, the pain of self-torture, like ritual washings and baptisms, changes the religious follower to make him or her ready to know more deeply the divine reality that is beyond the mundane world.

Perhaps in its transformative power, religious ritual comes closest to what we might call magic. But while the transformative ritual described above is about transforming oneself, some rituals are meant to transform the world. Religious ritual magic is, in a way, like technology, insofar as both magic and technology use powers that are understood perhaps only by a few experts (shamans and scientists) to change the world. But while technology uses the powers discovered by physics or chemistry, religious ritual magic uses more mysterious powers, the powers of spirits, souls, and gods. Here we might recognize the work of tribal shamans as they call upon spirits and ancestors to help heal the sick or to end a drought. There are also still examples today in India of Brahmin priests chanting the ancient Vedic scriptures and performing fire sacrifices in order to bring about a good harvest. The possibilities of how to use this divine power to change the world are literally endless.

Religious magic tries to use the power of the spiritual world to transform the world around us, ourselves, or the gods themselves.

There are many more transformative rituals, far more than we can here exemplify. Rituals that change wine into the Blood of Christ; chanting that brings the spirit of a god into the statue in a Hindu temple; sacrifices that cleanse people of sins, that appease gods or that bring rain—these are all efforts to use the "technology" of the Absolute to change the world, ourselves, and even the gods. Every effort to make a miracle, an effort that includes standard phrases, gestures, or other ritual actions, is transformative ritual. They may astonish us with their form, from bloody sacrifice to quiet contemplation, and they may promise miracles beyond reason. But they are a common and perhaps unavoidable part of religious life.

SEASONAL RITUALS AND HISTORICAL COMMEMORATION

Many religious rituals deal with the transitions associated with the changing seasons.

Just as there are rites of passage that mark the stages in an individual person's life, so there are also many rituals that mark the progress of time across the year. Many of these rituals are ancient and deal with the natural cycles of the seasons, while others are more recent and make their schedules according to more artificial calendars. Some are a combination of both.

■ SEASONAL RITUALS

Perhaps the most familiar seasonal ritual is Thanksgiving. The tradition in the United States, of course, has its supposed roots in the harvest feast of the Pilgrims and their native neighbors, and it can be depicted in a thousand rather unhistorical ways without any reference to religion. Yet, the very concept of giving thanks suggests the presumption of responding to the harvest as a gift of God. It implies a sense, therefore, that the natural cycle of growth and fruition that yields a wholesome harvest is not entirely "natural," in the sense of being taken for granted. It is also believed to be the work of God, one directly given to people as a gift. Perhaps humans need to be reminded occasionally that success and prosperity are not simply there to be taken. Perhaps in a very real sense, they are given.

Of course, the connection of the harvest to the actual giving of thanks to God would presume a concept of the Sacred like a Creator, as it was indeed for the Pilgrims. Yet, it is evident that other religious cultures, notably the native tribal cultures, are celebrating the cycles of nature and the changes of seasons. Ancient temples from the Incan culture in Machu Pichu (Peru) to the Mayan city in Chichen Itza (Mexico) or to Stonehenge (England) remarkably seem designed to mark the solstices and equinoxes that are the key points of the natural solar cycle. Somewhere around the 21st of December and June, of March and September, ancient peoples might well have gathered to celebrate the life and death of the sun itself, celebrating the return of life to the soil, the coming and passing of snow, the germination of seeds and the harvest of crops. And though not, perhaps, attributed to a single, benevolent Creator God, these changes would speak to them of the life of sun gods, spirits in tree and blossom, the power of Earth herself.

Modern Wicca has adopted such ideas, perhaps as unhistorically as Americans adopt the Pilgrims, to support a renewed interest in seasonal ritual. Here, the equinoxes and solstices figure as the prominent "Sabbaths," though interestingly, they are "lesser Sabbaths," when contrasted with the midpoints between each date, designated as the "greater Sabbaths" (Grimassi 309–310). These points along the solar calendar, as well as specified phases of the lunar cycle, thus become times of special spiritual energy and times for special religious rituals. The natural times for planting and harvest, animal procreation, the longest night of winter, and the longest day of summer all represent a close connection with the sacredness of land and nature itself. Thus, rituals are performed to draw this power into oneself, to obtain blessing or to worship. Such ritual is "a way of tuning into the seasonal cycle and celebrating the meaning of Goddess and God in our lives" (Hawke 108).

Such seasonal rituals clearly make a connection with a conception of the Absolute, understood to be part of, or intrinsically connected with, Nature itself. The spirits that animate objects, the power of the Goddess of nature or the mana of the land itself, are themselves sacred. By participating in the natural cycles, humans participate in the Absolute. For religions that do not find the Absolute in nature, such a direct connection with seasonal cycles would not be appropriate. In Judaism, as in the other Abrahamic faiths, it is considered idolatry to "serve the creature rather than the Creator" (Romans 1:25), and so the celebrations associated with natural cycles may themselves seem to be idolatrous. Nature for these religions may be a pointer *to* God but must not be worshipped *as* God.

The apparent logic of this point is only partly accurate. Certainly Judaism itself marked many of its early holidays according to seasons, with the Festival of Booths being a celebration of the barley harvest in early fall and even the Passover associated with the spring lunar cycle. And of course, as noted, there is Thanksgiving. But it is indeed notable that within Judaism, and likewise Christianity, the seasonal celebrations have counterparts in the annual festivals of commemoration.

■ COMMEMORATIONS

By "commemoration," we refer to the practice of commemorating, or simply remembering with celebration, some old but central historical event. The 4th of July, in the United States, is clearly a commemorative holiday, coming once a year to celebrate the signing of the Declaration of Independence in 1776. Being an annual holiday, it is like seasonal rituals, and indeed many American may well associate this holiday with the middle of summer. But of course there is nothing intrinsic to the meaning of this holiday that makes it seasonal. It is really a

mana—spiritual power

In many "nature" religions, participating in religious rituals at the times of seasonal change are especially powerful ways of participating in the Absolute.

remembering and a celebration of a historical event, one that might have taken place in the fall or winter.

We also easily note that Independence Day is not a religious holiday, precisely because it carries no intrinsic element of the Sacred. But Christmas or Easter for American Christians is indeed a sacred commemoration for the obvious reason that it connects the particular dates with something deemed holy. The birth of Jesus on (supposedly) December 25th and the resurrection of Jesus during the Passover celebration in the spring are generally taken by Christians to be real historical events, and they are celebrated by Christians like most people celebrate birthdays and other annual commemorations.

Already noted in Chapter 6: Myths, Stories, History were the various problems of interpreting historical language in various religions. The point here is not to consider whether Jesus really was born in a stable, visited by shepherds and "wise men." It is also quite unlikely that Jesus was born on December 25th at all. It seems indeed that this date was chosen in the fourth century CE to celebrate the Mass of Christ—Christmas—for rather unhistorical reasons. Some speculate that since the Spring Equinox is the renewal of life, Jesus must have been conceived near the end of March and, therefore, born near the end of December. More likely, the December date was chosen precisely because it could take over the pagan holiday of Sol Invictus, the winter solstice celebration of the sun's victory over darkness (Walker 155). This is not merely a case of someone "stealing" another's holiday; it rather marks how celebration of a season *per se* is quite appropriate for a religion that finds Sacred Reality within the natural cycles of the earth and sky, but seasonal celebration needs to change into historical commemoration for those religions whose Sacred Reality is a Creator, not nature, a Creator that nevertheless acts in history.

The relation of commemorative ritual to historical or presumed historical events should be evident. Again, that does not mean that there are no seasonal holidays in Christianity. Similarly, it does not mean there are no historical commemorations in other religions. Any religion that celebrates some event in the life of its founders or gods will have commemorative ritual. Thus, the **Vesak** (or Waisaka) festival in Buddhism celebrates all at once several great events in the life of the Buddha. In Sri Lanka, this holiday takes place at the first full moon of May and celebrates the Buddha's birth, death, and enlightenment (Fernando 66). In Islam, the whole month of Ramadan, given over to fasting during daylight hours, is a time chosen because it coincides with the time Muhammad received his first revelations from God (Esposito 91; see also the Holy Koran 2:183). This "Night of Power," in fact, is believed to have occurred on the 27th of that month, and for many Muslims, those nights are not only a time to break the fast of the previous day but also to stay awake in prayer, perhaps the whole night, in thoughtful remembrance of Allah's gift of the Holy Koran to humanity.

Two final points are worth noting. We can expect, given the logical connection between historical language and commemorative celebrations, that much commemorative ritual occurs on an annual cycle. That is precisely why it often overlaps and can be confused with seasonal ritual. An interesting exception is the Christian celebration of the Eucharist (or the Lord's Supper, Communion) as a commemorative ritual that, in some churches, occurs every week, even every day. Jesus, according to the biblical text, told his disciples to eat bread and drink wine as symbols of his body and blood. "Do this," Jesus told them, "in remembrance of me" (Luke 22:19). This the Christians have done for nearly 2000 years, not merely as an annual celebration of an event that, they believe, happened on a particular Thursday evening, but as a common and regular "remembrance."

Commemoration is also a case of reenactment ritual. Reenactment means that a ritual's basis is believed to lie in some prior event and that the modern ritual's form and content are intended to copy that event. In the Christian Eucharist, the participants break bread and drink wine in commemoration of Jesus' last supper; similarly, though no Muslim would claim to receive more revelations from Allah during their commemoration of the Night of Power, Muslims do mark the night with wakeful prayer, reenacting, as it were, Muhammad's own piety. Also similarly, many Buddhists mark the Visaka festival of the Buddha's awakening with long periods of deep meditation, hoping to find enlightenment as did the Buddha himself.

A classic case of reenactment ritual commemorating a past event is the Jewish **Passover**, or *Pesach*. This holy day is a commemoration of the liberation of the people of Israel from their slavery in Egypt. The well-known stories of that liberation (Exodus 12) include the ten plagues visited upon Egypt by God and eventually the coming of an "angel of death" that killed the first born of all the families of Egypt, except those who, in accordance with God's command, had prepared a special meal of lamb and put some of the lamb's blood as a mark on their doors. Today, Jews do not mark their doors with blood, but the Passover is celebrated with a special Seder meal that is "heavy with meaning" (Robinson 121), including explicit images that mark the events of that time. Bitter herbs represent their slavery, soft pillows mark their new freedom, lamb's meat and unleavened bread reconstruct that original, hurried meal, and readings of the events of the original story bring all pious Jews back into that sacred time. Thus, Jews for three millennia have been reminded of God's miracles and faithfulness in keeping His side of the covenant.

In such examples, we see that most commemorative ritual not only celebrates the religion's founding events with annual recognition but also celebrates with actions and words that replay, so to speak, those deep and formative events. As seasonal rituals point believers to the cycles of time and nature, so commemorative rituals point believers back and reenact the events. And both are religious rituals precisely because these actions, cycles, and events are the connection to the Absolute.

WORSHIP, PRAYER, AND MAGIC

It is valuable to note that the exact role of reenactment in religious ritual is probably much broader than only commemoration. The influential scholar of religion, Mircea Eliade (1907–1986), has argued that reenactment lies at the root of all ritual. Where historical language is not present to give the reenactment a commemorative quality, Eliade claims, mythic language is present to give ritual a kind of original form, a pattern that is repeated by contemporary people in current rituals. Especially among tribal peoples, he argues, myths about creation and ancestors give the living a model to follow, and the result is the rituals of dance and prayer, drama and recitation—even the rituals of daily life, like cooking and washing—that are believed to reenact what the original gods or ancestors accomplished (Beane and Doty 135). This is not, however, merely commemorative. It is powerful.

Rituals may bring believers into the presence of the Sacred Absolute.

Part of Eliade's point in this discussion is to note that rituals bring believers into the presence of the Sacred. When rituals are performed, the normal space and time is left behind and a connection with the Absolute is established.

■ WORSHIP

Perhaps it seems rather pointless, or perhaps it seems obviously important, that when one stands, so to speak, in the presence of the Sacred, one appropriate ritual behavior is simply to acknowledge its greatness. Worship is the ritual performance of proclaiming the value and greatness of the Sacred, declaring its worth and glory. Indeed, the etymology of the word "**worship**" contains the declaration of worth, the worth-ship of the divine. We see this word prominently in the Christian scriptural myth, the Book of Revelation, in which the citizens of heaven cry out, "'You are worthy, our Lord and God, to receive glory and honor and power, for you created all things, and by your will they existed and were created'" (Revelation 4:11). Here, in apocalyptic tradition, worshippers declare before God's throne His own worth. Christians all over the world reenact this worship in songs and liturgies within their churches and in their private thoughts.

The Holy Koran of Islam is perhaps even more replete with worship language throughout its text, inasmuch as this scripture bears repeated reminders that Allah is the only God, the only being worthy of allegiance and the only one whose word is final law. The traditional first chapter of the Holy Koran declares, "Praise be to God, Lord of the worlds! The compassionate, the merciful! King on the day of reckoning!" (1:1). God's unique position as the only God is thus declared here and at innumerable other places throughout the scriptures. These words in turn are taken up directly into the Islamic ritual of daily prayer (*salat*). In this formal, prescribed ritual, the words of scripture are quoted exactly as statements of God's worth. At the same time, postures of bowing and prostration (kneeling down and placing one's forehead on the ground) are physical manifestations of the acknowledgement of God's unique greatness and of one's own willingness to submit to that greatness. Thus, the Islamic ritual of *salat* both states and embodies worship.

Technically, it seems that worship is directed at God or gods, not at those forms of the Absolute that are impersonal. Although it is true that, for the Taoist, the Tao is the ultimate and uncreated reality, it makes little sense to imagine a Taoist worshiping the Tao in this sense. "O Tao, you are the great source of being," just does not seem to fit with the impersonal nature of the Tao. This may be especially evident in Hinduism, where deities like Vishnu and Shiva are commonly praised and invoked, but Brahman, the impersonal "One without a second," is not the object of prayer or worship. **Krishna** is clearly worshipped by **Arjuna** in the famous 11th chapter of the Bhagavad Gita, where, having seen the ultimate vision of Krishna's greatness, Arjuna exclaims, "Krishna, the universe responds with joy and rapture to your glory, terrified demons flee in far directions, and saints throng to bow in homage" (Miller 104). More commonly, however, the Bhagavad Gita urges people to offer Krishna a "leaf or flower or fruit or water" (9.26), and this ritual practice is precisely what can be observed in thousands of Hindu temples where images of gods and goddesses are surrounded with flowers and fruit. Yet, throughout India, there is no temple and no such ritual for Brahman, the ultimate oneness of pure being and consciousness. Ritual worship, therefore, seems clearly to be part of those religions that have a relational and potentially responsive deity and not of those religions for which the Sacred is a monistic whole.

We are forced to consider the somewhat ambiguous cases of Buddhism and Confucianism, in which there may or may not be "worship," but there is certainly a great deal of ritual "veneration." This term, ironically perhaps, seems to derive from the name of the goddess Venus, and therefore, hints at some kind of loving appreciation. Whatever the source of the word, we often use it to describe the common Buddhist ritual of "venerating" the Buddha or the equally common "veneration of ancestors" in Chinese religion. Here, there is some dispute about whether these beings are "worshipped," and perhaps, it is important to keep the terms distinct.

Such a distinction is not easy, however. One famous case involves the Jesuit Christian missionaries who worked with some success to bring Christianity to China in late 16th century. One brave pioneer missionary named Matteo Ricci made converts to Christianity among the Chinese and agreed that they could also offer incense to their ancestors, since this was not really the worship of other gods. But after 100 years, as other Roman Catholic missions grew up in China, the dispute about whether a Chinese convert could both worship the one God and worship his or her ancestors had to be brought before the Pope. In 1704, he decreed, "veneration of ancestors and even of their tablets (list of ancestors' names) was prohibited" (Smith 157). The issue here is not whether one may worship other gods besides the one Creator whom Christians acknowledge; that is clearly prohibited by the first commandment. The issue here is whether "veneration of the ancestors" is really "worship of other gods." Evidently, the answer is not straightforward.

Overall, the likely reason for the important distinction between worship and veneration is really to keep these ideas of the Sacred—the ancestors, the Buddha, and so on—distinct from their monotheistic counterparts. That is, one "venerates" the Buddha or one's ancestors, but one "worships" God or Allah precisely because the Buddha and the ancestors are not quite the same notion of the Absolute as the monotheistic deity of the Abrahamic religions. Such distinctions, we have noted throughout this text, are part of the logic of how religions make sense, and so this should come as no surprise.

A final point to note about worship, specifically worship as ritual, is its often very formal nature. We have defined ritual in general as sets of repeated and stylized actions done for a particular purpose. Notable in worship (and veneration) is that, for many religions, the methods and actions of worship are indeed quite structured. As is evident from the practice of *salat* in Islam, the prayers are very carefully structured, with each bow and prostration, each recitation of verses being prescribed and formalized. Thus, when one watches Muslims in prayer, one sees them lined up in precise rows, bowing, speaking, and kneeling in unison. This formality is given by tradition and by Islamic law; there are no deviations.

In some contexts, this formality is called liturgy. A liturgy is any body of ritual practices, the order of actions and words, prescribed for a public practice, especially formal worship. A worship liturgy may state exactly what prayers are to be said at which points in a ceremony, prescribing when the worshipers stand, sit, sing, or chant. Communal worship in many religions is often liturgical, precisely because it allows all participants to join in one voice and to understand the same value of the ritual. Admittedly, some people resist liturgical worship, desiring instead that worship be more individual and more spontaneous. Puritan Christians during the English Reformation, like many Protestants, for example, wanted to avoid what they perceived as the overly formal, magical, and meaningless repetition of the Roman Catholic Mass. At times, however, these Puritans argued, too, against the English *Book of Common Prayer*, the standard liturgy of the day. In the Admonition to the Parliament (1572), Puritan reformers demanded, "changes in the forms and substance of the prayers, the abolition of the word "priest," [and] the use of preaching instead of written homilies" (Howard 43). However, public worship needs a kind of order, and even in rejecting liturgical practice, such churches tended, and still tend, to replace them with different structures, outlines, and prescribed actions. Thus, liturgy, to some extent, seems almost inescapable in public worship.

We shall consider later some of the benefits and danger of formally structured worship and of formal ritual in general. For now, the emphasis will be on the practices of worship and veneration that are very common in the world's religions; even religions that might not want to say they are worshipping gods. And formality, too, is common in these public actions. Exactly how formal the practices are may tell something about how conformity and symbolic unity are considered in those religions. Whether one "worships" or "venerates" may tell something about how the followers conceive of the Sacred. Again, this should not be surprising. Worship is not a merely accidental occurrence within a random set of practices related to religious belief. It is an integral part of religions all over the world, a direct expression in many cases of what it means to stand in the presence of the Sacred.

■ PRAYER

It might already have been a bit confusing that we spoke about worship but used the Islamic ritual of *salat*, daily prayer, as a fundamental example. Is prayer the same thing as worship? Is worship always prayer? The answer is probably no. In fact, to explore this concept, we suggest that besides "worship" there is another subcategory of ritual, namely "prayer," that is somewhat distinct from worship. Of course, in one sense, these distinctions are fluid and the lines between practices like worship and prayer are perforated at many points. But in a way, Islamic *salat* constitutes a kind of worship precisely for its clear emphasis on Allah's greatness. And "prayer" for many people often means petition.

It would oversimplify the idea, of course, to say that all prayer is petitionary and that worship is not. Again, such harsh distinctions are usually incorrect. But

Puritan Christians—group of Christians requesting the simplification of worship and doctrine during the 16th and 17th centuries in England

Protestants—Christian members of those religious groups that separated from the Catholic Church in Rome during the Reformation (16th century) or their descendants

du'a—petitionary prayer, blessing, even curse

it may be helpful to emphasize that prayer, for many people, implies a sense of requesting something of a deity or other entity. "Petition" means request, and petitionary prayer, therefore, is that kind of prayer that asks something of God or gods or spirits or ancestors. From the elaborate Vedic pleas, "Indra, bestow on us the best of treasures, the spirit of ability and fortune, increase of riches, safety of our bodies, charm of sweet speech, and days of pleasant weather." (Kishore: *Rig Veda*, Book II, hymn 21: 6). In Islam, there is even a distinction between *salat* and *du'a*, where the first is the ritual worship we described in the previous section, while the second is clearly petitionary. Indeed, it should quite reasonably be expected that one may find some kind of petitionary prayer in any religion where there are believed to be deities that have the power and the concern to aid in the lives of followers.

Some may compare prayer to meditation. Indeed, "New Age" efforts to match religious concepts and to apply them especially to personal experience might conflate the two entirely. Thus, Sri Daya Mata of the Self-Realization Fellowship says, "In its pure and highest form, prayer is meditation. It means to withdraw ourselves from all objects of distraction and apply our attention one-pointedly to one idea. In meditation, that idea is God alone; in prayer, it is whatever idea is embodied in our affirmation or invocation" (5). This kind of interpretation may indeed say something about the psychological value of some prayer, but overall it misses the crucial distinction between a mental discipline and a petitionary conversation. As noted, meditation is a ritualized practice of personal transformation. Within the Indian religions, including the Hindu roots of Daya Mata's fellowship, meditation is a practice for cultivating specific states of consciousness and disciplines of concentration. Petitionary prayer, in contrast, is a request directed at a being with whom one is, in some sense, conversing. In meditation, the human being performs a ritual practice that transforms the mind. In prayer, the "wholly other" is engaged and the life is presented before him or her.

Prayer that includes petitions, therefore, is perhaps less like meditation than it is like worship. That is, prayer that requests of deities their aid and love may well acknowledge that God or gods need not respond. Ultimately, perhaps, the believer knows that the deity is altogether capable of not answering the prayer as hoped for. Thus, the prayer of Jesus in the **Garden of Gethsemane** adds at the end of his requests from God, "Yet, not my will but yours be done" (Luke 22:42). When one prays, therefore, as much as one is hoping to attain one's desire from the benevolence of the gods, one may also be giving up one's desire, insofar as one places it into the hands of sovereign deity.

Of course, not all deities are considered sovereign, and not all "deities" are even gods. In Hinduism, for example, prayers to the goddess Saraswati request her aid in school or with exams, as she is the goddess of education. But such prayer by no means presumes she is absolute or all-powerful. Such prayer does, of course, recognize her power and willingness to care for those who call her name, at least within the context over which she is divine. In Buddhism, the Mahayana sect called "Pure Land Buddhism," in particular, honors a great enlightened being named **Amitabha,** who created and inhabits a "Pure Land of the West." Those who recognize their own inability to achieve enlightenment may pray to Amitabha or even just call out his name, and receive from this gracious being automatic rebirth into his Pure Land. This Buddha, in one sense the object of veneration as is the historical Buddha himself, is here a celestial being to whom one may appeal for aid, especially aid in the final achievement of liberation from the realm of rebirth. The Buddha himself, in his final words to his disciples, said, "Take refuge in nothing outside of yourselves" (De Bary 29). If the Buddha of the Theravada sect is mostly a venerated teacher, guiding disciples in how to find their own salvation, here it seems the Buddha Amitabha is more like a god, granting favor in response to the prayers of the faithful.

All of these examples are to show how prayer is often a kind of request or petition that, in some sense, acknowledges the power or a being higher than ourselves. It also seems to presume that these gods or deities have some compassion for the lost and suffering humanity of earth. Thus, petitionary prayer in this sense refers most logically to personalized deities, not with concepts of the Absolute taken to be impersonal powers or abstract monisms. Indeed, prayer at its best, even as it requests the deity's aid, seems to recognize the deity's power, and so contains elements of worship. Worship and prayer are not, therefore, opposing notions of ritual but often are mingled and almost indistinguishable in the ritual practices of everyday believers.

■ MAGIC

If the goal in prayer is to move the spirits or gods to achieve one's own desire, and insofar as prayer is believed to be automatically effective, it takes on qualities of magic.

If petitionary prayer in one sense acknowledges the gods' authority, and so is similar to worship, it also seems to include, on the opposite end of the spectrum, a possible element of control and manipulation of spiritual power. In this way, prayer may resemble ritual magic. That is, insofar as one hopes with prayer to actually move the spirits and the gods to achieve one's own desire and insofar as the prayers are thought to be automatically effective whatever the will of the deity, the ritual of prayer has a kind of transformative power, not, like meditation, to transform one's own state of mind but to transform the world. This is religious magic.

We have already discussed religious magic as an example of transformative ritual, so there is no need to repeat the examples here. But it is valuable here to make a comparison with worship and prayer. For example, we noted the use of the hymns of the Hindu Vedas as transformative magic. Yet, we also noted that Vedic literature is worshipful and petitionary. It is indeed an interesting historical fact that there was what may be called a process in the evolution of Hindu scripture as it was, over time, transformed from the hymns of praise and prayer in the Rig Veda to the ritual formulas, chants, and mantras of the Yajur Veda and the Atharva Veda. That is, scholars seem to be able to trace the evolution of lines of scripture from being worshipful to being magical. As Thomas Hopkins notes:

> To perform his task properly the Brahman priest had to know the Rig, Sama, and Yajur Vedas, but he used as his special mantras those collected as the Atharva Veda. The function of these mantras as magical formulas was transferred to the ritual sacrifice, and the transformation of the sacrifice was complete. It now was a magical performance of cosmic proportions. (30, italics deleted)

Secularization is one of the trends associated with globalization. One expression of this process involves taking over religious principles and practices, then repackaging them separated from their religious roots. It is as if the practice is good, but the roots that supported the practice are rotten. A good example of this is the growing promotion of the health benefits of yoga.

A recent online edition of *Time Magazine* discussed just this issure. The feature article in "Health and Science" is about the Hindu practice of yoga. "A path to enlightenment that winds back 5,000 years in its native India," it declares, "yoga has suddenly become so hot, so cool, so very this minute. It's the exercise *cum* meditation for the new millennium, one that doesn't so much pump you up as bliss you out." Indeed, the phenomenon of yoga as a trend in the United States is all about health and exercise, the famous people of Hollywood who practice it, and the billion dollar industries that support it. According to the article, scientific research now indicates that the regular practice of formal posture and breathing techniques, mental focus and concentration, and even the manipulation of "life forces" and "energy centers," can help people to lose weight, relieve stress and even unclog arteries. As a medical development, it seems to be an improvement over invasive surgery and drugs; as a trend, it is advertised by high-profile actors and rock stars.

But, as the previous quotation notes, this practice is also part of India, its culture, and its religion. Indeed, the term "yoga" is woven throughout Hindu scripture. Generally, it means "discipline," suggesting a regular, devoted practice applied, at least in Hinduism, to the attainment of a spiritual goal. Famously described and debated in the Bhagavad Gita, the religious disciplines of good karmic works, meditative insight,

Such an example, and there could be many others, raises an interesting question about the effective role of ritual, or even about the "power of prayer." Are the gods moved to act? Does the prayer have to be said properly, with the right mind or the right words, to be answered? If so, it is at least intriguing to ask if this is still petitionary prayer, with its inherent element of worship, or if prayer has become magic.

Of course, the lines between elements of religion are not solid. Thus, hard distinctions between prayer and worship and magic are not to be used too aggressively. And as we noted above, it is the very nature of ritual that prayer, often interwoven with specific actions, almost inevitably becomes standardized, so that there is a "right" way to pray. We have seen that ritual in general has this element of regularity and repetition. But taken magically, we see that the actions and words of regular ritual become incantations, which, if spoken correctly, achieve their end by their own power. This possibility that the form of the ritual can overwhelm the spiritual wonder of the Absolute raises the problem of ritual prayer in particular, and of ritual in general. We shall consider this problem next. But for now, we should remember that prayer, even prayer focused on petitions and requests from the deity, can also be tantamount to worship and that petitions that acknowledge the great power and love of deity certainly seem to represent a strong sense of the Absolute. From the distance of a spectator, it is perhaps diffi-

and theistic devotion are all "yogas." Primarily, however, Hindu "yoga" referred to practices of concentration and the disciplines of the meditation. Of course the disciplines of the body, too, were important. In Panjali's *Yoga Sutras* (from around the beginning of the Common Era), careful disciplines of posture and breath control were ways of leading up to the mental disciplines that produce enlightenment. This enlightenment, in turn, is salvation, liberation from rebirth, the ultimate goal of spiritual awakening that leaves behind the blind, sensual world.

Here, then, is a religious ritual of India made into a trendy health ritual of the West. Globalization has made this possible. In one sense, it is a sign of the opening of the world that a first-century Indian religious ritual of enlightenment and liberation can become the twentieth-century health trend of the rich and famous. But in another way, it may seem like a corruption of religion. Certainly it seems the image of movie stars doing yoga in million-dollar homes is quite unlike the image of a Hindu ascetic developing and proving his detachment from sensual existence. It may have once been a religious ritual of Hinduism, but now it seems to be a very worldly "ritual" of personal health and well-being. Perhaps it is like Christmas, which is now celebrated all over the world, often without any religious meaning at all, and of course even in the United States there is often more about Santa than about Jesus. With yoga, one might argue that the physical disciplines that appear in the health trends of America have been shorn of their spiritual meanings or perhaps that spirituality is being taught in yoga courses whether they say so or not. Indeed, the claim that somehow we can make yoga a "mere" physical exercise seems to presume a strangely Western—not Hindu—division of body and spirit. Globalization, it seems, makes it possible to spread religious ideas from one continent to another, but whether they are still "religious" when they arrive remains open to debate.

Source: Richard Corliss. "The Power of Yoga." *Time Magazine Online.* April 15, 2001. http://www.time.com/time/health/article/0,8599,106356,00.html (accessed June 5, 2001).

cult to see in someone's ritual practices what is really worship, what is petition, and what is magic. Perhaps it is difficult to see even in our own practice.

THE PROBLEM OF RITUAL

We have defined religious ritual in this chapter as any series of repeated gestures and words that become an important part of the practice of a person's relation to the Absolute. We have been trying here to suggest why it is so valuable and important, indeed why, even though some religious practices might resist the formality of ritual, ritual remains a crucial element of religious practice. It offers unity to the community, a sense of identity to the people, guidance in stages of life, and a consistent relation to the Sacred. This is surely the value of ritual.

At the same time, there have been suggestions throughout this chapter that there can be some problem with formality and ritual. Indeed, in the very admission that some resist the use of ritual, we see that various religious thinkers have recognized a danger in the repetition and structure of religious ritual. We might suggest that there are two related dangers in ritual: formality, in contrast to spontaneity, and manipulation, in contrast to submission. We shall consider these problems briefly.

Form versus spontaneity means that in religious ritual the possibility of the practice becoming a merely repeated and automatic gesture, devoid of personal life and individual interest, is obvious. Certainly, if a religious follower has been educated in a ritual service and has practiced it her whole life, it can become a mere tedium, just "vain repetitions" (Matthew 6:7). Perhaps many religious followers all over the world can repeat prayers, follow liturgies, and generally "go through the motions" of a profound ritual without ever considering its meaning. That is one of the problems with repetition: It is repetitious.

Finally it might perhaps be presumptuous to think that somehow personal religious feelings and rituals can be as profound and beautiful as the prayers and actions developed over the centuries in various religious contexts. There is often beauty, wonderful poetry and music, deep significance and insight built into these rituals that have endured through many generations, that may add to one's own practice. In addition, as mentioned, the contact with history and with familiar forms is an important aspect of a community's religious identity. Therefore, if a ritual becomes merely empty and repetitious, that is perhaps not the fault of the ritual so much as the failure of the human being to pay attention to its relevance in the context of history and community.

Ritual not rooted in the relation to the Sacred Absolute Reality becomes meaningless action.

How much better is religious practice, we might say, if it could all be spontaneous and personal, instead of repetitious and communal? Certainly, we see the value of inner experience and personal spontaneity. But in this chapter, the value of repetition and uniformity for the sake of community has also been acknowledged. Watching, for example, a million Muslims bowing toward the Ka'aba during the Hajj in Mecca can give one a dramatic sense of the unity and identity of diverse people, united in honoring the one God, Allah. Similarly, imagine the comfort that would be felt by an immigrant from Japan when he finds, at last, a Pure Land temple, where he again can participate with many others in the familiar chanting of the name of Amitabha Buddha. Surely, finding familiar actions and familiar words in a new town or a new country can greatly enhance one's sense of belonging. These images, both of a united community and of personal belonging, highlight the value of ritual, even when, or especially when, it is not spontaneous.

A more significant problem for ritual might lie in its tendency to become magic, insofar as magic suggests that the power and wonder of the Sacred is, in the end, open to our own ritual manipulation. When the gods become pawns to ritual incantation, it is a problem, not merely for the spiritual experience, but for the very conception of the Sacred. Since Chapter 3: The Absolute, Ultimate, Holy, we have considered that the Sacred is absolute, the final and ultimate power and being, somehow beyond human understanding and beyond human control. It is precisely this "beyondness" that makes it mysterious and terrifying, as well as glorious and attractive (*mysterium tremendum et fascinans*). If ritual is too effective, if it is too successful in manipulating the Holy to human ends, then ritual becomes a weakening of religion instead of a tool of spiritual life.

Nevertheless, it is clear that magic, healing, incantation, purification, and many other ritualized forms of personal and miraculous transformation are integral parts of much religious practice. Moreover, the lines between magic and spiritual experience are often indistinct. Perhaps we must confess here a kind of tension, a paradoxical pull between the "otherness" of the Sacred and the need to have that power accessible, somehow with us as we are. Thus, we need prayer to approach God or meditation to cultivate enlightenment precisely because the Sacred is otherwise so great as to be utterly inaccessible.

It is the irony of ritual that its very repetitiveness can be abused, and in trying to avoid it, people often merely replace one ritual with another. It is likewise the irony of ritual that its formulaic effectiveness can seem to be a magical manipulation of the Absolute, while the ritual is also a necessary approach to that which is otherwise beyond human reach. This is perhaps why ritual is needed and it appears in almost unlimited forms. Just as we create ritualized ways to greet our friends, so humans construct ritualized ways to act in response to, and in the presence of, the Absolute. For religion is not only something people believe in or read about; it is also something people *do*.

GLOBALIZATION AND RELIGIOUS RITUAL

So far in this chapter we have discussed many aspects of religious ritual. We have noted that religious rituals carry meaning, relate those participating to the Sacred, may form the basis for day-to-day life, and may serve as a source of identity. At this point, we turn our attention to questions centering around globalization and religious ritual. We could look at how ritual interacts with religious rituals from other faiths or how religious ritual informs the quest for identity heightened by globalization. However, we have chosen to look at the interaction of religious ritual with one of the strongest forces in today's world—secularization. As usual, we cannot be a comprehensive analysis here but must be limited to a few suggestive remarks.

secularization— the tendency to view the world in nonreligious terms and to remove modern institutions such as education and government from the dominance of religion

By secularization, we mean the tendency to view the world in nonreligious terms and to remove modern institutions such as education and government from the dominance of religion. To illustrate, much of modern education is conducted by secular, state-run schools, and secular agencies now accredit education even in schools operated by various religions. In addition, the legitimatization of the modern state is not derived from religion as it was in traditional societies. So in democracies, the will of the people, not appeal to God, is what legitimates a country's government.

In modern societies, secular concepts legitimate the government, not the laws of God.

Most secular states try to keep religious and state activities separate.

The interaction between religions and secularization is complex, indeed. Visible are also a number of different interactions when the roles of religious ritual and secularism are analyzed. One interesting area involves the role of religious ritual in public life. Most secular states try to keep religion and state activities separate. For example, the First Amendment to the U.S. Constitution establishes separation of church and state. One interpretation of this separation would keep government-staged events free from religious ritual. Thus, in the United States, most public schools have had to remove religious items such as the Ten Commandments or the Bible from classrooms. Neither can they use prayer to open the school day, commencement, or athletic events. Likewise, nativity scenes and other religious enactment rituals have been removed from local town property across the country.

First modernization and then globalization have caused similar dilemmas for political entities worldwide. The predominantly Muslim country Turkey routinely forbids religious ritual from any governmentally sponsored event and has forbidden religious-based political parties. An interesting variation of this dilemma is playing out currently in the European Union at the time this chapter on ritual is being written. The European Union is currently drawing up a new constitution. The new draft constitution refers to examples of the common heritage of the European nations. Included in this discussion is a reference to Europe's common religious heritage in Christianity. A strong debate has broken out between those who want to keep reference to Christianity's past contribution to European identity and those who find offensive any mention of religion at all in the constitution of the secular-grounded European Union. Apparently, secularism religiously demands the writing of religion out of history as well as the avoidance of publicly sponsored religious ritual.

The separation of religion and the state does not mean that religion is removed entirely from governmental affairs.

Still, the interaction between religion and secularism is not as simple as removing religion from public life. In fact, religious ritual often is part of publicly sponsored observances in secular societies. For example, the U.S. Congress has government-paid chaplains and sessions of Congress are opened with prayer. Almost every politician, from the President to the local mayor, routinely sponsors "prayer breakfasts" where government and religious officials are photographed participating in religious observances. Additionally, the militaries of most countries have governmentally paid chaplains who lead troops in religious ceremonies. So it is that Muslim, Christian, and Jewish soldiers commonly go into battle after being blessed in their respective rituals to God even when doing battle for a secular state.

Political leaders often try to claim religious legitimacy for their actions and those of their governments.

In a similar way, secular religious leaders often participate in religious ceremonies covered by the news media as a way of swaying citizens' opinions and claiming religious legitimacy for their governments and their actions. So it is that an American president may like to be pictured attending church or conferring with religious leaders, largely for political purposes. And Saddam Hussein allowed Arab television to photograph him engaging in Muslim prayer during the spring of 2003 American-led war against his government. Since Saddam was never particularly religious, this appears to be a deliberate attempt to gather support for his cause in the Islamic world. We take a more in-depth look at the legitimating function of religion in Chapter 14: Religion and Society in a Global Age.

At this point, we need to mention a few other issues about religious, or religious-like, rituals in secular societies. In Chapter 3, we discussed the functional equivalents of religion. There it was noted that any system of beliefs and behaviors that claims ultimacy may be considered the functional equivalent of religion. Put simply, this means that any philosophy or system that claims final authority and demands a kind of absolute conformity to its beliefs, rituals, and practices can be considered religious even if it is markedly anti-religious. Using this approach, the modern state, along with its rituals, may be called "a religion." The claim of supremacy is a characteristic of secular states. More often than not, they claim that there is no authority higher than themselves, and one's personal loyalty to them must be placed above other loyalties like those to one's family or religion. Furthermore, secular states claim to be the primary identity for individuals. That is, people are to see themselves as primarily as Americans, Germans or Indians and secondarily as Christians, Buddhists, or Muslims.

Nation-states often employ religious-like rituals that enforce their supremacy.

Therefore it should not be a surprise that most nation-states organize elaborate performances and powerful rituals to enforce their claims of supremacy. Thus, the former Soviet Union organized massive parades and festivities celebrating socialism, touting the supposed achievements of the Soviet state, and glorifying founders like Karl Marx. Similar observances are staged in most nations around the world, including the United States. The rituals of the secular state try to give it a sacred meaning and to build that meaning into the lives of citizens. These rituals do not have to be as elaborate as a giant May Day or 4th-of-July parade. They may be as simple saluting the flag (a ritual of national devotion) and saying a pledge of allegiance or singing a national anthem. Other rituals commemorate sacred times, like those associated with a nation's founding, or sacred places, like those associated with battles for national liberation. Of course, some of the most powerful rituals are related to celebrating the sacred sacrifice of soldiers or ordinary citizens who have given their lives extending or defending national interests. While these rituals may or may not refer to traditional religions, there is little doubt one characteristic of the modern scene is the religion of nationalism and its attendant sacred ceremonies.

To a large extent, the nation-state and nationalism are the products of the Modern Period, while globalization promotes transnationalism. Here too, rituals and religions are emerging to build facets of global society into the lives of ordinary citizens. Whether we look at ceremonies and rituals conducted at the opening of the United Nations, employed in the World Court of Justice, or apparent in resolving a dispute before the World Trade Organization, rituals enforce the authority of entities that transcend nation-states.

At the same time, not all global rituals are tied up with politics or economics. For example, sports, along with their attendant ceremonies and rituals, have come to play a very important part in globalization. The Olympic Games were revived in the late 19th century as a deliberate attempt to promote peace through worldwide athletic competition. The elaborate ceremonies at the beginning and end of the games stress the theme of human unity even among the diversity of nations. This is very obvious at the opening ceremonies where representatives of athletes and judges alike ritually hold the Olympic flag and swear a sacred oath to uphold the universal standards of fair competition that supposedly transcend national loyalties.

In fact, some even argue that international athletic competition is the new world religion. In this, "religion" temples are replaced with stadiums, saints, and mythic heroes with dominant athletes, sacred ethics with rulebooks, and devotees with fans. It is interesting that the term "fan" used for an athletic or a rock star follower is derived from the word "fanatic" that historically has been applied to especially zealous religious persons. Rituals normally associated with religions seem to have their parallels in the sports world. There is stirring music, singing, dancing, chanting, focusing (meditation), sacred banners (team pennants), worship leaders (cheerleaders), and so on, all of which may lead to an altered state of consciousness such as euphoria when one's team wins a particularly important game. Are sports the new religion? Maybe so, maybe not. Are sports rituals religious rituals? Maybe so, maybe not.

Finally, it is important to note that there has been a global tendency for religious rituals to become secularized. As society has become more secular, there has been a trend to remove rituals and related sacred ceremonies from their religious roots. For instance, many of the rituals associated with Christmas originally had religious significance, but large numbers of people engage in ceremonies like gift giving long after they have ceased to be religious. So, it is that the Christian St. Nicholas of Myra (fourth century CE) came to be the patron saint of children who was known for "bringing" them gifts on his feast day of December 6. Over time, gift giving assumed a seasonal importance in and of itself.

The poor saint himself became St. Nick or Santa Claus, "a jolly, old elf," who brings gifts to good little boys and girls. People who are not religious continue to give Christmas gifts to their children in the name of Santa Claus. Even though secular schools cannot display religious images, they can promote Santa Claus with little fear of generating negative reaction. It is interesting that this secular understanding of Christmas has transcended the realm of traditionally Christian nations. Japan has imported Christmas as a season of giving as a way to increase business profits. All of this seems particularly ironic since the holiday originally celebrated the birth of the Christian savior in a lowly manger. Though examples could be multiplied, perhaps this serves to make the point that religious rituals may lose their meaning in different contexts or have that meaning distorted entirely.

CONCLUSION

Religious ritual, then, is a complex affair, especially when we see that religious rituals change into secular rituals and that secular rituals themselves may have elements of religious function. Indeed, as we saw, even if we could easily keep the religious elements of ritual clear in our minds and in our examples, the different kinds of religious rituals—transformative, commemorative, rites of passage, and so on—often overlap and mingle in how they express and function in religious life. But this complexity is itself one of the lessons of the study of religion. Religions are not "all the same," and neither are their rituals. But knowing how to label and explain rituals, knowing how they express historical elements or imply the distinction between an interrelational God to whom one prays and a nonpersonal Buddha Nature that one finds by meditation—these educated insights into religious similarities and differences help us to understand what religion is and how it functions in the lives of real individuals.

As religion cannot be ignored—even by the determined atheist—as a powerful social force throughout the world, so ritual cannot be ignored for the power it has in both religious and secular societies to unite people and to express their highest ideals. People who are willing to study the rituals of any religion, including their own, will inevitably learn something important about how religions in general work in people's lives to inspire awe, to sanctify stages of life, and to mark the calendar of important events. Perhaps most importantly, rituals like prayer, meditation, and worship also tell us something about how people actively respond to the Absolute itself. Religion is more than ritual, but ritual is one of the deepest and most powerful visible forms of religion.

■ INTERACTIVE EXERCISE

Please continue the exploration of ritual by going to the interactive exercise for this chapter online (**http://www.religion.wadsworth.com/richter**).

WORKS CITED

Beane, Wendell C., and William G. Doty. *Myths, Rites, Symbols: A Mircea Eliade Reader.* New York: Harper Colophon Books, 1976.

Burge, Gary M. "Are Evangelicals Missing God at Church?" *Christianity Today.* October 6, 1997. http://www.christianitytoday.com/ct/7tb/7tb20a.html.

Comstock, Gary L. *Religious Autobiographies.* Belmont, CA: Wadsworth, 1995.

Cragg, Kenneth. *The House of Islam.* Belmont, CA: Dickenson Publishing Co., 1969.

Daya Mata, (Sri). "Mastering the Life-Changing Power of Prayer." Self-Realization Magazine. Winter Winter 2002. http://www.yogananda-srf.org/writings/srm_w2002_a.htm. De Bary, William Theodore *The Buddhist Tradition in India, China, and Japan.* New York: Vintage, 1972.

Esposito, John L. *Islam: The Straight Path.* Oxford, UK: Oxford University Press, 1998.

Fernando, Anthony. "Contemporary Buddhism in Sri Lanka." in *Buddhism in the Modern World.* Ed. Heinrich Dumoulin. New York: Macmillan, 1976. 65–80.

Fisher, Mary Pat. *Living Religions.* 2nd ed. Englewood Cliffs: Prentice Hall, 1994.

Grimassi, Raven. *Encyclopedia of Wicca and Witchcraft.* St. Paul, MN: Llewellyn, 2000.

Hawke, Elen. *The Sacred Round.* St. Paul, MN: Llewellyn, 2002.

Hopkins, Thomas. *The Hindu Religious Tradition.* Belmont, CA: Dickenson, 1971.

Howard, Leon. *Essays on Puritans and Puritanism.* Albuquerque: University of New Mexico Press, 1986.

King, Winston L. *Theravada Meditation.* University Park: Penn State University Press, 1980.

Kishore, B. R. *Rig Veda.* New Delhi, India: Diamond, 1998.

Leggett, Trevor. *A First Zen Reader.* Ritland, VT: Charles E. Tuttle, 1960.

Leys, Simon (trans.). *The Analects of Confucius.* New York: Bantam Books, 1997.

Miller, Barbara Stoler (trans.). *The Bhagavad Gita.* New York: Bantam Classics, 1986.

Robinson, George. *Essential Judaism.* New York: Simon & Schuster Pocket Books, 2000.

Smart, Ninian, and Richard Hecht. *Sacred Texts of the World*. New York: Crossroads, 1990.

Smith, D. Howard. *Chinese Religions from 1000 B.C. To the Present Day*. New York: Hold, Rinehart, and Winston, 1968.

Suzuki, D. T. *Zen Buddhism*. Garden City, NY: Doubleday Anchor Books, 1956.

Tappert, Theodore G. *The Book of Concord: The Confessions of the Evangelical Lutheran Church*. Philadelphia: Fortress Press, 1959.

Thompson, Laurence G. *Chinese Religion: An Introduction*. 2nd ed. Encino, CA: Dickenson Publishing, 1975.

Corliss, Richard. "The Power of Yoga." *Time Magazine Online*. April 15, 2001 http://www.time.com/time/health/article/0,8599,106356,00.html (accessed April 29, 2004).

Walker, Williston. *A History of the Christian Church*. New York: Charles Scribners' Sons, 1959.

Warren, Henry Clarke. *Buddhism in Translations*. New York: Athaneum, 1982.

Watson, Burton(trans.). *Chuang Tzu: Basic Writings*. New York: Columbia University Press, 1964.

FOR FURTHER READING

Eliade, Mircea. *Rites and Symbols of Initiation: The Mysteries of Birth and Rebirth*. Trans. Willard R. Trask. New York: Harper & Row.1965.

McDaniel, June. *Offering Flowers, Feeding Skulls: Popular Goddess Worship in West Bengal*. Oxford, UK: Oxford University Press, 2004.

McVann, Mark. "Rituals of Status Transformation in Luke–Acts: The Case of Jesus the Prophet." In *The Social World Of Luke Acts: The Case of Jesus the Prophet*. Ed. Jerome Nerey. Massachusetts: Hendrickson, 1991. 333–360.

Segal, Robert A. *The Myth and Ritual Theory*. Malden/Oxford, UK: Blackwell, 1997.

Turner, Victor. *Process, Performance, and Pilgrimage: A Study in Comparative Symbology*. New Delhi, India: Concept, 1979.

———. *The Ritual Process: Structure and Anti-Structure*. Chicago: Aldine, 1969.

10 RELIGION, MORALITY, AND ETHICS

F or some religious people, morality and ethics *must* be based on religion; otherwise, they are suspect. Other religious people recognize problems with a morality or ethics based strictly on literal interpretations of scripture as a source of religious authority. Either way, there is little doubt that religion is at least a possible source of morality and ethics. The moral imperative of religion and related matters is presented in this chapter. For now, please look over the pictures found above and on the Web site (**http://www.religion.wadsworth**

.com/richter), and the following scriptural quotations, then consider the Introductory Questions that follow as a way to prepare for reading this chapter.

All that we are is the result of what we have thought: it is founded on our thoughts, it is made up of our thoughts. If a man speaks or acts with an evil thought, pain follows him, as the wheel follows the foot of the ox that draws the carriage. All that we are is the result of what we have thought. It is founded on our thoughts, it is made up of our thoughts. If a man speaks or acts with a pure thought, happiness follows him like a shadow that never leaves him.

—Buddhism: Dhammapada 1–4

These classes of living beings have been declared by the Jinas: earth, water, fire, wind; grass, trees, and plants; and the moving beings, both the egg-bearing and those that bear live offspring, those generated from dirt and those generated in fluids. Know and understand that they all desire happiness. By hurting these beings, people do harm to their own souls, and will repeatedly be born as one of them.

—Jainism: Sutrakritanga 1.7.1–2

The philosopher Kao said, "Man's nature is like the ke willow, and righteousness is like a cup or a bowl. The fashioning of benevolence and righteousness out of man's nature is like the making cups and bowls from the ke willow." Mencius replied, "Can you, leaving untouched the nature of the willow, make with it cups and bowls? You must do violence and injury to the willow before you can make cups and bowls with it. If you must do violence and injury to the willow in order to make cups and bowls with it, on your principles you must in the same way do violence and injury to humanity in order to fashion from it benevolence and righteousness! Your words, alas!, would certainly lead all men on to reckon benevolence and righteousness to calamities."

—Confucianism: Mencius 6.1.1–2

"Well then," said the Lord of the River, "what should I do and what should I not do? How am I to know in the end what to accept and what to reject, what to abide by and what to discard?"

Jo of the North Sea said, "From the point of view of the Way, what is noble or what is mean? These terms merely express excesses of contrast. Do not hobble your will, or you will be departing from the Way. What is few, or what is many? These terms merely express states of fluctuation. Do not strive to unify your actions, or you will be [in conflict with] the Way."

—Taoism: Chuang-tzu, book 17

You must not carry false rumors; you shall not join hands with the guilty to act as a malicious witness: You shall neither side with the mighty to do wrong—you shall not give perverse testimony in a dispute so as to pervert it in favor of the mighty— nor shall you show deference to a poor man in his dispute.

When you encounter your enemy's ox or ass wandering, you must take it back to him. When you see the ass of your enemy lying under its burden and would refrain from raising it, you must nevertheless raise it with him.

You shall not subvert the rights of your needy in their disputes. Keep far from a false charge; do not bring death on those who are innocent and in the right, for I will not acquit the wrongdoers. Do not take bribes, for bribes blind the clear-sighted and upset the pleas of those who are in the right.

You shall not oppress a stranger, for you know the feelings of the stranger, having yourselves been strangers in the land of Egypt.

—Judaism: Exodus 23:1–9

Jesus . . . taught them, saying: "Blessed are the poor in spirit, for theirs is the kingdom of heaven. Blessed are those who mourn, for they will be comforted. Blessed are the meek, for they will inherit the earth. Blessed are those who hunger and thirst for righteousness, for they will be filled. Blessed are the merciful, for they will receive mercy. Blessed are the pure in heart, for they will see God. Blessed are those who are persecuted for righteousness' sake, for theirs is the kingdom of heaven.

"Blessed are you when people revile you and persecute you and utter all kinds of evil against you falsely on my account. Rejoice and be glad, for your reward is great in heaven, for in the same way they persecuted the prophets who were before you."

—Christianity: Matthew 5:1–12.

They ask you about drinking and gambling. Say: "There is great harm in both, although they have some benefits for men; but their harm is far greater than their benefits." They ask you what they should give in alms. Say: "What you can spare." Thus God makes plain to you His revelations so that you may reflect upon this world and the hereafter. They question you concerning orphans. Say: "To deal justly with them is best. If you mix their affairs with yours, remember they are your brothers. God knows the just from the unjust. If God pleased, he could afflict you. His is mighty and wise."

—Islam: Holy Koran (Sura 2:219–20)

INTRODUCTORY QUESTIONS

The scriptures and pictures for this chapter deal with matters of morality: concern for personal righteousness, concern for the poor, and urgings against violence. Consider these examples and other ideas you may have about morality—especially religious morality—to respond to the following questions.

1. The Jain religion is justly famous for its doctrine of *ahimsa,* or nonviolence. It is based upon the idea that all living beings have "soul" and "desire happiness." Can you see how this belief implies the need to do no violence to any living thing, even bugs and trees? If you do not believe trees or mosquitoes have souls, does that change the moral idea?
2. The Judaic commands seem to insist on justice and good treatment even to one's enemies. Do you think this is realistic? The war picture is taken from the Israeli-Palestinian conflict. Can one be good to one's enemies in a situation of war? Do you think truly good, religious people would refuse to go to war?
3. Mencius was arguing in the third quotation that becoming a good and moral person could not be a matter of changing our own nature. Indeed, Mencius is famous for arguing that human nature is inherently good. Do you think that is true?
4. All three of the references from the Abrahamic religions talk about being concerned for the poor. Yet, as the picture shows, people are starving in this world. Do you think we all do have an obligation to save the poor? Why? Why does God care?
5. The Buddhist excerpt suggests the famous concept of *karma,* namely, that what we are now is the result of actions and thoughts done in the past. So in a sense, those who suffer now are feeling the effects of their own evils, and the main reason not to do evil now is so that a future life is not harmed. Do you think these ideas explain our motivations for moral actions? Do they, for example, help you care for the poor more, or less?

6. Chuang Tzu, like other Taoists, taught the ideal of nonaction. In the fourth excerpt, he is suggesting that in the larger reality of the Tao, the Way, there is no right or wrong. Why then should we bother with morality? Do you think that, in the big picture of things, morality does not really matter? Is this view religious in any way?

7. The Amish farmer is directed by his religious commitment to avoid modern technologies. The Amish are also traditionally pacifists. They also tend to stop education for their children at eighth grade. Ultimately, these are religious values for the Amish. Do you think he might be right about some and not about others? How might he decide if he can follow some moral ideals and not others? If there is some nobility in this way of life in obedience to God, how does it compare to the terrorist, who kills innocent people also, he believes, in obedience to God?

THE MORAL IMPERATIVE OF RELIGION

As we begin to think about the relationship between religion and morality and ethics, we can remind ourselves of something that was indicated in Chapter 2: What is Religion? There we noted that the etymology of the word "religion," either from *religare*, "to bind oneself," or *relegere*, "scrupulous observance," points directly to the virtually explicit understanding that religion includes action, whether doing something or refraining from doing something. This focus on action may be in the realm of thought, feeling, attitudes, or worldview, as well as in the realm of physical movement, which affects oneself and/or others. If we begin a casual conversation within a group of people, it is most likely that most of the individuals will think in terms of religion as a matter of belief or faith *and* what one should or should not do, usually in terms of ritual or moral obligations. "Oh, yes," one might say, "I'm religious (in my mind), but I don't practice it very much." Another might say, "You can't really call yourself religious if you don't go to church (or temple or mosque)." Or consider such moralistic claims as "Religion is fine as long as you don't try to impose it on others," or "What good is your religion if you don't try to apply it to your whole life and not just be a 'Friday Muslim' (or 'Saturday Jew' or 'Sunday Christian')?" Someone might even insist that "This country would be a lot better off if it were a truly Christian (or Muslim, or Jewish nation—as Orthodox Jews might say in Israel)," by which they would mean to describe the behavior and morality of the people as needing some religious guidance. In all these ways, we might hear people talk about religion and find that it naturally includes an emphasis on action.

Religion often is bound to concepts of what a person should or should not do (an ethic).

Thus, in a broad and general way, the very nature of religion implies an ethic: "Teacher, what good deed must I do to have eternal life?" (Matthew 19:16) This question was not only asked of Jesus but represents the quest of all religions as long as one treats "doing" and "eternal life" in the broadest of terms. "Doing" is understood broadly to include thinking and feeling, that is, mental activity, which is perhaps why Jesus added in other contexts that ". . . if you are angry with a brother or sister, you will be liable to judgment" (Matthew 5:22) and

"... everyone who looks at a woman with lust has already committed adultery with her in his heart" (Matthew 5:28). "Eternal life" can be understood broadly to parallel "becoming enlightened" or its analog in other religions (a parallelism we shall note in Chapter 12). Thus, with these broad understandings, the relation between religion and morality might change the question of Matthew 19 to "Teachers, what must we think and do in order to become true followers of this faith?" Or even more generally, we can pose the common, standard question of all ethics: "What is the morally right and/or good thing to do?"

Thus, we come in this chapter to discuss the relationship between religion and morality, a relationship both complex and powerful. In the words of David Chidester, "Any system of **religious ethics** weaves together a fabric of duties, responsibilities, and imperatives that produces a powerful sense of obligation. . . . Religion may therefore consist primarily in binding obligation and/or scrupulous observance of specific norms that govern behavior . . . in both ritual and [morality]" (23). Chidester's focus on behavior need not deny points already made in this text about the many aspects and functions of religious life: the originating experiences of the founders, the remembrance and retelling of the experiences in the form of myths or sacred stories, or the reenactment of the experiences, which come to be known as rituals. Indeed, previous chapters have stressed how the inspiration of any or all of these aspects may also find its way into the arts, especially music, dance, paintings, sculpture, poetry, and literature; the most significant and sacred of the latter two are then eventually called scripture. But however religion is experienced, another response it elicits is what it requires the individual, the community, or the larger group to do or refrain from doing in the realm of morality. And for some, this is the most important part of all religious life.

Religious behavior can be either moral or ritual. For some, ritual is the overriding obligation, the *sine qua non* of religion, without which morality is invalid. For others, however, morality is the greater, even the ultimate, test of "true" adherence to religion. This perspective is probably epitomized in the passage from the Tanakh (quoted in Chapter 2: What is Religion?), which emphasizes the rejection of mere ritual and God's demand for moral righteousness:

> *I hate, I despise your festivals, and I take no delight in your solemn assemblies. Even though you offer me your burnt offerings and grain offerings, I will not accept them; and the offerings of well-being of your fatted animals I will not look upon. Take away from me the noise of your songs; I will not listen to the melody of your harps. But let justice roll down like waters, and righteousness like an ever flowing stream. (Amos 5:21–24)*

Just as all human endeavor can be divided into theory and practice—thinking and acting—so also is there the parallel of ethics (systematic thinking about morality) and morality itself (action that is subject to moral judgment). **Morality** is usually thought of as coming first, and then ethics is the academic discipline within philosophy or religious studies, which attempts to understand, interpret, and critique morality and its sources. If one could take morality into a laboratory, to analyze and "dissect" it, one would be doing ethics. According to T. William Hall, Richard B. Pilgrim, and Ronald R. Cavanagh, morality is that "aspect of the religious life that prescribes how people ought to feel, think, and behave. . . . Morality is living according to standards of conduct" Ethics, by extension, "is the evaluation and interpretation of morality, often aiding in the establishment or revision of moral codes" (125). That is, morality is concerned with the day-to-day, lived-in reality of what we ought to do. But when we study that morality and wonder how to live by the larger, overarching principles they presume, we are doing ethics.

However, as Hall et al. go on to say, "morality and ethics . . . are not necessarily or automatically religious. They only become religious when they are understood as expressions of or responses to that which is experienced or perceived as ultimate or transcendent" (125–126). This is consonant with what we have urged all along, namely, that the specifically religious dimension of morality, like specifically religious myths and rituals, gains its religious quality from having some connection with the Absolute. Therefore, when we seek the overarching principles behind our religious moral duties, we shall unavoidably come to see the connection between what we ought to do and what we believe about the Holy. Thus, when we consider the Sacred, we almost unavoidably consider as well an ethical dimension, the intimate connection between what religion is about and what we ought to do.

The specifically religious dimension of morality is found in connection to the Absolute.

In most ancient societies, in fact, religion and morality were seen as one. The religion of the group was the source of its morality—both personal and public. Although anthropology has found a few cultures whose morality appears to be independent of religion, the vast majority of human societies base their morality and ethics on religion (Momen 338). Especially in "small-scale" societies, religion and the moral order of society are, to use the words of Ninian Smart, "effectively coterminous" (Smart 197). This means that being a "good person," as defined by a particular society, is often a matter of being an obedient member of that society's dominant religion.

However, there are classic examples of ". . . a divergence, and sometimes of an outright conflict, between . . . religious action-guides and . . . moral action-guides. . ." (Little and Twiss 67-68). Possibly the most famous example from the Bible is that of God commanding Abraham to sacrifice his son Isaac. This story describes a situation wherein the demands of God conflict with accepted, more humanitarian views of morality. Certainly, any religious person of today acting as if to kill his own child because "God told him to" would be deemed insane or immoral, and perhaps even Abraham himself suffered greatly under the internal religious conflict of needing to obey God's order to commit a heinous act (an internal passion that was most prominently focused on by **Søren Kierkegaard** (1813–1855) in his book *Fear and Trembling*). And yet, we know that still today religious individuals at times may feel themselves called to act contrary to social morality, and that the commands of God outweigh the morals of society. For them, the counterargument might be that the demands of the religious morality in question are not really contrary to human morality ". . . in the belief that the 'real' welfare of the affected parties is properly redefined in supernatural terms, and that the goal of a religious action-guide . . . is . . . 'really' other-regarding, even though the action works against the 'this-worldly' welfare of the affected party" (Little and Twiss 67–68). In other words, for some "extremely religious" people in some extreme cases, their perspective might be that "for your own benefit, for the sake of your ultimate salvation, we need to treat you in ways that

Religious persons may feel compelled to act against social morality.

society could find immoral." For it seems reasonable that the hope of eternity and the authority of God outweigh this-worldly benefits and the significance of human laws.

In some pre-modern societies, especially in the Middle and Far East, there is a complex symbiosis between religion, morality, and law. With the advent of Islam, the Holy Koran, which most Muslims believe is the literal word of God, and the Hadiths, traditionally the sayings and actions of Muhammad, are together seen as the foundational sources of the Shari'a, Islamic Law. This legal code, both religious and social,". . . explicitly aim[s] to regulate the whole of the community," says Ninian Smart, since "the aim of Islam is to be both the spiritual and temporal life-pattern" (Smart 197). Political science calls this a theocracy (Greek, *theos*, God; *cratia*, rule). In the West under the eventual influence of Christianity, the very name of the Holy Roman Empire makes explicit a similar relation between religion and social morality, in which being a good citizen of the empire was practically defined as being a good Christian. With the Renaissance and the Protestant Reformation of Martin Luther (1483–1546) and **John Calvin** (1509–1564), the seeds were planted for the possibility of the independence of reason and emotion from religion. However, not until relatively recent modern times, after the American and French revolutions, has there been an attempt to separate religious morality and state law. Thus it is only in the 18th and 19th centuries that we begin to see the work of the major secular theorists of morality in the West, philosophers like Immanuel Kant (1724–1804), **Jeremy Bentham** (1748–1832), and **John Stuart Mill** (1806–1873), who base morality and ethics on autonomous human reason. But more about that later.

The point so far has been to stress the power and the prevalence of religiously based moralities. It is arguable indeed that religions have framed and justified moral codes all over the world and that even today religious bases of moral rules inform our thinking and our behavior, even if we consider ourselves atheists and nonreligious. For good or ill, religion makes its power felt in guiding and, perhaps, misguiding human morality. This is only to state in another way a point we have made since the beginning of this text, namely, that religion is powerful and pervasive. This is all the more a good reason to consider carefully and in more detail the nature of religious morality.

To begin to construct a vocabulary for discussing religious ethics, we can use a medical analogy. If the description of a situation involving moral considerations is equivalent to the diagnosis of a disease, then the normative judgment about what ought to be done is the prescription or the medication to be applied. That is, it is one thing merely to describe the disease; it is another to try to explain what ought to be done to cure it. In philosophical terms, the "cure" is the normative or prescriptive element in ethics, which consists of the moral or ethical theories and/or principles that guide us in making our moral or ethical decisions, or which provide us with the "moral imperatives" in our lives. But now the question arises as to the origins or sources of these imperatives: On what authority— (whether religious or secular)—are our actions judged to be morally right or wrong, good or bad or evil? This question can be answered (1) historically, (2) along a continuum from "external" religious expressions or traditions to "internal" human experience, and (3) logically in terms of the categorization of sources (Hall et al. 126).

Shari'a—Islamic Law, based on the holy scripture of the Holy Koran and Hadith; considered divine law rooted in God's commandments

In pre-modern societies, religious laws and state laws were often the same, but in modern societies these have been separated.

HISTORICAL ORIGINS AND SOURCES OF MORALITY

Historically, the origin of morality is found in a people's effort to relate their rituals and right behaviors to their cosmogony.

Our English words "mores" and "morality" come from the Latin *moralis,* meaning the customs of the people. Likewise, our English words "ethos" and "ethics" come from the Greek *ethos,* meaning custom or character, and are related to the word "ethnic," referring to the people of a common culture. Thus, the morality of a people originally resides in their traditional common practices, and these in turn originate in their attempt to relate their cosmogony (theories of the origin of the universe, the generation or creation of the existing world order) to their religious rituals and morality. According to Robin Lovin and Frank Reynolds,

> *Such diverse ways of explaining and justifying moral imperatives may be taken as indications of a very general human effort to relate the changing requirements of action to a permanent and unchanging order of things. . . . [I]deas of "natural law" or of the "orders of creation" can be interpreted as systematic expressions of a far more widespread belief that truly significant actions recapitulate the primordial cosmogenesis or participate in a pattern established outside the flux of ordinary events. (1)*

Mircea Eliade (1907–1986), editor in chief of *The Encyclopedia of Religion* and one of the foremost historians of religion of the 20th century, demonstrated in his book entitled *Cosmos and History* "the pervasive effort of traditional cultures to relate the order of present action to cosmogony" (Lovin and Reynolds 2). Furthermore, these cosmogonic myths may provide

cosmogony—theory of the origin of the cosmos

> *. . . a pattern for human choice and action that stands outside the flux of change and yet within the bounds of human knowing. What unites the cosmogonies is this unifying function of bestowing on certain actions a significance that is not proportioned to their empirical effects or to the individual goals of their agents, but derives from their relation to an order of the world that begins with the beginning of the world as we know it. (5–6)*

Finally, religious and philosophical systems of ethics make explicit

> *. . . what Eliade discerns in the traditional civilizations that interpret the flux of history by "perpetually finding transhistorical models and archetypes for it." Interest in cosmogony marks a hope that despite the perpetual changes evident to traditional cultures and the diversity of beliefs apparent to moderns, some realities may be permanent and some things may be dependable enough to build a way of life on them. (6; compare Eliade, Cosmos 141)*

Morals, then, often find their origins in cultural traditions, although in these traditions themselves even deeper roots are sought in the very creation of the cosmos, where even the word "cosmos" in its original Greek presumes the ideal of an orderly and harmonious universe. Moving beyond the mere appeal to common sense—to be moral for the sake of order rather than chaos—more profound religious thinkers may realize that the way we ought to live needs to be tied in some mythic or philosophical way to the ultimate source of being. Indeed, this may be the basic appeal of any religiously based morals, namely, that they find their justification in something ultimate, in the Absolute itself. The effort to see the possible commonalities of religious and secular cosmogonies as a unifying factor in the current plethora of diverse and seemingly incompatible religious and moral or ethical perspectives may also be seen as an attempt to overcome another traditional problem for the study of religious ethics, namely, that of ethical relativism versus universalism or absolutism. But more about that later as well.

The effort to base morality in the Absolute may represent an attempt to overcome ethical relativism.

■ VERTICAL AND HORIZONTAL ASPECTS OF RELIGIOUS MORALITY

We have already seen the two dimensions of the practice of religion and their connections in the previous chapter. We noted there that an analysis of these practices reveals that they involve both ritual and moral practices. The rituals, we saw, such as worship or prayer, might be referred to as the vertical relationship to the object of devotion, as they look "up" to the Absolute. In contrast, the moral practices of religion seem primarily to involve what we might call the horizontal relationship towards one's fellow human beings, such as the extent to which one is or is not neighborly to one's neighbor in thought, word, deed, or feeling. These two dimensions are evident when Jesus says, ". . . love the Lord your God with all your heart, and with all your soul, and with all your mind. This is the biblical commandment [the vertical dimension]. And a second is like it: . . . love your neighbor as yourself [the horizontal dimension]" (Matthew 22: 37–39). However, the ritual dimension may not escape moral judgment either— to the extent that various rituals may be judged immoral by standards whose source may or may not be religious, such as ritual human sacrifice or animal sacrifice, ritual prostitution, rituals involving mind-altering substances (communion wine or peyote), or ritual circumcision or genital alteration, especially when practiced on females. Similarly, morals become ritualized in many cases as kindness or respect become practiced with formal greetings, honesty is emphasized by swearing on a Bible, or charity may be exercised in the passing of a plate or in a formal collection after the Islamic month of fasting (Ramadan). But for this chapter, we will be emphasizing how morality *per se* is connected to religion, as part of the natural implication that beliefs about the Absolute bear themselves into the world as moral action.

The ritual dimension may be seen as establishing a vertical dimension (humans to God), while morality involves the horizontal dimension (humans to humans).

Ramadan— twenty-nine or thirty days of fasting period in Islam

■ RELIGIOUS MORALITY AS A RESPONSE TO A FLAWED WORLD

Another way in which religion implies an ethics is that it acknowledges that human beings recognize—(whether originally by human insight or by religious "revelation"—(that there is a major discrepancy between the way human life *ought* to be lived ideally and the way it *is* lived. Of all the various definitions of religion we encountered in Chapter 2, perhaps one common element is the experience and recognition that all is not right with the world, and that in itself may be the religious dimension of human experience. This human but ultimately reli-

Religion often distinguishes between what is and the world and what ought to be.

gious experience is called fallibility, suffering, immorality, evil, sin, or alienation. Indeed, we saw in Chapter 7 that religions all over the world wrestle to different extents and answer in different ways a universal concern with the troubles of the world and of our own hearts. And as we shall see later, in Chapter 12, many religions offer visions of how to find release from the woes and ills of life, offering indeed a hope that all can be redeemed in this world or the next. This experience is inevitably a part of any understanding of what life is all about. How the individual or the group copes with this human condition constitutes what some scholars have called a "'vision of life'. . . a holistic interpretation of the meaning of life itself." This, in turn, they argue, inspires people to act, to move "from an understanding of the essential problem confronting life toward an 'ideal' goal by means of some mode of activity," —ritual or moral (Hall et al. 99). Thus, the religious sense that all is not right with the world and that somehow the human relation with the Absolute, and humans' relations with one another, are curiously torn moves us to religious acts deemed right or good. This again is the inherent connection between religion and morality.

We have by no means argued here that all morality is necessarily religious. Although moral thinking is powerful and pervasive in all human cultures, such that all the elements of our humanity—thought, action, passion or emotion or feeling, and will—are subject to moral judgment, the ultimate source of morality and ethical theories and principles, according to many scholars, can be (1) religion, (2) nature itself, albeit as interpreted by human beings, or (3) autonomous human nature, with a focus on one or more of the elements of humanity, especially reason. Representatives of these positions will be presented later in this chapter. But for now, even if not all morality and ethics are religious, we might want to argue that all religion inspires morality and ethics, though of course in different ways and to different extents. Certainly, one cannot merely conflate the two, as we have seen before, "reducing" religion to social concern or inner goodness, for it would be a mistake to lose sight of the Sacred in our desire to emphasize the value of moral action. But together religious piety and moral commands are a powerful and natural union, a force to be recognized and considered thoughtfully in the history of all human culture.

Though there may be a connection between religion and morality, it is a mistake to reduce religion to morality.

■ BUT WHY BE RELIGIOUS? WHY BE MORAL?

On our way toward another understanding of the historical origins of religious morality we may add what some consider to be the ultimate question for human beings who somehow recognize the religious dimension of human existence: Why be religious? Why try to do what religion calls for? And its concomitant question: Why be moral? (In modern parlance, this is a metaethical question, metaethics being another of the elements of philosophical ethics.) In yet other words, what are some of the religious motivations to be good and do what is morally right and to avoid what is morally wrong?

In order to provide a brief overview of some of the motivations for people of various religions to be religious, to be moral, or to be good, we shall follow the work of a major scholar in the field. In his book *Dimensions of the Sacred*, Ninian Smart summarizes the motivations some religions give "to ordinary people to be good and observant." If a religion believes in reincarnation, then moral or ethical conduct can generate "personal merit or karma" to move to a higher plane in a future life. Because of the nonfinality of this life, there can be moral progress, and this can provide a continuing motivation to engage in a program of what we might call "continuing education" to eventually "get it right." Those religions that believe in "a single life ending in the judgment of a God, as in the *Egyptian Book of the Dead* and in Western theisms, [give] being good or bad a more dramatic meaning" (198). From this perspective, there is an utter finality to the consequences of one's religiously motivated morality or one's irreligious immorality, especially in the most conservative understandings of Christianity and Islam.

A better rebirth or ultimate salvation may depend on moral behavior in this life, according to some religions.

But even so, within the Christian tradition the matter is not totally resolved because of the diverging interpretations of the tension between law—representing God's wrath and justice—and gospel (good news) or grace—representing God's love and mercy. This, in turn, raises the question of the appropriately faithful motivation: Should the believer be religious and thereby be good and do right in order to go to heaven "rather than out of true love of God," or does the believer try to be good and do right simply to avoid going to hell (Smart 198)? Yet another way of posing the problem is whether to be good and do right in order to earn or deserve heaven by obeying the law of God or whether the motivation for being good and doing what is right should be out of genuine, authentic gratitude for God's gift (grace) of salvation. Broadly speaking, this parallels, respectively, the situation within Christianity, which brought about the division between Roman Catholicism and Protestantism ("saved by grace through faith and not by works"), a discussion we will pursue more fully in Chapter 12. Here we can note that, according to the more Protestant emphasis on "salvation by grace," God is under no obligation to reward human beings for their "good works," since no one is truly holy except God himself. Yet God's justice is tempered by God's abundant and magnanimous love and mercy toward humankind. Consequently, some Jews and Christians interpret various passages of scripture as supporting a belief in universal salvation, that is, in the end all humankind will be saved. What then becomes of religious motivations for morality? For the Christian St. Paul, it was simply a matter of being "dead to sin" and "alive in Christ." Having once been "slaves to sin," he claims, the Christian saved by grace is now a "slave to God," serving God with moral action out of gratitude alone (see Romans 6).

Moral behavior may also stem from a grateful response to God's love.

Regarding the Confucian tradition, it can be seen as "the least 'religious' of the classical traditions," but "it takes ritual very seriously." As Smart points out, "Confucian *li* or proper behaviour . . . is crucial for the good life. But in addition ethics is clearly placed within a political frame: . . . Confucianism appeals to people to follow the moral life in order to ensure stability and prosperity in society" (199). Thus for Confucianism, the motivation for the moral life is both religious and worldly, a sense that the harmony of individual and social life is dependent on how the people cultivate virtue and good character. And this harmony in turn is a kind of mirror of the Tao.

li—proper behavior in the context with others

Religions such as Confucianism may stress proper behavior as a way of reaching harmony in this world and with the Ultimate.

Again, some of these points shall reappear when we talk of salvation in Chapter 12. Here, the point has been to emphasize that religion both guides and motivates morality for great numbers of the world's societies and the world's individuals. Religion ties a society's traditional guidelines to a deeper and more eternal order, offering a sense of order to those who feel religiously the flawed and troubled nature of the world. And in turn, religion motivates moral obedience with hopes for ultimate salvation, worldly order, or perhaps just an honorable sense of the greatness of the Absolute. However much we individually might or might not be guided by such ideas, we can see perhaps why religion is such a powerful force in the molding and maintenance of moral order.

EXTERNAL AND INTERNAL SOURCES OF RELIGIOUS MORALITY

Some people might think that religious and moral rules are "written in stone"; others may think they are not "written in stone" but are more a matter for interpretation according to one's own best, faithful understanding—in good conscience—given the changing circumstances throughout history. Interestingly, the phrase in quotation marks is a direct but sometimes unnoticed allusion to the book of Exodus in the originally Jewish scriptures in the Bible. There we find the story of God giving the famous Ten Commandments, a list of religious and moral directives said to have been written by God on two slabs of stone. In Islam a version of something like the Decalogue is given in the Holy Koran (Sura 17: 22–39). Insofar as this "law of God" is brought down from the sacred mountain by the prophet Moses, it may represent a classic case of what can be called an "external" source of religion and morality. We mean here that the moral rules are, in a sense, given from outside, there on the stone, or at least in the will and mind of a God external to ourselves. In some religious traditions this is a form of revelation, a revealing of God's moral direction for humankind. How we feel about these moral laws or how much our own internal conscience may or may not agree with these rules is, perhaps, irrelevant.

In Hinduism the external pole as the source for morality can be seen in the *varnasrama* system. This term comes from the Sanskrit words for caste (*varna*) and stage of life (*asrama*), which define, respectively, the social class into which one is born and the age and family status one has attained so far. That is, any Hindu will be born into a particular class (priest class, warrior class, merchant class, or servant class), and he or she is also in a particular family relationship based on age (student, householder, "forest dweller," and "renouncer"). It is from this combination of descriptive elements of one's life that Hindu tradition determines one's *dharma*, one's moral duties within society. These duties are in many ways socially constructed and simply handed down as tradition, but they were also well-developed in scripture, especially in the form of the Laws of Manu, written perhaps around 200 BCE. Here one finds that the initiation of a child into study (for example, of scripture) is done in the eighth year for Brahmins (priests), the eleventh year for Kshatriyas (warriors) and the twelfth year for Vaishyas (merchants). The Sudras (servants) are forbidden to read the scriptures. These laws declare what kinds of jobs each class may have, how wives are to revere their husbands, and when one may leave home to become a religious hermit (Fieser and Powers 44–51). It is all, in fact, so detailed and descriptive that it is difficult to summarize, yet it all makes sense within the Hindu sense of morality as the proper directives for individual life both within and away from society.

Some religious systems see morality as being fostered by an external source.

varnasrama— system of social organization in Hinduism

Brahmins—highest priestly class in Hinduism

Kshatriyas—warrior class in Hinduism

Vaishyas—merchant class in Hinduism

Sudras—servant class in Hinduism

Of course all of this "external" morality might seem foreign to people who would rather emphasize conscience as a source of morality instead of laws "written in stone." By "conscience," Jewish people might recall the prophecy of Jeremiah, in which God declares: "I will put my law in their minds and write it on their hearts" (Jeremiah 31:33). Interestingly, one sees here, alongside the Ten Commandments of Exodus (Exodus 20:1–17), two Jewish references that seem to point in contrary directions. That is, just as we described the "law" that is handed to humanity from the outside as having an "external" source, the law that seems to be a movement of one's own soul, the appeal of one's own conscience, might be called the "internal" source of morality as well. Thus it is curious, perhaps, that here in Judaism we see both, even though at times the two can seem to be in conflict,

Other religious traditions see morality emerging internally as the "law" is "written on the heart."

Hall et al. provide a paradigmatic example, also within Judaism, that illustrates both the external and internal poles of the sources of morality and their potential conflict. In the biblical book of Job, a distinction (and even tension) is set up between the Jewish tradition and its expressions (the external pole) on the one hand and direct experiences of God on the other, an experience unmediated by expressions (the internal pole). Three of Job's friends represent the "wisdom of the fathers" and hence the tradition's already-formulated expressions or responses to what Job is going through (that is, his inexplicable suffering). Job himself, however, soon discovers that this wisdom is not true wisdom; true wisdom, as the book says, begins in the "fear" or awe before God, and in the indwelling of the spirit of God (127). We have already talked about Job's suffering and the varying explanations for that suffering in Chapter 7. Here the point is that, morally speaking, two different perspectives are being taken on what Job ought to do. From the "outside," so to speak, it seems the rules declare that Job must repent and accept his sorrows as God's punishment for his sins; from the "inside," Job cries out for answers and asks God for explanations, which later appear to be "outside" the rules.

For Christians, the stories and the moral laws, especially the Ten Commandments, are an external source of morality, as they are for Jews and Muslims. But in the New Testament, Jesus seems most intent on pointing to the internal source of morality when he abandons Jewish laws regarding foods. These traditional laws were explicit about what kinds of foods make one "unclean," but Jesus denied the emphasis on what one "takes in" and replaced it with emphasis on what "comes out," such as, from within the human heart (compare Hall et al. 130). In Mark 7:18b–23, Jesus says:

> *Do you not see that whatever goes into a person from outside cannot defile, since it enters, not the heart but the stomach, and goes out into the sewer? (Thus he declared all foods clean.) And he said, "It is what comes out of a person that defiles. For it is from within, from the human heart, that evil intentions come: fornication, theft, murder, adultery, avarice, wickedness, deceit, licentiousness, envy, slander, pride, folly. All these evil things come from within, and they defile a person.*

marga—way in Buddhism

In Buddhism the external source of morality can be seen in the **marga**, one of the Four Noble Truths, better known as the Eightfold Path. This path consists of

The question of whether religion is necessarily tied to ethics or, stated differently, whether religion is necessary for a viable ethic has been debated for some time. However, it has taken on a new urgency when societies try to make religion an individual and private experience with no place in societal ethics or political debates. Author Hugh Heclo argues religion plays a vital role in social debates. He says,

. . . more is at stake than improving the forum for public debate. Religion also adds something vitally important to the content of what is being said. It asserts that a transcendent purpose gives meaning to who human beings are and what they do. The religious voice insists that God-inspired standards be taken seriously when a society governs itself, and that questions of right and wrong are more than matters of passing opinion. By its nature, religion rejects faint-hearted stabs at real virtue and dismisses the easy excuse that no one is perfect. Authentic religion insists that leaders—and everyone else—measure up rather than adjust the yardstick.

The point is not simply that religion is a powerful foundation for moral behavior . . . It's that religion can increase the fundamental humaneness of society. A religious outlook . . . contends with both the immortal grandeur and the tragic fallenness of humankind. It calls attention to the narrow ridge we must traverse between essential human worth and essential human humility . . .

Religion in the public square stirs up deep and troublesome issues. Yet it seems far healthier that our modern, policy-minded democracy endure the disturbance than dismiss it. If religion is absent from the public arena, humanity will invoke secular religions to satisfy its quest for meaning . . . [Perhaps it is worth remembering that throughout the 20th century] a succession of antidemocratic and antitheist political ideologies exploited people's yearning for meaning and social idealism. A godless faith in humanity as the creator of its own grandeur lay at the heart of communism, fascism, Maoism, and all the unnumbered horrors unleashed in that bloodiest of centuries. . . .

Source: Hugh Heclo. "The Wall that Never Was." *The Wilson Quarterly.* Winter 2003: 82.

---

sila—moral principles in Buddhism

vinaya—rules for the Buddhist monastic life

bodhi—enlightenment experience

prajna—enlightened wisdom

karuna—compassion

Right Speech, Right Action, Right Livelihood, Right View, Right Intention, Right Effort, Right Mindfulness, and Right Concentration. Traditionally, the first three are said to comprise the *sila,* or moral portion of the path. This moral order then becomes further specified as the "five precepts" of moral action: don't kill, don't lie, don't steal, don't misuse sex, and don't use intoxicants. For monks in particular, this moral practice became even more developed, evolving into the *vinaya,* literally hundreds of detailed rules for the proper behavior of monks and nuns (see Conze 73–77).

But Buddhism traditionally has its internal sources of morality as well. Perhaps especially within Mahayana Buddhism one finds an emphasis on *bodhi,* rather than on imposed rules, as the basis for one's conduct. A *bodhisattva,* an enlightened human being, is one whose *prajna,* enlightened wisdom, entails *karuna,* compassion, as the foundation for all human action for the benefit of all other beings. This "wise compassion" is the internal source of morality rather than any conformity to external rules. In Hinayana and Theravada Buddhism, the enlight-

metta—love for all beings

enment experience gives rise to the moral imperative of *metta*, love for all beings (compare Hall et al. 129–130).

In Confucianism, the external moral imperative is most famously expressed in the Analects with their emphasis on *li*, the traditional, carefully prescribed rules for respectful social behavior. Fung Yu-lan points out in his *Short History of Chinese Philosophy* that "the function of *li* is to regulate. The *li* provide regulation for the satisfaction of man's desires," but they also "give refinement and purification to man's emotions" (147). Rituals are therefore a form of social order and moral education. At the same time, Confucius seems himself to emphasize that it would be a mistake to think of social rituals as merely constrained from outside. While he says repeatedly in the Analects that rituals are ways to regulate society and oneself, he seems also to insist that sincerity is crucial. In Analects 3:12, it is said that when Confucius did the ritual offerings to his ancestors, he truly felt that they were truly present and that the ritual was therefore truly significant. He said, "If I do not participate in the sacrifice, it is as if I did not sacrifice at all."

Finally, in Islam the powerful "external source" of morality is the Shari'a, usually translated as "Islamic law." Codes of Islamic law were developed several centuries after the death of Muhammad, and they take as their sources not only moral direction drawn directly from the Holy Koran but also directions for daily life given in the traditions (*sunnah*) or examples of Muhammad's life. Islamic law then, by extending these lessons into other, analogous areas of life, came to provide moral directives for every aspect of a Muslim's life, a "straight path" for the right way of moral living. Indeed, Shari'a is better depicted, according to Snjezana Akpinar, in her article "The Ethics of Islam," as a "grand boulevard, the main street" of a system of life, noting that the Arabic word *shari'a* means "street" in English (56).

sunnah—Islamic law based on traditions about the life of Muhammad

Nevertheless, even here, Akpinar notes, the fact that medieval Islamic jurists had to think through and decide upon aspects of Islamic law provides in Islam an example of the beginnings of an internal source of morality, an internal source especially evident in the Islamic mystical tradition of Sufism. In this regard, Akpinar writes:

> *From the broad street of the Shari'a lead more inward paths. Known as tariqah, these paths lead individuals toward the center of their being. To follow a tariqah, then, is to undertake a personal quest. It is described as the cultivation and education of the self, the nafs, an Arabic word that denotes both soul and breath. Following one's tariqah teaches one to "breathe," or live, in a healthy manner, in harmony with the world and its rhythm. This aspect of religiosity, according to Islam, cannot be expressed in words or in rules and regulations. It is the gradual acquiring, through maintenance of a right lifestyle, of a supraknowledge, a gnosis, which allows us to acquire an insight into existence. In Arabic such an insight is known as ma'rifa. Cultivated within a human heart and expressed through one's behavior, ma'rifa enables us to harmonize with our surroundings and, indeed the whole universe. . . . [T]he method used in Islam to help one learn how to be at peace and at ease with one's self and one's surroundings is known as Sufism. (57–58)*

Sufism—mystical system in Islam

As a final example of an internal religious authority, one can refer to the unique personal religious experiences of Black Elk, an Oglala Sioux holy man. Though traditions of culture might offer an "external" guideline for native cultures, Black Elk found himself adrift in a changing world and faced with the white man's ever-advancing encroachment upon his homelands. In this need, he experienced dreams and visions that became the moral authority for the tribe's actions, a moral authority born from within (Neihardt 2; compare Hall et al. 130–131).

The point in these examples is that there do indeed seem to be both "internal" and "external" sources in religious moralities. In many ways, and perhaps in all these religions, both kinds of sources seem useful, perhaps even necessary. Even in the case of Jesus, it can be noted that, even while he stressed the "internal" aspect of morality, he claimed that he had not come to abolish the Jewish law "but to fulfill it" (Matthew 5:17).

Many, if not most, religious traditions recognize both external and internal sources of morality and see these as interacting with one another.

CATEGORIZATIONS OF THE SOURCES OF MORALITY

Religions may look to Divine commands or the "laws of the universe" as a source of morality.

Divine Command Theory—ethics that conforms with God's commands

As mentioned earlier, the sources of morality may be (1) religion, (2) nature, or (3) autonomous human nature. Within the religious sources of morality, there are generally two perspectives: conformity to the cosmic laws of the universe or conformity to God's commands. The appeal to the latter is often referred to as a Divine Command Theory ethics and seems most evidently derived through appeals to sacred writings or the scriptures in which God's commands are presumably given. In fact, however, both divine commands and the type of religious ethics that appeal to cosmic laws can be found in scriptures, as we shall see. Moreover, it should not be assumed that religious ethics in general is simply a matter of mindless obedience. Commensurate with the complexity of human life, much religious morality, for example, in Confucianism, Christianity, and Islam, requires ethical thinking and moral effort, which is ". . . both a conformity to the created order and the construction of a human order within it. Controversies arise as different interpreters decide how much weight should be given to each task" (Lovin and Reynolds 19).

Classic examples of Divine command moralities appear in Judaism, Christianity, and Islam, the Abrahamic religions. This should be no surprise since, as we have emphasized throughout this text, there is a logical consistency between the elements of religious belief and practice, such that, here, the idea of morality as obedience to God's commands fits very well with the idea of the Holy given in the three monotheistic religions. An example already noted but fundamental to all three religions would be the various versions of the Ten Commandments given in the Tanakh (Exodus 20:2–17, Deuteronomy 5:6–21) and in the Holy Koran (17:22–39). These ten rules of moral conduct represent both vertical and horizontal elements, both the behaviors expected toward God in the context of the sacred covenant (such as having no other gods), as well as our human duties toward other people, such as don't murder, don't steal, don't lie, don't commit adultery. These are relatively clear and direct commands of God according to the Jews, and by extension, to Christians and Muslims as well. Nevertheless, as the

*Even in Divine
Command ethics,
followers may
have to extend the
basic commands
into more elabo-
rate rules because
of the complexi-
ties of life.*

rabbis of Judaism sought to unpack and clarify the "Law of God" given in the Torah, the totality of their divinely given moral rules came to be 613 command-ments, "248 positive injunctions and 365 negative prohibitions" (Chidester 36). Even today these laws are seen by some Jews to be the entirety of God's will, encompassing everything from common rules against violence to rules on how to eat. Christians, too, have developed the commands of God beyond the Ten Commandments, based for them on the writings of the New Testament, espe-cially the words of Jesus, including the Sermon on the Mount, and of course for Muslims, the commands of Allah appear throughout the Holy Koran, which expands and details the proper commands of God for a good, moral human life. Examples of these Christian and Islamic developments of God's moral law appear in the opening quotations for this chapter.

*A perplexing
problem in Divine
command moral-
ity is what to
do when God
seems to demand
something that
is morally
repugnant.*

One of the more interesting and perplexing aspects of Divine command moral-ity appears when followers accept God's commands as utterly morally binding when, it seems, God may sometimes command actions that appear morally repugnant. The classic example, already mentioned and often discussed, is God's command to Abraham to sacrifice his only son Isaac (Genesis 22:1–14)—Ishmael in the Muslin tradition, based on an interpretation of Sura 37. While the modern terrorist who "obeys God" in committing heinous acts of violence against inno-cent lives seems clearly immoral, Abraham himself is praised as a true follower of God for being willing to kill his son in response to a divine command. Opinions about Abraham's obedience are divided: Immanuel Kant, the German rational ethicist, thought Abraham should have known better than to obey God, while Søren Kierkegaard, the Danish Christian existentialist of the 19th century, suggested Abraham's faith was simply something greater than most of us can understand. However impressive or repugnant we might find Abraham's willing-ness to obey God to this extreme, he remains a prime example of moral and spir-itual significance in all three of the monotheistic faiths. Thus, Abraham is the patriarch of all Judaism, the "father of faith" for Christians and an exemplary Muslim in Islam.

*Religions in which
the moral laws are
derived from the
very nature of the
cosmos are also
common.*

rita—natural
moral order
according to the
Vedas

Religions in which the moral laws are derived from the very nature of the cos-mos are also common. A primary example is the laws of *karma* in Hinduism and Buddhism. Karma does not seem to be any set of rules instituted by God, *per se,* as if given by commands. Perhaps in the case of Hinduism, the roots of the notion of *karma* do lie in divine creation, as the early Vedic God Varuna was said to have been the god of cosmic order. As such, he was responsible for the creation of *rita,* the natural moral order of things. By the time of the development of the later Vedas, however, and before the appearance of the Buddha around the 6th century BCE, Varuna's role was mostly forgotten, and the laws of *karma* were understood simply to be the way the world works. Indeed, for Buddhists the moral order is analogous to physical cause and effect. If one were to place one's hand in a flame, the resulting burn would not be the result of divine punishment but simply the causal result of the action; similarly, when one suffers sorrow for having caused pain to others, the result is not punishment but something more like physics. Somehow the cosmos just is the kind of place where a good thought or a good action echoes back with beneficent results. Again, refer to the opening quotations.

In some ways, a more-developed example can be found in Confucianism. Here, the Way of Heaven, the Tao, is the Ultimate Reality itself, the Holy (to use our text's terminology), as that which is absolute and uncreated. Yet the Way of Heaven, Confucius claimed, gives us a natural social order, with natural human relationships that correspond to natural human virtues. To be truly good, therefore, is no more and no less than to be truly natural, to follow the Way of Heaven. Mencius, Confucius's most famous follower, argued in fact that Heaven has built the natural virtues into the human heart, so that to be naturally moral is only a matter of following our own true nature. If a man goes bad, he claimed, that may be the fault of bad training, bad environment, or bad choices, but "it is not the fault of his native endowment." Rather, says Mencius, "benevolence, dutifulness, observance of the rites, and wisdom are not welded on to me from the outside; they are in me originally" (Mencius VI.A.6).

Whether following the commands of God or the Way of Heaven, appeals are made in religious ethics to what is Ultimate and Absolute. This indeed may be the very nature of religious ethics. We noted, however, that other sources of morality are possible. It is quite possible, for example, to appeal to nature as a source of moral direction without making nature into an absolute principle. When nature is seen as the source of morality, it may be via the innate human ability to discern moral values inherent in nature and not necessarily by any divine revelation. A classic example of this appears as the "natural law ethics" of Aristotle (384–322 BCE). In his view, expressed in his famous text, the *Nichomachean Ethics,* morality is a matter of understanding human virtues as the "mean" between extremes. For example, courage is somewhere between cowardice and foolhardiness. It takes wisdom and practice, but not necessarily religious insight, to understand and to become truly courageous, such as, to cultivate the virtue of courage.

Nature without any absolute principle also is seen as a source of morality.

Yet, although Aristotle's naturalistic ethics are not overtly religious, his views can be, and often are, bound to religious views. The 13th-century Christian theologian and philosopher Thomas Aquinas developed his ideas of Christian virtues directly from Aristotle, quoting "the Philosopher" any number of times as he considered the nature of virtue and value. Yet he added to Aristotle's ideas his own emphases on "infused virtues" and "theological virtues," alongside or even above the "cardinal virtues" of Greek philosophy (296–297). Certainly, in the Roman Catholic Church tradition, St. Thomas Aquinas's adaptation of Aristotle's natural law ethics for Christianity was seen as the quite reasonable marriage of natural law, the teleological organization of the universe, and divine commands (Munson 26–28; compare to Smurl 114–116).

Less evident perhaps is the potential within virtue-based ethics for compatibility with Buddhist ethics. Peter Harvey makes this point in his book *An Introduction to Buddhist Ethics.* Both Aristotle and Buddhism aim at human perfection by developing a person's knowledge and character, his or her "head" and "heart." In Buddhist terminology, this is done by eliminating both spiritual ignorance and craving, which feed off each other, by cultivating intellectual, emotional, and moral virtues sharing something of the qualities of the goal toward which they move. In both Aristotelian and Buddhist ethics, an action is right because it embodies a virtue, which conduces to and "participates" in the goal of human perfection (50; compare MacMillan 37-50; and Keown).

When autonomous human nature is seen as the source of morality, it may be with a focus either on reason or emotion, which may or may not be compatible with a religious perspective. Any detailed study of such nonreligious ethical theories would take us too far outside the scope of our text on religion, but a few classical examples of morality based on autonomous human reason can be noted. Immanuel Kant's deontological (duty ethics) approach set forth in his *Groundwork for the Metaphysics of Morals* and *Critique of Practical Reason* argued that pure reasoning alone could determine moral right and wrong based upon the simple idea that all truly moral action must be "universalizable." He claimed it was not necessary to see these rational moral guidelines as in any way commanded by God, although he admitted that one could accept morality as if it were divinely commanded. This yielded what he called "religion within the limits of reason alone," a gallant phrase that became the title of one of his last books.

Jeremy Bentham's *An Introduction to the Principles of Morals and Legislation*, and John Stuart Mill's *Utilitarianism* took a teleological approach to ethics and developed the idea that morals could be decided solely on the basis of the consequences of one's actions. Actions that tend to promote more pleasure than pain are good; those that do not are bad. Being concerned for other's pains and pleasures, Mill hoped, would be something we could all do without the help of any religion. He did suggest, however, that this was simply what was meant by Jesus' version of the Golden Rule: Love your neighbor as yourself (268).

Other examples of ethical theories without any evident religious basis can be noted. Examples of morality based on the element of emotion or sentiment or sympathy involved in the human affective response to moral situations (without excluding reason) as well as empirical observations of what human beings actually do espouse as moral ". . . in the full context of the rest of their beliefs and values . . ." (Lovin and Reynolds 9) are considered in **David Hume's** (1711–1776) *A Treatise of Human Nature*. More recently, the concept of an intuitive and more emotional form of ethical direction called "Care Ethics" has been developed on the basis of **Carol Gilligan's** study of women's moral development entitled *In a Different Voice*. **Nel Noddings** (1929–) in turn builds upon Gilligan's (1936–) work, writing *Caring: A Feminine Approach to Ethics and Moral Education*. Such efforts have been seen as somewhat of a counterbalance to the rather rigid rationalism of Kant's duty ethics.

As these latter examples show, one need not argue that only religious people are moral or have ethical theories. But we have also seen that there is something of a natural alliance between religion and morality. Again, it should not be surprising that religious moralities remain a prominent form of moral thinking and that what one thinks is moral often has a strong connection with what one thinks is Absolute. Indeed, this connection, along with the metaethical emphasis noted earlier and the general historical connection between religion and morality already stressed, re-emphasizes for us the power of religion in both guiding and motivating moral behavior.

MORALITY AND ETHICS AS AN EXPRESSION OF RELIGION AND CULTURE

However the source of religious—and thereby moral—authority is conceived and understood, whenever an action that is subject to moral judgment is taken and it is understood to be done ultimately as an expression of one's religious convic-

Autonomous human reason may be seen as another source of morality.

deontological approach to ethics—ethics that defines right action based on duty (that which is binding)

teleological approach to ethics—ethics based on the consequences of one's actions

Emotion, sentiment, and sympathy also have been proposed as the base of ethics.

tions, then for good or for ill that is a matter of religious morality and/or ethics. And insofar as religion becomes a central part of the definition of any culture, including (as we have seen) its myths and rituals and artistic expressions, there is inevitably a close and sometimes complicated relationship between what religious morals direct us to do and how society trains us to live. On the one hand, we often inherit from religion a code of behavior rooted (presumably) in the Absolute itself; on the other hand, society itself evolves with other habits and directives that demand our allegiance.

Religious codes and culture often give people their sense of morality.

The classic treatment of this inevitable and complex relationship between religious morality and social behavior, which must be worked out among the factors vying for our religious and moral allegiance, is **H. Richard Niebuhr's** (1894–1962) *Christ and Culture.* Obviously the title suggests that Niebuhr's discussion presumes a Western or Christian perspective, and yet more generally understood, it provides a typology of the relationship between whatever the religion may be and the culture in which it lives. Thus, other authors might have given us "Hinduism and Culture," "Buddhism and Culture," "Judaism and Culture," "Islam and Culture," and so on, and the typology would still hold true.

How to relate religion and culture often becomes a problem.

The "typology" we refer to here can be found in the way Niebuhr describes the different ways in which "Christ" relates to "culture." Substituting the word "religion" for the word "Christ" in Niebuhr's chapters, the typology can be seen broadly as the logically possible relationships between any religion and its culture. For example, when Niebuhr talks about "Christ Against Culture," we might discuss "Religion Against Culture" as the situation that recognizes the possibility of there being a conflict between a religion and its culture. This possible relationship between religion and culture is one of the more radical possibilities, acknowledging that sometimes the morality of a religion stands against the prevailing social codes. Pacifism, opposition to war or violence, and the refusal to bear arms may be the prime examples of this position as illustrated most famously in the lives of Mohandas Gandhi (1869–1948) and Martin Luther King Jr. (1929–1968). In contrast, "Religion of Culture" sees the possibility of agreement, perhaps to the point of assimilation, between the two elements as the other, least radical, pole of the relationship. The utter assimilation of German Christians into the Nazi Regime of Adolf Hitler (1889–1945) is the most tragic example of this possibility. The remaining positions represent some compromise or accommodation between the two. "Religion Above Culture" represents the possibility of the religion dominating the culture and yet somehow being virtually a product of its culture, as in the Holy Roman Empire of the Western Middle Ages or the contemporary examples of the theocracies of Iran and, until recently, Afghanistan under the Taliban. "Religion and Culture in Paradox" points to the potential dilemmas of attempting to maintain allegiance to both elements in ways that seem to be incompatible, such as loving one's neighbor (by "turning the other cheek") and yet having to protect oneself from the evils of one's neighbors, near and far as police and soldiers, respectively. Finally, a "middle way"—in the best sense of the term—is presented: "Religion the Transformer of Culture," which sees religion taking the best of what the culture has to offer and transforming it to the mutual benefit of the religion and the culture. In the words and genre of that once most-popular gospel song, "Oh Happy Day," what a happy day it would be indeed if the often troublesome relationship between religion, morality, and culture could be transformed to the mutual benefit of all.

Exactly how the morality of a religion and the accepted norms of a particular society do or do not coincide will, of course, vary from time to time and from place to place. Indeed, the happy conformity of a society to its religion might be a stable and comfortable habit for generations, but then, with the onset of new movements or developments—think of the '60s in the last century—the society changes and, necessarily, forces religion to redefine its own relation to its own culture. We shall see in the final chapter of this text that the response of religions to the developments of globalization are a perfect example of this need for religion to define itself as the world changes around it. For this chapter, it is perhaps enough to say that religion simply does exert uncommon force on people's moral ideals, defining and motivating moral behavior for millions of people. Yet it is also true that religious morality may find itself out of step with social changes. Shall a religious morality "written in stone" be changed to appease culture, or must culture yield to the authority of the Absolute? Evidently the answer to such a question is itself complex.

GLOBALIZATION, RELIGION, ETHICS, VIOLENCE, AND PEACE

One of the greatest failures of religions is their tendency to promote violence.

We would be remiss in a book dealing with religion and globalization if we did not discuss the very touchy topics centering around the relationship of religion to violence and peace. In fact, some would argue that the greatest ethical failures of contemporary religions are the tendency to promote violence along with the inability to produce peace. Obviously, we cannot go into this topic in any detail in the few remaining pages we have left in this chapter. We just offer a few suggestive ideas concerning the complex relation of religion to violence and peace to stimulate the reader's thought.

One set of issues centers on what we mean by violence and what we mean by religion's response to violence. Violence can take a number of different forms: physical violence (involving some type of bodily harm, from warfare to domestic abuse), political violence (where states undertake programs damaging persons), state-sponsored violence (violence against persons that falls outside of the legal system), structural violence (factors built into various social systems that in some fashion systematically abuse people or violate their rights), ecological violence (systematic damage of the environment), and liberative violence (violence carried on by persons in the effort to free themselves from oppression) (World Council of Churches).

Violence takes many forms.

Likewise, religion's response to violence is complex. On the negative side, one common response to violence is silence. Too often, religious communities simply say nothing when confronted with violence. Even worse, religions may sanctify (justify) violence. Often when religion is established in a position of privilege in a society, it is used to justify aggression against citizens or other societies. In this case, the religion's fate is usually tied with the aggressive state. Expansion is yet another response. Here, a given religion uses violence to expand its territories. Any number of varieties of religions, including Hinduism, Judaism, Christianity, and Islam, have used this method to incorporate new regions into their regimes (World Council of Churches). On the positive side, religions frequently have unmasked and opposed violence, have been instruments in limiting violence, and have served as models of nonviolence, especially Buddhism and the traditional "peace churches" of Christianity, such as the Society of Friends (better known as Quakers) and the Mennonites. Today, they can provide opportunity for encounter and solidarity among religions and societies, offer nonviolent resistance to violent regimes, counter extremism, and help heal abuses of the past (World Council of Churches).

Many religions have a vision of some kind of end-time when nature and humans live in harmony, where there is plenty and no violence. For instance, Judaism holds that time will end in the Kingdom of God, where reconciliation and peace prevail. The prophet Isaiah says: "The wolf shall live with the lamb, the leopard shall lie down with the kid. . . . The cow and the bear shall graze, their young shall lie down together; and the lion shall eat straw like the ox. . . . They will not hurt or destroy on all my holy mountain; for the earth will be full of the knowledge of the Lord . . ." (Isaiah 11:6–9).

Similarly, the Jewish prophet Micah predicts: "He shall judge between many peoples, and shall arbitrate between strong nations far away; they shall beat their swords into plowshares, and their spears into pruning hooks; nation shall not lift up sword against nation, neither shall they learn war any more" (Micah 4:3). This beautiful vision has been incorporated into Christianity and Islam as well. Interestingly, within these faiths this peaceful state is reached only after horrific battles between the forces of good and evil.

Whatever their vision for the future, it is clear that these faiths and most others see the current world situation as demanding some level of violence, at least under some circumstances. Hindu scholar Anatanand Rambachan notes that many people in the West associate Hinduism with *ahimsa* (nonviolence) largely because of the nonviolent resistance to British rule by Mahatma Mohandas Gandhi, who became the model for Martin Luther King Jr. (The Buddhists most consistently carry out the application of ahimsa by consistently abstaining from violence.) But this is hardly consistent with the violent attacks on Muslims seen in recent years carried out by Hindu mobs chanting religious slogans. Yet, the concept of nonviolence has existed side-by-side with *himsa* (violence) for centuries.

Not only was violence against animals called for in the early Hindu scriptures, but the use of violence against other humans was also sanctioned under certain circumstances. The *ksatriya*, or warrior-king caste, were specifically exempted from the requirements of *ahimsa*, as war might be a part of their duty. Hindu traditions also permit killing in self-defense and to implement religious injunctions. Additionally, there is recognition of a *dharma yuddha* in Hindu scripture. "A **dharma yuddha** is a war fought in defence of justice and righteousness and for the security and well being of the community" (Rambachan 1). While some Hindus may be obligated to fight a *dharma yuddha*, all are forbidden to engage in an *artha yuddha*, or a war carried out for the extension of power, greed, personal pleasure, and other such malevolent reasons. Clearly, Hinduism distinguishes between "holy" and "unholy" violence. Even when violence is justified, it is to be used only as a last resort when all means of peaceful resolution of disputes have been exhausted.

Christianity and Islam have inherited their ideas about "Godly violence" from Judaism, although, of the three Abrahamic faiths, Christianity theoretically should be the least violent. Though there are instances in the New Testament when Jesus seems to call for violence (for example, Matthew 10:10, 11:20–24), he appears to be a radical advocate of nonviolence in most cases (for example, Matthew 5:38–45, 48, 26:52). Certainly, the bulk of the New Testament image of Jesus is of a nonviolent Messiah, and this is the manner in which the early church interpreted the Christian way (Ariarajah 2). Early Christians were pacifists, refusing to take up arms against Rome or to serve in the Roman army.

Of the three Abrahamic faiths, theoretically Christianity should be the least violent.

This situation changed when Christianity became the official religion of the Roman Empire in the fourth century CE. At that juncture, the church had a vested interest in the power of the empire, in protecting Roman citizens and territory, and in deciding and enforcing justice within the empire. Under these conditions of social and political necessity, Christians had to reexamine their teachings on war and violence. It was under these conditions that the concept of Holy War was forged. From today's perspective, the most unfortunate historical examples of a Holy War were the Christian Crusades against the "Infidels" in the Muslim empires of that day.

Augustine of Hippo produced the foundation for Christian ideas about just war.

Augustine, Bishop of Hippo (354–430), produced the normative concept of when a Christian may wage war. According to him there were six conditions which must be met for a war to be just:

- The war must be declared by a legitimate authority.
- It must be undertaken with right intention, namely, to promote peace.
- It must be used only as the last resort . . . when all other means of resolving the conflict have been exhausted.
- It must be waged on the principle of proportionality, which means the evil and destruction perpetrated should not outweigh the good that comes out of it.
- It must have a reasonable chance of success, so that no wanton destruction is done when it is clear that the intention cannot be achieved.
- It must be waged with all the moderation possible, which means that violence unrelated to the battle (and to persons unrelated to the war) must be avoided. (Ariarajah 3)

However, these principles were so often abused and the power of the state was so often used to persecute minorities that Christian theologian and philosopher, Thomas Aquinas, declared in the 13th century that, even when war was waged for a just cause, it was sinful (Ariarajah 3). In spite of this, most Christian circles continue to recognize such instances as establishing justice, protecting the innocent, and resisting evil as situations wherein violence may be used in a just fashion.

Imam A. Rashied Omar presents a similar picture of violence in Islam. He notes that the Holy Koran permits war to prevent wrongful violence against Muslims as well as monasteries, churches, synagogues, and mosques (Sura 22:39–40); to preserve decent values (Sura 4:75, 22:40); and to stand for justice (Sura 4:135). As soon as the enemy sues for peace, the war must be halted. Although Islam recognizes the Torah's emphasis on revenge (an eye for an eye

In Islam, as in
Christianity, the
stress of holy
teachings is on
acting in love, not
violence, toward
one's enemies.

jihad—struggle or
just war

and a tooth for a tooth, etc.), Omar insists that the balance of Koranic teaching is on responding in charity to your enemies, as is also found in the Christian gospels (2).

Omar insists that the Islamic stress on *jihad* should not be interpreted as a call for holy war as it is often interpreted in the West and as currently misused by militant Islamicists. In Islam, war is never holy but is just or unjust. He explains it this way:

> *Jihad denotes any effort in pursuit of a commendable aim. Jihad is a comprehensive concept embracing peaceful persuasion (16:125), passive resistance (13:22; 23:96; 41:34) as well as armed struggle against oppression and injustice (2:193; 4:75; 8:39). Moreover, jihad is not directed at the other faiths. In a statement in which the Arabic is extremely emphatic, "There must be no coercion in matters of faith!" (2:256). More than this, the protection of freedom of belief and worship for followers of other religions has been made a sacred duty of Muslims. This duty was fixed at the same time when the permission for armed struggle (jihad al-qital) was ordained (22:39–40). (2)*

In Islam, war is
not holy but may
be just.

In spite of this, Omar insists that most Muslims do not see Islam as solely committed to a pacifist position but see violence as a mechanism for promoting legitimate ends. He also demonstrates that early Islamic tradition developed in a historical situation that encouraged dividing the world into two halves—the territory of Islam and the territory of war. While this division may have been a historical necessity, it may no longer be appropriate and does not represent the only historical model for Islamic societies relating to the nonIslamic world. Nevertheless, this simple dichotomy is firmly fixed in the minds of many Muslims. Omar believes that marginalized early models of peaceful coexistence now being recovered by Muslim scholars offer hope for relating positively to a pluralistic world (3).

Most religions
have a hard (vio-
lent) and a soft
(peaceful) side.

In short, most, though not all, religious traditions have a "hard side," which emphasizes a militant posture toward outsiders as well as those who raise questions within their own midst. The Holy is seen as demanding, powerful, and violent. They may also have a "soft side" in which the Holy is presented as forgiving, merciful, loving, and peaceful (Galtung). The former encourages an aggressive posturing, while the latter is more passive and accepting. In essence, the former emphasizes the masculine transcendent Absolute while the latter promotes the immanent feminine aspects of divinity. Most religions have within them both the seeds of destruction and healing, of violence and peace (Galtung). But religious violence seems to be on the increase.

RELIGIOUS MORALITY AND RATIONAL MORALITY

As a conclusion to this chapter, we shall take a brief look at the basic options available to us regarding how we might begin to rethink the relationship between religion, morality, and ethics. At the risk of stating these options in a rather cumbersome way, we might suggest three possibilities:

1. Religious Morality versus Rational Morality
2. Religious Morality completed by Rational Morality
3. Religious Morality Separate from but aesthetically related to Rational Morality

These subheadings already presuppose a philosophical approach to the problem rather than a possibly more appropriate phenomenological approach to the moral and ethical dimensions of religion. And yet this is simply a restating of the very phenomena in this area all religious and, potentially, even nonreligious, people face. In somewhat other contexts, it has been discussed as "faith versus reason" or "faith and reason," "science versus religion" or "science and religion," "sacred versus secular" or "sacred and secular,"—all of which are a partial reiteration of Niebuhr's classic typology of possibilities. Examples have already been given of religious morality in conflict with rational or secular morality. One of the most ambitious attempts to demonstrate the second of our subtitles is that of Ronald Green, presented in his *Religious Reason: The Rational and Moral Basis of Religious Belief*. There he attempts to show the "fundamental rational structures underlying religious belief" (108). And religious beliefs are concomitantly the logical outcome of human reason (121; see also "Morality and Religion," by Ronald M. Green in *The Encyclopedia of Religion*.) As summarized by Chidester, "Moral reason itself requires that we posit some supreme causal moral agency beyond our immediate experience"—Kant's moral argument for the existence of God. "The requirements of religious reason are also the requirements of reason" (60).

However, Chidester also points out the limits or objections to this approach to religious ethics, which the third of our subheadings refers to. For him, "reason is not the primary motive for responding to obligation with a system of religious ethics. . . . Reason plays a more subsidiary role within the dynamic, experiential process of responding to a sense of [religious] obligation" (60). Rather, "religious ethics is more aesthetics than logic"—indicating more of a separation between religion and reason, as does our third subheading. Chidester continues: "Although the ethical process involves considerable thought—we may think about what we do, reason about the best course of action, and rationalize our behavior—religious ethics engages a more fundamental process" (39). Chidester's irenic conclusion to our issue deserves to be quoted at length.

The philosopher Ludwig Wittgenstein (1889–1951) observed that "Ethics and Aesthetics are one and the same" (Chidester 40). A religious tradition embodies a certain picture of reality. The forms of life that are generated within that tradition are attempts to fit, match, or conform behavior to that picture. Religious ethics involves aesthetic experiments in harmonizing behavior with normative images of the sacred. This does not mean that ethics and aesthetics are both simply matters of taste, but they are both constituted by aesthetic qualities of order, image, metaphor, symbol, style, structure, pattern, and rhythm. These qualities represent the fundamental aesthetic impulses in religious ethics.

Religious ethics is then essentially a creative enterprise striving for harmony between images and actions. It begins with images of who we are and who we could be. These images, symbols, and metaphors are given within religious traditions. Systems of religious ethics create the conditions within which there might be an aesthetic fittingness between a person's (or a people's) sense of identity—

the self-image that is shaped through religious symbols, myths, and rituals—and behavior that visibly manifests that self (or corporate self) through action. People try to act in ways that fit their self-image. Religious ethics is a living drama. It provides a stage upon which human beings create a dynamic sense of self through the medium of action (40).

■ INTERACTIVE EXERCISE

Please continue your exploration of religion and ethics by going to the interactive exercise for this chapter online (**http://www.religion.wadsworth.com/richter**).

WORKS CITED

Akpinar, Snjezana. "The Ethics of Islam." *Religion East & West: Ecology & Ethics in Religious Traditions*. Vol. 2 (2002): 55–62.

Aquinas, Saint Thomas, and Mary T. Clark. *An Aquinas Reader*. Rev. ed. New York: Fordham University Press, 2000.

Ariarajah, S. Wesley. "Religion and Violence: A Protestant Christian Perspective." *The Ecumenical Review*. April 2003. http://www.findarticles .com/cf_O/m2065/2_55/106560166/p1/article.;html (accessed April 27, 2004). Aristotle. *The Nichomachean Ethics of Aristotle*. London: Oxford University Press, 1954.

Bentham, Jeremy, et al. *The Utilitarians: An Introduction to the Principles of Morals and Legislation*. Garden City, NY: Doubleday, 1961.

Chidester, David. *Patterns of Action: Religion and Ethics in a Comparative Perspective*. Belmont, CA: Wadsworth, 1987.

Conze, Edward (ed.). *Buddhist Scriptures*. Harmondsworth, Middlesex; Baltimore: Penguin, 1976.

Eliade, Mircea. *Cosmos and History: The Myth of the Eternal Return*. New York: Harper, 1959.

———. *The Encyclopedia of Religion*. 16 vols. New York: Simon & Schuster Macmillan, 1995.

Fieser, James, and John Powers. *Scriptures of the World's Religions*. Boston: McGraw Hill, 1998.

Fung, Yu-Lan, and Derk Bodde (ed.). *Short History of Chinese Philosophy*. New York: Free Press, 1966.

Galtung, Johan. "Religions, Hard and Soft." *Cross Currents*. Vol. 47, issue 4 (Winter 1997-1998), http://crosscurrents.org/galtung.htm (accessed April 27, 2004). Gilligan, Carol. *In a Different Voice: Psychological Theory and Women's Development*. Cambridge, MA: Harvard University Press, 1993.

Green, Ronald M. *Religious Reason: The Rational and Moral Basis of Religious Belief*. New York: Oxford University Press, 1978.

————. "Morality and Religion." In *The Encyclopedia of Religion*. Vol. 10, 92–106. New York: Simon & Schuster Macmillan, 1995.

Hall, T. William, Richard B. Pilgrim, and Ronald R. Cavanagh. *Religion: An Introduction*. San Francisco: Harper & Row, 1985.

Harvey, Peter. *An Introduction to Buddhist Ethics: Foundations, Values, and Issues*. New York: Cambridge, 2000.

Heclo, Hugh. "The Wall that Never Was." *The Wilson Quarterly*. Winter 2003: 68–82.

Huff, Peter A. "The Challenge of Fundamentalism for Inter-religious Dialogue." *Cross Currents*, 2000. http://www.crosscurrents.org/Huff.htm (accessed November 11, 2002).

Kant, Immanuel. *Critique of Practical Reason*. New York: Cambridge University Press, 1997.

————. *Groundwork for the Metaphysics of Morals*. New York: Oxford University Press, 2002.

Keown, Damien. *The Nature of Buddhist Ethics*. New York: Palgrave, 1992, 2001.

Little, David, and Sumner B. Twiss. *Comparative Religious Ethics*. New York: Harper & Row, 1978.

Lovin, Robin W., and Frank Reynolds. *Cosmogony and Ethical Order: New Studies in Comparative Ethics*. Chicago: University of Chicago Press, 1985.

MacMillan, Thomas F. "Virtue-Based Ethics: A Comparison of Aristotelian-Thomistic and Buddhist Approaches." *Religion East & West: Ecology & Ethics in Religious Traditions*. Vol. 2 (2002): 37-50.

Mencius, and D. C. Lau (trans.). *Mencius*. Harmondsworth, Middlesex: Penguin, 1970.

Mill, John Stuart. *Utilitarianism, on Liberty, Essay on Bentham. Together with Selected Writings of Jeremy Bentham and John Austin*. Cleveland, OH: World, 1962.

Momen, Moojan. *The Phenomenon of Religion: A Thematic Approach*. Boston: Oneworld, 1999.

Munson, Ronald. *Intervention and Reflection: Basic Issues in Medical Ethics*. 6th ed. Belmont, CA: Wadsworth, 2000.

Neihardt, John Gneisenau. *Black Elk Speaks: Being the Life Story of a Holy Man of the Oglala Sioux*. Lincoln: University of Nebraska Press, 1988.

Niebuhr, H. Richard. *Christ and Culture*. [50th anniversary expanded] ed. New York: HarperCollins, 2001.

Noddings, Nel. *Caring: A Feminine Approach to Ethics and Moral Education*. Berkeley: University of California Press, 1984.

Omar, Imam A. Rashied. "Islam and Violence." http://www.wcc.coe.org/wcc/what/interreligious/cd39-06html (accessed April 27, 2004).

Rambachan, Anantanand. "The Co-Existence of Violence and Non-Violence in Hinduism." http://www.wcc-coe.org/wcc/what/interreligious/cd39-05.html

(accessed April 27, 2004). Smart, Ninian. *Dimensions of the Sacred: An Anatomy of the World's Beliefs.* Berkeley: University of California Press, 1996.

Smart, Ninian, and Richard D. Hecht. *Sacred Texts of the World: A Universal Anthology.* New York: Crossroad, 1992.

Smurl, James F. *Religious Ethics: A Systems Approach.* Englewood Cliffs, NJ: Prentice-Hall, 1971.

World Council of Churches. *Religion and Violence: A World Council of Churches' Conference.* 2002. http://www.wcc-coe.org/wcc/what/interreligioius/cd39-08.html (accessed April 27, 2004).

FOR FURTHER READING

Aristotle. *The Nichomachean Ethics of Aristotle.* London: Oxford University Press, 1954.

Bentham, Jeremy, et al. *The Utilitarians: An Introduction to the Principles of Morals and Legislation.* Garden City, NY: Doubleday, 1961.

Chidester, David. *Patterns of Action: Religion and Ethics in a Comparative Perspective.* Belmont, CA: Wadsworth, 1987.

Green, Ronald M. *Religious Reason: The Rational and Moral Basis of Religious Belief.* New York: Oxford University Press, 1978.

———. "Morality and Religion." In *The Encyclopedia of Religion.* Vol. 10, 92–106. New York: Simon & Schuster Macmillan, 1995.

Hall, T. William, Richard B. Pilgrim, and Ronald R. Cavanagh. *Religion: An Introduction.* San Francisco: Harper & Row, 1985.

Hume, David. *A Treatise of Human Nature.* New York: Oxford University Press, 2000. Kant, Immanuel. *Religion Within the Boundaries of Mere Reason and Other Writings.* New York: Cambridge University Press, 1998

Little, David, and Sumner B. Twiss. *Comparative Religious Ethics.* New York: Harper & Row, 1978.

Lovin, Robin W., and Frank Reynolds. *Cosmogony and Ethical Order: New Studies in Comparative Ethics.* Chicago: University of Chicago Press, 1985.

Mill, John Stuart. *Utilitarianism, on Liberty, Essay on Bentham. Together with Selected Writings of Jeremy Bentham and John Austin.* Cleveland: World, 1962.

Momen, Moojan. *The Phenomenon of Religion: A Thematic Approach.* Boston: Oneworld, 1999.

Niebuhr, H. Richard. *Christ and Culture.* [50th anniversary expanded] ed. New York: HarperCollins, 2001.

Smurl, James F. *Religious Ethics: A Systems Approach.* Englewood Cliffs, NJ: Prentice Hall, 1971.

Winter, Gibson. *Social Ethics: Issues in Ethics and Society.* (esp. the "Introduction: Religion, Ethics, and Society.") New York: Harper & Row, 1968.

11 RELIGIOUS EXPERIENCE

Getty Images/PhotoDisc Collection

It is arguable that all religions rest on religious experience. Religious experiences vary from quiet affirmation to ecstatic and powerful. In spite of its importance to religion, religious experience is very difficult to deal with. It is almost impossible to transfer religious experience from one person to another, and it is questionable whether religious experience is a good guide for either theology or behavior. The picture found above and those on the Web site (**http://www.religion.wadsworth.com/richter**), along with the scriptural quotations show us a number of different religious experiences, some dramatic and some more everyday. Please look over these pictures and passages, and then consider the Introductory Questions that follow as a way to prepare for reading this chapter.

> *The Messenger of God said, "While I was sleeping in the Hijr,*
> *Gabriel [the angel] came and stirred me with his foot . . . He*

brought me out to the door of the shrine and there was a white animal, half mule half donkey, with wings on its side." The Messenger and Gabriel went their way until they arrived at the shrine at Jerusalem. There he found Abraham, Moses, and Jesus among a company of the prophets.

—Islam: Muhammad's "Night Journey" (Peters 65–66)

Beyond the senses, beyond the understanding, beyond all expression, is the Fourth [aspect of Self]. It is pure unitary consciousness, wherein awareness of the world and of multiplicity is completely obliterated. It is ineffable peace.

—Hinduism: Mandukya Upanishad (Prabhavananda and Manchester 51)

[Zen monk Koshu] went without food or sleep, giving himself up to constant zazen, often crying out in his torment . . . At last Koshu admitted his failure and, determined to make an end of it, advanced to the railing and slowly lifted a leg over it. At that very instant he had an awakening.

—Zen Buddhism: An enlightenment account (Stryk 398)

I was all by myself, left on the hilltop for four days and nights without food or water . . . Of course, when it was all over, I would no longer be a boy, but a man. I would have had my vision.

—Lakota Sioux Religion: Vision Quest account of John Fire Lame Deer (Comstock 51).

"About a quarter before nine, while [the preacher] was describing the change which God works in the heart through faith in Christ, I felt my heart strangely warmed. I felt I did trust in Christ, Christ alone, for my salvation; and an assurance was given me that He had taken my sins, even mine, and saved me from the law of sin and death."

—Christianity: John Wesley's conversion account (Pudney 51)

My soul thirsts for God, for the living God. When can I go and meet with God? My tears have been my food day and night, while men say to me all day long, "Where is your God?"

—Judaism: Psalm 42

"You may be an undigested bit of beef, a blot of mustard, a crumb of cheese, a fragment of an underdone potato. There's more of gravy than of grave about you, whatever you are."

—Ebenezer Scrooge to the ghost of Jacob Marley in Charles Dickens' *A Christmas Carol* (55–57)

INTRODUCTORY QUESTIONS

1. John Wesley seems to be describing a religious experience of regeneration, or being "born again." Could you describe this kind of experience in your own words? Have you had similar experiences, maybe not even religious ones? Do you know many people who have had religious experiences, or are they pretty rare?

2. Tradition says that Muhammad was taken away on a strange beast like a flying horse to Jerusalem, as related in the first quote. Look also at the picture of St. Francis receiving the stigmata. Could such stories be real? Could we verify them? Do we need to?

3. Note that the psalmist in the sixth quote talks of his thirst and unhappiness. Look also at the picture of the prophet Jeremiah, famous for his lamentations. Are some religious experiences not very pleasant? Are they still "religious" experiences?

4. In the second quote, the Hindu doctrine describes an awakening of deeper consciousness within oneself, completely apart from sensory, worldly, external experience. But St. Paul in the painting was knocked to the ground by a vision of Christ, thus dramatically changed, he would say, by something outside himself, namely Jesus. Is religious experience "inside" or "outside"? Is it something we do to ourselves or something done to us by an outside power? Is it both?

5. The Buddha in the picture sat in perfect peace and tranquility while around him danced the flames of Mara, the tempter. Similarly, Gomatesvara, the saint of Jainism, stood in perfect quiet for so long that vines grew up around him. Would you expect such peace and quiet to be a standard kind of religious experience? Or should religious experience be more exciting, more dramatic, and more passionate? Compare again to Jeremiah's sorrow or Muhammad's vision.

6. Koshu, the Zen Buddhist, achieved his enlightenment experience finally after days of hunger and struggle. The Vision Quest tradition of the Sioux Indians, too, includes fasting and isolation. Consider how much struggle and effort and self-deprivation goes into such experiences. Does this show how powerful our visions can be, or does it make them seem like matters of self-hypnosis?

7. In the famous line from Dickens' *A Christmas Carol*, Scrooge sees the ghost of Jacob Marley but attributes it to bad digestion. Might all religious experience similarly just be matters of physical changes in the body such as changes in brain chemistry? How could we tell? Is Scrooge reasonable, or is he too skeptical?

INTRODUCTION TO RELIGIOUS EXPERIENCE

In previous chapters, we have already talked about matters of religious language (Chapter 8), religious ritual (Chapter 9), and many other issues in which we have seen how differences within practices and expressions correspond to different approaches to the Sacred. It just makes sense that how one uses language and practices specific rituals, as well as what scriptures mean or how one practices religious morality, will have a direct logical connection with what one considers the Absolute to be like. Here in the chapter on religious experience, this two-pronged emphasis will be the same. That is, we will see that there are different kinds of religious experience, but we will also be able to relate those differences to varying concepts of the Holy.

In dealing with religious experience, however, we might first want to define just what we mean by religious experience in general. We can begin by noting, as a point of contrast, that in previous chapters we spoke of scripture and language, on the one hand, or spoke of rituals and ethics, on the other. We can say that we have been dealing here with two distinct parts of religion: what people believe and what they do. But perhaps in all this we have overlooked how people *feel*. So let us define **religious experience** as the noncognitive, emotional, and impassioned parts of religious life, not just what we think or do in religion but how we *feel* our religion. This is an imprecise definition—as perhaps it must be, since we are not dealing with doctrine and practice —but it may allow us to consider how important the experiential elements of religion are and how they differ from one religion to another.

THE IMPORTANCE OF RELIGIOUS EXPERIENCE

We have just suggested that, as we study religion, it is not enough to list beliefs or practices. Indeed, if one truly is religious, beliefs and practices might seem secondary considerations to what one experiences. Perhaps many people, in their own individual religious lives, might well agree that how they feel in their religion is the real basis for what they believe or what they do. We can consider the wisdom of this assumption later, but for now we can certainly see in a variety of ways that religious experiences have a profound effect on how religions come to be and on how individuals live their religious lives.

Religions often are based on the religious experience of a founder or founders.

For example, we might simply note that much of what we have explored before regarding many aspects of religion trace back to some basic founding experience, some important first experience of sages and prophets. We have already spoken of great founders, like the prophet Muhammad of Islam or Siddhartha Gautama, who became the Buddha, and for both, their original, powerful experience is what made them founders of religions.

Consider, for example, that Muhammad's career as a prophet begins with a dramatic experience, the call to hear and recite the words of God. Islamic tradition declares, in fact, that when Muhammad heard the angel tell him to "Recite!" he first protested, asking, "What shall I recite?" until the angel pressed on him and made him feel like dying. Then at last, the tradition says, Muhammad asked for the message, agreed to accept the role of "Messenger of God," if just to be delivered from the overwhelming pressure of the experience. Thus, finally Muhammad, after months in the mountains above Mecca, heard the angel say, "Recite in the name of thy Lord!" (Peters 51).

The Buddha, as we know from that title alone, became "The Awakened One" precisely through the experience of enlightenment. After days of deep meditation under the Bodhi Tree, he finally saw the truth, awakening to the fact of the "emptiness" of all things and so became free of all desire. Thus, after some days of "the bliss of emancipation," he said:

How blest the happy solitude of him who hears and knows the truth!
How blest is harmlessness towards all, and self-restraint towards living things!
How blest from passion to be free, all sensuous joys to leave behind!
Yet far the highest bliss of all, to leave the pride which says, "I am."
(Warren 87)

Bodhi Tree— pipal tree, variety of Indian fig tree, under which the Buddha enters the state of complete consciousness called *bodhi*

St. Paul, whose conversion experience we saw depicted in the pictures on the Web site, offers another dramatic example. As related in the Christian scriptures (Acts 9), this man, Saul of Tarsus, was on his way to the city of Damascus to arrest Christians when he was literally knocked from his horse by a powerful and blinding light. Then a voice asked him, "Saul, why do you persecute me?" This question came, according to the story, from Jesus himself. Saul, left blind and transformed by the experience, was finally healed and converted to the gospel of Jesus by one of the Christians he had gone to arrest. The experience clearly changed him radically from Christian hunter to Christian missionary.

Saul of Tarsus— Paul is also known as Saul in the book of Acts

The religious experience of founders is often life changing.

Religious experiences of rather dramatic kinds seem to be at the root of much of the founding of religion. Of course, as we often admit, such a generalization may not be universally true, as one could wonder what experience Confucius might have had that compares to that of the Buddha or St. Paul. But for the most part, powerful religious experiences can be found central to the beginning of the "call" of great founders. Clearly, those figures who sense a "call" in their encounter with the Holy are having what religious scholars label a commissioning experience; that is, their encounter leaves them feeling that they are to carry out some special mission in the name of the Holy. Thus, Moses' experience with the God in the burning bush (Exodus 3) left him with the mission to deliver the Israelites from bondage in Egypt. Paul's Damascus road experience compelled him to preach the gospel. Mohammad's experience with the angel Gabriel led him to recite the Holy Koran.

commissioning experience— an encounter with the Holy that leaves the believer with a sense that he must carry out a special mission

But we need not look only to great founders to see the importance of religious experience. Perhaps even in the religious life of more general believers and followers of different religions, the primary value behind their belief and practice is an experience, a kind of feeling about who they are and how they relate to the sacred. In a rather famous case, the great theologian Thomas Aquinas, who before the age of 50 had written scores of volumes of great philosophical work on Christian theology, came at last to a dramatic religious experience that changed his entire direction of life. According to the story, St. Thomas, even while still writing tremendous works of theology and philosophy, began to spend more and more time in quiet but emotional prayer, sometimes crying. Finally, the stories say, he was seen floating off the floor, and later, on December 6th of his last year, he had a vision that caused him to put away all his writing implements. Traditionally, stories say that he was asked why he would write no more, and he answered solemnly, "All that I have written seems to me like straw compared to what has now been revealed to me" (Weisheipl 322).

There is a central role for religious experience in most religions.

If Aquinas is right in general—and it is, of course, quite a leap to argue this point universally—it suggests that whatever doctrine or practice one pursues, there is also a central role in religious life played by religious experience. Thus, it is altogether possible that the central force—or at least one of the central elements—of religion is not about creeds or rituals but is about experience. But what do these experiences mean? How shall we understand such experience? Is any experience we want to call religious truly a good experience? Of course, it may seem unfair to turn back to ask questions of truth and goodness about issues of experience. But this is a textbook, after all, and not a devotional prayer book. So we may not, like Aquinas, hang up our writing implements and leave ourselves to personal visions of God.

Here is an approach we can use. There is a philosophical tradition of considering questions in three categories: God (or, for us, the Absolute), the self, and the world. In each of these areas, we can consider a list of different ways one might feel in a religious context. That is, one might talk about a direct experience of the Sacred, for example, about how one feels when confronted with some hierophany or appearance of the Absolute. How would one feel if one had a vision of God or the experience of Nirvana? Secondly, one can talk about how one experiences *oneself* in a religious way. That is, what do I feel about myself when I experience my religion? Thirdly, there may be different ways one experiences the world and others because of religious consciousness. We will examine these questions first, before we come to evaluating the meaning of such experiences.

hierophany—the vision or appearance of the Holy

EXPERIENCING THE HOLY

We can use Otto's "terrifying" and "fascinating" mystery to begin talking about religious experiences of the Holy.

When we first started talking about the Sacred, or the Holy, we used the Latin phrase from Rudolph Otto describing it as the *mysterium tremendum et fascinans*. Here, already, one can see an interesting division of feeling or experience about the sacred. The word *tremendum* suggests something scary and threatening, an external force that can crush in its powerful wildness. Yet, the word *fascinans* suggests loveliness and beauty, an attraction to the ultimate glory, perhaps a source of joy, peace, and rest. Thus, we can suggest a double list, two ways that one might describe a direct experience of the Sacred:

1. Fear, terror, wonder, awe, delight, awesome presence, worship of grandeur, confrontation, the Sacred as a raging storm
2. Peacefulness, quiet, restfulness, oneness, loss of identity, loss of language, the Sacred as a quiet ocean

Why two lists? Roughly, we have been guided by the *tremendum/fascinans* distinction already noted, but we might speculate as well that we could have different experiences of the Sacred based upon another fundamental distinction we saw long ago, namely the distinction between transcendent and immanent. The word "transcendent" describes the Absolute as beyond the world, "outside" creation, a distant power that enters the world as a kind of awesome intrusion. The "immanent" might be seen as "inside" creation, within the world as a kind of close presence. Thus, it makes some sense to see the connection between this division of experience and specific concepts of Sacred Reality: That which is utterly transcendent might feel to us like an awesome presence that breaks into the natural world with wonder and even terror; that which is fully immanent might seem an inner wholeness, a comforting presence.

The transcendent may be experienced as terror; the immanent as a comforting presence.

Examples of this difference are not hard to find. In Judaism, as we have noted before, the prophets do not often face the Almighty God without cringing in fear. Prophets cry out and seem convinced that they must die from having seen such power and greatness. Indeed, in the story of Moses it is related that, at one point, Moses requested to see God's glory. But God replied that Moses could only see a portion of God's goodness. "But you cannot see my face," God said to Moses, "for no one may see me and live" (Exodus 33:23). Similarly, we have already seen that those who witnessed the transfiguration of Jesus (Matthew 17), and Arjuna, when he saw the glory of Krishna (Bhagavad Gita, chapter 11), were terrified by the awesome glory they beheld. It was suggested in Chapter 3 (The Absolute, The Ultimate, The Holy), of course, that this terror is not really a fear of punishment or anger; it is rather a profound awe at the glory of what is revealed. That is why the wisdom literature of Judaism declares, "The fear of the Lord is the beginning of knowledge" (Proverbs 1:7).

transfiguration— Jesus' change to glorified appearance as described in Matthew 17

Such awestruck fear does not seem very prominent, however, when we speak of the Tao, and it would not make any sense at all when dealing with Nirvana or one's own Buddha Mind. These notions, let us remember, are also awesome, in the sense that they are beyond normal understanding; they are still the "otherness" that is beyond our ability to describe and to contain. Yet, in these cases, the Sacred is a harmony, recognized with a sense of calm participation. Thus, although it is vast as the ocean, Nirvana is also described as "unalloyed bliss," an ocean thus free of any evil or trouble, full only of purity and knowledge and freedom (Stryk 109, 115). In fact, according to the legends of the Buddha's life, his first disciples were earlier colleagues with whom he had practiced asceticism, and therefore, later, when they saw him coming toward them after his enlightenment, they resolved to show him no respect, since he had strayed from their spiritual practice. But, when he approached them, they could not help but find in him an attractive peace and equanimity. This was no transfiguration of awesome power but a manifestation of tranquility (Stryk 49).

The Sacred may be experienced as an awesome transforming power or a quiet tranquility.

affirmational experience—an encounter with the Sacred that leaves one feeling at home with oneself as well as with the spiritual and material realms.

The point, then, is that we might expect there to be at least this difference in religious experiences, that sometimes one finds an awesome and intimidating power, like a wild storm or a precipitous cliff, while at other times one experiences a calmness and peace, like an ocean at rest. And to a great extent, we find these two experiences associated with the Sacred that is, respectively, the transcendent "other" that breaks into life with glory and wonder, and the immanent presence that is somehow part of us or part of this world of harmony and order. It is this sense of the immanent presence that may lead to what scholars call an affirmational experience. An affirmational experience is a quiet encounter of the

Sacred that leaves the believer feeling secure and at home with him- or herself and within the spiritual and material realms.

Of course, this division between transcendence and immanency is not really quite so simple, and as we study varied examples we find a great amount of divergence. In the Upanishads, Brahman often is presented as "effulgent" and glorious, like a brilliant light. Yet, Brahman is an immanent concept as well. In contrast, there are many instances in the Hebrew scriptures of God being found in "sound, fury and might power." Yet, there are many examples of peace and quiet before the Judaic God, as when the prophet Elijah discovers God, not in fire, earthquake, or stormy winds, but in a "still, small voice" (I Kings 19). Maybe it is not so universally consistent that we have a basic fear/terror experience versus a happy/peaceful experience based on different concepts of Sacred Reality. In fact, one could have both experiences about the same concept of the Sacred. But, as usual, even though the lines are fuzzy or perforated, we make these distinctions to help us think over the religious concepts involved, and to see that not all religious experiences are the same.

■ MYSTICAL EXPERIENCE

But, perhaps we make this distinction between religious experiences—between the awesomeness of fearsome glory and the immanent peacefulness of inner harmony—on too low of a level. Perhaps only for "beginners" might it seem that Allah or Yahweh is a god of transcendent and awesome glory, while the experience of Nirvana or Brahman is less fearsome. Notably, some say the deepest experiences of Allah or Yahweh are very much like, perhaps identical to, those of Brahman or Nirvana. Perhaps even in Islam and Judaism, there is ultimately, for the spiritually mature, a sense of closeness and peace. This, at its most extreme, is a common claim of mysticism. **Mysticism** is a direct encounter with the Sacred that results in a strong sense of personal identity with the Sacred. Indeed, some even speak of "union" with the divine. Both mystics of the transcendent and of the immanent varieties speak of loss of individual identity and distinction, and a state of "being one with God."

The mystical experience may seem the same in all religions as an experience of union with the Sacred.

Examples are as common as mysticism itself. Martin Lings, in his study of Islamic mysticism, discusses the notion of "extinction" (fana) as a basic element of the Sufi experience. Quoting the mystic **Shustari**, Lings notes the paradoxical loss of identity in mystical experience in this poem:

fana—dissolution of the human will before God

> *After Extinction, I came out an I*
> *Eternal now am, though not as I.*
> *Yet who am I, o I, but I? (Lings 88)*

Mystical union with the Absolute may feel like a loss of the self.

Hindu mysticism is even more explicit about the loss of identity into the oneness of the Absolute, especially since the Ultimate, Brahman, is already identical with the deeper Self or Atman that is the eternal but impersonal soul of all beings. The Hindu mystic Shankara claimed that once one knows the Self as Atman, there is left no "self" as individual. "The know of Atman," he claimed, "has neither 'I'-notion nor desire for the result of action" (Mayeda 105). When I am one with the Absolute, there is no "me" to act or to think about.

But even on this level, where mystics of many kinds talk about "union with God," there may be useful distinctions to suggest. In Judaic traditions, this union often refers to an emotional, binding love, like sexual union. The sexual imagery is not uncommon (or inappropriate), as the divine "male" moves into the human and "female" soul. The Christian mystic Teresa of Avila (1515–1582) spoke of the "marriage" with God, in which God unites with the soul and is no longer separable. Indeed, in her original wording, God and the human soul join in spiritual union like two lovers whose marriage has been consummated (Peers 178). We need not be shocked at the imagery; it certainly seems to exist in the image of Israel as the wife of Yahweh, and Jesus as the husband of his "bride," the Christian Church. It may also exist in the sexual allegory of the Song of Solomon. But, we may note that this is a "spiritual" and emotional union, not an ontological union.

This term, ontological union, refers to the idea that the two beings that are united are, in fact, one being in a literal, material sense. Water from a glass that is poured into a pond does not merely become near, and certainly does not love, the waters of the pond. It literally *is* the pond; they are one substance. Thus ontological union, as opposed to something like a sexual union, is not easily consistent with religions focused on a transcendent Sacred in the theistic traditions, yet it is to be expected within monistic views of the Holy. "Oneness with Brahman," for example, might be seen as a submerging mingling of the self with the Absolute so that there is an identity of being. This is not two lovers intertwined but a wave slipping back into the ocean so that its waters become identical with the sea. Indeed, the Upanishads explicitly use the language of a river, the soul, which flows into the sea and thereupon is indistinguishable from it (Olivelle, Chandogya Upanishad 6:10). We *are* the sea; the Soul *is* Brahman.

Note the difference. Sexual union suggests distinct beings joined intimately, implying a great emotion and feeling, a marriage, a union of purpose, and mutual concern. Ontological union suggests one being, individuality melting away, and with that melting an emotion of peace, stability, and quiet rest. Two words from Latin have been used to suggest the difference in the religious experience. Exstasis, from which we get our common word "ecstasy," literally means "to stand outside oneself." Enstasis would be the opposite, suggesting an experience of standing "inside oneself," deeply within one's own consciousness. Thus, Mircea Eliade uses "enstasy" as a translation for the yogic concept of **samadhi**, a deep state of meditative insight common in the religions of India. Explicitly, then, there is no object of enstasy, no other being to love; rather, it is a state of mental absorption in oneself (Eliade 77n). The difference in the experiences of ecstasy and enstasy, then, would suggest the difference between absorption into the Ultimate Reality as opposed to a relation to the Ultimate. Perhaps in ecstasy one meets the glorious "other," while in enstasy one goes to find the Sacred in one's own identity, deep within oneself.

The point so far is that we can already see different kinds of emotions and experiences. Even where the one word "mysticism" covers a general notion of "union with the Absolute," there are differences of emphasis that might reflect differences in the way one understands the Sacred. Differences like peace, fear, wonder, silence, and so on are only part of it. Even at the deeper levels of mysticism, where the experience becomes overpowering and utterly self-defining, there

"Union with God" might feel like the union of lovers or a union of being: sexual union and ontological union in mysticism.

ontological union—the essence of "beings" united as one

The mystical experience may lead to a sense of oneness with the Holy.

exstasis—spiritual uplifting outside oneself

enstasis—submerging within one's own consciousness

In ecstasy one meets the other outside of oneself; in enstasy the Sacred within is found.

are similarities in the sense of union, "union with God," yet still there are important differences (such as sexual union, ontological union) rooted in the concept of Sacred Reality. For instance, one would not expect there to be a sense of ontological union with transcendent Sacred.

Some examples of a complete sense of oneness with the Holy even may be found in traditions with a strong transcendent focus.

But it *does* happen. There have been Muslim mystics, for example, that claim to *be* Allah, so deep is their mystic union. The infamous Muslim mystic, Husayn ibn Mansur, called al-Hallaj, at one point declared, "I am the Absolute Truth," so full was he of mystical "oneness" with God. But this is dangerous talk in Islam, and in the year 922 he was whipped, beheaded, and burned (Ahmed 92). Similarly, the Christian monk and mystic Meister Eckhart spoke in his spiritual ecstasy of Jesus being born in his soul. And since Jesus, the Son of God, is eternal, Eckhart concluded that the Father gave birth to the Son and to his, Eckhart's, own soul in exactly the same way. Thus, he declared, "He [the Father] gives me birth, his Son and the same son. I say more: He gives birth not only to me, his Son, but he gives birth to me as himself and himself as me and to me as his being and nature" (Eckhart 187). It is not surprising that such declarations of ontological unity with God would be condemned by the Church of the 14th century.

Nevertheless, some modern writers on mysticism find attractive the idea that maybe—way down deep—all mystic experiences are alike. Juan Mascaro, in his introduction to the Upanishads, quotes extensively from Asian mystics and European poets, finding declarations of Brahman's "pure being" even in Hamlet's "To be, or not to be." Thus, he concludes, "When by love the full communion of man with God has taken place, when man sees God in all and all in God, then man is one with Brahman, he has crossed the river of life and he has heard the songs of immortality welcoming him to the other shore. This is what all the masters of the Spirit tell us" (Mascaro 30). This may be a rather drastic generalization, but it seems to be based on the supposition that, perhaps at some "deep" level of mysticism or at some basic functional level, religious experiences *are* all the same. If Arjuna felt "awe" meeting Krishna and Moses felt "awe" meeting Yahweh, does that show Krishna *is* Yahweh or that both are legitimately labeled "God" in the same sense? Maybe, maybe not.

Even though mystical experiences are common in religion, we must be careful in assuming all of these are the same.

Intriguing as mysticism is, we must be careful in making Mascaro's universal conclusion. It has been suggested here, at any rate, that for all the talk of "union with the Sacred," there may be very important differences between experiences of the Holy, differences that are evident when we see the conceptual context within which those experiences occur. We shall examine later how religious experience and religious ideas continue to interact, changing and challenging one another, and we shall see that religious experience, vital and powerful as it is, is not necessarily the final arbiter of religious meaning.

EXPERIENCES OF ONESELF

Inner experience of the self is quite common in religions.

Besides there being a direct experience of meeting the Absolute or Sacred Reality, we can also note that a common religious experience is interior, especially one's experience of oneself in religion. That is, religion also gives us a feeling of our own spiritual health, our own value and purpose. Again, these experiences might be quite diverse.

- Self-acceptance, peace, inner assurance, and calm; a sense of inner growth, being the guide and master of one's own life; regular growth or steady relation to the Absolute; an unanalyzed constancy, wholeness, unity, with understanding, insight; spirituality as self-acceptance.
- Self-dislike, guilt, need for "rebirth;" anguish, or a sense of being a laborer, a worker, an ongoing moral and spiritual struggle; dramatic change, need for conversion; spirituality as the struggle for goodness.

Sick Soul and Healthy Soul experiences are two ways one feels about oneself in the presence of the Holy.

Might one have many of these experiences at once? Or are they distinct enough that they can be legitimately characterized into two groups? As is evident by the way these lists are divided, there is some suggestion that there are two different ways of feeling about oneself. This characterization is not, of course, absolutely binding but can be understood as a useful schema. Philosopher and psychologist William James, in his book *The Varieties of Religious Experience*, originally suggested it. There he talked about the "Sick Soul" and "Healthy Soul." This distinction is not intended to be an evaluative point but is merely descriptive. That is, he would not say that being a "sick" soul is worse than being a "healthy" soul; they are just different ways of experiencing who and what we are when faced with the presence of the Holy.

■ THE "SICK SOUL"

The sick soul experiences itself as inadequate, burdened, and divided.

For example, James says that the sick soul is one that faces the Sacred and feels itself inadequate, divided, or burdened. The person who experiences him- or herself as a sinner, for example, stands perhaps before the righteousness of God and knows his or her unworthiness. Or one could look within Buddhist traditions and find monks who labor long, as did **Koshu Sotaku** in the opening quotation, feeling only his failure and his ignorance of ultimate truth. One might feel separation from God, even being under the wrath of the gods; one could be locked in the "suffering" of *samsara* or burdened by ignorance. These describe some religious people's experience of themselves as something broken or burdened. This is the "sick" soul (we discuss sick-minded religion and conversion again in Chapter 13: Religion, Personality, and the Individual).

samsara—the cycle of birth and rebirth in Indian religions

In this picture, the Sacred is seen as somehow separate from the individual soul, beyond reach, or at least not yet realized. This is the experiential burden. Nevertheless, when the Sacred appears, when one's sin is forgiven or one finds enlightenment, then suddenly there is a new freedom from the bondage of sin or *samsara*. Thus, the "sick soul," according to James, may often come to experience a new breakthrough, an awakening of some kind that feels like a new and profound awakening to the Holy. Perhaps it includes a deep reliance upon the Sacred itself, as the old life gives way to new life. And so, there appears within various religions emphasis on the experience of enlightenment, awakening, rebirth, or conversion. As James says of Buddhism and Christianity, "[These] are essentially religions of deliverance; the man must die to an unreal life before he can be born to the real life" (James 162).

The "born again" experience may produce a radical change in one's life.

This may be what Christians often mean by saying they have experienced being "born again." A classic spokesperson for this idea of Christian conversion is the evangelist Billy Graham. In his book *How to be Born Again*, he describes many personal cases of individuals whose lives were a mass of philosophical confusion and moral corruption. Introduced to the redemption of Jesus, their lives were changed. In general, he says that the Biblical phenomenon of being "born again" creates in the convert a number of drastic changes: "from lust to holiness, from darkness to light, from death to resurrection, from stranger to the kingdom of God to now being its citizen." He concludes, "The Bible teaches that the person who is born again has a changed will, changed affections, changed objectives for living, changed disposition, new purpose. He receives a new nature and a new heart. He becomes a new creation" (Graham 151).

Of course, this is not a universal experience, even within Christianity. Indeed, even with such conversion, in some cases the battle is not yet over but only just begun. For "temptation is sure to come," Jesus told his followers, and one may repeatedly fall into sin. St. Paul, describing what it is like to desire to serve God, while still feeling the temptations of sin, cried out, "Oh, wretched man that I am! Who will deliver me from this body of death?" (Romans 7:24) Thus, there may be included in the "sick soul," even one "born again," a realistic need to deal with ongoing submission and struggle. This state of ongoing struggle against sin might be evident also in Islam, where the Muslim—which very name means "one who submits"—must put out some effort daily, even several times a day, to bring his or her will into submission to God. Here there is a long tradition of the "inner **jihad**," a "holy war," so to speak, that rages within one's own heart. It is the religious experience of struggle as one bows daily to God (Esposito 93).

Even "born again" people may continue to struggle with the "old self."

■ THE "HEALTHY SOUL"

The "healthy soul" feels itself to be generally good, at peace with the Holy or in a generally forward development of spirituality.

The healthy soul is consistent with those religions that stress cultivation of the self.

Contrasting to this view is the "healthy soul." Here one feels oneself to be not fully corrupt to begin with. One is less a sinner and more just "incomplete" perhaps. One needs only to move forward, and there is not so much a conversion as progress. The human self needs only to perfect itself, come to a gradual enlightenment or wisdom, or to a better insight into the law of God. James gives numerous examples of Christians who had no dramatic sense of sin nor any significant conversion experience. They might not describe themselves as "born again." In a broader study than James could do, we might find the "healthy soul" more consistent with those religions that require cultivation rather than conversion. Here the Confucian or Taoist would be an example. As noted briefly in Chapter 10 (Religion, Morality, and Ethics), Confucius emphasized the personal cultivation of virtue, developing habits of proper social behavior until one becomes a refined "Gentleman," the very reflection of the order of Heaven. Describing his own self-cultivation, Confucius himself claimed that he began his efforts at moral self-development when he was just 15 years old, and by the time he was 70, he said, "I follow all the desires of my heart without breaking any rule" (Analects 2:4).

Confucius, of course, was not confronted with the Absolute understood as a righteous and demanding God but as the "Way of Heaven," which is itself the order of peaceful and proper moral society. William James' discussion of the "healthy soul" uses examples that refer to God, but it can be argued that even here these western examples are far from orthodox Christianity. Many examples describe finding God within ourselves or indeed describe "God" as a "spirit of life and power" or "Divine Energy." Thus, indeed, these "Western" examples are perhaps more Hindu than Christian after all.

The general difference between the healthy soul and the sick soul is pretty evident. The application of this distinction to the Sacred, however, is difficult to specify. We have already seen that in James' book, he studies mostly Christian experiences, and though much of Christianity describes religious experience in "born again" terminology, there are many cases of the "healthy soul" within the Christian fold. Similarly, in Buddhism there are clear indications of both kinds. In Pure Land Buddhism, for example, the average person experiences him- or herself as needing outside assistance to come to fuller insight. "I shall never achieve liberation unless reborn into the "Pure Land" of Amida," one might say. Famously, Shinran (1173 –1262), the 13th century reformer of the Pure Land School of Buddhism, claimed that one would be saved from rebirth by the Buddha Amida just by saying his name once. Moreover, he declared, it is actually easier for a wicked person to find this salvation than for a "good" person, precisely because the wicked person is more aware of his need for help (Robinson and Johnson 254–255). This seems to echo Jesus' remark: "Those who are well have no need of a physician, but those who are sick . . . I have come to call not the righteous but sinners" (Matthew 9:12–13). Thus, apparently, knowing you have a "sick soul" is an important part of Pure Land Buddhism as well as Christianity.

At the same time, a great amount of Buddhist teaching emphasizes a "path," whether the Noble Eightfold Path of early Buddhism or the Bodhisattva Path of Mahayana schools. These paths are slowly cultivated, as insight and detachment from desire are gradually formed, until one at last, perhaps after lifetimes of effort, gains liberation from rebirth on the merits of one's own effort. Thus, Buddhism seems to have schools of teaching and practice for both the sick soul and for the healthy soul. This double possibility can be seen within the Zen school alone. In Rinzai Zen, the emphasis is on one's troubled, struggling fight against ignorance, which culminates in a sudden flashing insight called *satori,* or enlightenment. We have already seen such a case in our opening quotations. At the same time, Soto Zen emphasizes one's innate perfection in the present, stressing that you are now and always have been purely enlightened, and so you only need to practice being aware of it. Ironically, then, while the Rinzai master D. T. Suzuki stresses the vital centrality of *satori* and criticizes "quietism," the Soto master Shrunyu Suzuki hardly mentions it. What is important, says he, is simply to keep one's "beginner's mind."

The point here is, again, that we can note different kinds of experiences of the self. We could ask if a "rebirth" experience seems more consistent with some concept of Sacred Reality as transcendent, while "healthy soul" is more amenable to this-worldly religions, such as Taoism. We might also wonder if the sense of "rebirth" is necessary to *all* religion. Doesn't the religion have to *change* a person? Or, is this sense of oneself specific only to one religion or another, or to one concept of Sacred Reality? It seems from this brief look that we might not expect emphasis on a dramatic change, unless there is some sense of the greatness of the goal and the difficulty of overcoming barriers—whether sin or ignorance —to achieving that goal. This alerts us to the connection between this chapter and the next, where we shall talk of salvation.

Buddhism has schools emphasizing sick souls and those stressing healthy souls.

satori—the sudden flash of enlightenment, the goal of Zen, especially Rinzai Zen

D.T. Suzuki—prominent teacher of the Rinzai school of Zen Buddhism

Shrunyu Suzuki—prominent teacher of the Soto school of Zen Buddhism

EXPERIENCING THE WORLD

The world itself looks different and seems to have different value to people of different religious views.

One last area where one's experience of Absolute Reality has effect is in one's experience of the world and one's purpose in it. One may often have experiences of nature and the value or beauty (or disvalue and ugliness) of this world, and this experience of the world will have some connection to religion. That religion will also have a lot to say about what one is supposed to *do* in the world.

For example, the world might be experienced as a place of extreme beauty and harmony. Taoism (and its offspring in Zen) would very likely see the natural world as balanced, so that anything that happens is just part of the harmonious, all-embracing flow of Tao. In contrast, for Zoroastrians, the world is seen as a battleground between good and evil, a place where humans must choose whom and in whose army they will serve. Arguably, this is true for some Christians as well. For Jews, the world might be seen as an inhospitable place, in which the people of God are constantly at odds with the Gentiles, and in which the miracle of God's "chosen people" is evident simply in that the people survive. In much Indian religion (for example, Hinduism), the world is considered an illusion, a thin cover of deception over the single divine substance of Brahman.

How religions experience the world depends on their understanding of the world and its relation to the Holy.

Of course, such religious experiences may or may not change drastically how average people actually live in the world. Perhaps most people are just getting by in the world, where they work and live, enjoy what they can, and bear what they must. But the logic of how a religious view experiences the world can be understood in several ways:

1. If Sacred Reality is a God distinct from the world and the world is corrupted by sin, then the world is not my home, but I am rather a "sojourner." Thus in the Christian scripture, the writer of First Peter echoes the Jewish Psalmist urging Christians to live "as aliens and exiles [in the world]" (I Peter 2:11), while the Psalmists asks God for guidance precisely because "I live as an alien in the land [the world]" (Psalm 119:19).

2. In contrast, if all nature participates harmoniously in the wholeness of the Tao, then life, death, joy, and suffering are all just part of the system. Thus, as we saw in our discussion of the problem of suffering, the Taoist in Chuang Tzu's stories says, "I received life because the time had come; I will lose it because the order of things passes on. Be content with this time and dwell in this order and then neither sorrow nor joy can touch you" (Watson 81).

3. Similar to but more world-denying than Taoist thinking, Hindu philosophy that stresses the one reality of Brahman has tended to make its followers sense the world as a kind of trap or seduction. If the Sacred is one eternal substance, then the world with its plurality is a kind of mistake or an illusion, and our tendency to be embroiled in that illusion is precisely that from which we need to escape. Thus, the Upanishadic literature of Hinduism says, "Where one sees nothing but the One, hears nothing but the One, knows nothing but the One—there is the Infinite" (Prabhavananda and Manchester 73). Indeed the Katha Upanishad adds,

"From death to death he goes who sees here any kind of diversity" (Katha Upanishad ***Is this the Mascaro translation or the Olivelle version?4, 11). Thus, the world tempts us with its illusion of individuality and all the personal interests and enjoyments that go with that individuality. Ultimately, the world is a place to shun, and only those who renounce the world and its attractions can find salvation.

The point, then, is that the world around us just does not *look* the same to all people; it does not *feel* the same. For some, it is "home, sweet home," and for others, it is a foreign land or even a dangerous temptation.

■ WORLD AND ACTION

How one understands the world will affect how one acts in the world.

By the same token, these different views of the world may change the way one feels "called" to *act* in the world. Where there is a world of good and evil, one has a duty to join the fight, stand up, and speak out. Thus, some Christians offer their lives to the poor, serving worldwide anti-poverty missions and trying to save "the unborn" from abortion. Taoists, Zenists, and participants in primal cultures might understand themselves to be "called" by the beauty of the world simply to participate, to enjoy and live in harmony with whatever the world contains. Those living in the illusion of *samsara* may be "called" just to get through life and on to the next, or indeed to "renounce" this life and to live in austerity and anonymity. Notably, it is the Catholic, Mother Teresa, not the Hindu guru, who establishes the hospitals for the dying of Calcutta. Yet, from a Hindu perspective, the guru living in isolated self-denial may be more holy than the missionary doctor who lives in a relatively comfortable home. Perhaps all this harkens back to our Chapter 10: Religious, Morality, and Ethics, but it should not surprise us that how one feels about the world and how one acts in the world should be logically related and that both should be related to what one perceives to be the Ultimate Reality.

Of course, as with all our discussions, these generalizations are not necessarily what you will find in all cases. Early Christian monks ran from the pleasures of the world because they expected Jesus to return soon, and so the futility of the world was just a diversion from what is really important. Also, famous pictures during the war in Vietnam showed Zen monks who burned themselves alive in protest against South Vietnam's religious injustices and against the ugliness of the world around them. On the other hand, few people actually may change their lives drastically because of some dedication to religion. However, note that the way we perceive the world *is* likely to have *some* effect on how we live, and it

How we live ought to be consistent with the way we feel about Sacred Reality.

ought to be consistent with the way we feel the world is constituted by Sacred Reality. The illusory world is not one to become involved in; the battleground world is one to take sides in; the inhospitable world is one to defend oneself in.

As usual, part of a general point is that there is a consistency between religious concepts, here particularly between what one understands about the Sacred and the various religious experiences one might have. Whether one is experiencing the beauty or ugliness of the world, experiencing one's own inner joy or inner dissatisfaction, or directly experiencing the Holy itself, how one feels about these things may, and perhaps should, be influenced directly by what one thinks the Sacred *is*. Consequently, a different concept of Sacred Reality might well imply a different experience.

THE PROBLEM OF EVALUATING RELIGIOUS EXPERIENCE

It is evident that there are many different "kinds" of religious experience and that there may well be logical relationships between those kinds of experience and the Sacred Reality to which they appeal. But so what? What do such experiences mean? If I claim to have had a significant religious experience, does that mean I actually *did*? If one claims to have "felt God's presence," can we therefore say God really was present? Or, shall we say, that as long as I feel like it is true, it *is* true, or (to use a popular but problematic phrase) "true for me." Perhaps it is uncomfortable, but we can, and perhaps unavoidably must, raise an issue here of the legitimacy of religious experience. One could suggest that all such experience is utterly subjective, giving the experience an unfalsifiable personal validity, or we can ask if some experiences, in fact, might be false forms of self-deception. Remember in our opening quotations, Ebenezer Scrooge responded to even his own vision of Marley's ghost with a kind of natural skepticism, suggesting that his own experience of seeing ghosts was just a case of bad digestion: "There's more of gravy than of grave about you."

It is difficult to measure the legitimacy of religious experience.

Let us consider some examples of religious experiences to test some concerns about their nature and validity:

1. My friend was raised "Christian" but found it "boring." Finally, he discovered Buddhism and found peace of mind. Are Buddhist teachings therefore *true?*
2. My friend had a powerful conversion experience that had him weeping and shaking. He felt terrible burdens of sin until that day, and then he felt "born again." Does this indeed show, as he claims, that Jesus is alive and loves him?
3. My friend was a jerk; many people thought so. Then, upon being converted to a Hare Krishna group, we all agreed that he had become a remarkably nice guy. Does that make his religious claims about the divinity of Krishna more believable?
4. My friend was an alcoholic and then, upon going to a Pentecostal Christian meeting, was miraculously "healed." She has not drunk since. Is her faith in the power of the Holy Spirit therefore justified? Is her belief true?
5. I saw Jesus in a vision, walking down the road. Should anyone believe me? Does it make a difference that I am usually a very calm and reasonable person?
6. I and several other people saw this vision. What if there were three of us? What if there were 500? Does that make the claims about the vision, or about Jesus, more believable?
7. My friend had a cancerous liver. The priest went in and anointed her with oil, laid hands on her, and the next day the cancer was gone. Doctors were amazed. Is her religious belief therefore justified? True?
8. We have a video of the parting of the Red Sea. Does this prove that the Red Sea parted or, even if it did part, does the video prove God parted it?

Note that we have invented here different kinds of experiences, ranging from a vague inner sense of "peace" to what seem to be visions and miracles. The examples are listed in this order because there seems to be a fundamental difference between an occurrence that refers to nothing but one's own "inner feeling" and an experience that refers to something as evident as video footage and cancer cells in the liver. Surely, there is something more valid about an experience that others can check, or at least understand, than there is to an experience that refers only to my feeling. At the same time, some of the experiences above refer to "my friend's" experience, while others refer to "my" experience. Is it reasonable to think that my friend's experience could be merely his imagination but that my own is somehow believable? Remember, Scrooge doubted even his own experience. Should we trust any religious experience that is our own but doubt any that belongs to others? Or, should we trust experiences that many people had, versus those had by only one or a few? And who gets to decide, or on what criteria can we decide, what counts as valid experience and what does not? These are problems we have to consider in evaluating the meaning and validity of religious experiences.

■ THE PROBLEM OF SUBJECTIVITY

subjectivity—the application of an experience only to the person, the "subject," who had the experience

Subjective experience cannot be measured by external objective means.

Objectivity—the application of a claim or experience to a reality outside the person, application to the "object" and not only the subject of the experience

Objective experiences can be assessed by external means.

It is difficult for an external observer to know what another person's internal experiences mean.

The evident difference between experiences that only I or "my friend" might have had and those that involve aspects other people can witness or verify brings up the problem of subjectivity. An event or interpretation is said to be "subjective" when it is interior, hence just for the individual *subject* and not conveyed to or shared with others. Some obvious examples of subjective experiences are pain, happiness, love, and peace. These are subjective precisely because they belong only to the subject, the person having those experiences, and no one can check to see if the speaker "really" has the experience or has any basis for it. Obviously, no one feels my pain except me, and it makes little sense for anyone to deny any subjective claim I may want to make about my pain. If I say, "I have a terrible headache," it would be rather strange for someone else to say, "Oh, your headache isn't so bad."

The opposite of "subjective" is "objective." An experience is said to be objective when it refers to something exterior, to some reality in the *object*, so that the claim can be shared or shown. If I say, "I am six feet tall," I am making a claim about myself, but it is now an objective claim. Anyone with a measuring tape could verify it. In fact, I could claim to be eight feet tall, and someone could quite rightly say, "No, you aren't that tall!" Note the contrast with the case of the "terrible headache." For our religious experiences, the point is that there seem to be cases in the preceding list that are almost entirely subjective, while others are more objective. Specifically, "I have peace in my heart" seems to be subjective, but "I have cancer in my liver" seems to be objective.

The point of raising this distinction is not only to note that some experiences clearly seem to be more subjective than others. For the purposes of considering the meaning of religious experiences, we should also note that it seems that as experiences become more subjective, more interior, those people who are on the outside as mere observers have less chance of knowing what these experiences mean. Just as a bystander cannot know the extent of my headache, so no one can quite tell what the religious convert means by "peace of mind." Observing a friend, we might all admit that the person is now "nicer" or no longer getting drunk, but whether their religious experience has anything to do with the Holy Spirit or Krishna or Scrooge's "undigested bit of beef" is hard for us to recognize as true. Thus, the more subjective an experience is, the less likely others may be to take it seriously.

Let us look further at these examples, especially at the difference between scenarios 1 and 3, scenarios 3 and 4, and scenarios 4 and 8. Might we say that some of these claims are more impressive than others? Why? It seems indeed that some experiential claims are more forceful than others precisely because some are more objective than others are. That is, we have perhaps the very realistic sense that there is more validity to a claim based on an experience that we could check for ourselves. For example, scenario 4 and, especially, scenario 7 give us cases where the events under consideration are matters we might have observed for ourselves, given that alcoholism can be considered a genuine addiction and that cancer in one's liver is not merely a matter of feeling depressed or sinful.

In the case of a miracle as dramatic as the one mentioned in scenario 8, if indeed such things occur, seeing for oneself such an event would surely force one to consider the power of God or at least the almost equally dramatic possibility of mass hallucination (meaning that many people could have been tricked into verifying the case using what appeared to be objective data). Of course, when a religious history claims such miracles, and if we simply were not there to see it, at least we might look for objective evidence of this event, historical, archaeological, or even geological evidence that we could check for ourselves. But, if we talk of one's inner peace or self-assurance about God's love, there does not seem to be any way at all to check the "evidence" for such an event from the outside. Because such experiences are fundamentally subjective, the only "evidence" for such miracles as inner peace or conversion is the experience of the subject him- or herself. Thus, religious claims based on purely subjective religious experience may quite rightly leave us skeptical.

At the same time, we might also be quite uncomfortable with the thought that anyone could challenge someone else's religious experience. "If I say I feel God's presence, then I *do* feel God's presence," I might insist, and no one could say otherwise, just as it would seem odd for someone to ask for "evidence" that I have a headache. Perhaps we should, so to speak, let subjective religious claims be subjective and give up asking for, or being concerned about, objective "evidence." However, the problem here is that the kinds of religious claims that are often the result of religious experience certainly seem to be objective claims. Such claims are not merely, "I am happier today"; rather, they seem to be about God, about "Reality." When the Christian "born again" believer says, "Jesus lives!," he is not merely saying that he feels better. When the Buddhist gains enlightenment, he claims to see reality "as it truly is." We might be tempted to treat all such religious experiential claims as various ways of saying, "I am happier," but that does not seem—phenomenologically speaking—to be what the religions themselves want to say. Is this claim, "God lives here within my heart!" a statement about God, or only a statement about me? It looks objective, but from the outside perhaps we cannot help but look at it like it is subjective.

This is the problem of subjectivity. It is worth mentioning that much of the discussion of subjectivity, as well as the skepticism implied in our questioning, has become widely spread only in the modern period and is being spread with globalization. Much of the world is coming to trust objective data and place less trust in subjective data. Moreover, nonWestern cultures are following Western culture with its tendency to think of religion as something beyond argument or without "objective" concepts of truth. Religion is supposed to be especially interior, and hence the idea of objective evidence in religious belief is, to many people, irrelevant. This means on the one hand that what someone else sees from "outside" my experience has nothing to say about me but also that what I say from "inside" my experience has nothing to say about them.

With globalization, the Western idea that religion is beyond objective investigation or discussion is spreading.

There is an odd irony here. We think it very open-minded to believe that one person's experiential evidence is good "for him" but irrelevant to me, while mine is impressive to me but irrelevant to them. My experience is mine alone, we might say, and your experience is yours alone. We expect all religious experience to be equally subjective.

So why is this a problem? We want to say that all experiences of religion are equally subjective and nobody's experience can mean anything to anyone else. However, note that this means we will have an automatic mistrust of everyone else's experience (What can it say to me?) but an automatic trust of my own experiences (as my "truth"). Thus, if *you* find peace of mind in Amida Buddha, then I shrug and say, "Well, okay, but so what?" However, if I find that same peace, then I think something has become real to me, some reality has broken in on me. Indeed, we have noted all along that the Sacred is taken, not as an enjoyable illusion but as a sacred *reality*. Arguably, what looked like "open-mindedness" turns out in fact to be remarkably egotistical: My experiences are meaningful indicators of "reality," but yours are not.

The difficulty here seems to lie in the fact that religious experience is often considered to be "self-validating". That is, the common element in everybody's religious experience is that such experiences come with a kind of certainty. This is not just my vision of God but also a vision with assurance. That is not just your peace of mind but the certainty that such peace is the result of God or Nirvana. Ask the believer: How do you *know* this was God or Nirvana? The answer seems to be "I just know"; and maybe "You'd know too if it happened to you."

The problem of "self-validating" experience: Why should I think my inner feelings are meaningful if I don't think yours are?

The point is that religious experiences seem to come with their own built-in certainty and therefore are self-validating. But it is easy enough to believe that someone else may be speaking of "reality as it truly is," while for us it only means "I am happier today"; yet I allow my own experiences to make me believe that I have truly met God or seen reality. So, if we can doubt someone else's experience, would it be more honest if I were to doubt my own religious experiences, too? *Can* one doubt one's own religious experience? If we think again about Ebenezer Scrooge, it seems the answer is "yes."

■ THE PROBLEM OF SELF-INDUCED EXPERIENCE

This possibility of, and need for, doubting even one's own religious experience is further indicated by the fact that some experiences are apparently induced by something rather less holy than the Holy. Indeed, sometimes we might say that such experiences can be self-induced. Imagine a dramatic religious experience, such as the opening reference to Koshu's enlightenment noted in the quote at the

There seem to be artificially self-induced religious experiences.

Religion And The Brain. In the new field of "neurotheology," scientists seek the biological basis of spirituality. Is God all in our heads?

"That a religious experience is reflected in brain activity is not too surprising, actually. . . . Neurotheology is stalking bigger game than simply affirming that spiritual feelings leave neural footprints. . . . By pinpointing the brain areas involved in spiritual experiences and tracing how such experiences arise, the scientists hope to learn whether anyone can have such experiences, and why spiritual experiences have the qualities they do.

. . . just because an experience has a neural correlate does not mean that the experience exists "only" in the brain, or that it is a figment of brain activity with no independent reality. Think of what happens when you dig into an apple pie. The brain"s olfactory region registers the aroma of the cinnamon and fruit. The somatosensory cortex processes the feel of the flaky crust on the tongue and lips. The visual cortex registers the sight of the pie. Remembrances of pies past (Grandma's kitchen, the corner bake shop . . .) activate association cortices. . . . "The fact that spiritual experiences can be associated with distinct neural activity does not necessarily mean that such experiences are mere neurological illusions," Newberg insists. "It's no safer to say that spiritual urges and sensations are caused by brain activity than it is to say that the neurological changes through which we experience the pleasure of eating an apple cause the apple to exist." The bottom line, he says, is that "there is no way to determine whether the neurological changes associated with spiritual experience mean that the brain is causing those experiences ... or is instead perceiving a spiritual reality."

. . . In 1997, neurologist Vilayanur Ramachandran told the annual meeting of the Society for Neuroscience that there is "a neural basis for religious experience." His preliminary results suggested that depth of religious feeling, or religiosity, might depend on natural—not helmet-induced—enhancements in the electrical activity of the temporal lobes."

Source: Begley, Sharon, with Anne Underwood. *Newsweek,* May 7, 2001. http://www.American-buddha.com/religion.begley.htm (accessed February 19, 2004).

beginning of this chapter, or the description of Thomas Aquinas' vision of God. Imagine now that these great saints of religion returned from their experience full of the assurance of their visions, based on experiences inescapably self-validating, leading in turn to strong and certain convictions. Finally, imagine now that when these saints finally speak of their experiences, their friends laugh and admit that they put LSD into their tea. Does this change our sense of the validity of their experiences? Should it?

This scenario may seem silly or even unkind, but it raises some harsh and interesting questions about the validity of religious experience. The problem seems to be that, in fact, much religious experience is known to be related to behaviors that probably induce altered states of consciousness. For example, in the local tribal religions of Sri Lanka, women dance wildly for long periods of time in order to achieve trance states meant to prove that they are possessed by local gods. Thus, they hyperventilate and display ecstatic utterances, ultimately returning to their homes as acknowledged shamans (see "Buddhism: Footprint of the Buddha,"

Dervishes—members of a Muslim religious group, founded by Maulana Celaleddin Rumi (1207–1273); the group is especially known for the ritual performance of the sema, a mystical spiritual journey or prayer trance

peyote—plant with hallucinogenic powers used originally among the Indians of Mexico in religious ceremonies

soma—originally a substance with psychoactive power drunk by humans and deities during ritual actions

Dancing, chanting, the use of drugs and similar activities may produce "altered states of consciousness" that may be interpreted as religious experiences.

If religious experience is self-induced, is it always valid or invalid?

video series hosted by Ronald Eyre). Similarly, Muslim mystics called Sufis, or more explicitly the famed Dervishes, whirl and dance in literally dizzying formations, practices that include various aspects of breath control patterns and focused meditative attention disciplines. Such activity, interspersed with long repetitions of the name of God, traditionally helped one to enter a mystic trance and to experience feelings of peace and oneness with God (Friedlander 87–89). We might argue that similar examples are evident in modern American Pentecostalism, a branch of modern Christianity. In Pentacostalism, people dance, cry out, sing, and chant repetitive phrases until they develop the ecstatic experience of "speaking in tongues," the phenomenon of singing and speaking in "languages" unrecognizable, yet beautiful and deemed prophetic. The Pentecostal experience, as well as the Dervish and shamanistic experiences, are interpreted as real activities of the Holy Spirit, of Allah or of the gods. Yet, the skeptic might note that all such religious experiences seem to be dependent upon physical exercises that might simply be altering brain chemistry, giving us examples of self-induced religious experiences.

More remarkable might be those cases of religious experience that seem indeed to be intentionally induced by external conditions. For example, drugs have been used in many cultures to help induce religious experiences. Peyote is a prominent example, with roots of modern peyote rituals reaching back to Aztec times. Mexican tribal cultures, like the Huichol Indians, continue to use such natural intoxicants to foresee the future and to gain healing powers (Stewart 41). The modern ritual of the Native American Church mixes Christian symbolism with peyote use and is considered comparable to the Christian sacrament of bread and wine (Stewart 224). On the other side of the world, in India, there was also a famous drug called *soma,* used in religious practices as old as the Vedas. Soma was apparently a drug derived from a plant in India, and drinking the *soma* juice was supposed to help one attain the immortality of the gods. Indeed, *soma* was what made the gods themselves powerful. Thus, the entire ritualized process of extracting and drinking the *soma* juice appears as a significant ritual in the early Vedic scriptures. No one knows for sure what this plant was, but all agree that it was "highly intoxicating" (Zaehner 28).

Besides direct drug use, other means of altering one's brain chemistry are commonly used to establish and maintain religious experiences. We saw in an opening quotation a reference to the "Vision Quest" of some Native American tribal religions, in which isolation and exposure to the elements, as well as going without food or sleep for several days, result in a "vision." Fasting, sleep deprivation, hyperventilation, yoga, meditation, biofeedback, and other similar practices can be, and still are, used in well-established religious traditions to induce religious experience. How is the Vision Quest truly a vision, if it comes merely as the result of four days of being alone and exposed, without sleep or food? How is "speaking in tongues" a genuine experience of the Holy Spirit if it comes through hyperventilation and self-induced excitement?

Let us be intentionally skeptical: All these activities change brain chemistry and therefore induce religious experience. The question then is whether we should trust our own religious experience if we have to do such ritual works to achieve it. How is a religious experience any different from being stoned?

Perhaps it is reasonable to be skeptical about religious experience. Of course, one *feels* a sense of certitude with the experience, but the basic philosophical problem nevertheless is that we *might* be mistaken and self-deceived. Therefore, perhaps we should doubt even our own religious experience. The point of being so skeptical is that perhaps we should not take for granted that religious experiences are good evidence or good reasons to be religious, even for ourselves. Perhaps we should not take for granted that such experiences are somehow trump cards that outweigh statements of doctrine or the demands of morality. At the same time, it is not obvious that we should *always* be skeptical. Just because I have not experienced God in my life does not mean that there is no God to experience; it would be arrogant of me to believe that the U.S. President could not have called you on the phone just because he has not called me first. Both skepticism and automatic personal acceptance of religious experience may be unwarranted. This is why we should ask how one might tell a genuine religious experience from a deceptive one. This is why we should consider how religions themselves evaluate such experiences.

■ INTERTRADITIONAL EVALUATION OF EXPERIENCE

So, who has the right, we might demand, to say whose religious experience is legitimate and whose is not? Because of our modern conceptions of individualism, egalitarianism and "religious freedom," we might well bristle at the suggestion that anyone could evaluate and challenge anyone else's experience. Yet it seems that religious experiential self-deception and self-manipulation are possible, and if one feels so much certitude about one's own experience that one cannot doubt oneself, how shall we ask ourselves serious questions about validity? It seems we might *need* to have ways of checking ourselves or of having someone else offer criteria for what is and is not a valid experience.

Religions themselves have developed means for checking the validity of religious experience.

The fact is that there *are* checks and evaluations for "genuine" religious experience, and in most cases, those checks come from within the religions themselves. At the very least, we have seen that certain kinds of experiences seem to go best with specific religions. For example, the experience of being "born again" does not seem to fit very well with Taoism, nor does the mystical experience of ontological union coincide very well with Islam. Religions therefore develop traditional expectations of what kinds of experiences are right; as we might expect, there is and should be some consistency between the various aspects of a religion. Thus, the nature of religious experience is "checked" to the extent that it fits in with both the beliefs and the practices that are also part of the religion. Thus, just as there are "right beliefs" in a religion and just as there are "proper moral (or ritual) behaviors" in a religion, so we might speak of there being appropriate experiences in a specific religion. The latter seems for many of us the oddest of the three notions, and indeed there does not seem to be a proper word for the idea. But just as people speak of orthodoxy and orthopraxis (literally, straight doctrine and straight practice) within a religion, perhaps we could coin a new term, **orthopathos,** to refer to a religion's view of what is the right kind of experience.

Interestingly, where there seems to be some danger of religious experiences being deception, orthodoxy and orthopraxis actually offer ways of deciding if the experience was right. A notable example of this is the Christian mystic, Teresa of Avila, whom we noted referring to "spiritual marriage." In her autobiography, she admitted that not all experiences of mysticism are proper and that some "experiences of God" might really be deceptions of Satan. However, she noted that both doctrine and behavior offer useful tests to see if an experience is really from God. She wrote that "the soul must be convinced that a thing comes from God only if it is in conformity with Holy Scripture," and she in fact insisted that "even if it [the soul] were to see the heavens opened, [that] would not cause it to budge an inch from the Church's teachings" (Peers 238, 239). Thus, orthodoxy helps define orthopathos. In addition, practically speaking, she asserted that, if a soul sees a false vision, "it then becomes troubled, despondent and restless; loses the devotion and joy which it had before; and is unable to pray" (Peers 264). Thus, Teresa of Avila had tests for her own religious visions through orthopraxis as well, and these tests helped her to distinguish genuine from false experiences.

Orthodoxy may help us define orthopathos.

It seems, then, that, at least in this case of a Christian mystic, a religious experience, however powerful individually, should not contradict the teachings of the religion and, especially, of scripture itself. Some cases of how such tests can be or should have been applied can be drawn from a fascinating comparison of two other Christian mystics, Meister Eckhart (1260–1329) and Julian of Norwich (1342–1416). We have already noted earlier in this chapter that Meister Eckhart began to declare that Jesus had been reborn in his soul, and indeed that his own soul *was* the Son of God. To this, the orthodox teachers of the Church said, "No, you are mistaken!" "We do not deny that you may have had a powerful experience of God," the authorities might have said, "but you must be misunderstanding your own experience if it urges you to contradict the uniqueness of God." Similarly, Lady Julian had dramatic visions of Christ's love, feeling that love so intensely that she said she must never have sinned at all. However, in her careful orthodoxy, she declared that, of course that could not be true, since the Church and scripture teach otherwise. Thus, she changed the interpretation of her own experience to fit the teachings of her religion. She finally declared that her experience taught her Christ's love so deeply that it is *as if* she had never sinned. She said herself, "Yet in all things I believe as Holy Church preacheth and teacheth. . . . It was my will and meaning never to accept anything that could be contrary thereto. With this intent and with this meaning I behold the shewing [the visions] with all my diligence" (Walsh 61–62).

The point of this comparison is to suggest how Lady Julian, at least more so than Meister Eckhardt, exemplified the principle of challenging and interpreting one's own religious experience from within the orthodoxy of a religion. At least in religions where "straight belief" is important, it becomes reasonable that religious experience can be tested by conformity with higher authority. Thus, even today a devout Catholic might be guided to test his or her experiences of God by consistency with what the saints of old and the scriptures of the Church have taught.

There are means for testing religious experience even in religions not stressing orthodoxy.

Even in religions where "orthodoxy" is not so strictly enforced, and yet where religious experiences are and must be taken seriously, there can be traditional specific methods wherewith an experience can be tested for genuineness. For example, in the Zen tradition, one cannot merely stand up and claim to have experienced *satori* (enlightenment). The traditional relationship between the master and the student is precisely designed to offer teaching *and* to test the student's genuine understanding. The *koan*—odd questions, like "What is the sound of one hand clapping?"—are given to Zen students by their teachers as a focus of meditation and as a restraint on rationalization. However, they are not just games of intellect; they are rather exercises for training and creating religious sensitivity and, ultimately, religious insight. Thus, when the student has "seen through" the *koan*, discovered the transrational answer in the pure insight of enlightenment, he or she will claim to have had *satori*, the ineffable experience of Buddhist enlightenment. Yet this experience is not entirely unverifiable, for the teacher can, in some sense, verify the experience by seeing if the student has the "right" answer. So when the student comes before the teacher and is asked, "What is the sound of one hand clapping?," the master, whose mind already (we presume) sees with purity beyond reasoning, can tell if the student is struggling with mundane reasoning or if he or she truly sees with the Buddha Mind. In addition, when a student breaks through to genuine wisdom, the master will know it.

Religious experi-ence must pass the test of doc-trine, of scripture, and of higher authority in gen-eral.

These are examples of how religious experience can be tested and authorized by doctrine and by the higher wisdom of teachers. It seems evident that no mat-ter how powerful some personal experience might be, it should fit into the tradi-tion in which it occurs. And although it may seem strange to us that someone could say, "No, you don't really have a headache," it is not entirely strange that, from within a religious tradition, a teacher or some other higher authority can say, "No, you did not really experience the religious reality you think you saw." Such "testing" of religious experience may seem odd, but it may also be quite consistent with the internal coherence of established religion.

GLOBALIZATION, EXPERIENCING THE WORLD, AND THE ENVIRONMENT

The ongoing interplay among concepts, experience, and action has been a con-sistent theme in this chapter. We have noted that how one understands the world and its relation to the Sacred goes a long way in determining how a person (or a society) experiences and acts in the world. Nowhere is this phenomenon more apparent than when looking at contemporary ecological issues.

biosphere—those ecological systems necessary to sup-port life on this planet

Human activities associated with globalization are having a negative impact on the biosphere.

The human race is a "community of fate" that is in danger of having no future at all.

Modernization and globalization are processes that have had a tremendously detrimental impact on the biosphere, or those ecological systems that are neces-sary to support life on this planet. Human economic activity, industrial and agri-cultural pollution, the burning of fossil fuels, and the strain on resources pro-duced by ever-increasing population have combined to undermine the very biological systems that make life possible. These phenomena have locked human-ity in what political scientists David Held and Anthony McGrew call a "com-munity of fate" (40). That is, with the threat to the biosphere, all humans regard-less of nationality, religion, or gender are part of a single race whose future is not too bright. In fact, the activities associated with modern global society are so damaging that we humans are in danger of having no future at all.

Though ecological problems are widely discussed in a variety of disciplines, in this text we need to understand the interaction of religion with environmental concerns. In order to accomplish this, we must answer two questions: (1) Has religion somehow contributed to the current ecological crisis by affecting how people experience and act in the world? (2) Do religions have anything to offer in solving these problems? To begin to answer these questions, we draw upon materials mentioned earlier in this chapter regarding religious understanding and acting in the world. We also draw upon a number of concepts regarding globalization outlined in the first chapter (Religion in Global Society), including the two Axial Periods, the stress on rationalism along with rational instrumentality, the "dead" universe, reenchanting the universe, "communing" with nature, and so on.

The dominant paradigm associated with the Modern Period tends to view the universe as "dead" matter that has no sacred significance.

The dominant paradigm associated with the Modern Period tends to view the universe as "dead" matter that has no sacred significance. This has combined with rational instrumentality to make people believe that humans are superior to nature and that the sole purpose of nature is to serve human interests. So forests can be cut down, species made extinct, fisheries harvested to the last fish, insects poisoned, rivers dammed, mountains moved, canals dug, and the genetic structure of plants and animals altered. All of this may be done if it seems to serve the short-ranged purposes of people without regard to what impact these activities have on nature and ecological systems. Certainly, as modern ways of thinking have spread through globalization, the influence of Western ideas have extended far beyond the societies in which they originated.

Religion has played a key role in this spread and the subsequent environmental degradation. This is especially true of Christianity. As this dominant model became more prevalent, Christianity found support for its activities. For instance, in the Judeo-Christian perspective, humans are pictured as creatures (created beings), but they are at the peak of creation (the highest creature) as they alone are capable of communing with God. In essence, humans are at the crossroads between the material universe and the sacred cosmos since their bodies are matter and their souls are spirit. This distinction suggests a "lofty position," which is made even more significant by scriptural references like those found in the biblical book of Genesis where God is pictured as telling Adam and Eve: "Be fruitful, and multiply and fill the earth, and subdue it; and have dominion over the fish of the sea and over the birds of the air, and over every living thing that moves upon the earth" (Genesis 1:28).

Unfortunately, as Christianity interacted with emerging modernism, the sense of sacredness of the universe was lost. People also lost the sense that they were somehow embedded in nature—a condition that is implied in the Genesis accounts where people are "creatures" alongside other creatures in God's holy order. People were no longer seen as being part of the natural world but were separated from and above nature. The changing religious consciousness of humans' place in the spiritual and material worlds led people to interpret this indicative to "subdue the earth" as giving humans a free hand to use and abuse the material world. In essence, the dominant religious thinking encouraged humans to experience nature as "dead" and machinelike. It encouraged them to exploit nature without empathy or without understanding that destroying the natural world might have negative consequences for them as well. This tendency was enhanced by the rise of modern science, which stressed the objective over the subjective and encouraged humans to view themselves as detached objective observers of and masters over the material realm.

Historically, both Christianity and science have contributed to the notion that the universe is a "dead" thing to be manipulated.

It is common to trace this emphasis on dominion over nature to the rationalization of both religion and secular thinking that occurred through the European Renaissance and Enlightenment periods. However, religious writer Ewert

Cousins believes that the roots of the "dead" universe extend to the First Axial Period, where religions departed from the tribal religions' emphasis on living in harmony with nature in a spiritual universe.

Cousins believes that the roots for the separation of the material from the spiritual lies in the First Axial Period, when humans moved from religions based on achieving an experienced harmony with nature to those that focused on "heaven" (the spiritual) to the neglect of the "earth" (the material). He argues that for "some traditions this emergence of spiritual energy [released in the First Axial Period] caused a radical split between the phenomenal world and true reality, between matter and spirit, between earth and heaven" (162). This separation was made even more profound by the rise of science that ignores the spiritual altogether and focuses solely on the material. Thus, nature is detached from its living sacred base and becomes a dead material "thing" to be manipulated.

So these are some of the changes (many based in religious traditions) that got us into this contemporary ecological predicament; now what do we do about it? Should religion be involved in the solution to our problems? Does religion have anything special to offer in dealing with ecological issues? James Miller, a professor of East Asian Traditions, argues that religion is and must be deeply involved in the resolution of environmental issues. He notes,

> *What is necessary . . . is a way of revisioning the relationships that obtain between human beings and their environment. The goal of such a revisioning should be that human-earth relationships are viewed not solely as economic relationships in which what is important is how we obtain economic goods from the environment. Nor should these relationships be viewed solely as technical-scientific relationships that understand the fact of human interaction with the environment but not the moral value of such interactions. (1)*

An ecumenization and globalization of spiritual consciousness is underway that may provide a ground for dealing with our ethical responsibility toward the material world.

Instead, Miller argues that such a revisioning must be rooted in religions and the ethical systems related to them. What is needed is a new spiritual consciousness, which in fact is emerging. "The ecumenization and globalization of spiritual consciousness is one path that is opening up the possibility of practical ethical reasoning that is capable of dealing with the way in which we [are] transforming both negatively and positively the nature of our relationship with our very environmental matrix, our planetary mother" (3).

This transformation of spiritual consciousness does not eliminate diverse opinions for religious traditions but magnifies them.

Cousins believes that this new spiritual consciousness is part and parcel of the Second Axial Period now under way. Following Pierre Teilhard de Chardin, Cousins believes, "This new global consciousness will not level all differences among peoples; rather it [will] generate . . . creative unions in which diversity is not erased but intensified" (163). The resulting creative unions will cause "dialogic dialogue" where religions are forced to dig deep into their own religious traditions as well as to struggle with insights from other traditions as they seek to solve the pressing problems of humankind.

Cousins maintains,

> *We must recapture the unity of tribal consciousness by seeing humanity as a single tribe. And we must see this tribe related organically to the total cosmos. This means that the consciousness of the twenty-first century will be global from two perspectives: (1) from a horizontal perspective, cultures and religions must meet each other on the surface of the globe, entering into*

creative encounters that will produce a complexified collective conscious-ness; (2) from a vertical perspective they must plunge their roots deep into the earth in order to provide a secure base for future development. This new global consciousness must be organically ecological, supported by struc-tures that will insure justice and peace. (166)

The solutions to our ecological crises lie in a spiri-tual base that places humans in an organic web of life in an alive and sacred cosmos.

Thus, the solutions to our ecological crises must have a spiritual base that places humans within the organic web of life that reestablishes both the living and sacred nature of the cosmos. It is this reenchanted universe where humans do not seek to dominate nature but to live in harmony with the material world. It is this reenchanted universe where humans do not separate themselves from the natural world but embrace and commune with the material that offers the best possibility of successfully meeting our ecological challenges. Such a new global religious consciousness may cause humans to experience the universe differently and encourage them to act more positively in the world.

CONCLUSION

Religious experi-ences may be sub-jective in force but objective in con-tent.

Religious experi-ences may be so powerful that they drive a person outside of his or her religious tradi-tion into forming a new one alto-gether.

Religious experiences, in general, are powerful and personal. They seem often to be inherently subjective in force but apparently objective in content. That is, per-haps, why religious traditions of orthodoxy and orthopraxis often offer ways of helping to define what is a "proper" experience, what is "orthopathos." But of course, such tests and restraints on new and powerful religious experiences might fail. That is, a person might have a new and dramatic religious experience that failed to conform to previously accepted standards of doctrine or action, yet the one who is challenged might insist that the experience was valid even if it does not fit into the tradition. But when this occurs, we will find that the new experi-ence will drive the person out of his or her original religious tradition, and it is possible that a new and different religion is in the making. Consider, for exam-ple, the experiences of Joseph Smith or the Buddha. For both of these men, their new insights and visions were so new and so powerful that they broke from the original doctrine and started new religions. Thus, Buddhism emerged from Hinduism and Mormonism came from Christianity.

For those not sure of tradition and not bold enough to be new founders, the primary test of the meaning and validity of one's experience is tradition. Having had some great experience or even some more common and gentle inner feeling, one might (or should) ask what that experience seems to indicate, given the beliefs and practices that are described and historically common within a reli-gion. Shall I understand my subjective experience as forgiveness of sin, peace and oneness, ontological union with God, as *satori,* or as something else? One can be guided in such a question by whether specific interpretations are consistent with the given religious tradition. Is ontological union with God usually accepted by Christianity? In Islam? Probably not. In Hinduism? Almost certainly.

One might also simply choose to take on a certain amount of self-doubt and test the experience philosophically. Given some kind of "vision" of God, one can still ask if there are reasons to believe beyond the experience. What does belief in God imply in other areas of life? Does it make sense? For example, what does

*"Test the spirits."
Not everything
that feels like God
is God.*

ontological oneness with God (Brahman, Tao) imply in other areas of life? Can I live this way? The point here is that asking questions about others' and our own religious experience *can* be done. Indeed, it may even be necessary, though perhaps not comfortable. Thus, in the New Testament Christian church, converts were encouraged to "test the spirits." Not everything that feels like God *is* God.

At the same time, perhaps one should not, we have noted, take an exclusively skeptical attitude toward religious experience. It is presumptuous, and somewhat betrays our phenomenological approach, for us to try to stand utterly outside religious life and treat religious experience like some distant psychological aberration to be studied in a clinic. This is the quandary, the perplexity, of the whole issue. It would be easy just to accept all such experience as wonderful and "true" in some vague or subjective sense. It would be equally easy just to dismiss them all as some kind of mental illness or drug trip. The skeptic must realize that such experience brings all the religious talk—the myths and stories, the doctrines and beliefs, and even the ritual and morality—down to the inner core of individual life. Religious experience makes religion personal, makes it alive. Thus, as we have seen from the beginning of this text, religious experience is important, even indispensable. But the believer must, at the same time, realize that such experience will claim to be self-validating, while it may be self-induced or inconsistent. Therefore, religious experience is both vital and dangerous.

For our purposes in this text, the final job of weighing out the issue of the meaning and value of religious experience rests with the student. Which side of this perplexity shall I embrace? And why? Shall I tend to look at all religious experience as justified, even self-justifying? Or shall I adopt an intentional, overall skepticism about any religious feelings? Shall I or can I apply this acceptance or skepticism equally to my own experiences and the experiences of others?

Beyond the purely personal, how will my answer to these questions influence my relation to others and the world in which I live? Can I or must I change my understanding of where I fit into the spiritual and material worlds? Will a significant change in religious consciousness translate into the kind of activity in the world necessary to prevent ecological disaster? These are important questions to pose to ourselves. How we will answer these difficult and even dangerous questions may have profound impact on our personal religious experience and the world in which we live.

■ INTERACTIVE EXERCISE

Please continue your exploration of religious experience by going to the interactive exercise online (**http://www.religion.wadsworth.com/richter**).

WORKS CITED

Ahmed, Akbar S. *Discovering Islam.* New York: Routledge, 1992.

Avila, Teresa of. *The Interior Castle.* New York: Paulist, 1979.

Begley, Sharon, with Anne Underwood. *Newsweek.* May 7, 2001. http://www .American-buddha.com/religion.begley.htm (accessed February 19, 2004).

"Buddhism: Footprint of the Buddha." Video. Ed. David Thomas. London: BBC, 1973-1977.

Comstock, Gary L. *Religious Autobiographies*. Belmont, CA: Wadsworth, 1995.

Cousins, Ewert. "Religions on the Eve of the Twenty-first Century." In *The Community of Religions: Voices and Images of the Parliament of the World's Religions*. Eds. Wayne Teasdale and George Cairns. New York: Continuum, 1996.

Dickens, Charles. *A Christmas Carol*. St. Louis, MO: MCE Publishing, 1996.

Eckhart, Meister. *Meister Eckhart: Essential Sermons, Commentaries, Treatises, and Defense*. New York: Paulist Press, 1981.

Eliade, Mirceau. *Yoga, Immortality and Freedom*. Princeton, NJ: Princeton University Press, 1969.

Ernst, Carl W. *Sufism*. London: Shambala Press, 1977.

Esposito, John L. *Islam: The Straight Path*. Oxford, UK: Oxford University Press, 1998.

Friedlander, Ira. *The Whirling Dervishes*. New York: Macmillan, 1975.

Graham, Billy. *How to Be Born Again*. Waco, TX: Word Books, 1977.

Held, David, and Anthony McGrew. *Globalization./Antiglobalization*. Oxford, UK: Polity Press, 2002.

James, William. *The Varieties of Religious Experience*. 1902. New York: Macmillan, 1961.

Leys, Simon (trans.). *The Analects of Confucius*. New York: Bantam Books, 1997.

Lings, Martin. *What Is Sufism?* Berkeley: University of California Press, 1977.

Mascaro, Juan. *The Upanishads*. London: Penguin, 1965.

Mayeda, Sengaku. *A Thousand Teachings: The Upadesasahasri of Sankara*. Albany: State University of New York Press, 1992.

Miller, James. *World Religions and Global Climate Change*. http://rels.queensu.ca/jm/pubs.climate_change.htm (accessed August 6, 2003).

Olivelle, Patrick. *Upanishads*. Oxford, UK: Oxford University Press, 1996.

Peers, E. Allison. *The Autobiography of St. Theresa of Avila*. Garden City, NY: Doubleday Image Books, 1960.

Peters, F. E. *A Reader on Classical Islam*. Princeton, NJ: Princeton University Press, 1994.

Prabhavananda, Swami, and Frederick Manchester. *The Upanishads*. New York: Mentor Books, 1957.

Pudney, John. *John Wesley and His World*. New York: Scribner's, 1978.

Robinson, Richard H., and Willard L. Johnson. *The Buddhist Religion: A Historical Introduction*. 4th ed. Belmont, CA: Wadsworth, 1997.

Stewart, Omer C. *Peyote Religion*. Norman: University of Oklahoma Press, 1987.

Stryk, Lucien. *The World of the Buddha*. New York: Grove Weidenfeld, 1968.

Suzuki, D. T. *Zen Buddhism*. Garden City, NY: Doubleday Anchor Books, 1956.

Suzuki, Shrunyu. *Zen Mind, Beginner's Mind*. New York: Weatherhill, 1980.

Walsh, James. *The Revelations of Divine Love of Julian of Norwich*. St. Meinrad, IN: Abbey, 1975.

Warren, Henry Clarke. *Buddhism in Translations*. New York: Athaneum, 1982.

Watson, Burton (trans.). *Chuang Tzu: Basic Writings*. New York: Columbia University Press, 1964.

Weisheipl, James A. *Friar Thomas D'aquino*. Garden City, NY: Doubleday, 1974.

Zaehner, R. C. *Hinduism*. London: Oxford University Press, 1962.

FOR FURTHER READING

Eckhart, Meister. *Meister Eckhart: Essential Sermons, Commentaries, Treatises, and Defense*. New York: Paulist Press, 1981.

Held, David and Anthony McGrew. *Globalization./Antiglobalization*. Oxford, UK: Polity Press, 2002.

James, William. *The Varieties of Religious Experience*. 1902. New York: Macmillan, 1961.

Miller, James. *World Religions and Global Climate Change*. http://rels.queensu.ca/jm/pubs.climate_change.htm (accessed August 6, 2003).

Suzuki, D. T. *Zen Buddhism*. Garden City, NY: Doubleday Anchor Books, 1956.

Suzuki, Shrunyu. *Zen Mind, Beginner's Mind*. New York: Weatherhill, 1980.

Teasdale, Wayne, and George F. Cairns, eds. *The Community of Religions: Voices and Images of the Parliament of the World's Religions*. New York: Continuum, 1996.

Underhill, Evelyn. *Mysticism*. Oxford, UK: Oneworld, 1999.

12 SALVATION AND THE MEANING OF LIFE

Getty Images/PhotoDisc Collection

The picture found above and those on the Web site (**http://www.religion .wadsworth.com/richter**), although the following scriptural quotations suggest some very different religious views of what the ultimate purpose or goal of human life and human spirituality might be. They might also suggest different views on how to achieve that goal. Please look over these pictures and passages, and then consider the Introductory Questions that follow as a way to prepare for reading this chapter.

> *The sage leans on the sun and moon, tucks the universe under*
> *his arm, merges himself with things, leaves the confusion and*
> *muddle as it is, and looks on slaves as exalted. Ordinary men*
> *strain and struggle; the sage is stupid and blockish. He takes*

part in ten thousand ages and achieves simplicity and oneness. For him, all the ten thousand things are what they are, and thus they enfold each other.

—Taoism: Chuang Tzu (Watson 42)

The cessation of craving leads successively to that of grasping, of becoming, of birth, of old age and death, of grief, lamentation, pain, sadness and despair—that is to say to the cessation of all this mass of ill. It is thus that cessation is Nirvana.

—Buddhism: Questions of King Malinda (Conze 156)

These are they who are drawn nigh (to Allah), In the gardens of bliss. . . . On thrones decorated, Reclining on them, facing one another. Round about them shall go youths never altering in age, With goblets and ewers and a cup of pure drink; . . . And fruits such as they choose, And the flesh of fowl such as they desire. And pure, beautiful ones, The like of the hidden pearls: A reward for what they used to do.

—Islam: Holy Koran 56:11–23

Good Thunder now took one of my arms, Kicking Bear the other, and we began to dance. The song we sang was like this: "Who do you think he is that comes? It is one who sees his mother!" It is what the dead would sing when entering the other world and looking for their relatives who had gone there before them.

—Native American Religion: Black Elk Speaks (Neihardt 240)

For by grace you have been saved through faith, and this is not your own doing; it is the gift of God—not the result of works, so that no one may boast.

—Christianity: Ephesians 2:8–9

By the purified mind alone is the indivisible Brahman to be attained. Brahman alone is—nothing else is. He who sees the manifold universe, and not the one reality, goes evermore from death to death.

—Hinduism: Katha Upanishad (Prabhavananda and Manchester 21)

INTRODUCTORY QUESTIONS

1. The Islamic depiction of heaven in the third quotation is rather sensual, even sexual. Does this seem ideal as the literal, ultimate goal of religious salvation? How would you interpret such a depiction? Contrast it with Black Elk meeting his ancestors.

2. The famous picture from the Sistine Chapel shows the "Final Judgment," in which people are taken to heaven or to hell, based upon divine judgment. Do the ideas of heaven and hell seem fair to you? Does it seem mean of a god to condemn, or is it merely "justice" ?

3. How is Nirvana described in the Buddhist work? Do you think this is another way to describe the kind of heaven we find in the Islamic or Christian stories? How is it different? Is it attractive?

4. The Taoist idea described in the first quotation seems to be concerned with a free and easy life. Similarly, the depiction of the Chinese gods shows the ideal values of Prosperity, Longevity, and Posterity. Are such ideals "religious" ? What do they suggest about "Western" conceptions of heaven or hell?

5. What do you think St. Paul means by "grace" in the fifth quotation? What is the point of his contrasting it with "works"? Compare both concepts to the "purified mind" described in the Upanishads. What is achieved by these three things? How are they different?

6. One may find a kind of sensuality in the Islamic depiction of heaven, and the Taoist image of a free life may seem very worldly. Now look at the Wheel of Life. Note that for the Buddhist, all life, including the five realms of rebirth (depicted in the circle), are held in the claws of the demon of time. Generally, is the world something we should seek to escape from, or are its pleasures something religions should help us achieve?

7. In the "Final Judgment" picture, you get a sense that we all have one chance to make it into heaven or not. Yet the picture of reincarnation suggests lifetime after lifetime. Can you reconcile these views of life? How do they change one's view of the afterlife?

SALVATION AND THE MEANING OF LIFE

It should be evident by now that there is a great diversity of religious views on many issues that affect human life in various ways. We have seen in previous chapters the discussions of morality and ritual, art and experience, philosophy and language and scripture, and throughout the whole text these issues have been intimately interwoven with concepts of "the Absolute" as interpreted and described in the great religions of the world. We have seen moreover—as is evident even to a cursory look at world demographics or the local news—that religions change people's lives and that often these traditions, beliefs, and practices are the most formative parts of culture. It is no wonder that the issues of religion that we have considered all have significant effects on, and are significantly affected by, the reality of globalization.

But for all the power and relevance of religion across the globe, we might well come this far in our study with a general question: So what is the point? We might be asking why anyone should be religious in any way, or, more cynically perhaps, what is the ultimate payoff of the religious life. This question need not be quite so economic-sounding; it might rather be the very real question about the final goal and ultimate meaning of religious life. And since religious life is so often at the core of culture and human experience, it might be the question about the meaning of life in general.

Religions try to answer questions about the meaning of life.

An old cartoon depicts a student in a philosophy class saying to the professor, "This question on the meaning of life, is it essay or true-false?" The point of such humor, of course, is that the question itself seems necessarily to demand a kind of explanation. When one asks for "the meaning of life," what really is the question? "Why am I alive?" might be answered merely biologically, as if the question were merely concerned with how or why my parents conceived me. More likely, however, it is about what gives life its meaning, what makes life significant. In that sense, it is a question about the connection between life and some presumed object or goal. Thus, there is an attachment of the notion of "meaning" to something else. For our text, of course, the "something else" is "the Absolute," as we have seen it connected with many other aspects of life many times already. And here indeed, there is likely a logical connection between what one means by the "meaning" of life and what one considers Ultimate Reality.

What a person considers the meaning of life is related to how one conceives Ultimate Reality.

Indeed, we might proceed in a kind of logical discussion of religion as we proceeded when we first considered and defined the Sacred. In Chapter 3, we noted that sacredness in some objects (like the common wood of a statue or the water of Baptism) seems to be derived from something "higher," something more holy. That is, the wood or the water in itself is not holy, but it is made holy by something else, which in turn may be made holy by another. But ultimately, we suggested the sacredness of everything within a religious tradition may have to find its derivation from that which is sacred in itself, from "the Holy." In a similar way, in this chapter we might expect that "meaning," certainly an obscure notion in itself, needs to be defined precisely by the connection of life to the Absolute. "What is the meaning of life?" we ask. Religiously, we answer that it is a life made holy by its connection to the Holy.

For religion, the "meaning of life" is rooted in being connected to the Sacred.

The point of this definition is not to demean any nonreligious conceptions of the meaning of life. Indeed, there are certainly nonreligious ways of describing the meaning of life, from a personal dedication to a moral ideal or working to bring about a Marxist "classless society," or even some idealized hope to get drunk and have sex as much as is humanly possible. One might well pursue a philosophical debate about such conceptions of "meaning," considering whether they are honest or adequate, or perhaps too limited or demeaning. But such a debate would clearly be beyond the scope of this textbook. For our purposes, we may only need to presume that religious views of life describe "meaning" through their connection to the Absolute. Given that the Absolute is the Ultimate Being to religion, it is only reasonable to assume that finding a connection to the Absolute is the ultimate goal, the "meaning," of being religious.

The notion of finding a "connection to the Absolute," however, may be a bit vague. Thus, we may go on and describe what *kind* of "connection" we find in the various religions of the world. That is, we should be concerned within religion about what "connection to the Absolute" means. How shall we describe it? How is it achieved? Indeed, as we pursue such questions, we might find that the right kind of connection to the Sacred in one religion is as easy as praying; in another, it may require years, or even lifetimes, of meditation. In one religion, the "connec-tion" may be taken for granted, simply given with birth, while in another religion our connection with the Absolute may be obscure and difficult, as if the Ultimate Being is far away and inaccessible to all but the most holy human effort. We might in fact find that in many religions, the ultimate and perfected relation to the Holy cannot even be achieved in this life but awaits a kind of final perfection in death.

It may seem ironic that we can suggest seeking the ideal meaning of *life* only after life ends. Shall we presume that "heaven" or "final nirvana" can occur only in the "afterlife"? Certainly, for many religious people this is taken for granted. Nevertheless, as we will find, there are other religions that question this pre-sumption, and we have already mentioned the fact that many simply materialis-tic or "down to earth" people (like our Marxist or the "get drunk and have sex" person) might more readily insist on the meaning of life in *this* world. At the same time, we have seen in previous chapters—concerning ethics, the problem of evil, and so on—that there is a common notion in many religions that the world as we know it is not quite right. Consequently, in many religions, we return to the clear presumption that, whatever the nature of our current, earthly existence, and however good it might be, this world is not enough. And so, religions all over the world—though to different extents and in different ways—consider the afterlife.

When we think about the afterlife as the idea of a perfected relation to the Holy that is finally realized after death, we begin at last to suggest the concept of salva-tion. And indeed, "salvation" broadly understood could be a proper title for the ultimate goal of any religion. But as we have seen throughout this book, "broadly understood" means that we cannot immediately assume some Christian or Islamic notion of salvation that takes for granted the idea of a heavenly paradise populated by the believers who have "lived a good life." If "salvation" seems immediately to raise in one's mind the idea that "if you're good, you go to heaven," then salvation has not been "broadly understood." That is, this particular concept of salvation is only one of many, and we will find that in some religions, salvation has nothing to do with "heaven." And indeed, it may have little to do with "being good."

So for now let us indeed consider "salvation" very "broadly," as in a series of very different explanations and possibilities. In technical language, an integrated theory of what salvation means and how it is achieved can be called soteriology. From the Greek word for "savior" (*soter*) it implies that we will study a religion's salvation ideas as a coherent theory, an effort to discuss consistently how one is saved and what one is saved to. And we shall close by considering if this "salva-tion" might indeed be the ideal state of being for the religious person, for exam-ple, the meaning of life.

SOTERIOLOGICAL GOALS

The Greek philosopher Aristotle, and behind him a long line of important Western philosophers, argued that there can be only one ultimate goal of human action. If we ask why we behave in specific ways, we ultimately trace back our reasons to a final goal, an "end in itself." Thus, if we ask why we go to class, it might be in order to get course credit, and those credits in turn are for graduation, and graduation for getting a job, and getting a job for making money. But in the end, Aristotle argued, we all act for one end: happiness (Aristotle 316ff).

We might debate such a claim, of course, or it might seem obvious. In either case, it remains to be discussed exactly what makes for human happiness. Here we might well court a kind of subjectivism that just imagines anyone saying, "Happiness is whatever makes me happy." But this is again a rather trivial and unhelpful thing to say. Also, it may distract us from the greater issue, one that intrigued Aristotle as well as most religious thinkers: What *should* be the ultimate goal of humanity be? Thus, for Aristotle it was important to study human nature and to find out what qualities of human life should make for a healthy and happy human existence. It is a matter open for discussion, of course, but it is not a matter of arbitrary feelings.

In religion especially, we are offered some real answers to what makes for a full and happy existence. It is not merely a matter of being in a good mood: Indeed, even for Aristotle happiness could not mean only some extended state of being stoned, like a drug addict happily locked inside a cocaine dealer's house. Such a perpetually stoned life might be "pleasant" (as well as brief) to the addict, but it is also pitiful. For such a person failed to be what a person *can* be, and what a person *should* be. He may have been "happy," but he was not living a good life, a fulfilled and blessed existence.

In contrast, religions urge us to look for an ultimate ideal way of being, and they promise us a way of finding that life. It may indeed be a life outside of this world, but as we have already noted, we cannot presume that all religions teach, "If you're good, you go to heaven." For some religions, the ideal existence is very much within this world and is not expected merely after death. Commonly, teachers of religion have distinguished between "this-worldly" and "otherworldly" soteriological goals, such as those that emphasize an ultimate fulfillment of religious life before death and within the world, versus those who find the ultimate fulfillment in the afterlife or in some other kind of existence.

■ THIS-WORLDLY SALVATION

A great example of "this-worldly" religious goals is evident in Chinese religions. We have noted in Chapter 10, dealing with religious ethics, that Confucianism is a religion that emphasizes the rituals and virtues that create in us good character and create around us a healthy, prosperous society. Confucianism, we said, finds the model of all human relationships and of the virtuous human heart in the ideal of the Tao of Heaven. We see, then, that Confucianism, quite "religious" in its ultimate appeal to the Tao, is nevertheless focused almost entirely on what kind of person we become in this life. Indeed, Confucius himself rather famously asked the rhetorical question: "You are not yet able to serve men, how could you serve the spirits? . . . You do not yet know life, how could you know death?" (Leys 50) His point seems to be that the real issues of religious life are focused here on earth in our relations with the living. He would say indeed that our real religious duty is not to secure some otherworldly relation to gods and spirits but to become an excellent person here in a this-worldly life.

In religion we are given many answers about what makes a happy and full existence.

Religions can be defined as "this-worldly" or "otherworldly" depending on their soteriological goals.

"This-worldly salvation" is found in Confucianism.

For Confucius, as
for Aristotle, the
focus of salvation
is the cultivated
character and per-
sonal excellence.

For Confucius, the this-worldly goal of religious life might be encapsulated in the concept of the *Chun-tzu,* translated as the "gentleman" or the "superior man." Although the expression seems to focus on men in particular, as if moral excellence were an exclusively male quality, the point here, as it was for Aristotle, is to live a life of cultivated character and personal excellence. One follows the Tao of Heaven, according to Confucius, as the guide to how to live in relation to others, how to respect them, how to serve them properly, and how to develop integrity of character. And again, "Heaven" here refers not to the afterlife or to some other realm of spiritual existence but to the natural cosmic order of this world, and thus to how we as humans should behave. In the same way, therefore, one does not become the "superior person" in order to earn salvation in some distant other world but in order to live fully and blessedly here in this world. Recall that we depicted at the opening of this chapter three Chinese gods and that these deities represented not life in a heaven beyond the world but the very this-worldly ideals of prosperity, posterity, and longevity.

Not surprisingly, we would find a similar this-worldliness in the Taoist approach to an ideal life. Given that the Tao, the Way of Heaven, is met in the common flow of change in nature, the life of a true sage, according to Taoism, is to live life in harmony with the changes of time. The Tao Te Ching says, "In following the Tao, each day something is lost. Lost and again lost. Until there is nothing left to do. Not-doing, nothing is left undone. You can possess the world by never manipulating it" (McIntyre Chapter 48). This seems to claim that real wisdom lies in giving in to the flow of nature, following its way with "not doing." The result, then, is to "possess the world." In many of his famous parables, the Taoist writer Chuang Tzu emphasized that life lived simply and happily is the ideal goal of one who truly knows the Way. In one story, Chuang Tzu was asked to help rule a kingdom, but he refused.

In Taoism, the goal
is giving in to the
"flow of nature"
and thus, to live
life simply and
happily.

> *"I have heard that there is a sacred tortoise in Ch'u that has been dead for three thousand years. The king keeps it wrapped in cloth and boxed, and stores it in the ancestral temple. Now would this tortoise rather be dead and have its bones left behind and honored? Or would it rather be alive and dragging its tail in the mud?"*
>
> *"It would rather be alive and dragging its tail in the mud," said the two officials.*
>
> *Chuang-tzu said, "Go away! I'll drag my tail in the mud." (Watson 109)*

"This-worldly sal-
vation" is also
found in Judaism.

A similar, but perhaps more surprising example might be in the rather this-worldly notion of religious blessing we find in Judaism. The surprise here might be due to the fact that Judaism is, of course, the historical root of both Christianity and Islam, in which religions we find an apparently emphatic focus on heaven after death (as we shall discuss shortly). We might therefore have expected that Judaism would have emphasized salvation unto heaven, as did its offspring religions. But in fact, many Jews urge that our concern for the ideal religious life is here and now. Much like Confucius, the Baal Shem Tov, the founder of Hasidic Judaism, said, "If I can love God here and now, why do I need to worry about the life of the world to come?" (Borowitz 228)

To study this notion further within Judaism, we might look at the paradigm case of Abraham himself. This Patriarch, the one chosen by God to be the father of the whole Jewish people, was called into the "covenant," an agreement between him and God requiring devotion to, and the exclusive worship of, the one true God. Abraham, in return for his devotion, is not promised an afterlife of any kind, apparently. Rather, the covenant explicitly promises Abraham worldly blessings of land and progeny. "I will surely bless you," said God to Abraham, "and make your descendants as numerous as the stars in the sky and as the sand on the seashore. Your descendants will take possession of the cities of their enemies, and through your offspring all nations on earth will be blessed, because you have obeyed me." And finally, when Abraham dies, the scriptures rather unimpressively declare only that "Abraham was gathered to his people" (see Genesis 22:17–18 and 25:8).

As Judaism developed, an otherworldly concept of salvation also emerged.

This is not to say that there is no sense of "otherworldly" salvation in Judaism. As this religion evolves, it clearly seems to develop more and more a sense of otherworldliness, perhaps especially in response to the exile of the sixth century BCE. It is here that we find the great visions of Daniel and his prophecies of the end of the world. Thus, the angel tells Daniel:

But at that time your people shall be delivered, everyone who is found written in the book. Many of those who sleep in the dust of the earth shall awake, some to everlasting life, and some to shame and everlasting contempt. Those who are wise shall shine like the brightness of the sky, and those who lead many to righteousness, like the stars forever and ever. (Daniel 12:1–3)

From here the discussion within Judaism arises about the nature of the afterlife and about the resurrection of the dead. It is a discussion, interestingly, that appears even in the Christian scriptures as a point still disputed by teachers of Judaism. Some time after the death of Jesus, the Christian St. Paul was on trial before the Jewish council, when he referred to life after death and got the Jewish teachers to start arguing among themselves (see Acts 23:6–8).

By now, much Jewish teaching takes for granted the belief in the afterlife as a basic tenet of Judaism. But whether Judaism remains entirely this-worldly or not, the point so far has been to stress that religions around the world certainly do not always presume to find their ideal spiritual state in the afterlife. For many, the ideal result of spiritual practice, obedience, and wisdom is life here, in this world. Thus, one practices religion not in hopes of dying and going to heaven. Rather, it is more like the hope of the Vulcans in a *Star Trek* movie: "Live long and prosper."

■ OTHERWORLDLY SALVATION

"Otherworldly salvation" is a key principle in Christianity.

With Christianity itself, of course, there is no question about the final goal and its otherworldly character. With the death and resurrection of Jesus himself, Christianity finds an emphasis not necessarily on how successful life may be in this world but on the promise of heaven and an ultimate salvation in the presence of God. Jesus explicitly declares at his trial that his kingdom is "not of this world," and he just as explicitly promises his followers that he is going "to prepare a place" for them in heaven (see John 18:36 and 14:2). Many times he draws a contrast between what can be gained in this life only by losing the blessings of the next life, and with his self-sacrificial death and his reappearance to his disciples, this ideal otherworldliness is ideally exemplified. That is why early Christians could "rejoice" in their suffering and persecution, assured that later, they would be "overjoyed" by the presence of Jesus' glory (I Peter 4:13). That is also why Paul himself was torn between his desire to serve people on earth and his desire to be with Christ after death, saying, "For to me, living is Christ and dying is gain" (Philippians 1:21). And finally, that is indeed why there followed the first generation of disciples a host of martyrs whose blood, to quote the famous line of Tertullian, was "the seed of the church." In all such statements we see the effect of believing that real meaning and real life are beyond the joys and troubles of this world. There is an "otherworldly" goal.

There is much we could quote from the gospels and the teachings of Paul to emphasize the Christian belief in salvation after life and indeed the contrast between life now and life in heaven. The more detailed account of this afterlife, however, is famously taken from the book of The Revelation of John, or the Apocalypse, in which John is said to have received visions of the end of the world. Here there is judgment, the awful and glorious evaluation of all persons before the righteous throne of God. Here there are angels and strange heavenly creatures worshiping God and bringing upon the world its final devastations. But most importantly, here is the final vision of the City of God, the New Jerusalem, which drops out of heaven and descends to the earth to be the new habitation of the holy followers of God. With gates of pearl and streets of gold, the city's greatest glory is nevertheless the very presence of God and the Lamb (Jesus), who dwell with people and are the source of the "river of life." Indeed, as the vision declares, the city has no need of sun or lamp, "for the glory of God gives it light" ; nor does the city have a temple, "because the Lord God Almighty and the Lamb are its temple." (See Revelation 21:22–23, as well as surrounding verses and chapters.)

It can be argued, of course, that there is a this-worldly element to the otherworldliness of the Christian (and post-exilic Judaic) idea of the afterlife, inasmuch as it might be taken to emphasize not merely some overused image of winged harp players in heaven but also a hopeful ideal of heaven as "a new earth." Indeed, in the revelation to John, a loud voice from heaven declares of the New Jerusalem, "Now the dwelling of God is with men, and he will live with them" (Revelations 21:3). The return of Christ at the end of time might, moreover, indicate the redemption of this world, its re-creation as a world of justice and beauty. Indeed, this seems the point of the Jewish interpretation of the coming of the Messiah. This "anointed one" shall not merely lead people away from earth and to some distant, otherworldly heaven but shall redeem this world, make it right. Thus, when the Savior comes,

The wolf shall live with the lamb, the leopard shall lie down with the kid, the calf and the lion and the fatling together, and a little child shall lead them. The cow and the bear shall graze, their young shall lie down together; and the lion shall eat straw like the ox. The nursing child shall play over the hole of the asp, and the weaned child shall put its hand on the adder's den. They will not hurt or destroy on all my holy mountain; for the earth will be full of the knowledge of the Lord as the waters cover the sea. (Isaiah 11:6–9)

Here, and in a more worldly reading of the Christian heaven, there is some hope that the world of heaven is in some way like the world we know now. And yet we might stress that whatever world the afterlife promises, it is not this present world of pain and injustice. And it is, at least for most of us, "after life."

The otherness of this otherworldly model of salvation might be even clearer with an attempt to define and describe the concept of ideal existence from the religions of India. There (we might generalize) the religious ideals of renunciation and withdrawal from the world have for millennia suggested a need to deny and transcend the common ideals of earthly life. That is, there is a long tradition within Hinduism and Buddhism of becoming a *sannyasin,* literally "one who renounces" the normal pleasures and interests of the workaday world. Correspondingly, "salvation" has meant the permanent ability to escape the world, such as not returning to this world in any reincarnated form. Inasmuch as the soteriological problem consists of a karmic burden that forces the soul to enter again into flesh (the literal sense of "reincarnation"), salvation is liberation from this rebirth, explicitly *not* reentering this world. For example, even upon his birth, the infant Gotama, who grew up to become the Buddha, is said to have declared, "This is the last time that I have been born into this world of becoming" (Conze 36), and the Katha Upanishad of Hinduism declares that those who have reached purity of heart and mind are "born no more" (Prabhavananda and Manchester 19). Thus, one who reaches enlightenment achieves something beyond this world, indeed something that explicitly includes a denial of this world.

Both the mystical Hindu and the early Buddhist traditions use the term *nirvana* to describe this "other world," but exactly what this means is not easy to grasp. Certainly it is some kind of ideal existence, a perfect kind of being free of all desire and suffering. Quite literally, *parinirvana* is in fact "final nirvana," or "nirvana without remainder," in which all karmic force is extinguished and, at death, no rebirth is possible. But it is a mistake to think *nirvana* means something just like "heaven," and it is certainly not a recreated and purified "new earth." So even calling it another "world" is probably misleading. When asked exactly what he meant by *nirvana,* the Buddha seems to have avoided the question. As part of his famous "poisoned arrow" parable, he responded that any discussion of whether the Arhat, or enlightened monk, does or does not exist after death would be unhelpful. It is not really "life after death," but neither is it really nothing at all. Certainly it is not rebirth, given the general soteriology of the Indian religions, and certainly it is some kind of "extinction" (the literal meaning of *nirvana*), at least an extinguishing of the pains, sufferings, and evils of this world. Indeed, that was the clear point of one of our opening quotations for this chapter. But exactly what *nirvana* is remains mysterious.

Perhaps it must. In a celebrated passage from *The Questions of King Malinda,* the Buddhist monk Nagasena responds to the king's questions about nirvana. *Nirvana* (or here, *nibanna*), the monk insists, is unlike anything else, and it is impossible "to make clear the form or figure or age or dimensions of this *nibanna,* either by an illustration or by a reason or by a cause or by a method"

(Stryk 111). As we noted in Chapter 3 on the Absolute, this may be part of exactly what in Buddhism is meant by the tremendous and fascinating mystery of the "holy": that which is final and ultimate yet great beyond understanding.

Our point for this chapter, however, is not to reassert mystery but to describe what salvation might mean within the various religions of the world. And, as we have seen, there is great difference between what, for example, Confucianism might stress as an ultimate way of spiritual life in the world and what Christianity might indicate as the ideal state of being after death. Indeed, even though both the heavenly existence in the Christian's "New Jerusalem" and the possibly impersonal perfection of the mysterious existence of *nirvana* may both be described as "otherworldly," these, too, differ significantly in what they offer as the ideal result of spiritual life.

Of course, as is often the case in this text, the lines we draw to describe differences and similarities among the concepts of the world's religions are not sharp lines but are certainly sometimes bent and even broken. In one sense, the Buddha himself entered *nirvana* at age 35 and lived another 45 years in that blissful state. In another sense, he only entered "final *nirvana*" upon his death. In one sense, the purpose of life for the Confucian is the calm and proper dignity of the *Chun-tzu* (the "superior person"), though in another sense a spiritual life after death is taken for granted in the traditional Chinese focus on ancestor worship. Nevertheless, it can be useful to keep in mind as a tool for thinking through the nature of "salvation" in the world's religions, this distinction between "this-worldly" and "otherworldly" ideals. Certainly we can at least see that not all religions teach an ideal hope that "when you die, you go to heaven."

SOTERIOLOGICAL MEANS

We might have already noted that in a simple declaration of salvation, such as "If you're good, you go to heaven," there are really two important claims. The claim about "heaven" we have already discussed, emphasizing that there are many religious concepts of salvation along with the concept of "heaven" and that it would be a rather gross oversimplification to think that all religions mean the same thing when they talk about the ultimate goal of religious life. And in this section of our chapter, we need to point out that, in the same way, it is something of an oversimplification to think that all religions find their salvation by emphasizing "being good." Indeed, for some religions there is an explicit rejection of the notion that salvation is gained by "being good," at least insofar as that terminology suggests that morality or ritual behavior are somehow the decisive criteria in how one earns salvation. We shall therefore look at two other notions of how salvation is achieved: salvation by grace and salvation by gnosis, as well as the common notion of salvation by moral and ritual work.

Salvation is achieved in some religions by moral and ritual action (such as Judaism and Jainism).

■ SALVATION BY WORKS

Let us look first at the notion of salvation achieved by action. "Being good" might indeed be construed so broadly that it is meant to imply that any activity one pursues, and whereby one earns or gains salvation, is a matter of being good.

But we might emphasize here the focus on moral and ritual behavior. That is, we would hardly be surprised if a religious teacher would tell us that the righteous may stand with God in heaven but that sinners cannot enter. Or, we might find something similar in a teaching emphasizing *karma*, and the notion that one finds a better rebirth, or even escape from the cycle of rebirth, by self-purification. We have already noted in the chapter on religious ethics (Chapter 10) that there are many possible religious descriptions of exactly what "moral works" might be. For example, the "purity" demanded by Jainism may not be the same thing as the "purity" demanded by the Jewish law. For Jains, purity presumes the exhaustive renunciation of all violence toward any living thing—the ideal of *ahimsa*—and ultimately renunciation of all attachments to the sensory world itself. For Jews, purity means keeping the social and ceremonial law, all 613 commandments dealing with how to live in the world—including the proper eating of meat and proper sexual relations. Such differences, therefore, are evident in the content of moral ideals. But our point in this chapter is to note that their conclusions are similar in this: that it is only by the effort to keep the law and to purify the soul that anyone enters into the perfect state of salvation, whether it be the eternal kingdom of God's chosen people or the perfected state of the Tirthankara.

What is considered "moral behavior" varies, but many propose keeping the law and purifying the soul as one path to salvation.

The Tirthankara, we may recall, is a holy person of Jainism, one who has "found the ford," the way across the river of death and rebirth and achieved an ultimate perfection. Famous among the works of the Tirthankaras is the astounding act of self-purification, achieving a purity of existence cleansed of all bad *karma*, and indeed cleansed even of "good" *karma*. That is, for the Jains, *karma* is itself a kind of substance, like a fine dust, that covers the pure soul and keeps it bound to this world of birth and rebirth. The one who aspires to salvation, therefore, must purify himself, first by ceasing all actions that involve the heavier and cloying threat of bad *karma*, but eventually ceasing action of any kind. Thus, the moral perfection of the Jain saint involves, first of all, actions of self-restraint and care to avoid harming living things. It is the Jain doctrine of *ahimsa*, or nonviolence, that in fact inspires Jain monks to cover their mouths with cloth to avoid inhaling an insect, or to sweep the path before them with a broom in order to avoid accidentally stepping on a snail. And at its greatest, the Jain saint's self-control may include such rigorous self-denial that he can stand still and alone until he starves to death, like the great saint Gomatesvara. The Jain scriptures themselves declare that the *itvara*, the fast unto death, is a powerful moral action for gaining liberation from the world. The Acarangasutra, a portion of Jain scripture, states that "the monk, remaining true [to his vows], devoid of desires, successfully crosses over the ocean of cyclic existence, never doubting his ability to fulfill the fast, happily accomplishing [his goal], unaffected by circumstances" (Fieser and Powers 67).

itvara—in Jainism the ritualized fasting unto death of a Jain saint. It is not undertaken easily but requires years of preparation, although sometimes it may be chosen by a Jain saint as the culmination of an illness.

The saint of Jainism works for self-purification, first by nonviolence and later by self-denial, even to the point of self-starvation.

Salvation by moral obedience to God is a major theme in Judaism.

Moral perfection in the Judaic religions is not so much a form of asceticism or self-denial, but it is nevertheless a key element of salvation, inasmuch as moral action is understood fundamentally as obedience to God. Judaism asserts that God has spoken directly with prophets, especially Moses, and revealed His commands to His people. These commands constitute the Jews' side of "the Covenant," the agreement between Yahweh and the children of Abraham. "I will walk among you, and will be your God, and you shall be my people," God tells them (Leviticus 26:12). Here we see an emphasis on moral obedience, such that

God's promises to Israel are explicitly based upon them keeping God's law. The prosperity and peace of the nation (a this-worldly salvation) is directly tied to the people's ability and willingness to keep the law. In the book of Deuteronomy, Moses is told to relate to every succeeding generation that there is a purpose to the laws and precepts of God. "The Lord commanded us to obey all these decrees and to fear the Lord our God, so that we might always prosper and be kept alive, as is the case today," he declares. "And if we are careful to obey all this law before the Lord our God, as he has commanded us, that will be our righteousness" (Deuteronomy 6:24–25).

Human moral effort is clearly a key element in achieving salvation for both Jains and Jews. Similar cases can be made for Muslims and Hindus. For the former, willingness to bend one's own will to the will of God and the honest moral effort to give charity to the poor and to keep the fasts of the faithful are the decisive elements in the final judgment. Indeed, the very name of the religion, Islam, means "submission" to the will of God. For many Hindus, *karma* (meaning "action") remains the driving power of life, rebirth, and salvation, and it is only proper action that counts for good in the afterlife. Hindus must do right action, performing the proper duties of their age, gender, and social order (one's *dharma*) in order to have the "good *karma*" that causes a good rebirth. Both Hindus and Muslims would include in their good works certain ritual performances: the *puja*, or worship of Hindu gods, and the *salat*, or daily prayers of the Muslim. In all this, the "works" of the devotee are the crucial criteria for achieving heaven, or at least a better rebirth.

Of course, neither of these "ways" of salvation "by works" is entirely simple. That is, as we shall see, Hinduism can offer examples of several "ways" of salvation, and this "good works for better rebirth" ideal is only part of what Hindus seek. For Muslims, keeping the rituals and doing good works are important of course, but the grace and sheer forgiveness of Allah is a central hope. The same is true for Jews, who insist that although God can be angry at the disobedient, "The Lord is compassionate and gracious, slow to anger and abounding in loving kindness" (Psalm 103:8). Still, in all these examples, an emphasis can be found on action, especially moral and ritual action. For it is a simple point of justice (one might argue) that what one does should determine whether one finds salvation.

■ SALVATION BY GRACE

Salvation in Christianity is by grace.

Indeed, it may *seem* a "simple point of justice" that someone's salvation should depend upon his or her works. But a rather famous objection to the notion of salvation by "works" comes from the Christian St. Paul and has become a central doctrine of much Christianity, especially Protestant varieties. The issue of "justice" in matters of salvation, St. Paul might have argued, is that God's righteousness allows no sin or evil into His presence, and that His absolute justice requires that no one is "good enough" to go to heaven. The first great Christian missionary, Paul, wrote that "all have sinned and fall short of the glory of God" (Romans 3:23), and to this day, Christian evangelists quote Paul's point in order to emphasize that salvation simply *cannot* be gained by "being good." This would seem then to show that no one earns salvation and that heaven is empty of all beings but God himself, since after all God alone is truly righteous.

Box 12.1   Global Byte

Interreligious Dialogue and Salvation

In the first chapter, we discussed the global tendency toward universalism in religion as well as the Second Axial Period, where the religions of the world are coming together to deal with the pressing concerns of humankind. In part, these two trends are exemplified by the dramatic growth in interreligious dialogue. Interreligious dialogue means that different religions are gathering in a number of forums to discuss areas of agreement, disagreement, and cooperation.

The goal of such discussions is not to create one global religion to which everyone can adhere. Rather, they seek to foster understanding, growth, collaboration, and celebration of diversity. If such dialogue is to occur, there has to be a basic toleration of differences and a need to accept the legitimacy of one another's religions. There also has to be a willingness to admit the limits of one's religion and a drive toward critical examination of one's own faith. Such tendencies open participants to a willingness to learn from one another.

Given the dynamics of globalization we discussed in Chapter 1, it should not be difficult to imagine that such tendencies toward openness have generated particularistic responses in most of the world's major religions. Those who oppose interreligious dialogue see such efforts at best as a watering down of their traditional faiths and, at worse, a selling-out of their faith that threatens the very existence of their religion.

Even when believers are more tolerant and open to dialogue, there are often some sticking points in the process that make dialogue very uncomfortable. One of the most formidable of these entails questions involving salvation. Salvation frequently is a central doctrine of religions in general and may be even more key in the missionary religions that have spread from their places of origin to convert people of other religions and cultures. The major religions teach some kind of "eternal" salvation, though there is wide variation on what the ultimate state of that salvation looks like (that is, personal survival in some sort of paradise versus the complete absorption of the self to "become one with everything"). Moreover, religions also differ on how one is to attain salvation (that is, depending on some external god to save as opposed to inner journeying to find salvation within).

Given these differences, questions have to arise as to how a person deals with differing concepts regarding salvation in his or her faith as well as people from other religious traditions. Does the drive to dialogue and affirm the legitimacy of other people's religion mean I have to ignore my own faith's paths to salvation or, perhaps worse yet, to examine those ideas? If I am inclined to examine my own faith's concepts of salvation, does this examination mean that my own salvation is somehow threatened or lost?

Such issues become even more pressing when dealing with those interpretations of faith that call on people to share their faith with others and actively entreat others to convert to their religion. Many branches of Christianity, for instance, require active evangelism (efforts to convert others) on the part of their members. Should evangelism be abandoned for the sake of dialogue and harmony? Is not requesting such an abandonment disrespecting those Christians whose faith requires them to try to spread their ideas about salvation? Is it not questioning the legitimacy of their faith? Is it calling them to abandon their religious identity?

Globalization, salvation, universalism and particularism, dialogue, and evangelism—many questions, few clear answers.

But this is where Paul's soteriology emphasized "salvation by grace." The concept of grace is simply that salvation is given like a gift flowing from the unearned love of God, and it must be accepted like a gift, not worked for like a reward. We have already noted that concepts of the grace and mercy of God appear also in the soteriologies of Islam and Judaism. But in Christianity, this idea of grace comes to have a central place, based, of course, finally in the saving work of Jesus Christ. That is, for the Christians that emphasize the Pauline soteriology, there is a kind of logic and completeness to the salvation plan of God, a story that begins with the sin of Adam and ends with the perfect life and sacrificial death of Jesus. "No one is righteous," writes Paul (Romans 3:10), but he assumes the exception is Jesus, who is now capable of giving salvation as a gift of mercy to all who are willing to accept it. This acceptance is an act of "faith," trusting one's soul to the power of this Savior. Thus Paul summarizes: "By grace you are saved, through faith—and this is not from yourselves, it is the gift of God—not by works, so that no one can boast" (Ephesians 2:8–9).

Salvation by grace in Christianity is a radical departure from those soteriologies stressing people earning their way to heaven.

In the Christian soteriology, this emphasis on grace is taken as a radical departure from soteriologies in which people have to earn their way to heaven. It includes the elaborate theology of the person of Jesus and, therefore, much of the basis for debates about the Trinity. It concerns as well a notion of divine righteousness and the possibility of vicarious redemption, such as the idea that Christ could die in the place of sinners and that sinners could become "perfect" in the place of Christ. We have discussed some of these ideas in previous chapters, and this text is no place for an elaboration of the whole of Christian theology. But for Christians, salvation by grace remains a basic concept, and historically it has been the foundation for much of the theology we recognize as "Christian" today.

Salvation by grace is also found in Pure Land Buddhism.

There are other places in the world religions to find similar concepts of salvation by grace, although none of them develop the idea to the Christian extent nor place it within the context of the demands of a righteous God. Certainly, the similarities between the grace-focused soteriology of Christianity and the salvation offered in Pure Land Buddhism are striking. Developing in India in the early centuries of the Common Era, this Buddhist sect encourages devotion to the Buddha Amitabha, a great enlightened being who inhabits a "pure land of the west." This Amitabha, called Amida in Japan, has created this pure land out of the power of his own moral merit, so that, out of sheer compassion for the lost, he could provide salvation for those who call upon his name. Thus, those who chant or call the name of Amida are blessed to be reborn in the Pure Land in their next life. This is not quite "salvation," insofar as one must still, within the Pure Land, find enlightenment and liberation from rebirth altogether But certainly this ultimate salvation, liberation from all rebirth, is practically guaranteed, according to the teachings of Pure Land Buddhism, since, within the Pure Land, there is only beauty and no temptation. Even more, by being reborn in the Pure Land, one may sit at the feet of a Buddha and learn in its purity the doctrine of liberation (Robinson/Johnson 112).

In Japan, this doctrine of "salvation by grace" reaches its highest development (Robinson/Johnson 253–255). In the original scriptures of Indian Pure Land, it was declared that the devotee had to call upon the name of Amitabha 10 times and seek purity of life. Under the teaching of the Japanese developers of the Jodo (Pure Land) School, Honen and Shinran, the practice of chanting the name of

Amida became standardized and ritualized. And here, eventually it was declared that even one act of calling on the name of Amida was sufficient for salvation. And not only was it taught that "good works" are not necessary for such salvation, Shinran dramatically declared (somewhat like St. Paul) that those who consider themselves "good" are probably less likely to find this saving grace, precisely because they depend so much on their own goodness. Thus he wrote, "Even a good person attains birth in the Pure Land, so it goes without saying that an evil person will."

In the margin:

In Japan, Pure Land Buddhism's "salvation by grace" reaches its highest development in the Jodo School.

For a final example of "salvation by grace," we can look to Hinduism, specifically in the Bhagavad Gita, where there is significant statement of the limitation of "works" and the value of finding faith in Krishna. People can worship the gods, Krishna teaches in the ninth chapter, but, as is commonly taught in Indian religions, the "heaven" they earn is temporary and deceptive (9:21). "Good *karma*," then, offers only a temporary "salvation," and for true release from the cycle of rebirth, one must find a higher purity. Thus, to use the Christian terminology, it is not "works" but "faith" that is ultimately salvific. Or, to make the point in more truly Hindu terms, the devotee indeed ought to do his or her duties in society, but one finds salvation only by having one's mind focused on Krishna. By having a mind of devotion, one does one's good works not looking for the rewards of action but looking for the glory of the god Krishna. Krishna says to his follower Arjuna:

In the margin:

"Grace" salvation is found in Hinduism, especially from the teachings of Krishna in the Bhagavad Gita.

Whatever you do—what you take,
What you offer, what you give,
What penances you perform—
Do as an offering to me, Arjuna.
You will be freed from the bonds of action,
From the fruit of fortune and misfortune;
Armed with the discipline of renunciation,
Your self liberated, you will join me.
(Bhagavad Gita 9:27–28)

It is evident, of course, that Krishna is not another "suffering servant," as Jesus is sometimes described. Krishna is not a perfect savior whose righteousness is given to sinners so that they may gain salvation in the presence of a righteous God. Neither is he, technically, a Bodhisattva with his own "Pure Land." But the emphasis here on devotion does become for Hinduism a new form of salvation, alongside the traditional emphasis on karmic action. Thus Hinduism, besides having a soteriology focused on *karma-marga*, the path of salvation based upon the "works" of *karma*, also teaches the *bhakti-marga*, the "path of salvation based upon devotion."

As usual, it would be an oversimplification to say that Christianity, for example, has only an emphasis on "grace." Certainly Christians are expected to do "good works" as well. The Pure Land sect, too, as we saw, teaches a "salvation by grace," but only temporarily, inasmuch as one reborn in the Pure Land must then achieve salvation by finding enlightenment. And as we have seen, Hinduism seems to have more "paths" of salvation besides "grace." But we can make the point nevertheless that in some religions and some sects, this means of salvation "by grace" takes a central place and is indeed argued over and against "works."

■ SALVATION BY KNOWLEDGE

Salvation by gnosis, or knowledge, may be found in mystical Hinduism.

gnosis—knowledge, especially a mystical, religious kind of knowledge usually gained only by persons who obtain a special insight or enlightenment

The breadth and variability of Hinduism, with its *karma-marga* and *bhakti marga,* allow us to make a transition into the discussion of a third *marga,* or "path" of salvation, the *jnana-marga,* or the path of knowledge. This latter stresses what we might call gnosis, a special kind of knowledge or insight that is somehow liberating for the mystic soul. For the mystical branch of Hinduism, the emphasis is on knowing the union of the soul with Brahman. Simply to see the Atman, or the inner, absolute soul, is to know its unity with the totality of pure being, Brahman. And this knowledge at once liberates the soul from its bondage with the illusion of the world. In the Kena Upanishad it is written:

> *He truly knows Brahman who knows him as beyond knowledge; he who thinks that he knows, knows not. The ignorant think Brahman is known, but the wise know him to be beyond knowledge. He who realizes the existence of Brahman behind every activity of his being—whether sensing, perceiving, or thinking—he alone gains immortality. Through knowledge of Brahman comes power. Through knowledge of Brahman comes victory over death. (Prabhavananda and Manchester 31)*

In Buddhism, liberation may come from a special kind of knowledge.

This notion of salvation through special knowledge seems most common in religions that advocate a kind of enlightenment, as in the example from the Upanishads or, just as famously, from Buddhism. For the Buddha, too, taught that a special kind of understanding is the key to liberation. We are, after all, in bondage to the world of desires, he said, and yet those desires are themselves built upon "ignorance," the error of believing that the objects of our desires are real and substantial. Therefore, just by seeing that all things arise and decay and that nothing is permanent or worthy of desire, the craving for existence is broken, says the Buddha, and liberation is attained. Thus, salvation is attained by knowledge.

In later forms of Buddhism, such as Zen, the enlightenment experience is translated into a dramatic awakening called *satori,* a realization of "one's true nature." A Japanese term for this awakening is *kensho,* literally "seeing." This experience is necessarily "noetic," as D. T. Suzuki described it, meaning that the experience consists of a direct knowing of objects and, as he says, of the "Reality" that is behind them (83-108). It is a positive knowing of Ultimate Reality, yet it is beyond words. It is gnosis, and without it there is no liberation.

Gnostic salvation exists outside of India, as the debates about the "gnostic" aspects of early Christianity attest.

There have been gnostic elements outside the religions of India, of course, perhaps most famously in the early disputes about Christianity. From the New Testament letters of John to the current debates about the "Gnostic Gospels," there have been disputes about whether certain elements of "special knowledge" are a legitimate part of the Christian religion. In general, it seems that early Christian gnosticism tended to assert that the historical bases of faith in Jesus and the revelations to the Jews were less important than insight into the mysteries of the *Logos,* the "Word" or "Mind" of God. The world of flesh and blood, in general, was deceptive, and only a secret, spiritual insight into mysteries beyond the

*Christian
Gnosticism made
salvation less a
matter of grace
and more the
result of special
knowledge.*

world of perception was true knowledge. Harold Brown, a historian of Christian doctrine, claims that it is this appeal to secret knowledge, instead of the grace given through the historical person of Jesus, that makes Christian gnosticism a "heresy" (47). In contrast, Elaine Pagels would insist that Gnostic Christianity was a healthy sect "suppressed" by the Church authorities in the early centuries of the faith (102). Of course, any debate on this historical point is beyond the scope of our text and is probably more an evaluative than an historical argument. But by making "the Christ" more a spiritual and esoteric insight, this version of Christianity did seem to change salvation from a matter of "grace" to a matter of "knowledge."

Salvation within Christianity is, of course, a complex matter, even if "salvation by grace" seems to be the teaching derived from Paul. And in Hinduism, as we have seen, there are evidently many kinds of salvation paths that exist side by side. As usual, therefore, the presentation of these models of salvation is not meant to oversimplify the historical reality of how the different religions actually function. Instead, it is intended to suggest how one can explore and understand different strains and emphases within the world's religions, and even within one religion's various sects. The lines between these "means of salvation," like the lines between the concepts of "this-worldly" and "otherworldly" salvation goals, are, to some extent, flexible and perforated lines. It is an oversimplification to think that any given religion is simple and monolithic, just as it is an oversimplification to think all religions are alike. The terms and distinctions given in this chapter on salvation, therefore, like most of the concepts developed in this text, are meant to help keep the discussion going and to give us useful tools for making sense of the phenomenon of religion as it lives and breathes around us.

GLOBALIZATION, EVANGELISM, HUMAN RIGHTS, AND CULTURAL IDENTITY

evangelism— any effort to convert nonbelievers to religious faith or convert members of one religious faith to another

In Chapter 1 we first discussed globalization and some of its key concepts, such as particularism versus universalism and human rights. We have had occasion to return to these themes at several points in this book. We now use these ideas to look at another specific issue that is sometimes problematic on the contemporary religious scene, one that especially deals with the idea of salvation and the afterlife, namely evangelism. Evangelism is a term drawn from Christianity that has come to refer to any effort to convert nonbelievers to religious faith or members of one religious faith to another, presumably for the sake of the convert's own eternal happiness. A number of religions, such as Buddhism, Christianity, and Islam, are known as missionary religions. That is, they have been very active in their efforts to make converts, hoping to lead others to the salvation they offer. It is this effort that has assisted their growth beyond their cultures of origin to become "world religions" spreading to a number of different cultures.

There always has been some degree of conflict between established religions and newcomers. At times this has been a mild competition, but at other times the confrontation has turned violent. Although this conflict is not new, the emerging global society has given it some new twists. Some of these are found in complex questions involving universalism and particularism.

In Chapter 1, we mentioned the role religion played during the First Axial Period in the development of universal principles that transcended the particularistic tendencies of traditional religions. The tendency to universalism is especially apparent in missionary religions that assume that their concepts of the Absolute, their moral or social codes, and especially their understandings of salvation and paths to salvation have application for everyone. Yet, in one sense, these very claims to universal truths may be seen as particularistic in a world containing a multitude of religions, each with its claims to truth. Just whose idea of salvation are we to accept in a pluralistic world? The Jains? The Buddhists? The Muslims? The Christians? And what should be the reaction to evangelism that attempts to spread the particularistic doctrines of one religious faith into regions dominated by another religion?

These puzzling issues become even more complicated when we introduce concepts associated with human rights. The United Nations Declaration of Universal Human Rights recognizes people's right to practice their religion without undue interference from other people or governments. Does this, therefore, mean that those religions that teach the duty to spread their faith through evangelism have the right to attempt to convert others? Or does it mean that followers of a given religion have a right to be "protected" from those religions that would convert them? The Universal Declaration assumes that governments will protect freedom of religion. But which of these concepts of freedom of religion should dominate and under what circumstances? Can it be that one's free practice of religion interferes with another's free practice of religion?

Likewise, some argue that "peoples"—however "peoples" are defined—have the right to self-determination as well as to protection of their identity. So if a "people" constitutes the followers of a particular religion, do these "people" have the right to determine their own fate by pursuing practices and beliefs, including those centering around salvation, that may interfere with another religious people's right to determine the direction of their own religious way of life? Similarly, a people have a right to maintain their integrity by protecting their identity. But what if that identity as a people includes belonging to a particular religion? Does this mean that evangelism not only involves the possibility of religious conversion but is an attack on a people's culture as well?

Contemporary India presents an interesting example of how these assorted enigmas come into play. Technically, modern India is a democratic nation with freedom of religion and an upholder of human rights. Eighty-five percent of its people are said to be Hindu, although there are disputes about how the census of the country makes its count and defines its terms. Among the minority religions, Christianity is relatively small. Yet in recent years, this religion has been the focus of both press coverage and persecution because of its tendency to evangelism.

The quandary is this: If all religions are to be tolerated in India, then what shall we do with a religion that urges people to leave their religion and join another? Interestingly, some of the more conservative Hindus have proposed that, while the freedom to practice any religion is given by the constitution, it is possible to outlaw "conversion," so that it would be a crime only to encourage people to change religion. The irony, of course, is that while this view is, in one sense, tolerant of any religion, it clearly denies one religion its internal emphasis on teaching and spreading its view of salvation. This, in turn, may violate several human rights.

While India wants to preserve its Hindu cultural identity, it is also true that for Christians the act of offering the message of salvation to those outside the Christian fold is both a duty and an act of love. If salvation is indeed something of utter importance for the happiness of the human soul, then (at best) those who teach this salvation and offer its message to "the lost," are indeed agents of mercy, bringers of "good news," which is literally what "evangelist" means. And so, in a world increasingly crowded with cultural interactions governed by global norms, we will have to decide if the very proper "act of love" that evangelism tries to be must be interpreted as a threat to cultural unity and identity of people of different religions. In the world of the 21st century, such controversies may become more and more common.

CONCLUSION

Ideas about the nature of the human soul, community obligations, and the nature of the Absolute all tie into concepts of salvation.

We must make two more points about the significance and variety of religious notions of salvation to conclude our discussion. The first is the reiteration of a theme common in this text, namely that in studying and thinking about religious beliefs and practices one should look for the relationship between beliefs and practices within traditions. As we have said, religions are not haphazard collections of ideas and prescriptions but are unified sets of beliefs and practices that make sense in their own ways. Religions teach about morality, about rituals, about art and poetry and community and the nature of the human soul, just as they teach about salvation and ultimately about the Absolute itself. And within those religions, there is a consistency to be understood in how a specific moral direction is related to a concept of salvation or how the idea of the soul is related to directions on meditation. And in all religions, we have argued, there lies at the root something ultimate, something sacred, something final and absolute in itself. And whether we study Christianity or Islam, Hinduism, Taoism, or a dozen other, unique systems of action and belief, we can understand more and more by seeing why these ideas go together and by seeing what difference it makes.

Ideas about salvation have great import regarding the nature of religious life and the meaning of life in general.

The second point is more about the significance and meaning of such ideas. Insofar as the doctrines of salvation and the specifications of how salvation can be achieved tell us ultimately about the highest good and about the ideal existence of the human self, these ideas seem necessarily to carry with them a certain gravity and a certain implication about the importance of religious life. There is a story, for example, about a Christian missionary, C. T. Studd (1860–1931), who read the mocking words of a Marxist atheist about the doctrines of salvation. Without believing in the purported truth of the Christian soteriology, the Marxist claimed that, if it were true, it would be the most important message the world should hear. "Did I firmly believe, as millions say they do, that the knowledge and practice of religion in this life influences destiny in another, religion would mean to me everything," the atheist wrote. Therefore, he continued, if it were true, "I would esteem one soul gained for heaven worth a life of suffering. Earthly consequences would never stay in my head or seal my lips . . . I would strive to look upon eternity alone, and on the immortal souls around me, soon to be everlastingly happy or everlastingly miserable. I would go forth to the world and preach to it in season and out of season, and my text would be, 'what shall it profit a man if he gain the whole world and lose his own soul.'"

The point of the story, of course, is that this short declaration inspired Studd to work diligently at preaching the message of Christian salvation to the world. For our purposes, the point might be more general: Whatever one believes about the meaning of life and its ultimate purpose, if one truly believes it, then it bears in a person's life a deep significance beyond the flippant daily events of life. That is, if we are meant for heaven or if we find bliss only in unity with Brahman, if a life lived in fluid oneness with the Tao or in interrelational harmony with the world of spirits is the greatest life we could live, then there is an importance to religious life that outstrips our usual interest in jobs and homes and sports and entertainment. Regardless of how important our religious lives might be to us personally right now, there is a certain logic to the notion that religion is living and powerful, a motivating force and an ultimate meaning in the lives of innumerable people in the history of the world.

What is the meaning of life? Sometimes people ask such a question almost as a joke, taking for granted perhaps that there is no real answer, or at least nothing concrete. But religions throughout the world say otherwise, offering a variety of answers that at least appear to be offered seriously and with the utmost gravity. And if heaven or oneness with the Tao is indeed the ultimate goal of human life, then that life in turn is directed in certain ways, to certain beliefs and certain practices that reasonably become part of the devotion, dedication, and understanding that we call "religion." And ultimately, the "meaning of life" points us back to the Ultimate Reality, to God or Tao or Brahman, which is finally the source of holiness itself.

■ INTERACTIVE EXERCISE

Please continue your exploration of salvation by going to the interactive exercise online (**http://www.religion.wadsworth.com/richter**).

WORKS CITED

Aristotle. "Nichomachean Ethics." In *Introduction to Aristotle*. Ed. R. McKeon New York: McGraw/Hill, 1947.

Borowitz, Eugene. "We Cannot Know for Certain what Lies Beyond Death." In *Enduring Issues in Religion*. Ed. John Lyden San Diego: Greenhaven Press, 1995.

Brown, Harold O. J. *Heresies*. Grand Rapids, MI: Baker Book House, 1984.

Conze, Edward. *Buddhist Scriptures*. Baltimore: Penguin Books, 1959.

Fieser, James, and John Powers. *Scriptures of the World's Religions*. Boston: McGraw Hill, 1998.

Leys, Simon. *The Analects of Confucius*. New York: Norton and Company, 1997.

McIntyre, Stephen R. *Tao Te Ching*. October 29, 2001. Trans. James Legge. http://nothingistic.org (accessed September 12, 2002).

Miller, Barbara (trans.). *The Bhagavad Gita*. New York: Bantam Books, 1986.

Neihardt, John Gneisenau. *Black Elk Speaks: Being the Life Story of a Holy Man of the Oglala Sioux*. Lincoln: University of Nebraska Press, 1979.

Pagels, Elaine. *The Gnostic Gospels*. New York: Random House, 1979.

Prabhavananda, Swami, and Frederick Manchester. *Upanishads*. New York: Mentor Books 1957.

Shinran. *A Record in Lament of Divergences*. http://www.shinranworks.com (accessed February 12, 2003).

Stryk, Lucien. *World of the Buddha*. New York: Grove Weidenfeld, 1968.

Studd, C. T. http://www.hisword2.homestead.com/files/tcstudd.htm (accessed February 12, 2003).

Suzuki, D. T. *Zen Buddhism*. Garden City, NY: Doubleday Anchor, 1956.

Watson, Burton. *Chuang Tzu: Basic Writings*. New York: Columbia University Press, 1964.

FOR FURTHER READING

Brown, Harold O. J. "Structure and Variation." In *Heresies*. Grand Rapids, MI: Baker Book House, 1984.

Eliade, Mircea. *Yoga, Immortality and Freedom*. Princeton, NJ: Princeton University Press, 1969.

Graham, Billy. *How to Be Born Again*. NashvilleTN: Word Publishing, 1989.

Lyden, John (ed.). Chapter 4, "How Can One Find Meaning in Life," and Chapter 5, "What Lies Beyond Death?" Iin *Enduring Issues in Religion*. San Diego: Greenhaven Press, 1995.

Pagels, Elaine. *The Gnostic Gospels*. New York: Random House, 1979.

Raj, Sundar. *The Confusion Called Conversion*. Delhi: Traci Publications, 1988.

Shinran. *A Record in Lament of Divergences*. http://www.shinranworks.com (accessed February 12, 2003).

Thurman, Robert. *Tibetan Book of the Dead*. New York: Bantam, 1993. Top of Form

13 RELIGION, PERSONALITY, AND THE INDIVIDUAL

The pictures for this chapter found above and on the Web site (**http://www.religion.wadsworth.com/richter**), and the following scriptures deal with various issues concerning how religion affects who we think we are, our individual identity, close relationships, and, more generally, our mental health. Please look over these pictures and passages, then consider the Introductory Questions that follow as a way to prepare for reading this chapter.

> *We do not believe by ourselves, as individuals in isolation; we believe as part of a community of believers, whether the community is a Benedictine monastery, a communist cell, a Protestant congregation, a Jewish minyan, or a Hindu ashram.*

—Robert McAfee Brown on religious community: *Is Faith Obsolete?* (141)

Is there anyone among you who, if your child asks for bread, will give a stone? Or if the child asks for a fish, will give a snake? If you then, who are evil, know how to give good gifts to your children, how much more will your Father in heaven give good things to those who ask him!

—Christianity: Matthew 7:9–10

It is quite legitimate to argue from the analogy of human fatherhood to the "fatherhood" of God . . . we say that, just as a father is kind, careful, unselfish and forgiving in his dealings with his children, so is God in his dealings with men; that there is a true likeness of nature between God and man as between a father and his sons; because we are sons of our Father, we should look on all men as our brothers . . .

[We do not] deduce from the analogy that we are to imagine God as being a cruel, careless or injudicious father such as we may see from time to time in daily life.

— Dorothy Sayers commenting on common Christian/Judaic imagery (189–190)

[There is a middle path] that opens the eyes, and bestows understanding, which leads to peace of mind, to the higher wisdom, to full enlightenment, to Nirvana . . . Truly, it is this Noble Eightfold Path, that is to say: Right Views; Right aspirations; Right speech; Right conduct; Right livelihood; Right effort; Right mindfulness; and Right contemplation . . .

—Buddhism: The Benares Sermon (Van Voorst 84)

The Master said, "The superior man considers righteousness to be essentially everything. He performs it according to the rules of propriety. He brings it forth in humility. He completes it with sincerity. This is indeed a superior man."

—Confucianism: The Analects 15:17 (Van Voorst 140)

[Speaking to Nicodemus, a Pharisee, Jesus said] I tell you, no one can see the kingdom of God without being born from above [or born anew] . . . no one can enter the kingdom of God with being born of water and Spirit. What is born of the flesh is flesh and what is born of the Spirit is spirit.

—Christianity: John 3:1–6

INTRODUCTORY QUESTIONS

1. Brown argues that religion is always an affair of community. There can be no individual and private religion. Do you agree or disagree? Please support your position with your own argument. To what extent is your religion influenced by others around you such as family and friends?

2. The image of the Fatherhood of God is very important in Judaism, Christianity, and Islam. What feelings and understandings of God does this convey to you? Would the image of the Motherhood of God convey the same or different understandings? Why or why not?

3. Dorothy Sayers indicates that we do not draw upon the negative pictures that earthly fathers may also represent when describing God. Yet, our personal ability to respond to different analogies about the Holy is based upon our experience. If a person has an abusive father, what does this experience do to his or her understanding of God?

4. To what extent is the Confucian superior man like the Buddhist follower of the Nobel Eightfold Path? Is the way each achieves peace of mind similar or different? Would the superior man or the follower of the Nobel Eightfold Path be considered mentally healthy by today's standards?

5. The Buddhists and Confucians both believe that cleansing the mind and controlling the body are ways to obtain spiritual benefits. Jesus indicates that something more than proper attitude, discipline, and moral behavior is needed to obtain spiritual victory. What more is needed? How do his ideas compare with those of the Buddhists and Confucians? What do you think Jesus would say is the relationship between a healthy soul and mental health?

INTRODUCTION

It might seem that the question, "Who are you?" is a simple one, a question we often merely answer with our names. But of course in different contexts, "Who are you?" might be answered with one's relationship to another person ("I'm the brother of the groom") or with one's nationality ("I'm from the United States"). These are not exclusive answers; one can of course be the brother of the groom, from the United States, and named "Bob." But there are complex issues involved in putting together all of these identities into one, and each aspect of one's iden-

Religion plays a major part in forming our identity.

tity can be something that helps us or gets in the way of our mental health. One's religion, too, is part of one's identity. Indeed, even if we do not consider ourselves members of a particular religion, we are often influenced by religious views, attitudes, and ideas so much that the religion is part of who we are, whether we like it or not.

The Introductory Questions were intended to help us to begin to think about these complex relationships that exist between religion, individual identity, social identity, and mental health. As we proceed in this chapter, we shall consider the nature of individual personality and the factors that define personality and influence behavior. For our purposes, we shall especially emphasize the close relationship between individual personality and religion. A person's individual identity, though perhaps not formed entirely by religion, is certainly influenced by religion, and insofar as religion is itself a social phenomenon, this means that the individual identity also includes various social aspects. We are, after all, not only individuals but also members of groups, including religions and cultures, which interact with people's personalities, influencing their emotional and spiritual well-being. Thus, we are brought face-to-face with a fact noted way back in Chapter 1 (Religion in Global Society), namely that religion creates and maintains both personal and group identity, while at the same time those identities are challenged by the globalization process.

INDIVIDUALITY, THE SOUL, AND THE EXISTENTIAL SELF

We can begin to examine the concept of personal identity with a rather abstract, and yet rather well-known, notion. Arguably, every one of us knows who we are simply by the fact that we are aware of ourselves. We know ourselves as somehow a unity of experience, a unity of thoughts and ideas that are all (again, "somehow") mine, and this unity at least seems to us the wholeness of our personality, our integrity, the undivided self. Indeed, that seems to be at the root of the word "individual," knowing oneself as a single conscious being, as an integrated mind. The 17th century French philosopher Rene Descartes (1596–1650) famously declared, "I think, therefore I am," defining the "I," the self, simply as "a thing that thinks" (Descartes 84). His point here is to declare, he believes, something that all of us know already, namely that "I" refers to my own consciousness, the unique set of thoughts and experiences that I experience myself to be. For Descartes, as for many Western philosophers of his age and of previous ages, this "self" was understood as the "soul."

To follow through the various speculations of Western philosophy that tried to develop Descartes' point, and to express more carefully what is the "thing that thinks," would take us too far beyond the scope of religious studies. For our purposes, perhaps, the more important point is to see how Descartes considered a link between this "I" and the religious concept of the soul. For him, of course, this religious concept was a Christian concept, and he evidently worried that the theologians of his day would not take kindly to his philosophical analysis of their articles of faith. Thus, it was part of the self-defense of Descartes' philosophy, when presenting his views to religious authorities, that he claimed to have discovered philosophically nothing more than what Catholic Christianity had been teaching for centuries, namely that each of us has a unique soul, a soul that is a nonphysical spirit, a soul that lives beyond the death of the body (132).

It is debatable that Descartes' view of the soul is more like Plato's view than like that of the first Christians. But for our purposes, the point might be stressed that Descartes took for granted, as did many of his religious contemporaries, that what it means to be "me" is to be the mind that animates the body. Indeed, this verb "animate" comes from the Latin word for "soul," *anima*. Thus it is the soul, recognized as our own minds, that puts life into the body. This soul, then, is the bottom line, so to speak, that makes me, "me," inasmuch as it is this soul that stays pretty much the same over time. I am born a thoughtless, innocent baby; I

The soul is what makes us distinctive.

grow into a mischievous, playful child; I mature into a thoughtful, ponderous adult; and through it all, somehow, I am still me, indeed the same me, in some sense, through all the changes. For Descartes and, at least in his interpretation, the Catholic Church of the 17th century, the soul is the same "immaterial substance" that is identical over the course of my life. Thus the "identical" soul is precisely what gives me my "identity."

For Hinduism and other Indian religions (notably not Buddhism), finding identity in some deep, inner "soul" is an even more radical idea. That is, for the Hindus, the "self" that I find in my own thinking is still only a temporary phenomenon, and beyond it, deeper yet in the nature of the individual, is the "Self" (note the capital), the **Atman**. This "true Self" not only remains the same essence of being throughout "my" lifetime but even remains the unchanged soul within the many lifetimes of "my" reincarnations. As Patrick Bresnan says, "Sentient beings on Earth exist in a multitude of different kinds, a vast hierarchy stretching from the lowest forms of animal life to mankind, which we take to be the highest. Throughout all of this hierarchy, there is a constant cycling of death and birth. The body, being . . . material, dies. But the Atman . . . is eternal and never dies" (50). Thus, I may be a white American male in this lifetime, but "I" might also have been a Chinese female in the 18th century or even a giraffe a thousand years ago. Nevertheless, behind or beneath all these different "me's," there remains unchanged and unchanging the Atman, the eternal Self.

This concept presents many of us with a difficult problem: Since we know ourselves only in the form that appears in a given lifetime and then only at a particular moment in time, how can we know the Atman that lives through all lifetimes? Indeed, the point of the Hindu mystical soteriology (see previous chapter) was that one needs to draw oneself away from the seduction of one's temporary, finite identity and know oneself as the Eternal, as the Atman. For most of us, perhaps, the "finite identity," the self we think ourselves to be in this lifetime, is a difficult enough mystery, as all the "Who am I?" questions might suggest. For there, as we saw, "I am Bob" or "I am an American" or "I am the brother of the groom" are already a series of complicated possibilities that refer nonetheless only to this lifetime and the focus of today's experience. For Descartes, the soul is the single, unchanging identity of the individual that remains through all the changes of this life; for the Hindu mystics, the deeper soul is the single, unchanging identity that remains through all the changes of any life and indeed that ultimately denies all the self-identifications of "Bob," "American," or "brother of the groom."

Perhaps that is why the Western philosophical tradition has stressed the current conscious mind as the seat of identity. This focus culminates, in a decidedly nonreligious way, in the work of French existentialists like Jean Paul Sartre (1905–1980), for whom personal identity is emphatically described by our own minds' awareness of our own minds. That is, no one hears my thoughts except me; know one knows but you what you want for dinner. In this sense, the self, the individual "I," is a kind of isolated unit of consciousness that Sartre called "being for-itself," or the unique conscious mind that knows its own existence. This we might call the "existential self," your unique knowing of yourself, so to speak, from the inside. It is, the philosophers speculate, the locus of both identity

In Hinduism, the Soul is Atman, the True Self, which carries it through many reincarnations.

and free will, the place where you make choices and define who you are. The basis of one's own conscious identity, then, is for the individual mind "to be itself in the form of presence to itself" (Sartre 124). It is to know that I am myself.

Sartre's concept of the self, unlike Descartes', did not make any reference to the religious notion of the soul or the afterlife. Do I really have a soul? Or better, is it true that I am a soul? Perhaps for some these questions are even more difficult than the "Who am I?" that we started with, and perhaps that added difficulty lies precisely in the bothersome "religiousness" of the word *soul*. But even for Sartre, the idea of the self did contain a strong emphasis on free will and on the individual responsibility we all seem to bear for choosing the kind of people we want to be. And in a way, perhaps we all experience this *kind* of internal identity, the direct "existential" awareness of ourselves as an integrated consciousness. But we shall see that this unique and isolated "existential self" is perhaps not as unique and isolated as it seems.

Before passing on to discuss personality and social identity, however, it should be noted that even from some religious perspectives, this notion of a stable, unchanging "soul" cannot be presumed. The parenthetical reference to Buddhism barely alludes to the fact that the earliest teachings of that religion expressed the very opposite of the Hindu notion just described. Indeed, where the Hindus spoke of the Atman, the Buddha spoke of anatman, literally and explicitly "no-self." This Buddhist doctrine was founded on the simple claim that there is no evidence of an unchanging, eternal "self" within our experience of ourselves. I do not, the Buddhist might say, experience myself as an integrated individual but as a series of experiences, a series of moments of the "mind."

The more technical expression of the Buddhist doctrines of *anatman* proposed, instead of a notion of the soul, that "I" am merely a conglomeration of parts called the five skandhas. Literally, these five *skandhas* are "heaps" or collections of parts, each changing and varying with time, so that, in truth, there is never a situation in which I am the same "I" that I was even moments ago. Rather "I" at any moment refers only to that moment's collection of body parts, emotional states, sensory experiences, shifting thoughts, and roving consciousness. Thus, for the Buddha there is no "I" over time, no stable "me" that defines my identity throughout my life, let alone throughout many lifetimes. Rather "I" am only a name, a deceptive term used to label a collection of parts, like taking a coin collection and calling it "Henry." Thus "Bob," or "I," or any other term used to name oneself is merely a name conveniently coined to label the five *skandhas,* and like all names, these terms only fool us into thinking there is a stable, knowable identity of the self.

Similar skepticism about the reality of a stable "self" of any kind appeared in Western philosophers, such as David Hume (1711–1776), who similarly thought that "I" refers only to "a bundle or collection of different perceptions" (Hume 252). Other philosophers followed, some more or less religiously inclined to find and emphasize a "self" that could qualify as the soul and as the locus of one's true identity. This debate is not over, though current discussion has taken on perhaps a less religious tone and a more psychological vocabulary. Certainly, no discussion of the self in global society could be complete without looking at the findings of modern psychology.

For Buddhists, there is no single unchanging self or soul.

PERSONALITY, COMMUNITY, AND RELIGION

Personality is one of the key ideas coming from modern psychology that reflects on identity as well as a number of other understandings of the place and actions of an individual in our contemporary world. In this section we present a definition of personality, look at the type of religious communities that influence personality, and use these communities as a tool to investigate briefly the relation of the psychological self to the existential self. Concepts centering around the personality also will be used to investigate other issues regarding personality and religion. For instance, we discuss how factors influencing personality formation may impact our religious understandings.

■ PERSONALITY DEFINED

It is popular to talk about a person's personality and to assume that each personality is unique and relatively stable, perhaps indeed like the soul. People may in fact believe that personality is the key to understanding their lives as well as their relationship to other people. "This is the kind of person I am," we might think, "and that explains why I live as I do." A person may say, "I was sure I would do well at this job; I just have the personality for it." Or, sometimes we say, "I just can't stand that person's personality," or "I have such a good time with her because our personalities are so compatible." But exactly what is the personality? How does one get personality? Is it something we are born with or is it something we somehow acquire? Is it static or does it change between situations or over time?

There are many definitions of personality. Almost all of these try to get at the idea that people feel, think, and/or act in a fairly consistent fashion. That is, we can speak of a person's personality precisely because it does not change day to day or moment by moment. We can call a person "friendly," or "helpful," or "mean and nasty" because we have seen, and expect in the future to see, a kind of repeated pattern. However, three limits have to be placed on the "consistency" approach to defining personality.

First, some social scientists do not see the consistency being where most people would expect—inside of the individual. That is, we might expect that my self-definition could be rooted entirely in myself alone and that the consistency of what makes me, "me," is, again, that soul or self or mind that we investigated. However, in contrast to this image of the existential self as the source of the stability of the personality, psychiatrist Harry Stack Sullivan (1892–1949) held that the consistency (as in the personality) of the individual is found in a relatively stable pattern of relationships with other people. This is apparent when a person considers a key element of the personality—one's self-concept. The **self-concept** is an idea we develop about who we are and how we fit into the world around us. The self-concept also contains assessments about ourselves, such as value and moral judgments: "I am pretty or ugly," "I am good or bad," "People generally like me," or "I can be counted on to get a job done." Yet Sullivan's point, and something we have already noticed in this chapter, is that often when answering "Who am I?" we respond with relationships: "I am the son or daughter of . . .";"I am a student at . . ."; and so on. Even our preceding examples, "I am the brother of the groom" and "I am an American" are essentially descriptions of

Defining the self and the personality depends on a fairly stable pattern of relationships.

relationships in the world. In such responses, it seems evident that the very core of the personality includes the understanding of who a person is by placing a person in a particular set of relationships. Without this web of relationships, it could be argued, we do not know who we are. Alone, we have no distinct sense of self.

This brings us to a second limit on the idea of defining personality as an unchanging pattern of behaviors. Notably, we human beings are not as consistent in our behaviors, thought patterns, and attitudes as we think we are. There is a large body of research from the social and behavioral sciences that demonstrates people's behavior, attitudes, and the like change dramatically as they move from situation to situation and from relationship to relationship. For example, a college student will behave quite differently depending upon whether he or she is in class, in the student center "hanging" with friends, at a dance club, or in a religious service. People switch back and forth among behaviors that may be extremely different without ever realizing it.

Finally, the third twist to our questions about the stability of personality suggests that, although human behavior is very predictable, it is not absolutely fixed. To some extent, each person is a bundle of potentialities. This means that at birth we have the potential of becoming a number of different things. However, what we become may well depend on the type and extent of relationships we have with other people. For example, each baby has the potential to speak any language, but which language she speaks depends on what language she hears spoken early in life, when language normally develops. Moreover, it becomes more difficult later in life to learn a new language. Even if a person learns such a language, it is very difficult to speak it with the same accent as native speakers. If the potentialities to speak *any* language were not used at the proper stage of development, then these potentialities were lost or, at least, severely impaired.

So the personality, not as the existentially isolated but as the socially contextualized self, may be defined as follows: The **personality** is the total behavioral, thought, attitude, and potentiality patterns of a person interacting in a relatively stable set of relationships and in a variety of situations. Thus, personality is more complex, perhaps, than being an isolated individual, and insofar as who we are is dependent upon a social context, our identity will be influenced, if not genuinely created, by the religious community.

People behave differently in different situations.

Potentialities develop through interaction.

■ NATURAL AND VOLUNTARY RELIGIOUS COMMUNITIES

Insofar as our personality and identity depend on community membership, especially religious community membership, we should pause here and consider how membership in such communities is gained. That is, precisely because we simply are influenced and created by our community membership, we realize that our "existential self" is to a great extent not so independent and isolated. At the same time, it is also possible that we choose our relationship to a religious community, as seems to be the case when people change religious communities or join a religion having not been raised in that religion. But here, then, is a quandary: How can we be formed by a community and then stand outside enough to choose a new community? We shall find in answer to this question that some communities are more elective than others and that the relation between the individual and the community is dynamic and complex, not simple and one-dimensional.

We can see this complexity in the distinction between voluntary communities and natural communities. As the names suggest, **voluntary communities** are those that define their own membership as individuals who choose to join at a specific point in time. **Natural communities** are those in which membership is simply given; one may be simply "born into" the community—one did not join at a given time nor was one really given a choice. Both natural communities and voluntary communities are found within the world's religions.

Voluntary communities are ones we join; natural communities are ones into which we are born.

A fundamental example of a natural religious community can be found in Judaism. Technically, membership as a Jew is legally (as in within Jewish law) defined by descent from a Jewish mother. That is, if my mother was Jewish, then I am Jewish, and that defines my membership. This is true, in fact, of many tribal cultures in which membership in the tribe is completely coterminous with participation in the cultural traditions and the religious activities. The Aborigine individuals in Australia, for example, are simply born into that culture and follow the ways of the ancestors from birth. A Jew is a Jew by birthright, and consequently, as one commentator notes, "You can be a lapsed Jew, but you can never be an ex-Jew" (Judaism: The Chosen People).

In contrast, there is evidence in the scriptures of religious movements that, in some way or another, break away from dominant religions and that they see themselves as requiring one to make a choice, to join. Thus, Jesus is quoted rather dramatically as saying his teaching would be "a sword" that would rip apart families. He said, "For I have come to set a man against his father, and a daughter against her mother, and a daughter-in-law against her mother-in-law; and one's foes will be members of one's own household" (Matthew 10:35–36). Here we see an emphasis on the need to choose against one's family, at least under some circumstances. In Mecca, as Muhammad gave his revelations of the Holy Koran to the people, it was explicitly a "warning" for them to change from their worship of many gods to the worship of Allah. "Warn, therefore," God tells Muhammad, "for the warning is profitable: He that feareth God will receive the warning, and the most reprobate only will turn aside from it." (Holy Koran 87:9–11)

Similarly, though certainly less urgently, the Buddha in the Mahayana tradition is said to have offered his followers several "vehicles" for gaining enlightenment, and which vehicle one chooses is, apparently, dependent upon the individual's tastes and inclinations. Thus, in the famous Burning House Parable of the Mahayana scriptures, the gracious teacher calls children from the burning house by offering them different kinds of attractions, allowing them to choose according to their interests. In the same way, the parable claims, the Buddha teaches his doctrines in various ways, and different people choose to follow different methods, all three of them, of course, in contrast to the trap of seduction in the sensory world of desires. Thus, the Buddha urges followers of all kinds, saying "Flee from this Triple world, reach out for the three vehicles" (Conze 208).

Conversion implies voluntary communities.

Certainly the notion of voluntary religious affiliation is a common notion to any who have actually changed religions. We have already spoken of religious conversion in previous chapters, and it seems evident that some people at least very consciously choose their religious affiliations along lines suggested perhaps by the Christian, Muslim, and Buddhist ideas. But, of course, it is never as simple as saying that some religions are voluntary and others are natural communities. For people do convert to Judaism, and once a religious tradition becomes firmly entrenched in a particular community, we find that membership is often simply given, as is the case for many Christians and Muslims today, who are simply "born into" their religions by being natural members of the dominant society. As we have noted repeatedly in this text, the distinctions are seldom black and white; yet they are useful distinctions, we hope, for seeing in this case that religious membership can, at least, be more voluntary than natural, or more natural than voluntary. And with such terms in mind we can assess our own membership in our own religions. Indeed, it is perhaps ironic, but the more we proceed with such assessment, the more self-consciously we may find ourselves choosing our religion. And it is, of course, quite possible that one might voluntarily choose to recommit oneself to one's natural community. In this way, the self-awareness of the existential self and the socially formed personality coexist and overlap. And in the final analysis, it does not seem to be that we are either an individual self or a socially formed personality, but we appear to be both.

THE MIND, HUMAN BEHAVIOR, AND RELIGION

From all the discussion about the influence of relationships on the self and about the experience of being an individual, we see that an adequate understanding of a person's identity must take into account the complexity of factors that influence people and their personalities. We now look at some of the "minds" that motivate us in an attempt to understand the multitude of factors influencing behavior. (See Figure 13.1.) Developing such an understand is important for our study since the same factors that influence our behavior in general also impact our religious behavior and interpretations as well.

The idea of the mind has a long history, as philosophers, theologians, and social scientists have debated whether the mind exists, if the mind can be reduced to the brain, what are the characteristics of the mind, and a host of other questions. We do not intend to add to that debate here. Rather, we are using what scientists call an operational definition. That is, we are going to define "mind" in a particular way for the purposes of our study. For this discussion, "mind" will be defined as those factors that motivate us to think, feel, and act in a certain fashion. We also use behavior as a kind of shorthand for the behaviors, thought patterns, attitudes, and potentialities discussed previously.

Mind, as used at this point, indicates those factors that motivate the ways we think, feel, and act.

The motivators for human behavior are very complex. We have tried to illustrate these by noting four distinct minds. The first of these is the physical mind or those biological influences on human behavior. This would include a person's genes, hormones, and various chemicals, such as adrenaline or serotonin, that may change behavioral or attitudinal patterns. The physical mind also includes the physical structure of the brain itself. For example, the brain seems to have a region in it that responds when a person is having a religious experience (Newberg, d'Aquilli, and Rause). In the old nature-nurture debate (as in whether we are simply born to behave a certain way or we are trained to behave in that way), the physical mind represents the nature side.

The social mind represents those influences on people that are obtained by experience within the human group and stands for the nurture side of the nature-nurture debate. At least from the moment of birth on (if not before), an individ-

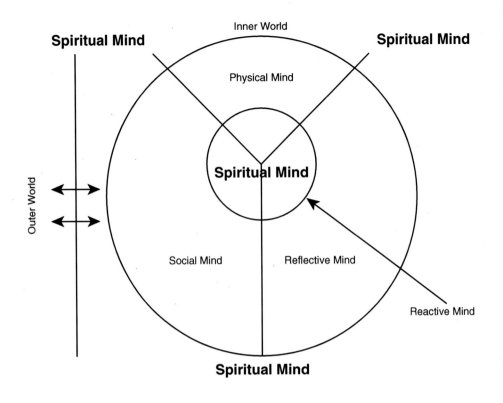

Spiritual Mind

Spiritual Mind

Inner World

Physical Mind

Spiritual Mind

Outer World

Social Mind

Reflective Mind

Reactive Mind

Spiritual Mind

Figure 13.1 The "Minds" that Motivate Our Behavior

Used by permission of R. Dean Peterson, College of DuPage

Social experience alters the physical structure of our brain.

ual has a number of experiences that profoundly influence the ways a person thinks, feels, and acts. The most important of these usually come from interaction with a person's family. However, experiences in other groups, such as a social class, age group, culture, religion, or even emerging global society, also play important roles. Arguably, the social mind, or the way that we internalize the behaviors, expectations, and teachings of others, is even more powerful than originally believed. We now know, for example, that how one learns, say, a language at an early age actually alters the physical structure of the brain. Thus in a very real way, the social mind *becomes* part of the physical structure of the brain and, as a result, becomes a component of our physical mind as well. In the same way, our religious experiences (positive or negative) may alter the structure of our brains. In a very real sense then, our religion becomes a part of us.

Human beings have experiences that are incorporated into our inner world, but we are not destined to be simply passive receptors of happenings. Instead, we actively think about what happens to us. This thinking element of our personality we call the reflective mind. Not only do we develop our self-concept, but we also build up other elements, such as moral principles and religious concepts, that may affect our behaviors. This reflection on our internal and external experience, in turn, may determine the future direction of our behavior. For instance, if some-

reflective mind—the thinking element of our personality

one comes to see himself as a caring, compassionate, and "godly person," then he likely will live his life in a fashion consistent with that understanding. In all likelihood, he will understand more about the compassion and love of God than the wrath and fury of God. On the other hand, if a person sees himself or herself as self-centered, ruthless, and evil, he or she will likely act out such ideas in his or her daily life and possibly will see more of the power, fury, and wrath of God than he or she will understand of the mercy, love, and gentle side of God.

While the elements of the reflective mind may result from our thinking about our experience, the conclusions we draw about ourselves may become so deeply engrained within us that we simply react or act out of them without further examination We call the "automatic" elements of our personalities the "reactive mind." The reactive mind represents those patterns of behavior that become so deeply seated within us that we act or react out of them without thinking or being aware that they are stimulating us. The most obvious illustration of this is driving a car. When we first learn to drive, we have to think through what we are doing, how to place the keys in the ignition, start the car, shift gears, drive out into the street, and so on. But after we have driven for some time, this driving-related behavior becomes entirely natural, and we do it without even thinking. Just as our driving behavior simply becomes a pattern of automatic responses, many of other types of interplay within ourselves and between us and the outer world assume a similar automatic character. It is likely that "religious reactions" get as deeply rooted in the reactive mind as other types of responses.

We have already noted that society influences one's self-development, practically constructing the "social mind." Likewise, the reverse is also true. Whatever is part of our reactive, reflective, social, or physical minds may be externalized and have influence on the outer world. The Thomas Theorem, developed by sociologists W.I. and Dorothy Thomas, states this as a general principle: If people believe something to be true, it is true in its consequences (572). In other words, if we believe something to be true, we act in ways that make the belief a reality. If people, whether they are from Buddhist, Muslim, or Christian traditions, experience religious conversions, they may believe they are changed people and act in ways that are different from their behavior before their religious experiences. (See Chapter 11: Religious Experience and Chapter 12: Salvation and the Meaning of Life.) People may see these changes and see the changed person in a different light. Thus, just as social ideas change us individually, so our individual behavioral alterations change the way society sees us.

Whatever is part of our reactive, reflective, social, or physical mind may have impact on the outer world.

Finally, from a religious point of view, humans also are immersed in a spiritual context that is both within us and outside of us. We call the inner and outer spiritual context in which people develop their characteristic patterns of behavior, the spiritual mind. In the diagram, the spiritual mind crosses over the boundaries between the other minds because any given religious response may simultaneously involve all elements of the inner world. For instance, a person may participate in a religious ritual. He or she has learned the ritual through experience in a particular religious community (social mind). She or he also may have thought about the meanings and obligations associated with the ritual (reflective mind). The experience also may elicit a powerful emotional response that involves the release of endorphins that give the person a "natural high" (physical mind) that the person thinks indicates an encounter with the Holy (reflective mind). If these experiences and interpretations occur fairly frequently, they may become so ingrained within the person that they become automatic responses to the stimulus of the ritual (reactive mind). In turn, the repetitive experience may become so embedded that it alters the brain and literally becomes part of the physical mind.

The spiritual mind is the thread that holds together and connects a person's other minds.

So the spiritual mind may be portrayed as the thread that runs through the other minds and connects them together. The spiritual mind also is shown in Figure 13.1 as outside of the other minds as well as part of the outer world. This is the case because the spiritual mind also points to the all-encompassing sacred matrix in which people are immersed. This sacred matrix forms the basis for life, is the factor that pulls the high and lows of life together, and is the backdrop against which our lives and deaths have meaning. In this vein, agreeing with unspecified Greek philosophers, the Christian apostle St. Paul said, "In Him [God] we live and move and have our being" (Acts 17:28).

The spiritual mind also is the matrix in which people are immersed.

The spiritual mind also interacts with the other minds at yet another level. It seems to be the case that humans are uniquely equipped, even physically, to interact with the spiritual dimension. For example, modern brain research is discovering indications of human spirituality in the structure of the brain itself. These structures appear to drive us toward relationship with the Holy. Internal spiritual experience, such as near-death experiences or mystical experiences, may have their proper place in the brain, as do perhaps the very ideas of "God" and/or "Ultimate Reality" that we find in societies globally. Religiously, this internal reality has been described by suggesting that humans are "made in the image of God," or, as noted in the case of Hinduism, that the infinite Brahman is found as *Atman* within us.

All of this discussion of the various "minds" that influence our behavior shows that our personalities contain both nature and nurture. These elements, in turn, are immersed in and penetrated by the spiritual. As we have already noted, although we are individuals, our individuality is rooted in interaction with others and in the relationships we have with them. Even the religious elements of the personality are based in relationships as well as the physical structure of the brain itself. It is no wonder that religion plays the powerful role it does in determining our personality and the health or weakness of our psychology.

RELIGION AND PERSONALITY

It should be obvious from all that has gone before in this chapter, as well as from the minds model in Figure 13.1, that religion may make up a portion of our personality. That is, most of us have experiences within the human group that have had an impact on the religious aspects of our personality, whether we are looking at learned behaviors, attitudes, beliefs, or morals. But we want to look here at a deeper, more fundamental aspect of the personality-religion interaction.

Some of the groundbreaking work on this issue was done by the American philosopher and psychologist William James. In his classic work, *The Varieties of Religious Experience,* James distinguishes between religion of "healthy mindedness" and religion associated with "sick souls." We already discussed how he developed these ideas in relation to conversion in Chapter 11. Here, we extrapolate from his underlying ideas as a way of looking at how basic personality traits interact with religion. The very pertinent question we may then ask is how much our basic human problems and perhaps their solutions are rooted in the sickness or healthiness of our religious minds.

■ PERSONALITY, EXPERIENCE, AND RELIGION

We have noted that, generally speaking, there is a dynamic, reciprocal relationship between personality and religion. That is, one's personality is influenced by his or her religion and one's religion is influenced by his or her personality. The vast majority of people in all cultures learn some kind of religion that may be incorporated directly into their personality structure. Their family, friends, and persons associated with their religion of membership convey values, behavioral expectations, rituals, and cosmologies. These traits are incorporated into their personalities to the point that the learned characteristics become second nature to them, as we noted in our discussion of the social mind.

At the same time, we have noted that people do make various choices about their religion. Thus, people's personality characteristics may lead them to choose a certain religion in cases where they have a choice. As adults, they may choose to stay with the religion in which they were reared, move into another religion, or abandon religion altogether. People likely will associate with other people in religions where their personality tendencies (positive or negative) are affirmed. If people stay in their childhood religion, they likely will change dramatically in their understanding of that religion as they go through various stages of their lives and as they mature emotionally.

For instance, as children, people may take the myths and stories of their religions to be literally true. Later in life, they may begin to question whether these stories are literally true or historically accurate. At that point, they have several choices. First, they can reject religion as nothing but "childless fairly tales" that have no relevance to real-life, adult situations. A second option is to maintain a literal, simplistic view of these stories as essential to their faith, perhaps even to make strong, conscious efforts to defend these stories from scripture or even from science. A third option is to decide that some of the religion's stories (for example, myths) are efforts to express deeper meanings or (as we saw in Chapter 7) that stories require interpretations and subtle explorations. In any of these cases, one's own personality will likely determine which direction one turns in order to produce a religious understanding capable of dealing with the complexities of day-to-day life.

Even when believers are in groups where theology and practice are diverse or not extreme, people's personalities, along with their experiences, come into play in how they understand and live out their faith. A good example of this can be seen in people who had a very negative, neglectful, or abusive relationship with their own father, especially relative to Christianity, where God is often referred to as "our Heavenly Father." By this phrase, Christians try to convey a relationship of dependency on God, whose function is to guide and discipline His children as an earthly parent might. "Heavenly Father" also attempts to convey God's loving concern and support for His earthly children as well as His willingness to place the children's good above that of His own.

Though many people have had good family experiences and can appropriate these tender views of God into their religious understanding, people who have had a negative experience with their own fathers may have no idea what is meant by this loving image of God. Worse yet, they can come to see the exact opposite in the concept of God as our heavenly Father. God may appear to them to be wrathful, vengeful, punishing, untrustworthy, and emotionally abusive. The Protestant reformer Martin Luther has been cited as an example of this phenomenon (Erickson). Early in his adult life, Luther could not experience God as a God of love, though his spiritual advisers tried to lead him in that direction. He only could see God as a God of wrath who had punishment in store for him because of his sins. Some scholars argue that Martin Luther's inability to see God as anything but vengeful and punishing stems from his strict upbringing by his father, where physical punishment and psychological abuse were handed out liberally. Even beginning to overcome the affects of negative childhood experience on Luther's religious life required a radical conversion event. One need not reduce Luther's religious insights to a mere psychological hang-up, but such examples do suggest that people with different personality structures will understand and live out the same religious teachings in quite divergent fashions.

People with negative experiences in family life may not be able to associate the positive meanings with the Christian teaching that God is their heavenly Father.

■ RELIGION AND PSYCHOLOGY

We discussed the various minds that influence our behavior earlier in this chapter. At this point, we combine that discussion with some material on religion and mental health. This is a topic that has been explored by any number of writers ever since modern psychology emerged as a scientific approach to understanding people's behavior. We cannot become deeply involved in this literature here in this textbook. Instead we mention briefly a few significant issues brought to the forefront by modern psychology.

Self-esteem, the Self, and Love of the Self

Modern psychology associates positive self-esteem with the healthy personality.

Self-esteem, a pivotal concept in modern psychology, is our evaluation of our self and our abilities. As a key component of the self-concept, positive self-esteem is believed to be the core of a healthy personality. A person with positive self-esteem believes in his or her own abilities, and this, some psychologists believe, leads a person to be confident, responsible, optimistic, loving, caring, moral, and respectful of others. Conversely, negative self-esteem may be at the heart of an unhealthy personality, leading to insecurity, lack of faith in one's abilities, irresponsible behavior, pessimism, inability to love, and negativity toward the self and others. People with positive self-esteem love themselves while those with negative self-esteem cannot love themselves.

A superficial review might lead to the conclusion that world religions prefer negative self-esteem.

Whether or not this popular psychological view of the importance of self-esteem is accurate, it is interesting to compare it to various religious perspectives. The question of self-esteem in the world's religions is complex indeed. A superficial review might lead to the conclusion that negative self-esteem is preferred by many religions. Followers are constantly cautioned against selfishness, exalting themselves, or placing their understanding of what is good above that of the

Holy. In Christianity, it is taught that "those who love their life lose it, and those who hate their life in this world will keep it for eternal life" (John 12:25). Indeed, later in the New Testament we hear St. Paul's declarations about the depths of sin and evil in the human heart: "There is no one who is righteous, not even one; there is no one who has understanding, there is no one who seeks God. All have turned aside, together they have become worthless" (Romans 3:10–12). Here, in fact, Paul seems to be quoting the Jewish scriptures, where other passages suggest similar lamentations: "The heart is devious above all else; it is perverse—who can understand it?" (Jeremiah 17:9).

In the Asian religions, especially perhaps those of India, we have already noticed a tendency toward a world-denying asceticism, and in many ways this can be taken as a poor attitude toward the self. Already noted in this chapter was the Hindu notion that the deeper soul, the Atman, is in some ways opposed to the individual self, the ego, and that true spirituality, therefore, lies in denying one's temporary, finite identity and seeking instead the Atman. Buddhists, in spite of the *anatman* or no-soul doctrine, similarly look forward to the day when we realize the illusion of individuality and therefore escape bondage to our own desires. All attachment to our own form, our own consciousness, and all the other *skandhas* is therefore the grave mistake that inhibits our spiritual liberation. The Buddha said, therefore, that the true disciple "becomes disgusted with form, and everything else, up to consciousness; disgusted, he sheds his greed for things [and] his dispassion sets him free" (Conze 188). For as long as the separate "self" survives, release from the endless cycle of birth and rebirth cannot be achieved nor the blessedness of *nirvana* experienced.

All these may seem to be purely negative views of the self, and therefore religions might seem to preach only a fundamentally bad form of self-esteem. But, unlikely as it may seem, the same Jesus who taught about "losing oneself" held a very Jewish belief that you should "love your neighbor *as yourself*" (Luke 10:27, emphasis added). Such a notion seems to take for granted that there is a natural and healthy concern for one's own welfare. But even more dramatically, the Jewish and Christian scriptures also, at least occasionally, re-emphasize the assertion that the human consciousness is, in some sense, made in the image of God, and that we are, as the Psalmist says, "fearfully and wonderfully made" (Psalm 139:14). Buddhists, too, while insisting upon the disappearance of the self, are taught to love others by starting first with a sense of a natural and healthy self-love. This "spirit of benevolent harmlessness," Winston King writes, "is to be universalized in the end, though one must begin on a lesser scale. As with other similar wish-thoughts, one begins first with himself, then proceeds to the respected, the loved, the neutral, the hostile and finally to the whole universe" (151). For the Buddhists, there may be no sense of being "fearfully and wonderfully made," but there is assumed a natural and valid self-concern. Even if the Indian religions teach a kind of ascetic self-denial, they also assume that one can take natural self-interest as a model for loving others.

Paradoxically, religions often teach loving both one's neighbor and one's self.

How can we resolve such an apparent paradox, where religions caution against and even strongly deny the self yet also assume the importance of being an individual with self-interest. Perhaps we can clarify this enigma by realizing that there are a number of types of emotional relations covered by the word *love*,

Religions see nar-
cissism as a
destructive form
of "self-love."

and perhaps the more dangerous and "unspiritual" kind of self-love is something more like an obsessive concern with the self that excludes all other people. This kind of love sometimes is called narcissism. Certainly the kind of self-love proclaimed by Christianity, for example, takes as a model Jesus himself, who, they believe, both declared himself the Son of God (hardly a humble declaration) and emphasized his own meekness and willingness to serve others and indeed to die for others on the cross. In a different way, Buddhists, too, stress that the denial of self also requires self-reliance, since, at least outside of sects such as Pure Land Buddhism (see the "grace" section of Chapter 11), Buddhist scriptures emphasize that an individual must be his or her own salvation. Thus the Dhammapada declares, "Oneself is one's own protector (refuge); what other protector (refuge) can there be? With oneself fully controlled, one obtains a protection (refuge) which is hard to gain" (Rahula 130).

This is perhaps a standing religious paradox, that we are regularly admonished to restrain ourselves, to doubt ourselves, and to deny ourselves, yet we are also vital and valuable spiritual beings, apparently worthy or capable of salvation. Soteriologically, the paradox may include the idea that we are "made in the image of God" but also "fallen sinners"; that we are wholly deluded by our own desires but must also be a "refuge to ourselves." Morally, the paradox plays out in the very practical notion that by learning to deny ourselves, we come to be more loving of others who are themselves worthy of love and service. We have spoken of the possible sources of our fallenness or ignorance in the chapter on suffering and evil (Chapter 7); we have spoken of enlightenment and salvation in the chapter on the meaning of life (Chapter 11). It should be no surprise that all these ideas are, within the religions of the world, intimately and carefully interwoven.

Sick Minds or Sick Souls

Though the previous statement about the healthy self and self-love may be true, it does not go deep enough in getting an accurate view of mental health and religion. We now turn to the question of "sick minds" or "sick souls" to further our understanding. We extended the term "mind" earlier in this chapter to include the spiritual realm. However, most contemporary psychologies focus solely on the various material and natural factors that motivate our behavior. These factors may lead to "sick minds." For our purpose, sick minds mean those pathological personality traits that result from natural, material sources. These traits may result in self-hatred, hatred of others, sick-minded religion, and destructive behavior.

sick minds—
those pathological
personality traits
that result from
natural, material
sources

The treatment of
sick minds is the
focus of most
modern psycholo-
gies as well as
some religions,
such as Buddhism
and Hinduism.

Generally, sick minds are the focus of treatment for most modern psychologies. These minds result from chemical, hormonal, or genetic deficiencies and/or from improper nurture and training by the families and friends who have the greatest impact on our psychological development. Treatment for such maladies involves counseling, psychotropic drugs, and self-correction through learning to change one's negative thoughts, perceptions, attitudes, and behaviors. The key assumption here is that sick minds and the natural influences that generate them *are* the problem. There is no deeper malady. Thus, correction of the problem comes through human intervention alone.

Far Eastern religions like Buddhism and Confucianism might well agree with this assessment. For Buddhists, the problem of human beings is our natural tendency to live in a world of *maya,* or illusion. We mistake the false for the real, the changeable for the unchangeable, the superficial for the important. We cling to things, people, and relationships when there is nothing to which we really can cling. Our lives are spent in the search for certainty when everything is uncertain. As we noted in Chapter 7, Buddhists do not attempt to explain why we are trapped in *maya* but accept that condition as a given for humanity. The solution to the dilemma of entrapment is to purify the mind through meditation and practices of self-control. This journeying can lead to a realization of the true nature of the self and of the world in which we live. This can lead to eventual release from the endless cycle of rebirth to the blessedness of *nirvana.*

As noted in the previous chapter, Confucianism is not concerned with eternal salvation but with how to live a moral and virtuous life in this world. Although Confucius was aware that evil people exist, he generally was optimistic about human nature. He believed that propriety, along with virtuous behavior, could be cultivated with proper instruction, devoted study, and self-discipline. Thus, to one degree or another, Buddhism and Confucianism teach that wrongmindedness could be replaced with rightmindedness without supernatural intervention. To use our jargon, sick-mindedness could be replaced with healthy-mindedness. The unhealthy mind is the core problem.

For the Abrahamic faiths, sick minds are a symptom of sick souls.

The Abrahamic faiths present another understanding of sick-mindedness. For them, sick minds are a symptom of sick souls. We use sick souls to represent the doctrine that human beings are alienated from the Holy in their spiritual center. The problems of human beings, their relationships, and their societies stem from a deeper spiritual source according to Judaism, Christianity, and Islam. As we noted in previous chapters, especially when discussing the myth of "The Fall" in Chapter 7 and Christian salvation in Chapter 12, the Hebrew scripture declares how human beings lost the originally pure and perfect state of existence and brought forth the sin and suffering and internal corruption we see in the world and in ourselves. We need not repeat the story except to emphasize that, according to this interpretation, we and our world are now alienated from God, which means we are alienated from our true selves, from one another and nature. Deception, shame, murder, and all manner of vice are thus an intrinsic part of human relations.

For the Abrahamic faiths, the healing of the soul through returning to a proper relation with God is necessary for having a truly healthy mind and physical health as well.

Perhaps the depth and extent of this corruption is stressed more in Christian teachings than in Judaic or Islamic views, but for all three of the Abrahamic faiths, repairing the damage done by sin starts with returning to a proper and submissive relationship with God. We are taught in the Abrahamic faiths to love our neighbors as ourselves, but this is impossible without first having a healthy obedience of, love for, or submission to God. Further, God has taken the initiative in repairing this relation as He reveals Himself to lost humanity in nature, history, and in His activities with specific human beings, such as His prophets. Acceptance of God's revelation and submission to His will is then the basis of the healing of minds, the repair of shattered personalities, and the destruction of evil in human's lives and their relationships. This and this alone heals sick souls, and only a healthy soul can give us a healthy mind.

Although the Abrahamic faiths generally believe that ultimately sick minds are embedded in sick souls, a word of caution is in order. It is evident from some tra-

Religious faith and healing have been closely associated throughout human history. For example, the traditional healer or "medicine man or woman" usually used herbs and compounds along with religious ritual to cure disease. Yet, with the rise of modern mechanistic, scientific medicine, a wedge has been driven between the two. In recent years, however, scientists are beginning to take a closer look at issues surrounding religion and health as these excerpts from *Newsweek* show.

In an effort to understand the health differences between believers and nonbelievers, scientists are beginning to parse the individual components that compose religious experience. Using brain scans, researchers have discovered that meditation can change brain activity and improve immune response; other studies have shown it can lower heart rate and blood pressure, both of which reduce the body's stress response. (Most religions incorporate meditative practices, like chanting or prayer, into their traditions.) Even intangibles, such as the impact of forgiveness, may boost health as well. In a survey of 1,500 people published earlier this year, Neal Krause, a researcher at the University of Michigan's School of Public Health, found that people who forgive easily tend to enjoy greater psychological well-being and have less depression than those who hold grudges. "There's a physiology of forgiveness," says Dr. Herbert Benson, head of the Mind/Body Medical Institute, and a host of the upcoming Harvard conference. "When you do not forgive, it will chew you up."

Using prayer to effect health is perhaps the most controversial subject of research. In (a) *Newsweek* Poll, 84 percent of Americans said praying for others can have a positive effect on their recovery, and 74 percent said that would be true even

Physical and mental health problems must be treated as real in spite of their origins in spiritual alienation.

ditional examples, such as the cases of epilepsy in the New Testament, that we must beware of taking every illness as a sign of spiritual affliction. In some stories of the Christian Gospels (for example, Matt 17:14–18), Jesus healed epileptics by "casting out demons," but today we treat it as a physical illness. Similarly, we should perhaps beware of the fact that healing one's soul by returning to faith in God and submitting oneself to His will may not automatically result in the curing of one's mind. People can restore their relationship with God, but some have been so deeply scarred during the development of their personalities that they struggle with unhealthy minds or even mental illness the rest of their lives.

This should not be too surprising when we consider two points. First, from the viewpoints of Judaism, Christianity, and Islam, humans are both spiritual and material. One's spiritual nature is real, but so is one's material nature. People not only are spirits (or souls), they also are bodies. These two elements making up humans are related, but they may also function somewhat independently of one another. Curing the soul does not automatically result in curing the mind or vice versa.

Second, what we have said in this section is consistent with the discussion with the minds model we presented earlier in this chapter. To a large measure, this model represents the "this-worldly" factors that influence healthy or unhealthy minds. The physical mind may contain genetic, hormonal, or chemical elements

if they didn't know the patient. But what does the science say? At a meeting of the American College of Cardiology last month, Duke researcher Dr. Mitchell Krucoff reported preliminary data on a national trial of 750 patients undergoing heart catheterization or angioplasty. A group of patients who were prayed for (by, among others, Roman Catholics and Sufi Muslims in the United States, Buddhist monks in Nepal and Jews at the Western Wall) did no better than a second group that received standard care or a third, which was given a special program of music, therapeutic touch and guided imagery. But there was one intriguing finding: a fourth "turbocharged" group, which received both prayers and the music program, had death rates 30 percent lower than any of the other patients. "Despite all the attention modern medicine has paid to new technology, it has neglected to ask what happens if you pay attention to the rest of the patient," says Krucoff.

Overall, the prayer studies have not shown clear effects, and even religious proponents are skeptical that it can ever—or should ever—be tested. So many people already pray for the sick that scientists cannot establish a control group; when the prescription is prayer, patients often get it whether doctors want them to or not. This "noise"—the extra prayers of mothers, fathers, sisters, brothers, friends, church members—may taint trial results. And the studies prompt questions that no one, not even the best scientists, will ever be able to answer: Can one extra prayer mean the difference between life and death? Can prayer be dosed, the way medicines are? Does harder praying mean better treatment by God? In the minds of many, especially theologians, those questions border on the sacrilegious. "To think that God would only respond to the group that was prayed for and leave the other group out in the dark is based on total misconceptions of how God responds to prayer," says Cynthia Cohen, a senior research fellow at the Kennedy Institute of Ethics at Georgetown University. "God is not a machine who responds mechanically."

Source: "Faith and Healing." *Newsweek.* 2004. http://www.msnbc..com/id/3339730/ (accessed April 26, 2004).

that predispose one to having a healthy mind, but it may also contain elements that create an unhealthy mind. Likewise, the social mind may incline a person toward either healthy-minded or sick-minded behavior. The reflective mind, which thinks about our experiences, may incline us toward mental health or illness. It is important to remember that we are not born with these minds; they develop through interaction with others. For instance, we are not born with a positive or negative self-esteem; we learn these through exchanges with people around us.

Once these minds are established, they become part of the reactive mind or our automatic responses to ourselves, to others, and to the world around us. This is even more telling when we recall that the learned patterns of behavior literally alter the physical structure of our brains. All-in-all then, patterns of behaviors, attitudes, and feelings that make up our various minds become powerful factors in and of themselves. Spiritual renewal may still leave these needing separate treatment if they are mentally unhealthy.

■ SOCIALIZATION AND RELIGION

Earlier in this chapter we discussed factors influencing the personality as well as how religion interacts with healthy and unhealthy personalities. We now want to look at the transmission of religious ideas along with how religion interplays with identity. For social scientists, socialization "is the process by which people learn the characteristics of their group—the knowledge, skills, attitudes, values, and actions thought appropriate for them" (Henslin GL-12). Most socialization occurs through specific individuals known as significant others (parents, family members, friends, teachers, and so on), though some socialization also results from indirect interaction with others via books, television, the Internet, and the like. Socialization leads to the creation of the social mind we discussed previously.

Religious ideas, beliefs, and practices are some of the elements that are transmitted to individuals through socialization. That is, most people receive some type of religious training (positive or negative—formal or informal) beginning in their childhood. This may come through parents and other family members along with formal instruction by various religious officials. In many countries, religious education is routinely conducted in public schools as well as in religious institutions. This early education stresses the basic teachings, beliefs, practices, and rituals of the child's religion. Many people do not move beyond this basic instruction; they never realize that more complex, "grown-up" understandings of their faith are possible. Such a childlike faith may be comforting and deeply traditional, or it may leave them ill-equipped to face more complicated religious, moral, and life dilemmas as they grow older.

The child's early religious socialization usually is accepted uncritically and becomes fixed in the social mind. Because of this, it generally reflects the views of a young person's significant others. This is true whether the significant others are intensely religious, mildly religious, or anti-religious. This brings us to another point that should be addressed. Scholars of religion often distinguish between extrinsic religion and intrinsic religion. **Extrinsic religion** involves religious beliefs, practices, and rules that are absorbed from "outside" of the individual. **Intrinsic religion** involves religious beliefs, practices, and ethical principles that result from a person critically examining religious views that, in turn, become a part of a person's religious makeup. Intrinsic religion functions from "within" a person.

At the risk of proposing an evaluative argument, we might suggest that there is a certain healthy development from extrinsic to intrinsic religion. For though a person's initial religious training is recorded in the social mind, it may still be understood only at a childlike level. There may even be injunctions against questioning these religious precepts. But we have already noted in our discussion of natural and voluntary communities that the more reflective activity of the existential self may, and perhaps should, come into play later in life, as a person receives additional education that allows him or her to develop a more sophisticated level of religious understanding. In this way, religion may become more intrinsic after precepts are questioned and accepted as one's own. Extrinsic religion is something received from others; intrinsic religion emerges when that which is received from others is examined and becomes one's own. As such, it resides initially in the reflective mind but with time may become part of the reactive mind. In this way, one does not only follow or mimic the religion of others, but rather, one's religion is "written on the heart." That is, one's faith can become personal and serve as a basis for the religious and moral activity that flows from a person's character.

One other point needs to be made before leaving the discussion of socialization. Much of what we have said assumes that an individual has some kind of

Most people receive some type of positive or negative religious instruction beginning in childhood.

With intrinsic religion, one's religious and moral activity flows from one's personal character.

Almost everyone has some degree of covert religious education because religion is deeply embedded in all cultures.

overt religious training, whereas in fact some people may never have received any religious education in their family or otherwise. This may be true, but almost everyone receives some degree of *covert* religious education. This is the case because religion becomes deeply involved with culture at any number of points.

By "covert religious education," we mean that even those members of a culture who have not been reared in overtly religious environments still may have received some kind of "religious education." For instance, almost all citizens of the United States who were reared in U.S. culture would conceive of God as singular, as only one God, and they would probably speak of God as masculine (He) as opposed to feminine (She). Additionally, they may be aware that God demands justice or obedience to His law. They likely are aware of the Ten Commandments and the Bible as "God's word." When people speak of the destructiveness of nuclear war or some other "end-of-the-world" scenario, they often refer to it as "Armageddon," as in the title of a recent movie. Most people are aware that this came from the Bible and somehow indicated the end of the Earth, though they may not have been aware that this refers to the great battle between the forces of God and Satan at the end of time pictured in the biblical book of the Revelation to St. John.

Similarly, in addition to the scientific cosmology regarding the universe, most citizens of the United States also receive a minimal religious cosmology. For example, they may conceive of a realm of reward for good behavior called "heaven" and a place of punishment for evil called "hell." Heaven is "up there" to most while hell is "down there." So it is that a football or baseball player who makes a good play may point up toward the sky (heaven) to express his thankfulness to God. These views are left over from the days when a religious cosmology dominated in which it was assumed that the Earth was the center of the universe with the realm of the dead below the surface of the Earth; the sun, stars, and moon revolved around the Earth; and heaven was above the firmament that held up the sky. Such religious ideas and cosmologies are transmitted in a covert fashion to most people as a part of "cultural literacy," even if they, their family, and their friends are not terribly religious.

IDENTITY, RELIGION, AND GLOBALIZATION

Earlier in this chapter we mentioned the importance of self-concept and discussed how our identity is rooted in relationships with other persons. In this section, we look at the role of religion in individual and group identity as well as how religion and identity interact with social change and globalization. For many people, religion is deeply involved in their psychological make-up at a number of different levels, and we have seen that the teachings of religion may encourage people to be either positive or negative about themselves. Similarly, religion may also lead people to have a positive or negative attitude toward the society in which they reside and/or to the universe itself.

Religion often serves as a powerful positive or negative force in establishing personal identity.

We have noted from the beginning of this chapter that religion becomes involved with our self-concept to the extent that it becomes a part of our identity. One person may say, "I am a Buddhist," another "I am a Muslim," or, yet another, "I am a Christian." For some, their religious identity is a key factor in their personalities. To deny their religious faith would be to deny who they are. Others may have only a vague religious identity. They may say, "I'm not an atheist, but I do not identify with any particular religion." Religion may also serve as a negative factor in the identity of some by showing what they are not. For example, one might claim, "I don't believe in any religion or God, since I am an atheist," or again, "Whatever else I may be, I am not a Christian." Thus, both positive and negative self-identifications in religious terms may be powerfully maintained.

Religion may also be directly involved as a positive or negative force in ethnic identity.

Religious identity also may become involved with ethnic identity. Most, though not all, Indians see themselves as Indian and Hindu. In their mind, being an Indian means being a Hindu. For the better part of the last one thousand years, to be a Russian was to be an Orthodox Christian. Likewise, for many Americans, being a citizen of the United States involves being part of a Christian nation—in spite of the fact that the United States has been a secular state from its inception. From a more sociological point of view, religion may serve an important group function by establishing and maintaining group boundaries. That is, it may be used to determine just who is in and who is out of a given group. Since religion supposedly roots its practices in the Absolute, the religious boundaries between groups may be especially emphatic, even specifying who is "damned" and who is "saved" or what categories of people are "friends of God" and "enemies of God." Additionally, they may lead people to act negatively toward "out" group members with particularly "holy" zeal.

Social change often threatens our identity. For instance, globalization causes dramatic shifts in identity, as we mentioned in Chapter 1, because more and more people are called upon to see themselves as members of a global society. In fact, when looking at economic, justice, and perhaps religious problems, people often are called upon to see themselves as "citizens of the world," as opposed to being members of an ethnic group, a nation-state, or a religion. That is, they may be required to look at complex environmental, social, economic, or religious problems from a perspective that is much wider than the usual sources of identity. More localized sources of identity, such as ethnic identity ("I am a Serbian"), national identity ("I am an American"), or religious identity ("I am a Muslim") may prevent finding solutions to global problems such as warfare, terrorism, pollution, or famine. If this is so, then one's religious identity, while being important and valuable as a way of understanding who one is, may also be challenged by and may get in the way of seeing things from a global perspective.

The changes associated with globalization threaten a person's very identity, which may cause him or her to retreat into religion to anchor his or her identity and way of life in the unchanging, the Eternal.

Social change may threaten us to the very core because our identity is at the very heart of who we are. This realization in turn may help us understand why first modernization, and now globalization, is so threatening to many people both in developed and developing nations. Not only does modernization undermine traditional commitments to such groups as family, village, or tribe, but it calls into question who a person is. As a result, modernization/globalization not only is a threat to a person's traditional way or life, but it also is destroying the very core of the individual by destroying who that individual sees him- or herself to be.

One way to "anchor" ourselves in a time of change is to project our identity into the Absolute. That is, we turn to our religion as a way of protecting ourselves against loss or change of identity. We might say, "Things change in society, but I do not change because God has made me a Muslim and I know that God and His law never change. Because of this, my society and my way of life also cannot change." At the same time, when global change impinges upon a person's way of life or identity, it also may seem to be an attack on his or her religion that is closely linked with the way of life and the personal identity. This realization may help us to understand recent events involving cultural/religious conflicts the world over. In addition, it might be a clue to interpreting reactions to the modern global society by some Muslims who consider globalization as an attack on their person, their way of life, and their religion. Thus, after the September 11, 2001, attacks in New York and Washington, the American President George W. Bush carefully specified that America's war on terrorism was not an assault on Islam, but this distinction was misunderstood by many Muslims who did not follow the modern logic that separates religion, culture, and the self. Bush's secular war on Islamic terrorists was still perceived as an attack on Islam. Similarly, to uproot a way of life (which globalization does) is at times perceived as an attack on religious traditions and their individual identity as well. It is probably safe to speculate that those who benefit least from globalization are most likely to have a strongly religious response against it.

Religion may play a positive role in personal and group identity. However, it may have some negative consequences as well. For one thing, the type of identity a person receives from religion may be destructive. For instance, if a person comes to see him- or herself as essentially evil, he or she may play that self-concept out in relation to his or her person as well as in relation to other people nearby. We discussed this matter earlier in the chapter under the heading of the reactive mind. That is, a negative self-concept (whether its source is religious or not) becomes a part of the way we react automatically to the world around us. This is not just a concept from the social sciences. Several thousands of years ago, the book of Proverbs from the Hebrew scriptures warned that as a person "thinks" in his heart, so he is (23:7).

Religion as part of group identity also can have dire consequences. We mentioned religion's role in boundary maintenance. Not only may religion help define who is in or out of one's group, but it also may help define who is in or out of a group's "moral universe." **Moral universe** is a term used by ethicists to designate who is deserving of ethical treatment. That is, a person who is a member of my religious group may be considered part of my moral universe and deserving of ethical treatment, but those outside of my religious group may not be considered as part of my moral universe and, therefore, do not deserve ethical treatment. In fact, if I am taught that those outside of my religious group are the "enemies of God," I may be bound by my faith to destroy them. This is not just idle speculation. Many could not understand how the people who attacked the World Trade Center in 2001 or how Timothy McVeigh who bombed the Federal Building in Oklahoma City in 1995 could have killed so many innocent people, including children. It is very simple. Both sets of terrorists were socialized in cultural and religious systems that defined anyone who did not agree with them politically and religiously as outside of their moral universe. The very fact that people were at the World Trade Center or the Federal Building meant that they were participating in an evil system that the terrorists were honor bound to destroy. No one, including children, was considered innocent.

Religion may define who is outside a group's moral universe and who may, therefore, be subject to abuse.

The implication of all of this is that, as globalization proceeds, we can expect religions of many kinds to continue to provide individuals with a strong element of their personal identity, sometimes in a way that gives individuals strength in times of uncertainty but sometimes also in a way that all the more feels threatened by change. We know well the power of religion in the face of change to give people strength or to arm them with anger and resistance. For good or ill, religion in a time of global change remains a force to be reckoned with.

CONCLUSION

In this chapter we have looked at the complex relationships among personality, experience, and religion. We have noted that a mutually effective relationship exists between religion and personality and that the personality is influenced by experience as well. This should not be surprising as people may be born with certain attributes but acquire many of their characteristics through social interaction.

We also have noted that religion is very much a two-edged sword. Religion often contributes to socially and emotionally healthy activities, but it is also a powerful force that may be destructive to individuals and to societies as well. Perhaps here it is good to recall Martin Marty's assertion, noted in our first chapter, that religion has caused more healing than perhaps anything else, while religion has also caused more bloodshed than perhaps anything else. Similarly, we might say that religion more than anything else makes us who we are and that it restricts us as we seek to form new relationships and to respond to a changing world. Again, we find that religion is a powerful force for good or ill, a force literally for defining who we are, and for creating the world we all will inhabit.

■ INTERACTIVE EXERCISE

Please continue your exploration of religion, personality, and the individual by going to the interactive exercise for this chapter online (**http://www.religion .wadsworth.com/richter**).

WORKS CITED

Bresnan, Patrick. *Awakening: An Introduction to the History of Eastern Thought.* 2nd ed. Upper Saddle River, NJ: Prentice Hall, 2003.

Brown, Robert McAfee. *Is Faith Obsolete?* Philadelphia: Westminster Press, 1974.

Browning, Don S. *Religious Thought and the Modern Psychologies: A Critical Conversation in the Theology of Culture.* Philadelphia: Fortress Press, 1987.

Conze, Edward. *Buddhist Scriptures.* Baltimore: Penguin, 1959.

Descartes, Rene. Meditations *Concerning First Philosophy.* New York: Bobs-Merrill, 1960.

Erickson, E. H. *Young Man Luther: A Study in Psychoanalysis and History.* New York: Norton, 1958.

"Faith and Healing." *Newsweek.* 2004. http://www.msnbc..com/id/3339730/ (accessed April 26, 2004).

Goodenough, Erwin R. *The Psychology of Religious Experiences.* New York: Basic Books, Inc., 1965.

Henslin, James M. *Sociology: A Down-to-Earth Approach.* 6th ed. New York: Allyn and Bacon, 2003.

Hinde, Robert A. *Why Gods Persist: A Scientific Approach to Religion.* New York: Routledge, Taylor, and Francis Group, 1999.

Hume, David. *A Treatise of Human Nature.* Ed. L. A. Selby-Bigge. New York: Oxford, 1964.

James, William. *The Varieties of Religious Experience.* New York: The Macmillian Company, 1961 (org. 1902).

Judaism: The Chosen People. Video recording. London: BBC-TV, 1977.

King, Winston L. *In the Hope of Nibbana.* LaSalle, IL: Open Court 1964.

Mead, George Herbert. *The Mind, Self, and Society.* Chicago: University of Chicago, 1934.

Newberg, Andrew B., Eugene G. d'Aquilli, and Vince Rause. *Why God Won't Go Away: Brian Science and the Biology of Belief.* New York: Ballantine, 2001.

Rahula, M. *What the Buddha Taught.* New York: Grove Press, 1974.

Sartre, Jean Paul. *Being and Nothingness.* New York: Washington Square Books, 1977.

Sayers, Dorothy L. "The Image of God." In *The World Treasury of Modern Religious Thought.* Ed. Jaroslav Pelikan. Boston: Little, Brown and Company, 1990.

Sullivan, H. S. *The Interpersonal Theory of Psychiatry.* New York: Norton, 1953.

Thomas, W. I., with Dorothy Swaine Thomas. *The Child in America.* New York: Knopf, 1928.

Van Voorst, Robert E. *Anthology of World Scriptures.* 4th ed. Belmont, CA: Wadsworth Publishing Company, 2003.

FOR FURTHER READING

Bakan, David. The *Duality of Human Existence: An Essay on Psychology and Religion.* Chicago: Rand McNally, 1966.

Browning, Don S. *Religious Thought and the Modern Psychologies: A Critical Conversation in the Theology of Culture.* Philadelphia: Fortress Press, 1987.

Descartes, Rene. *Meditations Concerning First Philosophy.* New York: Bobs-Merrill, 1960.

Jeeves, Malcom A. *Human Nature at the Millennium: Reflections on the Integration of Psychology and Christianity.* Grand Rapids, MI: Baker, 1997.

Marty, Martin E., and R. Scott Appleby. *Religion, Ethnicity, and Self-identity: Nations in Turmoil.* Hanover, NH: University Press, 1999.

Mead, George Herbert. *The Mind, Self, and Society.* Chicago: University of Chicago, 1934.

Newberg, Andrew B., Eugene G. d'Aquilli, and Vince Rause. *Why God Won't Go Away: Brian Science and the Biology of Belief.* New York: Ballantine, 2001.

Rahula, M. What the Buddha Taught. New York: Grove Press, 1974.

Sartre, Jean Paul. *Being and Nothingness.* New York: Washington Square Books 1977.

Sayers, Dorothy L. "The Image of God." In *The World Treasury of Modern Religious Thought.* Ed. Jaroslav Pelikan. Boston: Little, Brown and Company, 1990.

Shorto, Russell. *Saints and Madmen: Psychiatry Opens its Doors to Religion.* New York: Henry Holt, 1999.

Smith, Huston. *Forgotten Truth: The Common Vision of the World's Religions.* San Francisco: Harper, 1976.

Tart, Charles T., (ed.) *Transpersonal Psychologies.* New York: Harper and Row, 1975.

Taylor, Charles. *Varieties of Religion Today: William James Revisited.* Cambridge, MA: Harvard, 2002.

Yogananda, Paramahansa, et al. *A World in Transition: Finding Spiritual Security in Times of Change.* Los Angeles: Self-Realization Fellowship, 1999.

14 RELIGION AND SOCIETY IN A GLOBAL AGE

The pictures for this chapter found above and on the Web site (**http://www .religion.wadsworth.com/richter**), and the following quotations are intended to help students get into the complex interplay between religion and social factors in a rapidly globalizing society. Please look over these pictures and passages, then consider the Introductory Questions that follow as a way to prepare for reading this chapter.

> *Man makes religion, religion does not make man. . . .*
> *Religious misery is in one way the expression of real*
> *misery, and in another a protest against real misery. Religion*
> *is the sigh of the afflicted creature, the soul of a heartless*

world, as it is also the spirit of spiritless conditions. It is the opium of the people.

The abolition of religion as the illusionary happiness of the people is the demand for their real happiness. The abandonment of the illusions about their condition is the demand to give up a condition that requires illusion. Hence criticism of religion is in embryo a criticism of this vale of tears whose halo is religion.

—Marxist critique of religion: Karl Marx (286–287)

Do you not know that each of you (women) is also an Eve? . . . You are the Devil's gateway, you are the unsealer of that forbidden tree, you are the first deserter of the divine law, you are the one who persuaded him whom the devil was too weak to attack. How easily you destroyed man, the image of God! Because of the death which you brought upon us, even the son of God had to die.

—Christianity: Tertullian, Christian Church Father (*De Cultu Feminarum* 1:1.)

It is the nature of women to seduce men in this (world); for that reason, the wise are never unguarded in (the company of) females.

For women are able to lead astray in (this) world not only a fool, but even a learned man, and (to make) him a slave of desire and anger.

—Hinduism: Laws of Manu 2:213–214 (Bühler)

There will always be poor people in the land. Therefore I command you to be open-handed toward your brothers and toward the poor and needy in your land.

—Judaism: Deuteronomy 15:11

Duke Jing of Qi asked Confucius about government. Confucius replied: "Let the lord be a lord; the subject a subject; the father a father; the son a son."

—Confucianism: The Analects 12:11

There is no longer Jew or Greek, there is no longer slave or free, there is no longer male and female; for all of you are one in Christ Jesus.

—Christianity: Galatians 3:28

INTRODUCTORY QUESTIONS

1. Karl Marx believed that religion was a human creation resulting from workers being exploited by capitalism. Thus religion, he claimed, is a human creation with no basis in a spiritual world. It is only the "sigh" of people wanting a better life because economic oppression in this life is so bad. Do you think Marx is right? Could there be a sense in which Marx was both correct and incorrect? Please support your answer with your own argument.

2. The pictures show both the wealthy and the poorer classes at worship. What do such pictures tell you about how social and economic factors interact with religion? Do you think religion helps to unite people across economic classes? Consider these pictures in light of the command from Judaism.

3. Churches and temples often seem very ornate and decorated, even in places where poverty may be prevalent. In the pictures, does the gold or decoration seem unnecessary and wasteful? Do you think religions ought instead to "serve the poor"? Could religions consistently have both a concern for the poor and elaborate, decorated churches and temples? Explain your opinion.

4. Issues of gender equality (or inequality) are increasingly important in the world's religions of the global age. Tertullian's view about women is based on the story of the fall in the Hebrew Bible (Genesis 3:1–24). Do you agree or disagree with the way this story is interpreted by Tertullian? Compare it to the Laws of Manu excerpt. Within religion, is this apparently negative view of women common? Why? Do you think these interpretations are accurate? Support your claim with your own argument.

5. In light of the divisions between rich and poor, between the genders, and between races, how do you think Saint Paul hopes to find unity among Christian believers? Do other religions have similar hopes? Are they reasonable hopes that religion can unite people of various economic and social backgrounds? What do you think?

6. For Confucius, being "religious" might be nothing more—and nothing less—than knowing one's place in society. Do you think religion should control or define society? Or should religion be a purely private, internal matter? Defend your view.

INTRODUCTION

In the previous chapter we explored an important aspect of religion: the complex relationships among religion, personality, and the individual. In this chapter we look at religion as a phenomenon that has very complex interactions with the social setting in which it occurs. We began this task when we discussed religion and globalization in Chapter 1. In Chapter 4, on the origins of religion, we further elaborated on aspects of this interaction when we discussed various anthropological, sociological, and psychological approaches to religion. In that chapter we noted that many social and psychological factors play an important role in religion but that religion must not be reduced solely to sociological and psychological dynamics. At the close of our text, however, we come back at last to the study of religion's social dynamics, especially as "society" extends itself in our postmodern world to the global community.

One of the difficulties in understanding religion and society, especially religion and global society, is that modern societies tend to be individualistic. That is, much of modern life places a great deal of emphasis on the individual's private life, personal efforts, beliefs, desires, and rights. It is often believed that groups are nothing more than collections of individuals, but in fact this is not true. To a significant degree, we are the products of the groups to which we belong, or hope to belong. Nevertheless, the cultural stress on individualism with which many of us are familiar contributes to the process we noted in Chapter 1 of making religion an individual and private phenomenon. Yet, the truth is our religions are formed in groups. Most of us inherit our religions from our families or ethnic groups. Moreover, these groups interact with other elements of the societies in which they operate, as well as the forces such as globalization that influence the overall context in which they exist.

Even when people look at some of the social aspects of religion, they still may not realize the extent to which social forces interact with religious forces. Indeed, it may be an important part of a religion to believe that somehow their own beliefs are divorced from the social dynamics they see in other people's religions. For instance, we saw in previous chapters that for many religions, perhaps especially Islam, their holy scripture must be understood to be somehow delivered purely and perfectly to humanity, as if these words of God had no human influence or even human context. Thus, the conservative Muslim will contend that both Jews and Christians have allowed their scriptures to be perverted by human influence and consequently that only the Muslims truly follow the way of Abraham (Holy Koran 2:135). Society has influenced others' beliefs, the Muslim might argue, but our own has remained pure. Similarly, some Christians may feel their denominational views represent the "true gospel" or "the original church," while other Christian groups have been corrupted and their doctrine diluted by social change. While these must be taken seriously as sincere expressions of their respective beliefs, more detached views recognize how historical, social, economic, political, and psychological forces played out in the emergence of these faiths. Additionally, these forces play a significant role in how these religions developed and how they are lived out today. This chapter, then, takes a look at how religion interacts with society's elements and with the forces of change now sweeping the globe.

RELIGION AND CULTURE

There is a mutually effective relationship between religion and society.

There is a very complex set of relationships between religion and society in every religion and every time in history. We might describe this complexity more simply as the mutually effective relationship between religion and society. That is, religion has an effect on society and society has an effect on religion. The two do not exist in isolation from each other. However, we need to take a deeper look at this phenomenon for better understanding.

We need to review a few definitions to begin our inquiry. A **society** is a group of people who share a common culture. So what is it that makes nearly 300 million people, from different parts of the world and scattered over a large landmass, Americans? These millions of people are Americans because they participate in American culture. **Culture** is the shared way of life or lifestyle of a particular people. This includes a people's traditions, history, beliefs, and practices. It also includes a people's economic, educational, political, family, and religious systems. These are often referred to as the basic institutions of modern societies.

The complex patterns of relationships among these institutions and among other elements of society is known as the **social structure**. For example, the family structure of a given society is usually supported by, and in turn supports, religious beliefs and practices. For the last 10,000 years or so, most societies have been male-dominated, or patriarchal. This arrangement is reflected in religious systems where the chief gods are male as well as in teachings about husbands being the head of the household and women and children pictured as subservient to him. This pattern is reflected in the Hebrew scriptures in the second chapter of the book of Genesis, where Adam (man) is created first, and Eve (woman) is made for companionship with Adam. Further, God makes Adam from the dust of the earth, but Eve is made from the rib of Adam. Again, the hierarchical arrangement between men and women is reinforced as Adam is made directly by God and is dependent on Him for life, but Eve is dependent on Adam.

Interestingly, in the last 100 years the trend in modern societies has been toward more equal or egalitarian relationships between men and women. This has meant that in the home, the husband and wife are seen as equal partners. Supporters of this change also find religious justification for the new arrangements. For instance, they note that in the first chapter of the book of Genesis, the first man and woman are created at the same time with both being made "in the image and likeness of God." This shows that men and women are equal and equally reflect the very nature of God.

These points show that family structure is reflected in religious teachings. As the family structure changes, the interpretation of religion changes as a way to justify these. However, this is only part of the picture. Religion may also create or change existing social structure including the family system. A good example of this process is seen in the change of the status of women found in early Islam. Westerners often criticize the many restrictions on women in Islam as offensive to modern values and, perhaps, as violations of women's rights. But the picture looks a good bit different when the supposed restrictions of Islam are put in their historical and cultural context. At the time the prophet Mohammed was receiving his revelations, most women were seen as having a particularly low status. This was especially true among the desert tribes of what is now Saudi Arabia. The Holy Koran elevates women's status considerably above this miserable state. For instance, a man could have up to four wives, assuming he could treat each of them with equal affection and respect. Women also were given property rights and could institute divorce in an unhappy or abusive marriage.

The point here is not to discuss religious gender issues as such; that will be done later. For now, the point is to note how religion changes culture and is changed by culture. How we expect families to function, and how we define a "normal" family structure, is part of a culture, however much it may also be perceived as human nature. And such cultural structures do not exist apart from the other influences of culture, of which, as we have seen repeatedly, religion is one of the most powerful.

RELIGION, CULTURE, AND CIVILIZATION

The dynamics between religion and family are examples of much broader interactions. Numerous instances of religions incorporating cultural practices into their own system of symbols, rituals, ethics, and beliefs can be noted. For instance, Christmas trees and Easter eggs were originally pagan symbols for eternal life and fertility, respectively. When Christianity replaced the pagan religions of Europe, these symbols were brought into Christian practices. Likewise, female circumcision (or female genital mutilation) is a tribal practice from Africa that became incorporated into some forms of Islam—even though most Islamic scholars say it has nothing to do with Islam. Indeed, tribal Islam may look quite different from Egyptian, Iranian, and Indonesian Islam, just as American, Spanish, and Philippine Catholicism have many differences; Sri Lankan, Vietnamese, and Japanese Buddhism contain varied cultural elements; and so on. This diversity is due to the simple fact that religions absorb cultural elements.

The impact of religions on groups of cultures may be so profound that they help stimulate the creation of entire civilizations.

At the same time, religions often significantly alter cultures where they are introduced. Indeed, as religions spread, their impact on groups of cultures may be so profound that they help stimulate the creation of entire civilizations. By **civilizations,** we mean large geographical areas containing a number of diverse cultures, which, in spite of their differences, are bound together by common traditions, perspectives, cosmologies, ethics, religions, and philosophies. Civilizations are held together by more than religion, of course, but religions and related philosophies historically have been the foundation on which the great world civilizations rest. They often give diverse peoples a common source of identity and common values. For example, a large swath of territory stretching from North Africa through the Middle East into southern Asia contains numerous peoples and nations but still is considered the "Muslim world." Similarly, places as diverse as Western Europe, Greenland, Iceland, Canada, the United States, and the other countries of the Americas, Australia and New Zealand, can be considered part of Western Civilization, which continues to have its roots in Christianity, in spite of the secularization of modern times. In "the East," Chinese civilization has been, at least until the communist revolution, closely associated with the religious ideas of Taoism and, especially, Confucianism. The influence of Chinese Confucianism, moreover, has spread into Korea and Japan, becoming entrenched in those cultures as well.

In all such cases of religions extending into empires and civilizations, the religions help to define, as well as to legitimate and protect a society's or a civilization's institutions. Thus, the British may sing a hymn entitled "God Save the Queen," while Americans sing "America the Beautiful" with its own appeals to God's blessings, and both are sung to the same melody. Or even more to the point, first-century Roman emperors were considered gods, such that citizens were required to obey their emperors as both a political duty and religious obligation. Thanks to the Shinto religion, this was also true in Japan well into the 20th century.

RELIGION, CULTURE, AND THE WORLD

We discuss the issue of the interaction of civilizations with globalization later in this chapter. However, at this juncture we need to examine another interesting question: How do religions themselves understand their relationship to their own surrounding cultures? In some ways, as we have emphasized, religions are always deeply and inextricably interwoven with culture; yet in other ways, religions sometimes see the cultural practices of daily life with suspicion. Indeed, the term "secular," which often stands as the opposite of "sacred," comes from a Latin word meaning "the world." Following such usage, we will use the term "the world" to indicate cultural elements that may be viewed as somehow different from a given religion. How divergent religions understand their relationship to the world then varies widely. In fact, different groups *within* a given religion often dispute how their faith relates to the surrounding secular culture as well.

The classification scheme of H. Richard Niebuhr regarding religion's relation to the world seems to apply to many different religions.

As noted in Chapter 10, Christian theologian H. Richard Niebuhr has given us a typology with which to view religion and its relation to "worldly" culture. In that chapter, we referred to his classic book *Christ and Culture,* in which Niebuhr notes that historically, as well as currently, Christian groups have provided a number of answers as to how Christianity is to understand its link to the world. "Christ," he says (or, as Chapter 10 points out, religion in general), can be "Against Culture," such that a radical opposition and conflict exists between the faith and the world; or religion can be "Of Culture," such that a religion is virtually identified with its surrounding culture. These two options represent polar opposites in the relation of religion to culture: religion opposing and denying the world; religion absorbed into and supporting secular culture to the point that there remains virtually no division at all between secular and sacred.

We shall not develop here the three other positions in Niebuhr's scheme nor repeat the details of Chapter 10. Instead, our point here is to suggest that religions in general do seem to exist on a continuum between the polar opposite views, such that some religions seem to cooperate with the secular world very well and others do not. Our variation on Niebuhr's ideas is presented in Figure 14.1.

In our diagram, the letters along the bottom represent religions, some letters in fact representing divergent sects in the same religion. On the scale itself, at one extreme, A, religion is seen as in conflict with the surrounding social life. Religions are *not* involved in the secular society or may be even *against* social involvement. At the other extreme, B, religions are *very* involved in social organization, even determining the details of social structure. There may be a virtual identity between a religion and the surrounding culture. We will cite a few examples of different points along the continuum. On the left end, representing a certain degree of resistance to social involvement, there are three religions of India: Jainism, the Hinduism of the Upanishads, and early monastic Buddhism (J, UpH and B1). You might recall from Chapter 7 on "Suffering and Evil" that there is in the Indian religions a kind of mistrust of the sensual world, a sense that the world of "normal" social life can be a trap, even a seduction. We also saw in Chapter 12 that there is certainly a kind of "otherworldliness" to the sense of salvation in these religions, a view that one must leave this world to find purity. Indeed, the leaving of the world begins even in life for the truly devoted practi-

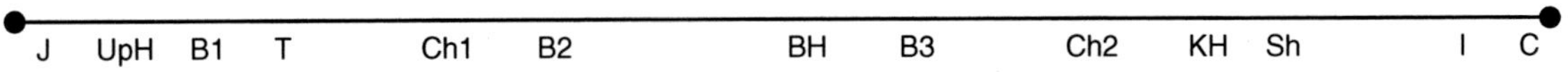

Figure 14.1   How Religion Relates to Culture

tioner of Jainism. The extreme practices of total nonviolence, for example, have inspired Jain saints to leave behind all ties to the sensual life, including eating wholesome food and having basic human relationships. In an extreme example, the Jain scripture, the Sutrakritanga, declares that "a person who is emotionally attached to relatives or friends is a fool who will suffer greatly" (Fieser and Powers 64). The Jain saint intent on liberation leaves home and family, perhaps (in some Jain sects) even going naked, eating only what has been thrown away by others. This is an extreme rejection of the secular realm.

In the three Indian religions, thre is a strong tendency toward renouncing the world.

The other two are not so extreme, but they still seem to require a rejection of normal social life, at least insofar as both religions emphasize the tradition of the *sannyasin*. **Sannyasin** in Indian religions refers to "one who renounces" all aspects of normal life to pursue spiritual liberation. Thus, literally this is a person who has renounced normal life of marriage and employment and has dedicated himself or herself to gaining liberation from the cycle of rebirth. According to this form of the Hindu religion, the world around us, with all its multiplicity and activity, is a kind of creative illusion, a distraction from the utter unity of Brahman, the Sacred Reality behind all things. For the Buddha, who rejected the notion of Brahman, there was still the need for monastic discipline. True monks and nuns were people who "renounced" the world, gave up possessions and family (especially sexual) relationships, and entered onto the path toward enlightenment. Nevertheless, in this form of Buddhism, for example, as one can still see it in Sri Lanka, the monks do tend to beg for their food in society, literally door-to-door, and the direct support of the monastic communities is quite visible. Buddhist monks also are often schoolteachers or other kinds of helpers in society. Nevertheless, since renunciation is clearly not something everyone can do, there remains in all three of these religious groups a relatively strong distinction between monks and laity, those who have renounced society to dedicate themselves to religious liberation in contrast to those who follow the practices as best they can but who have not fully renounced the world.

In Islam, faith demands the submission of the believer's heart and the effort to create a Godly social order.

At the other end of the scale, we find religions whose traditional relationship to society is very close indeed. Islam, for example, prides itself on being a system of belief and a guide of behavior for the whole of life. Islamic law makes no distinction between religion and society but governs all affairs, public and private, by the ideals derived from the Holy Koran and from the life of Mohammad. Indeed, in the person of Muhammad himself, the role of religious prophet, military leader, and political authority were combined. Therefore to be Muslim includes, ideally, being part of a Muslim society. At its beginning, the justification for the Islamic conquest of the Byzantine lands and northern Africa was not to force conversion but to set in place an Islamic order. For "submission" is a matter of the heart, but social order is a command of God. (See Esposito 28–29.)

Confucianism represents such a marked union of religion and social order that some might consider it only a social system and not a religion at all. We have argued in the opening chapters that there is some justification for seeing in Confucius' use of the concept of the Tao that basic idea of the Absolute that is (at least for our purposes) a defining mark of religion everywhere. But it is true that the significant point for Confucius was precisely that the Tao of Heaven is mirrored in human society. That is, for Confucius to follow the Tao is to belong to society and to cultivate the virtues of character that help one to conform to society's natural order, the order given in its natural relationships. Thus, the secret to a healthy and well-governed state is, as noted in our opening quotations, to "let the lord be a lord; the subject a subject; the father a father; the son a son." (The Analects 12:11.)

On the scale, there are still a wide variety of religious views about society between the two extremes we have suggested, and to describe them all in detail would be, perhaps, tedious. But just to understand the drawing and its justifications, consider these points:

> T = Taoism. Taoism is unconcerned with or, even disdainful of, social structures. Certainly social relationships and living peacefully in society, enjoying its pleasures, were still quite acceptable, even encouraged. But it is interesting to note how Taoists were chided by Confucians for their apathetic attitude toward society.
>
> Ch1 = Early Christian. Some early Christian apocalyptic thinking assumed the Kingdom of God would soon arrive and replace the corrupt world. As a result, some Christians were encouraged not to marry, and early monastic movements tried to distance themselves from "worldly" and "fleshly" corruption. Because many early Christian communities took very seriously the idea that Jesus would return soon to end the world, involvement in the world was not very important.
>
> B2 = Mahayana Buddhism. Mahayana Buddhist thinking moves a step away from a strict denial of the world by including "householders." That is, in some stories, even married and "worldly" persons were enlightened teachers. Thus, the Mahayana sect tended to recognize a "broader community" committed to Buddhist principles. At the same time, overall Indian Mahayana Buddhism is still monastic, and becoming a monk or a nun may still be expected of those who are truly devout.
>
> BH = Bhakti Hinduism. Bhakti Hinduism emphasizes the worship of gods instead of renunciation, and thus it maintains social involvement. Indeed, the possibility and the superior value of devoted worship without losing one's place in society seems to be the emphasis in, for example, the Bhagavad Gita.
>
> B3 = Socially Engaged Buddhism. Socially Engaged Buddhism is a modern Buddhist movement stressing the importance of practicing involvement in social issues under the guidance of Buddhist ideas of compassion and peace. One finds this movement inspired by the mixture of social critique and alternative spirituality arising in the United States in the 1960s.
>
> Ch2 = Moral and Social Christianity. Moral and Social Christianity stresses the need to actively serve God in the service of others. Even in the earliest years, some Christians emphasized also the need to serve the community in the name of Jesus. One may consider Jesus' call to be "in the world, but not of the world" (see John 17:14–18) as part of this tendency.

KH = Karmic Hinduism. Karmic Hinduism, especially as seen in the Laws of Manu, stresses the necessity of social duties. Responding, perhaps, both to the world-renouncing ideals of Upanishadic Hinduism and to the devotional side of the Bhakti Hinduism of the Bhagavad Gita, later texts reasserted the proper roles of caste and gender and the strict social organization these entail.

Sh = Shinto. Shinto produces a very strong identity between the religion and Japanese ethnicity. In a very real sense, to be Japanese is to be Shinto. This was especially true when Shinto was official state policy, and failure to be involved in Shinto ritual was tantamount to treason against the state. Even today, many Japanese practice Shinto so much as simply a part of social tradition that they themselves often do not recognize it as religion.

Of course these summary claims are not entirely careful, and one could find ways to disagree with them at various points. Nevertheless, it seems evident in general that religious views justify individual involvement in "secular" society to widely different extents. Indeed, as we see in Figure 14.1 and in the preceding explanations, even within one religion there may be quite different emphases on social relations that direct believers to be more or less withdrawn, more or less involved in social and personal relationships. It is precisely these differences, however, that make for interesting analysis. What is it in a belief system or in a particular doctrine that urges a believer to withdraw from society or to be all the more actively engaged in it? We may find that how one views the Absolute will have a dramatic effect on how one engages in social life and that how much one engages in social life is likely to affect one's idea of the Absolute.

How one understands the Absolute will have a dramatic impact on how he or she relates to the world.

RELIGION AND SOCIAL STRUCTURE

Besides his work in *Christ and Culture,* H. Richard Niebuhr also discussed the interaction between religion and various elements of the social structure in a classic book called *The Social Sources of Denominationalism.* In this work, he notes that people usually stress the theological disagreements as the source of the denominations. However, Niebuhr demonstrated that, in the United States, social factors such as social class, regional sectionalism (such as the division between the North and South), immigration from different areas of Europe from which immigrants brought their brands of Christianity, and race actually produced the various types of Christianity found in America. There is ample reason to believe that similar social forces helped to shape the religions of the world. We do not have space to discuss these interactions in detail. Instead, we present some sample cases by considering religion and the power structure, official religion versus popular religion, and religion and gender.

The same social forces which influenced Christian religion likely affected other religions as well.

■ RELIGION AND THE POWER STRUCTURE

Every society has some type of power structure, but these structures are varied indeed. Some societies have a clan type of ruling structure based on family ties and inheritance: others are ruled by despots. Some are ruled by a small group of individuals (an oligarchy), others by monarchs, and others with democratic systems. It is beyond the scope of this book to delve deeply into the many governance systems, much less the myriad of religious organizations that might interact with these systems. We look at a few general patterns.

The first pattern may be seen when religion legitimates the power structure, for example, when religion serves to justify the existing social, economic, and political structures of society. In fact, this role is so powerful and prevalent that no other secular ideologies, like modern democracies or Marxism, have been completely successful at replacing this function of religion in modern times (Momen 411).

Religion may be used to legitimize the power structure.

Broadly speaking, there are two basic approaches to this legitimization process. In the first of these, religion dominates the power structure of society. The classic example is some type of "theocracy." A **theocracy** is a society run according to religious laws. Religious officials also may be religious functionaries, though they may be separate from political officials but serve as interpreters of the meaning and application of religious laws. Examples of this are seen in the rule of "the first four caliphs of Islam, the Fatimid caliphate in Egypt, [John] Calvin's Geneva [in the 16th century], the Dalai Lamas' rule in Tibet from 1642 to 1959, and Ayatollah Khomeini's regime in [modern] Iran" (Momen 412).

Legitimization may come in the form of theocracy or rulers seeking religious support for their actions.

A second approach is found where a religion legitimates the political structure but is not seen as identical to this structure. Rulers often seek the authority of the dominant religion for their actions. A good example of this is found in the theory of the Divine Right of Kings in Medieval Europe, where the king was seen as placed on the throne by God and claimed the Deity's authority for his rule. In our times, religious leaders often pray at the beginning of parliamentary sessions (as they do in the U.S. Congress) or bless the activities of state leaders even when they go to war. In return for this support, state authorities grant privileges to religious functionaries and help maintain their status. This cozy relationship may backfire on religious leaders if the society is particularly unjust. If unpopular political leaders are overthrown, the religion that supported them may also be displaced.

Religion may undermine the existing social structure.

On the other hand, religion may serve to undermine the legitimacy of social and political structures. This often happens in various groups of persons who are in some fashion "disinherited," that is, groups that are religiously, socially, politically, and/or economically marginalized in the existing system. One kind of reaction is relatively passive in relation to the system. Some religious groups composed of marginalized persons simply seek to insulate themselves from the "world" (the social/political structure). Examples of this may be found in what Niebuhr called the "churches of the disinherited." For Niebuhr, these are composed of economically and/or racially disadvantaged groups who developed a "pie-in- the-sky" kind of religion. Their religion emphasizes rewards in the afterlife as compensation for their lowly status in this life. Although the existing social and political system may be seen as somehow illegitimate (ungodly) and the source of suffering, their religion does not lead them to directly challenge the system, at least not on the level of somehow trying to replace it. Rather, followers are encouraged to endure suffering in this world for the sake of rewards in the next.

However, other groups of disinherited people may actively challenge or even attack the existing system on the basis of religious convictions. Good examples of this tact may be seen in Mahatma Gandhi's challenge of British imperial rule in India in the 1940s, the American Civil Rights Movement in the 1950s and 1960s, and those fundamentalist groups that attack political and economic power structures in the 2000s. In each of these cases, the system is seen as illegitimate because of injustice, immorality, or other failures to conform to religious dictates. It is worth mentioning that the more pragmatic social, political, or religious institution may have difficulty in dealing with this variety of disinherited religious groups because they claim the authority of the Absolute for their position. If their position represents the Absolute, then there can be no compromise, even though compromise often is portrayed as the lifeblood of modern political processes.

■ OFFICIAL RELIGION AND POPULAR RELIGION

The contrast found in most societies between official religion and popular religion is another example of the interaction of religion and the social structure. Most societies have a number of different levels of religious belief and practice even when there is a single, dominant religion. Discussions of these levels usually limit themselves to a contrast between two categories: some kind of overt, generally accepted set of religious ideas and practices versus the more covert patterns associated with how most people actually live out their religion in day-to-day practice. Scholars have used a variety of terms to describe this contrast, including "normative" and "operative," "cognitive" and "affective," and "Great Tradition" and "Little Tradition." We have chosen to label this contrast "official" and "popular" religion, following the logic of Moojan Momen.

There often is a difference between official religion (what the religion is supposed to practice) and popular religion (how ordinary people live it).

By **official religion**, Momen means the "formal orthodox religion" as taught and practiced by "religious professionals," such as priests and monks, while **popular religion** is "the religion as it is actually practiced" (386). The discrepancy between official religion and popular religion may result from several different factors. The individual may depart from official practices because of his or her personality traits, experiences in groups to which he or she belongs, or circumstances in life. For instance, the person who has a negative self-concept may find it difficult to believe in the essential goodness of God, or the family in which a person is reared may teach him or her to be less devout than is officially accepted, or a person whose religion teaches him or her to accept adversity without complaint may feel it necessary to complain when he or she is battered by the negative experiences of life.

Likewise, one's place in the social structure also has an impact on how religion is lived out. People who are comfortable in their middle-class lives often believe that the primary purpose of religion is to teach them how to reach their potential in this world. That is, religion teaches one how to live authentically, ethically, and happily in their daily existence. However, those whose lot in life is less comfortable may believe that this world is a "vale of tears," where the primary purpose of religion is to prepare for the next world.

In a similar vein, official religion may not have a great deal of practical applicability to real-life situations for most people. For example, Buddhism teaches developing a detachment from this life as a prerequisite for release into Nirvana and is atheistic in that there are no gods to whom one may appeal for assistance. Yet, people still have to make a living, rear their children, assure success, and deal with crises. As a result, many Buddhists have gods to whom they pray and rituals that are employed to assure success in everyday living or to cope with crises.

Finally, even religions that claim to be universal, thus transcending all local customs, actually incorporate local practices into their popular religious practice. For example, many practices that are considered Christian actually are adapted from the European, African, or Native American religions that preceded them. "Similarly, in Buddhist countries, spells and magical formulas are used. Their power is attributed to Buddha. This is despite the formal doctrinal position that such things can have no effect on the workings of the laws of karma" (Momen 389). It should be noted that even when departing from the official religion, most people continue to see themselves as loyal followers of their religion. This is true even when their practices are denounced by representatives of official religion.

The point perhaps to recognize from these facts is that religion within a society, even when it is officially accepted and sanctioned, has its own internal divisions. Just as religion may or may not support an existing political and economic power structure, so too an official religion may or may not actually reflect what the people believe and practice. The political, economic, and educational differences that exist within a society and within that society's religion are not entirely escapable, and they will surface in the way a religion is interpreted and practiced by its followers.

The individual, political, economic, and educational differences influence how people "do religion."

■ RELIGION AND GENDER

Alongside the social influence of political/economic power structures and the division between the teachings of official religion and the day-to-day needs of the people practicing that religion, one of the most fundamental divisions in most cultures is between men and women. We briefly alluded to religious teachings on women earlier in this chapter. Now we need to look more carefully at a topic that has come to demand utmost attention in the global age—the role of gender in religion. In the center of the debate is the question of how religious belief influences the ways women are perceived in a certain culture and society. Since the roles of women in modern societies are undergoing remarkable changes, it is apparent that their role in religious contexts also is being reconsidered. What is the reason for the fact that the founder figures of the major religions are male? Is it significant that God in the Christian tradition is often portrayed as male? Why were women not allowed to be ordained as nuns in Theravada Buddhism throughout most of the centuries? Why are women considered to be the original source of evil in some Judeo-Christian and Islamic views? Questions like these are raised frequently in the current debate about gender and religion, and the answers vary widely. But we shall see that both the language of religious myth and the tremendous influence of religious art have been powerful forces in constructing and maintaining ways in which women are perceived by culture.

Women's Nature

One religious story that has significantly influenced past and present paradigms for what has been considered the nature of women in the Judeo-Christian and Islamic traditions is Genesis 3: 1–24, the narrative about the fall of humanity. As we noted in the chapter on myths and stories (Chapter 6), this myth deals with the disobedience of human beings against God. Since Adam and Eve eat from "the tree of the knowledge of good and evil," both reject the will of God and consequently are banished from the garden and punished. Moreover, each is cursed in accordance with the role he or she is seen to play for all humanity. Thus Adam, whose name means "man," must work the soil "by the sweat of his brow" to produce food, and Eve, whose name means "life," has to bear children in pain and long for her husband, who is given dominion over her (Genesis 3:16). The story therefore provides an important blueprint for the structure of Judeo-Christian and Islamic societies. Men and women have a designated role that, at least according to Genesis 3:1–24, has its roots in the failure of human beings to follow God's commands. While man will labor to provide food, woman is responsible for bearing the children and submitting herself to her husband's authority. Such a division of responsibility certainly reflects the structure of a society different from the modern Western world but one quite in keeping with a common way of life in ancient Israel.

Some interpretations of Genesis 3 blame women for the fall of humanity.

The point of noting the biblical story of the fall is to recognize how it has influenced longstanding authoritative views of the role of women in both Christian and Islamic societies. In one influential example, Tertullian, a Christian church father of the second and third centuries CE, used reference to the story of the fall to address a group of nuns, advising them according to the proper garment to be worn:

> *And do you not know that you are (each) an Eve? The sentence of God on this sex of yours lives in this age: the guilt must of necessity live too. You are the devil's gateway; you are the unsealer of that (forbidden) tree: you are the first deserter of the divine law: you are she who persuaded him whom the devil was not valiant enough to attack. You destroyed so easily God's image, man. On account of your desert—that is, death—even the Son of God had to die. (Tertullian I:1)*

In this Christian interpretation, the woman has become the sole origin of evil. Her power to seduce her husband even surpasses the power of the devil itself. Adam, apparently, would have been without fault if it had not been for the woman. Tertullian effectively designates the nature of women as evil by emphasizing specific aspects of the story in a literal interpretation of the events in the garden Eden.

A very similar interpretation can be found in Michelangelo's famous painting of the fall in the Sistine Chapel in Rome. Although Michelangelo (1475–1564) painted his influential image more than a thousand years after Tertullian, it effectively portrays the sinfulness of the female gender in the stunning body of the serpent, the biblical symbol for temptation in Genesis 3:1 as well as other scripture passages. Its head is the torso of a woman. Epitomized in this visual interpretation, again evil itself is identified with the female gender. Evident from these two Christian examples is the influence of interpretation on the role of women. While the biblical story of the fall does not provide a clear indication that the gender is the decisive aspect for the nature of evil, later interpreters seemingly found evidence for such an interpretation in the text.

One of the ongoing conflicts in global society centers around the proper place of religion in a secular world. This conflict is pointed to by the continuing controversy in France over the issue of young Muslim women wearing their traditional head covering, or *hijab*, in public schools.

In December 2003, in a televised speech following months of debate, the French President Jacques Chirac called for a new law in public schools banning the wearing of "conspicuous" religious symbols, while "discreet" ones may still be worn. Among these symbols are the Islamic headscarf and large Christian crosses, as well as skullcaps for Jewish boys. The goal of the law, if passed, is to assist in preserving the division between the secular state and religious institutions.

France today houses a growing Muslim community. Since the headscarf is often viewed as a religious display, its presence in public schools of a secular state has become an especially fiercely debated issue. Polls show that a large majority of French people support the proposed ban. Yet many Muslims, as well as Muslim leaders, argue that the wearing of *hijab* is not a choice nor a political action but a religious duty for them. They maintain that it becomes an increasingly difficult task for them to raise children and pursue their freedom to practice Islam in a secular state like France. Other voices, like the grand sheik of al Azahar, Muhammad Sayad Tantawi, disagree with this position, contending that even though the wearing of the headscarf is a religious duty, it is not mandatory if this violates the law of a non-Muslim country. In a similar manner, Muslims are also not required to follow dietary restrictions if they are not able to without fault of their own.

Source: "Muslim Leader Says France Has Right to Prohibit Head Scarves." *New York Times* (December 31, 2003): A5.

It is interesting to see that the Koranic passages, which also mention the story of the events in the Garden (for example, in Sura 7:19–25), seem to have undergone a very similar fate. The famous Holy Koran commentary by Al-Tabari (d. 923) and his collection of many traditions provides insights into many interpretations that blame the seductiveness of Adam's wife for his downfall. He writes that "Adam refused to eat from the tree, but Eve came forward and ate. Then she said: Eat, Adam! For I have, and it has done me no harm" (al-Tabari, 1989). As in Tertullian's interpretation, the origin of disobedience is the woman; Adam alone could not have been persuaded to eat from the tree. Herein lies a reason why women need to be guarded in particular with respect to their very dangerous power to seduce men. One can easily see how such underlying characteristics of women would play a role in securing the treacherous potential of the female gender in any given society. Codes of behavior and clothing certainly have been influenced by such an assessment of the nature of woman.

Some authoritative interpretations of the Holy Koran also blame Eve (woman) for the Fall.

What becomes obvious in the interpretations of both Koranic and Biblical texts is the adaptation of the messages to their immediate social context. That is, the general view of men as morally superior to women seems to have come through in these interpretations, a superiority that generally reflects the customs of the countries in which the Judaic religions originated. In turn, these authoritative voices offering interpretation of holy scripture tended to solidify and perpetuate the gender differences common to the age. The influence of such statements that essentially define the nature of woman as evil should not be underestimated for the power they had to define the role of women in these societies.

Subordination of Women

While the preceding examples were taken from the Judeo-Christian and Islamic tradition, this does not mean that other religious contexts treated women in a very different manner. Since, with very few exceptions, societies throughout the world were predominantly patriarchal systems, religious contexts generally reflect those traditions. In the Hindu religion, the Laws of Manu was written around 200 BCE as a book of rules and regulations concerned with prescriptions for the ideal Hindu society. It says,

> *Women must be honored and adorned by their fathers, brothers, husbands, and brothers-in-law, who desire their own welfare. Where women are honored, there the gods are pleased. . . . >[3.55] Nothing must be done independently by a girl or woman, or by an old woman, even in her own house. In childhood a female must be subject to her father, in youth to her husband, and when her husband is dead to her sons. A woman must never be independent . . . [5.147] She must always be cheerful, clever in household affairs, careful in cleaning her utensils, and economical expenditure. She shall obey the man to whom her father may give her . . . The husband who wedded her with sacred texts always gives happiness to his wife, both in season and out of season, in this world and in the next. Although he may be destitute of virtue, or seek pleasure elsewhere, or lacking good qualities, yet a husband must be constantly worshipped as a god by a faithful wife [150]. (Laws of Manu 1886)*

The definition of women as evil has powerful influence on how women have been treated, especially in patriarchical societies.

In this passage, the woman's responsibility to care for the household in traditional Hinduism, as in many other historical societies, is an honorable task. Her nearest male companions are required to adorn her, an obligation for men given by the gods (see Laws of Manu 3:56–60). The honorable position of women in the family and household gives her a respected place in the Hindu society. Yet as the ensuing verses make clear, this role is in the context of a patriarchal society, in which the relations of power are distributed differently for men and women. The woman is subjected to complete obedience in regard to her immediate male relatives. Any stage of her life is overseen and decided by a male relative, and it is expected that she will cheerfully submit to any difficulties that life might provide for her, even if the husband is "destitute of virtue." It cannot be ignored that the law protects an asymmetrical power structure, which makes women subjugated to their male relatives. This becomes also evident in the requirement for widows to abstain from marriage after the death of their husband and to follow an ascetic lifestyle (Laws of Manu 157–165).

Women's Spiritual Qualities

In some cases, the presumed moral inferiority and the subordination of women to men may result in the suggestion, or even the doctrinal assertion, that women in general do not possess the spiritual qualities necessary to practice religion. For example, Hindu women, along with members of the lower castes, were forbidden to learn or study the Vedas. In the Jain tradition, especially in the Digambara sect where the devout renunciant is required to go naked (having renounced all forms of property), women cannot achieve liberation and must accumulate good *karma* in this life in order to be reborn a man in some future existence (see the Sutraprabrita in Fieser and Powers 62).

The role of women in the Theravada Buddhist tradition has also been problematic throughout history. According to tradition, Mahapajapati approached the Buddha to institute an order for nuns. Initially the Buddha declined this request. However, when his (male) disciple Ananda asked about the ability of women to attain the fruits of a spiritual life, the Buddha acknowledged this possibility. While this story provides the foundation for the ordination of Buddhist nuns, nevertheless orders of women died out in the Theravada Buddhist tradition and in Tibet. This is of utmost importance in the Theravada Buddhist tradition since liberation can only be achieved from the status of monkhood (King 513). While there were orders of nuns present in East Asia, they were explicitly subjected to the most junior monk status in the monastic system according to the "Eight Chief Rules" that had to be accepted by women during their initiation (see *Vinaya Texts,* part 3). The hierarchies of monastic life therefore, even where it was formally allowed for women, meant an inferior standing in comparison to monks.

In Theravada Buddhism, women nuns are possible, but are still held in an inferior position to male monks.

There are, of course, exceptions to these cases of gender hierarchy in the world's religions, but they are relatively rare. Ironically, in fact, there are examples where the religion does offer prominent roles to women and may have female goddesses, without those facts changing the relatively lowly status of women. Hinduism is one example; Japanese Shinto is another. There have been many famous female mystics in the Christian tradition, and Mary Baker Eddy became famous as the founder of the Christian Science sect in the late 19th century. Nevertheless, prominent and egalitarian roles for women in religion remain rare, and it has been our point to show that religion can and does have great effects on how a society functions and creates its internal divisions and hierarchies. Yet much of this is changing today, and we shall have to reconsider the place of women and hierarchical social structures under the force of globalization.

THE CHANGING CONTEXT: RELIGION AND GLOBALIZATION

The underlying argument in this book is that modernization and globalization have been radically altering the context for "doing religion." To some extent, these forces have energized religions. For example, movement by Indians into the West along with "missionary" activities by Hindu organizationsm has found a whole new market for branches of Hinduism in Western societies. Likewise, the spread of the marshal arts have helped increase acceptance of Far Eastern precepts in Western societies.

More importantly, the forces of change themselves have energized religious responses. These responses are largely psychological and sociological in their origins and results, as we have seen at several points in this textbook. In this final section, we look at several more changes associated with globalization that underlie some of the more visible social/religious issues today. Specifically, we look at the changing status of women, issues of war and peace, and the problems of universalism and particularism, including fundamentalism. We shall conclude with some observations about how religions change or do not change in response to a changing world.

■ GLOBALIZATION AND REDEFINING WOMEN IN RELIGIOUS TRADITIONS

Female religious scholars and theologians are helping redefine understanding of women in various religious traditions.

One of the issues that thoughtful religious people will be dealing with in the global age is the role of women in society and in religion itself. We have already discussed at length the socially problematic interpretations of gender in the world religions, where we noted that most of the sacred texts were developed in patriarchal societies where males dominated. The changes in the status of women associated with modernism and globalization are therefore causing a reinterpretation of these holy documents. Female feminist scholars and theologians, as well as many male thinkers, argue that the patriarchal elements of scriptures were associated with the historical settings and cultural contexts in which they developed. Thus, they should not be considered binding in today's world. These scholars and theologians insist that the male-dominated language, along with negative images of women, must be removed so that the true essence of spiritual teachings applying to all persons can be understood. Such a redefinition of religious teachings is well underway in most Western societies, though the more extreme forms of gender-neutral applications remain controversial. Even in Western societies,

Efforts to redefine women in religion often result in a backlash from conservatives.

very conservative groups continue to insist that male-dominated models are essential, not superficial, to the nature of religious teachings. To change such "eternal" concepts is to deny the very unchanging teachings of God. They often insist that the supposed decay of modern societies is a result of humans denying the revelation God has given by conceding too much to the whims of contemporary times.

Evidently, there is hidden here a dispute between those who read their scriptures conservatively and those who interpret their scriptures more in historical context. Beyond this theological argument, however, we may stress at this point that the changing status of women not just a religious question but is a global sociological trend, one that is not welcomed everywhere. Many societies and individuals feel very threatened by the challenges to patriarchy, and as the social structures change, religion will still be used to anchor traditional gender relations in spiritual authority. Thus, the sociological changes likely will continue to be seen as a threat to the cosmological and spiritual orders.

At the same time, it is equally likely that advocates for change, including improving the status of women, will find spiritual justification for their position as well. Being awakened to the need for an egalitarian view of gender relations, some will reread their scriptures and critique their own traditional doctrines in order to find and emphasize the bases within religion for a higher view of women than we saw in Tertullian or in Digambara Jainism. Some will change gently, like "Evangelicals for Biblical Equality"; others, like the feminist theologian Mary Daly, will assert change more radically. And whether change comes easily or with rage and scorn, or indeed even if many continue to hold onto the traditional gender roles and try not to change at all, the issue is forced upon us by the development of modern and global society, and no one can escape the discussion for long.

■ Universalism, Particularism, and the Rise of Fundamentalism

We noted in the first chapter that religious phenomena were related to their social and historical contexts. We also noted that the current context seems to be a period of *kairos,* where modernism is giving way to some sort of global society through the process of globalization. Certainly, it is in this context that today's religion must be understood. Additionally, we noted that a given social change can produce diametrically opposed reactions. The movements toward universalism and particularism were mentioned as especially important examples of these reactions. The changes associated with globalization threaten traditional social relations, cherished values, and personal and group identities. Reactions to all these changes often assume a personal and intense religious reaction.

All of this is said to remind the reader that numerous factors besides theological differences often affect religious expressions, though theology may be used to justify these expressions. The twin forces of universalism and particularism are good examples of the interaction of social trends and religious trends. Universalism involves searching for things that diverse groups have in common. Ideally, this entails finding principles, experiences, ethics, and the like that would apply to all humankind. Particularism, on the other hand, involves the assertion of a given group's distinctive characteristics, emphasizing the group's distinctive identity, against universalistic claims and the identifying claims of other groups.

Universalism and particularism function in a wide range of areas, including religion. Two of the most important trends in modern religion are interreligious dialogue on a global scale and the rise of worldwide fundamentalism (Huff 1). The former embraces discussion as a way to understanding, pluralism in religions and cultures, finding common ground, and cooperation in meeting the world's pressing social, cultural, and ethical concerns. The latter emphasizes the distinctiveness of its religious tradition, the value of its tradition relative to others, and the possibility of universal adoption of its religious program for the sake of meeting the world's needs.

Therefore, **religious universalism** encompasses those religion-based reactions to modernization and globalization that stress the unity of humankind along with the necessity of finding common ground for religious and social cooperation. This trend represents the "coming together" aspects of Ewert Cousin's Second Axial Period, discussed in Chapter 1. The finding of common ground may be based on assumptions that humans share a common nature, that they have the Divine within, or that they are all tied to a common fate, such as the threat of environmental destruction. They often stress the necessity of finding peaceful ways for societies and religions to interact, in contrast to what appears to be the culture of war so prevalent in secular society as well as some aspects of religious tradition. Such efforts have dramatically increased over the last two centuries. Bat Shalom: Women's Center for Peace and Social Justice, the Institute for Interreligious/Intercultural Dialogue, the Center for Global Ethics, the Global

Ethics Foundation, the Institute for Ecumenical Studies, and a Parliament of the World's Religions represent but a small fraction of those movements and organizations dedicated to interreligious dialogue and action.

In the midst of such efforts to find common ground between religions, some might criticize the universalistic approach for its failure to maintain the value of particularity. That is, while a universalist might be seeking unity, some Muslims might feel that they are being asked to deny the finality and uniqueness of the Holy Koran, or a Christian might feel she is being told that Jesus cannot be considered the unique Savior of mankind. Religious universalism, for all its embracing of the global climate, may be in danger of forcing its own version of "world peace" on those whose unique religious traditions are denied by its universalistic goals.

Thus "religious particularism" is the opposite reaction to globalization. **Religious particularism** involves those forms of religious expression that stress their own uniqueness, along with a desire to remain separate from other religions and their cultural expressions. That is, the particularist will insist that we must retain and protect, even spread and defend the unique claims of a specific religion, resisting the "temptation" to dilute the exclusive truth claims and evangelistic mission of particular religions. We may all want world peace, the religious particularist might say, but we cannot deny the uniqueness and finality of the Islamic/Christian/Buddhist message.

Perhaps the most common type of religious particularism in the world today, and certainly the most infamous, is fundamentalism. **Fundamentalism** is a socioreligious reaction to modernism and globalization that stresses the uniqueness of a particular religious tradition, rejects selected aspects of the contemporary world, and proposes its vision of a religiously based society as a solution to the perceived inadequacies of contemporary culture. As a self-conscious effort to maintain and encourage the spread of the "fundamentals" of the faith (which is the historical origin of the term), fundamentalism may be only a strong and motivated form of religious particularism. Unfortunately, as the nightly news sometimes conveys, fundamentalism today—whether Islamic, Christian, Hindu, or Japanese—can also be violently reactionary.

Fundamentalists accept certain aspects of the contemporary world but reject others. For instance, they usually accept technology and may even use this technology to further their ends, such as using television to spread the Gospel. However, like any concerned particularist, they usually reject such modern notions as secularism and religious or cultural pluralism. At their worst, their mistrust of globalization may result in the denial, or at least severe questioning, of equality for women, political democracy, and even perhaps the ideals of universal human rights. The most extreme of fundamentalist groups can even become aggressive and militant in their posturing toward other religions, as well as against those in their own faith who do not share their zeal.

At their worst, fundamentalist approaches to globalization and to other changes of the modern world can be paranoid. Modern changes may be seen as an attack on their cherished way of life or religion, while contemporary society itself is seen as being in moral and spiritual decline. The cause of the decline may be projected on "secular humanists," Americans, "one-worlders," Jews, Christians, Muslims, Hindus, or whoever may be identified as a supposed malevolent out-group. Therefore, the fundamentalist may conclude, the contemporary situation must be radically altered by the recovery of an imagined time when religion, society, and human behavior were in harmony and the world was a better place. Indeed, in order to recover the imagined ideal society of the past, and to reestablish the holy society of the future, the use of force may be advocated, and thus the language of war and "holy struggle" appears in many fundamentalists' vocabulary, even those that are not violent. Ironically, even as some fundamentalists struggle to recover the true tradition of their faith, they may very well be creating an entirely new tradition, which is responding to global society.

Of course, the dangers of such violent language, and indeed of the occasional violent actions that can be born of fundamentalism, are clear, especially now that we have created weapons that have the possibility of destroying all life on earth. Thus, the more liberal religious traditions are all the more inspired to emphasize the moral and emotional power of religion to create a "culture of peace" in the contemporary world. And so the paradox of globalization leads to universalists seeking human unity while relying on the particular traditions of the past, while particularists seek to protect and even expand their traditions in a world that, more than ever, needs to learn to settle its controversies without resorting to violence.

Paradoxically, globalization creates religious movements that seek the common unity of humankind while it generates religious movements that foster differences.

In the end, then, we see the importance of understanding religion, even as was noted in Chapter 1. Certainly government officials, and even ordinary people, cannot afford to ignore the power of religion in dealing with others. Of course, as we enter the global community, factors other than religion will underlie various conflicts around the world, and yet we can expect that the people involved in these conflicts will continue to define them in religious terms. To ignore the religious elements in these conflicts is a serious mistake. For instance, in the late 1970s, the American CIA failed to understand the depth of resentment toward the Shah of Iran's regime, along with the power of religious opposition that produced a successful rebellion and led to the establishment of an Islamic republic hostile to the United States. In a similar way, unless we understand how religion informs the minds and moves the hands of people all over the globe, we may not be able to interact fairly and peacefully in the worldwide community. Thus, it may well be that the political leaders of the 21st century will have to be skilled in theological debate.

CONCLUSION

In this book we have taken a phenomenological approach to religion by reviewing many aspects of what religion is and how it functions in the lives of people all around the world. We have demonstrated that religion is a powerful factor in people's individual lives as well as a prime determinant of the interactions associated with sociological and historical change. And behind it all are concepts of the Absolute, the holy "Something" that gives life, action, relationships, and societies their meaning. This is true of the past and continues to be true in the contemporary world.

Part of contemporary thinking includes the secularization thesis, which proposes that, as modern societies become more secular, religion will disappear as a social entity and become more and more relegated to the private sphere of peoples' lives. While there is no doubt that societies in the West have become more secular, ideas presented in this book demonstrate that religion is by no means disappearing, and indeed religion is making a vigorous comeback in global society. The fact is that religion must be understood and dealt with effectively if we are to live peacefully with our neighbors as well as build a healthy and just future.

We have seen where the world's religions disagree on important topics but also where there is agreement, along with some degree of commitment, within the world's religious communities to work for a just and peaceful future. We have seen that within most religious traditions there exist both the seeds of violence and the grounds for peace. Perhaps the best way to conclude this book is to remind the reader of a point Christian historian Martin Marty made in our first chapter: Religion has caused more killing than any other factor in history, but it also has produced more healing than any other force. This remains the case today. Yet we might hope that those who take the time to study religion will find ways to understand their own and others' religious traditions, to cultivate honest and sincere commitment, and to find peaceful ways of dealing with the changes brought about by globalization.

■ INTERACTIVE EXERCISE

Please continue your exploration of religion in global society by going to the interactive exercise for this chapter online (**http://www.religion.wadsworth.com/ richter**).

WORKS CITED

Al-Tabari. *The History of Al Tabari; General Introduction and From the Creation to the Flood.* Trans. Franz Rosenthal. Albany: State University of New York Press, 1989.

Bourdieu, Pierre. *Language and Symbolic Power.* Trans. Gino Raymond and Matthew Adamson. Cambridge, MA: Harvard University Press, 1991.

Bühler, George (trans.). "Laws of Manu." *Sacred Books of the East,* Vol. 1. 1886. http://www.sacred-texts.com/hin/ (accessed April 4, 2004).

Durkheim, Emile. *The Elementary Forms of the Religious Life.* Trans. J. W. Swain. London: George Allen and Unwin, 1976.

Esposito, John L. *Islam, The Straight Path.* Oxford, UK: Oxford University Press 1998.

Fieser, James, and John Powers. *Scriptures of the World's Religions.* Boston: McGraw/Hill, 1998.

King, Sallie. "Awakening of Zen Buddhist Women." In *Buddhism in Practice.* Ed. Donald S. Lopez, Jr. New Jersey: Princeton University Press, 1995: 513–16.

Laws of Manu, Sacred Books of the East. Vol. 25. Oxford, UK: Oxford University Press, 1886.

Leys, Simon. *The Analects of Confucius.* New York: W. W. Norton, 1997.

Marx, Karl. *The Essential Marx: The Non-Economic Writings—A Selection.* Ed. and trans. Saul K. Padover. New York: The New American Library, 1979.

Momen, Moojan. *The Phenomenon of Religion: A Thematic Approach.* Oxford, UK: One World Publications, 1999.

"Muslim Leader Says France Has Right to Prohibit Head Scarves," *New York Times* (December 31, 2003): A5.

Niebuhr, H. Richard. *Christ and Culture.* New York: Harper and Row, 1975.

———. *The Social Sources of Denominationalism.* New York: Meridian Books, 1957 (org.1929).

Pagels, Elaine. *Adam, Eve and the Serpent.* New York: Vintage Books,1989.

Tertullian, *De Cultu Feminarum 1:1.* Trans. Rev. S. Thelwall (last updated 02/03/1998). http://www.tertullian.org/anf/anf04/anf04-06.htm#P265_52058 (accessed May 29, 2001).

———, *On the Apparel of Women.* Trans. Rev. S. Thelwall (last updated 02/03/1998). http://www.tertullian.org/anf/anf04/anf04-06.htm#P265_52058 (accessed May 29, 2001).

Vinaya Texts, Part 3, Chapter 8. Trans. T.W.R. Davids and H. Oldenberg. Oxford, UK: Clarendon, 1885.

Wahud, Amina. *Koran and Woman: Reading the Sacred Text from a Woman's Perspective.* Oxford, UK: Oxford University Press, 1999.

FOR FURTHER READING

Ahmed, Leila, *Women and Gender in Islam.* New Haven, CT: Yale University, 1992.

Ariarajah, S. Wesley. "Religion and Violence: A Protestant Christian Perspective." http://wcc.coe.org/wcc/what/interreligious/cd39-04.html (accessed November 11, 2002).

Galtung, Johan. "Religions, Hard and Soft." *Cross Currents.* 2002. http://www.crosscurrents.org/galtung.htm (accessed November 11, 2002).

Niebuhr, H. Richard. *The Social Sources of Denominationalism.* New York: Meridian Books, 1957 (org.1929).

Schottroff, Luise, and Marie-Theres Wacker. *Feminist Interpretation: The Bible in Women's Perspective.* Trans. Martin and Barbara Rumscheidt. Minneapolis, MN: Fortress Press, 1998.

Smith, Huston. *Why Religion Matters: The Fate of the Human Spirit in an Age of Disbelief.* San Francisco: HarperSanFrancisco, 2001.

Stowasser Freyer, Barbara. *Women in the Koran, Traditions, and Interpretation.* New York: Oxford University Press, 1994.

World Council of Churches. *Religion and Violence: A World Council of Churches' Conference.* 2002. http://www.wcc-coe.org/wcc/what/interreligioius/cd39-08.html. (accessed November 11, 2002).

GLOSSARY

Abraham—Biblical patriarch

Aditi—Vedic goddess, venerated for her creative powers

Advaitin theories—philosophy that claims the oneness of Ultimate Reality, Brahman is Atman (Soul)

Amitabha—Buddha of infinite life, lord of the western regions of the heavens (Pure Land)

Anabaptists—group of Protestant sects that denied infant baptism and advocated social-economic reforms as well as the separation between church and state

anatman—"without atman"; no soul based on the realiztion that nothing, including the image of oneself, is permanent in Buddhism

ancestor spirits—belief in the spirits of ancestors possessing supernatural powers

animism—belief in the spiritual character of natural phenomena and the universe itself

anomie—literally "without rules," the impression that something in life is chaotic, uncontrolled, and dangerous. For Peter Berger, "anomie" refers to situations in life that are troubling enough to force us to look for higher meaning

apostolic succession—unbroken succession from the apostles to bishops and priests and the pope

Aquinas, Thomas—medieval theologian and philosopher

Aristotle—Greek philosopher

Arjuna—hero of the Bhagavad Gita

Arthur Schopenhauer—German philosopher (1788–1860)

atheist—person rejecting the belief in a personal God/gods

Atman—conceptualization for the eternal Self or soul in humans according to the Hindu Upanishads

Augustine of Hippo—Christian Church Father

avatar—in Hindu polytheism, a god's "descent" into physical form, e.g., when Vishnu becomes Krishna or Rama; thus an avatar is one of many possible forms of a particular god

Averroes—Islamic philosopher

axial period—an era of time around which subsequent history rotates

Baha'ullah—Founder of Bahai religion

Bar Mitzvah/Bat Mitzvah—Jewish rite of passage for boys and girls in which boys and girls learn to read the Torah in Hebrew and are recognized as full members of the religious community

Bentham, Jeremy—British philosopher, leading theorist with regard to Anglo-American ethics

Bhagavad-Gita—famous dialogue between Krishna and Arjuna, part of the Mahabharata, sacred Hindu text in which the nature of the soul and its liberation is expounded

bhikku/bhikkuni—Buddhist monk/nun

Bodhidharma—founder of Zen Buddhism

bodhi—enlightenment experience

Brahman—impersonal, ineffable Ultimate Reality in Hinduism, identical with Atman, the individual self as world soul

Brahmins—highest priestly class in Hinduism

Buddha Mind, Buddha Nature—enlightenment

Calvin, John—French reformer and theologian

Calvinists—followers of John Calvin (1509–1564), a theologian and leader during the reformation

Christian Trinity—one God in three persons (Father, Son, and Holy Spirit)

chronos—Greek term for the step-by-step ordering of time

Chuang Tzu—Chinese sage and philosopher

Church Fathers—leaders in the early Church whose writings are considered authoritative texts in Christianity

Cicero—Roman statesman and philosopher

circumcision—religious rite among Jews and Muslims in which the foreskin is removed

civilizations—large geographical areas containing a number of diverse cultures that, in spite of their differences, are bound together by common traditions, perspectives, cosmologies, ethics, religions, and philosophies

Confucius—Chinese leader and philosopher and acclaimed founder of Confucianism

Constantine—Roman emperor established Christianity as state religion (272–337 CE)

Creator—describing the Ultimate Being as one who forms the existence of the natural world outside himself/herself; *see* **contrast with emanation**

creed—authoritative formula of belief

culture—shared way of life that binds people together into a society

dharma—in Buddhism, a general term for the "truth" or "law" of the Buddha, thus all that the Buddha taught and exemplified

doctrine—a principle or system of teachings

dualistic—in a two-fold manner

Durkheim, Emile—French sociologist and philosopher

Eddy, Mary Baker—founder of Christian Science

Ekaku, Hakuin—Zen teacher (1685–1769)

emanation—literally, an act of proceeding out from the Ultimate Reality

European Enlightenment—18th century philosophical movement

exclusivism—claim that a religious belief excludes contradictory claims

experience of the sublime—that which we sense, yet which our sense cannot really contain; it is beyond our senses, yet hinted at by the greatness of what we see or hear; as such it both awes us and challenges us

extrinsic religion—religious beliefs, practices, and rules that are absorbed from "outside" the individual

fana—dissolution of the human will before God

Feuerbach, Ludwig—German philosopher

First Axial Period—period in history focused on knowing oneself and personal development

Freud, Sigmund—psychologist, founder of psychoanalysis

functional equivalent of religion—a nonreligious system that organizes and gives meaning to people's lives like a religion does

fundamentalism—socio-religious reaction to globalization that stresses the uniqueness of a particular religious tradition, thus an effort to maintain, encourage, and spread the "fundamentals" of a particular faith

Gandhi, Mahatma Mohandas—Indian political leader

Ganga Ma—the Ganges personified as a deity

Garden of Gethsemane—garden near Jerusalem believed to be the site of Jesus' agony and betrayal

Gilligan, Carol—American psychologist

globalization—a massive process of social change resulting from the growing interconnectedness of human social, cultural, economic, and religious life that is realtering human activities on a planetarywide scale

Gnostics—early Christian group, emphasizing mystic-spiritual knowledge

Gospels—the initial four books of the Christian Bible, describing the life and death of Jesus the Christ

Hadith—collection of sayings and deeds by Mohammad and his followers

Heilsgeschichte—"salvation history" that does not merely describe events in time and space but also interprets them as acts and intentions of God

heterodox—not conforming with the accepted teachings

Hindu caste system—social system rooted in religious tradition in which human beings are separated into different classes

Hitler, Adolf—German fascist political leader of Nazism, responsible for the Holocaust

Hui-neng—founder of Zen Buddhism

humanism—a philosophy which believes that humans, along with their well-being, needs, and happiness determine the nature of good and evil

Hume, David—Scottish philosopher

icon—sacred image

identity—the way individuals and peoples understand themselves along with the ways they see themselves relating to other peoples, the natural world, and the spiritual world

idolator—someone worshipping idols, images, or objects that are representative of a god/gods/God

immanent—within a certain context

inclusivism—claim that what is considered truth in a religious context is truth in other religious contexts as well

individualistic worldview—focus on individual versus collective interests

Indra—Hindu god of rain and thunder

intrinsic religion—religious beliefs, practices, and ethical principles that result from a person critically examining religious views that, in turn, become a part of a person's chracter and "natural behavior"

jihad—struggle or just war in Islam

Judaeus, Philo—Jewish philosopher and theologian

kairos—Greek term for a moment in history "pregnant with expectancy"

Kant, Immanuel—German philosopher

karma—literally "action"; refers to the notion that one's actions produce effect in the cosmos that return to affect that soul's future. A kind of moral cause and effect, such that those actions performed by a specific soul come back and affect how that soul lives, dies, and is reincarnated

karuna—compassion (Buddhism)

Kierkegaard, Søren Aabye—Danish philosopher and theologian

koan—exercise in which the student rejects a pardoxical thought

Krishna—incarnation of Vishnu

Kshatriyas—warrior class in Hinduism

Lao Tzu—acclaimed Chinese philosopher and founder of Taoism

Li Hongzhi—Founder of Falun Gong

li—proper behavior in the context with others (Chinese)

Luther, Martin—German theologian and key figure initiating the Reformation

Mahabharata—Indian epic including the Bhagavad Gita

Mahavira—legendary teacher in Jainism

mana—a pantheistic concept of native Polynesian religion suggesting a force or power in nature and powerful people or spiritual leaders

marga—way in Buddhism

Martyr, Justin—church historian

Marx, Karl—German philosopher, economist, socialist, and father of communism

Marxist-Leninist-Stalinist communism—political system based on a theory in which all property and wealth is in the hands of the community or state

Mecca—sacred place for Muslims

mechanistic, materialistic vision of the cosmos—view of the universe that sees the universe as a big machine composed of dead matter

Mencius—Chinese sage and philosopher

Mennonites—members of an evangelical Protestant denomination

metta—love for all beings in Buddhism

Midrash—collection of commentaries on the Hebrew Bible

Mill, John Stuart—British philosopher, student of Jeremy Bentham

modern and postmodern culture—culture influenced by modernism and postmodernism; movements often characterized by the rejection of traditional beliefs, values, methods, and forms of expression; while modernism generally tends to strive for a coherent worldview and universal meaning (for example, the ideas of humanism or knowledge based on reason and rationality), posmodernism rejects the idea of "totality" and the "grand narratives," embracing incoherence, chaos, and fragmentation

monism—belief that all reality is part of a single ultimate principle

monotheism—belief in one all-encompassing God

moral universe—a term used by ethicists to designate who is deserving of ethical treatment

morality—action that is subject to moral judgment

Mohammad—prophet and founder of Islam

Moses—Jewish prophet

mystic—person claiming insights into mystery transcending common reality and human knowledge

mysticism—a direct encounter with the Sacred that results in a strong sense of personal identity with the Sacred

myths—stories that try to communicate deep mysteries of the world and its relation to the Sacred

Nakayama, Miki—female founder of Tenrikyo

Nanak—founder of Sikhism

Nicomachean Ethics—work by the philosopher Aristotle

Niebuhr, H. Richard—American Protestant theologian

Nirvana/Nibbana—in Buddhism, the freedom from suffering in enlightenment; in Hinduism, the unification of Atman and Brahman

Noddings, Nel—American philosopher

numinous—characterized by a sense of the mysterious or supernatural; spiritually elevated or sublime

objective globalization—the increasing planetary interconnectedness of human social activity and the worldwide effects or repercussions of that activity

official religion—the formal orthodox religion as taught and practiced by religious professionals such as priests and monks

orthodox—literally, straight doctrine or the officially correct beliefs of a doctrinal religion

orthopathos—the validation of spiritual experience in a given religious context

Osceola—leader of the Native American Seminole tribe

Otto, Rudolph—Christian theologian

Pali—language of early Buddhist scripture

pantheism—belief that identifies God with the cosmos

pantheon of gods—a list of gods, "all the gods," or a temple dedicated to all of the gods

papal infallibility—claim that authoritative teachings spoken by the pope *ex cathedra* are absolute truth

Parvati—Hindu goddess, consort of Shiva

Passover/Pesach—Jewish holiday commemorating the liberation of the people of Israel from slavery

People of the Book—religious traditions dating back to Abraham (Judaism, Christianity, Islam)

personality—the total behavioral, thought, attitude, and potentiality patterns of a person interacting in a relatively stable set of relationships and in a variety of situations

phenomena—aspects perceivable via sensory experience

phenomenological approach—phenomenological approach to religion—analysis of religion by describing beliefs, practices, and expressions using comparison in the search for essential characteristics of religion

Plato—Greek philosopher (429–347 BCE)

pluralism—claim that there are many truths in religious contexts

polytheism—belief in many gods

popular religion—the religion as it is actually practiced

prajna—enlightened wisdom

prophet—person speaking in the name of God

Purusha—cosmic man whose sacrifice brings about the world

Quakers—(officially: The Religious Society of Friends) members of a Christian community opposed to violence

rabbi—Jewish scholar, leader of Jewish congregations

Ramadan—twenty-nine or thirty days of fasting period in Islam

Ramakrishna—Hindu mystic teacher

Ramayana—Indian epic

Rand, Ayn—philosopher and writer

rational instrumentality—belief that human reason can be used to manipulate the universe and its component parts to suit human needs and desires

reader-response criticism—critical method that interprets the text taking the perspective of the reader into consideration

reductionistic definition of religion—definition that reduces religion to merely human invention or psychological needs

re-enchanting the universe—a strong tendency to see the material universe as alive with spirit

reincarnation—the belief that the spirit of a deceased person can be reborn in another living being

religious ethics—system of moral principles, teachings, and norms in its respective religious context

religious experience—the noncognitive, emotional, and passionate parts of religious life; how we *feel* our religion

religious founders—people initiating and/or establishing a religious belief

religious particularism—religious reactions that stress their own uniqueness and specific identity

religious universalism—religious reactions that stress the unity of humankind and the necessity of finding common ground among religions

rites of passage—rituals that acknowledge, bless, and sanctify, through ritual contact with the holy, the natural changes of life, such as birth, death, puberty, marriage, and so on

ritual—practice or prescribed pattern performed in a set form (for example, shaking hands, burial practices, worship)

Roman Catholicism—teachings, doctrines, faith of the Roman Catholic Church

Rothko, Mark—Latvian/American painter

Rudra—Hindu god ruling powers of nature

sadhus—Hindu holy men who exercise asceticism

salat—daily prayer in Islam

samadhi—state of meditative insight (Buddhism)

samsara—in a general sense, the process of reincarnation into different mortal beings

Samyutta Nikaya—part of the Buddhist scriptures containing *sutras* or discourses, either of the Buddha or his close disciples

sannyasin—in Indian religions, "one who renounces" all aspects of normal life to pursue spiritual liberation

Sanskrit—language of religious Hindu texts

satori—transformative experience of enlightenment found in Buddhism and some branches of Hinduism

Schleiermacher, Friedrich—German philosopher and theologian

scientific history—the approach to history based on the assumption that history is composed of factual events that can be investigated using objective data

scripture—sacred text

Second Axial Period—period in history resulting in a convergence of religions and human consciousness

secularism—a philosophy that seeks to remove society from under the dominance of religion and to place it under the guidance of rational humanism

secularization—the tendency to view the world in nonreligious terms and to remove modern institutions such as education and government from the dominance of religion

Seder—elaborate dinner, performed by Jews to commemorate the Exodus from Egypt and slavery

self-concept—an idea we develop about who we are and how we fit into the world around us

Septuagint—Greek translation of the Hebrew Bible and Apocrypha

shahadah—Islamic declaration of the belief in the one and only God, Allah

Shakespeare, William—English dramatist and poet

Shankara—Hindu philosopher

Shari'a—Islamic Law, based on the holy scripture of the Holy Koran and Hadith; considered divine law rooted in God's commandments

shirk—in Islam, the association of anything or anyone with the oneness of God

Shustari—Shi'ite writer

Siddhartha Gautama—the founder of Buddhism

sila—moral principles in Buddhism

skandhas—components of the self

social structure—the complex patterns of relationships among these institutions and among other elements of society

society—a group of people who share a common culture

Socrates—Greek philosopher

Sotaku, Koshu—famous teacher in the Rinzai school

soteriology—study or analysis of salvation, explaining a religion's view of how salvation occurs and what it achieves

subjective globalization—the social redefinition of identities and worldviews that emerges from the human confrontation and dialogue caused by objective globalization

Sudras—servant class in Hinduism

Sufism—mystical system in Islam

Sufis—mystic Muslim sect

sunnah—Islamic law based on traditions about the life of Mohammad

Sunni—member of one of the Islamic divisions

sutra—original text pertaining to the ritual practice of the Vedas, in time forming fundamental texts of Hindu law in Hinduism and in Buddhism, the Buddha's words, providing the basis for Buddhist scripture

Talmud, Torah—scripture of Judaism. Torah (Law or Teaching) especially refers to the five books of Moses and is the primary authoritative scripture. Talmud is the collected arguments of rabbis from 200 BCE to 400 CE, and these become the primary focus of the development of how to understand and apply the Torah.

Tanakh—Jewish sacred texts composed of the Torah, the five books of Moses, the Neviim, the prophets, and the Ketuvim, sacred writings. In Christian context, the Tanakh is generally referred to as the Old Testaments or Hebrew Bible

Tertullian—Christian theologian

theism—belief in God/gods as Ultimate Reality

theocracy—a society run according to religious laws

theory of evolution—biological theory that explains the variety of forms of life as the result of changes occurring from generation to generation (e.g., mutation, natural selection)

Tirthankaras—spiritual teachers in the Jain tradition

Torah—*see* **Talmud, Torah**

transcendent—to be above a certain context

transformative rituals—rituals that initiate change through the power of the Sacred

trickster—mischievous figure in Native American oral tradition that appears in many manifestations (for example, coyote, raven) creatively transforming the world; one who thwarts or bungles human hopes for cosmic order and relief that fail to keep death away

Tripitaka—early Buddhist scriptures written in Pali

Upanishads—philosophical texts in Hinduism composed between eighth and sixth centuries BCE

Vaishyas—merchant class in Hinduism

value system—the desired patterns of life, states of being or outcomes of social life by which individuals and collectives measure the quality of their existences and the direction of their activities

Vedas—oldest group of sacred texts in Hinduism

Vendanta—Hindu philosophical school based on the Upanishads

Vesak/Wesak/Waisaka—festivals celebrating three major events in the life of the Buddha (birth, enlightenment, death)

Vinaya—discipline and rules for the *sangha* or Buddhist monastic order

Vulgate—Latin translation of the Bible

Wang Yang-ming—Confucian philosopher

Weber, Max—German economist and sociologist

worship—the ritual performance of proclaiming the value and greatness of the sacred

Zoroaster—founder of Zoroastrianism

INDEX

Book of Mormon, 52
Bothner, Hans-Casper von, 125
Brahman, 66, 68, 78, 79, 80, 178,
    206, 237, 287
    experiencing the world, 293
    oneness with, 288
    as sage, 96
Brahmins, 263
Bresnan, Patrick, 335
Bromley, David, 55
Brown, Harold, 131, 326
Buddha, 93
    religious experience of, 284
    as sage, 96
    Truth of, 96
Buddha Amida, 292, 324
Buddha Amitabha, 324
Buddha Mind, 42
Buddha Nature, 42
Buddhism, 6
    art of, 210
    balance and acceptance in, 187
    canonization of scripture in, 120
    and dukkha, 185
    ethics of, 269
    experience of the Holy in, 286
    explanation for evil and suffering
        in, 175
    external and internal morality in,
        264, 265
    founders of, 93
    four noble truths of, 131, 186
    and healthy soul, 292
    Hinayana, 120, 265
    historical commemorations in, 235,
        236
    as historical religion, 155
    ignorance and, 178
    impermanence in, 186
    instructional language in, 159
    Jodo School of, 324, 325
    karma in, 268
    lists in, 132
    on love and self-love, 347
    maya in, 349
    Nichiren, 98
    Nichiren sect of, 98
    other-worldly salvation in, 319
    paths of, 292
    prayers in, 240
    Pure Land, 292, 324
    relation to culture, 366
    religious community in, 340
    responses to suffering in, 189
    salvation by grace in, 324
    salvation by knowledge in, 326
    scriptures of, 115, 117
    second-generation authors of, 98
    spiritual qualities of women in,
        375

sutras of, 116, 117, 155
Tantric, 210
Theraveda, 120, 210, 231, 241,
    265
Three Refuges in, 131
Tibetan art in, 200
worship in, 238
Zen. See Zen Buddhism
Burmese animism, 183
Byzantine art, 209

calligraphy, 200, 210
Calvin, John, 99, 258
Calvinism, 229
canon, 119
capitalism, 40
caste system, 184, 263
Chalcedonian Creed of 451, 131
chanting, 201
Chardin, Pierre Teilhard de, 20, 305
charismatic leader, 52
Chidester, David, 256, 276
Children of God, 55
China
    oppression of Falun Gong in, 53
    religion of, 104
Christ, 82
Christian Crusades, 274
Christian Science, 93
Christianity, 7, 76
    acting in the world, 294
    art in, 200
    belief in, 131
    commemorations in, 235
    concepts of violence in, 274
    divine command theory in, 267
    early, 294, 367
    and environmental degradation,
        304
    experiencing the world in, 293
    external and internal morality in,
        264
    faith and healing in, 350
    founders of, 93
    as historical religion, 154
    imaging the divine in, 208
    instructional language in, 158
    interpretation of origins of evil in,
        176, 177
    Jesus as founder of, 99
    missionaries of, 238
    moral and social, 367
    morality in, 262
    original language of texts in, 142
    origins of, 89
    other-worldly salvation in, 317
    prophets of, 94, 95
    reaction to Holocaust, 191
    religious community in, 340
    response to suffering in, 189, 190

response to violence in, 273
salvation by grace in, 322
scientific history and, 164
second-generation authors of, 98
sick-mindedness in, 349
splitting of church in, 127
suffering in, 181
transformative rituals in, 233
triune God of, 73, 99
worship in, 237
Christians
    born again, 290
    fundamentalist, 165
    modernist, 165
Christmas, 235
    secularization of, 248
chronos, 11
Chuang Tzu, 98, 161, 178, 187, 293,
    316
Chun-tzu, 97
Church, Forrest, 77
church fathers, 209
Church of Latter Day Saints
    (Mormons), 52
churches of the disinherited, 369
church-type organization, 51
Cicero, 32
circumcision, 229
Civil Rights movement, 370
civilization, religion and, 364
clockmaker god, 105
commemorations, 234
commissioning experience, 284
Communion, 235, 236
communism, Marxist-Leninist-
    Stalinist, 40, 44
community, 338
    of fate, 303
Confucianism, 6
    canon of, 120
    external and internal morality in,
        266
    founders of, 93
    humor in, 161
    li in, 262, 266
    morality in, 262
    other-worldly salvation in, 320
    puberty rituals in, 230
    relation to culture, 366
    second-generation authors of, 98
    sick-mindedness in, 349
    source of morality in, 268, 269
    this-worldly salvation in, 315
    worship in, 238
Confucius, 12, 93
    and healthy soul, 291
    religious experience of, 284
    as sage, 96, 97
consumerism, 18
contingent, 67

idolator, 80
idolatry, 208
ignorance, 178
Iliad, The, 74
illusion, religion as, 44
incarnation, 99
inclusivism, 82
India, toleration of religions in, 328
individual, 332–358
    religion and, 46
individualism, 14
individuality, 334
Indra, 67, 74
Indus Valley, 89, 102
ineffability, 66, 133
instruction regarding belief and
        practice, 158
integrity, 47
intrinsic religion, 352
Isaac, 257, 268
Isaiah, 24, 95
Ishmael, 268
Isis, 74
Islam, 7, 76
    architecture in, 214
    calligraphy in, 214
    concepts of violence in, 274
    divine command theory in, 267
    external and internal morality in,
        266
    faith and healing in, 350
    historical commemorations in, 235
    as historical religion, 155
    Iblis (devil) in, 177
    interpretation of origins of evil in,
        176, 177
    law of, 258
    mysticism in, 287, 289
    peaceful end-time of, 273
    personal interpretation by, 130
    prayer in, 239
    prohibition against imaging the
        divine in, 209
    prophets of, 94
    relation to culture, 366
    religious community in, 340
    response to violence in, 378
    rituals of, 244
    salvation by grace in, 324
    salvation by works in, 322
    scripture of, 117
    sick-mindedness in, 349
    statements of belief in, 131
    suffering in, 181
    Sufi dervishes of, 300
    view of Jesus of, 219
    worship in, 237, 238
itvara, 189, 321
Izanagi, 74
Izanami, 74

Jainism, 6
    hero of, 93
    responses to suffering in, 189
    salvation by works in, 321
    spiritual qualities of women in,
        375
James, William, 43, 290, 291, 344
Japan
    religion of, 103
    salvation by grace in, 324
Jeremiah, 24, 95, 264
Jesus
    art depicting, 209
    as founder of Christianity, 93, 99
    on love and self-love, 347
    as Messiah, 96
    Muslim view of, 219
    prayer in Garden of Gethsemane,
        240
    as prophet, 95
    Sermon on the Mount of, 268
    transfiguration of, 286
    as Word of God Incarnate, 99
jihad, 275, 379
jnana-marga, 326
Job's story, 181, 264
Joel, 95
Judaism, 7, 76
    chronicles of, 95
    concepts of violence in, 273
    divine command theory in, 267
    experience of the Holy in, 286
    experiencing the world in, 293
    external and internal morality in,
        263, 264
    faith and healing in, 350
    founders of, 93
    gentle mockery in, 161
    Hasidic, 316
    as historical religion, 151, 154,
        157
    imaging of the divine in, 207
    instructional language of, 159
    interpretation of origins of evil in,
        176, 177
    nature in, 105
    original language of texts in, 142
    origins of, 89
    peaceful end-time of, 273
    personal interpretation in, 130
    prophets of, 25, 36, 94, 95
    puberty rituals in, 230
    religious community in, 340
    salvation by grace in, 324
    salvation by works in, 321
    seasonal rituals as idolatry in, 234
    sick-mindedness in, 349
    suffering in, 180
    this-worldly salvation in, 316
Julian of Norwich, 302

just war theory, 378
justice, 188

kachina dolls, 217, 218
kairos, 11, 12, 19
Kali, 66, 74, 76, 100, 104, 207
kami, 93, 103
Kant, Immanuel, 65, 203, 204, 213,
        258, 276
    deontological ethical approach of,
        270
karma, 183, 184, 268, 321, 322
karma-marga, 325
karuna, 265
Keay, John, 157
Kelly, J. N. D., 130
Kierkegaard, Søren, 176, 257
Kilmer, Joyce, 145
King, Martin Luther, Jr., 271, 273
King, Winston, 347
kinship, 14
koan, 161, 302
Koranic scripts, 125
Krishna, 82, 100, 156, 237, 286, 325
kshatriyas, 263, 273
Küng, Hans, 72
Kuo Hsiang, 104

Lai, Master, 187
Lakshmi, 207
land, as origin of religion, 103
language
    art as, 200
    historical, 153, 156
    humor in, 160
    instructional, 155, 158
    mythic, 146, 147
    poetic, 148
    silence as, 162
    text and, 142
language games, 143, 144
    art as, 202
Lao Tzu, 11, 93
    as founder of Taoism, 100
    as sage, 97
laws
    of Buddha, 96
    of Manu, 263
    of universe, 267
legends, 156
Leggett, Trevor, 211
Lewis, C. S., 181
Li Hongzhi, 53
life, meaning of, 310–331
Lings, Martin, 287
literal meaning, 125, 145
liturgy, 239
living dead, 75
logos, 99
Long, Charles, 150

Lord's Supper, 235, 236
Lucifer, 183
Luther, Martin, 12, 99, 258, 346
    reforming New Testament, 119
    translation of New Testament by,
        143

Ma, Anandamayi, 102
mad cow disease, 35
Magee, John B., 39
magic, 233, 236, 241, 244
Mahabharata, 101, 116, 156, 231
Mahavira, 24, 93
Mahayana Buddhism, 120
    external and internal morality in,
        265
    path of, 292
    prayers in, 240
    relation to culture, 367
    religious community in, 340
mana, 68, 79, 234
mandala, 211
Mansur, Husayn ibn, 289
mantra, 207
marga, 264
Marty, Martin, 8
Martyr, Justin, 74
martyrs, 189
Marx, Karl, 9, 44, 90, 190
Marxist-Leninist-Stalinist
    communism, 40, 44
Mata, Sri Daya, 240
materialism, 15
maya, 349
meaning of life, 310–331
meaning-giving activity, 39
Mecca, 35, 244
mechanism, 15
media imperialism, 218
meditation
    prayer compared with, 240
    rituals for, 231
Mencius, 98, 269
Mennonites, 273
messengers, 94
Messiah, 164
messianic prophecy, 95
metta, 266
Mexican tribal cultures, self-induced
    experiences of, 300
Micah, 95
Michelangelo, 200, 215, 372
Midrash, 123
Mill, John Stuart, 258, 270
Miller, James, 305
Milton, Kay, 21
mind, 341
    motivating behavior, 342
    physical, 341
    reactive, 343

reflective, 342
sick, 348
social, 341
spiritual, 343
miracles, testing of, 297
Mitra, 74
modern culture, 217
Modern Period, 12
    mechanistic view of religion in,
        105
modernism, 12, 13
modernists, 165
Moggallana the Great, 185
Mohammedanism, 93
Momen, Moojan, 43, 370
monism, 78
monotheism, 76
    suffering and, 180
monothetic, 34
Moonies, 55
moral behavior, 321
moral conduct, religion as, 36
moral universe, 355
morality, 18, 251–279
    in ancient societies, 257
    based on emotion, sentiment, and
        sympathy, 270
    defined, 256
    derived from nature of cosmos,
        268
    as expression of religion and
        culture, 270
    historical origins and sources of,
        259
    human nature as source of, 269
    reasons for considering, 261
    religious and rational, 275
    secular, 261
    sources of, categorization of, 267
Mormons. See Church of Latter Day
    Saints
Moses, 68, 93, 151
    experience of the Holy, 286
    historical research on, 107
    as prophet, 94, 95
    religious experience of, 284
    speaking with God, 321
Mother Goddess, 104, 106
    and globalization, 105
Mother Teresa, 294
movies
    and globalization, 218
    religious themes in, 218
Muhammad, 12, 93
    as prophet, 94
    religious experience of, 283
multicultural analysis, 4
Munch, Edvard, 202
Muslims. See Islam

mysterium tremendum et fascinans,
    38, 65, 71, 204, 244, 285
mystic, 46
mystical experience, 287
mysticism, 287
mythic vision, 149
myths, 139–168
    cosmogenic, 259
    to explain suffering and evil, 172
    explaining origins of evil, 175
    false or true, 150
    and history, 151
    modern, 150
    performance of, 148
    performed or spoken, 148
    poetry and, 151
    social dimension of, 149
    trickster, 177

Nagasena, 319
Nakayama, Miki, 93, 103
Nanak, 93, 108
Narasimha, 100
Narayan, Swami, 102
narcissism, 348
Nathan, 95
nationalism, 40
nation-states, rituals enforcing
    supremacy in, 246
Native American religions
    art in, 217
    Caddo legend of, 177
    puberty rituals in, 230
    trickster in, 160
    vision quest of, 300
native religions, nature spirits in, 182
nats, 183
nature
    in Chinese religion, 104
    cruelty of, 174
    inanimate objects of, 104
    in Judaism, 105
    personification of, 75
    power of, 64
nature religions, return to, 106
nature spirits, 182
Navajo sand paintings, 75
Nazi regime, 191, 271
Neshat, Shirin, 220
neti-neti, 68, 79, 162
neurotheology, 299
Neusner, Jacob, 192
Nevi'im, 95
New Testament, 119, 123, 268
    concepts of violence in, 274
    external and internal morality in,
        264
Nicholas, St., 248
Nichomachean Ethics, 269

vaishyas, 263
value system, 22
Varanasi, 230
varnasrama, 263
Varuna, 268
Vasubandhu, 81
Vedas, 67, 74, 93, 102, 114, 241, 268
Vedic, 102
Vedic pleas, 240
Vedic times, 104
veneration, 238
verifiable evidence, 15
vinaya, 155, 265
violence, 272, 377
Virgin Mary, art depicting, 202
Vishnu, 82, 102, 206, 237
    avatars of, 100
visions, mythic, 149
Visuddhimagga, 231
Vulgate Bible, 143

Wakan, 172
Wallace, Anthony F. C., 34
Wang Yang-ming, 132, 160
wars, 190
Weber, Max, 9, 39, 51
Weitz, Morris, 202
Western Civilization, spread of, 20
wheel of life, 186
Whitehead, Alfred North, 46
Wicca, 106, 234
Wiesel, Elie, 192
Wilber, Ken, 15
will to detachment, 205

wisdom literature, 159
wise people, 96
Witch Doctors, 90
witch doctors, 75
Witches, 106
Wittgenstein, Ludwig, 144, 276
Wolpe, David, 151
women
    nature of, 371
    redefining of by globalization, 376
    roles of, 219
    spiritual qualities of, 374
    status of, 363, 371
    subordination of, 374
Word, The, 99
Word of God, 118
words
    connotative meaning of, 126
    denotative meaning of, 126
    limits of, 133
    literal meaning of, 125
    meanings of, 144
world
    acting in, 294
    experiencing, 293, 303
world building, 49
world maintenance, 49, 135
world religions, comparison of, 6, 7
world scriptures, 111–138
World War II, 20, 191
worlds, changing, 134
worldviews
    clash of, 220
    of various societies, 13, 14

worship, 33, 236
    as ritual, 238

Yahweh, 76, 81, 287
Yao, Emperor, 104
yin and yang, 187
yoga, 242
Yoruba religion, 76
Youlin, Lin, 104
Yu, Hsu, 104

Zen Buddhism, 98, 302
    acting in the world, 294
    Americans' attraction to, 219
    Chinese, 115
    empty circle in, 201, 211
    humor in, 161
    humorous art in, 211
    language and words in, 133
    poetry in, 152, 212
    Rinzai, 292
    salvation by knowledge in, 326
    silence in, 162
    Soto, 292
    tea ceremony in, 211
    Vietnamese monks of, 294
Zeus, 74
Zoroaster, 24
Zoroastrians, experiencing the world,
    293